ADMINISTRATIVE LAW

General Editor

Abhinandan Malik

BA, LLB (HONS.) (NALSAR), LLM (UNIV. OF TORONTO)

Administrative Law

Prof. (Dr) I.P. Massey

LLM (Lko), LLM (Calif., Berkeley), PhD

Formerly Professor and Chairman, Department of Law
and Dean, Faculty of Law
Himachal Pradesh University, Shimla,
Member, State Legal Services Authority, (H.P.),
Member, State Human Rights Commission, (H.P.),
Fellow, Indian Institute of Advanced Study, Shimla,
Visiting Professor of Law,
Hidayatullah National Law University Raipur (Chhattisgarh)
Presently Professor of Law and Dean, Faculty of Law,
National Law University, Jodhpur (Rajasthan)

Foreword by

Justice P.N. Bhagwati

Chief Justice of India

With an Introduction by

Prof. Upendra Baxi

EBC

Lucknow | Delhi | Prayagraj | Guwahati
Bengaluru | Ahmedabad | Nagpur | Kolkata

EBC

Website: www.ebc.co.in, E-mail: sales@ebc-india.com, Webstore: www.ebcwebstore.com

Lucknow (H.O.): 34, Lalbagh, Lucknow-226 001
Phones: +91–522–4033600 (30 lines), Fax: +91–522–4033633

Delhi: 1267, Kashmere Gate, Old Hindu College Building, Delhi-110 006
Phones: +91–11–23917616, +91–9313080904, Fax: +91–11–23921656

Bengaluru: 25/1, Anand Nivas, 3rd Cross, 6th Main, Gandhinagar,
Bengaluru-560 009, Phone: +91–80–41225368

Prayagraj: Manav Law House, Law Publishers & Booksellers, Near Prithvi Garden,
Opp. Dr Chandra's Eye Clinic, Elgin Road, Civil Lines, Prayagraj-211 001
Phones: +91–532–2400877, 2422023, Fax: +91–532–2623584

Ahmedabad: Satyamev Complex-1, Ground Floor, Shop No. 7
Opp. High Court Gate No. 2 (Golden Jubilee Gate)
Sarkhej—Gandhinagar Highway Road, Sola, Ahmedabad-380 060
Phones: +91–9228012539, +91–7567903245

Nagpur: F-9, Girish Heights, Near LIC Square, Kamptee Road, Nagpur-440 001
Phones: +91–712–6607650, +91–7028924969

Guwahati: Advika, Unit No. 205, 2nd Floor, M.G. Road, Pan Bazar, Guwahati-781 001
Phone: +91–8736091956

Kolkata: Ground Floor, Malik House, 7, Hare Street, Kolkata-700001
Phone: +91–033–48089874, +91– 9170413377

www.scconline.com/blog
Facebook: Eastern Book Company | SCC Online
Twitter: @ebcindia | @scconline_
Instagram: @scconline_ | @ebcwebstore
Linkedin: Eastern Book Company | SCC Online
YouTube: @easternbookcompany | @thescconline

First Edition,	1980	Fifth Edition,	2001	Eighth Edition,	2012
Second Edition,	1985	*Reprinted*,	2003	Ninth Edition,	2017
Third Edition,	1990	Sixth Edition,	2005	Tenth Edition,	2022
Fourth Edition,	1995	*Reprinted*,	2007	*Reprinted*,	2023
Reprinted,	1998	Seventh Edition,	2008		

Reprinted, 2024

9 788119 868322

Published by Eastern Book Company, 34, Lalbagh, Lucknow–226 001 under licence from EBC Publishing (P) Ltd., Lucknow

Printed and Produced by Media Network, A-388, Sarita Vihar, New Delhi–110 076

Dedicated to
My Parents

Law as a discipline that keeps growing simultaneously with the developments in society, has to be learnt continuously and consistently with the times.

Chief Justice of India

Foreword to the Second Edition

I am very glad that Dr I.P. Massey has brought out a really useful book on administrative law. The concept of administrative law has assumed great importance in the last three decades and has witnessed remarkable advances in recent times. It is a branch of law which is being increasingly developed to control abuse or misuse of governmental power and keep the executives and its various instrumentalities and agencies within the limits of their power. The rule of law, which runs like a golden thread through every provision of the Constitution and indisputably constitutes one of its basic features, requires that every organ of the State must act within the confines of the powers conferred upon it by the Constitution and law; and administrative law is that branch of law which seeks to ensure observance of the rule of law.

We are at present living in a modern welfare state and its chief characteristics are: 1) a vast increase in the range and detail of government regulation of privately owned economic enterprise; 2) the direct furnishing of services by government to individual members of the community—the economic and social services as social security, low-cost housing, medical care, etc.; and 3) increasing government ownership and operation of industries and businesses which, at an earlier time, were or would have been operated for profit by individuals or private corporations. In short, as pointed out by Friedmann in his well-known book, *Law in a Changing Society*, the State performs five different functions and three out of these functions result from the activities of the State as provider, entrepreneur and economic controller.

In the welfare state, public power becomes an instrumentality for the achievement of purposes beyond the minimum objectives of internal order and national defence. It is not sufficient that the State be secure against internal disorder and external aggression; a State can be secure and well ordered and yet lack the attribute of distributive justice. But as social justice becomes the conscious end of State policy, as is the case in India under our Constitution, there is a vast and inevitable increase in the frequency with which ordinary citizens come into direct relationship with the wielders of power. An ordinary citizen's significant encounter is not so much with the policeman or magistracy as with the officers representing regulatory authorities, dispensers of social services, managers of public sector undertakings, etc. It is this dramatically increased incidence of encounter that set the task of the rule of law in the welfare state. It should be the goal of rule of law to see that these multifarious and diverse encounters are fair, just and free from arbitrariness. This was precisely what was pointed out by me, speaking on behalf of the Supreme Court, in *Ramana Dayaram Shetty* v. *International Airport Authority of India*[1] (*Airport Authority*) as:

> Today with tremendous expansion of welfare and social service functions, increasing control of material and economic resources and large scale assumption of industrial and commercial activities by the State, the power of the executive Government to affect the lives of the people is steadily growing. The attainment of socio-economic justice being a conscious end of State policy, there is a vast and inevitable increase in the frequency with which ordinary citizens come into relationship of direct encounter with State power-holders. This renders it necessary to structure and restrict the power of the executive Government so as to prevent its arbitrary application or exercise.

It is also an important factor which cannot be ignored that a modern welfare state entails the conferment of discretionary powers on the administration to effectuate wide socio-economic goals. In any area of socio-economic regulation, discretionary power over valuable interests is perhaps inevitable. The theory that the legislature must delineate the policies and that administrators must have no discretion, except to apply the legislative policies, has to yield to the stark reality that legislatures cannot possibly anticipate and provide for all situations. As Aristotle said, "The generality of law falters before the specifics of life." Moreover, quite often, the legislation is skeletal, leaving many gaps and conferring powers on the administration to act in a way it deems "necessary" or "reasonable" or if it "is satisfied"

1. (1979) 3 SCC 489.

or "is of opinion" and so on. The legislature often bestows more or less unqualified or uncontrolled discretion on the executive. Discretion is a tool for individualisation of justice. The administration has to apply statutory provisions, which may be seemingly vague or indefinite, according to the fact situations as they arise with a view to effectuating legislative policy. As Davis has said:

> All governments in history have been governments of laws and of men. Rules alone, untempered by discretion cannot cope with the complexities of modern government and of modern justice. Discretion is our principal source of creativeness in government and in law.

It, therefore, becomes necessary to confine structure and check discretion in order to uphold the principle of rule of law in administration. The judiciary has over the years evolved rules for controlling and structuring the exercise of discretionary power which, having regard to the complexities of modern economy, has necessarily to be vested in different instrumentalities and agencies of the State, so that the discretionary power does not degenerate into arbitrary power. There is often antithesis between power and justice, and by administrative law, this antithesis is sought to be removed and power is sought to be controlled and channelised for bringing about a just result. Administrative law is, in fact, a potent weapon for bringing about harmony between power and justice.

There are several principles of administrative law which have been evolved by the courts for the purpose of controlling the exercise of power so that it does not lead to arbitrariness or despotic use of power. These principles are intended to provide safeguard to the citizens against abuse or misuse of power by the instrumentalities or agencies of the State. One of the most important of these principles is the rule of natural justice which consists of two major constituent principles, namely, the principle of *audi alteram partem* and the principle that no one shall be a judge in his own cause. The principle of *audi alteram partem* requires that no one shall be condemned unheard, and it has received its finest flowering in recent times in the decisions of the Supreme Court in *Mohinder Singh Gill* v. *Chief Election Commr.*[2] (*Gill*) and *Maneka Gandhi* v. *Union of India*[3] (*Maneka Gandhi*). The Supreme Court has held that if in a given case prior hearing would frustrate the object and purpose of the exercise of the power, it can be dispensed with, but, in that event, it must be substituted by post-decisional

2. (1978) 1 SCC 405.
3. (1978) 1 SCC 248.

hearing. This is a striking advance made by the Supreme Court on the English Law because there the law is that the requirement of prior hearing may be dispensed with if it would frustrate the object and purpose of the exercise of the power and in such a case, there need be no hearing at all, but in India, the Supreme Court has introduced the necessity of post-decisional hearing in such a case. Sometimes, an attempt is made by lawyers appearing on behalf of the government to contend that even where prior hearing is not given, the exercise of the power does not become bad and it can be cured by post-decisional hearing. But this is a gross misunderstanding of the decisions of the Supreme Court in *Gill*[4] and *Maneka Gandhi*[5], because it is clear law that if prior hearing is required to be given as part of the rule of natural justice, failure to give it would indubitably invalidate the exercise of the power and it cannot be saved by post-decisional hearing. It is only where the necessity for prior hearing cannot be read into the statute because to do so would be to defeat the object and purpose of the exercise of the power, that post-decisional hearing is required to be given and if that is not done, the exercise of the power would be vitiated. The other principle that no one shall be a judge in his own cause has also been recognised and developed in Indian jurisprudence in several decisions of the Supreme Court. The Supreme Court has also held that every quasi-judicial tribunal must give reasons for the decisions it makes, and necessity to give reasons is a part of the principles of natural justice. Dr Massey has very perceptively dealt with these rules of natural justice as evolved in various decisions of the Supreme Court as well as courts outside India.

One other development which has revolutionised administrative law in India owes its genesis to the decisions of the Supreme Court in *Airport Authority*[6] and *Ajay Hasia* v. *Khalid Mujib Sehravardi*[7]. These decisions have laid down that not only the State Government but also every instrumentality or agency of the State Government is subject to the constitutional limitations imposed by fundamental rights, and one of the limitations so imposed is that every action of the State or its instrumentality or agency must be reasonable and non-arbitrary. The Supreme Court has imposed the requirement of reasonableness and non-arbitrariness in every action, whether it be of the government or any of its instrumentalities or agencies, and laid down that the yardstick of reasonableness must be found

4. (1978) 1 SCC 405.
5. (1978) 1 SCC 248.
6. (1979) 3 SCC 489.
7. (1981) 1 SCC 722.

in the directive principles of state policy. This principle has invested the courts with immense power to scrutinise the action of the executive and its instrumentalities and agencies for the purpose of determining whether such action is reasonable and non-arbitrary. If the court finds that the action is not based on any principle or norm, but is arbitrary, the court would be under the plainest duty to strike it down. This principle has also been adequately discussed by Dr I.P. Massey in this book.

One other question which has bedevilled administrative law is the question of State liability for the unconstitutional acts of its servants. What is the extent of liability of the State for the wrongful acts of the administration? There are decisions of the Supreme Court which seem to indicate that where there is gross violation of the right to life and the principle enshrined in Article 21 of the Constitution by any government servant, the State may be held liable to pay compensation to the victim or his dependents. The Supreme Court in *Rudul Sah* v. *State of Bihar*[8] directed compensation in the sum of ₹30,000 to be paid to Rudul Sah for his detention in jail contrary to the mandate of Article 21. So also the Supreme Court in *Sebastian M. Hongray* v. *Union of India*[9] directed the State to pay a sum of ₹1 lakh each to the wives of two citizens who were arrested by the armed forces, but who did not return back. This is a developing branch of law and it remains to be seen how far the Supreme Court will go in awarding compensation for violation of Article 21 of the Constitution.

Dr I.P. Massey's book contains a lucid exposition of administrative law in all its aspects and dimensions and offers a highly perceptive and critical analysis. I have no doubt that this book will be of immense use not only to law students but also to lawyers and administrators and men in public life.

May I once again congratulate Dr I.P. Massey on bringing out a really critical and refreshing book on administrative law.

—P.N. BHAGWATI

3, Janpath
New Delhi
16 August 1985

8. (1983) 4 SCC 141.
9. (1984) 3 SCC 82.

Preface to Tenth Edition

Administrative law is a highly complex and constantly evolving discipline, hence, makes regular revision imperative. Generally, this text was being revised after every five years but I was surprised when EBC asked me to revise after three years! I express my gratitude to all the readers of the book for their continued interest, which keeps me going.

Although this Tenth Edition comprehensively updated the text, yet in size and structure it remains unchanged. In this revision, effort has been made to contextualise the concepts, doctrines and principles of administrative law for a better understanding of the subject. Special emphasis has been put on remedial issues. I continue to hope that this revised treatise will be useful to the students and other scholars of administrative law.

I would like to say "Thank You" to Mr Surendra Malik, Chief Editor, Supreme Court Cases for his continued interest and assistance. My sincere thanks to Mr Abhinandan Malik, General Editor and his team of experts and editors, including Ms Primisha Tripathi and dedicated workers at Eastern Book Company, Lucknow, for bringing out this edition with the required speed and accuracy. For moral support my thanks to my wife Dr Meera Massey for her sustained support during this revision process.

August 15, 2021 —I.P. Massey

About the Author

Prof. I.P. Massey, formerly, was the Professor and Chairman, Department of Law and Dean, Faculty of Law, Himachal Pradesh University, Shimla. From 1996 to 1999, he was the Fellow at the Indian Institute of Advanced Study, Shimla. He was appointed member of the Himachal Pradesh State Human Rights Commission in 1996 for a period of five years. He has been appointed member of Himachal Pradesh State Legal Services Authority. He was Visiting Professor of Law, Hidayatullah National Law University, Raipur, Chhattisgarh.

Prof. Massey has received his LLM degree from Lucknow University and also from the School of Law (Boalt Hall) University of California, Berkeley, US with specialisation in constitutional and administrative law. He obtained PhD in law from the Kurukshetra University. He has widely travelled and delivered lectures at Indiana University, Fort Wayne campus, US and MART Institute of Technology and in TMT/MICIA Co-operative Programme in Malaysia. He has written extensively on constitutional and administrative law. He participated in various national and international seminars and conferences. His research articles have been published in reputed journals and books.

Presently, he is Dean, Faculty of Law, National Law University, Jodhpur (Rajasthan).

Brief Contents

Contents

6. TRIBUNALISATION OF JUSTICE

7. PRACTICE AND PROCEDURE OF ADMINISTRATIVE ADJUDICATION: RULES OF NATURAL JUSTICE

8. JUDICIAL REVIEW OF ADMINISTRATIVE ACTIONS: PRINCIPLES

JUDICIAL REVIEW OF ADMIN. ACTIONS: PRINCIPLES (*Contd.*)

9. JUDICIAL REVIEW OF ADMINISTRATIVE ACTION: MODES

LIABILITY OF THE ADMINISTRATION (*Contd.*)

12. STATUTORY AND NON-STATUTORY PUBLIC UNDERTAKINGS

13. CITIZEN AND ADMINISTRATIVE FAULTS

14. CONSTITUTIONAL PROTECTION TO CIVIL SERVANTS AND THE ADMINISTRATIVE SERVICE TRIBUNAL

15. GLOBAL ADMINISTRATIVE LAW

Table of Cases

B

C

D

E

F

G

H

I

J

K

L

M

N

O

P

Q

R

S

T

U

V

W

Y

Z

Introduction[*]

Prof. Upendra Baxi

The Myth and Reality of the Indian Administrative Law

1. PREFATORY OBSERVATIONS

At the outset, I wish to thank Prof. I.P. Massey and the publishers for their invitation to continue to associate myself with the seventh edition of this work. Prof. Massey's admirable textbook has stood the test of time. This edition continues to provide a reliable overview of extensive and intensive judicial decisions and doctrinal developments. Telling stories of these developments in a short compass remains an arduous task, indeed, and Prof. Massey accomplishes this admirably well. Among the notable changes, this edition offers, is a most welcome addition via its brief but important chapter concerning global administrative law (Chapter 15).

While appreciative of the demands made by many readers that no re-write may surrender some "inspirational" or "critical" elements in its earlier versions, I still proceed to recompose this introduction substantially to specifically peruse the following tasks: 1) contrasting conventional legal understanding of the Indian administrative law (IAL) with historical and sociological narratives of it; 2) understanding elements of continuity and change in the IAL; 3) addressing some "tragedies" of the IAL; 4) re-visiting the normative developments; and 5) developing some threshold standards for the appraisal of judicial role and function.

2. UNDERSTANDING INDIAN ADMINISTRATIVE LAW

Administrative law is no doubt a conceptually awkward and fuzzy notion and, yet at the same moment, an ever-growing doctrinal sphere because it has no fixed terrain. The IAL is not really a subject or discipline of law like, say, torts, property, company law, and at times invades administration of the criminal justice system. The IAL principles emerge across the board,

* Introduction to the Seventh Edition, 2008.

and are to be found, discovered, and even invented, wherever allegations of arbitrary exercise of power are raised and judicially dealt with. One may reasonably specialise in studies or in practice in a specific area of law, but it strains belief that one may ever specialise in the IAL as such. To understand the stuff of which the IAL is made, one has to understand relevant domains of "substantive" law to which courts apply the more general principles of legality and fair play.

This, of course, is not a widely shared view, as for the most part it is believed that the IAL constitutes an autonomous genre or a new disciplinary field. Many scholars, including Prof. Massey, claim some singular place for it. By common convention, the IAL is regarded as "public law" because it deals with the relationships between citizen and State; the IAL becomes an integral part of the constitutional law of India, reflecting it but also shaping it. The IAL, in a special sense, constitutes the common law of the Constitution, as for the most part it is uncodified, though it is clear that regulatory agencies and tribunals always concurrently making their own "law" have always existed and are now growing apace.

Different images of the IAL emerge from the varied constituencies of law persons. If for justices, the IAL emerges as a field for the exponentially growing judicial review or adjudicatory powers, it constitutes for legal practitioners a virtual (in a pre-digital sense) gold mine. The literally fantastic growth of the IAL is "big business" for the legal profession, augmenting their affluence, prestige, and power. For law reformers, the IAL is an untidy and messy field which needs constant landscaping and the law academics stand, offered by the IAL, some unusual challenges for teaching and research; further, as with lawyers, academic eminence stands built upon successful performances of narrating doctrinal development. Law students not merely improve their knowledge-base by studying the IAL but also improve their competitive credentials for public service and judicial examinations. This diversity of interests that generate and sustain the IAL development also signifies that many different material or institutional interests are at play in conventional approaches towards its understanding.

Put together, the different images under gird a distinctly legal liberal ideology. The IAL, like administrative law formations in all liberal societies or constitutional democracies, celebrates the values of a "rule of law" based State and society. The social meaning of the rule of law is just this: The rule of law means that *power must always be rendered accountable here-and-now, governance be made progressively just, and the State incrementally ethical.* Understood this way, the IAL offers as a series of success and failure stories about the attainment of the rule of law based governance and society. Its jurisprudential meaning has been expounded rather well in Chapters 1–2 of this work. What the rule of law means in action, varies from time to time depending on how courts may interpret technical and complex doctrines such as the separation of powers, arbitrariness, natural justice, reach and limits of judicial review powers. This technical and complex understanding of the rule of law is important but not enough.

3. TOWARDS A SOCIOLOGICAL AND HISTORICAL UNDERSTANDING OF THE IAL FORMATIONS

The conventional understanding of the IAL is necessary but not sufficient. Alternate frameworks situating the IAL development in time and space do not deny its importance but rather enrich it. Administrative law primarily unfolds via judicial decisions; hence, these furnish the raw material for understanding how justices and courts arrive at the sense of the limits of executive/administrative decision-making power and of their own judicial review powers. This sense of limits cannot be grasped via case citations and mechanical narration of the principles enunciated by the judicial decisions as offering timeless truths.

Such doctrinal narratives via the practices of citation history overlook that it is not the same as contextual history; these ignore the obvious fact that courts as institutions (always exposed to changes in their structure, composition, role, and function over time) and justices as individual decision-makers (who bring to their task differing world views on State, Constitution, law, rights and development) act in changing historical contexts. Nor does citational history bring to public, and even to scholarly consciousness, the differential identities of litigants and lawyers who problematise State action and conduct in terms of arbitrariness or denial of fair play (now in the "neoliberal" jargon, the "level playing field"). The conventional IAL narratives (in this case and in that case type narratives) do a singular injustice to changing adjudicatory policies and styles, gestated within changeful political, social, and economic (in short, the historical) circumstance. Nor do they help us to understand how the client-bound lawyerly activities incrementally contribute to the cultural production called the IAL.

To understand this, we need to recourse to historical and sociological perspectives. Historical understanding of the IAL entails context-sensitivity. One way to attain this is by the device of periodisation, which always remains a contentious enterprise. "Dating" doctrinal developments remains co-equally difficult. Yet, the question is not whether we should do this but how may we best proceed! I offer here distinctions between "old", "new", and "contemporary" IAL formations by reference to four very diverse historical moments. In each of these, the "business" of arguing and deciding IAL cases proceeds differently, even when the principles and doctrine of natural justice and fair play continue to provide a common language and rhetoric.

Very tersely these are put as:

(1) The long Nehruvian moment of Indian constitutional planned economic development, and further the transition from a planned economy to the emergence of the State finance capitalist formation (with Indira Nehru Gandhi's bank nationalisation and abolition of the privy purses plus the rhetoric of *Garibi Hatao*).

(2) The authoritarian State formation of the internal Emergency of 1975–1976.

(3) The cathartic judicial populism in the wake of lifting of the Emergency maturing, subsequently, in new forms of judicial action, crystallised by social action litigation (SAL) (1977–1989).

(4) Beginning with the 90s, the era of new economic reforms, which now almost wholly immunises macro-economic policies and associated "developmental" measures from any strict constitutional and human rights oriented scrutiny.

The "old" IAL developed during the first two historical moments, the new forms of IAL developed distinctly in the third, and the contemporary IAL formations has began to occur in the fourth moment.

These four moments or phases invite us to more fully consider some wider political economy type considerations, an obviously difficult task at least for two reasons. *First*, as noted, historical periods dovetail into each other, making any "neat" demarcation illusory. *Second*, one should remain anxious about any reprehensible suggestion that courts and justices decide live cases and controversies by reading political manifestos and electoral results. Granting this, it may still not be gainsaid that overall political and economic contexts present both opportunities and constraints for judicial law-saying. Deciphering these is never an easy task, and all I can do in the next few sections of this brief introduction is to offer some narrative contrasts between the three IAL formations.

Like historical understanding, sociological understanding of the IAL still awaits its maternal labour pains, and this introduction constitutes merely its first spasm! There are many traditions of doing theoretical and empirical sociological studies of law (for example, the law-in-society tradition compared with the law-and-society genre). Collapsing these differences remains necessary for the present purpose to understand the large range of related but distinct questions, thus, opened up for understanding the IAL.

First, there is an assumption (now partly displaced by SAL) that the IAL petitioners or plaintiffs recourse to courts for the protection of their specific and, at times, strategic interests. Sociologically, then the question matters: Which sorts of parties or litigants recourse to courts? And what classes of aggrieved persons infrequently or even rarely go to courts? Which classes or groups stand most to benefit from this activation of judicial review power and process, and to which actual short and long term results? In the early decades, the IAL has developed largely by four types of litigants: companies and other business entities, trade unions or individual work persons, those subjected to preventive detention and varieties of dragnet security laws, and Article 311 citizens (that is civil servants). More players were later included with the rise of SAL (still miscalled "public interest litigation"). It would be useful, to say the least, that posing this question in the reading of the work will enliven the study of IAL, beyond the elaboration of the binding law and principles offered asymmetrically by judicial decisions and leading administrative law treatises.

Second, how may we understand differential responses by justices and courts to cases and controversies brought before them? How or why is the case that the many maxims/precepts/"standards"/"rules" of natural justice constantly vary in everyday application? Does this have to do with the changing social profiles of justices and lawyers who "develop" the ILA forms and techniques? Or, does this relate to the ways in which the artificial languages of the IAL develop (such as standing/justiciability, the maxims of "natural justice", and "due process")? What social functions, indeed if any, may be signified by the distinctions between "administrative" and "quasi-judicial" power and function, and superfine distinctions between "conditional delegated legislation" and the "rule-making" delegation of power to the executive,[1] and the difference between "policy" and "law"[2]?

Third, how may we understand the (and at times rather abject) dependence of lawyers and justices on foreign precedents, especially from the old Commonwealth law and the US jurisprudence, set against the relative insularity of the latter? Why is it that the remarkable originality of the judicially developed IAL has little resonance elsewhere? Why or how does it come to pass that the Indian justices and courts are so remarkably hospitable to Euro-American justices and so little informed by the administrative jurisprudence of the Global South? This is not just the question about judicial and forensic argumentative cultures (the Indian Bar is perhaps the most entrenched preserve in the world of Euro-American legal cultures) but also about the colonial nature of the post-colonial Indian IAL (for example, see Chapter 10, speaking of the difficulties of eradicating the vestiges of the doctrine of sovereign immunity for the tortious acts of its officials and agents).

Fourth, how may we understand constantly reiterated fact that the legal and other officials of the Union and State Governments remain so inveterately fairness-challenged? How may we understand their minuscule IAL-IQ, which constantly fails to grasp the elementary rules of natural justice or fair play in governmental action and conduct? Is it the case that the IAL jurisprudence as developed remains a response to the ways of governmental lawyering? As each and every SAL petitioner knows poignantly well, State counsel simply decline, despite repeated judicial reminders, to file responsive affidavits on time; the implementation of interim orders and directions remains tardy and indifferent; State-caused delays in final disposition of social action matters often exhaust the energies as well as the staying power of even the most tenacious SAL petitioners (and I here speak in terms of my own experience as SAL citizen-in-person petitioner!) How may we understand the litigational State conduct save as a kind of war *of attrition* waged on them?

Further, *fifth*, what difference has the liberalisation and democratisation of rules of standing via the SAL (see Chapter 10), made from the perspectives of the plights and rights of the constitutionally worst-off project, affected peoples? Has the SAL made any impact on the means and ends pursued by

1. As to this, see, *Vasu Dev Singh* v. *Union of India*, (2006) 12 SCC 753, para. 16.
2. *Directorate of Film Festivals* v. *Gaurav Ashwin Jain*, (2007) 4 SCC 737, para. 16.

the managers of Indian economic development? In this context, especially, how may we understand the "greening" of the IAL—that is the ways in which ecological and environment judicial sensibilities stand enacted and enhanced? How far, further, does the IAL remain gender-sensitive and equitous?

Sixth, if the IAL is to be understood as a prime instrumentality, overall, to monitor and arrest the carcinogenic growth of untrammelled executive power, how far may we tell stories of this having actually happened? Has the IAL rescued large masses of Indian citizens from brute powers of domination, that is, governance bereft of principles? The raising of this question "sociology of the IAL" constitutes at the same moment the sociology of Indian governance. How is that courts and justices as holders of State power speak in a forked tongue, articulating both the specific content of sovereign power as well as its interrogation in terms of human rights values, standards, and norms. At what point of time does the differentiation State powers may serve only the reinforcement of the centralised unity of State power, and at what point of time may it mark any authentic site for democratic articulation of popular sovereignty?

I begin this journey with you with an advance apology for the introduction of several acronyms: OIALF (old IAL formation), NIALF (the new IAL formation) and CIALF (contemporary IAL formation) and NJ (or natural justice). Some more acronyms will unfortunately further erupt; these crudities of language still may save forests and be otherwise ecologically justified!

4. THE OLD IAL FORMATION (OILAF)

In the main, the OIALF understandably develops in an era of the assertion of parliamentary sovereignty. Despite contention over the then actually existing right to property (Article 31), the Indian Supreme Court (hereafter "ISC") accommodates the assertion of the plenary powers of Parliament to amend the Constitution. The constitutional *samskaras* of Indian IAL are forged in two leading decisions. Vast powers of delegated legislation recognised and affirmed in *Delhi Laws Act, 1912, re*[3] with a principled caveat that the "essential features" of legislative power—identified as the power of policy-making accompanied with annexation of sanctions—may not be delegated away. And this caveat is seldom brought into play by the

3. 1951 SCC 568: AIR 1951 SC 332.

ISC. By "essential" features of legislative powers, the court does not, from early on, mean "non-negotiable" features; or, put another way, it remains for courts and justices to decide what "essential features" may mean in each IAL developmental phase.[4]

My own favourite text of the OIALF is the decision in *Ram Jawaya Kapur* v. *State of Punjab*[5]. This remarkable decision on the one hand recognises the importance of the doctrine of separation of powers—the Indian Constitution does not contemplate assumption of any one organ or part of functions that *essentially belong to the other*[6]—yet on the other hand, already and early on expands the realm of judicial review powers. When a bunch of Punjab school text publishers, led by no less than Rai Bahadur Ram Jawaya, impugned an executive order "nationalising" the publication of prescribed school textbooks, the ISC had some clear choices to make. It could have said either that a fundamental right was here violated by State policy without the authority of legislation, or that no such right was violated. But, Their Lordships had equivocated. They said that if a policy of nationalisation violated Article 19 rights, surely this would be questionable under Part III. Then they said that the policy did not violate any fundamental right because no one was forbidden to publish "textbooks"; the policy only related to what the school boards or department of education may prescribe as mandatory texts! However, the issue was here not book publishing relevant to school education, but rather concerned the right to publication of prescribed textbooks. Disturbed by the fact or possibility that this may open wide doors for "nationalisation" policies, they proceeded to say that such measures required the authority of law prescribing reasonable restrictions subject to judicial review. Alarmed in turn by the implication of such an enunciation in the instant case, the ISC said that even assuming otherwise, this policy was authorised by statutory law because the annual allocation of budgetary grants of various departments of the government stood approved by the legislature! Realising further no doubt that recognising the annual budget as a law, that may justifiably authorise "reasonable restrictions" on Part III rights to freedom, may deprive the court of all potency of judicial review power, it merely said that this may not always be thus construed! If so, what sense may we make, if any, of this decision that in one swift stroke conceives the acts of appropriation as general legal frameworks, authorising

4. *See infra*, the heading "Judicial control" in Chap. 4.
5. AIR 1955 SC 549.
6. *Ibid*, para. 12. *See infra*, Chap. 2.

executive-framed economic policies and, simultaneously, also places these beyond any constitutional or judicial strict scrutiny? Put another way, if annual budgets are "law" justifying "reasonable restrictions", justices and courts may not look any further in their everyday tasks of judicial control over administrative policy action. Clearly, the ISC was unwilling to go thus far; it wished to acknowledge large executive power and, yet, desired to retain the power to make adjudicatory policy imposing constitutional control. This means two sorts of diverse things. Justices and courts may not in principle, at one moment, make decisions that influence national budget-making (say via specific human rights based requirements in the implementation of Part IV) and at another moment, precisely thus, require by providing for monetary damage awards for the violation of fundamental rights (Chapter 10). How may we understand this replenishing all along of an infinite reservoir of executive power thus placed beyond the scope of judicial review of administrative actions, yet also entailing strict constitutional scrutiny?

Since it is beyond the bounds of this introduction to subject each case narrative to such detailed examination, may I say generally that what makes the IAL interesting and contradictory is that from its inception it signifies a one-step-forward-two-steps-backward adjudicatory movement! I may at least urge that you read the book in your hands as exemplifying this judicial see-saw! Perhaps, all this may be grasped only via the recognition of the fact that the first generation of the Indian Supreme Court justices recognised the need to repose complete trust in the first generation of nationalist movement Indian political leaders. This was also the time of recuperation from the massive trauma of the Indian Partition and a time for sustaining the charismatic model of Indian development, under the leadership of Pandit Jawaharlal Nehru.

Yet, in the nature of things, the fabrication of constructive trust could not mean abdication of judicial responsibility directed to develop a sense of limits of the reach of administrative power. The ISC thus, and variously, proceeds to discipline everyday or routine exercises of power. The first device it deploys requires that quotidian administrators ought to follow the letter and spirit of the statutory powers vested in them. Thus, the ISC insists in *State of Bombay* v. *K.P. Krishnan*[7] that statutory powers to make reference of an industrial dispute to Labour Courts may only be exercised

7. AIR 1960 SC 1223.

within its stated purpose and ambit and for no ulterior purpose or motive. Thus stands enwombed the doctrine of ultra vires: administrators vested with constitutional and/or legislative powers act within its four corners; they may not act outside jurisdiction or in bad faith or mala fides. This latter requirement becomes merely evidentiary; that is, the burden of proof that the action is such lies heavily on the administrative law petitioner. Rarely can such an overwhelming burden be discharged, although in the CIALF perhaps the administrative openness ushered in by the Right to Information Act may yet prove somewhat helpful.

Significantly, the OIALF develops some basic norms concerning administrative adjudication via the requirement that duties arise to act judiciously when administrative decision vested with power to decide disputes (judicial powers) acts to the prejudice or detriment of any person.[8] I say "judiciously" because the ISC does not require administrators to behave as justices, yet it seeks to impose on administrators a minimal discipline of fair play; later, this requires constant judicial and juridical elaboration of when action is merely administrative or "quasi-judicial" (*see* Chapters 8–9).

These germinal decisions of the first two decades of the jurisprudence of the ISC no doubt represent a golden era of the IAL. For one thing, these were the days when justices knew and perfected the art of writing chiselled judicial prose. They were master-craftspersons of legal prose and rhetoric. They knew, in complete plain words, how best to write judgments, unfortunately more than can be said of the contemporary judicial style, even generously recognising some rare exceptions. Yet so early on, the judicial rhetoric and reasoning also at the same moment constitute an adjudicatory "hands-off" posture. Historical understanding of the IAL suggests fully that judicial review simultaneously *opens up* as many spaces for the interrogation of arbitrary exercise of public power as it also *encloses*. All this deserves fuller dignity of discourse than here possible to the incipient judicial signals, which inaugurally find and found the notions of "law" beyond any IAL type judicial review.

8. *Board of High School and Intermediate Education* v. *Ghanshyam Das Gupta*, AIR 1962 SC 1110. This landmark decision preceded *Ridge* v. *Baldwin*, 1964 AC 40: (1963) 2 WLR 935 (HL), a fact scarcely acknowledged by the anglophile ways of Indian lawyering and scholarship. I am delighted that Massey now, in agreement with me, so fully highlights this notable advance.

The OIALF elaborates NJ doctrine as a vector of integrity in public decision making. Courts and justices begin to foundationally insist on the virtue of what we now name as governance transparency. Overall judicial strategies, though evolved case by case, did not deny the investment of vast discretionary powers in State officials and public authorities; rather, justices variously insisted that the various decision-makers follow some minimal rules of fair play. This task remained easy enough to name but difficult to fully enunciate. Even as the OIALF rather patiently yet fully elaborates what must be named as distinctive forms of the Indian constitutional common law, it does not always fully mitigate the inequities inherent to the exercise of administrative discretion.

To say this is not at all to deny the achievements of the OIALF. The Constitution clearly did not explicitly write the texts of NJ maxims and doctrines such as *audi alteram partem* (the obligation to afford a hearing or listening to the adversely affected interests); *nemo judex in causa sua* [the obligation requiring that administrative decision-makers must reach their decisions without personal (self-interested) or pecuniary bias (see Chapter 6)]. These were the munificent bounties bestowed on us by the first generation ISC justices, even when they stopped short of insistence that the Indian rule of law enacts not merely the idea of the *rule by reason* but also the rule *of reason*.

The rule by reason means generally that the public authorities making executive or administrative decisions that prejudicially affect rights or interests of the affected party should be as far as possible "speaking" decisions. The caveat is important because statutes may legitimately exclude the rule in situations that require immediate or urgent action. Thus, from early on emerges a distinction between the *normal time* of IAL adjudication, contrasted with the *state of exception* marking situations in which the IAL normativity may never fully extend!

In the OIALF, what mattered more was the development of the doctrine of reasoned decision making. What counted as such posed a difficult threshold. The ISC preciously as well precariously denied the sway of the doctrine of "subjective satisfaction" for arriving at a decision. This meant that the executive decision-makers may not simply decide as they please; rather, they ought to arrive at publicly reasoned decisions (the test of "objective satisfaction"). This requirement made (and continues to make) good sense because nothing remains of IAL if courts and justices have no material before them otherwise to scrutinise the indictment of arbitrary State action. Judicial review ends when "subjective satisfaction" reigns supreme. It begins when courts and justices stand provided with reasons for decision, which may in turn be contested before them; thus begins the long itinerary of judicial superintendence over the myriad forms of administrative action, which of necessity open up the grounds for objective satisfaction via the duty to give reasons. So far so good; but seldom good enough as well because what may count as "good" reasons, consistent with the letter and spirit of the Constitution, varies from time to time. The rule by reason presenting a terrain of growth of indefinite and indeterminate adjudicative State power always falls short of the rule of reason.

In any evaluation, however, of the OIALF judicial role and function, we need always to remember that courts and justices may not act alone, but rather in partnership with the Bar. The OIALF developed in a tradition of lawyering where some outstanding jurist-lawyers who mimed as well as mined the Anglo-American jurisprudence as a resource, perfecting it for their own individual credentials, while still acting also truly as officers of the court advancing responsible and responsive judicial decision-making cultures. They served their clientele rather well but within a discipline of argumentative tradition, a discipline that has since then been almost altogether dissipated; that is, the Bar has ceased to act as a learned profession guiding justices and courts to assist them to achieve the best possible performance of constitutional justicing and reincarnates itself as conduit of legal business, promoting the worst forms of pressing partisan interests. This becomes clearly manifest, as we note later, in the CIALF.

Far from constituting a vulgar jibe at the changing character of the Indian Bar, I offer this observation by way of a complex sociological remark. When the practice of law becomes primarily profit and power-oriented business, courts and justices remain severely lonely in speaking to some higher principles addressing the future of Indian constitutionalism, beyond the instant imprisonment of meanings of fair play vociferously urged before them by the Bar. We may accordingly benefit a great deal at the outset by essaying an understanding of the changing histories and forms of the IAL formations as markers of incarceration or capture of judicial power by vested or special interests, and of the practices of judicial or juridical submission as well as resistance against this. A most fruitful way of reading this admirable book is to ask at every turn of its page a simple question: How far the changing composition and character of the Indian Bar, in ways amnesic of its own constitutional and social responsibility, may be said to have affected the IAL judicial beings and doings? This question remains particularly poignant in the contemporary lawyerly and judicial IAL practice.

Leaving this momentarily aside, the old administrative law petitioners comprised at least four types of paradigmatic litigants, namely, economic actors contesting an era of control and command economy, the later forms of Indian State finance capitalism, Article 22 citizens contesting the preventive detention regime, Article 311 Indian citizens contesting the privileges of political masters over civil servants, and Article 31 citizens seeking to protect their property rights. I later elaborate how an engagement with who uses the IAL, for what purposes, and what resultant effects remain imperative for understanding the itineraries of the IAL development.

5. THE NEW IAL FORMATION (NIALF)

The NIALF preserves as well as reconstitutes past doctrinal or normative judicial achievements. The first phase occurs in the post-Emergency era of cathartic and populist judicial activism.[9] In part, *Kesavananda Bharati* v. *State of Kerala*[10] (*Kesavananda Bharati*) enunciation inaugurates this era. The languages of essentiality, of "essential features" (especially via *Delhi Laws Act, 1912, re*[11]) now travel so far as to prescribe some difficult limits for the amendatory powers of Parliament, acting under Article 368. *Kesavananda Bharati* marks a "merger and acquisition" (to use the gracious languages of corporate law) fully assimilating the doctrines of IAL into a new judicial re-writing of the Indian Constitution. What thus comes to pass remains in some respects simply incredible!

Maneka Gandhi v. *Union of India*[12] (*Maneka Gandhi*) and its immensely varied progeny continues to re-write the text of Articles 14 and 21, thus recasting altogether the adjudicatory policy postures of the OILAF. The equality before the law and equal protection of law under Article 14 auspices means in this era that IAL writ-petitioners may no longer be required to discharge any evidentiary thresholds showing violation of the

9. *See*, Upendra Baxi, *The Indian Supreme Court and Politics* (Eastern Book Company, Lucknow 1980) and *Courage, Craft and Contention: The Indian Supreme Court in Mid-Eighties* (N.M. Tripathi, Bombay 1985); and *generally see*, S.P. Sathe, *Judicial Activism in India* (OUP, Delhi 2002).
10. (1973) 4 SCC 225.
11. (1978) 1 SCC 248.
12. *Ibid.*

enumerated rights under Part III of the Constitution. All that they now need to do is to chant the mantra of arbitrary and unreasonable State action! No more, do the old Article 14 doctrine of reasonable State action (via the devices of "reasonable classification" which so much animated the OIALF) discipline the ways of constitutional and IAL lawyering; all that matters is the forensic outcry of "arbitrariness". The justices, in turn, proceed to all the rest of the work on their own furnishing, as it were the very being or soul of judicial activism! Much the same remains entailed in the judicial rewriting of Article 21, which now runs a constitutional cursor over the phrase "procedure established by law" and entirely substitutes it by the full judicial interpretive plenitude of the "due process of law". From then on, the ISC remarkably proceeds with sincere constitutional intensity in mandating many new disciplinary imperatives on State action. Fair play NJ doctrines thus remain immortally constitutionalised with, and since, *Maneka Gandhi*. Nothing now escapes strict constitutional scrutiny of the manifold forms of dispensation of State largess (as Chapters 5–10 illustrate so well).

Via the NIALF itineraries, the ISC remarkably extends judicial discipline over the forms of constitutional executive action, especially as concerns even the deployment of Article 356 powers. It thus reinvents the doctrine of basic structure via the decision in *State of Rajasthan* v. *Union of India*[13] holding, overall, that because lacking any "reasonable nexus" between the reasons disclosed and the "satisfaction" of the President of India, the exercise of these powers is in fact mala fide. *S.R. Bommai* v. *Union of India*[14] further epitomises the NIALF. And the democratisation of standing via SAL declares an open door for all kinds of social actors, who crowd the courts complaining about arbitrariness of the exercise of State discretionary power, well beyond the already identified principal groups that dominated the landscape of the "old" IAL. The constitutionally-worst off peoples now occupy the centre stage of the theatres of IAL (*see,* Chapter 10 and some concluding remarks later in this introduction).

Much more needs to be said concerning the NIALF. Space constraints allow me only one reference to the extraordinary sway of *Ramana Dayaram Shetty* v. *International Airport Authority of India*[15] (*Shetty*)

---

13. (1977) 3 SCC 592.
14. (1994) 3 SCC 1 carries this logic further by its insistence that basic structure doctrine authorises full judicial review of Art. 356 powers. The recent Bihar dissolution case, [*Rameshwar Prasad (6)* v. *Union of India*, (2006) 2 SCC 1] carries the complex unfolding even further.
15. (1979) 3 SCC 489.

which now brings a large number of administrative authorities, as Prof. Massey puts this, in the "gravitational orbit" of the term State in Article 12 of the Constitution.[16] Clearly, larger the notion of "State", the greater also remains the scope of judicial review over administrative action. However, even in this first explosive NIALF moment and in the hands of even so imaginative a justice as Praful Bhagwati, corporate identity and power continues to escape constitutional and human rights obligations. Prof. Massey acutely laments this (and I fully agree) that the ISC has consistently "missed a unique opportunity" for insisting that "the corporate device will not be allowed to be used as a barrier... ousting the Constitutional Control of Fundamental Rights"[17]. The interesting structural question is of course not whether but rather why this opportunity was missed or not fully seized, when it remained entirely judicially possible to do so.

The question thus posed is of supreme importance: Should constitutional and related IAL interpretive techniques and imagination altogether leave out "non-State" but also many "State-like" actors, who exercise powers of life and death over citizens and peoples? Prof. Massey is entirely justified in asking why the ISC failed to follow the US Supreme Court decisions enunciating a doctrine of "State action" which travelled so far as to frontally attack racial segregation in zones of otherwise non-State entities and operations ruling, for instance, that because the State licenses places of entertainment, public facilities such as parks, pubs, and related public places, these may not remain immune from strict constitutional scrutiny. Somehow, the judicial metaphysic of what constitutes the "State" under Article 12 remains fully aborted in the NIALF; remarkably, it fails to more fully reach out to human rights responsibilities of business entities and corporations. This furnishes, at least for my purposes, as good a starting point as any for further grasp of transition from the "new" to the "contemporary" IAL formation.

6. CONTEMPORARY IAL FORMATION (CIALF)

CIALF formation begins to take shape with the new economic policy—the NEP—directed towards the relaxation in one sense, and the near-total liquidation in another sense, of the control and command economy models. The NEP measures/policies are driven by a desire to promote faster economic growth which also propels India to the status of a major economic world

16. *See infra,* Chap. 8.
17. *M.C. Mehta* v. *Union of India*, (1987) 1 SCC 395, 413.

power. The varied processes of liberalisation of the economy are guided by the standard "neoliberal" agenda pursuing vigorously policy measures, which include the following:

(1) *Denationalisation*: a process of privatisation of resources earlier owned, managed or controlled by the State as a lead economic actor, State assets.
(2) *Disinvestment*: that is, sale of State property and assets in the market overt to private bidders.
(3) *Deregulation*: that is, dismantling of legislation and administrative action that earlier entailed some serious-minded engagement by the government to ensure that the constitutionally worst-off Indians are not entirely sacrificed at the altar of high economic growth rate; the most important policy here is the pursuit of "flexible labour markets" (that is, a continuing diminution of the rights of the organised and disorganised working/labouring peoples).
(4) *De-reservation*: that is, no constitutional obligation for the so-called "weaker sections of society" may constitute any part of Indian and multinational corporations' inheritance of erstwhile State assets [the ISC remains insistent in its most recent ruling in *Ashoka Kumar Thakur* v. *Union of India*[18] that private education institutions may not as yet, indeed if ever, attract the discipline of the newly announced regime of the OBC reservations].
(5) *De-juridicalisation*: that is, via the constitution of new forms and formats of independent regulatory agencies which now control and shape the agendum for judicial review.
(6) *De-politicisation*: that is, claims of new economic rationalism which insist that neither judicial nor human rights/social movement actors may have the competence, nor even a modicum of the legitimacy to interrogate neoliberal policies and programs.
(7) *De-constitutionalisation*: that is, the articulation of the sovereign executive policy for economic development under whose auspices "development" remains best defined by regimes of executive policy, responsible to the community of direct foreign investors (and their normative cohorts such as the international financial institutions and the Northern governmental aid and development bureaus) rather

18. (2008) 6 SCC 1.

than *primarily* to the Indian citizens, especially the constitutionally worst-off.

These several "Ds" constitute the constitutive contexts of CIALF. Obviously, Indian courts and justices now declare NJ very differently. A wide, and indeed constitutionally vast, margin of appreciation is now accorded to executive discretion which shapes macroeconomic policy, including trade and investment decisions. The ISC now variously declares itself incapable of reviewing acts of such policy. The question stands now posed no longer in terms of applying strict constitutional scrutiny of "the lush field of administrative law", but rather entails forms of accelerated ways of judicial exit out of these.[19] The major figure here is the "policy" realm over which justices now relinquish all judicial review control.

As before, the ISC says that the choice of policy is for the [executive] decision-maker and not [for] the court.[20] This in itself remains an unexceptionable observation. But the question always has been how may courts speak to this realm when confronted by the claim that acts of policy stand indicted of violation of binding law and constitutional rights? Despite some manifest, despite judicial sound-bytes to the contrary,[21] the ISC in effect now tells us (in a recent decision in *M.P. Mathur* v. *DTC*[22]) that "once public interest is accepted as a superior equity", it can "override individual equity" and if aggrieved individuals could be said to have anticipated revision or change in policy, they may not crowd the courts with a complaint either that their legitimate expectations stand violated nor may they claim any promissory estoppel (both judicially crafted IAL doctrines).[23] The facts of the case further suggest that the creditor (Government of India) constrained in part the debtor [Delhi Transport Corporation (DTC)] to resile from an earlier beneficial policy and concurred further with the DTC policy change.[24] The federal creditor-debtor rationality thus enacted as "superior equity" now.

19. See, *State of Arunachal Pradesh* v. *Nezone Law House*, (2008) 5 SCC 609, 614 (*per* Dr Arijit Pasayat J, emphasis added).
20. *Ibid*, 615.
21. The doctrine of "proportionality" makes the test of unreasonable or arbitrariness even more complicated than before, as now it has two judicially enunciated components described as "balancing" and "necessity" tests: see, *Coimbatore District Central Coop. Bank* v. *Employees Assn.*, (2007) 4 SCC 669, paras. 18, 19, 21 (*per* C.K. Thakkar J). The "necessity" "test" *requires infringement of human rights to the least restrictive alternative* [SCC 678, para. 19 (emphasis added)].
22. (2006) 13 SCC 706.
23. *Ibid*, para. 13. *See also*, paras. 12, 13, 14, 15, 17, 18.
24. *Ibid*, para. 12.

Further, a new CIALF understanding now seeks to guide us to an understanding that the old NJ doctrines are no more than fungible instruments of adjudicatory policy. NJ conceptions are now presented frankly as a series of "recruits" to a long list of concepts fashioned by the courts for the review of administrative actions.[25] Some conceptual recruits thus may be summarily court-martialed as well! This happened clearly in *Indian Airlines Officers' Assn.* v. *Indian Airlines Ltd.*[26], where the employees of the Indian Airlines were held not denied NJ because of non-consultation with them. The ISC is candid, "The employees of Indian Airlines did not and could not have any say in policy-making." Even when their rights and interests may be adversely affected, they did not have any NJ right to be heard prior to policy enunciation and even, as turns out, subsequent to it! "Non-participation" of the employee association "would not be fatal to policy decision"[27]. All this happens as if Article 43-A, directive principle, mandating worker participation in management was excised away by judicial interpretation.

I may not further (given space constraints) elaborate the judicially promoted exclusions from the "lush fields of administrative law" save to fully note that every time a departure is made from the OIALF or NIALF, Their Lordships are careful to emphasise that their decisions remained based on "the facts and circumstances of the case". Prima facie, of course, this makes a lot of sense when the IAL stands conceived as constitutional common law. However, this remains a curious fact, to say the very least, because taken seriously, such judicial averments actually diminish the ISC to the dimensions of a trial court, the ISC thus problematises its own scaling some dizzying heights in making and declaring constitutional law under Articles 141 and 142 powers! This further underscores the need for the restoration of the constitutional dignity of the summit court.

One may well ask, "What thus remains by way of the normative stuff of the IAL?" The short answer is: nothing or very little! I know that this is a strong statement, yet, reading Prof. Massey's account of some recent IAL developments, it leaves no better alternative. Deciding on the facts and circumstances of each case, without simultaneous affirmation of the vital NJ principles, facilitates the CIALF aggressively free-market friendly, rather than human-rights friendly, postures. The development of

25. *State of Arunachal Pradesh* v. *Nezone Law House*, (2008) 5 SCC 609, 615, para. 15.
26. (2007) 10 SCC 684.
27. *Ibid*, para. 38.

the constitutional muscle now favours the communities of direct foreign investors and constituencies of the global capital over the bleeding-heart human rights talk of the NIALF. In complete plain words, justices and courts now seem to pursue a new IAL adjudicatory policy taking-off the register of high adjudicative power any active citizen recourse confronting the seven Ds. No doubt, the CIALF continues to lisp the alphabet of natural justice; yet this now comprises a different narrative altogether, as compared and contrasted with the old and the new IAL formation.

7. IAL, GLOBAL ADMINISTRATIVE LAW (GAL) AND GLOBALISING ADMINISTRATIVE LAW (GOAL)

A new genre of IAL has thus emerged via a network of regulatory institutions, and the attendant cultures of administrative adjudication, directed more to the goals of regulatory efficiency and less to conceptions of constitutional justice. The erstwhile judicial control over administrative powers is now slowly slipping into new and complex relationships between the ISC and the new regulatory agencies. If so, how may we address at all fully the distinction between the "old", "new", and "contemporary" forms of the IAL? May it be the case that the CIALF will steadily supplant the "old" and "new" IAL formations in the next decade or so? Put another way; given the seven Ds—overall summating the shift from public into privatised realms of Indian governance—would the IAL as we once-upon-a time knew it survive at all? Chapter 16 does at least implicitly raise this question.

7.1 The GAL

GAL, clearly a theoretical construct and a research field developed by relatively disinterested and autonomous academicians interested in legal comparison, always sensitive to legal and adjudicative histories yet articulating some commonalities across cultures. It offers some terms of decent respect for human rights languages and the transcendent claims and aspirations for global justice. The nascent GAL movement suggest ways for the redirection and renewal of the potential of national administrative power and law formation towards a more effective pursuit of human rights (as internationally and constitutionally recognised). GAL, further, opens up some creative activist spaces, directing attention to a fine regard for the principles of natural justice in global and transnational administrative law systems (whether in the theatres of the United Nations system, European

Union, or multilateral trade and investment regimes). Prof. Massey captures this mood, method, and message admirably when he observes (in the concluding sentences of Chapter 14) that "... the demand for a global administrative law based on freedom, equality, justice, and accountability" remains "... imperative for a new world order based on inclusiveness and equity" always directed to well being of the worst-off peoples.

7.2 The GOAL

In contrast what I here name as GOAL (globalising administrative law) remains pervasively dedicated to foster the ends of "free-market" economy and fully directed towards fashioning some new forms of inherently market-friendly regulation. In GOAL, overall, what decisively matters is business/economic efficiency conceived as the kernel of social justice. This means, in sum, that the new regulatory agencies should more effectively promote the aims of efficient privatisation of the ownership of means of production. GOAL further translates the very notions of citizenship in terms of "financial", "market", and "consumer", forms; thus citizenship becomes increasingly less a political conception and more a device interlinking the emergent universal globalising middle classes.[28] Citizenship is either perceived in the imagery of stakeholders or that of consumers that is reconfigured as the new "citizens" of a "free" global marketplace.

I may here only invite your attention to two pioneering studies:

(1) Navroz K. Dubash and D. Narasimha Rao, *The Practice and Politics of Regulation Regulatory Governance in Indian Electricity*[29]; and

(2) Vikram Raghavan, *Communications Law in India: Legal Aspects of Telecom, Broadcasting and Cable Services.*[30]

28. *See*, for these notions, Frank J Garcia, "The Global Market and Human Rights: Trading Away the Human Rights Principle", (1999) 25 Brooklyn Journal of International Law 51–97; John Braithwaite, and Peter Drahos, *Global Business Regulation* (Cambridge University Press, Cambridge 2000); Stephen Gill (2000), "The Constitution of Global Capitalism", <www.theglobalsite.ac.uk> (last accessed 28-5-2003); Stephen Gill, *Power and Resistance in the New World Order* (Palgrave-McMillan, New York 2003); David Schneiderman, "Investment Rules and the New Constitutionalism", (2000) 25 Law and Social Inquiry 757–86; and Schneiderman, *Constitutionalizing Economic Globalization: Investment Rules and Democracy's Promise* (Cambridge University Press, Cambridge 2008). *See further*, James Thuo Gathii, "International Justice and the Trading Regime", (2005) 19 Emory International Law Review 1407–30; Robert McCorquodale and Penelope Simons, "Responsibility Beyond Borders: State Responsibility for Extraterritorial Violations by Corporations of International Human Rights Law", (2007) 70:4 Modern Law Review 597–635; and Upendra Baxi, *The Future of Human Rights* (3rd Edn. OUP, Delhi and Oxford 2008) Chap. 9.
29. (Macmillan, Delhi, India 2007).
30. (Lexis-Nexis, Butterworths, Delhi 2007).

Both these works now fully complicate any fuller understanding of the futures of the old IAL and its already heavily battered adjudicatory futures.

A wholly new GOAL-directed intermix/remake of IAL is now fully under way. As Dubash and Rao rather fully illustrate, GOAL invites full deliberative attention to the privatisation of regulatory governance "beyond the legal [the IAL constituted] framework" towards "regulation in practice, its politics"[31]. GOAL-directed IAL accentuate the technical over the political element; its "apolitical façade" produces a state of affairs in which "politically driven investment choices [manage] to escape scrutiny of regulators and stakeholders"[32]. The IAL thus no longer names a field of tension, marking the relationship between the State actors and citizens. A new category of regulatory and finance/corporate citizenship thus stands incarnated, dissipating the idea of the constitutional citizenship. Neither the regulators, nor the stakeholders (nor also the globalised consumer classes) remain constitutionally sincere citizen-actors who may fully contest the logics and languages of macro-developmental, neoliberal, or hyper-globalising economic policies. Vikram Raghavan, overall, offers a different, and a constitutionally hopeful, take in which IAL languages and doings still remain central, even when not finally decisive.

Thus, unfolds a new ledger of distinction among the elected (oathed citizens) and the unelected (the un-oathed citizens). Unlike Indian judicial actors, regulatory agents remain relatively uncluttered by the obligations of oath which prescribe fidelity to the Indian Constitution. The oathless Indian citizens who operate the logics and languages of privatised regulation no doubt stand confronted occasionally by oath-taking Indian judicial citizens. Yet, it increasingly remains the case that the emergent new regulatory agencies and actors now systematically overshadow, for weal or woe, the adjudicatory prowess of a sphere hitherto known as the IAL, constituted by fully-oathed citizen-justices. Perhaps, Prof. Massey, as well as his readers, may ponder more fully the rather uncertain futures of the "old" IAL already thus constituted.

8. WHO WINS AND WHO LOSES UNDER THE RULE OF LAW?

Regardless of the majestic promises of the rule of law (ROL) talk, not everyone remains its equal beneficiary. Yet, we are commonly told that

31. Navroz K. Dubash and D. Narasimha Rao, *The Practice and Politics of Regulation Regulatory Governance in Indian Electricity* (Macmillan, Delhi, India 2007) ix.
32. *Ibid*, xiii.

even those who are not equal beneficiaries of the ROL goods should believe that it is a better sort of society than the "non-rule-of-law" societies, characterised by the fact of no accountability of the rulers to the ruled. In contrast, the ROL societies do proclaim, in theory, much greater scope of accountability. Those who are ruled are thus said to be not entirely at the mercy of those who rule. But there is a difference between regimes of general as contrasted with specifically detailed regimes of political accountability/responsibility. That is why even in a ROL society, there remains scope for grave and continuing excesses of power, whether spectacular or routine. Thus, fully emerge some jurisprudential needs to evolve specific and concrete mechanisms of accountability in addition to the diffused and general ones like elections, impeachment, public opinion, etc. It is this search for new and effective mechanisms to make holders of public power adhere to the law and justify the exercise of power in terms of law, policy and constitutional values, which distinguishes a ROL society from others. The basic expectation in a ROL society is, as this narrative would have us believe by sheer narrative power or force of repetition, that the holders of public power and authority must be able to publicly justify their action as legally valid and even socially wise and just.

In modern societies, wide powers vest with legislators, judges and administrators. Each group can act, if it so wished, quite arbitrarily in any or all of the ways thus far specified. Or, as also happens, one group may quite arbitrarily assume control over the functioning of the other; often enough it may not be the group, but just one single person. In this latter case, we speak of dictatorship or tyranny. When one group with a strong leader concentrates all powers in itself, we speak of "authoritarianism". When power is dispersed in dominant institutions of governance and when those affected by power can, in theory, hold their rulers accountable (in one way or the other), we speak of a liberal democracy or a "rule-of-law society". This type of society basically seeks to ensure that grants of power to the rulers are at the same time charters of accountability for the ruled.[33]

Naturally, this effort does not wholly or even substantially succeed. But what matters is, we are constantly told, that the effort is made at all

33. The distinction between forms of polity made in the text is rather simplistic. Concepts like "authoritarianism" and "liberal democracy" have acquired rich and diverse historic meanings. We must accept the fact that even forms of democracy vary; there exist "non-liberal democracies" with rather distinctive mechanisms of political accountability. See, C.B. MacPherson, *The Real World of Democracy* (Clarendon Press, Oxford 1972); S.E. Finer, *Comparative Government* (Penguin, London 1970).

and the underlying conviction is that such an endeavour is worthwhile and necessary. And one would like to think that one general result of such an effort in the long run would be to help diminish arbitrariness in the exercise of public power. This progressive diminution of arbitrariness in the exercise of public power is ultimately what the rule-of-law notion is all about.[34] Indeed, in one sense, that is what we mean, and ought to mean, by a "civilised society".

Precisely because the IAL celebrates this ideology, it becomes necessary to pose the question of winners and losers. Of course, even this talk remains confined to those with access to courts and legal professionals; those priced out of legal services and judicial markets are as it were "born losers". I would urge you to just look at the name of the parties in the case citations in order to understand who activate the IAL jurisdiction the most in each IAL formation; now, it remains for me to briefly elaborate four categories of the regular or systemic users of the IAL in each phase.

My first category of super-citizens comprise Article 311 citizens or more broadly the civil servants (a category to which many young readers of the book aspire to as would-be civil servants!) As a class, these are beings who marshal unto themselves (at least until superannuation) the "sovereign" power to harm and hurt the ordinary citizens. A related second category comprises the elected public officials and those belonging to political parties, possessed of a similar capacity to cause hurt and harm to *aam admi* (the lay folks). And these include some evergreen political actors who somehow continue to "represent" India. Both classes resent the growth of IAL judicial power at least while in office; both also applaud this public virtue when out of power. Thus, the super-citizens develop an ambivalent (love/hate) relationship with the forms of constitutional judicial review powers and processes. The tragedy of IAL consists in just this fact. The in service Article 311 super-citizens derive the maximal advantages of the doctrine of natural justice (fully protecting their security of tenure and other unwelcome intrusions—such as arbitrary postings) and, yet, routinely deny this to ordinary citizens caught within the web of their administrative powers. They maintain that the very advantages they seek for themselves may yet be difficult of a fuller extension to ordinary citizens, given the dynamics of exigent public administration and regulation, in turn a sphere best protected by immunity from judicial review. Even so, they have no

34. *Cf*, Philip Selznick, with the collaboration of Philippe Nonet and Howard M. Vollmer, *Law, Society and Industrial Justice* (Russell Sage Foundation, New York 1969).

compunction whatsoever in invoking these processes and powers to defend their own rights and interests versus their "political masters". What at one moment is represented as an unwarranted and capricious exercise of judicial power becomes at another moment a legitimate function, nay even a duty, of adjudicatory power! This kindergarten see-saw perspective of role and function of IAL jurisprudence stands fully illustrated poignantly by these Article 311 ILA-induced formations.[35]

The third category of super-citizens are people I would like to name as "Gurubhai" citizens, in recognition of a recent Bollywood blockbuster production entitled "Guru". These represent an ensemble of trade, business and industrial citizens, who otherwise fully and strategically allied with the political (ruling) classes, yet crowd the courts presenting themselves as vulnerable citizen-victims of "arbitrary" administrative action! One way to tell stories about the IAL remains just this: a class of super-citizens who otherwise specialise in the denial of fair play and human rights of the working "classes" appear as IAL litigants, constituting a series of *vulnerable* social groups! The producer of the recent mega-movie indeed remained innocent of reading administrative law treatises; however, no student of the IAL may afford to ignore the message of the film as providing an entrepreneurial classes' critique of State regulatory action. In the concluding scenes of the film, addressing the tribunal investigating unethical and unlawful business practices and some huge public interest violations, Gurubhai in effect conveys the following powerful message: The energy of capitalist classes in making a new India may not be dammed by laws and enquiries; when we can get way with cajoling and corrupting the ruling classes, we will do so; otherwise, we will kick lustily at the doors closed by the so-called regime of law and regulation. Not merely the audience at the tribunal lustily applauds this statement, even the tribunal is moved to conclude the proceeding by an award of symbolic fine! Not being a film critic, or a social theorist of the mass media, puts me at disadvantage in estimating the overall social effects of this powerfully constructed message but, as a student of Indian law, it is clear that the IAL practitioners and even some justices are listening closely!

In saying thus, I do not mean to contest the experienced social fact that civil servants and businesspersons actually feel exploited or harassed or unjustly treated. No doubt, a microscopic community of conscientious civil servants and honest industrialists often feel discriminated against, and even

35. *See,* U. Baxi (Ed.), *Rama Jois' Civil Services Under the State* (1989 Edn. N.M. Tripathi, Bombay 1989).

persecuted, by arbitrary State action. And their sense of victimage thus experienced is quite real, and the IAL serves some valuable sites for the vindication of their due process rights-claims. Yet, it also remains the case that a majority of Article 311 and "Gurubhai" citizens also remain entirely constitutionally insincere because the duties of fair play they claim for themselves (a theatre maximising their profit and power) they remain loathe to extend to the constitutionally worst-off peoples. What these classes have in common is just this: for these, the IAL constitutes no transcendent moral pedagogy, no actually operative ethic of everyday governance power, and no messages for corporate governance and related business practices. The exceptions, as always, prove the rule!

The fourth category signifies a rather miscellaneous category of the Indian middle classes, who indeed enjoy and manipulate the blessings of IAL developments in different moments of Indian constitutional development. They have exploited, fascinatingly, every nook and cranny of an indeterminate development of IAL jurisprudence, naturally, to their own advantage. Perhaps, "middle classes" is too amorphous a term[36] as some salient illustrations help us to understand:

(1) Systemic recourse by university students who regularly invoke administrative law jurisprudence to stay action against them on manifest grounds of discipline or unfair means (*i.e.* cheating at exams) or admissions to professional courses.[37]

(2) Some spectacular recourse towards self-promotion even by university teachers![38]

---

36. *See*, Upendra Baxi, "The Avatars of Judicial Activism: Explorations in the Geography of (in) Justice" in S.K. Verma and Kusum (Eds.), *Fifty Years of the Supreme Court of India* (Indian Law Institute, New Delhi 2000) 159–209.

37. Of the latter category, the most recent example was furnished by an elaborate *inquisition of* the Law School Admission Test conducted by Delhi University and actual admissions made in a particular year. In one proceeding, I was directed to file an affidavit, as the Vice-Chancellor of Delhi University. The Delhi High Court orders and judgments indicate that universities are *suspect* institutions and that any person—student or aspiring student need not meet even the *slightest* burden of proof at the stage of admission. What is more, such persons and their lawyers seem India wide to enjoy impunity from even judicial strictures or reprimands, let alone credible sanctions for perjury.

38. The most spectacular writ in this regard was by a Delhi law teacher before the Delhi High Court insisting that the UGC Merit Promotion Scheme, which considered "equivalent publications" as an alternative to a Ph.D. in Law, *in effect* estopped the university from saying that he was not *constructively* holding a Ph.D. degree of Delhi University. *See*, *Shyam Sunder Vats* v. *Delhi University*, a writ petition continued without disposal by the Delhi High Court for a number of years and finally withdrawn. The petitioner, no doubt, had obtained a letter from the Registrar saying that for purposes of merit promotion his publications were, under the relevant guidelines, equivalent to Ph.D. degree. What Their Lordships would have finally decided is *unknowable*. But for that entire period, a candidate duly selected as a Professor

(3) Judicial cloning of a hybrid of stay-order Indian humanity, manifest in situations where students, academics, highly designated government officials, even stay-order Vice-Chancellors (as Shri Hardwari Lal's court-extended tenures at Maharshi Dayanand University at Rohtak) assume or occupy statuses created by chaotic judicial interim orders and even verdicts.

(4) Successful deflection of all sensible regulatory efforts advantaging industries as shown in *Workers* v. *Rohtas Industries Ltd.*[39] and *LIC* v. *Escorts Ltd.*[40]

(5) Empowerment of eco-enemies (forest contractors, miners, dam builders, polluters of Holy Ganges and manifestly corrupt politicians), which stymie the reach of rectificatory action by appealing to various tragic-comic invocations of natural justice maxims and principles.

(6) Deployment by political actors and parties of the grounds of natural justice that contest the Election Commission's decisions on re-polling[41] and related matters.

Prof. Massey understandably endorses a conception of the activist IAL adjudicatory postures, wherein the "chances of injury" of arbitrary action by powerful, economic, and governance (political) interests "must be eliminated"[42], rather than merely "punished". I cannot agree more with Massey's wish-list, as it were. However, the histories of IAL adjudication also show, even in the hands of India's most gifted and socially compassionate justices, the IAL developments as constituting an epic of sorrow for the vast masses of the suffering Indian humanity. The typically formatted IAS narratives comprise some combinatory elements of fairy tales and horror stories.

held his post subject to final orders. And the status of the highest degree a university could confer remained indeterminate!

The petitioner, an able law teacher, was subsequently merit-promoted by the university to the Chair. Obviously, the Delhi University's decision was based on its due process of academic appointments. The possibility which the High Court raised by its entertaining the petition was that courts could issue *mandamus* to universities for conferment of constructive doctorates, and that too in *law*!

39. 1994 Supp (2) SCC 359.
40. (1986) 1 SCC 264.
41. *Mohinder Singh Gill* v. *Chief Election Commr.*, (1978) 1 SCC 405. Of course, this citation has a slightly musty air because since then the Election Commission has evoked cooperation of the Supreme Court to reinforce its autonomy as well contested its jurisdiction in defence of its own autonomy. Even as this introduction goes to press, the Commission has successfully persuaded the court to the view that even it lacks power to stay Rajya Sabha polls once announced by the Commission.
42. *See infra*, Chap. 5.

9. ENGAGING THE BHOPAL CATASTROPHE AS A WAY OF PARADIGMATIC UNDERSTANDING OF THE IAL

There are in fact several Bhopal catastrophes starting with the devastating catastrophe of 2–3 December 1984 Bhopal catastrophe, further replicated by a second Bhopal catastrophe that occurred with the judicial settlement orders immunising the Union Carbide Corporation, the third catastrophe constituted the callous and long-drawn disbursement of the compensation amount, and the fourth catastrophe comprised of a never-ending story of official neglect and political indifference towards the sorrowful plight of the Bhopal victims. The Bhopal "victims" underwent a ceaseless IAL/GOAL directed process of adjudicatory fashioned re-victimage.

Each and every Bhopal catastrophe violated IAL. Indian citizen knows a few cruel truths concerning the much-vaunted tradition of doing IAL justice, Indian-style. Indian humanity has experienced, at each step of its unfolding tragic life in the aftermath of these severally and jointly constructed catastrophes, the cruel hollowness of the commanding doctrines of the IAL, otherwise superbly crafted by some of India's (and the world's) gifted justices. If the canonical IAL doctrine and craft required that public decisions ought to be taken in consultation with affected interests, at no stage in the past two-plus decades have the Bhopal victims enjoyed the blessings of this maxim. They were denied the right of being heard, even when parties to proceedings, when the Supreme Court arrived at a settlement, wholly adverse to their claims, interests, and dignity. The post-decisional hearing accorded to them after the settlement only aggravates the initial judicial default: it does not cast on the Union Carbide Corporation beyond the initial settlement amount any legal responsibility for the amelioration of their plight; nor are the governments of the Union of India and the State of Madhya Pradesh required systematically to redress the continuing human rights violation of the Bhopal victims. The *Bhopal case* demonstrates extraordinary judicial paternalism that erases all the way the languages of human rights, justice, and core due process obligations.[43] Much the same IAL governance stories remain cruelly replicated for the survivors of the 1974 Sikh genocide and 2002 Gujarat riots,[44] not to here

43. *See*, Upendra Baxi, "The 'Just War' for Profit and Power: The Bhopal Catastrophe and the Principle of Double Effect" in Lene Bomann-Larsen and Oddny Wiggen (Eds.), *Responsibility in World Business: Managing Harmful Side-Effects of Corporate Activity* (The United Nations University Press, Tokyo 2004) 175–201.

44. *See*, as concerns Gujarat 2002, Upendra Baxi, "The Gujarat Catastrophe: Notes on Reading Politics as Democidal Rape Culture" in Kalpana Kannabiran (Ed.), *The Violence of Normal Times: Essays on Women's Lived Realities* (New Delhi) 332–83.

mention the judicially mandated demolition drives of human habitats for the Indian impoverished in several 2007 judicial decisions.

How may we fully grasp the erosion of administrative norms in the Bhopal saga and related theatres of mass atrocities and disasters? How may we thus even begin to tell the different stories about the IAL-led, and also caused, citizen-victimage? The GOAL-directed IAL performances continue to determine the contexts, conditions, and circumstances in which fundamental abrogation of doctrines of natural justice are regarded as fully legitimate; how, on this register, may GAL-type understanding further assist the Indian impoverished and disenfranchised citizen-peoples? In any event, how may forms of creative judicial empathy develop, given the fact that overall neither eminent justices nor lawyers—those who impart authority to the IAL doings—may stand to overall benefit but never suffer from these performances?

The everyday producers of IAL norms and standards remain distant from the victimage that they recurrently produce. Put another way, and rather starkly, their life projects remain seldom affected by the IAL decisions they make for other Indian co-citizens. Nor do those who tell the IAL stories—these epistemic communities that produce knowledges about that something named as "administrative law",—do necessarily bear in their individual lifetimes the brunt of its costs. Of course here again the exceptions prove the rule! Thus, even some justices of the Supreme Court in the *Bhopal case* complained that they were being "victimised"[45], when all that happened was the appeal by Bhopal victims that Their Lordships adhere to their own natural justice jurisprudence, proclaimed most notably in *A.R. Antulay* v. *R.S. Nayak*[46] (*Antulay*)![47] And in (the first and the last instance in independent India) *Sarojini Ramaswami* v. *Union of India*[48], the impugned justice claimed several violations of natural justice by his own Brethren.[49] Think, for a moment, about hundreds of thousands of Bombay (now Mumbai) pavement-dwellers. In *Olga Tellis* v. *Bombay*

45. Confronted with victim, activist and media criticism, often strident, of the Bhopal settlement orders, and especially by description of the settlement orders as constituting a second Bhopal catastrophe, E.S. Venkataramiah J at one point stated, in the open court, that public expression of outrage was worse than facing an impeachment!
46. (1988) 2 SCC 602.
47. For analysis of the Antulay discourse, *see*, U. Baxi, *Liberty and Corruption: Antulay Case and Beyond* (Eastern Book Co., Lucknow 1990).
48. (1992) 4 SCC 506.
49. *See*, S. Sahay, *Gone At Last?: The Story of V. Ramaswani's Impeachment* (Har-Anand Publications, New Delhi 1993).

Municipal Corpn.[50], a paradigmatic judicial decision which still ails to yield a considered reasoned "judgment"[51], the Indian Supreme Court, while affirming Article 21 life and liberty rights as inclusive of the right to housing and shelter decided, in effect, that no rights of theirs would be violated if the Municipal Commissioner of Bombay was, even without a hearing, to throw them with their belongings to the sea! And in *Union Carbide Corpn.* v. *Union of India*[52], Their Lordships quoted Macbeth to Bhopal victims who urged that a settlement, which denies even a modicum of hearing to them, is legally flawed by the very jurisprudence developed by the Supreme Court. Their Lordships said, "'To do a great right' after all, it is permissible sometimes 'to do a little wrong'."[53] In complete plain words, when the claims of justice of a mighty multinational (a "great right") are pitted against those of hundreds of thousands of children, women and men, radically MIC-infected (a "little" wrong), the "great right" has to prevail![54]

On this perspective, administrative law in India emerges as an archive of production of human rightlessness for the Indian "masses" and a saga of solicitude for the Indian middle "classes"[55]. The superbly crafted doctrines and principles of administrative justice ensure that the Indian rule-of-law notions provide moments of solace to the Indian middle classes against the amorality of the political/executive combine. Doctrines such as promissory estoppel[56] and the more recent doctrine of legitimate

50. (1985) 3 SCC 545.
51. I have consistently maintained that if by a "judgment" we mean a discourse where reasons or grounds of decision have at least *some* bearing on the final result or order, *Olga Tellis* cannot be dignified with that description. The result there so contradicts the operative order as to make it *insensible*, both legally and logically. Not all documents signed by justices and published in law reports necessarily become binding judgments. Undoubtedly, situations in which one would have to take such a stance as I do with respect to *Olga Tellis* would be rare. But when they occur, it is our duty to explain that as a matter of fact *no* "judgment" appears despite a *purported* act of issuing it and our right to insist that the court deliver a *judgment*.
52. (1991) 4 SCC 584.
53. *Charan Lal Sahu* v. *Union of India*, (1990) 1 SCC 613, 705.
54. Note that "little wrong" consisted in (*a*) denying a pre-decisional hearing to victims in the court-approved settlement orders; (*b*) in offering, after a great struggle by victims, a post-decisional fairness hearing, only to hold that the rules of natural justice are not absolute; (*c*) in upholding the settlement amount of $470 million but striking down criminal immunities, without any explanation of how a bargain represented in the settlement can be severed; (*d*) in not retrospectively legitimating, by explicit invocation, the principle of absolute multinational/economic enterprise liability which would avoid future Bhopals. *See*, my "Introduction" to U. Baxi and A. Dhanda (Eds.), *Valiant Victims and Lethal Litigation: The Bhopal Case* (N.M. Tripathi, Bombay 1990).
55. I realize that in deploying the contrast thus, I remain open to the charge that I am using obsolete vocabulary in these halcyon days of globalisation. But for any Indian *human* being, the contrast between "classes" and "masses" must surely be a *livid one*.
56. *See infra*, Chap. 11, and in particular judicial meanderings in *Jit Ram Shiv Kumar* v. *State of Haryana*, (1981) 1 SCC 11.

expectations of economic enterprises,[57] the judicial disinclination to sustain governmental "blacklisting" economic entities without giving them some kind of opportunity of being heard,[58] the requirement of fairness in the award of government contracts[59] continue to favour the middle classes or the constitutional haves. Those urban impoverished recently subjected to massive demolition drives in Delhi and other parts of India may not ever expect to benefit from the doctrine of promissory estoppel (even when they were promised a title in their slums and *bastis*), nor may the hawkers and other street children have any benefit of the extension of the doctrine of "legitimate expectations"! The question how far the worst-off citizens may benefit from the IAL developments remains answered in the negative in several contexts.

First, the constitutionally worst-off peoples are put at a disadvantage in alleging mala fide action by the political rulers and highly placed government officials because the impoverished petitioner must discharge a nearly impossible onus of proof;[60] and doctrines such as acting on "irrelevant considerations"[61], "mechanically or without due care"—a fluctuating corpus of considerations—or even outside powers duly conferred not amounting to acting mala fide simply do not extend to respond to their woes. *Second*, ordinary citizens may not question as excessive delegation the transfer of power of rule-making and adjudication to administrative officials, because the justices say that belief in good faith of administrators is an important marker of a healthy democratic society and polity and distrust of politics, as well as distrust of governments, augurs ill for democracy.[62]

Third, the new CIALF developments continue privileging business entities and interests in more explicit ways than ever before. The "old" LA requirement insisting on consultation with the adversely affected interests

57. *Union of India* v. *Hindustan Development Corpn.*, (1993) 3 SCC 499; *Madras City Wine Merchants' Assn.* v. *State of T.N.*, (1994) 5 SCC 509. I am not as sanguine about the doctrine of legitimate expectations as the author. *See infra*, Chap. 8.

58. *V. Punnen Thomas* v. *State of Kerala*, 1968 SCC OnLine Ker 110: AIR 1969 Ker 81; *Erusian Equipment & Chemicals Ltd.* v. *State of W.B.*, (1975) 1 SCC 70; *Ramana Dayaram Shetty* v. *International Airport Authority of India*, (1979) 3 SCC 489.

59. *See infra*, Chap. 11. The "deficient" development of the doctrine is perhaps inevitable given the admixture or commingling of the realm of "private" (civil) law with "public" (administrative) law.

60. The iron law of onus is embodied in *S. Partap Singh* v. *State of Punjab*, AIR 1964 SC 72.

61. *Ibid.*

62. *Gwalior Rayon Silk Mfg. (Wvg.) Co. Ltd.* v. *CST*, (1974) 4 SCC 98.

Unprincipled adjudicative tolerance of delegated legislation marks (in the present view) a retreat from democracy as well as justice. If making laws consonant with the mandate of the Constitution remains the paramount obligation of legislatures (with attributions of

is held judicially incapable of extension to require that the employees and workers have any "say" concerning decisions about denationalisation and disinvestment. Take further the judicially crafted, and rather finely nuanced, doctrine of "reasoned decision". Who may, after all, decide momentous matters concerning the "reason" and the "unreason" of disinvestment decisions? Should the governmental decisions and decision-making conduct and processes remain subject to any sort of judicial review? Should the ISC under the received IAL doctrine and craft entertain SAL petitions fully impugning executive decisions concerning "disinvestment", even of profit-making statutory corporations/undertakings? Should they further entertain SAL petitions challenging as arbitrary the methods of valuation at which public sector undertakings may be sold (the distinction usually involves contrast between book value of assets and their real market value) and further proceed also to invigilate procedures for international bids of national economic assets to such sale? Or, ought they to leave alone the processes and outcomes of "macroeconomic" choices that elected officials may make from time to time, regardless of their manifest human rights violative short term and long run impact? How may the ISC proceed to invigilate excesses and abuses of hyper-globalising acts of public power? Should judicial performance hold deregulation as rigorously accountable as regulation once was? The old Article 31 jurisprudence imposed, howsoever problematic, the regime of constitutional discipline on arbitrary State conduct taking away or abrogating the right to property without due compensation. Why does it remain the case that the CIALF now remains disinclined to recognise some "new" property rights regimes of the project affected peoples (whether exemplarily and cruelly now constituted by Narmada/Tehri Dam and related iconic figurations) as well as of the urban

representation, accountability, and legitimacy), how does it become *unworkable* to demand, even in a modern state, that legislators make it their prime, if not sole, duty to attend to the business of legislation? One has just to consult the archives of the Lok Sabha Debates to see what minuscule amounts of time are dedicated to the actual form and content of laws wil ly-nilly enacted. I suspect that an easy-minded acceptance of delegated legislation has, after all, virtually left Indian legislators off the hook! Much of the gifts of legislative time and talent remains dedicated to feats of *politicking* (in some very pejorative senses of that term). There is simply no way of avoiding the question: Would Indian democracy have been more substantial a human achievement than it is now, if the Indian judiciary had held delegated legislation to the strictest scrutiny of legislative application of mind to the infinite detail, and labour, of legislation? Reference to the Commonwealth, West European or American experience does not simply help, given the longer and different traditions and histories of their legislation (and democracies). Third, and in any event, judicial abdication monitoring excessive delegation of legislative powers produces a result where legislators who ought to be accountable of their default stand absolved, whereas administrators (who are accountable only to their political superiors) are asked to be the prime agents of the rule-of-law society.

global cities type "infrastructure" development projects? How indeed does it now comes to pass that the new Resident Welfare Associations (RWAs) now stand judicially authorised by SAL-type recourse to fully demolish the life prospects of the urban impoverished citizen-peoples? How may the Indian judiciary help contest the blind-spots of the Indian globalising political elite, which has comprehensively forgotten the ideals that animated struggles for Indian Independence and some of the finest hours of Indian democracy at work? How far, workers made more secure against unfair labour practices by the dynamic interpretation in the new IAL formation may now at all proceed to contest the judicial dismantling of their rights—illustrated in leading decisions such as *State of Karnataka* v. *Umadevi (3)*[63] and the related case law? What prospects of fairness may the hapless Indian citizenry, now further re-constituted and re-crucified by the régime of the constitutional lawlessness of the law and policy regimes of special economic zones, may expect from the CIALF? It is pointless to multiply these instances. The otherwise acknowledged virtuoso judicial feats of the enunciation of the majestic IAL values, norms, and standards, overall, continue to disproportionately benefit the constitutional "haves" to the continuing and eventual detriment of the constitutional have-nots.

10. JUDGING THE JUDGES: FAIRNESS, EFFICIENCY, AND JUDICIAL DISCRETION

Much of the IAL, as well as the SAL, in particular, and constitutional interpretation in general of courts and justices remain just this; they fail themselves to practice what they preach to others; put another way, they do not extend to their own work the maxim, "Wherever there is power, there is responsibility." There is no question that this maxim must extend to the judicial makers of the IAL. This introduction has so far (and the book in many places) expressed deep disappointment with some actual decisions and specific decisional IAL trends because courts and justices have failed to follow some foundational principles of natural justice that they have themselves enunciated. I believe that while judging the judges is a serious enterprise, it remains inevitable as a part of Article 51-A fundamental duty of all citizens to develop "scientific temper" and "spirit of critical enquiry", and further to develop "excellence" in all walks of life.

A larger question is thus raised: What may be the import of these constitutional duties for judging the judges? Put another way, how may

63. (2006) 4 SCC 1.

our criticism remain socially and constitutionally responsible (hereafter "SCRC")? This is of particular importance with regard to feats of judicial creativity and the styles of judicial activism manifest in the SAL justicing. The legitimacy of the SAL is now much questioned and not only by the occasional recent pronouncements of the Prime Minister, Manmohan Singh, but also the Speaker for the Lok Sabha, Somnath Chatterjee; and has been valiantly defended by the former Chief Justice of India, K.G. Balakrishnan J. I do not burden this text with full citations to this exchange, easily available in the newspaper archives, save to say, that we have been there before, that is, similar criticism have occurred many a time earlier in governance rhetorics. Now, in the circumstance of the Indian hyper globalisation, this acquires a poignant edge, because this genre of criticism is aimed at what I have described (in my keynote address at the Golden Jubilee Celebrations of the Indian Law Institute, 2008) as the "structural adjustment of judicial activism".

There is simply no single way in which to describe the tasks and nature of the ECRC of courts and justices at work. Nor is it possible for this introduction to speak about the varieties of approaches to understanding judicial role and function.[64] I have elsewhere argued that

(1) there is no *universal* theory about what judges ought or ought not to do (judicial role);

(2) most purported theories of the judicial role, on deeper analysis, turn out to be relevant to, and drawn from, the experience of the First World societies, and that those may not be uncritically extended to our experience;

(3) the inherited categories of distinction between "legislation" and "adjudication", are, to say the very least, questionable and ought to be questioned[65] *especially when corrupt or intransigent ruling classes tend to relegate the constitutional normativity into a historic dustbin.*

64. *See* for a more recent statement, Ronald Dworkin, *Justice in Robes* (Harvard University Press, Mass. Cambridge 2007; 1st Indian Edn., Universal Law Publishing Co., New Delhi 2007); Upendra Baxi, "A Known but an Indifferent Judge: Situating Ronald Dworkin in Contemporary Indian Jurisprudence", (2003) (1) I.CON: International Journal of Constitutional Law 557–89.

65. U. Baxi, "On How Not to Judge the Judges: Notes Towards Evaluation of Judicial Role" (1983) 25 JILI 212; U. Baxi, "The Travails of Stare Decisis in India" in A.R. Blackshield (Ed.), *Legal Change: Essays in Honour of Professor Julius Stone* (Butterworths Sydney 1982) 34–51. *See also*, Upendra Baxi, "The Avatars of Judicial Activism: Explorations in the Geography of (in) Justice" in S.K. Verma and Kusum (Eds.), *Fifty Years of the Supreme Court of India* (Indian Law Institute, New Delhi 2000) 159–209.

In the main, three related arguments are presented concerning the "proper" limits of judicial role and function. The first argument is best called the "usurpation" or the "fine line" position, which says that justices ought to be careful lest their work trespass on the legitimate province and function of the co-equal branches of governance. The second argument is the efficiency argument, which says that even the most constitutionally sincere and human rights ardent justices may not efficiently pursue the tasks they undertake because they lack expertise necessary to achieve their ends. The third argument concerns the limits of effective judicial action. Even at the risk of expanding the scope of this introduction, it remains necessary to address briefly these grounds of criticism as concerns the SAL.

10.1 The usurpation argument

This usually proceeds on some essentialist conceptions of the doctrine of separation of powers (SOP), a view under which the task of the legislature is to make laws, that of the executive is to implement the laws, thus made, and to make policies, and that of the justices and courts is to decide disputes and controversies coming before them. In contrast, one may narrate SOP in more dynamic terms, a view in which the tasks are not so neatly divided but often overflow the conventional boundaries thus established. It is this fluidity that informs the development of the IAL—the ISC has thus broadly approved vast delegation of the rule-making power and even adjudication to the administrative or statutory authorities, left relatively untouched some archaic forms of the power coded by the law of parliamentary privileges, and generally respected the executive prerogative to make or not to make policies save when these may be said to have fallouts on the integrity of fundamental rights under Part III of the Constitution. What sense may we make then of the usurpation argument, especially on a more fluid, functional or dynamic SOP versions?

Should courts and justices remain mute spectators when the executive does not implement its statutory and constitutional obligations, in response to an adequate showing to this effect by the SAL petitioners? Should they not feel constitutionally constrained to intervene when police do not enforce the law to prevent buying and selling of women in market overt; when superintendents of prisons do not and will not prevent torture and brutalisation of prisoners; when police and pubic prosecutors fail to bring thousands of undertrials to expeditious trial; when governments fail to carry out release and rehabilitation of bonded labourers mandated by the

Constitution and laws; when the officials responsible for the administration of minimum wages, contract labour, migrant labour, and labour safety legislations flout their statutory obligations; and when governments fail to perform the mandatory duties of rehabilitation and resettlement of a vast number of project affected peoples? This listing is merely illustrative of a legion of stark governance failures and manifest human rights violations. Are justices and courts usurping, in any sense of that word, the powers of other institutions of governance in issuing orders and directions to cease and abate from unlawful and unconstitutional administration on the part of the executive?

Perhaps, then, the argument is that justices and courts should not take policy initiatives which is the primary function of the executive; as noted for the most part, the ISC has consistently agreed. However, it is also true that acting under vastly expanded understanding of Article 21 rights, the ISC (and some High Courts as well) have launched some major policy initiatives (for example, vehicular and noise pollution, protection of forests, fragile ecosystems and endangered species, inter-linking of river systems, authorised spaces of urban living and the urban master plan policies, reservation policies for the socially and educationally backward classes and the other backward class, and occasionally some livelihood policies for the constitutionally worst-off peoples). The Indian judiciary has done this, for the most part, in open public hearing, with full contestation by relevant parties appearing before them including government counsel, guided by consensually agreed expert socio-legal commissions of enquiry and detailed judgments giving rights-based justification for policy initiatives thus adopted. The last feature is especially important because it is a well-known fact that executive policy making quite systemically ignores constitutional and internationally adopted human rights considerations in framing national policies. How may SCRC of judicial performance proceed is an important question, but not properly raised by the glib version of usurpation argument only because the national government has far too often accepted SAL judicial leadership and at times even acted upon it.

A further kaleidoscopic turn of this argument reveals a different strand which now insists that SAL jurisdiction may not extend to making legislative policies (such as concerning campus ragging, or elections, the reform of the colonial Police Act, prison reform, consumer rights, right to information) or even binding enunciation of the law, as in *Vishaka* v. *State of Rajasthan*[66] (*Vishaka*). The same features described in the preceding paragraph ought to more fully inform this twist in the tale. The ISC in all these contexts acts on a rights-based approach. It pushes the frontiers of judicial responsibility no doubt but does so in the face of an overwhelming demonstration by the SAL petitioners that the government's own committees and commission recommendations have been for decades gathering dust. Is nudging a callous legislative or executive combine to attend to its constituted wisdom and to act upon its "usurpation"? I accept that some of these legislative initiatives emanate directly from the ISC (such as campus policies and sexual harassment at workplace). But even in such contexts, the court makes law pending further initiative by Parliament. *Vishaka* thus declared law concerning sexual harassment in workplaces about a decade ago subject to further parliamentary legislation; none has followed. Is this constitutional endeavour to protect women's rights as human rights a constitutionally unforgivable judicial transgression? Does this not further rescue the dilapidated "legitimacy" of the Indian representative institutions that have so little time to attend to its specific task—that of making law?

Turn the kaleidoscope a bit further and you reach the heart of usurpation argument in the context of some ISC performance in invigilating corruption in high political places. All was well when the ISC finally proceeded to deal with corruption indictments of public officials under the Prevention of Corruption Act, 1947, because the decision to grant sanction for prosecution was exercised in a way that rarely extended to the top echelons of the bureaucracy and rarely its political masters. *Antulay*[67] (which I have analysed fully in my book *Liberty and Corruption*) breached this carefully constructed political impunity but not with any enduring effect. The situation begins to change in the recent years given the active jurisdiction exercised by the ISC decisions now in relation to some former Prime Ministers and Chief Ministers (including among the latter some incumbent ones and some incumbent Union Ministers). Understandably, the judicial tolerance of sting operations via the SAL and especially in *Vineet Narain* v. *Union of India*[68], where the ISC takes over the administration of the Central Bureau of Investigation and the National Vigilance Commission, remains both irksome to political masters and raises some questions about judicial overreach. So do some decisions were the ISC actually monitors the pace of investigation or of actual trial and deals with pleas of transfer

66. (1997) 6 SCC 241.
67. *A.R. Antulay* v. *R.S. Nayak*, (1984) 2 SCC 500.
68. (1998) 1 SCC 226.

of cases from one jurisdiction to another. I may not elaborate this in any detail here (because of space constraints) save saying that the usurpation argument overstates its point here because leading political actors charged with corrupt activities have not always been hurt or harmed by the court's intervention. Emprises of adjudication apart, is the activist judicial call for a judicially monitored investigation of corruption in high political places an act of impermissible judicial transgression, or an endeavour to restore a modicum of transparency in "democratic" governance? Without being uncharacteristically dogmatic, I think that no two answers here remain possible.

In sum, the usurpation argument is no argument at all, but rather narrates some contextual politically-minded, knee-jerk responses. What is troublesome about these is the fact that such responses fail to take account of the ways in which judicial activist practices contribute to fashioning some ways out of the legitimation crises of contemporary Indian governance. If these practices lend to SCRC, this may consist in saying radically that it is no part of judicial role and function to thus legitimate forms of unconstitutional governance. This sounds nice, even chic, in the absence of the realisation, or at least an appreciation, of the fact that some human rights-based approaches to Indian governance also stand enacted in the process.

10.2 The efficiency argument

This criticism is based on the proposition that judges ought not to undertake tasks, which they cannot effectively accomplish. This is an old idea, which insists that jurisdiction must be related with effectiveness. And the ISC has in some contexts recognised it fully.[69] However, outside the test of extraterritorial effectiveness, this idea is invoked by all and sundry, but when some incumbent justices and renowned social activists reiterate it, we need to attend to it rather carefully.

One way to do this is to ask some leading questions concerning the notion of "efficiency". The standard economic way of thinking about efficiency is provided by the rational actor model thus,

69. For example, it very recently declined to entertain a petition by the Sikh Legal Foundation praying for some direction to the French Government to reconsider the ban on wearing turbans in workplaces. More important, it is not unlikely that the Bhopal settlement orders passed in chambers without hearing the victim petitioners were influenced by the suggestion that any damage award may not be effective being subject to a local New York court's assessment on whether it complied with due process standards.

> [R]ational agents are self-interested maximisers of utility; ... utility can be best understood ... as a single item varying only in quantity; ... utility is best analysed in terms of preferences; ... preferences are ... not significantly shaped by law and institutions; and ... ends adopted by an agent cannot be the subject of rational deliberation, although agents may deliberate about instrumental means to ends.[70]

Put another way, efficiency consists in the means-ends relationship; once you decide the ends or purposes, the question is how to achieve these best by rational means, and those means are rational which involve the least transaction costs. However, as John Rawls has notably demonstrated what an actor considers as *rational* may not always be *reasonable*.[71] In our context, we may revert to a number of examples. It was thus "rational" for Union Carbide Corporation to have provided no state of art security system at Bhopal (such as it provided for in its West Virginia plant) and to ignore its own safety audit team recommendation or downplay the causes and effects of the catastrophe and insist on a pittance of settlement amount, but the questions that the review petitions on settlement orders raised were concerns about "reasonableness" of such acts of corporate "governance" conduct. It is "rational" for the State of Madhya Pradesh, in the current Narmada proceedings, to claim that special rehabilitation package is a "rational" substitute for land based compensation under the Narmada Water Dispute Tribunal award, but the contest is whether it is "reasonable". It would be rational for the ISC at some future date to revert to the old conceptions of standing and thus close doors to remedies and processes initiated via the SAL because of increase in workload, complexity of issues presented, etc.; but would it be "reasonable" to so do?

If the rational in the above examples refers to some specific calculation of utility maximisation, how may we conceive its other—"reasonableness"? Both in the ILA and the SAL, justices and courts have been saying that what constitutes "reasonableness" are constitutional thresholds of fair play

70. Martha Nussbaum, "Flawed Foundations: The Philosophical Critique of (A Particular Kind of) Economics", (1997) 66 U Chi L Rev 197–214.
71. John Rawls has consistently guided us to think this difference. Reason signifies relating means to an end. But not every decision or choice that is rational remains reasonable. Rational actors chose to maximise their power, influence, or authority but doing so may not always be reasonable. The Bhopal settlement orders were rational in this sense but they were not reasonable. The decision in *Shiv Kant Shukla* denying habeas corpus even on grounds of mistaken identity was "rational" in terms of furthering the ends of Emergency Rule, but was not reasonable. It would be interesting to study the jurisprudence of the duty to give reason from this perspective. *See further*, the interesting discussion on the contributions in David Dyzenhaus (Ed.), *The Unity of Public Law* (Hart Publishing, Oxford 2004).

in governmental action and State conduct in relation at least to citizens affected; no policy should ignore these rights-based considerations; in other words, efficiency considerations are important, but so are fairness and human rights considerations. As a matter of principle, the ISC (and the State High Courts) remain justified in promoting a constitutional value-based notion of efficiency. The point of criticism should be not that the justices and courts thus adversely affect cost-benefit analysis by introducing fairness, but rather that they all too often yield to it!

Second, argument from efficiency often dramatise the cost-escalation for public projects caused by the IAL/SAL type judicial intervention or invigilation. It is clear that even regardless of judicial intervention some elephantine time and resource gestation costs may go in planning and execution of public projects. For example, the Narmada Dam project which consumed nearly a decade and a half constitutionally ordained wrangling before the Narmada Inter-State River Disputes Tribunal. The escalations of financial costs thus otherwise fully ignored become an issue only when the adversely affected citizens begin to challenge developmental decisions. As indeed has happened, the Indian Supreme Court has, at the end of the day, converted the constitutional issue of the legality/legitimacy of the Dam into merely an affair of dispensation of the accompanying relief and rehabilitation policy measures. Has the constitutional litigation time thus invested imposed any unreasoned costs on the pursuit of that project? Likewise, is it the case that the Tehri Dam proceedings (where the Supreme Court neither admitted nor dismissed a well-worked out petition; at the end of about three years, declining even an issue of an interim order) escalated any developmental costs by simply urging the Tehri Dam Virodhi Sangharsh Samiti (social action group of local communities) to hold discussions with the federal government? It indeed further minimised the costs by its unwillingness to address the question as to how local communities may effectively discuss issues with the government without full and complete access to information, which has been, from time to time, proclaimed rhetorically as a human, and a fundamental, right! The judicial performance on location of nuclear plants has constantly declined even to consider by acts of unreasoned judicial decision, terminating some fully reasoned public anxieties about the location of civilian nuclear energy plants.

Have the acts of judicial hearing, finally declining any SAL relief, escalated costs? In any event, the readers of the reports of the Comptroller General of Audits and Accounts or the Parliamentary Public Accounts Committee would know that cost overruns are all too common even without the factor of judicial stay order type intervention. Further, the States always complain that project clearance by the Union of India takes unreasonable time and is often moved by political rather than "rational" considerations. Even so, an impression is created that the SAL/IAL consideration is a serious cause of delays in implementing public projects. This impression is not based on any empirical analysis, yet the creation of this impression in the public mind is considered to provide a good tool for SCRC. As having appeared often as petitioner in person and as a student of the judicial process for well over 30 years, I am able to say that the shoe is on the other foot, as it were; State counsel take large slices of time even for filing relevant affidavits and the less said about the quality of these affidavits, the better it is! They also remain quite adjournment happy. It is unnecessary to multiply instance to say that the SAL type consideration aggravates project costs, makes a political rather than scientific statement.

A third strand in the efficiency argument is an epistemic claim that some public officials know better or the best mix of efficiency and fairness than others; in particular, the elected ones know better than the unelected officials. The elected officials, acting in the company of unelected bureaucrats/technocrats, remain best placed to develop national policies and legal regimes that match the policy "ends" with the "means" necessary to achieve these. Courts and justices may never fully know, for example, well enough whatever constitutes a proper mix of efficiency considerations in evolving, say, suitable forest, energy, sustainable development, water, housing, tax, urbanisation, industrial and labour policies. Their attempt to insert conceptions of constitutional "reasonableness" remains out of line/synch with the conceptions of "rational" and often with allegedly disastrous impact on "national" development.

Attractive as the argument is in the abstract, it is also true that the political exponents of this argument have little hesitation suggesting that only the ISC can best handle complex matters of historical evidence, such as the identification of the historic birth site of Lord Rama[72] and currently, the Ram Sethu controversy before the court. In what respect, pray, is the opinion of Dr Jeevan Reddy J holding that mixing of religion and politics

72. *M. Ismail Faruqui* v. *Union of India*, (1994) 6 SCC 360. Here for the first time the ISC declined the reference for advisory opinion.

stands constitutionally proscribed[73] is less complex than any adjudicatory feat on location of nuclear power plants or large-scale irrigation projects? At the end of the day, the so-called difference between judiciary's power to pronounce on profound political issues and deep scientific/technocratic ones is a difference without distinction. Both sets of issues pose architectonic challenges of conceptualising and articulating the play of public power on the images and futures of human rights. The enunciation of the latter is typically the province and function of judicial power.

Further, time and again, the SAL jurisprudence has shown as a matter of objective record that governmental policy decisions, bereft of public participation, remain based on ignorance, masquerading as official knowledge. Activist knowledge, as "certified" by the ISC/SAL doings, have repeatedly shown that policy experts remain simply ignorant of the obligations imposed by law and the Constitution. Legions of example fully demonstrate this! Should you doubt this, please ask yourself the following questions, by way of example:

(1) Was it the ISC or the executive/legislative combine that invented the notion that the category of "bonded" labour includes workers denied minimum wages?

(2) Was it not the ISC, rather than the legislative/executive combine that led to a series of policy decisions concerning the use of CNG that notably reduced the adverse health impacts in Delhi and other global Indian cities?

(3) Is it not the case, despite some obvious NBA–Tehri-dam type disappointments, that the ISC not merely afforded legitimate spaces against undemocratic official repression of anti-mega irrigation projects articulating the constitutional obligation of the Indian State towards a just resettlement and rehabilitation policies for the project affected urban, rural, and forest-dwelling denizens of India? Would the so-called national declarations on forest, environment, and suchlike policies have been at all possible outside the citizen-ISC paradigmatic interaction informing the orders of a new reasonableness, pitted against the myriad forms of State irrationality?

In so illustrating this movement, I am not at all saying that the ISC has done any thing better, and always, for the rights and plights of the constitutionally worst-off peoples. Starkly put, it could have done a whole lot better. Even

73. *S.R. Bommai* v. *Union of India*, (1994) 3 SCC 1, 236, para. 310.

so, it has created more spaces for participatory citizen action than have the cumulative performances of the elected officials. In this sense, we all must still count our thus offered constitutionally activist judicial blessings.

10.3 The impact argument

In general, this argument develops the conventional aphoristic wisdom that courts and justices command neither the power of the "purse" nor the "sword". It would be silly to maintain otherwise. But it would also be silly to deny that the SAL performances have not in fact significantly influenced national planning or budgetary decisions and, in this sense, the acts and conduct of the elected officials,[74] or to insist that in *no case* they *ought* to do so.[75] In any event, the ISC has been relatively accommodating on this score; rarely has contempt notice been issued on the ground that a particular direction of the ISC enforcing Article 21 rights has not been enforced because of resource constraints.

The more specific line of argument here is that the SAL directions suffer from a lack of governmental compliance and because long-term defiance of judicial orders, directions, and dispositions tends to undermine the constitutional and moral authority of the ISC, it should tread warily. This is an argument even made by the ISC justices themselves in the history of the SAL: most notably by R.S. Pathak J in *Bandhua Mukti Morcha* v. *Union of India*[76], Venkataramiah J in *Sudipt Mazumdar* v. *State of M.P.*[77], and recently more dramatically by Markandey Katju J in *Common Cause* v. *Union of India*[78]. The ISC (and the High Courts) have developed a series of responses to address the problem:

(1) As noted earlier, the founding justices insisted that the SAL is a cooperative rather than adversarial jurisdiction; they typically used the language of "hope and trust" in passing orders and directions rather than mandate compliance on the pain of contempt.

74. The ISC adjudicatory concerning constitutionally legitimated reservations for educationally and socially backward classes and other backward classes has triggered a vast release of national funds for enabling institutions of "higher" learning. Never before in Indian educational scenario has such massive resource-flows have occurred! Via SAL processes the ISC has also revised the salaries and facilities of the district judiciary.

75. If only because in general, enforcement of Part III rights always entail forms of public expenditure and specifically because SAL directions that statutory or constitutional duties should be strictly implemented may not be resisted silly on the ground that budgetary allocations have not been made.

76. (1984) 3 SCC 161.

77. (1983) 2 SCC 258.

78. (2008) 5 SCC 511.

(2) The device of keeping the matter on board for considerable periods of time (or continuing mandamus) has meant that the State lawyers must publicly justify their indifference or inaction, a rather difficult enterprise.

(3) By ordering that relevant high profile civil servants be in attendance at court hearings constitutes an irksome demand on their self-images and bureaucratic time, which often has the effect of achieving the exercise of soft disciplinary judicial power.

(4) By the issuance of verbal strictures during the course hearings, which of course make 24x7 headline news for the print and electronic mass media, has the effect of both naming and shaming them.

(5) The explicit incorporation of some dire judicial strictures in the judgment, and also in interim orders, often generates important political fallouts or consequences to a point of triggering governance exit by some leading public or political figures.

(6) Strictures during the course of hearings often tend to be very sharp indeed and when directed against the Solicitor General of India has the effect of moving things alone.

(7) Occasional impositions of heavy costs on the government and even directions that a particular civil servant has to bear the costs from his/her individual sources of income has the effect of inducing more voluntarily-based compliance.

(8) The evolution of new techniques such as the development of the doctrine of juristic activism[79] fosters some important ways of inducing compliance. In this practice, some activist justices, especially on the Supreme Court, try to get around judicial helplessness by writing judgments in such a way as would lay down general propositions or lines of thought and enquiry not strictly germane to cases at hand but of considerable relevance to the future development of the law. I have described this phenomenon elsewhere. Particularly noteworthy are the performances of Mathew J in *Sukhdev Singh* v. *Bhagatram Sardar Singh Raghuvanshi*[80] and Bhagwati J's opinions in *Maneka Gandhi*[81]

79. U. Baxi (Ed.), *Justice K.K. Mathew on Democracy, Equality and Freedom* (1978) xxxviii *et. seq.*
80. (1975) 1 SCC 421, 447.
81. (1978) 1 SCC 248.

and *Shetty*[82], as well as Krishna Iyer J's opinion in *Nawabkhan Abbaskhan* v. *State of Gujarat*[83].

It is clear, at least to me as an active participant in the SAL process, that compliance is not, as usually portrayed, an all-or-nothing phenomenon but rather a continuing spectrum of processes of creeping jurisdiction[84] through which judicial power proceeds to craft some unconventional notions of implementation. Clearly, disappointed SAL petitioners justly complain that this process does not yield legitimately expected results. And a sustained chorus of public disappointment always remains an important democratic resource for future SAL developments, both in terms of intensifying "creeping jurisdiction" and related techniques described above, but also as productive of an additional set of judicially devised mechanisms monitoring compliance.

This being fully said, it also needs saying further that Indian political and constitutional development without the SAL, directed towards an incremental promotion of ethics of human rights and justice friendly cultures of Indian governance, would have been very different than now is the case. The same remains true of the contribution of activist justices around the world whose exertions mark some valiant triggering/steering contributions towards democratic capability directed at promoting new cultures of responsive and responsible governance. Indian IAL/SAL scholarship has much to learn from comparable judicial developments in the third and the post-socialist judicial worlds.[85] It is true that these adjudicative exertions always fall short of generating a new ethic of power. But it is also the case that such judicial struggles mark as well as make a historically pertinent difference. Granting this comparative fact of resurgent "juristocracy", it also remains true in the Indian case that what is at stake is the cultivation of a culture which extols *influence* over power.

This distinction is indeed important as we know from the Indian political conjecture where leading public figures ever since Mahatma Gandhi have sought to cultivate ethically-based *influence* rather than pursue the oath of

82. *Ramana Dayaram Shetty* v. *International Airport Authority of India*, (1979) 3 SCC 489.
83. (1974) 2 SCC 121.
84. U. Baxi, "Taking Suffering Seriously: Social Action Litigation Before the Supreme Court of India", (1979–80) 8–9 Delhi LR 91; extended and revised in U. Baxi (Ed.), *Law & Poverty: Critical Essays* (N.M. Tripathi, Bombay 1989).
85. *See* as to the latter, Bill Bowring, *The Degradation of the International Legal Order? The Rehabilitation of Law and the Possibility of Politics*, 83–98 (Routledge-Cavendish, London 2007); *see also*, William Abresch, "A Human Rights Law of Internal Armed Conflict: the European Court of human rights in Chechnya", (2005) 16 EJIL 741–67.

wielding political power. I have said often that each and every contemporary activist Indian justice is a lineal descendent of Jay Prakash Narain's Total Revolution Movement, whether or not this specific debt is consciously acknowledged.

I read Prof. Massey's treatise, replete with provocative live insights,[86] as a step forward towards this kind of understanding. Indeed, what is striking about this book is the insistence that "courts" must exercise its power for the protection of the "little man" or, to vary this imagery, the perennial historic victim of carcinogenic concentration of public power in dominant institutions of governance. Neither the ISC nor the High Courts have been unaware of the perils of an uneven combat with the recidivist forms of official or administrative deviance. Yet, they necessarily proceed to check the arrogance of power by the supreme executive. The Indian experience shows that justices may at best seek to educate elected and unelected public officials towards a more constitutionally sincere exercise of public power, and the SAL justices may compel but only as a last resort.

SAL has initiated a dialogue subversive of our tame certainties and pet dogmas concerning the judicial role. SAL, and judicial review generally, is an ongoing aspect of the struggle to realign the balance of power between the Governors and the governed. It is an effort to make the rule-of-law notions, which have pre-eminently served the strategic interests of the Indian *rulers,* to increasingly serve as well the *ruled* of India. In this sense, it is not the political parties or representative institutions but rather the courts and justices who now emerge as what Antonio Gramsci named, in his *Prison Notebooks*, as the "Modern Prince".

To conclude, the SAL endeavour will be effective, in its vast socio-political significance, only when the well-endowed few are made to begin to fight for the disadvantaged, dispossessed, and deprived millions of Indians. It offers

86. For example, Massey suggests that for purposes of Art. 12 invocation, there is no justification for courts to take the view that "private individuals and bodies are not amenable". He suggests that the "correct approach" to Art. 12 is that "every authority or person who pose a threat to fundamental rights should be amenable to the jurisdiction of the court". The relevant test, he maintains, should not be the "type of agency" but rather the "threat to fundamental rights". [*Infra*, Chap. 8].

Similarly, he observes that "in a country like India where people have no right to know, judicial process grinds slow and other grievance procedures are feeble and inefficient, perhaps the discretion to disobey may provide an effective check on the operation of the government machinery in a reckless manner". [*Infra*, Chap. 13].

Massey is also the first Indian administrative law specialist to explicitly say that the notion of the rule of law has an "ideological" content as well (*see infra*, Chap. 2).

the call for the thinking humanity to suffer by the suffering humanity, to begin to think. As Karl Marx memorably said:

> The existence of a suffering humanity which thinks and of thinking humanity which is oppressed will necessarily be unpalatable for the passive animal and the world of Philistines.... The longer circumstances give thinking humanity time to reflect and suffering humanity time to rally, the more finished when born will be the product that the world carries in its womb.

—UPENDRA BAXI[87]

87. Professor of Law, University of Warwick; Vice-Chancellor, University of Delhi (1990–94); University of South Gujarat (1982–85); Professor of Law, Delhi University (1973–96). I dedicate this introduction to luminous memory of Prof. S.P. Sathe.

CHAPTER 1

Introduction to Administrative Law

1. DEFINITION AND SCOPE OF ADMINISTRATIVE LAW

Administrative law is a heuristic science. It is a branch of public law which is essentially anti-authoritarian. It is a "Dharma" of the administration. It strives to develop a rule of law society based on fairness, reasonableness and justness. In the 21st century due to economic liberalisation and globalisation, administrative law has assumed transnational significance as it tries to bring rule of law in global administrative space. In this context administrative law is not merely a legal discourse, it has become a civilisational discourse.

Administrative law as a separate branch of legal discipline, especially in India, came to be recognised only by the middle of the 20th century. Today the administration is ubiquitous and impinges freely and deeply on every aspect of an individual's life. Administrative law as a component of public law imposes duties and responsibilities on public authorities to serve public interest better and for this purpose it deals with a variety of legal processes and techniques for controlling the misuse of power by public authorities. In this direction courts play a central role which makes administrative law an ever-evolving discipline. Therefore, administrative law has become a major area for study and research.[1] Principles of administrative law are not extra-constitutional, they emerge from various provisions of the Constitution.

In administrative law, the term "Administration" is used in its broadest possible sense and covers within its reach

(1) all executive actions, its programmes and policies;
(2) all administrative aspects of Parliament and judiciary;
(3) all actions of State like actors (agency and instrumentality of State);
(4) all actions of non-State actors (private entities) exercising public functions.

---

1. The first seminar on administrative law was organised by the Indian Law Institute, New Delhi in December 1957 right after its inauguration. Since then the major area of activity of the Institute has been administrative law.

It is a harsh fact of life that the phenomenal growth of administrative power as a by-product of an intensive form of government, though necessary for development and growth, at times spells negation of people's rights and values. Profligate and pachydermic administration emboldened by the anesthetised public conscience does not hesitate to trample upon the civil liberties of the people. Thus, administrative adventurists impatient of democratic process may slip into authoritarianism, making all material growth a pretence for tyranny. Here comes the need, importance and purpose of administrative law. Administrative law thus becomes dharma which conduces to the stability and growth of society, maintenance of a just social order, and welfare of mankind by reconciling power with liberty. It seeks to channelise administrative powers to achieve the basic aim of any civilised society, that is, "growth with liberty". Thus, administrative law goes beyond legalism and represents a principled regulation of administrative space, whether domestic or global, which can be practically regulated for the expansion of human freedoms. Therefore, today, administrative law represents the way of conceptualising and articulating a new domestic and global socio-economic order.

Against this backdrop, administrative law has a tremendous social function to perform. Without a good system of administrative law any society would die because of its own administrative weight like a Black Hole—which is a dying neutron star that collapses due to its own gravity. Administrative law, therefore, becomes that body of reasonable limitations and affirmative action parameters which are developed and operationalised by the legislature and the courts to maintain and sustain a rule of law society.

Thus, four basic bricks of the foundation of any administrative law may be identified as: 1) checking abuse or detournement of administrative power; 2) ensuring citizens an impartial determination of their disputes by officials; 3) protecting citizens from unauthorised encroachment on their rights and interests;[2] and 4) making those who exercise public power accountable to the people.

Nevertheless, for a student "administrative law" defies definition. The reason seems to be that in almost every country, irrespective of its political philosophy, the administrative process has increased so tremendously that today we are living not in its shade but shadow. Therefore, it is impossible to attempt any precise definition of administrative law which can cover the entire range of administrative process. Perhaps this was the reason why Dr F.J. Port, who published the first book bearing the title "Administrative Law" in England in 1929, did not venture to define the term. He simply attempted to describe administrative law as follows:

2. *See*, Julius Stone, *Social Dimensions of Law and Justice* (1966) 711. There the reference is to judicial review.

> Administrative law is made up of all these legal rules—either formally expressed by statute or implied in the prerogative—which have as their ultimate object the fulfilment of public law. It touches first the legislature, in that the formally expressed rules are usually laid down by that body; it touches judiciary, in that *a*) there are rules which govern the judicial action that may be brought by or against administrative persons, *b*) administrative bodies are sometimes permitted to exercise judicial powers; thirdly, it is of course essentially concerned with the practical application of law.

Even this attempt to describe administrative law rather than to define it is not without difficulty. Administrative law besides touching all branches of government, touches administrative and quasi-administrative agencies, *i.e.* corporations, commissions, universities and sometimes even private organisations. Furthermore, administrative law is made up not only of legislative and executive rules and a large body of precedents but also of functional formulations, for every exercise of discretion forms a rule for future action.

Early English writers did not differentiate between administrative law and constitutional law and, therefore, the definition they attempted was too broad and general.

Sir Ivor Jennings defines administrative law as the law relating to administration. It determines the organisation, powers and the duties of administrative authorities.[3] This formulation does not differentiate between administrative and constitutional law. It lays entire emphasis on the organisation, power and duties to the exclusion of the manner of their exercise. A student of administrative law is not concerned with how a Minister is appointed but only with how a Minister discharges his functions in relation to an individual or a group. How the Minister of Housing and Rehabilitation is appointed is not the concern of administrative law, but when this Minister approves a scheme for a new township, which involves the acquisition of houses and lands of persons living in that area, questions of administrative law arise. Jennings' formulation also leaves many aspects of administrative law untouched, especially the control mechanism.

A.V. Dicey, like Jennings, belongs to that group of English writers who did not recognise the independent existence of administrative law. According to Dicey's formulation, administrative law relates to that portion of a nation's legal system which determines the legal status and liabilities of all State officials, defines the rights and liabilities of private individuals in their dealings with public officials, and specifies the procedure by which those rights and liabilities are enforced.[4]

Dicey was obsessed with the French "Droit Administratif" and, therefore, his formulation mainly concentrated on judicial remedies against State officials. Therefore, this definition excludes the study of every other aspect of administrative law.

---

3. Jennings, *The Law and the Constitution* (5th Edn.) 217.
4. Dicey, *Law of the Constitution*, 329.

The American approach is significantly different from the early English approach, in that it recognised administrative law as an independent branch of the legal discipline. According to Kenneth Culp Davis, administrative law is a law that concerns the powers and procedure of administrative agencies, including especially the law governing judicial review of administrative action. Within his formulation, Davis includes the study of administrative rule-making and rule adjudication but excludes rule application which according to him belongs to the domain of public administration.[5]

However, even this classification by Davis cannot be considered complete because he excludes from his control mechanism, the control exercised by the legislature, higher administrative authorities, and the mass media representing public opinion, and also the vast area of administrative action which is neither quasi-legislative nor quasi-adjudicative.[6]

The unenviable diversity in definitions of the term "administrative law" is also due to the fact that every administrative law specialist tries to lay more emphasis on any one particular aspect of the whole administrative process, which according to his own evaluation deserves singular attention. Prof. Upendra Baxi thus lays special stress on the protection of the "little man" from the arbitrary exercise of public power.[7] According to him, administrative law is a study of the pathology of power in a developing society. Accountability of the holders of public power for the ruled is thus the focal point of this formulation:

> The basic expectation in a rule-of-law society is that holders of public power and authority must be able to publicly justify their action as legally valid and socially wise and just. [Therefore,] administrative law is one part of this valiant enterprise of accountability. In any rule-of-law society general forms of accountability do exist. Legislators go to polls periodically, errant judges could be impeached, bureaucrats are responsible to the elected politicians. These forms of general accountability become very feeble in any developing society because of poverty, illiteracy and ignorance of the masses. Consequently, the study of administrative law assumes special significance in any developing society for the development of more specific forms of accountability.[8]

Against this backdrop of the situation prevailing in India, administrative law today remains only as an "instrument of middle-class Indians to combat governmental power through courts"[9].

For our purposes, we may define administrative law as that branch of *public law* which deals with the *organisation and powers of administrative and quasi-administrative* agencies and *prescribes principles and rules* by which an *official action* is *reached* and *reviewed* in relation to *individual liberty and freedom*.

---

5. Davis, *Administrative Law Text* (1959) 2.
6. *See generally*, Chaps. 8 and 10 of this book, *infra*.
7. *See*, Introduction by Prof. Upendra Baxi to this book.
8. *Ibid.*
9. *Ibid.*

Thus defined, administrative law attempts to regulate administrative space, domestic and global, in order to infuse fairness and accountability in the administrative process necessary for securing equity and inclusiveness in the domestic and world order.

An analysis of this formulation would not only give us an acceptable definition of administrative law but would also identify its nature and scope:

(1) Administrative law is a law, but it is not a law in the lawyer's sense of the term like property law or contract law. It is a law in the realist's sense of the term which includes statute law, administrative rule-making, precedents, customs, administrative directions, etc. It also includes the study of something which may not be termed "law" in the true sense of the term such as administrative circulars, policy statements, memoranda and resolutions, etc. Besides this, it includes within its study "higher law" as well, like the principles of natural justice. However, in India, administrative law, basically and wholly, remains a judge-made law and, thus, suffers from "the frailties and benefits from the strengths of judicial law-making"[10]. Consequently, personal and institutional constraints make the growth of administrative law vulnerable to judicial meanderings and tentativeness.

(2) Administrative law is a branch of public law in contradistinction to private law which deals with the relationships of individuals inter se. Therefore, administrative law primarily deals with the relationship of individuals with the organised power.

(3) Administrative law deals with the organisation and powers of administrative and quasi-administrative agencies. The stress on the study of organisation is only to the extent that it is necessary to understand the powers, characteristics of actions, procedure for the exercise of those powers and the control mechanism provided therein. The study includes not only administrative agencies but also the quasi-administrative agencies such as corporations, firms, autonomous agencies, individuals, and civil society institutions, both national and global, and the like operating in public space and exercising public functions.

(4) Administrative law includes the study of the existing principles and also of the development of certain new principles which administrative and quasi-administrative agencies must follow while exercising their powers in relation to individuals, *i.e.* the principles of natural justice, reasonableness and fairness.

(5) Administrative law primarily concerns itself with the official action which may be
   (*a*) rule-making or quasi-legislative action,
   (*b*) rule-decision or quasi-judicial action,
   (*c*) rule-application or administrative action, or
   (*d*) ministerial action or pure administrative action.

10. *See*, Introduction by Prof. Upendra Baxi to this book.

Besides these main actions, the actions which are incidental to the main action are also covered within its study. Such incidental actions may be investigatory, supervisory, advisory, declaratory and prosecutory.

(6) One of the main thrusts of the study of administrative law is on the procedure by which the official action is reached. If the means (procedure) are not trustworthy, the end cannot be just. There is a bewildering variety in the procedure which the administrative agencies follow in reaching an action. Such procedure may be laid down
   (*a*) in the statute itself under which the administrative agency has been created;
   (*b*) in the separate procedure code which every administrative agency is bound to follow, *i.e.* Administrative Procedure Act, 1946 in the US and Tribunals and Enquiries Act, 1958 in England.

However, in many more cases either the administrative agency is left free to develop its own procedure or it is required to render its actions according to the minimum procedure of the principles of natural justice.

(7) Administrative law also includes within its study the control mechanism by which the administrative agencies are kept within bounds and made effective in the service of the individuals. This control mechanism is technically called the "review process". An administrative action may be controlled by
   (*a*) courts exercising writ jurisdiction through the writs of habeas corpus, mandamus, certiorari, prohibition and quo warranto;
   (*b*) courts exercising ordinary judicial powers through suits, injunctions and declaratory actions;
   (*c*) statutory authorities like ombudsman, Human Rights Commissions, and other investigative agencies;
   (*d*) higher administrative authorities;
   (*e*) public opinion, and mass media in the 20th century is also an important control on any administration which a student of administrative law cannot lose sight of. In the US, opinion polls and mass media exercise much more effective control on the administration than any other single control inasmuch as this control mechanism has the potentiality of pre-empting any adverse administrative decision.
   (*f*) Civil society and interest representations also play an important role in controlling the arbitrary exercise of public power, both at the pre-natal and post-natal stages. Though in India this form of control is still at the take-off stage, yet organisations such as Consumer Protection and Research Society, Society for the Protection of Civil Liberties, Chipko Movement and other consultative and advisory bodies have played a significant role in this direction.

(g) "Easy access to justice" also provides an effective check on bureaucratic adventurism in the exercise of public power. If the access to justice is easy and quick, it may deter administrative instrumentalities from developing an attitude which has been termed as "fly-now-pay-later"[11]. "Easy access to justice" includes procedural facility which is cheap, speedy and less formalistic, legal aid, availability of advocates for public interest litigation, intellectual capacity of the party and active participation of the judges. Uncontestably, this control mechanism in India is too weak to provide any effective check on recidivist administrative deviance. Procedural law and practice is highly formalistic, dilatory and expensive, and legal aid is merely a concept. Very few advocates are available to take up public interest litigation. Lately, advocates and journalists are coming forward to sponsor public interest litigation. Cases in the courts relating to the illegal felling of trees, environmental pollution, flesh trade, prison torture are some of the illustrations. Recently, judges have also showed some signs of active participation. The Supreme Court has demonstrated its eagerness to stretch its long arms, and in very many situations it has treated a mere letter as a writ petition. All this will go a long way in influencing the behaviour of the custodians of public power.

(*h*) Right to know, right to reply and discretion to disobey also have inherent potentialities of proving effective, though indirect, in providing a check on administrative behaviour.

(8) The study of administrative law is not an end in itself but a means to an end. The focal point of the study of administrative law is the reconciliation of power with liberty. When the administrative process started rising after the death of laissez faire at the birth of the 20th century, the stress on the study of administrative law was on circumscription of administrative powers. But now when the administrative process has come to stay, the emphasis has shifted to the regulation of administrative powers. The paradox of the 21st century is the prolific growth in the powers of private sector, which on the one hand is necessary for the promotion of human economic growth and freedom, but on the other hand threatens to endanger individual freedom. Thus, courts must extend administrative law principles to private sphere also. Therefore, the main task of the students of administrative law is to evolve certain principles and rules by which an ideal equilibrium between the powers of the administration and the dictates of individual liberty can be sustained.

The above formulation, however, only delineates the scope of administrative law as is commonly accepted in the common-law world. Administrative

11. *See*, Introduction by Prof. Upendra Baxi to this book.

law specialists in England and India mainly focus their attention on various aspects of judicial control of administrative decisions and actions. In the study of such topics as tribunals and enquiries, the emphasis is likely to be between these institutions and the courts as alternative methods of controlling administrative action. These specialists rarely delve into administrative process itself to consider how government departments and other administrative agencies actually operate, or how and why their procedures and structures differ from the judicial model of decision-making, or how the administrative process could be made more effective and efficient by reform from within. Such matters are usually left to political scientists, and administrative lawyers are content to debate the question of proper role of courts in reviewing administrative action. On the contrary, American administrative law specialists discard such a limited vision. In the US, administrative law is seen to be as much concerned with what goes on inside the fourth branch (administration) of the government as it is with judicial scrutiny of the administrative process.

James O. Freedman[12], therefore, felt concerned with the legitimacy of administrative process rather than the legitimacy of judicial review of administrative action. In his study of administrative law, he includes his concern for 1) failure of the administrative agencies to conform to the constitutional parameters; 2) public ambivalence towards the substantive policies sought to be achieved by some agencies; 3) departure made from judicial procedure in decision making; 4) scepticism about administrative expertise and bureaucratic expansion; 5) apparent absence of direct political accountability; and 6) problems created by the broad delegation of legislative powers.[13]

Viewed against this perspective, administrative law becomes an all-pervasive legal discipline. Principles of administrative law emerge and develop whenever and wherever any person becomes the victim of the arbitrary exercise of public power. And the allegation of arbitrary exercise of power can be raised in almost all areas of substantive law. Therefore, it will not be incorrect to say that no one can specialise in administrative law.[14]

Today, the emerging patterns of global governance as a consequence of globalised interdependence in such fields like trade, development, environment, communication, banking, migration and security has thrown new challenges before this discipline of law which requires an organised action for research and practice.

This transnational administrative and regulatory regime which has consequences for the people of the world, especially those living in the developing countries, needs a strong system of international administrative law to reconcile growth with justice and free competition with fair competition. Certainly growth for the sake of growth is no growth; it is cancerous

12. Freedman, *Crisis and Legitimacy* (1978).
13. *See*, "Introduction", (Oct. 1981) 30 Int'l & Comp LQ, Part 4, 880.
14. *See*, Introduction by Prof. Upendra Baxi to this book, p. 1.

growth, unless it is tempered with social justice. Only a good body of administrative law can fill this growing space at the national and transnational level with advantage by enforcing probity, responsibility and accountability within the area of administrative process. Development of these new norms of administrative law jurisprudence still remains the unfinished agenda of globalisation. This makes administrative law an excellent area of study, research and practice.

Administrative law is not a branch of philosophy of law but of sociology of law.

Philosophy of law deals with the cosmos of law, its object being to formulate features which every established legal order must necessarily possess, and which were derived by the sheer force of logic and deduction or through divine ordination. The jurisprudence thus developed assigned a mechanistic role to a judge based on neutral principle. Sociology of law, on the other hand, is a science of practical application which requires an analysis of diverse functions of law in their application to particular situations. Thus, the spirit of law becomes experience and not logic which runs close to the rule of life. In this realm, law cannot afford to become divorced from the socio-economic realities of society. It must become people oriented, weighted in favour of the weaker sections of society. In this context, administrative law and its utility and vitality depends on its capacity to solve the just expectations of the neglected segments of society. Against this backdrop, administrative law must run very close to the lives which we daily live.

2. REASONS FOR THE GROWTH OF ADMINISTRATIVE LAW WITH SPECIAL REFERENCE TO INDIA

Administrative law is a by-product of intensive form of government. During the last century, the role of the government has changed in almost every country of the world, from laissez faire to paternalism and from paternalism to maternalism. Though presently, under the force of globalisations, the role of governments is fast changing and a government is seen more as an enabler, facilitator and regulator than as provider, yet in developing countries role of the government as provider still remains important. Today the expectation from government is not only that it will protect its people from external aggression and internal disturbance, but also that it will take care of its citizens from the cradle to the grave. Therefore, the development of administrative process and the administrative law has become the cornerstone of modern political philosophy.

Today there is a demand by the people that government must solve their problems rather than merely define their rights. It is felt that the right of equality in the US Constitution will be a sterile right if the black is the first to lose his job and the last to be re-employed. In the same manner, the equality clause in the Indian Constitution would become meaningless unless the government comes forward to actively help the weaker sections of society to bring about equality in fact. This implies the growth of administrative law and process.

In the same manner today, the people recognise all problems as solvable rather than political controversies. There was a time, before the industrial revolution in England during the heyday of laissez faire, when it was considered that the employer–employee conflict was a political controversy and the government would do well by keeping away. But today everyone feels that it is the duty of government to resolve this conflict and maintain industrial harmony, which is essential for economic growth. Likewise, the regulation of the patterns of ownership, production and distribution is considered the responsibility of any good government to guarantee the maximum good of the maximum number. This again has led to the growth of administrative law and process.

Phenomenal growth in science and technology which started from 20th century has placed a counter-balancing responsibility on a modern government to control the forces which science and technology have unleashed. Modernisation and technological developments produce great structural changes and create crucial problems such as cultural conflicts; haphazard urbanisation; ruthless exploitation of natural resources; environmental pollution (water, air and sonic); rapid transport and traffic chaos; automation and consequential unemployment; erratic production and distribution; concentration of economic power; dismal health, education, employment and training conditions; incessant labour strikes and lockouts; staggering inflation; accelerated smuggling; pervasive corruption; adulteration; tax evasion; commercial malpractices; violence; inadequate management of sea and space; and many others. Growth of global administrative space has further multiplied such problems. These multi-dimensional problems with varied social, economic and political ramifications cannot be solved except with the growth of administration and law regulating administration.

The inadequacy of the traditional type of courts and law-making organs to give that quality and quantity of performance which is required in the 20th century for the functioning of a welfare and functional government is the biggest single reason which has led to the growth of administrative process and law. Like medicine, in law also there is a shift from punitive to preventive justice. Today litigation is not considered a battle to be won but a disease to be cured. Inadequacy of the traditional courts to respond to this new challenge has led to the growth of administrative adjudicatory process. Furthermore, the traditional administration of justice is technical, expensive and dilatory. It is unworkable where the subject-matter is dynamic and requires not only adjudication but development also, as in the cases of industrial disputes. Therefore, in cases where the need is fair disposition and not merely disposition on file, administrative adjudicatory process seems to be the only answer.

For the same reason, because of limitation of time, the technical nature of legislation, the need for flexibility, experimentation and quick action, the traditional legislative organs cannot pass that quality and quantity of laws which are required for the functioning of a modern government. It is said, perhaps rightly, that even if our Parliament sits all the 24 hours and all the 365 days in a year, it cannot possibly pass all the laws needed by the government today. Therefore, the inevitable growth of administrative legislative process.

No list of causes, howsoever lengthy it may be, can be exhaustive. Nevertheless, a modern functional government in the backdrop of socialism was the main force behind the growth of administrative law and process in the 20th century.

Recent growth in global administrative space and the emerging intergovernmental regulations by global agencies with tremendous national consequences has further added new focus to administrative law with global dimensions necessary to make new world economic order inclusive and equitable. This has added to the scope of administrative law as an outsourced, policy-delivery mechanism to enforce responsibility and accountability in global governance not only on States but also on corporations, firms, autonomous agencies, individuals and civil society institutions.

2.1 Growth of administrative law in India

There existed in India from very early times a system of both administrative legislation and adjudication. The object of early British administration was to maximise profit, and for this efficiency in the administration was the chief necessity. Therefore during the Company days, the courts were tools in the Company's hands. The executive had overriding powers in matters of administration of justice. However, the establishment of the Supreme Court at Calcutta in 1774 under the provisions of the Regulating Act, 1773 inaugurated an era in independent judicial administration. But with the passage of the Act of Settlement, 1781, the era came to an end and all the later developments in the judicial system during the Company's time worked to the detriment of the native population.

From the Battle of Plassey in 1757 until Independence, one significant advantage that the Indian administration had from a centralised but undemocratic form of government, was the facility to make laws. During that period, the executive was invested with such wide powers to make rules as a modern democratic legislature cannot even imagine. Even prior to the famous Code of Civil and Criminal Procedures known as Cornwallis Code of 1793, Elphinstone Code of 1827 and many other regulations were in operation. These regulation laws aimed mainly at the regulation of the powers of the administration and their control. Thus, expansion of the administrative powers and provisions of some kind of control went hand in hand. For instance, Regulation 10 of 1822 which codified the law regarding the excise on salt, opium, and general custom dealt mainly with the powers of administrative agencies (salt chowkies) and also the control of these agencies. It made provisions regarding power of confiscation, procedure in the proceeding of confiscation and the control to be exercised by the courts. Section 108 of the Regulation of 1822 reminds of one of the provisions of the Administrative Procedure Act, 1946 when administrative agencies were required to record facts, evidence and the decision. Judicial relief was made available only after the exhaustion of administrative remedies. The courts, though had ample powers to set aside an administrative action, yet paid great respect and attention to their decisions.

Till the end of the British rule in India, the government was concerned with the most primary duties only, and the functions of a welfare state were not discharged. However, increasing and rapid strides in the fields of communication and transport in the West resulted in the need for the control of administrative agencies through regulatory bodies and tribunals like the Inter-State Commerce Commission in the US and the Railways and Canal Commission in England. Finally, the two World Wars brought in a plethora of administrative agencies exercising control over almost every aspect of individual life.

When India became independent, the philosophy of welfare state was made the creed of the Indian Constitution. The Preamble of the Constitution laid down that the Constitution aims at establishing a sovereign, socialist, secular, democratic republic, so as to secure to all its citizens social, economic and political justice; liberty of thought, expression, belief, faith and worship; equality of status and of opportunity; and to promote among them all fraternity assuring dignity of the individual and the unity of the nation. Article 38 further provides that the State shall strive to secure a social order in which social and economic justice shall inform all institutions of national life. Article 39 requires the State to direct its policy towards securing an order in which citizens have equal rights to an adequate means of livelihood; that the ownership and control of the material resources of the community are so distributed as best to subserve the common good; that there is no concentration of wealth; and that means of production are not used to the common detriment; and that there is equal pay for equal work.

Articles 39-A and 41 oblige the State to provide for equal justice and free legal aid; to work within its economic capacity and development making effective provision for securing the right to education, assistance in old age, unemployment and other contingencies. Articles 43 and 43-A enjoin upon the State to secure work for the workers, a living wage, a decent standard of living and participation in the management of industries. Article 45 obliges the State to provide free and compulsory education for children up to the age of 14 years. Article 47 enjoins upon the State to regard the raising of the level of nutrition, the standard of living of its people, and the improvement of public health as among its primary duties. Article 48-A imposes a duty upon the State to protect and improve the environment.

This is in brief a blueprint for the development of future India and the motif of socialism which looms large in constitutional text and context.[15] These welfare and socialistic aims and objects cannot be achieved by the State without the growth of the administrative process. Articles 323-A and 323-B were added to the Constitution to facilitate the establishment of special tribunals to meet the needs of administrative justice, which the growth of administrative process had created. From 1990s onwards with the adoption of the policy of economic liberalisation and globalisation of economy, huge regulatory space had been created which was to be administered by creating various regulatory agencies. Corporatisation of economy has given further impetus to the growth of administrative process in India.

Besides providing for a functional government and consequential growth in the administrative process, the Constitution has also provided for an elaborate control mechanism so that the water may not overrun its banks. Under Articles 32 and 226, the Supreme Court and the various High Courts have been invested with powers to issue writs of certiorari, mandamus, quo warranto, prohibition and habeas corpus to check the excesses of the government and the administrative agencies. Article 300 gives a right to individuals to file a suit against the government for torts committed by its servants. Article 311 protects government servants from arbitrary actions of the government in the matters of dismissal, termination and reduction in rank. In the same manner, Article 136 confers power on the Supreme Court to grant special leave to appeal from any judgment, decree, determination, sentence or order passed or made by any court or tribunal in India. Article 227 further invests the High Courts with the power of superintendence over all courts and tribunals within their jurisdiction.

All legislative actions of the administration have been expressly brought by the Constitution within the purview of Article 13 by defining "law" as including "order", "bye-law", "rule" and "notification", etc. having the force of law. Therefore, the rule-making action of the administration can be challenged not only on the ground that it is ultra vires the delegating statute but also on the ground that it violates the fundamental rights guaranteed under the Constitution.[16] An administrative act will also be void if it contravenes any other provisions of the Constitution outside Part III of the Constitution, *i.e.* Articles 301, 311, 314 or 365.[17] In the same manner

15. *See*, Prof. Upendra Baxi, "Pre-Marxist Socialism and the Supreme Court", (1983) 4 SCC J-3; a paper submitted to a seminar on Company Law under the auspices of the Indian Law Institute and the J.C. College of Law, Bombay.

16. *Dwarka Prasad Laxmi Narain* v. *State of U.P.*, AIR 1954 SC 224; *Zafar Ali Shah* v. *Custodian*, AIR 1967 SC 106; *Bidi Supply Company* v. *Union of India*, AIR 1956 SC 479; *State of Bombay* v. *Bombay Education Society*, AIR 1954 SC 561; *Kameshwar Prasad* v. *State of Bihar*, AIR 1962 SC 1166; *Mervyn Coutindo* v. *Collector of Customs*, AIR 1967 SC 52; *Kharak Singh* v. *State of U.P.*, AIR 1963 SC 1295; *Maneka Gandhi* v. *Union of India*, (1978) 1 SCC 248.

17. *Firm Ghulam Hussain Haji Yakoob and Sons* v. *State of Rajasthan*, AIR 1963 SC 379; *Atiabari Tea Co. Ltd.* v. *State of Assam*, AIR 1961 SC 232; *S. Sukhbans Singh* v. *State of Punjab*, AIR 1962 SC 1711; *Accountant General* v. *N. Bakshi*, AIR 1962 SC 505.

when the action of the administration is quasi-judicial, it can be challenged not only on the ground that it is ultra vires the Constitution but also on the ground that the delegating act is itself unconstitutional.[18] Thus, within the fabric of tremendous growth in the administrative process in almost every field, an effective control mechanism has been woven.

Besides the growth of administrative process, which is possible through legislation and executive actions, the Constitution itself provides for the establishment of some administrative agencies to regulate a particular field, *i.e.* Article 263, creation of Inter-State Council; Article 280, Finance Commission; Article 262, Inter-State Water Dispute Authority; Article 315, Public Service Commissions of India; and Article 324, Election Commission.

Today in India, the administrative process has grown so much that it will not be out of place to say that today we are not governed but administered. In this context, the Law Commission of India rightly observed:

> The rule of law and judicial review acquire greater significance in a welfare state...the vast amount of legislation which has been enacted during the last three years by the Union and the States, a great deal of which impinges in a variety of ways on our lives and occupations. Much of it also confers large powers on the executive. The greater, therefore, is the need for ceaseless enforcement of the rule of law, so that the executive may not, in a belief in its monopoly of wisdom and its zeal for administrative efficiency, overstep the bounds of its power and spread its tentacles into the domains where the citizen should be free to enjoy the liberty guaranteed to him by the Constitution.[19]

Observations of Law Commission are no less relevant today when India has adopted the policy of liberalisation, privatisation and globalisation in which administrative law has developed international dimensions. Though State is now withdrawing from business, yet its functions as a facilitator, enablor and regulator are bound to increase. Growth of new centres of economic power which often exercise power in total disregard of the fundamental rights of people, especially of the disadvantaged sections of society, will put emphasis on the development of new norms of rule of law and judicial review for reconciling economic growth with social justice.

To appreciate the principles of administrative law, a good knowledge of social economic, political, and cultural realities is necessary and these realities are: chaotic exercise of public power; corruption and lack of accountability; factionalism based on caste, religion, language and region; and low performance by public authorities. These realities make the study of administrative law significant and vital. People have not lost faith in the system, they want it to perform and administrative law plays a vital role in the system performance.

18. *Bidi Supply Company* v. *Union of India*, AIR 1956 SC 479; *Express Newspapers (P) Ltd.* v. *Union of India*, AIR 1958 SC 578.
19. Fourteenth Law Commission Report, Vol. II, 672.

3. DIFFERENCE BETWEEN CONSTITUTIONAL LAW AND ADMINISTRATIVE LAW

Constitutional law and administrative law are parts of the public law. While constitutional law is anti-majoritarian, administrative law is anti-authoritarian. In every constitutional democracy, power is limited by express or implied constitutional limitations and values. In administrative law exercise of constitutional power is limited by the norms and principles of administrative law of fairness, reasonableness and justness. In this manner administrative law is the common law of the Constitution which fills the Constitution in the same manner as equity filled the law in Britain. Administrative law makes constitutional governance public-centric and the State incrementally ethical.

To the early English writers on administrative law there was no difference between administrative law and constitutional law. Therefore, Keith observed:

> It is logically impossible to distinguish administrative from constitutional law and all attempts to do so are artificial.

However, according to Holland, the constitutional law describes the various organs of government at rest, while administrative law describes them in motion.[20] Therefore, according to this view, the structure of the legislature and the executive comes within the purview of constitutional law, but their functioning comes within the sphere of administrative law. Maitland, however, does not agree with this classification for, in that case, powers and prerogatives of the Crown would be relegated to the arena of administrative law.[21]

According to another view,[22] administrative law deals with the organisation, functions, powers and duties of administrative authorities while constitutional law deals with the general principles relating to the organisation and powers of various organs of the State and their mutual relationships and relationship of these organs with the individual. In other words, constitutional law deals with fundamentals while administrative law deals with the details.

It may also be pointed out that constitutional law deals with the rights and administrative law lays emphasis on public needs. However, a dividing line between constitutional law and administrative law is a matter of convenience because every student of administrative law has to study some constitutional law.[23]

In countries which have written constitutions, the difference between constitutional law and administrative law is not so blurred as it is in England. In such countries, the source of constitutional law is the Constitution while

20. Holland, *Constitutional Law of England* (1st Edn.) 506.
21. Maitland, *Constitutional History of England* (1908) 526.
22. Jennings, *The Law and the Constitution* (5th Edn.) 217.
23. *See*, Benjafield and Whitmore, *Principles of Australian Administrative Law* (4th Edn.) 12.

the source of administrative law may be statutes, statutory instruments, precedents and customs.

Whatever may be the arguments and counter-arguments, the fact remains that today administrative law is recognised as a separate, independent branch of the legal discipline, though at times the disciplines of constitutional law and administrative law may overlap.

The correct position seems to be that if one draws two circles of administrative law and constitutional law, at a certain place they may overlap and this area may be termed as the "watershed" in administrative law.

In India, in the watershed one can include the whole control mechanism provided in the Constitution for the control of administrative authorities, *i.e.* Articles 32, 136, 226, 227, 300 and 311. It may also include the study of those administrative agencies which are provided for by the Constitution itself, *i.e.* Inter-State Council, Article 263; Finance Commission, Article 280; Inter-State Water Dispute Authority, Article 262; Public Service Commissions, Article 315; and Election Commission, Article 324. It may further include the study of constitutional limitations on delegation of powers to the administrative authorities and also those provisions of the Constitution which place fetters on administrative action, *i.e.* fundamental rights.

4. DROIT ADMINISTRATIF

In France, Droit Administratif can be defined as a body of public law which determines the organisation and the duties of public administration, and regulates the relations of the administration with the citizens of the State.

Droit Administratif is associated with the name of Napoleon Bonaparte. Before the Revolution in 1789, there was a constant see-saw struggle for power going on in the French politics between the traditionalist Bonapartists (who supported the executive power even in judicial matters) and reformist parliaments (who supported the jurisdiction of ordinary courts). In pre-revolutionary France, Conseil du Roi advised the King in legal and administrative matters. This body can be compared with Curia Regis and the Privy Council in Britain during feudalistic days. Conseil du Roi also discharged judicial functions such as deciding disputes between great nobles. Ordinary courts (Parlements) became jealous and not only interfered with the functioning of the executive but also tried to impede the growth of the measures which the monarchy wanted to introduce.

After the Revolution in 1789, a major breakthrough was made in this deadlock. The first step taken by the revolutionists was to curtail the power of the executive which was done on the theory of separation of powers by the famous 16–24 August 1790 Law. Conseil du Roi was abolished and the King's powers were curtailed. Napoleon, who became the first Consul, favoured freedom for the administration and also favoured reforms. He wanted an institution to give relief to the people against the excesses of the administration. Therefore, in 1799 Conseil d'Etat was established. The main aim of the institution was to resolve difficulties which might occur in the course of the administration. However, in due course of time it started exercising judicial powers in matters involving administration. In the beginning it was not an independent court but an appendage of the executive. Its main task was to advise the Minister with whom the complaint was to be lodged. In fact the Minister was the judge, and the Conseil d'Etat administered only advisory justice. It did not have public sessions. It had no power to pronounce judgments. It represented the government's point of view. It was this aspect of the Conseil d'Etat which was against Dicey's concept of the rule of law.

In 1872, its formal power to give judgment was established. The Arrets (Executive Law) Blanco, 8 February 1873 finally laid down and settled that in all matters involving administration, the jurisdiction of the Conseil d'Etat would be final. It laid down, among other things, the principle that questions of administrative liability would be within the jurisdiction of administrative courts, and that the liability was subject to special rules different from those of Droit Civil. In 1889, it started receiving direct complaints from the citizens and not through Ministers.

Droit Administratif does not represent principles and rules laid down by the French Parliament; it consists of rules developed by the judges of the administrative courts. Droit Administratif, therefore, includes three series of rules:

(1) *Rules dealing with administrative authorities and officials.*—These relate to appointment, dismissal, status, salary, and duties, etc.

(2) *Rules dealing with the operation of public services to meet the needs of citizens.*—These services may be operated either wholly by public officials or under their supervision or they may assist private agencies to provide public utility services.

(3) *Rules dealing with administrative adjudication.*—If any injury is done to a private citizen by the administration, the matter would be decided by the administrative courts. Conseil d'Etat is the highest administrative court. This system of administrative adjudication developed in France due to historical reasons in order to avoid encroachment by the courts on the powers of the administrative authorities and prevent intrusion by the judges into the business of the administration.

In case of conflict between the ordinary courts and the administrative courts regarding jurisdiction, the matter is decided by the Tribunal des Conflicts. This tribunal consists of an equal number of ordinary and administrative judges and is presided over by the Minister of Justice.

There is no Code of Droit Administratif like the Code Civil. The Conseil d'Etat has developed and elaborated the doctrines on its own. This has been done neither to justify the arbitrary powers of the administrative officials nor to narrow the field of citizens' liberty but to help citizens against the excesses of the administration. Sometimes these new doctrines created by the Conseil d'Etat have been adopted in the Civil Code through Parliament.

From the above discussion, the following characteristics of the Droit Administratif in France may be noted:

(1) Matters concerning the State and administrative litigation are decided by the administrative courts and not by the ordinary courts of the land.
(2) In deciding matters concerning the State and administrative litigation, special rules as developed by the administrative courts are applied.
(3) Conflict of jurisdiction between ordinary courts and administrative courts are decided by the agency known as Tribunal des Conflits.
(4) It protects government officials from the control of the ordinary courts.
(5) Conseil d'Etat which is the supreme administrative court is not a priori invention but is the product of historical process with deep roots. It is not merely an adjudicatory body but is also a consultative body. In 1979, it considered 147 draft laws which were placed before Parliament in 1980 and also considered 489 draft decrees.[24]

The early common criticism of the Droit Administratif in France has been that it cannot protect the private citizen from the excesses of the administration. However, later researches have shown that no single institution has done so much for the protection of private citizens against the excesses of the administration as has been done by the Conseil d'Etat.[25]

POINTS FOR DISCUSSION

1. There is a great divergence of opinion regarding the definition or concept of administrative law. How did it arise?
2. Difficulties in attempting a uniform agreed definition of administrative law with special reference to different constitutional structurisations and claim patterns.
3. Analysis of cause and effect theory common to all administrative development patterns in various jurisdictions of the world.
4. "Administrative law is the study of the pathology of governmental power." This formulation may be discussed against the backdrop of the grant and the exercise of public power in "authoritarian", "liberal" and "non-liberal'" societies.
5. Administrative law is a valiant endeavour to help reduce and diminish arbitrariness in the exercise of public power. Students may discuss the general and specific forms of accountability of the rulers to the ruled. Discussion may include constitutional, legislative, judicial and other informal forms of accountability.

24. William Dale (Tr.), Bernard Ducamin, "Role of Conseil d'Etat in Drafting Legislation", Int'l & (Oct. 1981) 30 Comp LQ, Part 4, 882.
25. Hamson, *Judicial Control of Administrative Discretion. See also,* Waline, *Droit Administratif*, Chap. I.

6. "Easy access to justice" is considered an important form of accountability. This may include informal procedure, speedy and less expensive trial, legal aid, public interest litigation, easy bail, and active participation of judges. This form of control mechanism may be discussed with special reference to India with a view to suggest improvements.
7. Administrative law in India is wholly a judge-made law which has all the "strengths and frailties of judicial law-making". These strengths and frailties may be discussed with special reference to a trade-off between executive arbitrariness and judicial arbitrariness inherent in judicial review.
8. Administrative lawyers in the common-law world are content to debate the question of the proper role of the courts in reviewing administrative action. Whereas, the US administrative law is seen to be as much concerned with what goes on inside the administration as it is with judicial scrutiny of the administrative process. Against this backdrop, the proper scope and nature of the administrative law may be discussed.
9. Administrative law is said to be "an instrument in the hands of middle-class Indians to combat administrative authoritarianism through the instrumentality of courts". Students may discuss the constituency, input, output and compliance factors of the judicial process with a view to suggest measures which can make administrative law a shield for the majority of Indians living below or slightly above the poverty line.
10. Relevance of French administrative law in a system of intensive form of government.
11. Overlapping boundaries between constitutional law and administrative law with reference to the obsession of the early English writers to acknowledge administrative law as a regular member of the legal community.
12. Rise of global administrative law with the growth of global administrative space with a view to infuse equity, inclusiveness and accountability in the administrative process may be discussed with special reference to developing world.

SUGGESTED READINGS

1. A.V. Dicey, *Law and Public Opinion in England* (1962) 126–210.
2. A.V. Dicey, *Law of the Constitution* (1950), Appendix by E.C.S. Wade, 175–544.
3. Abhishek Dubey, "The Relationship Between Constitutional Law and Administrative Law: An Indian Perspective", (2006) PL August 7.
4. Benjafield and Whitmore, *Principles of Australian Administrative Law* (4th Edn.) Chap. I.
5. Brown and Garner, *French Administrative Law* (1967) Introduction.
6. Brown Jethro, *The Underlying Principles of Modern Legislation* (1971) 156–280.
7. C.B. MacPherson, *The Real World of Democracy* (1972) Chap. I.

8. C.J. Hamson, *Executive Discretion and Judicial Control: An Aspect of the French Conseil d'État* (1954).
9. C.K. Thakker, *Administrative Law* (Eastern Book Company, 2012) Chap. I.
10. Denning, *Freedom Under the Law* (1949) 124–29.
11. F.A. Hayek, *The Road to Serfdom* (1956) 76–80.
12. Fourteenth Law Commission Report (1958) 674–76.
13. Freund, *Cases on Administrative Law: Selected from Decisions of English and American Courts*, (1911) Chap. I.
14. Griffith and Street, *Principles of Administrative Law*, Chap. I.
15. Jain and Jain, *Principles of Administrative Law*, Chap. I.
16. Jennings, *The Law and the Constitution* (1955) 215–19.
17. Joseph Minattur, "French Administrative Law", 16 JILI (1974) 364.
18. Lord Hewart, *The New Despotism* (1929) Chap. I.
19. M.A. Fazal, *Judicial Control of Administrative Action in India and Pakistan: A Comparative Study of Principles and Remedies* (1969) Chap. I.
20. Maitland, *Constitutional History* (1908) 526–39.
21. Mauro Cappelletti (Ed.), *Access to Justice* (1979) 79.
22. P. Selznick, *Law, Society and Industrial Justice* (1969) Chap. I.
23. Parker, "The Historic Basis of Administrative Law", (1958) 1 Rutgers L Rev 449.
24. Prettyman, "Nature of Administrative Law", (1958) 44 Va L Rev 685.
25. Ramaswamy, "Rule of Law in a Planned Society", (1959) 1 JILI 31.
26. Robson, *Justice and Administrative Law: A Study of the British Constitution* (1951) Chap. I.
27. S.A. de Smith, *Constitutional Law and Administrative Law* (1977) 511–22.
28. S.E. Finer, *Comparative Government* (1970).
29. S.N. Jain, "Law, Justice and Affirmative Action", (1979) 21 JILI 262.
30. Schwartz, *American Administrative Law* (1962) Chap. I.
31. Schwartz, *French Administrative Law and the Common-Law World* (1954) Vanderbilt's Introduction, XIII.
32. Thio Li-ann, "Administrative and Constitutional Law", (2014) 15 SALAnnRev 1.
33. Timothy Endicott, *Administrative Law* (Oxford University Press 2015).
34. Upendra Baxi (Ed.), *Mathew's Democracy, Equality and Freedom* (1978) XXXVIII ff.
35. Upendra Baxi, "Mass Copying: Should Courts Act as Controllers of Examination?" Delhi LR 144 and "The Supreme Court Under Trial: The Supreme Court and Undertrials", (1980) 1 SCC J-35.
36. Wade, *Administrative Law* (1971) Chap. I.
37. William Dale (Tr.), Bernard Ducamin, "Role of Conseil d'Etat in Drafting Legislation", (Oct. 1981) 30 Int'l & Comp LQ Part 4, 882.

CHAPTER 2

Conceptual Objections against the Growth of Administrative Law

1. CONCEPT OF THE RULE OF LAW

While in Europe, administrative law has been, for a century and a half, a separate branch of law and a subject for academic study, it is only during the last few decades that, in the US and the common-law world, it has attained full stature as a "respectable" field of study for the law students and practitioners.[1] The reason seems to be that the people had a mistrust regarding the growth of administrative process, and hence did not recognise its independent existence. The weapon which the people in England used to strike at the growth of administrative law was Dicey's formulation of the concept of the rule of law.

"Rule of law" is the supreme manifestation of human civilization and culture and is a new "lingua franca" of global moral thought. It is an eternal value of constitutionalism and an inherent attribute of democracy and good governance. The core task of administrative law is to impose the rule of law on public authorities in order to achieve the objective of good and responsible government. Thus, rule of law is a principle of exercise of power by the government whereas the doctrine of separation of powers is a principle of allocation of power. Both the principles are mutually exclusive.

The concept of the rule of law is an animation of natural law and remains as a historical ideal which makes a powerful appeal even today to be ruled by law not by a powerful man.

"Rule of law" is to be understood neither as a "rule" nor a "law". It is generally understood as a doctrine of "state political morality" which concentrates on the rule of law in securing a "correct balance" between "rights" and "powers", between individuals, and between individuals and the State in any free and civil society. This balance may be drawn by "law" based on freedom, justice, equality, and accountability. Therefore, it infuses law with moral qualities.[2] "Rule of proper law balances the needs of society and the individual."[3]

1. Benjafield and Whitmore, *Principles of Australian Administrative Law* (1971) 1.
2. Alex Carrol, *Constitution and Administrative Law*, 40 (2nd Edn., 2002).
3. Aharon Barak, "Begin and the Rule of Law" (Fall 2005) 10(3) Israel Studies 1–28.

The term "rule of law" is derived from the French phrase *la principe de legalite* (the principle of legality) which refers to a government based on principles of law and not of men. In this sense the concept of *la principe de legalite* was opposed to arbitrary powers.

Early Greeks located the concept of the rule of law in "right reason" which must inform all State actions. Aristotle (384–322 BC) made a difference between procedural justice and moral justice. Rule of law can be located in moral justice. Thomas Aquinas and St. Augustine located it in Laws of God; Hobbes, Locke, Rousseau located it in secular traditions of "social contract" in which a State is formed only to protect the life, liberty and dignity of the individual. Dicey located it in right-based liberalism and judicial review. Modern writers like Richard Fallon locate it in quality of law which includes clarity, efficacy, stability, authority and impartial justice. Nevertheless, Edward Coke is said to be the originator of this concept when he asserted that king must be under God and law and, thus, vindicated the supremacy of law over pretensions of the executive.

James M. Buchanan[4] distinguishes between "law" and the "rule of law". All primitive and non-democratic societies had "law", but all liberal and progressive societies having "rule of law" are not necessarily lawless societies. According to him "generality" is at the centre of rule of law, besides fairness, prospectivity and due process. Generality as an ingredient of law forecloses many majoritarian options, but classification is still possible provided it is reasonable and in public interest. Generality, as a normative principle of rule of law, makes law more acceptable and there are less chances of oppression and discrimination. Generality provides for more liberty and freedom for action and protects human rights of the people.

Rule of law, as a higher law, provides an ideal which societies can emulate. It thus provides a criterion with references to which one can evaluate law and legal structures of governance of any society. Rule of law is possible only in democratic societies, where it puts restraints on majoritarian rule. The term "rule of law" can be used both in normative and functional sense. A society may be a rule of law society in normative sense but may not be in realist or functional sense of the term. Therefore, realistic and functional approach to the rule of law concept is articulated over more abstract and normative approach.

If put in perspective, "rule of law" mandates that power must be made accountable, governance progressively just and equal, and State incrementally ethical.

In India, the concept of the rule of law can be traced to the Upanishads. It provides: "Law is the King of Kings. It is more powerful and rigid than they (Kings). There is nothing higher than law. By its powers the weak shall prevail over the strong and justice shall triumph." Thus in monarchy, the

4. James M. Buchman, *Criteria for a Free Society: Definition, Diagnosis and Prescription, In collected works of Buchman* (2001).

concept of law developed to control the exercise of arbitrary powers of the monarchs who claimed divine powers to rule. In a democracy, the concept has assumed different dimensions and means that the holders of public powers must be able to justify publicly that the exercise of power is legally valid and socially just. Prof. A.V. Dicey later developed on this concept in the course of his lectures at the Oxford University. Dicey was an individualist; at the end of the golden Victorian era of laissez faire in England, he wrote about the concept of the rule of law. That was the reason why Dicey's concept of the rule of law contemplated the absence of wide powers in the hands of government officials. According to him, wherever there is discretion, there is room for arbitrariness.[5]

The rule of law is a viable and dynamic concept and, like many other such concepts, is not capable of any exact definition. This, however, does not mean that there is no agreement on the basic values which it represents. The term rule of law is used in contradistinction to "rule of man" and "rule according to law". Even in the most autocratic forms of government there is some law according to which the powers of the government are exercised, but it does not mean that there is the rule of law. Therefore, rule of law means that the law rules, which is based on the principles of freedom, equality, non-discrimination, fraternity, accountability and non-arbitrariness, and is certain, regular and predictable, using the word "law" in the sense of "jus" and "lex" both. In this sense the "rule of law" is an ideal. It is a modern name for natural law. In history, man has always appealed to something higher than that which is his own creation. In jurisprudence, Romans called it "jus naturale"; Mediaevalists called it the "Law of God"; Hobbes, Locke and Rousseau called it "social contract" or "natural law"; and the modern man calls it the "rule of law".

The basic concept of the rule of law is not a well-defined legal concept. The courts generally would not invalidate any positive law on the ground that it violates the contents of the rule of law. However, in *ADM, Jabalpur* v. *Shivakant Shukla*[6], popularly known as *Habeas Corpus case*, an attempt was made to challenge the detention orders during the Emergency on the ground that it violates the principles of the rule of law as the "obligation to act in accordance with rule of law... is a central feature of our constitutional system and is a basic feature of the Constitution". Though the contention did not succeed and some justices even went on to suggest that during an emergency, the emergency provisions themselves constitute the rule of law, yet if the reasoning of all the five opinions is closely read, it becomes clear that the contention was accepted, no matter it did not reflect in the final order passed by the court.[7] Therefore, despite the unfortunate order to the effect that the doors of the court during an emergency are

5. Dicey, *Law of the Constitution* (8th Edn.) 198.
6. (1976) 2 SCC 521.
7. *See*, Upendra Baxi, "Developments in Indian Administrative Law" in A.G. Noorani (Ed.), *Public Law in India* (1982) 134. See also, *The Indian Supreme Court and politics* (1980).

completely shut for the detenus, it is gratifying to note that the concept of the rule of law can be used as a legal concept.

In the opinion of some of the judges constituting the majority in *Kesavananda Bharati* v. *State of Kerala*[8] (*Keşavananda Bharati*), the rule of law was considered as an "aspect of the doctrine of basic structure of the Constitution, which even the plenary power of Parliament cannot reach to amend".[9]

In *Indira Nehru Gandhi* v. *Raj Narain*[10] (*Indira Nehru Gandhi*), in which the Supreme Court invalidated clause (4) of Article 329-A inserted in the Constitution by the Constitution (39th Amendment) Act, 1975[11] to immunise the election dispute to the office of the Prime Minister from any kind of judicial review, Khanna and Chandrachud JJ held that Article 329-A violated the concept of basic structure.[12] Other justices though did not go to this extent but certainly held that Article 329-A, clause (4) offends the concept of the rule of law. Ray CJ held that since the validation of the Prime Minister's election was not by applying any law, therefore it offended the rule of law.[13] According to Mathew J, clause (4) of Article 329-A offended the rule of law which postulates the pervasiveness of the spirit of law throughout the whole range of government in the sense of excluding arbitrary official action in any sphere.[14] Referring to the same constitutional provision, Beg J observed that the jurisdiction of the Supreme Court to try a case on merits cannot be taken away without injury to the basic postulates of the rule of law and of justice within a politically democratic constitutional structure.[15] "A study of *Kesavananda*, *Indira Gandhi* and other *Habeas Corpus* cases", writes Prof. Baxi,

> provides a distillation of Indian judicial thought on the conceptions of the Rule of Law, which has evolved well over a quarter century. References to western theories and thinkers from Dicey onwards abound in these opinions; but these occur by way of rhetorical flourishes, masking the typically Indian approaches.[16]

Taking a cue from its earlier decisions, the Supreme Court in *P. Sambamurthy* v. *State of A.P.*[17] categorically stated that Article 371-D(5) (proviso) of the Constitution clearly violates the rule of law which is a basic structure and essential feature of the Constitution. This provision had authorised the Andhra Pradesh State Government to nullify any decision

8. (1973) 4 SCC 225. See also, *Mohinder Singh Gill* v. *Chief Election Commr.*, (1978) 1 SCC 405, 431, para. 38.
9. *Ibid*, para. 133 (SCC).
10. 1975 Supp SCC 1.
11. Art. 329-A was *omitted* by the Constitution (Forty-fourth Amendment) Act, 1978.
12. *See*, Upendra Baxi, "Developments in Indian Administrative Law" in A.G. Noorani (Ed.), *Public Law in India* (1982) 134.
13. *See*, 1975 Supp SCC 1, para. 59.
14. *Indira Nehru Gandhi* v. *Raj Narain*, 1975 Supp SCC 1.
15. *Ibid*, para. 623.
16. *See*, Upendra Baxi, "Developments in Indian Administrative Law" in A.G. Noorani (Ed.), *Public Law in India* (1982) 134.
17. (1987) 1 SCC 362.

of the administrative services tribunal. Declaring the provision unconstitutional, the court maintained that it is a basic principle of the rule of law that the exercise of power by the executive or by any other authority must not only be conditioned by the Constitution but must also be in accordance with law and the power of judicial review as conferred by the Constitution with a view to ensuring that the law is observed and there is compliance with the requirement of law on the part of executive and other authorities, and it is through the power of judicial review that the rule of law is maintained and every organ of the State is kept within the limits of law. The Supreme Court rightly observed in *Som Raj* v. *State of Haryana*[18] that the absence of arbitrary power is the first postulate of the rule of law upon which whole constitutional edifice is based. If the discretion is exercised without any principle or without any rule, it is a situation amounting to the antithesis of the rule of law.

Anyone who surveys the decisional law in this area will come to the conclusion that the concept of the rule of law has developed many facets which are not only negative providing constraints on governmental action but affirmative also imposing an affirmative duty of fairness on the government. These various negative and affirmative facets have been summarised by Prof. Upendra Baxi thus:

> One is that power should not be exercised arbitrarily. This has meant that it should be exercised for the purpose for which it has been conferred. It also means that power should be exercised within the statutory ambit; and purported exercise of it would not just be ultra vires, but in a true sense of the term arbitrary. Simple negation of arbitrariness is, however, not enough to preserve the Rule of Law values. Indian courts have gone further to insist on specific positive content of the Rule of Law obligations. These include the rules of natural justice which have to be followed not just in quasi-judicial action but often also in purely administrative action. The scope and content of the requirements of natural justice have varied from time to time according to the judicial interpretation, but the broad insistence remains. In addition, access to information as to the grounds of decision has remained an important preoccupation of the Indian judiciary, as any impediments to it have the tendency of obstructing judicial review of administrative action. This means that the courts have from time to time insisted that exercise of administrative power be accompanied by reasons, although the exact status of the obligation to give reasons is as yet indeterminate. The Rule of Law notion has been in addition consistently extended to secure for the individual fair dealing by the State in its economic activities. For example, the government is held bound by its assurance to individuals in business transactions by way of estoppel. The State has to follow some of the rules of natural justice before reaching a decision that it would not trade with certain contractors or before blacklisting them. In matters involving government contracts, the courts have been increasingly keen to insist that the ambit of fair play is not lessened in view of the dominating capacity of the State over the individuals. In the area of losses and injury arising out of State economic

18. (1990) 2 SCC 653, 658–59.

> entrepreneurial function, courts have tended to restrict the scope of the defence of sovereign immunity in favour of the affected individuals.[19]

It is heartening to see that the courts are making all concerted efforts to establish a rule of law society in India by insisting on "fairness" in every aspect of the exercise of power by the State. Some of the recent decisions of the Supreme Court are clear indicators of this trend. In *Sheela Barse* v. *State of Maharashtra*[20], the court insisted on "fairness" to women in police lock-up and drafted a code of guidelines for the protection of prisoners in police custody, especially female prisoners. In *State of M.P.* v. *Ramashanker Raghuvanshi*[21], the court secured "fairness" in public employment by holding that reliance on police reports is entirely misplaced in a democratic republic. Thus, the efforts of the courts in legitimising "due" administrative powers and illegitimising "undue" powers[22] by operationalising substantive and procedural norms and standards can be seen as a high benchmark of judicial activism for firmly establishing the concept of the rule of law in India.

The term "rule of law" can be used in two senses: 1) formalistic sense; and 2) ideological sense. If used in the formalistic sense, it refers to organised power as opposed to a rule by one man; and if used in an ideological sense, it refers to the regulation of the relationship of the citizens and the government and in this sense, it becomes a concept of varied interest and contents.

In its ideological sense, the concept of rule of law represents an ethical code for the exercise of public power in any country. Strategies of this code may differ from society to society depending on the societal needs at any given time, but its basic postulates are universal covering all space and time. These postulates include equality, freedom and accountability. "Equality" is not a mechanical and negative concept but has progressive and positive contents which oblige every government to create conditions: social, economic, and political; where every individual has an equal opportunity to develop his personality to the fullest and to live with dignity. "Freedom" postulates absence of every arbitrary action, free speech, expression and association, personal liberty, and many others. These basic rights of any society may be restricted only on the ground that the claims of these freedoms would be better served by such circumscription. The basic idea behind "accountability" is that the rulers rule with the deference of the people and, therefore, must be accountable to them in the ultimate analysis. Forms of accountability may differ, but the basic idea must remain the same that the holders of public power must be able publicly to justify the exercise of public power not only as legally valid but also socially just, proper and

19. *See*, Upendra Baxi, "Developments in Indian Administrative Law" in A.G. Noorani (Ed.), *Public Law in India* (1982) 134–35.
20. (1983) 2 SCC 96. See also, *Veena Sethi* v. *State of Bihar*, (1982) 2 SCC 583.
21. (1983) 2 SCC 145.
22. *See*, M.P. Jain, *Changing Face of Administrative Law, India and Abroad* (1982) 3.

reasonable.[23] In this manner the concept of the rule of law represents values and not institutions and connotes a climate of legal order which is just and reasonable, wherein every exercise of public power is chiefly designed to add something more to the quality of life of the people. Every legislative, executive and judicial exercise of power must, therefore, depend on this ideal for its validity. Consequently, it is the rule of law which must define law rather than the law defining the rule of law.[24]

Dicey's formulation of the concept of "rule of law", which according to him forms the basis of the English constitutional law, contains three principles:

(1) Absence of discretionary power in the hands of the government officials. By this Dicey implies that justice must be done through known principles. Discretion implies absence of rules, hence in every exercise of discretion there is room for arbitrariness.

(2) No person should be made to suffer in body or deprived of his property except for a breach of law established in the ordinary legal manner before the ordinary courts of the land. In this sense, the rule of law implies

   (*a*) absence of special privileges for a government official or any other person;

   (*b*) all the persons irrespective of status must be subjected to the ordinary courts of the land;

   (*c*) everyone should be governed by the law passed by the ordinary legislative organs of the State.

(3) The rights of the people must flow from the customs and traditions of the people recognised by the courts in the administration of justice.

Dicey developed the contents of his thesis by peeping from a foggy England into a sunny France. In France, Dicey observed that the government officials exercised wide discretionary powers, and if there was any dispute between a government official and a private individual, it was tried not by an ordinary court but by a special administrative court. The law applicable in that case was not the ordinary law but a special law developed by the administrative court. From this Dicey concluded that this system spelt the negation of the concept of the rule of law which is the secret of Englishmen's liberty. Therefore, Dicey concluded that there was no administrative law in England.

The first principle of Dicey's rule of law is the recognition of a cardinal principle of democratic governments as opposed to arbitrary and autocratic governments which lays down that no functionary of the government should have wide arbitrary or discretionary powers to interfere with the liberty and freedom of the people. But here Dicey was not referring to a wide measure of discretion which is inescapable in any modern government. He

23. *See,* Introduction by Prof. Upendra Baxi to this book.
24. *Ibid.*

was certainly indicating the position in some countries where police authorities exercised wide arbitrary or discretionary power of imprisonment and punishment outside the ordinary legal system.

The second principle of Dicey's rule of law also enunciates a democratic principle of equal subjection of all persons to the ordinary law of the land as administered by the ordinary courts. This does not mean that the law must be the same for everybody irrespective of functions or service. Dicey's insistence was that a government officer must be under the same liability for acts done without legal justification as a private individual. Thus, he contrasts the English legal system with that of France where government officials were protected by special rules in special administrative tribunals.

The third principle of Dicey, in fact, does not lay down any legal rule but merely explains one aspect of the British constitutional system where common law is the source of fundamental freedoms of the people. He thus distinguishes the British system from that of many other countries which had written constitutions with a chapter on individual rights. Dicey feared that if the source of the fundamental rights of the people was any document, the right could be abrogated at any time by amending the Constitution. This is what happened in India during the 1975 Emergency when the Supreme Court ruled that even illegal acts of the government could not be challenged in a court because it was found that the source of personal liberty in India was Article 21 of the Constitution, which had been suspended by the Presidential Proclamation, and not any common law of the people.[25]

Evaluation of Dicey's thesis.—It has become a fashion to criticise Dicey. Sir Ivor Jennings did it most effectively. But in order to be fair to Dicey, one must understand his personality and the compulsions of the times when he developed his thesis. Until lately, nothing was known about Dicey's inner self. Researches mainly concentrated on his contribution in the field of constitutional law. However, Prof. R.A. Cosgrove[26] gives a unique insight into various facets of Dicey's personality. The portrait of Dicey which Prof. Cosgrove paints shatters all images which students of constitutional law and administrative law have built of this great scholar. Prof. Cosgrove has explored the voluminous correspondence of Dicey with friends like Bryce and Strachey. He discovers in Dicey a sombre, uncompromising and artless figure, lacking in confidence as a scholar and frustrated in his political ambitions. He is painted as a remote figure for whom passing years brought increasing disillusionment with the world where politics of party supplants politics of country, where trade unions are above law, and where socialist dogma is gaining ground. As a lawyer of the Victorian era, he was highly individualistic and advocated a referendum for giving self-rule to the people of Ireland. This iconoclastic description of Dicey's personality goes a long

25. *ADM, Jabalpur* v. *Shivakant Shukla*, (1976) 2 SCC 521.
26. R.A. Cosgrove, *Rule of Law*; Albert Venn Dicey, *Victorian Jurist* (1980). Professor Cosgrove's evaluation of Dicey can be accepted only with a pinch of philosophy that idols invariably must possess feet of base clay.

way in explaining his attitudes towards Droit Administratif of France and his rule of law doctrine. His total insistence on the institution of judges for the control of administrative action is clearly referable to his disillusionment with politics and politicians. Letters also confirm that Dicey never fully grasped the merits of administrative law.

Dicey believed that administrative law as it existed in Europe should have no place in the UK. One Mr Barthelemy, Dean, Law Faculty, Paris University asked Dicey, who was on holiday in France: What is the status of administrative law in England? He retorted, "In England we know nothing about administrative law and we wish to know nothing." However, it existed then and has grown today.

By administrative law Dicey meant only a single aspect of the French Droit Administratif, namely, administrative jurisdiction to the exclusion of ordinary civil and criminal process. Dicey admitted, after 1901, that he conceived his idea of the nature and existence of administrative law from de Tocqueville, who himself later admitted his ignorance about the actual working of the Droit Administratif in his own days.[27] Therefore, like de Tocqueville, Dicey also viewed the system as a historian rather than as a lawyer. He thus reached a natural conclusion, for he found a similarity between the system of French administrative law of his days and the institutions of ancient autocratic monarchy.

Dicey was historically correct up to the time of 1873, when Arrets (Executive Law) Blanco finally settled the jurisdiction of the Conseil d'Etat in all questions involving administrative matters. Among other things, the Blanco decision firmly laid down that questions of administrative liability would be within the jurisdiction of administrative courts and that this liability was subject to special rules different from those of droit civil. After the 1789 Revolution, the Conseil Du Roi which acted as an advisor to the King in all executive and judicial matters in France, like the Curia Regis of England, was replaced by the Conseil d'Etat in order to give relief to the people against the excesses of the administration. In the beginning, its function was only to resolve difficulties which occurred in the course of administration, but subsequently it entered the judicial sphere too. Prior to 1873, it was not an independent court but an appendage to the executive. It did not receive direct complaints from the public but through Ministers. It did not hold open sessions and represented the government's point of view. In fact, a Minister was the judge and the Conseil d'Etat thereby merely administered advisory justice. Therefore, writing against this backdrop at the end of the 19th century, Dicey entertained doubts, which was natural for an Englishman, and was dubious whether the administrative courts could give protection to the individual against administration.

However, Dicey misconceived the administrative law because he thought that the French system is administrative law, when administrative law

27. Dicey, *Introduction to the Study of the Law of the Constitution* (9th Edn., 1950) 392.

is more than that. In fact Dicey was concerned not with the whole body of law relating to administration, but with a single aspect of it, namely, administrative adjudication. His comparison was between the favourable position of an Englishman when in conflict with the State in contrast to that of a Frenchman. It may be emphasised that the difference between judicial and administrative agencies is not fundamental. Both apply the law to individual cases and thereby exercise discretion. But if the safeguards which protect the exercise of judicial functions are applied to administrative bodies, the quality of adjudication will be the same.[28] It is not the case that Dicey failed to realise that all lawful authority within the State is legal authority, but he relied upon one organ, the courts, to restrain the illegal excesses of the administration and did not examine the latter's lawful power to the full extent. It is upon this limited view of the administration that his interpretation of the rule of law rests.[29] Dicey was also not right when he said that there is no administrative law in England because even during Dicey's time the Crown and its servants enjoyed special privileges on the basis of the doctrine that "the King can do no wrong". There were also in existence special courts in England, *i.e.* ecclesiastical and admiralty courts. There were special tribunals established under the Poor Law Amendment Act, 1834 where Poor Law Boards were exercising legislative and adjudicatory powers. In the same manner, the Constables Protection Act, 1750 gave special immunity to police officers. Government officials enjoyed wide discretionary powers under the Public Health Acts to enter private properties. However, inspired by the decisions of the House of Lords in *Local Government Board* v. *Arlidge*[30] and *Board of Education* v. *Rice*[31], wherein the administrative agency was authorised to decide even a question of law, Dicey himself recognised his mistake and observed that there exists in England a vast body of administrative law. Even towards the end of his life he doubted whether official law, *i.e.* "administrative law", could be as effectively enforced by the courts as by "a body of men who combine official experience with legal knowledge", provided that they are entirely independent of the government.[32]

Even in the sense in which Dicey used his formulation of the rule of law, there is no essential contradiction between rule of law and administrative law. If the central thesis of Dicey's formulation is the absence of arbitrariness and equality before the law then in that sense there is no contradiction with administrative law.

---

28. Lauterpacht, *The function of law in the international community* (1933) Chap. 19, S. 2.
29. Dicey, *Introduction to the Study of the Law of the Constitution* (1959) Introduction by E.C.S. Wade, CIV.
30. 1915 AC 120 (HL).
31. 1911 AC 179 (HL).
32. Dicey, "The Development of Administrative Law in England", (1915) 31 LQR 148. Though in the final analysis, Dicey asserted that it is not a true administrative law because the supremacy of ordinary courts prevails. Dicey, *An Introduction to the Study of the Law of the Constitution* (9th Edn.) Introduction by Wade, LXIX.

Administrative law developed not to sanctify executive arbitrariness but to check it and protect the rights of the people against the administration's excesses. Therefore, the central theme of administrative law is also the reconciliation of liberty with power. Administrative law and the rule of law are not discrete series. Both aim at the "progressive diminution of arbitrariness and fostering a discipline of fairness and openness in the exercise of public power"[33]. However, though Dicey's distrust of the administrative process and administrative adjudication has been proved wrong in the French context, it is still valid in the Indian situation where administrative action is often arbitrary and based on extraneous considerations and administrative justice is an euphemism for the denial of justice.[34]

The modern concept of the rule of law is fairly wide and, therefore, sets up an ideal for any government to achieve. This concept was developed by the International Commission of Jurists, known as Delhi Declaration, 1959, which was later on confirmed at Lagos in 1961. According to this formulation, the rule of law implies that the functions of the government in a free society should be so exercised as to create conditions in which the dignity of man as an individual is upheld. This dignity requires not only the recognition of certain civil or political rights but also creation of certain political, social, economical, educational and cultural conditions which are essential to the full development of his personality and the protection of his dignity. For this purpose the Declaration puts emphasis on independence of the judiciary and effective government.

During the last few years, the Indian Supreme Court has developed some fine principles of Third World jurisprudence. Developing the same new constitutionalism further, the Supreme Court in *Veena Sethi* v. *State of Bihar*[35] extended the reach of the rule of law to the poor and the downtrodden, the ignorant and the illiterate, who constitute the bulk of humanity in India, when it ruled that the rule of law does not exist merely for those who have the means to fight for their rights and very often do so for the perpetuation of the status quo, which protects and preserves their dominance and permits them to exploit a large section of the community. The opportunity for this ruling was provided by a letter written by the Free Legal Aid Committee, Hazaribagh, Bihar drawing its attention to unjustified and illegal detention of certain prisoners in jail for almost two or three decades.

33. *See,* Introduction by Prof. Upendra Baxi to this book.

34. A classical recent illustration of arbitrary action is provided by the Punjab Engineering College, Chandigarh, where admissions for vacant seats were made not from the waiting-list according to merit but from amongst those candidates who perchance were present on the campus. The High Court of Punjab and Haryana quashed the action with the remark that the judicial bar against arbitrary action could not be outflanked by instant whimsicality. *Indian Express*, 15-9-1982, 9. (Supreme Court upheld the decision of the High Court. *Indian Express*, 5-3-1983).

35. (1982) 2 SCC 583, 586.

The Commission divided itself into certain working groups which tried to give content to the concept in relation to an individual's area of activity in a society:

(1) Committee on Individual Liberty and the Rule of Law, which laids down
 (*a*) that the State should not pass discriminatory laws;
 (*b*) that the State should not interfere with religious beliefs;
 (*c*) that the State should not place undue restrictions on freedoms.

(2) Committee on Government and the Rule of Law
 Under this the rule of law means not only the adequate safeguards against abuse of power but effective government capable of maintaining law and order.

(3) Committee on Criminal Administration and the Rule of Law
 Rule of law here means
 (*a*) due criminal process;
 (*b*) no arrest without the authority of law;
 (*c*) presumption of innocence;
 (*d*) legal aid;
 (*e*) public trial and fair hearing.

(4) Committee on Judicial Process and the Rule of Law
 Under this the rule of law means
 (*a*) independent judiciary;
 (*b*) independent legal profession;
 (*c*) standard of professional ethics.

In 1957, the University of Chicago held a conference on the rule of law as understood in the West. It was attended by 11 countries including two communist countries. The Secretary of the colloquium described the broad areas of agreement as follows:

(1) The rule of law is an expression of an endeavour to give reality to something which is not readily expressible; this difficulty is primarily due to identification of the rule of law with the concept of rights of man—all countries of the West recognise that the rule of law has a positive content, though that content is different in different countries; it is real and must be secured principally, but not exclusively, by the ordinary courts.

(2) The rule of law is based upon the liberty of the individual and has as its object the harmonising of the opposing notions of individual liberty and public order. The notion of justice maintains a balance between these notions. Justice has a variable content and cannot be strictly defined, but at a given time and place there is an appropriate standard by which the balance between private interest and the common good can be maintained.

(3) There is an important difference between the concept of rule of law as the supremacy of law over the government and the concept of rule

of law as the supremacy of law in society generally. The first concept is the only feature common to the West, connoting as it does the protection of the individual against arbitrary government—different techniques can be adopted to achieve the same end and the rule of law must not be conceived of as being linked to any particular technique. But it is fundamental that there must exist some technique for forcing the government to submit to the law; if such a technique does not exist, the government itself becomes the means whereby the law is achieved. This is the antithesis of the rule of law.

(4) Although much emphasis is placed upon the supremacy of the legislature in some countries of the West, the rule of law does not depend upon contemporary positive law—it may be expressed in positive law, but essentially it consists of values and not institution; it connotes a climate of legality and legal order in which the nations of the West live and in which they wish to continue to live.[36]

The Secretary General of the United Nations in its 2004 Report (5/2004/616) described rule of law to contain principles of governance and the measures necessary to ensure adherence to those principles.[37]

(1) *Principles of governance include*: Accountability of all persons, institutions and entities, public and private including State, to law which is publicly promulgated, equally enforced, independently adjudicated and is consistent with the human rights values, norms and standards.
(2) *Measures necessary to enforce these principles of governance may include*: Supremacy of law based on the above principles, equality before law and equal protection of law, fairness in the application of law, separation of powers, participation in the decision-making, legal certainty, avoidance of arbitrariness, procedural transparency and accountability to law.

Everyone agrees that rule of law is an important political ideal but there is a lot of disagreement on what that ideal is. According to R. Dworkin[38], there are two different conceptions of rule of law: 1) rule-book conception, 2) rights' conception. Rule-book conception provides that no State power be exercised against any individual except in accordance with the rules clearly laid down in the law-book available to all. State and individual both must be bound by these rules unless changed. This conception of rule of law is silent about the contents of law.

The second conception, "rights' conception", is an ideal of a just society which assumes that people have some moral rights and duties inter se and political rights against the State. These rights form the contents of rule

36. *See*, Goodhart, "The Rule of Law and Absolute Sovereignty", (1958) 106 Pennsylvania Law Review 946–63. Countries which attended the conference were the UK, West Germany, Italy, Canada, Sweden, Turkey, Brazil, Mexico, Israel, USSR and Poland.
37. *See* generally, Lord Bingham, *Rule of Law* (2003).
38. R. Dworkin, *A Matter of Principle* (Oxford University Press 1985).

of law which must be enforced against one another and the State by the courts. In this sense, the rule of law becomes an ideal of a just society. Moral rights of the citizens refer to pre-existing rights recognised under positive law, so that these may be enforced against individual and the State on demand by a citizen through courts or other judicial institutions.

Chief Justice of India N.V. Ramana, while delivering 17th Justice P.D. Desai Memorial Lecture on Rule of Law[39], identified four components of rule of law and ably brought out the difference between rule of law and rule by law. According to him, rule by law was the law with which India was governed during British rule and rule of law is what we fought for, *i.e.* law based on justice and equity.

CJI Ramana identified four principles of rule of law:

1. Law must be clear and accessible to the people.
2. Equality before law. This may include:
    (*a*) Law must be the same for the people who are equally circumstanced. Like must be treated alike.
    (*b*) Equal access to justice which may imply:
        (*i*) Equal capacity to enjoy and enforce rights.
        (*ii*) Gender equality which may include legal empowerment of women as bias and prejudice lead to injustice.
        (*iii*) Law must be inclusive of social conditions of the people.
3. Right to participate in the creation and refinement of law either directly or indirectly through their elected representatives.
4. Judiciary as a guardian of the Constitution and protector of the fundamental rights of the people and enforcer of rule of law. For this purpose the judiciary must be strong and independent. Power of judicial review as a basic feature of the Indian Constitution cannot be curtailed by Parliament even by amending the Constitution. Judicial independence and freedom is necessary to ensure proper checks and balances. However, he cautioned that judiciary cannot completely disassociate from the happenings in the society. Judges cannot live in "ivory castles". Judges must be free from executive pressures and inducements and must discharge their duties without fear or favour and be true to their oath.

The Chief Justice of India gave wider social and economic meaning to the concept of rule of law when he quoted "a nation is not merely a territory. A nation is essentially its people. Only when its people progress, the Nation progresses."[40]

In civil law jurisdiction (Germany), the concept of rule of law is comprehended in material and formal sense. In material sense, it implies that all State powers be subjected to substantive basic values of the Constitution

39. "Rule of Law in Democracy", (2021) 5 SCC J-1.
40. Telugu Mahakavi and Reformist Gurajada Apparao, taken from the excerpts published in the *Indian Express*, 2-7-2021.

(Basic Law) which includes: human dignity; democratic federal and welfare order; people participation in government formation; pre-eminence of basic rights of the people; State accountability under law and unamendability of these values. In formal sense, the rule of law implies procedural fairness; principles of equity, proportionality, contextuality and independence of the judiciary.

Thus, rule of law doctrine is a complicated and demanding criteria for evaluating the legitimacy of governance in any State. Nevertheless, it cannot be a ground to ignore it if benefits of a constitutional democracy are to be secured for the present and future generations of people.

Recent aggressive judicial activism can only be seen as a part of the efforts of the constitutional courts in India to establish a rule of law society which implies that no matter how high a person may be, the law is always above him. Court is also trying to identify the concept of rule of law with human rights of the people. The court is developing techniques by which it can force the government not only to submit to the law but also to create conditions where people can develop capacities to exercise their rights properly and meaningfully. The public administration is responsible for effective implementation of the rule of law and constitutional commands which effectuate fairly the objective standards laid down by law.[41] Every public servant is a trustee of society and is accountable for due effectuation of constitutional goals.[42] This makes the concept of rule of law highly relevant to our context.

Though the concept of rule of law has all the merits, the only negative side of the concept is that respect for law degenerates into legalism from which its very rigidity works injury to the nation.

2. DOCTRINE OF SEPARATION OF POWERS

Though the doctrine is traceable to Aristotle[43], but the writings of Locke[44] and Montesquieu[45] gave it a base on which modern attempts to distinguish between legislative, executive and judicial power are grounded. Locke distinguished between what he called

(1) discontinuous legislative power,
(2) continuous executive power, and
(3) federative power.

He included within "discontinuous legislative power", the general rule-making power called into action from time to time and not continuously. "Continuous executive power" included all those powers which we now call executive and judicial. By "federative power" he meant the power

41. *State of Punjab* v. *G.S. Gill*, (1997) 6 SCC 129.
42. *UT of Chandigarh* v. *Kuldeep Singh*, (1997) 9 SCC 199.
43. Aristotle, *Politics*, Vol. IV, 14.
44. *The Second Treatise of Civil Government*, Chaps. 12 and 13.
45. *L'esprit des lois* (1748) Chap. 12.

of conducting foreign affairs. Montesquieu's division of power included a general legislative power and two kinds of executive powers: an executive power in the nature of Locke's "federative power", and a "civil law" executive power including executive and judicial power.

Locke and Montesquieu derived the contents of this doctrine from the developments in the British constitutional history of the early 18th century. In England after a long war between Parliament and the King, they saw the triumph of Parliament in 1688 which gave Parliament legislative supremacy culminating in the passage of the Bill of Rights. This led ultimately to a recognition by the King of legislative and tax powers of Parliament and the judicial powers of the courts. At that time, the King exercised executive powers, Parliament exercised legislative powers and the courts exercised judicial powers, though later on England did not stick to this structural classification of functions and changed to the parliamentary form of government.

Writing in 1748, Montesquieu said:

> When the legislative and executive powers are united in the same person, or in the same body of Magistrates, there can be no liberty; because apprehensions may arise, lest the same monarch or senate should enact tyrannical laws, to execute them in a tyrannical manner. Again, there is no liberty, if the judiciary power be not separated from the legislative and executive. Were it joined with the legislative, the life and liberty of the subject would be exposed to arbitrary control; for the judge would be then the legislator. Were it joined to the executive power, the judge might behave with violence and oppression.
>
> There would be an end of everything, were the same man, or the same body, whether of the nobles or of the people, to exercise those three powers, that of exacting laws, that of executing the public resolutions, and of trying the causes of individuals.[46]

The doctrine of separation of powers is an animation of the rule of law and its roots also lie in the concept of natural law because both aim at progressive diminution of the exercise of arbitrary power necessary for protecting the life, liberty and dignity of the individual. It is an organic flexible doctrine which can be moulded to suit the requirements of governance, but its inherent fundamentals and rationality must not be compromised, *i.e.* "accumulation of power" is a definition of tyranny.

Brandeis J scientifically explained the purpose of this doctrine when he said that the purpose of the separation of powers doctrine is not to promote efficiency in the administration but to preclude the exercise of arbitrary power. He further emphasises that its purpose is not to avoid friction amongst various organs of the State by keeping them separate but to protect people from autocracy by means of inevitable friction due of distribution of powers. Therefore, the basic purpose of the doctrine of "separation

46. Nugent (Tr.), *The Spirit of the Laws,* 151–52 quoted in C.K. Thakker, *Administrative Law* (Eastern Book Company 1992) 31.

of power" is to divide governance against itself by creating distinct centres of power so that they could prevent each other from threatening tyranny.

The practical import is that no significant deprivation of life, liberty and dignity of any person can take place unless all the organs of the government combine together. If a person is to be put in jail, then a legislature has to pass a law making his action illegal, executive has to execute the law and judiciary must find him guilty. However, if a person is to be set free then any branch can do it. In Westminster type of democracy where legislature and executive are not separate, judiciary must be separated from the rest. Executive always demands power, at times by threatening insecurity among the people and legislature would always oblige because it is controlled by the executive. In such situation, judiciary, if separate, would apply brakes and save people from tyranny. It is for this that judiciary has now been separated from Parliament in the UK.

The doctrine of separation of powers is based on four different principles:

(1) Exclusivity principle which suggests structural division in all the three organs of State, as it is in the US.
(2) Functional principle which prohibits amalgamation and usurpation but not interaction of all the organs of State.
(3) Check and balance principle, meaning, thereby, that each organ of State may check the other to keep it within constitutional bounds.
(4) Mutuality principle which aims at creating concord not discord, cooperation not confrontation, engagement not estrangement amongst different organs of State to create a society of constitutional image, which is a free, equalitarian, inclusive and rule of law society.

This doctrine can be further used in two senses: 1) negative sense, in which this doctrine puts limits on the exercise of power by each organ of State; and 2) positive sense, in which it not only demarcates limits but also defines the minimum contents of power within those limits which a court can enforce to achieve constitutional values.[47]

Though the doctrine of separation of powers in its classical structural form is not followed in any country, not even in the US, yet logic behind it is still valid—logic of polarity because "threat to liberty arises not from blended powers but unchecked powers". Interaction of power facilitates liberty and freedom.

The theory of separation of powers signifies three formulations of structural classification of governmental powers:

(1) The same person should not form part of more than one of the three organs of the government. For example, Ministers should not sit in Parliament.
(2) One organ of the government should not interfere with any other organ of the government.

47. See, *State of U.P.* v. *Jeet S. Bisht*, (2007) 6 SCC 586.

(3) One organ of the government should not exercise the functions assigned to any other organ.

It may be pointed out that in none of these senses does a separation of powers exist in England. The King, though an executive head, is also an integral part of the legislature and all his Ministers are also Members of one or the other Houses of Parliament. Therefore, in England the concept of "parliamentary executive" is a clear negation of the first formulation that the same person should not form part of more than one of the three organs of the government. As regards the second formulation, it is clear that the House of Commons ultimately controls the executive. The judiciary is independent, but the judges of the superior courts can be removed on an address from both Houses of Parliament. As to the exercise by one organ of the functions of the other organs, no separation exists in England. Though with the establishment of the UK Supreme Court, judiciary has now been separated from Parliament, yet legislative and adjudicatory powers are being increasingly delegated to the executive. This also distracts from any effective separation of powers. Thus, in parliamentary form of government, separation of powers simply means independence of the judiciary as the legislature and executive are rolled into one.

The doctrine of separation of powers was gospel to the settlers who were obsessed with the violation of their life, liberty and dignity by the monarchs in England, who combined all the powers. Consequently, drafters of the US Constitution made this doctrine the basic brick of the Constitution. Madison said, "Accumulation of power, legislative, executive and judicial, in the same hand, whether one, a few or many, whether hereditary, self-appointed or elected may be justly pronounced as the definition of tyranny." Jefferson also emphasised, "Concentration of legislative, executive and judicial powers in the same hand is precisely the definition of despotic government. It would be no alleviation that these powers will be exercised by plurality of hands and not by a single person. 173 despots would surely be as oppressive as one."

Thus, this doctrine forms the foundation on which the whole structure of the US Constitution is based. Article I, Section 1 vests all legislative powers in the Congress. Article II, Section 1 vests all executive powers in the President of the US. Article III, Section 1 vests all judicial powers in the Supreme Court. It is on the basis of this theory of separation of powers that the US Supreme Court has not been given power to decide political questions, so that the court may not interfere with the exercise of power of the executive branch of the government. The US Constitution has also not given overriding power of judicial review to the US Supreme Court. It is a queer fact of American constitutional history that the power of judicial review has been usurped by the court. However, American constitutional developments have shown that in the face of the complexity of modern government, strict structural classification of the powers of the government is not possible. The President of the US interferes with the exercise of powers by the Congress through the exercise of his veto power. He also exercises the law-making power in exercise of his treaty-making power. The President also interferes with the functioning of the Supreme Court through the exercise of his power to appoint judges. In fact, President Roosevelt did interfere with the functions of the court when he threatened to pack the court in order to get the court's support for his New Deal legislation. In the same manner, Congress interferes with the powers of the President through vote on budget, approval of appointments by the Senate and the ratification of treaty. Congress also interferes with the exercise of powers by the courts by passing procedural laws, creating special courts, and approving the appointment of judges. In its turn, the judiciary interferes with the powers of the Congress and the President through the exercise of its power of judicial review. It is correct to say that the US Supreme Court has made more amendments to the US Constitution than the Congress itself.

Though no separation of powers in the strict sense of the term exists in England and the US, yet the curious fact is that this doctrine has attracted the makers of most modern constitutions, especially during the 19th century. Thus in France, the doctrine has produced a situation in which the ordinary courts are precluded from reviewing the validity not only of legislative enactments but even of the actions of the administration. The void has been filled by the establishment of special administrative courts.

In India, the doctrine of separation of powers has not been accorded a constitutional status. Only executive power is vested in the President and Governor. Other powers are not so vested. Apart from the directive principle laid down in Article 50 which enjoins separation of judiciary from the executive, the constitutional scheme does not embody any formalistic and dogmatic division of powers.[48] The Supreme Court in *Ram Jawaya Kapur* v. *State of Punjab*[49] held:

> Indian Constitution has not indeed recognised the doctrine of separation of powers in its absolute rigidity but the functions of the different parts or branches of the government have been sufficiently differentiated and consequently it can very well be said that our Constitution does not contemplate assumption, by one organ or part of the State, of functions that essentially belong to another.

In *Indira Nehru Gandhi*[50], Ray CJ also observed that in the Indian Constitution there is separation of powers in a broad sense only. A rigid separation of powers as under the US Constitution or the Australian Constitution does not apply to India. However, the court held that though the constituent power is independent of the doctrine of separation of powers to implant the theory of basic structure as developed in *Kesavananda*

48. Upendra Baxi, "Developments in Indian Administrative Law" in A.G. Noorani (Ed.), *Public Law in India* (1982) 136.
49. AIR 1955 SC 549.
50. 1975 Supp SCC 1.

Bharati[51] on the ordinary legislative powers will be an encroachment on the theory of separation of powers.[52] Nevertheless, Beg J added that separation of powers is a part of the basic structure of the Constitution. None of the three separate organs of the Republic can take over the functions assigned to the other. This scheme of the Constitution cannot be changed even by resorting to Article 368 of the Constitution.[53]

In India, not only is there a functional overlapping but there is personnel overlapping also. The Supreme Court has the power to declare void the laws passed by the legislature and the actions taken by the executive if they violate any provision of the Constitution or the law passed by the legislature in case of executive actions. Even the power to amend the Constitution by Parliament is subject to the scrutiny of the court. The court can declare any amendment void if it changes the basic structure of the Constitution.[54] When the court decides a case and lays down a law, it is exercising legislative function. When the High Courts exercise the power of supervision over the lower judiciary, they are exercising administrative function. Power to transfer a case from one court to other under Article 228 is also an administrative power.[55] The President of India in whom the executive authority of India is vested exercises law-making power in the shape of ordinance-making power and also the judicial powers under Articles 103(1) and 217(3), to mention only a few. The Council of Ministers is selected from the legislature and is responsible to the legislature. The legislature besides exercising law-making powers exercises judicial powers in cases of breach of its privilege, impeachment of the President, and removal of the judges. The executive may further affect the functioning of the judiciary by making appointments to the office of Chief Justice and other judges. One can go on listing such examples, yet the list would not be exhaustive.

Apart from the difficulties inherent in the enforcement of any strict doctrine of separation of powers in the functioning of a modern government, there is also the inherent difficulty in defining in workable terms the division of powers into legislative, executive, and judicial.[56] Even the Supreme Court has often refrained from delving into this quagmire except that in *Indira Nehru Gandhi*[57], it held that adjudication of a specific dispute is a judicial function which Parliament, even acting under a constitutional amending power, cannot exercise.

The Constitution has invested the constitutional courts with the power to invalidate laws made by Parliament and State Legislature transgressing

51. (1973) 4 SCC 225.
52. 1975 Supp SCC 1, 61, para. 136.
53. 1975 Supp SCC 1, 61, 210, para. 555.
54. *Kesavananda Bharati* v. *State of Kerala*, (1973) 4 SCC 225.
55. *Buhari Sons (P) Ltd.* v. *State of T.N.*, 2014 SCC OnLine Mad 1512: (2014) 4 CTC 113.
56. *See*, Upendra Baxi, "Developments in Indian Administrative Law" in A.G. Noorani (Ed.), *Public Law in India* (1982) 136.
57. 1975 Supp SCC 1; *see also*, Upendra Baxi, "Developments in Indian Administrative Law" in A.G. Noorani (Ed.), *Public Law in India* (1982) 137.

constitutional limitations. Where an Act made by the legislature is invalidated by the courts on the ground of legislative incompetence, the legislature cannot enact a law declaring that the judgment of the court shall not operate; it cannot overrule or annul the decision of the court. But this does not mean that the legislature which is competent to enact that law cannot re-enact that law. Similarly, it is open to a legislature to alter the basis of the judgment. The new law or the amended law so made can be challenged on other grounds but not on the ground that it seeks to ineffectuate or circumvent the decision of the court. This is what is meant by "check and balance" inherent in a system of government incorporating separation of powers.[58]

From the above discussion it becomes clear that the doctrine in its classical sense which is structural rather than functional cannot be literally applied to any modern government because neither the powers of the governments can be kept in watertight compartments nor can any government run on strict separation of powers. Nevertheless, in the US, people criticised the growth of administrative law on the ground that it violates the principles of the doctrine of separation of powers. The criticism became more intense at the growth of statutory commissions to regulate the new areas of activity. These commissions were given wide legislative, executive and judicative powers. Regulatory powers exercised by regulatory authorities such as Inter-State Commerce Commission, Civil Aeronautics Board, Federal Communication Commission, Federal Power Commission, and Security Exchange Commission represented an amalgam of functions devised with little regard to constitutional theory of separation of powers because the control of concentrated industrial power through concentrated governmental power had become inescapable.[59] This led to the appointment of Attorney General Committee to review the entire growth of administrative process. The Committee saw no danger to the personal liberty in the growth of administrative process if the control mechanism is activated properly. On the recommendations of this Committee, the Administrative Procedure Act, 1946 was passed. The Act "represents a moderate adjustment on the side of fairness to the citizens in the never-ending quest for a proper balance between governmental efficiency and individual freedom"[60]. This never-ending quest further led to the appointment of the Task Force of the Second Hoover Commission which also recommended an effective control mechanism to safeguard the liberty of the people in the face of growing administrative process.

Before all these commissions the main problem was: How to reconcile the delegation of legislative and judicial powers to administrative agencies with the doctrine of separation of powers? First attempt at such reconciliation was made by using the word "quasi". It was pointed out that what the

58. *P. Kannadasan* v. *State of T.N.*, (1996) 5 SCC 670.
59. Bernard Schwartz, *Administrative Law* (1976) 13.
60. Byse, "The Federal Administrative Procedure Act", (1958) 1 JILI 89, 92.

administrative agencies exercise is only a quasi-legislative and quasi-judicial power. No matter, to soften a legal term by a "quasi" is a time-honoured lawyer's device, yet, in the sphere of administrative process it becomes illogical to grant legislative and judicial powers to administrative agencies and still deny the same.[61] Therefore, now it is being increasingly realised that the "cult of quasi" has to move from any theoretical prohibition to a rule against unrestricted delegation circumscribed by the power of judicial review under the compulsions of modern government.[62]

If the doctrine of separation of powers in its classical sense, which is now considered as a high school textbook interpretation of this doctrine, cannot be applied to any modern government, this does not mean that the doctrine has no relevance in the world of today. The logic behind this doctrine is still valid. The logic behind this doctrine is of polarity rather than strict classification, meaning thereby that the centre of authority must be dispersed to avoid absolutism. In the same manner Prof. Wade writes that the objection of Montesquieu was against accumulation and monopoly rather than interaction.[63] Montesquieu himself never used the word "separation". Therefore, not impassable barriers and unalterable frontiers but mutual restraint in the exercise of power by the three organs of the State is the soul of the doctrine of separation of powers. Hence the doctrine can be better appreciated as a doctrine of "check and balance" and in this sense, administrative process is not an antithesis of the doctrine of separation of powers.

In *Indira Nehru Gandhi* v. *Raj Narain*[64], Chandrachud J (as he then was) also observed that the "... political usefulness of the doctrine of separation of powers is now widely recognised ...." No constitution can survive without a conscious adherence to its fine checks and balances.

> Just as courts ought not to enter into problems entwined in the 'political thicket', Parliament must also respect the preserve of the courts. The principle of separation of powers is a principle of restraint which 'has in it the precept innate in the prudence of self-preservation ... that, discretion is the better part of valour'.[65]

In *Supreme Court Advocates-on-Records Assn.* v. *Union of India*[66], the Supreme Court held that separation of powers or distribution of powers is the tectonic structure of the Constitution of India. Various checks and balances are provided only for maintaining a proper equilibrium amongst the structures and that is the supreme beauty of our Constitution. Under our constitutional scheme, one branch does not interfere impermissibly with the constitutionally assigned powers and functions of another branch. The permissible areas of interference are the checks and balances but there are certain exclusive areas for each branch which are its "core functions" or its

---

61. Bernard Schwartz, *Administrative Law* (1976) 32.
62. *National Cable Television Assn.* v. *United States*, 39 L Ed 2d 370: 415 US 336 (1973).
63. Wade, *Administrative Law* 251.
64. 1975 Supp SCC 1, 260, paras. 686, 688.
65. Julius Stone, *Social dimensions of law and justice* (1966) 668.
66. (2016) 5 SCC 1.

powers central. There shall be no interference with powers central of each branch.

In conclusion, "doctrine of separation of powers" in today's context of liberalisation, privatisation and globalisation cannot be interpreted to mean either "separation of powers" or "check and balance" or "principle of restraint", but "community of powers" exercised in the spirit of cooperation by various organs of the State in the best interest of the people.

Closely allied to the doctrine of separation of powers is the doctrine of "subsidiarity" which also deals with allocation of powers of the State. It suggests that State powers be assigned at the right level. It prescribes that no governmental power be given at the level which is very remote from the people because administrative authorities can exercise tasks effectively and reasonably at a level closer to people whom the authority is required to serve. It is for this reason the European Union Constitution allocates "international trade" at the Central level and subjects like criminal law and family law at the local level.

POINTS FOR DISCUSSION

1. Dicey's personality and his historical perspective may be discussed in order to appreciate the origin of the contents of his rule of law doctrine.
2. Dicey's concept of the rule of law and its reconciliation with the growth of the administrative process.
3. Development of the doctrine of rule of law from a political ideal to a juridical concept designed to keep the administration within bounds. Visible trends in Indian jurisprudence.
4. Rule of law has ideological contents also. Against this backdrop some ideological parameters may be discussed with special reference to the Indian situation.
5. Dicey had a misconception about administrative law. He was concerned more with institutions than values. Reasons for this misconception may be discussed with reference to the growth of administrative law in France and England.
6. Modern meaning of the rule of law, especially its relevance in Western and Communist societies, common law, civil law countries and global context.
7. Recent aggressive judicial activism as an effect to usher in a rule-of-law society.
8. The virtues of the doctrine of separation of powers do not evoke much enthusiasm today. Is it because the doctrine has accepted a harder core of generally accepted meaning or because some constitutions survive adequately without relying on it for sustenance?

9. The relevance of logic behind the doctrine of separation of powers and the growth of administrative process to a point that we are living not in its shade but shadow.

SUGGESTED READINGS

1. A.V. Dicey, *Introduction to the Study of the Law of the Constitution* (9th Edn.) Chaps. IV and XII.
2. A.V. Dicey, *Victorian Jurist* (1980).
3. Arndt, "The Origins of Dicey's Concept of the 'Rule of Law' ", (1957) 31 ALJ 116.
4. Benjafield and Whitmore, *Principles of Australian Administrative Law* (4th Edn.) Chap. IV.
5. C.K. Allen, *Law and Order* (1965) 1.
6. C.K. Davis, "English Administrative Law—An American View", (1962) Public Law 139.
7. C.K. Thakker, *Administrative Law* (Eastern Book Company 2012) Chap. II.
8. Davis, *Administrative Law Treatise* (1958) Chap. I.
9. Denning, *Freedom Under the Law* (1949) 77–78.
10. Devi Prasad Singh, "Sovereignty, Judicial Review and Separation of Power", (2012) 7 SCC J-1.
11. Dicey, "The Development of Administrative Law in England", 31 LQR 148 (1915).
12. E. Freund, *Administrative Powers Over Person and Property: A Comparative Survey* (1939).
13. F.H. Lawson, (1959) Political Studies 200.
14. F.H. Lawson, "Dicey Revisited", (1959) 7 Political Studies 109.
15. F.M. Marx, "Administrative Ethics and the Rule of Law", (1949) APSR 1119.
16. "First Report of the Public and Administrative Law Reforms Committee", (1968) 3 New Zealand Universities L Rev 351.
17. Friedmann, *Law in a Changing Society*, Chap. XVI.
18. *Functions of Law in the International Community* (1933) Chap. XIX.
19. Goodhart, "The Rule of Law and Absolute Sovereignty", 106 Pennsylvania L Rev 946.
20. Griffith and Street, *A Case Book of Administrative Law* (1967) 15–16.
21. H.W.R. Wade, "Anglo-American Administrative Law: Some Reflections", (1965) 81 LQR 357.
22. J.D.B. Mitchell, "The Causes and Effects of the Absence of Public Law in the United Kingdom", (1965) Public Law 95.
23. J.F. Garner, *Administrative Law* (1967) 12.
24. Jeffrey Jowell, "The Rule of Law and Its Underlying Values" in Jeffrey Jowell and Dawn Oliver, *The Changing Constitution* (2007) Chap. 1.
25. K. Sangeetha, "Rule of Law and Indian Constitution", CNLU LJ (8) [2018–19] 126.
26. Lord Bingham, *Rule of Law* (2003).

27. M.J.C. Vile, *Constitution and The Separation of Powers.*
28. MacDermott, *Protection from Power Under English Law*, 60.
29. Nettheim, "Legislative Interference with the Judiciary", (1966) ALJ 221.
30. R.A. Cosgrove, *Rule of Law.*
31. Rabindra Kr. Pathak, "The Virtue of Rule of Law", 7 RMLNLUJ (2015) 121.
32. Robson, *Justice and Administrative Law* (3rd Edn., 1951).
33. Sawer, "The Separation of Power in Australian Federalism", (1961) 35 ALJ 177.
34. Schwartz, "Legislative Control of Administrative Rules and Regulations: The American Experience", (1955) 30 NYU L Rev 1031.
35. Street, *Justice in the Welfare State* (1968).
36. Sehaj Singh Cheema, "Inseparate Powers & De Facto Offices of Profit: The Contorted Reality of Constitutional Ideals", 9.2 NLIU LR (2020) 374.
37. V.S. Deshpande, "Standing and Justiciability", 13 JILI (1971) 153.
38. W.H. Jones, "The Rule of Law and the Welfare State in Essays on Jurisprudence", 1963 Col LR 400.
39. Waseem Ahmad Bhat, "Rethinking Ram Jawaya Kapur : How far the Executive can go without Legislative Authorisation?", (2020) 10 GJLDP (October) 77.

CHAPTER 3

Anatomy of Administrative Action

1. CLASSIFICATION OF ADMINISTRATIVE ACTION

Administrative action is a comprehensive term and defies exact definition. In modern times the administrative process as a by-product of intensive form of government cuts across the traditional classification of governmental powers and combines into one all the powers which were traditionally exercised by three different organs of the State. Therefore, there is a general agreement among the writers on administrative law that any attempt of classifying administrative functions on any conceptual basis is not only impossible but also futile. Even then a student of administrative law is compelled to delve into the field of classification because the present-day law, especially relating to judicial review, freely employs conceptual classification of administrative action. Thus, speaking generally, an administrative action can be classified into four categories:

(1) Rule-making action or quasi-legislative action.
(2) Rule-decision action or quasi-judicial action.
(3) Rule-application action or administrative action.
(4) Ministerial action or pure administrative action.

1.1 Rule-making action or quasi-legislative action

Legislature is the law-making organ of any State. In some written constitutions, like the US and Australian Constitutions, the law-making power is expressly vested in the legislature. However, in the Indian Constitution, though this power is not so expressly vested in the legislature, yet the combined effect of Articles 107 to 111 and 196 to 201 is that the law-making power can be exercised for the Union by Parliament and for the States by the respective State Legislatures. It is the intention of the constitution makers that this law-making power must be exercised by those bodies alone in whom this power is vested.[1] But in the 21st century today, these legislative bodies cannot give that quality and quantity of laws which are required for the efficient functioning of a modern intensive form of government.

1. *Delhi Laws Act, 1912, re*, 1951 SCC 568: AIR 1951 SC 332.

Therefore, the delegation of law-making power to the administration is a compulsive necessity. When any administrative authority exercises the law-making power delegated to it by the legislature, it is known as the rule-making action of the administration or quasi-legislative action.

Rule-making action of the administration partakes all the characteristics which a normal legislative action possesses. Such characteristics may be generality, prospectivity, and a behaviour which bases action on policy consideration and gives a right or a disability. These characteristics are not without exception. In some cases, administrative rule-making action may be particularised, retroactive and based on evidence. According to Chinnappa Reddy J, a legislative action has four characteristics: 1) generality; 2) prospectivity; 3) public interest; and 4) rights and obligations flowing from it.[2] Elaborating the characteristics of a rule-making action of the administrative authority, the Supreme Court in *State of Punjab* v. *Tehal Singh*[3] held that 1) where the provisions of a statute provide for the legislative activity, *i.e.* making of a legislative instrument or promulgation of a general rule of conduct or a declaration by a notification; 2) where the power exercised by the authority under a statute does not concern the interest of an individual but relates to the public in general, or concerns a general direction of a general character and is not directed against an individual or to a particular situation; and 3) lays down a future course of action, such action will generally held to be quasi-legislative action of the authority. Applying this test, the court held that on making of a declaration determining the territorial area of a Gram Sabha and, thereafter, establishing a Gram Sabha for that area is a quasi-legislative act of the administration.

It is on the basis of these characteristics that one can differentiate between quasi-legislative and quasi-judicial action. A quasi-judicial action in contradistinction to a quasi-legislative action is particularly based on the facts of the case and declares a pre-existing right. However, in certain situations, like wage or rate fixing, it is not capable of easy differentiation. In *Express Newspapers (P) Ltd.* v. *Union of India*[4], the Supreme Court left the question open as to whether the function of the Wage Commission under the Working Journalists and Other Newspaper Employees (Conditions of Service) and Miscellaneous Provisions Act, 1955 is quasi-judicial or quasi-legislative. However, the delegation to the government of the power to fix the price of levy sugar was held to be a quasi-legislative function.[5] In *Essar Steel Ltd.* v. *Union of India*[6], the Supreme Court of India held that even though price-fixing is a legislative function, the same can be delegated and can be fixed by way of executive orders as well (particularly when there was no legislation holding the field concerned). Effect of a statute cannot

2. *Union of India* v. *Cynamide India Ltd.*, (1987) 2 SCC 720.
3. (2002) 2 SCC 7.
4. AIR 1958 SC 578.
5. *Shri Sitaram Sugar Co. Ltd.* v. *Union of India*, (1990) 3 SCC 223. See also, *Shri Malaprabha Coop. Sugar Factory Ltd.* v. *Union of India*, (1994) 1 SCC 648.
6. (2016) 11 SCC 1.

be circumvented by an office memorandum of the department.[7] From this it appears that the distinction between legislative and administrative functions is difficult in theory and impossible in practice. According to Wade:

> They are easy enough to distinguish at the extremities of the spectrum: an act of Parliament is legislative and a deportation order is administrative. But in between is a wide area where either label can be used according to taste, for example, where ministers make orders affecting large number of people....[8]

In the same manner, the Committee on Ministers' Powers which was appointed in England in 1928 distinguished between administrative and quasi-legislative action on the ground that where the former is a process of performing particular acts or of making decisions involving the application of general rules to particular cases, the latter is the process of formulating a general rule of conduct without reference to particular cases and usually for future operation.[9]

Though the rules of natural justice do not apply to legislative actions, yet reasonableness and fair play in action must be observed as Article 14 of the Constitution equally applies to legislative actions.[10]

Administrative rule-making action is controlled by Parliament and the courts. A detailed study of these control mechanisms has been made in Chapter 4.

1.2 Rule-decision action or quasi-judicial action

Today the bulk of the decisions which affect a private individual come not from courts but from administrative agencies exercising adjudicatory powers. The reason seems to be that since administrative decision-making is also a by-product of the intensive form of government, the traditional judicial system cannot give to the people that quantity and quality of justice which is required in a welfare state.

For an act of an administrative body to be characterised as quasi-judicial: 1) there must be legal authority; 2) this authority must be to determine questions affecting the rights of citizens; and 3) there must be a duty to act judicially. Further held, the absence of a lis between the parties would not necessarily lead to the conclusion that the power conferred on an administrative body would not be quasi-judicial. So long as the aforesaid three tests are satisfied, the power is quasi-judicial.[11] Quasi-judicial order can generally be varied or reviewed when obtained by fraud or when power therefor is conferred by relevant Act or Rules.[12]

---

7. *ESIC* v. *Mangalam Publications (India) (P) Ltd.*, (2018) 11 SCC 438.
8. Wade, *Administrative Law* (6th Edn.) 848.
9. Command Paper 4060 20 (1948).
10. *Shri Sitaram Sugar Co. Ltd.* v. *Union of India*, (1990) 3 SCC 223.
11. *NSDL* v. *SEBI*, (2017) 5 SCC 517.
12. *Industrial Infrastructure Development Corpn. (Gwalior) M.P. Ltd.* v. *CIT*, (2018) 4 SCC 494.

In *Chintpurni Medical College & Hospital* v. *State of Punjab*[13], the Supreme Court held that Section 21, General Clauses Act, 1897 is not applicable to exercise of quasi-judicial power. Where the law requires that an authority before arriving at a decision must make an enquiry, such a requirement of law makes the authority a quasi-judicial authority. Also when the authority is required to act according to rules and not dictated by policy or expediency, the authority performs the quasi-judicial function and not an administrative function.

In some jurisdictions the term "quasi-judicial" is used to denote administrative, adjudicatory or decision-making process. But because the term "quasi-judicial" is vague and difficult to define, it is falling in disuse. Therefore, the use of this term is being carefully avoided.

Administrative decision making may be defined as a power to perform acts administrative in character, but requiring incidentally some characteristics of judicial traditions. On the basis of this definition, the following functions of the administration have been held to be quasi-judicial functions:

(1) Disciplinary proceedings against students.[14]
(2) Disciplinary proceedings against an employee for misconduct.[15]
(3) Confiscation of goods under the Sea Customs Act, 1878.[16]
(4) Cancellation, suspension, revocation or refusal to renew licence or permit by licensing authority.[17]
(5) Determination of citizenship.[18]
(6) Determination of statutory disputes.[19]
(7) Power to continue the detention or seizure of goods beyond a particular period.[20]
(8) Refusal to grant "no objection certificate" under the Bombay Cinemas (Regulations) Act, 1953.[21]
(9) Forfeiture of pensions and gratuity.[22]
(10) Authority granting or refusing permission for retrenchment.[23]
(11) Grant of permit by regional transport authority.[24]
(12) Registration of a political party by the Election Commission.[25]

13. (2018) 15 SCC 1.
14. *Bhagwan* v. *Ram Chand*, AIR 1965 SC 1767.
15. *Calcutta Dock Labour Board* v. *Jaffar Imam*, AIR 1966 SC 282.
16. *East India Commercial Co. Ltd.* v. *Collector of Customs*, AIR 1962 SC 1893.
17. *Fedco (P) Ltd.* v. *S.N. Bilgrami*, AIR 1960 SC 415; *Raman and Raman Ltd.* v. *State of Madras*, AIR 1959 SC 694; *D. Natraja Mudaliar* v. *State Transport Authority*, (1978) 4 SCC 290.
18. *Mohd. Ayub Khan* v. *Commr. of Police*, AIR 1965 SC 1623.
19. *CST* v. *Super Cotton Bowl Refilling Works*, (1989) 1 SCC 643.
20. *P.L. Lakhanpal* v. *Union of India*, AIR 1967 SC 1507; *I.J. Rao* v. *Bibhuti Bhushan Bagh*, (1989) 3 SCC 202.
21. *State of Gujarat* v. *Krishna Cinema*, (1970) 2 SCC 744.
22. *State of Punjab* v. *Iqbal Singh*, (1976) 2 SCC 1.
23. *Workmen* v. *Meenakshi Mills Ltd.*, (1992) 3 SCC 336.
24. *Mithilesh Garg* v. *Union of India*, (1992) 1 SCC 168.
25. *Indian National Congress (I)* v. *Institute of Social Welfare*, (2002) 5 SCC 685.

1.2.1 *Attributes of administrative decision-making action or quasi-judicial action and the distinction between judicial, quasi-judicial and administrative action*

Generally speaking, an administrative action/decision is one that is taken to give effect to the policy of the government, and judicial or quasi-judicial decision is one that decides a dispute or declares a legal status. However, these actions, at times, may overlap. Nevertheless, in both situations, the authority is bound to act fairly and reasonably and follow the dictates of law.

The Donoughmore Committee on Ministers' Powers (1932) analysed the characteristics of a "true judicial decision" and summed up the attributes, the presence or absence of which stamped a decision as administrative decision-making or quasi-judicial action. The Committee was of the view that a true judicial decision presupposes a *lis* between two or more parties and then involves four requisites:

(1) Presentation of the case.
(2) Ascertainment of questions of fact by means of evidence given by the parties.
(3) Ascertainment of questions of law on the basis of submission of legal arguments.
(4) A decision which disposes of the whole matter by applying the law to the facts.

A quasi-judicial decision involves the first two determinants, may or may not involve the third, but never involves the fourth determinant, because the place of the fourth determinant is in fact taken by administrative action, the character of which is determined by the Minister's free choice involving expediency, discretion and policy considerations.

Decisions which are administrative stand on a wholly different footing from quasi-judicial as well as from judicial decisions. In administrative decisions, there is no legal obligation to consider and weigh submissions and arguments, or to collect any evidence, or to solve any issue. The grounds upon which the action is taken and the procedure for taking the action are left entirely to the discretion of the authority.

This approach of the Committee seems fallacious because the judges cannot be regarded as mere norm-producing slot machines, they do take into consideration policy, socio-economic and political philosophy, expediency, and exercise discretion while deciding a case. In the 21st century, it is admitted at all hands that the judiciary is like any other branch of the government because litigation like legislation and administration is a stage in the accommodation of interests. On the other hand in certain areas of administrative adjudication, like tax, the administration applies law to the facts in the same manner as sometimes the judges do. Therefore, it is wrong to suggest that any admixture of policy in the virgin purity of a judicial determination immediately reduces it to the rank of quasi-judicial decision.[26]

As the English "law and policy" determinant is devoid of sufficient classification, in the same manner, the American "position-of-the-judge" approach is not without exception. In the American approach, a court is where a judge sits as arbiter—impartial and with no interest in the suit between the two parties. The institution and presentation are the responsibilities of the parties. In an administrative decision, on the other hand, the judge is rarely one who is disinterested in the case and sits detached like a judge. One may be tempted to argue and rightly so, that this classification matrix would also fail in the case of independent tribunals where the presiding officer does sit in judge-like detachment.

Therefore, only that classification determinant can be reasonable which is institutional rather than functional. There are administrative agencies exercising adjudicatory powers which are like full courts—it is only the will of the legislature that these are not classified as courts.

However, it does not mean that because purple is the confused mixture of red and blue, so there is no distinction between red and blue.[27] Administrative decision-making action is not required to follow the elaborate judicial procedure; it is sufficient if, in the absence of any statutory requirement, the action is rendered by following the minimum procedure of natural justice.

There was a time when the view prevailed that the rules of natural justice have application to a quasi-judicial proceeding as distinguished from an administrative proceeding. The distinguishing feature of a quasi-judicial proceeding in this behalf is that the authority concerned is required by law under which it is functioning to act judicially. Duty to act judicially was spelt out in *R.* v. *Electricity Commissioners*[28] by Lord Atkins thus:

> Whenever any body of persons having legal authority to determine questions affecting the rights of the subjects, and having the duty to act judicially, acts in excess of its legal authority, they are subject to the controlling jurisdiction of the King's Bench Division.

Lord Hewart CJ in *R.* v. *Legislative Committee of Church Assembly, ex p Haynes Smith*[29] read this observation of Lord Atkin to mean that the duty to act judicially should be an additional requirement existing independently of the "authority to determine questions affecting the rights of subjects"—something superadded to it. This gloss placed by Lord Hewart CJ, on the dictum of Lord Atkins LJ, to use the words of Krishna Iyer J bedevilled the law for a considerable time and stultified the growth of the doctrine of natural justice. Therefore, the court held that

26. (1952) 1 SCC 1: AIR 1952 SC 75.
27. H.W.R. Wade, "Quasi-judicial and its Background", (1949) 10 Cambridge LJ 216.
28. (1924) 1 KB 171 (CA).
29. (1928) 1 KB 411.

the duty to act judicially need not be superadded and it may be spelt out from the nature of the power conferred, the manner of exercising it, and its impact on the rights of the person affected.[30] The court was constrained in every case that came up before it to make a search for the duty to act judicially, sometimes from tenuous material and sometimes in the services of a statute, and this led to oversubtlety and over-refinement resulting in confusion and uncertainty in the law.[31]

In India, the judicial search for the duty to act judicially was sometimes made within the corners of the statute[32] under which the authority exercised power, and sometimes in the tenuous material, remote and extraneous, such as *lis inter partes* including proposition and opposition,[33] implications arising from the nature of the functions, and the rights affected thereby.[34]

This doctrinal approach of the courts in India and England not only made the law confused and uncertain but also eluded justice in many cases.

However, in England, a turning point came with *Ridge* v. *Baldwin*[35] (*Ridge*) when Lord Reid pointed out that the gloss of Lord Hewart was based on misunderstanding of the observations of Lord Atkins. Lord Reid observed:

> If Lord Heward meant that it is never enough that a body has a duty to determine what the rights of the individual should be, but that there must always be something more to impose on it a duty to act judicially, then that appears to me impossible to reconcile with the earlier authorities.[36]

Lord Reid held that the duty to act judicially must arise from the very nature of the function intended to be performed, and it need not be shown to be superadded. Krishna Iyer J quoted Prof. Clark from his article, "Natural Justice: Substance and Shadow"[37], who is of the view that the observation of Lord Reid has restored light to an area "benighted by the narrow conceptualism of the previous decade".

This development of law is traceable in India also where the Supreme Court even earlier than *Ridge*[38] was of the view that if there is power to decide and determine to the prejudice of a person, the duty to act judicially

30. *Maneka Gandhi* v. *Union of India*, (1978) 1 SCC 248.
31. *Ibid.*
32. *Province of Bombay* v. *Kusaldas S. Advani*, 1950 SCC 551: AIR 1950 SC 222; *Radheyshyam Khare* v. *State of M.P.*, AIR 1959 SC 107.
33. *Gullapalli Nageswara Rao* v. *A.P. SRTC*, AIR 1959 SC 308.
34. *Babul Chandra Mitra* v. *Patna High Court*, AIR 1954 SC 524; *Raman and Raman Ltd.* v. *State of Madras*, AIR 1959 SC 694; *Board of High School and Intermediate Education* v. *Ghanshyam Das Gupta*, AIR 1962 SC 1110; *Shivji Nathubhai* v. *Union of India*, AIR 1960 SC 606; *Board of Revenue* v. *Vidyawati*, AIR 1962 SC 1217; *Dwarka Nath* v. *ITO*, AIR 1966 SC 81; *P.L. Lakhanpal* v. *Union of India*, AIR 1967 SC 1507; *Rampur Distillery Co. Ltd.* v. *Company Law Board*, (1969) 2 SCC 774; *Indian Sugar and Refineries Ltd.* v. *Amravathi Service Coop. Society Ltd.*, (1976) 1 SCC 318.
35. 1964 AC 40: (1963) 2 WLR 935 (HL).
36. Quoted in Wade, *Administrative Law* (6th Edn.) 848.
37. 1975 PL 27.
38. 1964 AC 40: (1963) 2 WLR 935 (HL).

is implicit in the exercise of such power.[39] In fact, the foundation of applying natural justice in administrative actions had been laid down in the dissent of Subba Rao J in *Radheyshyam Khare* v. *State of M.P.*[40] It is significant to note that he held:

> ... incompetency carries a stigma with it and what is more derogatory to the reputation of the members of the Committee than to be stigmatised as incompetent to discharge their statutory duties? Would it be reasonable to assume that public men in a democratic country are allowed to be condemned unheard?[41]

This dissent became strikingly pronounced in *A.K. Kraipak* v. *Union of India*[42] (*Kraipak*). In this case the Supreme Court held that though the action of making selection for government services is administrative, yet the selection committee is under a duty to act judicially. The court observed that the dividing line between an administrative power and quasi-judicial power is quite thin and is being gradually obliterated.[43] For determining whether a power is quasi-judicial or administrative, regard must be had to 1) the nature of the power conferred; 2) the authority on whom the power is conferred; 3) frameworth of the law conferring that power; 4) the consequences ensuing from the exercise of that power; and 5) the manner in which that power is expected to be exercised.[44] In *D.K. Yadav* v. *J.M.A. Industries Ltd.*[45], the Supreme Court further observed that the distinction between quasi-judicial and administrative action which had become thin is now totally eclipsed and obliterated. Proceeding a step further the Supreme Court clearly held in *Chandra Bhavan Boarding and Lodging* v. *State of Mysore*[46] that it is not necessary to classify an action of the administrative authority as quasi-judicial or administrative because the administrative authority is bound to follow the principles of natural justice in any case. In this case, the question was whether the power to fix a minimum wage under the Minimum Wages Act, 1948 is quasi-judicial or administrative.[47]

In *Indian National Congress (I)* v. *Institute of Social Welfare*[48], the Supreme Court once again defined the meaning and attributes of a quasi-judicial function. In this case the question was: Whether function of the Election Commission to register a political party is quasi-judicial or administrative? The court held that the legal principle as to when an act of a statutory authority would be a quasi-judicial act is where 1) a statutory authority empowered under a statute to do any act, 2) which would prejudicially

39. *Board of High School and Intermediate Education* v. *Ghanshyam Das Gupta*, AIR 1962 SC 1110.
40. AIR 1959 SC 107.
41. *Ibid.*
42. (1969) 2 SCC 262.
43. *A.K. Kraipak* v. *Union of India*, (1969) 2 SCC 262.
44. *Automotive Tyre Mfg Assn.* v. *Designated Authority*, (2011) 2 SCC 258.
45. (1993) 3 SCC 259.
46. (1969) 3 SCC 84.
47. See also, *DFO* v. *Ram Sanehi Singh*, (1971) 3 SCC 864.
48. (2002) 5 SCC 685.

affect the subject, 3) although there is no *lis* or two contending parties and the contest is between the authority and the subject, and 4) the statutory authority is required to act judicially under the statute, the decision of the said authority shall be quasi-judicial. The court further elaborated that where the law requires that an authority before arriving at a decision must make an enquiry, such a requirement of law makes the authority quasi-judicial authority. In other words if an authority is required to act according to rules, its functions will be quasi-judicial. Therefore, if the authority has power to summon witnesses, enforce their attendance, examine them on oath and requires discovery and production of documents, its functions will be quasi-judicial.[49]

Elaborating the law further, the court identified three characteristics of a quasi-judicial action:

(1) it is in substance a determination upon investigation of a question by the application of objective standards to facts found in the light of pre-existing legal rules;
(2) it declares rights or imposes upon parties obligations affecting their civil rights; and
(3) that the investigation is subject to certain procedural attributes contemplating an opportunity of presenting its case to a party, ascertainment of facts by means of evidence if dispute be on questions of fact, and if the dispute be on question of law on the presentation of legal argument, and a decision resulting in the disposal of the matter on findings based upon those questions of law and fact.[50]

Applying the above characteristics, the court concluded in *Manju Varma* v. *State of U.P.*[51] that the power exercised by the Chief Justice of the Allahabad High Court under paragraph 14 of the United Provinces High Courts (Amalgamation) Order, 1948 to transfer a writ petition from Lucknow Bench to Allahabad Bench in administrative capacity is quasi-judicial power subject to review by the higher forum. The court observed that the Chief Justice could not have allowed the plea without hearing the affected party and without determining on objective criteria and upon investigation whether the case is transferable and should be transferred. The decision of the Chief Justice would have direct bearing on the right of the appellant to choose "forum convenience", hence the action is quasi-judicial subject to review by the higher forum.

1.3 Rule-application action or administrative action

Though the distinction between quasi-judicial and administrative action has become blurred, yet it does not mean that there is no distinction between the two. If two persons are wearing a similar coat, it does not mean that

49. *State of Maharashtra* v. *Marwanjee F. Desai*, (2002) 2 SCC 318.
50. *Manju Varma* v. *State of U.P.*, (2005) 1 SCC 73.
51. *Ibid.*

there is no difference between them. The difference between quasi-judicial and administrative action may not be of much practical consequence today but it may still be relevant in determining the measure of natural justice applicable in a given situation.

In *Kraipak*[52], the court was of the view that in order to determine whether the action of the administrative authority is quasi-judicial or administrative, one has to see the nature of power conferred, to whom it is conferred, the framework within which it is conferred, and the consequences. In *State of A.P.* v. *S.M.K. Parasurama Gurukul*[53], replying to the question whether the power of the government to appoint trustees under Section 15 of the A.P. Charitable and Hindu Religious Institutions and Endowments Act, 1966 is quasi-judicial or administrative, the court held the function as administrative and laid down that if there is *lis* between the parties, and the opinion is to be formed on objective satisfaction, the action is quasi-judicial, otherwise administrative. In the same manner in *Govindbhai Gordhanbhai Patel* v. *Gulam Abbas Mulla Allibhai*[54], the court came to the conclusion that since there is nothing in the Act to show that the Collector has to act judicially or in conformity with the recognised judicial norms, and as there is also nothing requiring the Collector to determine questions affecting the rights of any party, the function of the Collector in giving or withholding permission of transfer of land to a non-agriculturist under Section 63(1) of the Bombay Tenancy and Agricultural Lands Act, 1947 is administrative. The Delhi High Court applying the same parameters held that the function of the Company Law Board granting authority to shareholders to file a petition in the High Court is an administrative and not a quasi-judicial function.[55] Moving forward in the same direction, the Supreme Court further held that the function of the government under Sections 10, 12(5) and 11-A to make or refuse a reference to the Industrial Tribunal[56] and the power to grant or refuse a licence[57] are administrative in nature. In fact, in some cases, an administrative authority may determine questions of fact before arriving at a decision which may affect the rights of a person, even then such function shall continue to be administrative in character. In the same manner if the authority is dictated by the policy and expediency, its function will be administrative.[58]

Therefore, administrative action is the residuary action which is neither legislative nor judicial. It is concerned with the treatment of a particular situation and is devoid of generality. It has no procedural obligations of collecting evidence and weighing argument. It is based on subjective

52. (1969) 2 SCC 262.
53. (1973) 2 SCC 232.
54. (1977) 3 SCC 179.
55. *Sri Krishna Tiles & Potteries (P) Ltd.* v. *Company Law Board*, 1978 SCC OnLine Del 200: ILR (1979) 1 Del 435, *per* V.S. Deshpande CJ.
56. *Ram Avtar Sharma* v. *State of Haryana*, (1985) 3 SCC 189.
57. *State of U.P.* v. *Raja Ram Jaiswal*, (1985) 3 SCC 131.
58. *Indian National Congress (I)* v. *Institute of Social Welfare*, (2002) 5 SCC 685.

satisfaction where decision is based on policy and expediency. It does not decide a right though it may affect a right. However, it does not mean that the principles of natural justice can be ignored completely when the authority is exercising "administrative powers". Unless the statute provides otherwise, a minimum of the principles of natural justice must always be observed depending on the fact situation of each case. This requirement to follow a minimum of the principles of natural justice imposes a duty on the administration that while taking "administrative action" the authority must act "fairly"[59].

No exhaustive list of such actions may be drawn; however, a few may be noted for the sake of clarity:

(1) Issuing directions to subordinate officers not having the force of law.[60]
(2) Making a reference to a tribunal for adjudication under the Industrial Disputes Act, 1947.[61]
(3) Internment, externment and deportation.[62]
(4) Granting or withholding sanction to file a suit under Section 55(2) of the Muslim Wakf Act, 1954.[63]
(5) Granting or withholding sanction by the Advocate General under Section 92 of the Civil Procedure Code, 1908.[64]
(6) Fact-finding action.[65]
(7) Requisition, acquisition and allotment.[66]
(8) Entering names in the surveillance register of the police.[67]
(9) Power of the Chancellor under the U.P. State Universities Act, 1973 to take decision on the recommendation of the selection committee in case of disagreement of the executive council with such recommendation.[68]
(10) Functions of a selection committee.[69]
(11) Decision to extend time for anti-dumping investigation.[70]

Administrative action may be statutory, having the force of law, or non-statutory, devoid of such legal force. The bulk of the administrative action is statutory because a statute or the Constitution gives it a legal force, but in some cases it may be non-statutory, such as issuing directions

59. *See*, C.K. Thakkar, "From Duty to Act Judicially to Duty to Act Fairly", (2003) 4 SCC J-1.
60. *B.N. Nagarajan* v. *State of Mysore*, AIR 1966 SC 1942.
61. *State of Madras* v. *C.P. Sarathy*, AIR 1953 SC 53.
62. *A.K. Gopalan* v. *State of Madras*, 1950 SCC 228: AIR 1950 SC 27.
63. *K.M. Abdul Kasim* v. *P.M.N. Mohamed Dawood*, 1960 SCC OnLine Mad 183: AIR 1961 Mad 244.
64. *A.K. Bhaskar* v. *Advocate General*, 1961 SCC OnLine Ker 71: AIR 1962 Ker 90.
65. *Raja Narayanlal Bansilal* v. *Maneck Phiroz Mistry*, AIR 1961 SC 29.
66. *Province of Bombay* v. *Kusaldas S. Advani*, 1950 SCC 551: AIR 1950 SC 222.
67. *Malak Singh* v. *State of P&H*, (1981) 1 SCC 420.
68. *Neelima Misra* v. *Harinder Kaur Paintal*, (1990) 2 SCC 746.
69. *National Institute of Mental Health and Neuro-Sciences* v. *K. Kalyana Raman*, 1992 Supp (2) SCC 481.
70. *Designated Authority (Anti-Dumping Directorate)* v. *Haldor Topsoe A/S*, (2000) 6 SCC 626.

to subordinates not having the force of law, but its violation may be visited with disciplinary action.[71] Though by and large administrative action is discretionary and is based on subjective satisfaction, however, the administrative authority must act fairly, impartially and reasonably.

1.4 Ministerial or pure administrative action

A further distillate of administrative action is ministerial action. Ministerial action is that action of the administrative agency which is taken as a matter of duty imposed upon it by the law devoid of any discretion or judgment. Therefore, a ministerial action involves the performance of a definite duty in respect of which there is no choice. Collection of revenue may be one such ministerial action. Furthermore, if the statute requires that the agency shall open a bank account in a particular bank or shall prepare the annual report to be placed on the table of the Minister, such actions of opening of the bank account and the preparation of the annual report shall be classified as ministerial. However, the area of such action is highly limited because any efficient discharge of a governmental function presupposes at least some discretion vested in the administrative authority. Gordon classifies the functions of administrative authorities into judicial and non-judicial. Judicial functions involved the decision of rights and liabilities so that an investigation and application of fixed legal standards was a material part of the functions. Non-judicial functions are further divided into administrative and ministerial functions. Ministerial functions are exercised by taking active, often coercive measures, and administrative functions by meting out policy and expediency with unfettered discretion. When an administrative agency is acting ministerially, it has no power to consult its own wishes, but when it is acting administratively its standards are subjective and it follows its own wishes.[72]

2. ADMINISTRATIVE INSTRUCTIONS

Subject to the provisions of the Constitution, the executive power of the Union and the States extends to all matters in respect of which Parliament or State Legislatures have power to make laws.[73] The executive power includes both the determination of policy as well as carrying it into execution. Thus the power to issue instructions flow from the general executive power of the administration.

In any intensive form of government the desirability and efficacy of administrative instructions issued by the superior administrative authorities to their subordinates cannot be overemphasised. "Administrative instruction" is a most efficacious technique for achieving some kind of uniformity

71. *Raman and Raman Ltd.* v. *State of Madras*, AIR 1959 SC 694. See, *A.K. Kraipak* v. *Union of India*, (1969) 2 SCC 262.

72. D.M. Gordon, "Administrative Tribunals and the Courts", (1933) 49 LQR 94, 419.

73. Arts. 73 and 162 of the Indian Constitution.

in administrative discretion, and to manipulate in an area which is new and dynamic. These instructions also give a desired flexibility to the administration devoid of the technicalities of the rule-making process.

Administrative instructions may be specific or general, and directory or mandatory. What kind of instruction it is depends largely on the provisions of the statute which authorises the administrative agency to issue instructions. The instructions which are generally issued not under any statutory authority but under the general power of administration are considered as directory, and hence are unenforceable, not having the force of law. In *G.J. Fernandez* v. *State of Mysore*[74], the court held the Mysore Public Works Department Code of Instructions as not having the force of law because this is issued under no statutory authority but in exercise of general administrative power. However, though the violations of such instructions may not be enforceable in a court of law, yet their violation may expose the officer concerned to disciplinary action. The determination of statutory or non-statutory source of administrative direction is a complex question.[75]

Even in those situations where administrative instructions have a statutory source, their binding character depends on multiple factors. In *Raman and Raman Ltd.* v. *State of Madras*[76], the Supreme Court came to the conclusion that the administrative instructions, despite their issuance under Section 43-A of the Motor Vehicles Act, 1939, do not have the force of law. However, another decision of the Supreme Court in *Jagjit Singh* v. *State of Punjab*[77] sets the pace in a new direction. In this case, the State Government requested the Punjab Public Service Commission to select and recommend six candidates for filling six vacancies in the Punjab Civil Services (Executive Branch). A competitive examination was held and the appellant, who was a member of the Scheduled Caste (SC), secured third position among the SC candidates. Since only 20 per cent of the reserved quota was available, the first two successful candidates were issued appointment letters. Later on, one of the candidates was selected in the Indian Administrative Service and he resigned. Since the appellant was next in merit on the selection list, he applied to the government for appointment in the vacancy. This claim was based on the State Government's instructions contained in a circular. The claim was rejected by the government and a petition filed in the High Court was dismissed. The Supreme Court, allowing the appeal, held that the government instructions not only deprecate the existing practice of including the resultant vacancy in the normal pool but go on to lay down in unmistakable terms that if the services of a government servant belonging to SC or ST are terminated, the resulting vacancy should not be included in the

74. AIR 1967 SC 1753.
75. *I.N. Saksena* v. *State of M.P.*, AIR 1967 SC 1264; *Kumari Regina* v. *St. Aloysius Higher Secondary School*, (1972) 4 SCC 188.
76. AIR 1959 SC 694.
77. (1978) 2 SCC 196. See also, *Jayantilal Amratlal Shodhan* v. *F.N. Rana*, AIR 1964 SC 648; *Ellerman Lines Ltd.* v. *CIT*, (1972) 4 SCC 474; *Indian Airlines Corpn.* v. *Sukhdeo Rai*, (1971) 2 SCC 192.

normal pool but should be filled up on an ad hoc basis from the candidates belonging to those categories. In the face of these clear instructions, nothing contrary from the State Government can be accepted. The thrust of the case is that if the administrative instructions do not run counter to the statutory rules, they are binding and their violation can be enjoined through a court of law. Undoubtedly, the government in exercise of its executive authority cannot supersede a statutory rule or regulation, but it can certainly effectuate the purpose of a regulation by supplementing it.[78]

The law relating to the statutory status and the enforceability of administrative instructions or directions is in a highly nebulous state because the approach of the courts has so far been residual and variegated. Judicial meanderings in this area of high legal visibility is scathing. Three decisions of the Supreme Court clearly depict court legerdemain. In *V.T. Khanzode* v. *RBI*[79], the question before the court was whether the staff regulations issued by the Reserve Bank of India, fixing the basis of seniority of its employees, could be modified by a mere circular issued by it later on. The court reiterated the well-settled proposition that administrative instructions, which by their very nature do not have statutory force, cannot modify statutory rules and regulations, and held that since the staff regulations were not issued under Section 58 of the Reserve Bank of India Act, 1934, they were not rules but merely administrative directions which could be amended by any administrative circular.

However, a different position was taken by the court in *Amitabh Shrivastava* v. *State of M.P.*[80], where the court allowed the enforceability of administrative instructions even in view of the fact that they modified statutory rules. In this case the State Government had prescribed certain qualifying marks by statutory rules for admission to medical colleges in the State. The petitioner did not qualify for admission on the basis of these rules. Subsequently, the qualifying percentage of marks was lowered by an executive order, on the basis of which the petitioner became eligible for admission. The Supreme Court allowed admission to the petitioner by enforcing an administrative instruction as against the rules. The only justification which the court found for its ruling appears to be that the government did not object to the enforceability of an administrative direction at the instance of an individual. However, in subsequent decisions the Supreme Court held that exclusive instructions can supplement a statute or cover areas to which the statute does not extend. But they cannot run contrary to statutory provisions or whittle down their effect.[81] Thus, in *Mahadeo Bhau Khilare* v. *State of Maharashtra*[82], the court held that a

78. *Gurdial Singh Fijji* v. *State of Punjab*, (1979) 2 SCC 368.
79. (1982) 2 SCC 7.
80. (1982) 1 SCC 514.
81. *State of M.P.* v. *G.S. Dall and Flour Mills*, 1992 Supp (1) SCC 150; *C.L. Verma* v. *State of M.P.*, 1989 Supp (2) SCC 437.
82. (2007) 5 SCC 524.

scheme framed by an administrative instruction in violation of statutory rules cannot be sustained.

In *Veerendra Kumar Dubey* v. *Chief of Army Staff*[83], it was held by the Supreme Court that executive orders cannot supplant rules framed under the proviso to Article 309 of the Constitution but can only supplement them. When rules, regulations or executive instructions are contrary to any statutory provision, the statutory provision shall prevail and rules or executive instructions so far as they are contrary to statutory provisions would fail.[84]

The administrative directions issued by a body incorporated under a statute are certainly not laws, no matter if these are issued under statutory provisions. At best these may be compared with the articles of association of a company which have no force of law.[85]

Even if administrative instructions have no force of law but if these are consistently followed for a long time, the government cannot depart from it at its own sweet will without rational justification because this would be a clear violation of Articles 14 and 16 of the Constitution.[86]

However, no specific instructions can be issued to any administrative authority exercising quasi-judicial power or any other statutory power, laying down the manner in which this power is to be exercised. It has always been considered as an interference in the independent exercise of power by the agency and also is against the principles of administrative due process.[87]

If administrative instructions are intended to make a representation to the people then anyone who acts on the representation can hold the agency bound by it on the ground of equitable estoppel.[88]

Even if the administrative instruction is binding, the effect of its non-compliance on the legality of the decision would depend on the fact situation. Therefore, administrative instruction to obtain prior permission of government for making an award under the Land Acquisition Act, 1894, if the value exceeds ₹20,000 per acre, though binding, yet it was held that the violation thereof does not constitute an infirmity in the acquisition of land itself.[89]

In *Union of India* v. *Charanjit S. Gill*[90], the law was summarised thus:

(1) Notes and administrative instruction issued in the absence of any statutory authority has no force of law, nor can supplement any provision of law, Act, or rule and regulation.

83. (2016) 2 SCC 627.
84. *Lok Prahari* v. *State of U.P.*, (2016) 8 SCC 389.
85. *Coop. Central Bank Ltd.* v. *Industrial Tribunal*, (1969) 2 SCC 43.
86. *Amarjit Singh Ahluwalia* v. *State of Punjab*, (1975) 3 SCC 503.
87. *B. Rajagopala Naidu* v. *STAT*, AIR 1964 SC 1573; *Sri Rama Vilas Service Ltd.* v. *Road Traffic Board*, 1947 SCC OnLine Mad 269: AIR 1948 Mad 400.
88. *Union of India* v. *Indo Afghan Agencies Ltd.*, AIR 1968 SC 718. *See*, Jain, *Principles of Administrative Law* (1973) 494–505.
89. *Collector* v. *Narra Venkateswarlu*, (1996) 7 SCC 150.
90. (2000) 5 SCC 742.

(2) By administrative instructions government has power to fill up gaps in the rules if the rules are silent on the subject and are not inconsistent with the existing rules.
(3) If administrative instructions are not referable to any statutory authority, they cannot have the effect of taking away rights vested in the person governed by the Act.

3. ADMINISTRATIVE DISCRETION/ SUBJECTIVELY WORDED POWER

Discretion in layman's language means choosing from amongst the various available alternatives without reference to any predetermined criterion, no matter how fanciful that choice may be. A person writing his will has such discretion to dispose of his property in any manner, no matter how arbitrary or fanciful it may be. But the term "discretion" when qualified by the word "administrative" has somewhat different overtones. "Discretion" in this sense means choosing from amongst the various available alternatives but with reference to the rules of reason and justice and not according to personal whims. Such exercise is not to be arbitrary, vague and fanciful, but legal and regular.[91] For Edward Coke once said that discretion is a science or understanding to discern between falsity and truth, between right and wrong, and not to do according to will and private affection.

The problem of administrative discretion is complex. It is true that in any intensive form of government, the government cannot function without the exercise of some discretion by the officials. It is necessary not only for the individualisation of the administrative power but also because it is humanly impossible to lay down a rule for every conceivable eventuality in the complex art of modern government. But it is equally true that absolute discretion is a ruthless master. It is more destructive of freedom than any of man's other inventions.[92] Therefore, there has been a constant conflict between the claims of the administration to an absolute discretion and the claims of subjects to a reasonable exercise of it. Discretionary power by itself is not pure evil but gives much room for misuse. Therefore, remedy lies in tightening the procedure and not in abolishing the power itself.

There is no set pattern of conferring discretion or subjectively worded power on an administrative officer. Modern drafting technique uses the words "adequate", "advisable", "appropriate", "beneficial", "competent", "convenient", "detrimental", "expedient", "equitable", "reputable", "safe", "sufficient", "wholesome", "deem fit", "prejudicial to safety and security", "satisfaction", "belief", "efficient", "public purpose", etc. or their opposites. It is true that with the exercise of discretion on a case-to-case basis, these vague generalisations are reduced into more specific moulds, yet the

91. *Susannah Sharp* v. *Wakefield*, 1891 AC 173 (HL).
92. Douglas J in *United States* v. *Wunderlich*, 1951 SCC OnLine US SC 93: 96 L Ed 113: 342 US 98, 101 (1951).

margin of oscillation is never eliminated. Therefore, the need for judicial correction of unreasonable exercise of administrative discretion cannot be overemphasised.[93]

3.1 Judicial behaviour and administrative discretion in India

Though courts in India have developed a few effective parameters for the proper exercise of discretion, the conspectus of judicial behaviour still remains halting, variegated and residual, and lacks the activism of the American courts. Judicial control mechanism of administrative discretion is exercised at two stages:

(1) Control at the stage of delegation of discretion.
(2) Control at the stage of exercise of discretion.

Control at the stage of delegation of discretion.—The court exercises control over delegation of discretionary powers to the administration by adjudicating upon the constitutionality of the law under which such powers are delegated with reference to the fundamental rights enunciated in Part III of the Indian Constitution. Therefore, if the law confers vague and wide discretionary power on any administrative authority, it may be declared ultra vires Articles 14 and 19 and other provisions of the Constitution.

Control at the stage of exercise of discretion.—In India, unlike the US, there is no Administrative Procedure Act providing for judicial review on the exercise of administrative discretion. Therefore, the power of judicial review arises from the constitutional configuration of courts. Courts in India have always held the view that judge-proof discretion is a negation of the rule of law. Therefore, they have developed various formulations to control the exercise of administrative discretion. These formulations may be conveniently grouped into two broad generalisations:

(1) That the authority is deemed not to have exercised its discretion at all, or there is failure on its part to exercise discretion.
(2) That the authority has not exercised its discretion properly, or there is an excess or abuse of discretion.

These clauses are, however, not mutually exclusive. They may overlap and at times run into each other.

(1) *That the authority is deemed not to have exercised its discretion at all.*—Under this categorisation, courts exercise judicial control over administrative discretion if the authority has either abdicated its power or has put fetters on its exercise, or the jurisdictional facts are either non-existent or have been wrongly determined. The authority in which discretion is vested can be compelled to exercise it, but not to exercise it in a particular manner.

93. Freund, *Administrative Powers over Persons and Property: A Comparative Study* (1928) 71. List given above has been further added to.

Purtabpore Co. Ltd. v. *Cane Commr. of Bihar*[94] is a notable case in point. In this case the Cane Commissioner, who had the power to reserve sugarcane areas for the respective sugar factories, at the dictation of the Chief Minister, excluded 99 villages from the area reserved by him in favour of the appellant-company. The court quashed the exercise of discretion by the Cane Commissioner on the ground that he abdicated his power by exercising it at the dictation of some other authority; therefore, it was deemed that the authority had not exercised its discretion at all. Thus, the exercise of discretion in compliance with instructions of some other person amounts to failure to exercise the discretion altogether. It is immaterial that the authority invested with the discretion itself sought the instructions.[95]

However, this does not mean that the administrative authority cannot frame broad policies for the exercise of its discretion. In *Shri Rama Sugar Industries Ltd.* v. *State of A.P.*[96], Section 21 of the A.P. Sugarcane (Regulation of Supply and Purchase) Act, 1961 gave power to the administrative authority to exempt from payment of tax any new factory which has substantially expanded. The government framed a policy granting exemption only to factories in the cooperative sector. The Supreme Court, negativing the contention that the adoption of this policy has fettered the exercise of discretion, held that a body endowed with a statutory discretion may legitimately adopt general rules or principles to guide itself in the exercise of its discretion provided such rules are not arbitrary and not opposed to the aims and objectives of the Act. The court further remarked that by adopting such rules the agency must not disable itself from exercising genuine discretion in individual cases. Mathew and P.N. Bhagwati JJ, however, gave a dissenting opinion on the ground that the adoption of policy, as has been done in this case, predetermines the issue.[97]

(2) *That the authority has not exercised its discretion properly.*—This is an all embracing formulation developed by courts in India to control the exercise of discretion by the administrative authority. Improper exercise of discretion includes everything which English courts include in "unreasonable" exercise of discretion and American courts include in "arbitrary and capricious" exercise of discretion. Improper exercise of discretion includes such things as "taking irrelevant considerations into account", "acting for improper purpose", "asking wrong questions", "acting in bad faith", "neglecting to take into consideration relevant factors"or "acting unreasonably".

94. (1969) 1 SCC 308. See also, *Commr. of Police* v. *Gordhandas Bhanji*, 1951 SCC 1088: AIR 1952 SC 16; *State of Punjab* v. *Suraj Parkash Kapur*, AIR 1963 SC 507.
95. *Anirudhsinhji Karansinhji Jadeja* v. *State of Gujarat*, (1995) 5 SCC 302.
96. (1974) 1 SCC 534.
97. *See*, Baxi's "Introduction" in Mathew, *Democracy, Equality and Freedom* XLVIII-XLIX and S.P. Sathe, "Discretion and Policy: A Note on *Shri Rama Sugar Industries Ltd.* v. *State of A.P.*" See also, *U.P. SRTC* v. *Mohd. Ismail*, (1991) 3 SCC 239.

In *Indian Railway Construction Co. Ltd.* v. *Ajay Kumar*[98], elaborating the law on this point, the court held that in general, a discretion must be exercised only by the authority to which it is committed. The authority must genuinely address itself to the matter before it; it must not act under the dictates of another body or disable itself from exercising discretion in each individual case. In the purported exercise of discretion, it must not do what it has been forbidden to do, nor must it do what it has not been authorised to do. It must act in good faith, must have regard to all relevant considerations and must not be influenced by irrelevant considerations, must not seek to promote purposes alien to the letter and spirit of the legislation that gives it power to act, and must not act arbitrarily or capriciously. The distinctive features of some recent cases signify the willingness of the courts to scrutinise the factual basis on which discretion has been exercised. One can classify these grounds of judicial control of administrative discretion into "illegality", "irrationality" and "procedural impropriety". To characterise an exercise of discretion as "irrational", the court apply Wednesbury Test of Reasonableness and see whether discretion is "so outrageous" as to be in total defiance of logic and moral standards. Exercise of discretionary power can be set aside if there is manifest error in the exercise of such power, or the exercise of such power is manifestly arbitrary or mala fide or unreasonable. The decision could be of many choices open to the authority, it is open to the authority to exercise its choice and the court would not substitute its view. In this way, courts have widened the scope of judicial review of administrative discretion restricting the doctrine of immunity from judicial review to class of cases which relate to deployment of troops, and entering into international treaties, etc.

3.1.1 *Notable instances: Administrative discretion and Article 14*

State of W.B. v. *Anwar Ali Sarkar*[99].—In this case, in order to speed up the trial for certain offences, Section 5(1) of the West Bengal Special Courts Act, 1950 conferred discretion on the State Government to refer any offence for trial by the special court. Since the procedure before the special court was stringent in comparison with that for normal trials, the respondents asserted its unconstitutionality on the ground that it violates the equality clause in Article 14. The court held the law invalid on the ground that the use of vague expressions, like "speedier trial", confers a wide discretion on the government and can be a basis of unreasonable classification.

98. (2003) 4 SCC 579.
99. (1952) 1 SCC 1: AIR 1952 SC 75.

State of Punjab v. *Khan Chand*[100].—In this case, the truck of Khan Chand was requisitioned by the District Magistrate, Rohtak for famine relief work. He challenged the constitutionality of the East Punjab Requisition of Movable Property Act, 1947, under which the action was taken, on the ground that it violates the provisions of Article 14 of the Constitution. The court, upholding the contention, held that the Act confers wide discretionary powers upon authorities by not laying down the guidelines for requisitioning movable property. Even the words "public purpose" are not used. Therefore, arbitrariness and power to discriminate are writ large on the face of the Act and fall within the mischief which Article 14 seeks to prevent. It would be wrong to assume an element of judicial arrogance in the judicial behaviour striking down the statute.

Manhar Lal Bhojilal Shah v. *State of Maharashtra*[101].—In this case and many others, signs of judicial humility or withdrawal in judicial behaviour on account of administrative convenience are strikingly visible. In this case, Section 187-A of the Sea Customs Act, 1878 gave wide discretionary power to the authorities to either refer a case of smuggled goods to a magistrate or to look into the matter themselves. The court upheld the constitutionality of the statute on the ground that as this discretion is to be exercised by senior officers, that will stand as a guarantee against its misuse. This kind of judicial behaviour aimed at preserving wide discretionary powers may ultimately end up in destroying it.

Monarch Infrastructure (P) Ltd. v. *Ulhasnagar Municipal Corpn.*[102].—In this case, Municipal Corporation had invited tenders for appointment of agents for the collection of octroi. However, one of the eligibility conditions was deleted after the expiry of time for submission of tenders but before opening thereof. Thereafter, tender was awarded to one who did not fulfil the deleted condition. The Supreme Court held award of tender arbitrary and discriminatory.

3.1.2 *Notable instances: Administrative discretion and Article 19*

Article 19 contains six freedoms [the freedom to acquire, hold and dispose of property—Article 19(*f*)—has been deleted by the Constitution (44th Amendment) Act, 1978]. These freedoms are not absolute and are subject to reasonable restrictions. The courts have always taken the view that the vesting of wide discretionary power in the administrative authorities to curtail these freedoms is unreasonable and hence unconstitutional.

100. (1974) 1 SCC 549. *See*, M.P. Jain, "Administrative Discretion and Fundamental Rights", (1958–59) 1 JILI 247–48.
101. (1971) 2 SCC 119. See also, *Pannalal Binjraj* v. *Union of India*, AIR 1957 SC 397; *R. Chitralekha* v. *State of Mysore*, AIR 1964 SC 1823.
102. (2000) 5 SCC 287. See also, *Mohd. Riazul Usman Gani* v. *District and Sessions Judge*, (2000) 2 SCC 606.

Himat Lal K. Shah v. *Commr. of Police*[103].—Rule 7 under Section 44 of the Bombay Police Act, 1951 gave unguided discretionary power to the Police Commissioner to grant or refuse permission for any public meeting to be held on a public street. The Supreme Court struck down Rule 7 as being an unreasonable restriction on the exercise of a fundamental right.

State of Madras v. *V.G. Row*[104].—Section 15(2)(*b*), Criminal Law Amendment Act, 1908 as amended by Madras Act, 1950 gave wide discretionary powers to the State Government to declare any association as unlawful. The court struck down Section 15(2)(*b*) as being unconstitutional because it allows the administrative authority to exercise this discretion on subjective satisfaction without permitting the grounds to be judicially tested.

State of M.P. v. *Bharat Singh*[105].—The M.P. Public Security Act, 1959 invested the District Magistrate or the State Government with wide discretion, uncircumscribed by procedural safeguards, to extern a person from any area and to intern him in any specified place if his activities were prejudicial to the security of State or maintenance of public order. The Supreme Court held the relevant provision unconstitutional on the ground that it invests the government with such wide discretion without procedural safeguards that a person could even be interned in a place which could render him a destitute without any means of livelihood.

Harakchand Ratanchand Banthia v. *Union of India*[106].—The Gold Control Act, 1968 invested administrative authority with blanket discretionary power to grant or refuse licence to any dealer in gold ornaments. Though the Act had provided that such power was to be exercised with reference to the number of existing dealers, anticipated demand, suitability of the applicant and public interest, the court struck down the law on the ground that such vague expressions may result in the arbitrary exercise of power.

State of Maharashtra v. *Kamal Sukumar Durgule*[107].—In this case the legislature had given the power to the competent authority to declare a land vacant and then to acquire it. The power had been given without laying down any guidelines for the exercise of this discretion, and no provision had been made of any notice and hearing to the owner. Quashing Sections 3(1) and 4(1) of the Land Acquisition Act, 1894, the Supreme Court held that because law confers arbitrary powers on the government, hence it violates Article 14 of the Constitution. The court further observed that the fact that the exercise of this power has been given to officers of high echelon makes

103. (1973) 1 SCC 227.
104. (1952) 1 SCC 410: AIR 1952 SC 196. See also, *S. Ramakrishnaiah* v. *District Board, Nellore*, 1951 SCC OnLine Mad 295: AIR 1952 Mad 253.
105. AIR 1967 SC 1170. See also, *State of M.P.* v. *Baldeo Prasad*, AIR 1961 SC 293.
106. (1969) 2 SCC 166.
107. (1985) 1 SCC 234.

no difference to the position and is not a palliative to the prejudice which is inherent in the situation.

In certain situations, the statute, though it does not give discretionary power to the administrative authority to take action, may give discretionary power to frame rules and regulations affecting the rights of citizens. The bestowal of such a discretion can be controlled by the court on the ground of excessive delegation.[108] This aspect of "discretion" has been discussed in detail in the chapter on administrative rule-making.

3.1.3 *Notable instances*

Barium Chemicals Ltd. v. *Company Law Board*[109].—This case shows a definite orientation in the judicial behaviour for an effective control of administrative discretion in India. In this case, the Company Law Board exercising its powers under Section 237 of the Companies Act, 1956 ordered an investigation into the affairs of Barium Chemicals Ltd. Under Section 237, the Board is authorised to order investigation if in its opinion the business of the company is being conducted with intent to defraud its creditors or members, etc., or the management of the company is guilty of fraud, misfeasance or other misconduct, or the members of the company have not been given full information about the affairs of the company. However, the basis of the exercise of discretion for ordering investigation was that due to faulty planning the company incurred a loss, as a result of which the value of the shares had fallen and many eminent persons had resigned from the Board of Directors. The court quashed the order of the Board on the ground that the basis of the exercise of discretion is extraneous to the factors mentioned in Section 237 for such exercise of discretion. This case also stands for the proposition that mere executive declaration that there was material for forming an opinion will not save the exercise of discretion from judicial scrutiny.

M.A. Rasheed v. *State of Kerala*[110].—In this case, the Kerala government issued a notification to prevent high consumption of coir in mechanised industry because the traditional sector was starving, causing unemployment. The main ground of challenge was that there was no reasonable basis for the exercise of this discretion. The court observed:

(1) Whenever a public authority is invested with the power to make an order which prejudicially affects the rights of an individual, then, whatever may be the nature of the power, whatever may be the procedure prescribed and whatever may be the nature of the authority, the proceedings of the public authority must be regulated by the analogy of rules governing judicial determination of disputed questions.

108. *Hamdard Dawakhana* v. *Union of India*, AIR 1960 SC 554.

109. AIR 1967 SC 295. See also, *Rohtas Industries Ltd.* v. *S.D. Agarwal*, (1969) 1 SCC 325.

110. (1974) 2 SCC 687.

(2) Where powers are conferred on the executive authority based on subjective satisfaction, the courts will not readily defer to the conclusiveness of an executive authority's opinion as to the existence of a matter of law and fact upon which the exercise of power is predicated.
(3) Administrative decision in exercise of powers even if conferred in subjective terms is to be made in good faith based on relevant considerations. The courts can inquire whether a reasonable man could have come to the decision without misdirecting himself on law and fact. The standard of reasonableness may range from the court's own opinion of what is reasonable to the criterion of what a reasonable man might have decided. The courts will find out whether conditions precedent to the forming of opinion have a factual base.
(4) Where reasonable conduct is expected, the criterion of reasonableness is not subjective but objective.

S.R. Venkataraman v. *Union of India*[111].—The appellant, a Central Government officer, was prematurely retired from service in "public interest" under Rule 56(*j*)(*i*) on attaining the age of 50 years. Her contention was that the government did not apply its mind to her service record, and that in the facts and circumstances of the case the discretion vested under Rule 56(*j*)(*i*) was not exercised for furtherance of public interest, and that the order was based on extraneous circumstances. The government conceded that there was nothing on record to justify the order. The Supreme Court, quashing the order of the government, held that if a discretionary power has been exercised for an unauthorised purpose, it is generally immaterial whether its repository was acting in good faith or bad faith. An administrative order based on a reason or facts that do not exist must be held to be infected with an abuse of power. The court quoted with approval Lord Esher in *R.* v. *Vestry of St. Pancras*[112] as:

> If people who have to exercise a public duty by exercising their discretion take into account matters which the courts consider not to be proper for the guidance of their discretion, then in the eye of the law they have not exercised their discretion.

Ramana Dayaram Shetty v. *International Airport Authority of India*[113].—It is heartening to see the law catching up with the vagaries of the State's dealings in the exercise of its discretion. In this case the issue was the awarding of a contract for running a second-class restaurant and two snack bars by the International Airport Authority, which is a statutory corporation. The tenders were invited from "registered second-class hoteliers", and it was clearly stipulated that the acceptance of the tender would rest with the Airport Director who would not bind himself to accept any tender and reserved to himself the right to reject all or any of the tenders

111. (1979) 2 SCC 491.
112. (1890) LR 24 QBD 371, p. 375 (CA).
113. (1979) 3 SCC 489.

received without assigning any reason. The highest tender was accepted. The only snag was that the tenderer was not a hotelier at all. A writ petition was filed by a person who was himself neither a tenderer nor a hotelier. His grievance was that he was in the same position as the successful tenderer because if an essential condition could be ignored in the tenderer's case why not in the petitioner's? The Supreme Court accepted the plea of locus standi in challenging the administrative action. Bhagwati J, who delivered the judgment of the court, held:

(1) Exercise of discretion is an inseparable part of sound administration and, therefore, the State, which is itself a creature of the Constitution, cannot shed its limitation at any time in any sphere of State activity.
(2) It is a well-settled rule of administrative law that an executive authority must be rigorously held to the standards by which it professes its actions to be judged, and it must scrupulously observe those standards on pain of invalidation of an act in violation of them.
(3) It is indeed unthinkable that in a democracy governed by the rule of law, the executive government or any of its officers should possess arbitrary powers over the interests of an individual. Every action of the executive government must be informed with reason and should be free from arbitrariness. That is the very essence of the rule of law and its bare minimal requirement.
(4) The government cannot be permitted to say that it will give jobs or enter into contracts or issue quotas or licences only in favour of those having grey hair or belonging to a particular political party or professing a particular religious faith. The government is still the government when it acts in the matter of granting largesse and it cannot act arbitrarily. It does not stand in the same position as a private individual.

This case is not an attempt in judicialising the administrative process but only reiterates that the exercise of discretion must not be arbitrary, fanciful and influenced by extraneous considerations. In matters of discretion the choice must be dictated by public interest and must not be unprincipled or unreasoned.

It has been firmly established that the discretionary powers given to the governmental or quasi-governmental authorities must be hedged by policy, standards, procedural safeguards or guidelines, failing which the exercise of discretion and its delegation may be quashed by courts. This principle has been reiterated in many cases.[114] The courts have also insisted that before the exercise of discretion, the administrative authority must also frame rules

---

114. *R.R. Verma* v. *Union of India*, (1980) 3 SCC 402; *Ramakanyadevi* v. *State of Karnataka*, 1980 SCC OnLine Kar 105: AIR 1980 Kar 182; *Subhash Chandra* v. *State of U.P.*, (1980) 2 SCC 324; *Chandrabhan Chunilal Gour* v. *Shrawan Kumar Khunnolal Gour*, 1979 SCC OnLine Bom 76: AIR 1980 Bom 48; *State of Punjab* v. *Gurdial Singh*, (1980) 2 SCC 471; *Accountant General* v. *S. Doraiswamy*, (1981) 4 SCC 93.

for the proper exercise of the discretion. Courts have emphasised that even the power of the President or the Governor to grant pardon and suspend, remit or commute sentences, or the power of the Chief Minister to allot cement, plots or houses from discretionary quota or make nominations to medical or engineering colleges must conform to this norm. The Himachal Pradesh High Court had struck down the nomination of three students to the State Medical College made by the Chief Minister out of his discretionary quota for 1982–1983. The main thrust of attack in a bunch of petitions challenging these nominations was that no guidelines have been prescribed for the exercise of discretion, and hence the power is uncanalised and liable to be abused and may be subject to political pulls and pressures. Quashing these nominations, the court emphasised that while the college prospectus leaves nominations to the discretion of the Chief Minister, it has not provided any clear policy or guidelines with reference to which the Chief Minister was to exercise his discretion.[115] However, it is not necessary that the guidelines must be ex facie found. It is sufficient if guidelines could be gathered on wholesome reading of the statute and rules, regulations, orders or notifications issued thereunder.[116] Nevertheless in order to meet the challenge of arbitrariness, clear and unequivocal guidelines, criteria, rules or regulations must be predetermined and published for the public and action should be taken accordingly. Reason and justice and not arbitrariness must inform every exercise of discretion.[117] In the same manner when no guidelines were prepared for the selection of dealers of fair price shops, and the selection was left entirely to the whims of the individual officer holding interview, the court held that the exercise of such unbridled power is violative of Article 14 of the Constitution.[118] Thus, within the area of administrative discretion, the courts have tried to fly high the flag of rule of law which aims at the progressive diminution of arbitrariness in the exercise of public power.

Nevertheless, the Supreme Court has reiterated that the judicial invigilation of administrative decision should not extend as far as reviewing the actions on merit. In *P. Kasilingam* v. *P.S.G. College of Technology*[119], the court held that a High Court transgresses its jurisdiction under Article 226 if it enters upon the merits of the controversy by embarking upon an enquiry into the facts.

115. *Indian Express*, 20-11-1982. The Bench consisted of V.D. Misra CJ and H.S. Thakur J. Two of the three nominees had appeared for the Pre-Medical Test of the H.P. University, but failed to qualify for admission. The Supreme Court not only upheld the decision of the High Court but also directed on appeal the Union Government and the State Government that they must refrain from making such nominations without proper guidelines. *Indian Express*, 10-2-1983.
116. *M.J. Sivani* v. *State of Karnataka*, (1995) 6 SCC 289.
117. *New India Public School* v. *HUDA*, (1996) 5 SCC 510; *Gajraj Singh* v. *STAT*, (1997) 1 SCC 650.
118. *Y. Srinivasa Rao* v. *J. Veeraiah*, (1992) 3 SCC 63.
119. (1981) 1 SCC 405.

Elaborating the same principle, the Supreme Court in *Air India Ltd.* v. *Cochin International Airport Ltd.*[120] observed that it is the decision-making process and not decision which is amenable to judicial review. In this case, Cochin International Airport Authority wrote letters to certain firms for quotations for ground handling services. Cambata Aviation quoted higher offer and thus was recommended by the evaluation committee. However, Board of Directors decided to negotiate with Air India, being a public sector undertaking. After negotiation it increased its offer, and hence contract was awarded to Air India. Declining to interfere in the exercise of discretion of the authority, the court observed that the State can choose its own methods or various factors of commercial viability, therefore, court should not interfere with the decision unless dire public interest so requires. The court further observed that even if some defect is found in the decision-making process, the decision should not be interfered with unless it is unreasonable, mala fide or arbitrary, and overwhelming public interest requires so.

Following the same line of reasoning which allows administration necessary flexibilities, the Supreme Court in *Muni Suvrat-Swami Jain S.M.P. Sangh* v. *Arun Nathuram Gaikwad*[121] held that it cannot direct administrative authority to exercise its discretionary powers in a particular manner. In this case, a writ was filed in the High Court against inaction of the Municipal Corporation in demolishing the unauthorised structure. The High Court issued mandamus directing the authority to demolish the entire illegal and unauthorised structure. Before the Supreme Court, the Municipal Corporation took the stand that the Temple Trust has made a fresh application for regularisation of the structure and the same would be disposed of in accordance with law. Allowing the appeal, the Supreme Court held that the Bombay Municipal Corporation Act, 1888 gives discretion to the authority whether or not to demolish the unauthorised construction, therefore, court cannot impede the exercise of that discretion by any mandatory order. Thus, exercise of discretion cannot be clogged by any mandatory order of the court, though court can compel the authority to exercise its discretionary powers when it refuses to exercise it.

In the same manner, the Supreme Court speaking through Sinha J rightly stressed that possibility of abuse of discretionary powers cannot ipso facto be considered as violative of Article 14 of the Constitution on ground of arbitrariness.[122] Nevertheless, it is settled law that reasonableness and non-arbitrariness are the hallmarks of any action by the State even in contractual relationship. This was clearly stated by the Supreme Court in *Bharat Petroleum Corpn. Ltd.* v. *Maddula Ratnavalli*[123]. Burmah Shell was acquired by the government. The lease which this oil company

120. (2000) 2 SCC 617.
121. (2006) 8 SCC 590.
122. *Hardev Motor Transport* v. *State of M.P.*, (2006) 8 SCC 613.
123. (2007) 6 SCC 81.

held before acquisition could be renewed under Section 5(2) of the Burmah Shell (Acquisition of Undertakings in India) Act, 1976 if so desired by the government. The court opined that the State must act fairly and reasonably. Simply that a discretionary power has been given to an authority does not mean that it can exercise it in any manner it likes. Every State power is a public trust and must be exercised in the best interest of the people. Thus administrative discretion, though is based on subjective satisfaction, but must be exercised on objective criteria.

The court has developed a kind of caste-based hierarchical view of administrative responsibility when it presumes that "high" authority is unlikely to use its discretionary power injudiciously or arbitrarily. This presumption is certainly conjectural and hence not tenable.[124] This makes the judicial review of administrative discretion marginal and feeble. However, even where the court would not look into exercise of discretionary power by a high functionary on merit, it would certainly interfere if the exercise of power is arbitrary, mala fide or in absolute disregard of constitutionalism. Thus in *Swaran Singh* v. *State of U.P.*[125], the court remanded the case back to the Governor who had granted remission of sentence in a situation when adverse material against the petitioner was not brought to his notice. The Supreme Court deviated from its earlier view that there is a presumption against abuse of power vested in a high-ranking official.[126] Even the constitutional authorities cannot claim that either there is no discretion in the matter or the discretion is unfettered.[127] Discretionary power has to be exercised to advance the purpose for which the power has been given.

4. ABSOLUTE DISCRETION IS CONSTITUTIONAL BLASPHEMY—DOCTRINE OF IMPLIED LIMITATION

In a pace setting judgment in *State of Punjab* v. *Salil Sabhlok*[128], the Supreme Court re-invented a core principle of administrative law which provides without exception that in the exercise of all constitutional or statutory powers there is an implied requirement that every exercise of power/direction must be fair, reasonable and just and must also be guided by public interest. Thus, there cannot be any thing like absolute and final exercise of discretion in a constitutional democracy. This re-invented principle is not extra constitutional but emerges from the provisions of Article 14 of the Constitution itself.

In this case, the government had appointed a person as Chairman of the Punjab Public Service Commission in exercise of its discretionary powers

124. *See*, Upendra Baxi, "Developments in Indian Administrative Law" in A.G. Noorani (Ed.), *Public Law in India* (1982) 150; M.P. Jain, *Changing Face of Administrative Law in India and Abroad* (1982) 31; *State of Punjab* v. *Dial Chand Gian Chand & Co.*, (1983) 2 SCC 503.
125. (1998) 4 SCC 75. See also, *Satpal* v. *State of Haryana*, (2000) 5 SCC 170.
126. *Accountant General* v. *S. Doraiswamy*, (1981) 4 SCC 93.
127. *Shiv Sagar Tiwari* v. *Union of India*, (1997) 1 SCC 444.
128. (2013) 5 SCC 1.

under Article 316 of the Constitution. It was alleged that the appointee had neither competence nor integrity required for the job. The appointment was challenged before the High Court which quashed it, hence appeal before the Supreme Court.

The State pleaded that Article 316 of the Constitution confers absolute discretion to the State to appoint any person of its choice as Chairman of the Public Service Commission inasmuch as Article 316 does not lay down any qualification, suitability criteria or procedure for appointment. Upholding the decision of the High Court, the Supreme Court clarified that any discretion given to a public authority cannot be absolute in the sense that it can be exercised on the whims and sentiments of the authority. There is always an implied limitation that the exercise of discretion must be based on relevant considerations of necessary qualifications, competence and integrity necessary for holding any public office. The court clarified that if Article 316 does not lay down any qualification or procedure for appointment, it does not mean that a constitutional power cannot be regulated by law and appointment can be made on the grounds of political affiliation and pliability. The Supreme Court rightly asserted that if discretionary power is influenced by considerations that cannot be taken into account or by the disregard of relevant considerations required to be taken into account either expressly or by necessary implications, the court can quash it and to this end the Constitution confers wide powers on the constitutional courts to reach arbitrariness and unreasonableness wherever found.

However, in *Manoj Narula* v. *Union of India*[129], the Supreme Court refused to interfere with the choice of a ministerial candidate who also lacked competence and integrity on the ground that it is a choice purely based on political considerations and that principles of comity and subsidiarity oblige the court to act with self-restraint. Nevertheless, the Supreme Court clarified that this does not mean that the discretion is absolute and not limited by the principles of implied limitations. The fundamental principle that emerges is that in a constitutional democracy, no public power can be absolute, unlimited and unfettered. Every power, no matter discretionary in nature, is limited by the constitutional limitations, express or implied, and also by the norms of fairness and reasonableness of the administrative law.

In England, where Parliament is supreme and can confer any amount of discretion on the administrative authority, the courts have always held that the concept of "unfettered discretion" is a constitutional blasphemy. Besides requiring that the discretion must be exercised in conformity with the general policy of the Act and for a proper purpose, courts insist on its "reasonable" exercise. Thus the judicial control of administrative discretion in the US, England, and India converges on the same point despite divergent constitutional structurisations.

129. (2014) 9 SCC 1.

The decision of the House of Lords in *Padfield* v. *Minister of Agriculture Fisheries and Food*[130] lays down the parameters of judicial control of administrative discretion in England. In this case under the statutory milk-marketing scheme, the prices paid to milk producers in different areas are fixed by the Milk Marketing Board which consists of representatives of the producers. The producers near the area of London complained that though they were in proximity of the London market, yet the price paid did not reflect the higher value of their milk, and requested the Minister to refer the matter to the Statutory Committee for Complaints. To direct or not to direct a complaint to the Committee was the sole discretion of the Minister. The Minister in exercise of his unfettered discretion refused to direct the complaint. One of the reasons given by the Ministry was that the Minister would be in a difficult political position if, despite the Committee's acceptance of the complaint, the Minister should take no action. The House of Lords held that the Minister's reasons were unsatisfactory and his decision was unreasonable. The purpose of the Act was that every genuine complaint must be forwarded to the Committee and anything contrary to this would frustrate that purpose.

R. v. *Metropolitan Police Commr., ex p Blackburn*[131] is another classical example of judicial control of administrative discretion. Illegal gambling had increased considerably in London, but because of shortage of police personnel, the Police Commissioner issued confidential instructions that the observation of gambling clubs was to cease. Thereafter, a policy of not prosecuting these clubs was adopted. Mr Blackburn, a private individual, applied for a writ of mandamus to direct the police to do their duty and enforce the law. Though the writ lapsed because the Police Commissioner reversed his policy, yet the court held that the discretion of the police was not absolute and uncontrollable in the sense that no means were available for enforcing this duty. Therefore, in England, the long arm of the court reaches out to administrative discretion to correct its abuse in the same manner as it does in India and the US.

In the US, besides the judicial review of administrative discretion which is available in the "due process clause" and the general grant of constitutional judicial power, the Administrative Procedure Act, 1946, in Section 10, provides that the reviewing court shall "hold unlawful and set aside agency action, findings, and conclusions found to be arbitrary, capricious, an abuse of discretion, or otherwise not in accordance with law". This entails that if administrative discretion is exercised arbitrarily or capriciously, the courts would intervene. Section 10 also provides for a dangerous exception to the rule of judicial review in cases "where agency action is by law committed to agency discretion". However, courts have interpreted this exception in a manner not to cover arbitrary or capricious exercise of discretion.

130. 1968 AC 997: (1968) 2 WLR 924 (HL).
131. (1968) 2 QB 118: (1968) 2 WLR 893 (CA).

In *Citizens to Preserve Overton Park Inc.* v. *A. Volpe*[132], the Secretary of Transportation had authorised the use of federal funds for the construction of a highway through the public park. The statute gave discretion to the Secretary to allow such a construction only if a "feasible and prudent" alternative route did not exist. The Supreme Court did not accept the contention of the Secretary that the determination of "feasible and prudent" alternative route is committed to his absolute discretion and hence is not subject to judicial review. The court did not allow the exception to Section 10, Administrative Procedure Act, 1946 to reign supreme. In the same manner, in *Barlow* v. *Collins*[133] where the statute authorised the Secretary of Agriculture "to prescribe such regulations as he may deem proper to carry out the provisions of this Chapter", the court did not accept the contention that the contents of the regulation were committed to the absolute discretion of the Secretary which was not subject to judicial review.

In the US, judicial activism has entered the area of administrative discretion also, and courts not only substitute their discretion to the discretion of administrative authority but sometimes exercise discretion which is vested in an administrative authority. In *Boreta Enterprises Inc.* v. *Deptt. of Alcoholic Beverage Control*[134], the agency revoked the liquor licence because the licencee employed topless waitresses. The agency exercised its discretion on the ground that the licencee's conduct was contrary to public morals and might lead to socially deleterious conduct. The California Supreme Court held the exercise of discretion invalid on the ground that it is not a legal exercise of discretion covered within the requirement of the "good cause" clause for revocation of licence. In the same manner in *United States* v. *Professional Air Traffic Controllers' Organisation*[135], the court ordered the controllers of air traffic to end a strike and return to work. The order of the court also laid down that the Federal Aviation Authority (FAA) will impose no penalty of suspension or dismissal, no matter that the question of discipline in case of strike was within the sole discretion of the FAA.

In France, the administrative courts exercise power of judicial review over administrative action if the administrative authority abuses its discretionary powers. The term "abuse of power" includes everything which the term "unreasonable exercise of power" includes in England and "arbitrary and capricious exercise of power" includes in the US. From the above analysis it becomes clear that though some discretion is necessary to keep the giant wheels of administration moving in this age of an intensive form of government, if the power is misused the arms of the court are long enough to reach it.[136]

---

132. 1971 SCC OnLine US SC 46: 28 L Ed 136: 401 US 402 (1971).
133. 1970 SCC OnLine US SC 54: 25 L Ed 2d 192: 397 US 159 (1970).
134. 2 Cal 3d 85: 84 Cal Reptr 113 (1970).
135. 438 F 2d 79 (2nd Cir 1970).
136. *Maneka Gandhi* v. *Union of India*, (1978) 1 SCC 248, 294.

POINTS FOR DISCUSSION

1. Is there any need left to study the classification of administrative action after the Supreme Court's decision in *Kraipak*[137]?
2. Place of administrative finality in the constitutional structurisation in India. Evaluation of judicial behaviour.
3. Desirability and efficacy of the strategy of administrative instructions to bring uniformity in the area of administrative discretion.
4. What possible parameters can be developed to identify the binding character of administrative instructions.
5. Administrative discretion has a value of its own in the form of individualisation of administrative action but it is a ruthless master also. Are the norms developed by the courts to regulate administrative discretion at the stage of delegation and the exercise of it adequate to eliminate administrative arbitrariness?
6. Do you think that the court ought to exercise power of judicial review over exercise of discretion of the Prime Minister in appointing a Minister and also in appointing a member of the Public Service Commission by the government?

SUGGESTED READINGS

1. Alok Kumar, "Administrative Adjudication : A Comparative Understanding With Special Reference to Tribunals", 1 SML L Rev 105 (2018).
2. Alice Jacob, "Judicial Insistence on Fairness in Administrative Process", 25 JILI (1983) 195.
3. Alice Jacob, "Requirement of Findings of Fact in Administrative Determinations—Judicial Experience in India and the United States", 8 JILI (1966) 54.
4. Baker, "Policy by Rule or Ad Hoc Approach—Which should it be?", (1957) 22 Law & Contemp Probs 657.
5. C.K. Thakker, *Administrative Law* (Eastern Book Company 2012) Chaps. 3 and 9.
6. Committee on Ministers' Powers, Reports, 4, 5, 23, 51–52 (1932).
7. D.M. Gordon, "Administrative Tribunals and the Courts", (1933) 49 LQR 94.
8. D.M. Gordon, "What did the Anisminic Decide?" 34 Mod L Rev 1 (1971).
9. Freund, *Administrative Powers Over Persons and Property: A Comparative Study* (1928) Chap. I.
10. Griffith and Street, *Principles of Administrative Law* (1963) Chap. II.
11. H.W.R. Wade, "Constitutional and Administrative Aspects of Anisminic Case", (1969) 85 LQR 178.

137. (1969) 2 SCC 262.

12. H.W.R. Wade, "Quasi-judicial and its Background", (1949) 10 Cambridge LJ 216.
13. M.P. Jain, *Indian Constitutional Law* (1970) 474–668.
14. M.P. Jain, "Judicial Response to Private Clauses in India", (1980) 22 JILI 1.
15. M.P. Singh, "Duty to Give Reasons for Quasi-Judicial and Administrative Decisions", 21 JILI (1979) 45.
16. Megarry "Administrative Quasi-legislation", (1948) 60 LQR 125.
17. R.F. Fuchs, "Procedure in Administrative Rule-Making", (1938) 52 Harv L Rev 259.
18. R.S. Gupta, "Administrative Discretion and Judicial System", (1980) Indian Journal of Public Admn. 1100.
19. Ramaswam, "Detournement de Pouvoir in Indian Law", (1961) 3 JILI 1.
20. S.N. Jain, "Administrative Discretion in the Issue of Import Licences", (1968) 10 JILI 121.
21. S.N. Jain, "Legality of Administrative Directions", (1966) 8 JILI 349.
22. S.N. Jain, "Legal Nature of Administrative Instructions under the Income Tax Act", (1972) 14 JILI 383.
23. S.N. Jain, "Legal Status of Administrative Discretions: Three Recent Cases Add to the Confusion", (1982) 24 JILI 126.
24. S.N. Jain, "New Trends of Judicial Control of Administrative Discretion", (1969) 11 JILI 544.
25. Sathe, *Administrative Law* (3rd Edn.) Chap. II.
26. Schwartz, "Administrative Finality in England", (1948) 26 Can BR 1072.
27. Sri. Prabu Natarajan, "Judicial Review of Administrative Action—an Analysis", (1993) 2 LW (JS) 42.
28. Timothy Endicott, *Administrative Law* (Oxford University Press) Chaps. 7, 8, 9.
29. Treves, "Administrative Discretion and Judicial Control", (1946) 10 Mod L Rev 276.

CHAPTER 4

Rule-making Power of the Administration

Quasi-legislative action or delegated legislation or outsourcing of law-making power

With the growth of the administrative process in the 20th century, administrative rule-making or delegated legislation has assumed tremendous proportions and importance. Today, the bulk of the law which governs people comes not from the legislature but from the chambers of administrators. The fact is that the direct legislation of Parliament is not complete, unless it is read with the help of rules and regulations framed thereunder; otherwise by itself it becomes misleading.

In the present day context of free market economy, there has been a tremendous growth of administrative and regulatory forces which has made outsourcing of law-making power to the administrative authorities a compulsive necessity. Therefore, legislature limits its functions to merely laying down policies and guidelines of the law, outsourcing all ancillary law-making power to the administrative authorities to make law relevant to the needs of the people.

The term "delegated legislation" is difficult to define. However, if defined, in a simple way, delegated legislation refers to all law-making which takes place outside the legislature and is generally expressed as rules, regulations, bye-laws, orders, schemes, directions or notifications, etc. In other words, when an instrument of a legislative nature is made by an authority in exercise of power delegated or conferred by the legislature, it is called subordinate legislation or delegated legislation.[1] Salmond defines delegated legislation as "that which proceeds from any authority other than the sovereign power and is, therefore, dependent for its continued existence and validity on some superior or supreme authority"[2]. The term delegated legislation may be used in two senses: 1) the exercise of law-making power by the administrative authority delegated to it by the legislature; or 2) the actual exercise of law-making power itself in the forms of rules and regulations, etc.[3]

1. *Halsbury's Laws of England*, Vol. 44 (4th Edn.) 981–84.
2. Salmond, *Jurisprudence* (12th Edn.) 116.
3. *See*, Jain and Jain, *Principles of Administrative Law* (1986) 26.

1. NEED FOR ADMINISTRATIVE RULE-MAKING

Delegated legislation is not a new phenomenon. Ever since the statutes came to be made by Parliament, delegated legislation also came to be made by an authority to which the power was delegated by Parliament. Going back into history one can find the Statute of Proclamation, 1539 under which Henry VIII was given extensive powers to legislate by proclamations. This proves the fact that there was and will always be the need for delegated legislation. The exigencies of the modern state, especially social and economic reforms, have given rise to delegated legislation on a large scale, so much so that a reasonable fear arises among the people that they are being ruled by the bureaucracy.[4]

The Indian Parliament enacted from the period 1973 to 1977 a total of 302 laws; as against this the total number of statutory orders and rules passed in the same period was approximately 25,414. Corresponding figures for States and Union Territories are not available, but the number of rules issued under the delegated powers may well be astronomical.[5]

The modern trend is that Parliament passes only a skeletal legislation. A classical example may be the Imports and Exports (Control) Act, 1947 which contains only eight sections to provide through the rule-making power delegated to it under legislation and delegates the whole power to the administrative agencies to regulate the whole complex mechanism of imports and exports. The examples may be multiplied. This trend brings us to the need matrix of the phenomenon of delegated legislation or administrative rule-making.

The basis of need matrix of administrative rule-making lies in the fact that the complexities of modern administration are so baffling and intricate and bristle with details, urgencies, difficulties, and a need for flexibility that our massive legislatures may not get off to a start if they must directly and comprehensively handle legislative business in all their plenitude, proliferation and particularisation. Therefore, the delegation of some part of legislative power becomes a compulsive necessity for viability. If the 525-odd parliamentarians are to focus on every minuscule of legislative detail leaving nothing to subordinate agencies, the annual output may be both unsatisfactory and negligible. Law-making is not a turnkey project, ready-made in all detail and once this situation is grasped, the dynamics of delegation easily follows.[6] From the above generalisation, the factors leading to the growth of administrative rule-making may be particularised as follows:

(1) Legislation on ever-widening fronts of a modern welfare and service state is not possible without the technique of delegation. It is trite but correct to say that even if today Parliament sits all the 365 days in a

4. *Agricultural Market Committee* v. *Shalimar Chemical Works*, (1997) 5 SCC 516.
5. Statement from the working paper presented by Professor Upendra Baxi, quoted in *Avinder Singh* v. *State of Punjab*, (1979) 1 SCC 137, 160.
6. From the judgment of Krishna Iyer J in *Avinder Singh* v. *State of Punjab*, (1979) 1 SCC 137, 147.

year and all the 24 hours, it may not give that quantity and quality of law which is required for the proper functioning of a modern government. Therefore, delegation of rule-making power is a compulsive necessity. It also gives an advantage to the executive, in the sense that a Parliament with an onerous legislative time schedule may feel tempted to pass skeleton legislation with the details to be provided by the making of rules and regulations.[7]

(2) Today, legislation has become highly technical because of the complexities of a modern government. Therefore, it is convenient for the legislature to confine itself to policy statements only, as the legislators are sometimes innocent of legal and technical skills, and leave the law-making sequence to the administrative agencies.

(3) Ordinary legislative process suffers from the limitation of lack of viability and experimentation. A law passed by Parliament has to be in force till the next session of Parliament when it can be repealed. Therefore, in situations which require adjustments frequently and experimentation, administrative rule-making is the only answer.

(4) In situations where crisis legislation is needed to meet emergent situations, administrative rule-making is a necessity because the ordinary law-making process is overburdened with constitutional and administrative technicalities and involves delay.

(5) In some situations it is necessary that the law must not be known to anybody till it comes into operation. For example, in case of imposition of restrictions on private ownership, it is necessary that the law must be kept secret till it comes into immediate operation, otherwise people could arrange their property rights in such a manner as to defeat the purpose of the law. This secrecy can be achieved only through administrative action because the ordinary legislative process is always very open.

(6) Where government action involves discretion, *i.e.* expansion of public utility services, administrative rule-making is the only valid proposition.

(7) Today there is a growing emergence of the idea of direct participation in the structurisation of law by those who are supposed to be governed by it because indirect participation through their elected representatives more often proves a myth. Therefore, administrative rule-making is a more convenient and effective way and provides for this participation.

One may go on multiplying the factors responsible for the growth of administrative rule-making, yet the list may not be exhaustive. It will suffice to say that the technique of administrative rule-making is now regarded as useful, inevitable and indispensable.[8]

7. *Agricultural Market Committee* v. *Shalimar Chemical Works Ltd.*, (1997) 5 SCC 516.
8. Committee on Ministers' Powers, Report 45, 23, 51, 52 (1932).

However, one must not lose sight of the fact that though the technique of administrative rule-making is useful and inevitable, yet constitutional legitimation of unlimited power of delegation to the executive by the legislature may, on occasion, be subversive of responsible government and erosive of democratic order.[9] At times, the legislature passes only skeletal laws without laying down even a policy in clear terms, and leaves everything else to the discretion of the administrative agency. Therefore, the administration armed with the law-making power threatens to overwhelm the little man by trampling upon his liberty and property. The technocracy and the bureaucracy which draft subordinate legislation are perhaps well-meaning and well-informed but insulated from parliamentary audit and isolated from popular pressure and may, therefore, make law which is socially less communicable, acceptable and effective.

Furthermore, if law-making is taken over by the government, it may make its administration by barrel of the secretariat pen.[10] Therefore, if the technique of administrative rule-making is to serve its laudable task, the norms of the jurisprudence of delegation of legislative power must be dutifully observed. These norms include a clear statement of policy, procedural safeguards and control mechanisms.

Moving in the same direction in *Rojer Mathew* v. *South Indian Bank Ltd.*[11], the Supreme Court held that principles laid down in judicial precedents can provide the necessary guidance, as the delegate is as much bound to comply with judicial precedents as it is bound to comply with legislative policy. The delegate is bound to act strictly in conformity with the applicable binding judicial precedents. It is always open to a constitutional court on challenge made to the delegated legislation framed by the executive, to examine whether it conforms to the parent legislation and other laws, including the applicable judicial precedents, and apply the "policy and guidelines" test and if found contrary, can be struck down without affecting the constitutionality of the rule-making power itself.

2. CLASSIFICATION OF ADMINISTRATIVE RULE-MAKING POWER OR DELEGATED LEGISLATION

Administrative rule-making or delegated legislation in India is commonly expressed by the term "statutory rules and orders". However, this classification is not exhaustive as it appears in other forms also, *i.e.* regulation, notification, bye-law, scheme and direction. These terminologies are confusing because different words are used for the same thing and same words are used for different things.

9. *Avinder Singh* v. *State of Punjab*, (1979) 1 SCC 137, 160.
10. *Ibid.*
11. (2020) 6 SCC 1.

2.1 Title-based classification

(1) *Rule*: The term "rule" is defined in the General Clauses Act, 1897 as a rule made in exercise of power conferred by any enactment and shall include a regulation made as a "rule" under any enactment. These rules may be made applicable to a particular individual or to the general public. It may include rules of procedure as under the Atomic Energy Act, 1948, and also the rules of substantive law as in the Defence of India Rules (now repealed).

(2) *Regulations*: This term is not confined to delegated legislation. It means an instrument by which decisions, orders and acts of the government are made known to the public. But in the sphere of administrative rule-making, the term relates to a situation where power is given to fix the date for the enforcement of an Act, or to grant exemptions from the Act, or to fix prices, etc.

(3) *Order*: This term is used to cover various forms of legislative and quasi-judicial decisions. Orders may be specific or general. The former refers to administrative action while the latter refers to administrative rule-making.

(4) *Bye-laws*: The term has been confined to rules made by semi-governmental authorities established under the acts of legislatures.

(5) *Directions*: The term is used in two senses. The Constitution gives powers to the Central Government to give directions to State Governments for the execution of its laws. In this sense it has no application to delegated legislation. In the second sense, the term "direction" is an expression of administrative rule-making under the authority of law or rules or orders made thereunder. These may be recommendatory or mandatory. If mandatory, these have the force of law.

(6) *Scheme*: The term refers to a situation where the law authorises the administrative agency to lay down a framework within which the detailed administrative action is to proceed.

The Committee on Ministers' Powers has recommended for the simplification of the nomenclature, confining the term "rule" to the statutory instrument regulating procedure, the term "regulation" to describe the substantive administrative rule-making, and the term "order" to instruments exercising executive and quasi-judicial decisions.

2.2 Discretion-based classification (conditional legislation)

Another classification of administrative rule-making may be based on discretion vested in the rule-making authority. On the basis of "discretion", administrative rule-making may be classified into subordinate and contingent or conditional legislation. This classification is linked with the leading case of *Field* v. *Clark*[12], where the impugned Act authorised the President by proclamation to suspend the operation of an Act, permitting free introduction into the US of certain products, upon his finding that the duties imposed upon the products of the US were reciprocally unequal and unreasonable. The US Supreme Court upheld the validity of the Act on the ground that the President is a mere agent of the Congress to ascertain and declare the contingency upon which the will of the Congress will prevail. The court further held that the Congress cannot delegate its power to make a law, but it can make a law to delegate the power to determine some factors or state of things upon which the law intends to make its own action depend. Therefore, contingent or conditional legislation may be defined as a statute that provides control but specifies that they are to go into effect only when a given administrative authority finds the existence of conditions defined in the statute itself. In subordinate legislation, the process consists of the discretionary elaboration of rules and regulations. The distinction between the two is of "discretion". Contingent or conditional legislation is fact-finding and subordinate legislation is discretionary. In conditional legislation, the gun and the gunpowder is provided by the legislature and the administrative authority is only required to pull the trigger, but in subordinate legislation the administrative authority is to manufacture the gunpowder also. It may be noted that this distinction is hardly real. In contingent or conditional legislation also, a certain amount of discretion is always present. The contingent legislation formula is a fiction developed by the US court to get away from the operation of the doctrine of separation of powers.

It is thus obvious that in conditional legislation, the legislation is complete in itself but its operation is made to depend on fulfilment of certain conditions, and what is delegated to an outside authority is the power to determine according to its own judgment whether or not those conditions are fulfilled. In case of delegated legislation proper, some portion of the legislative power is delegated to the outside authority, in that the legislature, though competent to perform both the essential and ancillary legislative functions, performs only the former and parts with the latter, *i.e.* the ancillary functions of laying down details in favour of another authority for executing the policy of the statute enacted. The distinction between conditional legislation and delegated legislation exists in this that whereas conditional legislation contains no element of delegation of legislative power and is, therefore, not open to attack on the ground of excessive delegation, delegated legislation does confer some legislative power on some outside authority and is, therefore, open to attack on the ground of excessive delegation.[13]

12. 1982 SCC OnLine US SC 74: 36 L Ed 294: 143 US 649, 692 (1892).
13. *State of T.N.* v. *K. Sabanayagam*, (1998) 1 SCC 318. See also, *Vasu Dev Singh* v. *Union of India*, (2006) 12 SCC 753.

In *King Emperor* v. *Benoari Lal Sarma*[14], the Privy Council for the first time upheld the validity of the Governor General's Ordinance of special courts, which had delegated the power to extend the duration of the ordinance on provincial governments in case of an emergency, on the ground of conditional legislation. The Privy Council observed that it was a piece of conditional legislation as the legislation was complete and what had been delegated was the power to apply the Act on the fulfilment of certain conditions. The Supreme Court also in *Inder Singh* v. *State of Rajasthan*[15] upheld the validity of the Rajasthan Tenants' Protection Ordinance on the ground that it is conditional legislation. The Ordinance was promulgated for two years, but Section 3 had authorised the Governor to extend its life by issuing notification if required. In the same manner in *Tulsipur Sugar Co. Ltd.* v. *Notified Area Committee*[16], the Supreme Court upheld the validity of a notification issued under Section 3 of the U.P. Town Areas Act, 1914 on the ground that it is not a case of "subordinate legislation" but of "conditional legislation". In this case by a notification under the Act, the limits of Tulsipur town had been extended to the village Shitalpur where the sugar factory of the plaintiff was situated. In *I.T.C. Bhadrachalam Paperboards* v. *Mandal Revenue Officer*[17], the court held that power conferred on government to bring an Act into existence to grant exemption under it is a conditional legislation and not delegated legislation. In *Union of India* v. *Shree Gajanan Maharaj Sansthan*[18], the court was of the view that statute providing that a certain provision thereof would come into force on a date to be notified by the government is a conditional legislation, and such a power did not enable the government to decide whether to bring or not to bring that provision into force. However, no mandamus can be issued against the government to consider whether the provision should be enforced and when the government would be able to do it.

Conditional legislation is classified into three categories: 1) statute enacted by legislature, future applicability to a given area left to the subjective satisfaction of the delegate as to the conditions indicating the proper time for that purpose; 2) Act enforced, but power to withdraw the same from operation in a given area or in given cases delegated to be exercised on subjective satisfaction or objective satisfaction of the delegate as to the existence of requisite condition precedent; and 3) power exercisable upon the delegate's satisfaction on objective facts by a class of persons seeking benefit of the exercise of such power to deprive the rival class of persons of statutory benefits. Last category of conditional legislation attracts principles of natural justice.[19] Thus, though delegated legislation as such did

14. 1944 SCC OnLine PC 32: (1944–45) 72 IA 57: AIR 1945 PC 48.
15. AIR 1957 SC 510.
16. (1980) 2 SCC 295.
17. (1996) 6 SCC 634.
18. (2002) 5 SCC 44.
19. *State of T.N.* v. *K. Sabanayagam*, (1998) 1 SCC 318.

not attract the principles of natural justice but it applies in the case of conditional legislation where a person is deprived of his statutory rights.

2.3 Authority-based classification (sub-delegation)

Another classification of administrative rule-making is based on the position of the authority making the rules. Sometimes the rule-making authority delegates to itself, or to some other subordinate authority, a further power to issue rules; such exercise of rule-making power is known as sub-delegated legislation. Rule-making authority cannot delegate its power unless the power of delegation is contained in the enabling Act. Such authorisation may be either express or by necessary implication. If the authority further delegates its law-making power to some other authority and retains a general control of a substantial nature over it, there is no delegation as to attract the doctrine of "delegatus non potest delegare". Therefore, if the administrative authority which has been delegated the power to impose and collect tax, delegates only the collection part to some other agency, it will not be a case of sub-delegation.[20] Thus, though rule-making power cannot be delegated unless authorised by parent Act, yet administrative power can be delegated. The maxim "delegatus non potest delegare" indicates that sub-delegation of power is normally not allowable though the legislature can always provide for it. Courts have always taken the position that sub-delegation is invalid unless authorised by the parent Act. A classical illustration is *A.K. Roy* v. *State of Punjab*[21]. In this case, the power to initiate prosecution for offences under Section 20(*i*) of the Prevention of Food Adulteration Act, 1954 had been given to the State Government. The Act had not authorised sub-delegation of power. Nevertheless, under Rule 3 of the Prevention of Food Adulteration (Punjab) Rules, 1958, the power of prosecution was delegated to the Food Inspector. The court held sub-delegation as ultra vires the parent Act. In *State* v. *Amir Chand*[22], the court further held that authorisation of sub-delegation must be express, it cannot be inferred. Under the Employees' State Insurance (Central) Rules, 1950, Rule 16(2) had provided for two types of sub-delegations: 1) Director General was empowered to delegate the powers conferred on him by the said rules; 2) Director General was further empowered to delegate his powers and duties under any resolution of the corporation or the standing committee. The court held sub-delegation in the second case as invalid on the ground that conferment of powers and duties under a resolution of the corporation could be by way of delegation to the corporation, and empowering

20. *M. Chandru* v. *Chennai Metropolitan Development Authority*, (2009) 4 SCC 72.
21. (1986) 4 SCC 326. See also, *Ganpati Singhji* v. *State of Ajmer*, AIR 1955 SC 188; *Ajaib Singh* v. *Gurbachan Singh*, AIR 1965 SC 1619; *Naraindas* v. *State of M.P.*, (1974) 4 SCC 788; *Barium Chemicals Ltd.* v. *Company Law Board*, AIR 1967 SC 295; *Sahni Silk Mills (P) Ltd.* v. *ESI Corpn.*, (1994) 5 SCC 346.
22. 1952 SCC OnLine Punj 44: AIR 1953 Punj 1.

the Director General to further delegate such powers is impermissible.[23] Thus, if power to delegate rule-making power is obtained by the authority by its own rule-making power, it will not be valid if not authorised by the parent Act.[24]

The Essential Commodities Act, 1955 provides a unique example of sub-delegation where sub-delegation is authorised at two stages. Section 3 of the Act empowers the Central Government to make rules, but Section 5 authorises sub-delegation of powers to the State Governments who have been further empowered to sub-delegate powers to their officers.

It is now almost settled that the legislature can delegate its powers of law-making after indicating the policy. Therefore, the maxim "delegatus non potest delegare" which means that a delegate cannot further delegate is not attracted in case of delegation by the legislature, but certainly applies in case of sub-delegation. The maxim was originally invoked in the context of delegation of judicial powers and implied that in the entire process of adjudication, a judge must act personally except insofar as he is expressly absolved from his duty by a statute. Therefore, the basic principle behind the maxim is that a discretion conferred by the statute on an authority must be exercised by that authority alone unless a contrary intention appears from the language, scope, or object of the statute. However, keeping in view the imperatives of modern administration, courts are slow in applying the maxim when there is question of exercise of administrative discretionary powers.[25]

The mechanism of sub-delegation makes parliamentary control illusory, postpones the rule-making process, and makes publication of rules difficult, therefore, it must be resorted to only in unavoidable circumstances. It is against this backdrop that the Committee on Subordinate Legislation in India suggested that sub-delegation in very wide language is improper and some safeguard must be provided before the delegate is allowed to sub-delegate his authority.

2.4 Nature-based classification (exceptional delegation)

Classification of administrative rule-making may also be based on the nature and extent of delegation. The Committee on Ministers' Powers distinguished two types of parliamentary delegation:

(1) Normal delegation

- (*a*) *Positive*.—Where the limits of delegation are clearly defined in the enabling Act.
- (*b*) *Negative*.—Where power delegated does not include power to do certain things, *i.e.* legislate on matters of policy.

23. *ESI* v. *T. Abdul Razak*, (1996) 4 SCC 708.
24. *M. Chandru* v. *Chennai Metropolitan Development Authority*, (2009) 4 SCC 72.
25. *Sahni Silk Mills (P) Ltd.* v. *ESI Corpn.*, (1994) 5 SCC 346.

(2) Exceptional delegation—Instances of exceptional delegation may be:
(*a*) Power to legislate on matters of principle policy.
(*b*) Power to amend Acts of Parliament of existing law.
(*c*) Power conferring such a wide discretion that it is almost impossible to know the limits.
(*d*) Power to make rules without being challenged in a court of law.

Such exceptional delegation is also known as Henry VIII clause to indicate executive autocracy. Henry VIII was the King of England in the 16th century. He imposed his autocratic will through the instrumentality of Parliament, so he is described as a "despot under the forms of law". Under this clause, very wide powers are given to administrative agencies to make rules, including the power to amend and repeal. Instances of exceptional delegation may be found in Section 20 of the States Reorganisation Act, 1956 (now repealed) where power was given to the executive to make changes in the existing law. This type of delegation is delegation running riot. Even extraordinary conditions do not justify delegation outside the sphere of constitutional authority.

A classical illustration of Henry VIII clause is found in the Constitution itself. Under Article 372(2) of the Indian Constitution, the President has been delegated the power to adapt, amend and repeal any law in force to bring it in line with the provisions of the Constitution, and the exercise of such power has been made immune from the scrutiny of courts. The court also found Henry VIII clause in Regulation 34 of the West Bengal State Electricity Regulation which had authorised the Board to terminate the services of any permanent employee on three months' notice or pay in lieu thereof. The Supreme Court observed that the naked "hire and fire" rule of Regulation 34 is parallel to Henry VIII clause so familiar to administrative lawyers.[26] Exceptional delegation has always been held to be ultra vires the Constitution.

3. CONSTITUTIONALITY OF ADMINISTRATIVE RULE-MAKING OR DELEGATED LEGISLATION

The term "constitutionality of administrative rule-making" means the permissible limits of the constitution of any country within which the legislature, which as the sole repository of law-making power, can validly delegate rule-making power to other administrative agencies. Today the necessity to aid the transition from laissez faire to a welfare and service state has led to the tremendous expansion of government authority. The new role of the State can be fulfilled only through the use of greater power in the hands of the government which is most suited to carry out the social and economic tasks before the country. The task of enhancing the power of the

26. *W.B. SEB* v. *Desh Bandhu Ghosh*, (1985) 3 SCC 116; *Central Inland Water Transport Corpn.* v. *Brojo Nath Ganguly*, (1986) 3 SCC 156.

government to enable it to deal with the problems of social and economic reconstruction has been accomplished through the technique of delegation of legislative power to it. This delegation of legislative power raises a natural question of its constitutionality.

In England, Parliament is supreme and, therefore, unhampered by any constitutional limitations, Parliament has been able to confer wide legislative powers on the executive. However, sovereignty of Parliament does not mean that there are no principles to which the practice of delegation must conform. The Committee on Ministers' Powers in its third recommendation has suggested that the precise limits of law-making power which Parliament intends to confer on a Minister should always be expressly defined in clear language by the statute which confers it—when discretion is conferred, its limits should be defined with equal clearness. Laying down of limits in the enabling Acts within which executive action must work is of greater importance to England than to any other country, because in the absence of any constitutional limitation, it is on the basis of those parliamentary limits alone that the power of judicial review can be exercised.

In the US, the rule against delegation of legislative power is basically based on the doctrine of separation of powers and its necessary corollary "delegatus non potest delegare". In the US, the doctrine of separation of powers has been raised to a constitutional status. The US Supreme Court has observed that the doctrine of separation of powers has been considered to be an essential principle underlying the Constitution, and that the powers entrusted to one department should be exercised exclusively by that department without encroaching upon the powers of another.[27] Therefore, legislative powers cannot be delegated. Hence, the syllogism of Prof. Cushman[28]:

> *Major Premise*: Legislative powers cannot be constitutionally delegated by Congress.
> *Minor Premise*: It is essential that certain powers be delegated to administrative officers and regulatory commissions.
> *Conclusion*: Therefore, the powers thus delegated are not legislative powers.

However, it is accepted at all hands that a rigid application of the doctrine of separation of powers is neither desirable nor feasible in view of the new demand on the executive. This has been seen by Marshall CJ who, perceiving that there are powers of a doubtful nature which need not be arbitrarily fitted into the Montesquieuian trichotomy, held that it was within legislative competence to assign their exercise to the executive branch. The court further observed that the line has not been exactly drawn which separates those important subjects which must be entirely regulated by the legislature itself from those of less importance in which a general provision may be made and power be given to those who are to act under such general provisions to fill up the details.[29] Therefore, in the US, courts have made

27. *Field* v. *Clark*, 1982 SCC OnLine US SC 74: 36 L Ed 294: 143 US 649, 692 (1892).
28. C.K. Thakker, *Administrative Law* (Eastern Book Company 1992) 74.
29. *Wayman* v. *Southard*, 1825 SCC OnLine US SC: 6 L Ed 253: 23 US 1 (1825).

a distinction between what may be termed as "legislative powers" and the power to "fill in the details". This distinction has created a real dilemma for courts and the balance has been swinging left and right depending upon the facts and need matrix. Two decisions of the US Supreme Court arising under the National Industrial Recovery Act, 1933—a New Deal legislation—may be noted which turned the balance to the left.

Panama Refining Co. v. *Ryan*[30] is a case based on Section 9 of the National Industrial Recovery Act, 1933. Section 9 authorised the President to prohibit the transportation in inter-State and foreign commerce, petroleum and the products thereof produced or withdrawn from storage in excess of any State law or valid regulation. The President authorised the Secretary of the Interior to exercise all powers under Section 9. Regulation V provided that every purchaser and shipper should submit the details of the purchase and sale of petroleum. Panama Refinery Company challenged Section 9 of the National Industrial Recovery Act, 1933 as unconstitutional delegation of legislative powers. The Act laid down that the policy of the law is "to encourage national industrial recovery" and "to foster fair competition". The US Supreme Court held the Act as unconstitutional on the ground that the adequacy of prescribed limits of delegation of legislative power is not satisfied by laying down a vague standard for administrative action. Hughes CJ observed that an executive order must, in order to satisfy the constitutional requirement, show the existence of particular circumstances and conditions under which the making of such an order has been authorised by the Congress.

In *Ala Schechter Poultry Corpn.* v. *United States*[31], the Corporation, which was engaged in live poultry operations, challenged the constitutionality of Section 3 of the National Industrial Recovery Act, 1933 on the ground of unconstitutional delegation of legislative power. Section 3 of the Act authorised the President to approve "Codes of Fair Conduct" laying down the standard of fair competition for a particular trade or industry. The Act made violation of the Code punishable. Hughes CJ held Section 3 as unconstitutional on the ground that it supplies no standard besides the statement of the general aims of rehabilitation, correction and expansion described in Section 1. Therefore, in the opinion of the court it was a case of virtual abdication of legislative powers by the Congress.

Since the decision in this case the balance has tilted in the other direction, perhaps because of social and economic imperatives. Thus, pragmatic considerations have prevailed over theoretical objections.[32] Hence, the court has allowed a wide margin to the Congress in laying down a valid standard. If the delegation is of a regulatory nature, the court has upheld constitutionality of the delegation of legislative power even in the absence of any

30. 1935 SCC OnLine US SC 3: 79 L Ed 446: 293 US 388 (1935).
31. 1935 SCC OnLine US SC 118: 79 L Ed 1570: 295 US 495 (1935).
32. Jain and Jain, *Principles of Administrative Law* (1986) 34.

specified standard. Therefore, in *Lichter* v. *United States*[33], the Supreme Court held the delegation valid observing that the statutory term "excessive profits" was sufficient expression of legislative policy and standards to render it constitutional. In this case, the Reorganisation Act, 1942 had empowered administrative officers to determine whether the prices were excessive and to recover profits which they determined to be excessive.

3.1 Constitutionality of administrative rule-making in India

The question of permissible limits of the Constitution within which law-making power may be delegated can be studied in three different periods for the sake of better understanding.

3.1.1 *When the Privy Council was the highest court of appeal*

The Privy Council was the highest court for appeal from India in constitutional matters till 1949. The question of constitutionality came before the Privy Council in the famous case of *R.* v. *Burah*[34]. An Act was passed in 1869 by the Indian legislature to remove Garo Hills from the civil and criminal jurisdiction of Bengal, vesting the powers of civil and criminal administration in an officer appointed by the Lieutenant Governor of Bengal. The Lieutenant Governor was further authorised by Section 9 of the Act to extend any provision of this Act with incidental changes to Khasi and Jaintia Hills. One Burah was tried for murder by the Commissioner of Khasi and Jaintia Hills and was sentenced to death. The Calcutta High Court declared Section 9 as unconstitutional delegation of legislative power by the Indian legislature on the ground that the Indian legislature itself is a delegate of British Parliament, therefore, a delegate cannot further delegate. The Privy Council on appeal reversed the decision of the Calcutta High Court and upheld the constitutionality of Section 9 on the ground that it is merely a conditional legislation. The decision of the Privy Council was interpreted in two different ways. One interpretation was that since the Indian legislature is not a delegate of British Parliament, there is no limit on the delegation of legislative functions. According to the other interpretation, it was argued that since the Privy Council has validated only conditional legislation, therefore, delegation of legislative power is not permissible.

The doctrine of conditional legislation was again applied by the Privy Council in *Benoari Lal*[35] when it upheld the constitutionality of an ordinance passed by the Governor General for the establishment of special courts, and delegated power to the provincial governments to declare this law applicable in their provinces at any time they deem fit.

---

33. 1948 SCC OnLine US SC 91: 92 L Ed 1694: 334 US 742 (1948); see also, *Fahey* v. *Mallonee*, 1947 SCC OnLine US SC 114: 91 L Ed 2030: 332 US 245 (1947).
34. 1878 SCC OnLine PC 17: ILR (1879) 4 Cal 172: (1878) LR 3 AC 889.
35. 1944 SCC OnLine PC 32: (1944–45) 72 IA 57: AIR 1945 PC 48.

Therefore, during the period the Privy Council was the highest court of appeal, the question of permissible limits of delegation remained uncertain.

3.1.2 *When Federal Court became the highest court of appeal*

The question of constitutionality of delegation of legislative powers came before the Federal Court in *Jatindra Nath Gupta* v. *Province of Bihar*[36] (*Jatindra Nath*). In this the validity of Section 1(3) of the Bihar Maintenance of Public Order Act, 1948 was challenged on the ground that it authorised the provincial government to extend the life of the Act for one year with such modifications as it may deem fit. The Federal Court held that the power of extension with modification is unconstitutional delegation of legislative power because it is an essential legislative act. In this manner for the first time it was laid down that in India legislative powers cannot be delegated. However, Fazal Ali J in his dissenting opinion held that the delegation of the power of extension of the Act is constitutional because according to him it merely amounted to a continuation of the Act.[37]

3.1.3 *When Supreme Court became the highest court of appeal*

The decision in *Jatindra Nath* created doubts about the limits of delegation of legislative powers. Therefore, in order to clarify the position of law for the future guidance of the legislature in matters of delegation of legislative functions, the President of India sought the opinion of the court under Article 143 of the Constitution on the constitutionality of three Acts covering three different periods: 1) Section 7 of the Delhi Laws Act, 1912; 2) Section 2 of the Ajmer-Merwara (Extension of Laws) Act, 1947; and 3) Section 2 of the Part "C" States (Laws) Act, 1950.

Section 7 of the Delhi Laws Act, 1912 delegated to the provincial government, the power to extend to Delhi area with such restriction and modification any law in force in any part of British India. Section 2 of the Ajmer-Merwara (Extension of Laws) Act, 1947 delegated the power to the government to extend to the province of Ajmer-Merwara any law in force in any other province with such modification and restriction as it may deem fit. Section 2 of the Part "C" States (Laws) Act, 1950 delegated power to the Central Government to extend to Part "C" States, with such modification and restriction as it may deem fit, any enactment which was in force in any Part "A" State. It also empowered the government to repeal or amend any corresponding law which was applicable to Part "C" States. *Delhi Laws Act, 1912, re*[38] is said to be the Bible of delegated legislation. Seven judges heard the case and produced seven separate judgments. The case was argued from two extreme positions. M.C. Setalvad argued that

36. 1949 SCC OnLine FC 23: AIR 1949 FC 175.
37. *Ibid*, 194.
38. 1951 SCC 568: AIR 1951 SC 332.

the power of legislation carries with it the power to delegate and unless the legislature has completely abdicated or effaced itself, there is no restriction on delegation of legislative powers. The learned Counsel built his arguments on the theory of separation of powers and "delegatus non potest delegare", and tried to prove before the court that there is an implied prohibition against delegation of legislative powers. The Supreme Court took the via media and held:

(1) Doctrine of separation of powers is not a part of the Indian Constitution.
(2) Indian Parliament was never considered an agent of anybody, and therefore the doctrine of "delegatus non potest delegare" has no application.
(3) Parliament cannot abdicate or efface itself by creating a parallel legislative body.
(4) Power of delegation is ancillary to the power of legislation.
(5) The limitation upon delegation of power is that the legislature cannot part with its essential legislative power that has been expressly vested in it by the Constitution. Essential legislative power means laying down the policy of the law and enacting that policy into a binding rule of conduct.

On the basis of this reasoning, the Supreme Court came to the conclusion that

(1) Section 7 of the Delhi Laws Act, 1912 is valid;
(2) Section 2 of the Ajmer-Merwara (Extension of Laws) Act, 1947 is valid; and
(3) Section 2 of the Part "C" States (Laws) Act, 1950 is valid except that part of the section which delegated power of repeal and modification of legislative policy, as it amounted to excessive delegation of legislative powers.

Even though seven judges gave seven separate judgments, but it will not be correct to hold that no principle was clearly laid down by the majority of judges. Anyone who surveys the whole case comes to an inescapable conclusion that there is a similarity in the views of the judges at least on three points: 1) that the legislature cannot give that quantity and quality of law which is required for the functioning of a modern state, hence delegation is a necessity; 2) that in view of a written constitution the power of delegation cannot be unlimited; and 3) that the power to repeal a law or to modify legislative policy cannot be delegated because these are essential legislative functions which cannot be delegated. The Supreme Court has now made it abundantly clear that the power of delegation is a constituent element of legislative power as a whole under Article 245 of the Constitution and other relative articles.[39]

39. *Agricultural Market Committee* v. *Shalimar Chemical Works Ltd.*, (1997) 5 SCC 516.

After the decision in this case, the main controversy in every case involving delegation has, therefore, been the question of determination of what is essential legislative function which cannot be delegated and that which is non-essential and can be delegated.

3.2 Excessive delegation is unconstitutional

It is now firmly established that excessive delegation of legislative power is unconstitutional. The legislature must first discharge its essential legislative functions (laying down the policy of the law and enacting that policy into a binding rule of conduct) and then can delegate ancillary or subordinate legislative functions which are generally termed as power "to fill up details". After laying down policy and guidelines, the legislature may confer discretion on administrative agency to execute the legislative policy and to work out details within the framework of the policy and guidelines.

Whether a particular legislation suffers from "excessive delegation" is a question to be decided with reference to certain factors which may include 1) subject-matter of the law, 2) provisions of the statute including its Preamble, 3) scheme of the law, and 4) factual and circumstantial background in which the law is enacted.[40] Elaborating further, the Supreme Court held that while determining "excessive delegation", the court must take into consideration the nature of the administrative body. If the administrative body is representative and responsive, the court may allow a wide margin of delegation. The court may also take into consideration if the subordinate legislation is necessary for implementing the purpose and object of the Act.[41]

When a statute is challenged on the ground of excessive delegation, there is a presumption in favour of its vires and if two interpretations are possible, one that makes it constitutional is to be adopted. Courts may also read down and interpret the law in a way as to avoid its being declared unconstitutional.[42] This is being done in view of the fact that today delegation of legislative power has become a "compulsive necessity".

In *Rojer Mathew* v. *South Indian Bank Ltd.*[43], the Supreme Court held that no doubt the legislature cannot self-efface its personality and make over in terms the plenary and essential legislative functions but complexities of modern administration are bafflingly intricate and present themselves with urgencies and difficulties and the need for flexibility, which the direct legislation may not provide. Delegation is, therefore, inevitable and an administrative necessity. Thus, while essential legislative policy cannot

40. *St. Johns Teachers Training Institute* v. *National Council for Teacher Education*, (2003) 3 SCC 321.
41. *Rojer Mathew* v. *South Indian Bank Ltd.*, (2020) 6 SCC 1.
42. *St. Johns Teachers Training Institute* v. *National Council for Teacher Education*, (2003) 3 SCC 321–322.
43. (2020) 6 SCC 1.

be delegated, inessentials can be delegated over to relevant agencies. Policy and guidelines test can be applied for effecting this.

3.3 What is an essential legislative function and where is the policy of the law to be found

The opinion of the Supreme Court in individual cases is to be analysed in order to determine the extent of permissible delegation.

Rajnarain Singh v. *Patna Admn. Committee*[44].—Section 3(1)(*f*) of the impugned Act empowered the Patna local administration to select any provision of the Bengal Municipality Act, 1884 and apply it to Patna area with such restrictions and modifications as the government may think fit. The government picked up Section 104 and after modification applied it to the town of Patna. The Supreme Court declared the delegation ultra vires on the ground that the power to pick out a section for application to another area amounts to delegating the power to change the policy of the Act which is an essential legislative power, and hence cannot be delegated.

Harishankar Bagla v. *State of M.P.*[45] (*Harishankar Bagla*).—Section 3 of the Essential Supplies (Temporary Powers) Act, 1946 authorised the Central Government to make rules for the purpose of maintaining or increasing supplies of essential commodities and for securing equitable distribution at fair price. Section 6 further provided that the orders made thereunder shall have effect notwithstanding anything contained in any law for the time being in force. The Supreme Court held the delegation valid on the ground that Section 3 lays down the legislative policy with sufficient clarity within which the government can operate. The court also upheld the validity of Section 6 on the ground that it is not a delegation of power to repeal but only an attempt to bypass difficulty.

Edward Mills Co. Ltd. v. *State of Ajmer*[46].—The impugned Act authorised the administrative agency to set up minimum wages for certain industries specified in the schedule and further empowered the authority to vary the schedule by adding other industries to the list. The Supreme Court upheld the validity of the delegation on the ground that the legislative policy which was to guide in the selection of industries is clearly indicated in the Act, namely, to avoid exploitation of labour due to unequal bargaining power or other reasons. This case also stands for the proposition that the rule of the exercise of essential legislative function by the legislature is applicable to all types of delegation including conditional legislation.

Hamdard Dawakhana v. *Union of India*[47] (*Hamdard Dawakhana*).—Parliament passed the Drugs and Magic Remedies (Objectionable

44. AIR 1954 SC 569.
45. AIR 1954 SC 465.
46. AIR 1955 SC 25.
47. AIR 1960 SC 554.

Advertisements) Act, 1954 to check the mischief being done to innocent patients suffering from certain incurable diseases through advertisements claiming magic remedies for such diseases. Section 3 laid down a list of diseases for which advertisements were prohibited and authorised the Central Government to include any other disease in the list. This is the first case in which the Supreme Court struck down an Act on the ground of excessive delegation of legislative powers. The court held that nowhere had the legislature laid down any policy for guidance to the government in the matter of selection of diseases for being included in the list. The decision of the court is certainly not in line with its earlier approaches because the clear mention of certain diseases in the list could have supplied the standard and criteria for the selection of other diseases. Furthermore, the title of the Act lays down sufficiently the policy of the Act.

Jalan Trading Co. (P) Ltd. v. *Mill Mazdoor Sabha*[48].—Section 37 of the Payment of Bonus Act, 1965 authorised the Central Government to provide by order for removal of doubts or difficulties in giving effect to the provisions of the Act. The court held Section 37 ultra vires on the ground of excessive delegation and observed that the Act authorised the government to determine for itself what the purposes of the Act are which in substance would amount to exercise of legislative power that cannot be delegated.

Gammon India Ltd. v. *Union of India*[49].—Section 34 of the Contract Labour (Regulation and Abolition) Act, 1970 provided that if any difficulty arises in giving effect to the provisions of the Act, the Central Government may make such provisions, not inconsistent with the provisions of this Act, as appeared to it to be necessary or expedient for removing the difficulty. The Supreme Court held that Section 34 does not amount to excessive delegation as it does not contemplate any alteration in the Act. It simply authorises the removal of difficulties which may arise in the implementation of the law.

Kerala SEB v. *Indian Aluminium Co. Ltd.*[50]—In this case, the validity of the Kerala State Electricity Supply (Kerala State Electricity Board and Licensees Areas) Surcharge Order, 1968 was in question. The order was passed in exercise of the powers conferred by Section 3 of the Kerala Essential Articles Control (Temporary Powers) Act, 1961. The Act in Section 2(*a*) defined "essential article" as meaning any article which may be declared by the government by notified order to be an essential article. The purpose of the Act is to provide, in the interest of the general public, for the control of the production, supply and distribution of, and trade and commerce in certain articles. Section 2(*a*) was challenged on the ground of excessive delegation. The court upheld the constitutionality of Section 2(*a*) on the ground that the Act lays down sufficient policy to guide

48. AIR 1967 SC 691.
49. (1974) 1 SCC 596.
50. (1976) 1 SCC 466.

the discretion of the administrative authority. However, Gupta J disagreed with the majority decision on the ground that the Act contains no specific standard or policy with reference to which an article may be declared as an "essential article".

Avinder Singh v. *State of Punjab*[51].—In this case, the Supreme Court has taken a very liberal view on the question of the laying down of legislative policy in the Act by the legislature. In this case the petitioners were licence-holders for trade in foreign liquor. The State of Punjab in view of the powers vested in it by Section 90(4) of the Punjab Municipal Corporations Act, 1976, required various municipal bodies in the State to impose a tax at the rate of ₹1 per bottle. Since municipalities failed to take any action, the State itself issued a notification imposing the tax. Section 90(1) of the Municipal Corporations Act, 1976 sets out certain items for taxation and lays down that the tax so collected is to be utilised "for the purpose of the Act". Imposition of the tax was challenged on the ground, among others, that the legislature has not laid down any purpose and policy of the Act with reference to which the rate of tax is to be determined, and, therefore, it is a case of excessive delegation. The court held that the words "for the purpose of the Act" laid down a clear policy of the Act, and, therefore, it is a valid delegation of legislative powers. The court observed that the words "for the purpose of the Act" are pregnant with meaning. It sets a ceiling on the total quantum that may be collected. It canalises the objects for which the fixed levies may be spent. It brings into focus the functions of municipal bodies and the raising of the resources necessary for discharging those functions. In the case of a body like the municipality with functions which are limited and the requisite resources which are also limited, the guidelines contained in the expression "for the purpose of the Act" are sufficient. This may not be sufficient in the case of a State Government whose functions are not so limited. One would agree that this is going too far to find the legislative policy.

A.V. Nachane v. *Union of India*[52] (*A.V. Nachane*).—The Life Insurance Corporation of India Class III and Class IV Employees' (Bonus and Dearness Allowance) Rules, 1981 were made by the Central Government on 2 February 1981 in exercise of the powers conferred by Section 48 of the Life Insurance Corporation Act, 1956 as amended by the Life Insurance Corporation (Amendment) Ordinance, 1981. The rules were challenged on the ground that Parliament has not laid down any legislative policy for the guidance of the rule-making authority. The Supreme Court found legislative policy in the Preamble of the Amendment Act which provided that

> for securing the interests of the Life Insurance Corporation of India and its policy-holders and to control the cost of administration, it is necessary that

51. (1979) 1 SCC 137.
52. (1982) 1 SCC 205.

revision of the terms and conditions of services applicable to the employees and agents of the Corporation should be undertaken expeditiously.

The court further met the challenge of excessive delegation of legislative power on the ground that Section 48(3) of the Act which provided for the laying of the rule on the table of Parliament subject to a resolution of modification or annulment perfectly indicates that Parliament has in no way abdicated its authority, but is keeping strict vigilance and control over its delegate.[53] In *Charan Lal Sahu* v. *Union of India*[54], the court found the legislative policy in the purpose of the Act. In this case, the Bhopal Gas Disaster (Processing of Claims) Act, 1985 had been challenged on the ground that without laying any policy and guidelines the government has been authorised to conduct suits and enter into compromises.

Applying the same principle, the Supreme Court declared the Tamil Nadu Private Educational Institutions (Regulation) Act, 1966 as ultra vires because the legislature did not lay down any policy or guideline with reference to which the power to regulate and control private educational institutions can be exercised by the government.[55]

However, if the power delegated to the administrative authority is quasi-judicial then guidelines are not required.[56]

However, according to K.K. Mathew J, this effort on the part of the Supreme Court to somehow find the legislative policy from somewhere was undignified for any judicial process. He observed that "... the hunt by court for legislative policy or guidance in the crevices of a statute or nook and cranny of its preamble is not an edifying spectacle"[57]. In his dissenting opinion in *Gwalior Rayon Silk Mfg. (Wvg.) Co. Ltd.* v. *CST*[58] (*Gwalior Rayon*), he propounded a new test to determine the constitutionality of delegated legislation. According to him, so long as a legislature can repeal the enabling Act delegating law-making power, it does not abdicate its legislative function and, therefore, the delegation must be considered as valid no matter howsoever broad and general the delegation may be. However, the majority led by Khanna J did not agree to this "abdication test" and reiterated the already well-established test of "policy and guidelines". Nevertheless, Mathew J ignoring the majority opinion applied his own test in 1975 in *M.K. Papiah* v. *Excise Commr.*[59] (*Papiah*). Thus, the court's decisions in *Gwalior Rayon* and *Papiah* took two different and conflicting views on the question of constitutionality of delegated legislation. Added to this, the Supreme Court's decision in *Registrar of Cooperative Societies* v.

53. (1982) 1 SCC 205, 218–19.
54. (1990) 1 SCC 613.
55. *A.N. Parasuraman* v. *State of T.N.*, (1989) 4 SCC 683.
56. *Workmen* v. *Meenakshi Mills Ltd.*, (1992) 3 SCC 336.
57. See, *Gwalior Rayon Silk Mfg. (Wvg.) Co. Ltd.* v. *CST*, (1974) 4 SCC 98. *See also*, Upendra Baxi, "Developments in Administrative Law" in A.G. Noorani (Ed.), *Public Law in India* (1982).
58. (1974) 4 SCC 98.
59. (1975) 1 SCC 492. *See also*, M.P. Jain, *Changing Face of Administrative Law, India and Abroad* (1982) 26.

K. Kunjabmu[60] (*Registrar, Coop. Societies*) though upholds the "policy and guideline" test, yet creates an impression that this test is tentative and can be reopened. The court observed:

> We do not wish in this case to search for the precise principles decided in the *Delhi Laws Act case*, nor to consider whether N.K. Papiah beats the final retreat from the earlier position. For the purposes of this case we are content to accept the 'policy' and 'guidelines' theory....[61]

Whatever may be the test to determine the constitutionality of delegated legislation, the fact remains that due to the compulsions of modern administration, courts have allowed extensive delegation of legislative powers, especially in the area of tax and welfare legislation. In *Registrar, Coop. Societies,* the court upheld the validity of Section 60 of the Madras Cooperative Societies Act, 1932, which was a "near Henry VIII clause"[62]. Section 60 provided:

> The State Government may, by general or special order, exempt any registered society from any of the provisions of this Act or may direct that such provisions shall apply to such society with such modifications as may be prescribed in the order.

The law on the constitutionality of delegated legislation was summed up by the Supreme Court in *Mahe Beach Trading Co.* v. *UT of Pondicherry*[63]. The court held:

> If there is abdication of legislative power or there is excessive delegation or if there is a total surrender or transfer by the legislature of its legislative functions to another body then that is not permissible. There is, however, no abdication, or surrender of legislative functions or excessive delegation so long as the legislature has expressed its will on a particular subject matter, indicated its policy and left the effectuation of the policy to subordinate or subsidiary or ancillary legislation, provided the legislature has retained the control in its hand with reference to it so that it can act as a check or a standard and prevent or undo the mischief by subordinate legislation....[64]

The same principle was reiterated by the Supreme Court in *Agricultural Market Committee* v. *Shalimar Chemical Works Ltd.*[65] The Supreme Court observed that in order to meet the challenge of complex socio-economic problems, Parliament often finds it convenient and necessary to delegate subsidiary or ancillary powers to delegates of its choice for carrying out the policy laid down in the statutes. The essential legislative function consists

60. (1980) 1 SCC 340. The court held that the "power to legislate carries with it the power to delegate" but "excessive delegation may amount to abdication" and "delegation unlimited may invite despotism uninhibited". Therefore, the principle of delegation remains: "The leg islature cannot delegate its essential legislative functions. Legislate it must by laying down policy and principle and delegate it may to fill in detail and carry out policy." *See*, M.P. Jain, *Changing Face of Administrative Law, India and Abroad* (1982) 25–26.

61. *Ibid*, 342.

62. *Per* Chinnappa Reddy J.

63. (1996) 3 SCC 741.

64. *Ibid*.

65. (1997) 5 SCC 516.

of the determination of the legislative policy, and the legislature cannot abdicate essential legislative functions in favour of another. Power to make subsidiary legislation may be entrusted by the legislature to another body of its choice, but before delegation the legislature should enunciate, either expressly or by implication, the policy and the principles for the guidance of the delegate. The effect of these principles is that the delegate has to work within the scope of authority and cannot widen or restrict the scope of the Act or the policy laid down thereunder. It cannot in the garb of making rules, legislate on the field covered by the Act and has to restrict itself to the mode of implementation of the policy and the purpose of the Act.[66] In this case, the Agricultural Market Committee created under the A.P. (Agricultural Produce and Livestock) Markets Act, 1966 had been given power to levy market fee only on the sale or purchase of agricultural produce within the notified area. The Committee imposed a fee on dry coconut purchased from Kerala and received in Hyderabad by truck on the plea that the sale was taking place in Hyderabad and not in Kerala. The court held that Rule 74(2) framed under Section 34(1) is ultra vires the Act because the Act had empowered the Committee to levy a fee on produce moving out of a notified area after sale or purchase, but Rule 74(2) provided for levying tax even if the produce is weighed, measured or counted there no matter if sale may have taken place elsewhere.[67]

Validation of extensive delegated legislation thus continues unabated in India on the ground of administrative necessity.[68] However, Prof. Baxi is of the view that in India there is no a priori ground compelling the conclusion that such untrammelled powers of executive law-making are essential for the attainment of the goals of the Constitution or for attaining administrative efficiency, although this is offered, parrotlike, as the justification for such powers. On the other hand, there is ample indication that people affected by exercise of delegated legislative power have no real access to executive law which may determine their status adversely.[69] It may be noticed that the broad delegation of legislative powers in the US are counterbalanced by the effective procedural and legislative controls which are very feeble in India.

Constitutionality of delegated legislation has always been very contested issue. Breaking new ground, the Supreme Court, in *Southern Agrifurane Industries Ltd.* v. *CTO*[70], held that while deciding the constitutionality of the delegated legislation, court may take into consideration the context in which the rule-making power has been exercised. In this case in order to rehabilitate the appellant sick company, acting under the provisions of the

66. *Agricultural Market Committee* v. *Shalimar Chemical Works Ltd.*, (1997) 5 SCC 516.
67. *Ibid.*
68. *See*, Upendra Baxi, "Developments in Indian Administrative Law" in A.G. Noorani (Ed.), *Public Law in India* (1982) 137–41.
69. *Ibid*, 140.
70. (2005) 2 SCC 575.

Sick Industrial Companies (Special Provision) Act, 1985, the government had issued notification for deferring sales tax without specifying amount. This notification was subsequently amended modifying the sum and the government gave it a retrospective operation. The company contended that quantifying the amount of sales tax in the second notification amounts to retrospectively denying it the benefit of deferment of the entire tax liability given under the first notification. The Supreme Court amplified that in order to determine the constitutionality of delegated legislation, the context and the background in which rule was made can be taken into consideration and, therefore, company is entitled to the sales tax deferment only to the extent it was necessary to take it out of the sickness and any further deferment would be beyond the powers of the government under Section 17 of the T.N. General Sales Tax Act, 1959.

However, the court was quick to emphasise that no straitjacket approach is desirable and intensity of public law review in delegated legislation area will depend on the subject-matter in each individual case.[71] Thus in *Food Corporation of India* v. *Bhanu Lodh*[72], the court emphasised that while deciding on the constitutionality of delegated legislation "proportionality" approach may produce better results in cases involving serious violation of public interest. In this case, Section 6(2) of the Food Corporation Act, 1964 had empowered government to issue "policy instructions" to the Board of Directors of the Corporation. In the exercise of this power, the government issued policy instructions regarding recruitment policy. However, after receiving complaints of corruption in appointments, the government issued further instructions declaring those appointments as void. The question before the court was: Whether these later instructions are within the power of the government under the Act and hence constitutional? Upholding the constitutionality of instructions, the court opined that policy instructions may include instructions not only with regard to the organisation and management but also with regard to corruption in recruitment as it would in the long run may affect the interest of the consumers and producers for whom the Food Corporation of India is established.

Developing a fine principle of delegation jurisprudence, the court in *Ishwar Singh* v. *State of Rajasthan*[73] held that sub-delegation of rule-making power does not imply parting with the power or authority. It points rather to the conferring on a subordinate officer the power to do something which otherwise that officer would have done himself. Therefore, the delegator of power does not denudes or divests himself of all the powers. Delegating authority will retain not only the power to revoke the grant of power but also the power to act concurrently on matters within the area of its authority, except insofar as it may have bound himself by an act of his delegatee.

71. *Food Corporation of India* v. *Bhanu Lodh*, (2005) 3 SCC 618.

72. *Ibid.*

73. (2005) 2 SCC 334.

Though the fundamentals of administrative law relating to outsourcing of law-making power by the legislature to the administrative authorities have, more or less, achieved finality, yet they require restatement in the context of new emerging situation. In *Kerala Samsthana Chethu Thozhilali Union* v. *State of Kerala*[74] (*Kerala Samsthana Chethu Thozhilali Union*), the Supreme Court restated these principles in a new context. In this case, the State of Kerala had banned the sale of arrack (a kind of liquor) in 1966, but later on took a policy decision to rehabilitate the retrenched workers of the trade. For this purpose, the government framed Kerala Abkari Shops Disposal Rules, 2002, under the Kerala Abkari Act (1 of 1077) which imposed conditions on every toddy shop to employ one retrenched arrack worker. This was challenged by the licence-holders of the shops and the toddy workers. The High Court held that the State has power to make rules under the Kerala Abkari Act (1 of 1077) to interfere with the employment contract, hence appeal before the Supreme Court.

Appellants before the Supreme Court contended:

(1) The State in making the rule relating to compulsory employment of arrack worker in each toddy shop transgressed powers delegated to it under the parent Act as it did not conform to any provision requiring adoption of welfare measure by the State.

(2) The special purpose (compensating retrenched workers) for which said rules were framed is governed by the Industrial Disputes Act, 1947, a Central legislation, therefore, the State had no power to make such rules which have the effect of modifying the existing law.

(3) The rules in question cannot impose any unreasonable condition on the free exercise of fundamental right [Article 19(1)(*g*)].

(4) The compulsory employment rule also violates Article 14 of the Constitution being arbitrary.

On the other hand the State contended that

(1) imposition of compulsory employment condition was within the domain of the State in terms of Sections 18-A, 24(*c*) and 29 of the enabling Act and also under Articles 39, 42 and 43 (Directive Principles of State Policy) of the Constitution;

(2) rule of compulsory employment for arrack workers in toddy shops has reasonable nexus with the purpose of the enabling Act and hence, not beyond the policy and purpose of the Act;

(3) while considering the validity of rules, not only the object and purpose of the enabling Act but also the purpose served thereby must be taken into consideration;

(4) since the trade in liquor is *res extra commercium*, the licencee could not contend that the conditions imposed for the grant of licence were onerous.

74. (2006) 4 SCC 327.

Speaking on behalf of the court, S.B. Sinha J gave new direction to law relating to the constitutionality of administrative rule-making.

The court restated the principles of delegation of law-making power by the legislature to the administrative authorities and held:

(1) Under the common law and also under the provisions of the Specific Relief Act, 1963, there is freedom to the employer to employ any person as per his choice, therefore, it is well settled that no person can be thrust upon an unwilling employer except in accordance with the provisions of a special statute operating in the field. Such provisions cannot be made by the State under its delegated rule-making powers unless the same is expressly conferred by the statute.

(2) An administrative rule is not only required to be made in conformity with the provisions of the enabling Act but at the same time must be in conformity with the provisions of any other existing law. A subordinate legislation cannot be violative of any plenary legislation made up by the legislature.

(3) The power of the State to make rules under Section 29 of the enabling Act is limited only for the purpose of "carrying out the purpose of the Act". Therefore, rules cannot be framed in matters not contemplated under the Act. Rules must conform to the legislative policy and are subject to the provisions of the enabling Act. Rules must not also be framed in contravention to any constitutional provision or legislative measure.

(4) The purpose of the rule for compulsory employment to one arrack worker in each toddy shop in preference to other toddy workers is beyond the policy of the enabling Act. The object of the rule is to rehabilitate the former retrenched employees of the arrack shop which is not within the policy and object of the enabling Act.

(5) In order to determine whether the rules are within the policy and object of the enabling Act, nexus between the rules and the policy and purpose of the Act is the determining factor. In the instant case, there is no nexus between the excise policy of the State and the rehabilitation of workers.

(6) Any rule framed beyond the policy and purpose of the Act is an unconstitutional exercise of rule-making power of the State. Therefore, rule-making power must be exercised within the confines of the delegating statute. Administrative authority cannot travel beyond the confines of the enabling Act and create any substantial right, obligation and disability.[75]

(7) In case an industry is closed, the rights of a workman are governed by the Industrial Disputes Act, 1947. Thus by the exercise of its rule-making power, authority cannot repeal the provisions of any special existing law.

75. *Indian Young Lawyers Assn. (Sabarimala Temple–5J.)* v. *State of Kerala*, (2019) 11 SCC 1.

(8) Contracts of employment are governed by the Contract Act, 1872 and Specific Relief Act, 1963 and, therefore, so long as contract employment in a particular trade is not prohibited in terms of statutory or constitutional provisions, State in exercise of its rule-making power cannot modify these existing laws.

(9) Administrative rules and regulations in order to be valid must not be violative of any provisions of the Constitution. Therefore, administrative rule-making must satisfy the requirement of reasonableness of Articles 14 and 19 of the Constitution. Thus any condition imposed in order to be valid must not be arbitrary. "Take it or Leave it" condition imposed by the administrative rules is arbitrary. It is well settled that every executive action including rule-making, which operates to the prejudice of any person without the authority of law, is invalid.

Basing its decision on the above principles of law, the Supreme Court ruled that the Rule 4(2) relating to "compulsory employment" made by the State under the rule-making power delegated to it by the enabling Kerala Abkari Act (1 of 1077) is ultra vires the enabling Act and also Article 14 of the Constitution.[76]

Delegated legislation can be declared unconstitutional only in case of clear violation of a statute or the Constitution beyond all reasonable doubts. In *Hinsa Virodhak Sang* v. *Mirzapur Moti Kuresh Jamat*[77], where a resolution of the Municipal Corporation was passed under the Bombay Provincial Municipal Act, 1949, closing slaughters houses for nine days during Jain festival, and was challenged on the ground that it violates the fundamental right of butchers under Article 19(1)(*g*), the court held that since the restriction is for a short period of time, it did not amount to excessive, unreasonable or disproportionate restriction on fundamental rights.

Thus, "Rules" be read in equitable manner while deciding on the constitutionality of rules and regulations. However, only technical violations or such violations which are not substantial and do not go to the roots of the matter can be condoned by the court.[78]

3.4 Norms of jurisprudence of delegated legislation emerging from the decisions analysed

(1) The power of delegation is a constituent element of the legislative power as a whole under Article 245 of the Constitution and other relative articles. Delegation of some part of legislative powers has become a compulsive necessity due to the complexities of modern legislation.

76. (2006) 4 SCC 327, 337. See also, *State of T.N.* v. *P. Krishnamurthy*, (2006) 4 SCC 517. Held, State cannot make rule to terminate all private quarrying in sand unless the enabling Act provides for it, *Bombay Dyeing and Mfg. Co. Ltd.* v. *Bombay Environmental Action Group*, (2006) 3 SCC 434.

77. (2008) 5 SCC 33.

78. *Walaiti Ram Charan Dass* v. *State of Punjab*, (2019) 9 SCC 779.

(2) Essential legislative functions cannot be delegated by the legislature.
(3) Essential legislative functions mean laying the policy of the Act and enacting that policy into a binding rule of conduct. In other words, the legislature must lay down legislative policy and purpose sufficient to provide a guideline for administrative rule-making. The policy of law may be express or implied and can be gathered from the history, preamble, title, scheme of the Act or object and reason clause, etc.
(4) After the legislature has exercised its essential legislative functions, it can delegate non-essentials, however numerous and significant they may be.
(5) In order to determine the constitutionality of the delegation of legislative powers, every case is decided in its special setting.
(6) Courts have travelled to the extreme in holding very broad general statements as sufficient policy of the Act to determine the question of constitutionality.
(7) There are various forms of administrative rule-making. However, the parameter for determining the question of constitutionality is the same, namely, the legislature must lay down the policy of the Act.
(8) The delegated legislation must be consistent with the parent Act and must not violate legislative policy and guidelines. Delegatee cannot have more legislative powers than that of the delegator.[79]
(9) Sub-delegation of legislative powers in order to be valid must be expressly authorised by the parent Act.
(10) The delegated legislation in order to be valid must not be unreasonable and must not violate any procedural safeguards if provided in the parent Act.
(11) In determining the validity of delegated legislation, if it is within the competence of the authority, motive of the delegated legislation is not taken into account.
(12) When the law allows delegation of administrative power by an officer to another officer subordinate to him, he does not divest himself of all the power. The delegating authority will retain not only the power to revoke the grant but also the power to act concurrently on matters within the area of delegated authority, except insofar as it may already have bound himself by an act of the delegate.
(13) While deciding on the constitutionality of delegated legislation, court may take into consideration relevance of context and background in which power of rule-making has been exercised.
(14) Court has imported the principle of "proportionality" in determining the constitutionality of delegated legislation especially in cases involving serious violation of public interest where this new doctrine may produce better results.

79. *Indian Oil Corpn.* v. *Municipal Corpn., Jullundhar*, (1993) 1 SCC 333.

(15) If the parent Act is repealed, notification issued under it would also stand repealed unless saved by the repealing Act.
(16) Rules and regulations validly made by the administrative authority become part of the parent Act.[80]
(17) Court decision cannot be nullified by the administrative authority by changing its rules. It would amount to contempt of court.[81]
(18) Power to repeal and amend (in essential respect) cannot be delegated.
(19) Unless a delegated legislation is specifically challenged by the party, the court has no power to take suo motu cognizance and quash delegated legislation and hold the rules unreasonable and arbitrary.[82]
(20) Rules to be read in equitable and humane manner but only technical violations can be condoned and not violations that go to the root of the matter.[83]
(21) Where the legislature has not provided for any notice and hearing before framing rules and regulation, it will not be permissible to read principles of natural justice into such legislative activity.[84]

3.5 Constitutionality of delegation of taxing power

Power to tax is an inherent power of any State. It is also considered as an essential legislative function. Power to tax can be exercised not only for raising revenue for the State but also for regulating the social, economic, or political structure of the country. Therefore, the delegation of taxing power by the legislature deserves special attention. The permissible limits of a valid delegation of taxing power can be comprehended by analysing the following decisions of the Supreme Court:

(1) *Orient Wvg. Mills (P) Ltd.* v. *Union of India*[85].—In this case the Supreme Court upheld the constitutionality of the delegation of power to the government to exempt any excisable item from duty.
(2) *Banarsi Das Bhanot* v. *State of M.P.*[86]—The delegation of power to the government to bring certain sale transactions under the Central Provinces and Berar Sales Tax Act 21 of 1947 was upheld against the challenge of excessive delegation.
(3) *Devi Das* v. *State of Punjab*[87].—The delegation of power to the executive to determine the rate of tax between the maximum and minimum laid down in the enabling Act was upheld. The Terminal Tax on Railway Passengers Act, 1958 authorised the executive to impose

80. *Kalyani Mathivanan* v. *K.V. Jeyaraj*, (2015) 6 SCC 363.
81. *Bihar State Govt. Secondary School Teachers Assn.* v. *Ashok Kumar Sinha*, (2014) 7 SCC 416.
82. *State of Kerala* v. *Shibu Kumar P.K.*, (2019) 13 SCC 577.
83. *Walaiti Ram Charan Dass* v. *State of Punjab*, (2019) 9 SCC 779.
84. *Cellular Operators Assn. of India* v. *TRAI*, (2016) 7 SCC 703.
85. AIR 1963 SC 98.
86. AIR 1958 SC 909.
87. AIR 1967 SC 1895.

sales tax at a rate between 1 per cent to 2 per cent. The court held that the discretion in fixing the tax rate is too limited to hold it to be excessive delegation.

(4) *MCD* v. *Birla Cotton, Spg. & Wvg. Mills*[88].—In this case the power delegated to the Corporation to impose electricity tax without prescribing any maximum limit was upheld on the ground that the Corporation is also a representative and responsive body which stands a guarantee against the misuse of the power.

(5) *Corpn. of Calcutta* v. *Liberty Cinema*[89].—In the same manner, in this case, the constitutionality of the delegation of power to the Corporation to levy a licence fee on cinema at such rate as may be prescribed by the Corporation was upheld.

(6) *Cantonment Board Poona* v. *Western India Theatres Ltd.*[90].—The power given to the Corporation (of the City of Pune), in terms very wide, to levy "any other tax" came to be considered from the point of view of abdication of legislative functions. The negation of this argument was based on the key words of limitation contained therein, namely, "for the purpose of the Act", and it was held that this provides sufficient guidance for the imposition of the tax.

(7) *Jullundur Rubber Goods Manufacturers' Assn.* v. *Union of India*[91].—The court in this case further upheld the constitutionality of Section 12(2) of the Rubber Act, 1947 which empowered the Rubber Board to levy an excise duty either on the producers of rubber or the manufacturers of rubber goods. The court negatived the challenge of excessive delegation on the ground of inherent checks on the exercise of such power, namely, the representative character of the Board and the control of the Central Government. The Act had provided that tax can be levied only according to the rules made by the government subject to the laying procedure.

(8) *Avinder Singh* v. *State of Punjab*[92].—In this case, the Supreme Court upheld the constitutionality of delegation of taxing power even in the face of a broad statement which was considered as sufficient guidance. The State of Punjab acting under Section 90(4) of the Punjab Municipal Corporations Act, 1976 required various municipalities to impose a tax of ₹1 per bottle of foreign liquor. On the failure of the municipalities to take action in the matter, the Government of Punjab imposed the same tax. The power to impose tax was challenged on the ground of excessive delegation. The contention was repelled on the ground that the words "for the purpose of the Act" lay down sufficient guideline for the imposition of tax. Section 90(2)

88. AIR 1968 SC 1232.
89. AIR 1965 SC 1107.
90. 1953 SCC OnLine Bom 13: AIR 1954 Bom 261. Also see, *N.J. Nayadu & Co.* v. *Administrator of the City of Nagpur*, 1968 SCC OnLine Bom 48: AIR 1970 Bom 59.
91. (1969) 2 SCC 644.
92. (1979) 1 SCC 137.

of the impugned Act enables the Corporation to levy "any other tax" which the State Legislature has the power to impose under the Constitution. Sub-section (3) leaves the rate of levy to the determination of the State Government. Sub-section (5) empowers the State Government to notify the tax which the Corporation shall levy. The court observed that these provisions show that the levy of taxes shall be only "for the purpose of the Act", an expression which sets a ceiling on the total quantum that may be collected and also canalises the objects for which levies can be spent and, therefore, it provides a sufficient guideline. Constitutionality of delegation was reinforced by the argument of the responsive and representative character of the Municipal Corporation. Applying the same principle, the Supreme Court in *Darshan Lal Mehra* v. *Union of India*[93] held Section 172(2), U.P. Nagar Mahapalika Adhiniyam, 1959 as constitutional. This section had authorised the municipalities to impose taxes mentioned in the Act "for the purpose of the Act". The court held that the words "for the purpose of the Act" lay down sufficient policy for the guidance of the municipalities to impose tax and, therefore, so long as the tax has reasonable relation to the purpose of the Act, the same cannot be held to be excessive delegation. It may be pointed out that even in the US, courts have made an exception in favour of municipalities on the question of constitutionality of delegated legislation.[94]

From an analysis of the above case-laws, the following general principles can be developed:

(1) Taxing power is an essential legislative power that cannot be delegated.
(2) However, the power to levy tax can be delegated only subject to the legislature itself exercising essential legislative function, namely, laying down the policy of the Act which permits sufficient guideline for the imposition of tax.
(3) Wide expressions like "for the purpose of the Act" have been held to be sufficient guidelines for the imposition of the tax.
(4) Wide expressions like "for the purpose of the Act" are sufficient policy matrix only when power is delegated to a responsive and representative authority.
(5) Within these limitations, the following powers may be validly delegated:
    (*a*) Power to exempt any item from tax.
    (*b*) Power to bring certain items within the ambit of tax.

93. (1992) 4 SCC 28. See also, *Agricultural Market Committee* v. *Shalimar Chemical Works Ltd.*, (1997) 5 SCC 516.
94. Gellhorn and Byse, *Administrative Law*: *Cases and Comments*, 128.

(*c*) Power to determine rate of tax within the minimum and the maximum laid down in the Act.
(*d*) Power to determine rate of tax where no maximum and minimum limits are prescribed.
(*e*) Power to select different rates of tax for different commodities, provided there is a rational justification for it.
(*f*) A charge under a taxing statute can only be under the Act and not under the rules.[95]

These principles show that direct control of Parliament over taxing power is on a decline. In this context one must remember the fact that the first big battle of democracy was fought in Britain on the question of the right of the King to impose taxes on his subjects at will. The people won at the end of a long and hard struggle and the world saw the birth of a fundamental canon of democracy: no taxation without representation. It is curious that in India instead of strengthening its grip over taxing, Parliament is weakening it by allowing the delegation of wide taxing power to administrative authorities.

3.6 Retrospective operation of delegated legislation

Before the pacesetting judgment of the Supreme Court in *B.S. Yadav* v. *State of Haryana*[96], the simple proposition for retrospective operation of delegated legislation was that an administrative authority can make its rules and regulations with retrospective effect if the parent statute authorised it either expressly or by necessary implication. For example, Section 36-A of the Administrative Tribunals Act, 1985 expressly authorises the rule-making authority to frame rules with retrospective effect. Section 36-A provides:

> The power to make rules under clause (*c*) of sub-section (2) of Section 35 and of clause (*b*) of Section 36 shall include the power to make such rules or any of them retrospectively from a date not earlier than the date on which this Act received the assent of Parliament....

As far as Article 309 is concerned, the highest Bench ruled that the article was wide enough to include the making of rules with retrospective effect.[97] Power to pass retroactive law may be inferred from legislative intention also. Therefore, when the Act is declaratory in nature, the presumption against retrospectivity is not applicable. The Supreme Court in *Mithilesh Kumari* v. *Prem Behari Khare*[98] held that the Benami Transactions (Prohibition) Act, 1988 shall apply to all pending suits including appeals as it serves a just public purpose. The same principle can be applied to subordinate legislation also. However, now, under the Yadav ruling it is not enough that the statute should authorise retrospective operation of the delegated legislation,

95. *State of Kerala* v. *Madras Rubber Factory Ltd.*, (1998) 1 SCC 616.
96. 1980 Supp SCC 524.
97. *B.S. Vadera* v. *Union of India*, AIR 1969 SC 118.
98. (1989) 2 SCC 95.

the authority must also show that there was sufficient, reasonable and rational justifications for applying the rules retrospectively. In this case the Governor of Punjab in exercise of his legislative powers under Article 309 of the Constitution had amended the seniority rules on 31 December 1976 but gave them retrospective operation from 9 April 1976. The effect of this amendment was that the "date of confirmation" which was the basis to determine seniority in the judicial services was replaced by the "length of continuous service in a post" criteria. This amendment when given retrospective operation disturbed the seniority of many persons. The Supreme Court struck down the retrospective operation of the rule on the ground that there was no nexus or rational relationship between the rule and its retrospectivity. This ruling of the Supreme Court is certainly a welcome step in the area of administrative law.[99] The same principle was reconfirmed by the Supreme Court in *Haribans Misra* v. *Railway Board*[100]. In this case certain employees were promoted according to the existing rules but, thereafter, a correction slip was added which wiped out not only promotions but even the length of service for about nine years with retrospective effect. The rule was struck down on the ground that it was made to meet exigencies of service and there was no real purpose or objective behind it.

However, by giving rules a retrospective effect or by applying the rule to existing persons, a right which is vested cannot be divested. In *Raj Soni* v. *Air Officer Incharge Admn.*[101], the petitioner was appointed as a teacher under the Delhi Education Code, then in force, which provided for retirement at the age of 60. However, thereafter the Delhi Education Act, 1973 and the Delhi Education Rules, 1973 fixed the retirement age at 58 years. The petitioner was retired at the age of 58 years. The Supreme Court held that since the petitioner was an existing employee when the Act and Rules of 1973 were enacted, he could not be retired at the age of 58 years. The Committee on Subordinate Legislation in India, therefore, suggested that rules should not be given retrospective operation, unless such a power has been expressly conferred by the parent Act, as they may prejudicially affect the vested rights of a person.

In *Union of India* v. *G.S. Chatha Rice Mills*[102], the Supreme Court held that the delegated or subordinate legislation does not have retrospective effect unless the statutory provision under which it is framed allows retrospectivity either by the use of specific words to that effect or by necessary implication. Furthermore, the fact that subordinate/delegated legislation may have been framed in pursuance of a resolution passed by the legislature or that it may have to be placed on the table of the legislative body,

99. *See*, S.N. Jain, "Validity of Retrospective Delegated Legislation—The Court Develops a New Principle", (1981) 23 JILI 102. See also, *K.V. Subba Rao* v. *State of A.P.*, (1988) 2 SCC 201.

100. (1989) 2 SCC 84.

101. (1990) 3 SCC 261. However, the court sounded a different note in *K. Jagadeesan* v. *Union of India*, (1990) 2 SCC 228.

102. (2021) 2 SCC 209.

held, does not lead to an inference that the legislature had authorised the framing of subordinate legislation with retrospective effect. Retrospective operation of notification issued under Section 8-A, Customs Tariff Act, 1975, as in the present case, with effect from midnight/00:00 hours on 16 February 2019 is not permissible, the same being in the nature of delegated legislation and the Customs Tariff Act, 1975 not providing for retrospective operation of notifications issued under Section 8-A either expressly or by necessary implication.

Moving in the same direction, the Supreme Court further emphasised that the doctrine of promissory estoppel applies to delegated legislation and by giving a retrospective operation to delegated legislation, administrative authority cannot take away a right be it accrued or vested in a person. Therefore, where the government announced policy incentives by way of tax exemptions, same cannot be withdrawn without assigning any reason with retrospective effect. The Supreme Court is unanimous on the point that if law does not provide for it, administrative authority cannot give delegated legislation any retrospective operation.[103] Thus, retrospectivity of delegated legislation is subject to the provisions of the Constitution [Article 20(1)] and also to legislative authorisation either expressly or by necessary implication. Unless there are words in the statute sufficient to show intention of the legislature to affect existing rights, delegated legislation shall be deemed to the prospective only. However, where a delegated legislation deals merely with a matter of procedure and not with any substantive rights, the delegated legislation is normally presumed to be retrospective unless such construction is textually inadmissible.[104]

4. CONTROL MECHANISM OF ADMINISTRATIVE RULE-MAKING IN INDIA

The control mechanism of administrative rule-making comprises three components, namely, parliamentary control, procedural control, and judicial control. These controls will now be discussed in detail.

4.1 Parliamentary control

Every delegate is subject to the authority and control of the principal, and the exercise of delegated power can always be directed, corrected, or cancelled by the principal. Hence, parliamentary control over delegated legislation should be a living continuity as a constitutional necessity.[105] The fact is that due to the broad delegation of legislative powers and the generalised standard of control also being broad, judicial control has shrunk, raising the desirability and the necessity of parliamentary control.

103. *M.D. University* v. *Jahan Singh*, (2007) 5 SCC 77.
104. *Collector* v. *K. Govindaraj*, (2016) 4 SCC 763.
105. *Avinder Singh* v. *State of Punjab*, (1979) 1 SCC 137.

In the US, the control of the Congress over delegated legislation is highly limited because neither is the technique of "laying" extensively used nor is there any Congressional Committee to scrutinise it. This is due to the constitutional structurisation in that country in which it is considered only the duty of courts to review the legality of administrative rule-making. There is even authority that the negative resolution technique so widely used in Britain would be unconstitutional in an American legislature.[106]

In England due to the concept of parliamentary sovereignty, the control exercised by Parliament over administrative rule-making is very broad and effective. Parliamentary control mechanism operates through "laying" techniques because under the provisions of the English Statutory Instruments Act, 1946, all administrative rule-making is subject to the control of Parliament through the Select Committee on Statutory Instruments. Parliamentary control in England is most effective because it is done in a non-political atmosphere and the three-line whip does not come into operation.

In India parliamentary control of administrative rule-making is implicit as a normal constitutional function because the executive is responsible to Parliament.

4.1.1 *Direct general control*

Direct but general control over delegated legislation is exercised

(1) through debate on the Act which contains delegation. Members may discuss anything about delegation including necessity, extent, type of delegation, and the authority to whom power is delegated;

(2) through questions and notices. Any Member may ask questions on any aspect of delegation of legislative powers, and if dissatisfied can give notice for discussion under Rule 59 of the Procedure and Conduct of Business in Lok Sabha Rules;

(3) through moving resolutions and notices in the House. Any Member may move a resolution on motion if the matter regarding delegation of power is urgent and immediate, and reply of the government is unsatisfactory;

(4) through vote on grant. Whenever the budget demands of a ministry are presented, any Member may propose a cut and thereby bring the exercise of rule-making power by that ministry under discussion;

(5) through a private Member's Bill seeking modifications in the parent Act, or through a debate at the time of discussion on the address by the President to the joint session of Parliament, Members may discuss delegation. However, these methods are rarely used.

106. Schwartz, "Legislative Control of Administrative Rules and Regulations: The American Experience", (1955) 30 NYUL Rev 1031.

4.1.2 *Direct special control*

This control mechanism is exercised through the technique of "laying" on the table of the House rules and regulations framed by the administrative authority.

As mentioned earlier in this chapter in the US, the control of the Congress over the exercise of delegated legislation is feeble; however, it does not mean that the technique of "laying" is non-existent. The notable use of this technique was made in the Reorganisation Acts of 1939 to 1969, which authorised the President to reorganise the executive government by administrative rule-making. The Acts of 1939 and 1945 provided that the Presidential organisation plans were not to have any effect for a specified period during which they could be annulled by the Congress through a concurrent resolution of both Houses. A classic annulment through this process has been the rejection by the Senate of President Truman's Plan to abrogate the provisions of the Taft-Hartley Act, 1947 providing for a separation of functions between the National Labour Relations Board and the independent Office of General Council.[107] In six States (Connecticut, Kansas, Michigan, Nebraska, Virginia and Wisconsin), provisions exist for the annulment of administrative rules either by the concurrent resolution of two Houses or by the resolution of one.[108]

In England the technique of laying is very extensively used because all the administrative rule-making is subject to the supervision of Parliament under the Statutory Instruments Act, 1946 which prescribes a timetable.[109] The most common form of provision provides that the delegated legislation comes into immediate effect, but is subject to annulment by an adverse resolution of either House. Other provisions for laying defer the operation of delegated legislation for a specified period; require affirmative resolutions of the House before the delegated legislation can operate; allow the delegated legislation to operate immediately, but require affirmative resolution for subsequent continuance in operation; postpone operation until approved by affirmative resolutions.

By Section 4 of the Statutory Instruments Act, 1946, where subordinate legislation is required to be laid before Parliament after being made, a copy shall be laid before each House before the legislation comes into operation. However, if it is essential that it should come into operation before the copies are laid, it may so operate but notification shall be sent to the Lord Chancellor and the Speaker of the House of Commons explaining why the copies were not laid beforehand.

Where a statutory instrument is subject to annulment by resolution of either House, Section 5 provides that it shall be laid in accordance with

107. Schwartz, "Legislative Control of Administrative Rules and Regulations: The American Experience", (1955) 30 NYUL Rev 1031.

108. *Ibid*, 1038.

109. Ss. 5–7.

Section 4, and if, within 40 days, a prayer for annulment is presented to Her Majesty, no further proceedings shall be taken under the delegated legislation after the date of resolution and Her Majesty may revoke the delegated legislation.

Under Section 6 where it is provided that a draft of any statutory instrument shall be laid, but there is no prohibition of making of the rules without the approval of Parliament, then the rules shall not be made until the expiration of 40 days from the laying of the copies before each House of Parliament, nor shall further proceedings be taken on the draft if either House resolves that the rules be not made.

"Laying" may take various forms:

(1) *Laying with no further direction.*—In this type of laying, the rules and regulations come into effect as soon as they are laid. It is simply to inform the House about the rules and regulations.

(2) *Laying subject to negative resolution.*—In this process the rules come into effect as soon as they are placed on the table of the House, but shall cease to have effect if annulled by a resolution of the House.

(3) *Laying subject to affirmative resolution.*—This technique may take two shapes:

(*a*) that the rules shall have no effect or force unless approved by a resolution of each House of Parliament; and

(*b*) that the rules shall cease to have effect unless approved by an affirmative resolution.

In both these processes, it is the duty of the government to move a resolution.

(4) *Laying in draft subject to negative resolution.*—Such a provision provides that when any Act contains provision for this type of laying, the draft rules shall be placed on the table of the House and shall come into force after 40 days from the date of laying unless disapproved before that period.

(5) *Laying in draft subject to an affirmative resolution.*—In this type of laying, the instruments or draft rules shall have no effect unless approved by the House.

The earliest instance of the laying provision found in India is in the Immigration Act, 1922. Between 1929 to 1939, only three Acts made provisions for laying, namely, the Insurance Act, 1938, Agriculture Products Act, 1938 and the Motor Vehicles Act, 1939. After a gap of five years, the Central Excise Act and Salt Act, 1944 and the Aircraft Act, 1934 made provisions that the rules framed thereunder must be laid on the table of the House. Only in a few Acts, *i.e.* Insurance Act, 1938 and Aircraft Act, 1944 provision was made for laying subject to a negative resolution. The negative resolution procedure differs from its counterpart in England, as in India it includes the power of modification also.[110] Three other Acts, namely, Representation of the People Act, 1951; All-India Services Act, 1951; and Indian Development and Regulation Act, 1951 contain only the right of modification of the rules and not annulment. The period during which the rules could be modified varies from seven days to one month. It may be noted that in England this is a uniform period of 40 days. The Indian Tariff (Amendment) Act, 1950 provides an illustration where rules are made subject to laying with affirmative resolution.

By the Delegated Legislation Provisions (Amendment) Act, 1983, our Parliament has amended 50 Indian statutes and inserted provisions for laying before State Legislatures and Parliament where there were no such provisions and in other instances, provided for annulment or modification within a specified period. A typical clause reads as follows:

> Every rule prescribed or sanctioned by the Central Government under this Act shall be laid, as soon as may be after it is prescribed or sanctioned, before each House of Parliament, while it is in session, for a total period of thirty days which may be comprised in one session or in two or more successive sessions, and if, before the expiry of the session immediately following the session or the successive sessions aforesaid, both Houses agree in making any modification in the rule or both Houses agree that the rule should not have effect, the rule shall thereafter have effect only in such modified form or be of no effect, as the case may be; so, however, that any such modification or annulment shall be without prejudice to the validity of anything previously done under that rule.

In the State of Uttar Pradesh, an identical provision is made applicable to rule-making by the U.P. government under all the U.P. and Central Acts by adopting a convenient method of inserting it in the U.P. General Clauses Act, 1904, thus, making it a rule of uniform application without having to add or amend the individual U.P. or Central Act.

In the absence of any general law in India regulating laying procedure, the Scrutiny Committee made the following suggestions:

(1) All Acts of Parliament should uniformly require that rules be laid on the table of the House "as soon as possible".

(2) The laying period should uniformly be 30 days from the date of final publication of rules.

(3) The rule will be subject to such modification as the House may like to make.[111]

4.1.2.1 *Legal consequences of non-compliance with the laying provisions*

In England the provisions of Section 4(2) of the Statutory Instruments Act, 1946 makes the laying provision mandatory for the validation of statutory

110. *See*, S. 5(3)(1), Muslim Women's (Protection of Rights on Divorce) Act, 1986; and S. 26, Employees' Provident Fund Act, 1986.

111. *See*, C.K. Thakker, *Administrative Law* (Eastern Book Company 1992) 152.

instruments.[112] In Australia also, the provisions of the Interpretation Act, 1984 provide that the failure to comply with the laying provision would render the rules void.

In India, however, the consequences of non-compliance with the laying provisions depend on whether the provisions in the enabling Act are mandatory or directory. In *Narendra Kumar* v. *Union of India*[113] (*Narendra Kumar*), the Supreme Court held that the provisions of Section 3(5) of the Essential Commodities Act, 1955 which provided that the rules framed under the Act must be laid before both Houses of Parliament, are mandatory and, therefore, clause 4 of the Non-Ferrous Metals Control Order, 1958 has no effect unless laid before Parliament.

However in *Jan Mohd. Noor Mohd. Bagban* v. *State of Gujarat*[114], the court deviated from its previous stand. Section 26(5) of the Bombay Agricultural Produce Markets Act, 1939 contained a laying provision, but the rules framed under the Act could not be laid before the provincial legislature in its first session as there was then no functioning legislature because of World War II emergency. Nevertheless, the rules were placed on the table of the House in its second session. The court held that the rules remained valid because the legislature did not provide that the non-laying at its first session would make the rules invalid.

This decision may not be considered as a deviation from the *Narendra Kumar* rule because of the very special circumstances attending the case. This becomes clear from the decision of the Supreme Court in *Hukam Chand* v. *Union of India*[115]. In this case, Section 40 of the Displaced Persons (Compensation) Act, 1954 empowered the Central Government to make rules and required them to be placed before Parliament subject to a negative resolution. The government added an *Explanation* to Rule 49 and gave it retrospective operation under which non-urban land could be allotted to displaced persons. The Supreme Court held that out of the three recognised types of laying, it comes in the second category which is a mandatory provision of the law. Therefore, the rules were struck down as ultra vires the powers of the administrative agency.

In *Atlas Cycle Industries Ltd.* v. *State of Haryana*[116], the Supreme Court, however, held the impugned provision of law which provided that every order by the Central Government or its officer or authority "shall be laid before both Houses of Parliament as soon as may be after it is made" as merely directory and did not make "laying" a condition precedent to the making of the order. According to the court, the word "shall" in Section 3(6) of the Essential Commodities Act, 1955 is not conclusive and decisive of the matter, and the court is to determine the "true intention"

112. *R.* v. *Sheer Metalcraft Ltd.*, (1954) 1 QB 586: (1954) 2 WLR 777.
113. AIR 1960 SC 430.
114. AIR 1966 SC 385.
115. (1972) 2 SCC 601.
116. (1979) 2 SCC 196.

of the legislature. The two considerations for regarding a provision as directory are 1) absence of any provision for meeting the contingency of the provision not being complied with; and 2) serious general inconvenience and prejudice that would result to the general public if the act of the government is declared invalid for non-performance with the particular provision. Section 3(6) provides for simple laying in which Parliament has no power either to approve or disapprove the order. Therefore, simple laying is merely directory and non-laying would not make the order void.

Even if the requirement of laying is only directory and not mandatory, the rules framed by the administrative authority without conforming to the requirement of laying would not be permissible if the mode of rule-making has been consciously violated. It is on this line of reasoning that the rules framed by the Inspector General under Section 21(3) of the Railway Protection Force Act, 1957 without complying with its laying requirements were held ultra vires the powers of the administrative agency. In the same manner, Parliament had to pass the All India Services Regulations (Indemnity) Bill, 1972 to indemnify the government and its officials from the consequences arising out of the omission to comply with the laying provisions under the All-India Services Act, 1951. However, laying would not cure any invalidity of the rules.

4.1.3 *Indirect control*

This control is exercised by Parliament through its committees. In 1950, the Law Minister made a suggestion for the establishment of a committee of the House on the pattern of the Select Committee on Statutory Instruments, 1944 to examine delegated legislation and bring to the notice of the House whether administrative rule-making has exceeded the intention of Parliament or has departed from it or has affected any fundamental norm or principle. Such a committee known as the Committee on Subordinate Legislation of Lok Sabha was appointed on 1 December 1953. The Committee consisted of 15 Members nominated by the Speaker for a period of one year. The Chairman is appointed by the Speaker from amongst the Members. If the Deputy Speaker happens to be a Member then he shall act as Chairman. In England, the healthy tradition is that the Leader of the Opposition is always appointed as Chairman. The Committee has the power to appoint sub-committees and may refer any matter for its consideration. It also has the power to compel the attendance of any person and to compel the production of documents and records. The powers of the Indian Committee are much wider than its counterpart. In England, the Committee can only ask government departments to send memos or to depute a person to appear before it as witness.

According to Rule 223 of the Lok Sabha Rules of Procedure, the main functions of the Committee shall be to examine the following:

(1) Whether the rules are in accordance with the general object of the Act.
(2) Whether the rules contain any matter which could more properly be dealt with in the Act.
(3) Whether it contains imposition of tax.
(4) Whether it directly or indirectly bars the jurisdiction of the court.
(5) Whether it is retrospective.
(6) Whether it involves expenditure from the Consolidated Fund.
(7) Whether there has been unjustified delay in its publication or laying.
(8) Whether, for any reason, it requires further elucidation.

This Committee has, between 1953 and 1961, scrutinised about 5300 orders and rules, and has submitted 19 reports.

There is also a similar committee of the Rajya Sabha which was constituted in 1964. It discharges functions similar to the Lok Sabha Committee.

The Committee on Subordinate Legislation has made the following recommendations in order to streamline the process of delegated legislation in India:[117]

(1) Power of judicial review should not be taken away or curtailed by rules.
(2) A financial levy or tax should not be imposed by rules.
(3) Language of the rules should be simple and clear and not complicated or ambiguous.
(4) Rules should not be given retrospective operation, unless such a power has been expressly conferred by the parent Act, as they may prejudicially affect the vested rights of a person.
(5) Legislative policy must be formulated by the legislature and laid down in the statute, and power to supply details may be left to the executive, and can be worked out through the rules made by the administration.
(6) Sub-delegation in very wide language is improper and some safeguards must be provided before a delegate is allowed to sub-delegate his authority to another functionary.
(7) Discriminatory rules should not be framed by the administration.
(8) Rules should not travel beyond the rule-making power conferred by the parent Act.
(9) There should not be inordinate delay in making of rules by the administration.
(10) The defects pointed out to the administration should be cured as soon as possible.
(11) The rules framed by the administration and required to be laid before the House by the parent Act should be laid before Parliament as soon as possible, and whenever there is inordinate delay, an explanatory note giving the reasons for such delay should be appended to the rules so laid.

117. *See*, C.K. Thakker, *Administrative Law* (Eastern Book Company 1992) 154–55.

(12) The final authority for interpretation of rules should not be with the administration.
(13) Rules should contain short titles, explanatory notes, references to earlier amendments for convenience of location, ready reference and proper understanding.
(14) Sufficient publicity should be given to the statutory rules and orders.

If in India parliamentary control of administrative rule-making is to be made a living continuity as a constitutional necessity, it is necessary that the role of the Committees of Parliament must be strengthened, and a separate law like the Statutory Instruments Act, 1946, providing for uniform rules of laying and publication, must be passed. The Committee may be supplemented by a specialised official body to make the vigilance of administrative rule-making more effective.

In Britain, the Committee on Ministers' Powers suggested the appointment of a Special Standing Committee of both Houses of Parliament for the supervision of delegated legislation. This was implemented in 1944 by the setting up of a Select Committee for the House of Commons and Special Orders Committee (1925) in the House of Lords. The duty of the committees was to bring to the notice of the House if its special attention was needed relating to delegated legislation on any of the following grounds:

(1) That it imposes a charge.
(2) That it excludes challenge in courts.
(3) That it purports (without specific authority in the parent Act) to have retrospective effect.
(4) That there has been unjustifiable delay in publication or laying before Parliament or in sending a notification to the Speaker when the instrument comes into operation before it has been laid.
(5) That its form or purport calls for elucidation.
(6) That it appears to make some unusual or unexpected use of the powers conferred by the statute under which it is made.[118]

From 1944 to the end of 1959, the Scrutiny Committee had seen some 10,000 instruments, and had drawn the attention of the House to 120 of these.[119]

4.2 Procedural control

Parliamentary control over administrative rule-making is admittedly weak because legislators are sometimes innocent of legal skills. A constant search, therefore, is on for an alternative mechanism which, besides providing effective vigil over administrative rule-making, can guarantee effective people participation for better social communication, acceptance and effectivity of the rules.

118. Report of the Select Committee on Delegated Legislation (1953) XIII.
119. Kersell, *Parliamentary Supervision of Delegated Legislation* (1960) 58.

Procedural control mechanism has the potential to meet the abovenoted requirements for allowing specific audit of rules by those for whose consumption they are made. Procedural control mechanism operates in three components:

(1) Drafting.
(2) Antenatal publicity.
(3) Consultation.
(4) Post-natal publicity.

4.2.1 *Drafting*

The drafting of delegated legislation by an expert draftsman who is, at the same time, in a position to advise whether the proposed rules and regulations are intra vires is obviously a valuable safeguard. It is no denying the fact that, in the absence of this safeguard, in India poorly drafted rules, in many situations, create great hardship for the people by increasing avoidable litigation. Therefore, the Committee on Subordinate Legislation in India rightly recommended that the language of rules should be simple and clear and not complicated or ambiguous. In *Daiichi Sankyo Co. Ltd.* v. *Jayaram Chigurupati*[120], the Supreme Court emphasised that "Object and Reason Clause" must also be introduced in delegated legislation, as it would help in proper interpretation of administrative rule-making. Throughout Australia the bulk of delegated legislation is either drafted or checked by parliamentary draftsmen. By a long-standing convention, all delegated legislation to be made or approved by the Governor of New South Wales is submitted for the opinion of the Attorney General as to its validity.[121]

4.2.2 *Antenatal publicity*

In India there is no separate law governing the procedure of administrative rule-making, and the parent Act may or may not provide for procedural requirement. However, in some cases the parent Acts have provided for antenatal publicity. Section 15 of the Central Tea Board Act, 1949, Section 30(3) of the Chartered Accountants Act, 1949 and Section 43 of the Co-operative Societies Act, 1912 may be cited as examples where it was provided that the rules must first be published in draft form to give an opportunity to the people to have their say in the rule-making.

Antenatal publicity required by the enabling Act attracts the application of Section 23 of the General Clauses Act, 1897 which requires

(1) that the rules be published in draft form in the Gazette;
(2) that objections and suggestions be invited by a specific date mentioned therein; and

120. (2010) 7 SCC 449.
121. *See*, Benjafield and Whitmore, *Principles of Australian Administrative Law* (1976) 106.

(3) that those objections and suggestions be considered by the rule-making authority.

It may, however, be noted that the procedure prescribed in the General Clauses Act, 1897 applies only to rules, regulations and bye-laws, and the administrative rule-making appearing under any other name is not governed by it.

The American experience shows that antenatal publicity is most beneficial in practice because those subject to administrative regulations tend to be members of trade or business organisations which perform the routine task of scanning the Federal Register and alert their members about the proposed rule-making. It may be noted that in the US "lobbying" is an institution and vigorous efforts are made to support the organisation's viewpoint before the administrative agency. Keeping in view the utility of antenatal publicity, Section 4 of the Federal Administrative Procedure Act, 1946 provides for the publication of proposed rules in the Federal Register. The agency concerned must then afford an opportunity to the interested persons to participate in the administrative rule-making through submission of written data, views or arguments, with or without opportunity of being heard orally. The Act also provides an escape clause where this procedure can be dispensed with in cases of its impracticability, or it being unnecessary or contrary to public interest. It may be noted that the requirements of Section 4 apply only to substantive rules and, therefore, has no application to interpretative rules, general statements of policy, rules of agency, organisation, procedure and practice. The American experience shows that the escape clause has been used in very few cases and it has not been abused.

In Britain, unlike in the US, the emphasis is on informal procedural requirements. The original rules of antenatal publicity and prior consultation laid down in the Rules Publication Act, 1893 have been repealed by the Statutory Instruments Act, 1946 which now provides for publication of rules. In England, the law contains no general requirement for antecedent publicity or any right to hearing. However, in individual cases, Parliament may provide for antenatal publicity and prior consultation. The Factories Act, 1961 may be cited as an illustration where antenatal publicity of rules, people's participation through consideration of their objections by individual or public hearing, were provided by Parliament. It does not mean that antenatal publicity and people's participation are absent in England. In England these are provided as a matter of unavoidable administrative necessity. It is correct to say that today it is almost unthinkable that the Minister of Health can run the National Health Service through his rule-making power without consulting the medical professionals. Britain, therefore, abandoned its attempt to judicialise rule-making the same year as the US enacted the Administrative Procedure Act, 1946 which laid down an ambitious programme of public participation.

4.2.3 *Consultation with affected persons*

This control mechanism makes administrative rule-making a democratic process and, therefore, increases its acceptability and effectivity.

In India there is no general law which provides for prior consultation with affected persons before rules and regulations are framed by administrative authorities. Therefore, the provision of prior consultation is sometimes provided in the enabling Act itself. Such a provision if contained in the enabling Act is considered as mandatory and its violation is visited with the invalidity of rules.[122] However, if the prior consultation has not been made mandatory by the parent Act, failure to consult will not affect the validity of the rules. Prior consultation shall be considered mandatory when some consequences are provided in the absence of such consultation. Section 16(5) of the Electricity (Supply) Act, 1948 makes provision for consultation with the State Electricity Consultative Council before raising tariffs. The Supreme Court in *Hindustan Zinc Ltd.* v. *A.P. SEB*[123] held that the failure to consult does not render the exercise of power invalid because consultation with the council has not been made mandatory, in the sense that no consequence is provided in the absence of such consultation. In India, the provisions for prior consultation made in the enabling Act may be grouped into five possible headings:

(1) *Official consultation with a named body.*—The Banking Companies (Acquisition and Transfer of Undertakings) Act, 1970 provides for prior consultation with Reserve Bank of India before making rules under the Act.

(2) *Consultation with administrative boards.*—The Mines Act, 1901 sets up Administrative Boards to advise the government and makes obligatory prior consultation with the boards before the Central Government can make rules under the Act.

(3) *Consultation with a statutory board in charge of a particular subject.*—Under the Tea Board Act, 1949, the Tea Board has been constituted as a statutory body in charge of the whole subject of tea cultivation, development, marketing, etc. The Act makes it obligatory to consult this Board before the government can frame rules under the Act.

(4) *Consultation with interested persons.*—Law authorised the municipalities to frame rules for the imposition of tax, but made it obligatory to publish draft rules in a Hindi daily and consult the inhabitants of the area who are to be affected by such tax. Amendments to the Food Adulteration Rules and standards for food items are similar for drugs and cosmetics as well as rates of minimum wages call for representations and suggestions from the general public by publishing the draft rules in the Official Gazette. Similarly, under the Industrial

122. *Banwarilal Agarwalla* v. *State of Bihar*, AIR 1961 SC 849.
123. (1991) 3 SCC 299.

Development and Regulation Act, 1951 representations from industry and the public are invited. Post-decisional representations in matters of excise rates, sales tax rates, and customs duty is also provided. This growing awareness of the need to invite people's participation is certainly a healthy development in administrative rule-making in India.

(5) *Preparation of rules by the affected interests.*—In order to guarantee complete efficacy and acceptability, the Mines Act empowers the owners of mines to draft rules themselves for the safety and prevention of accidents in mines and submit the draft rules to the inspector of mines. Such rules become operative on being approved by the government. In the same manner the Forward Contracts (Regulation) Act, 1952 gave power to a recognised association to make draft rules and submit them to the government. The rules become effective on approval by the Central Government with such modifications as it may deem fit.

As mentioned earlier, in England the Statutory Instruments Act, 1946 does not mandate prior consultation. However, there is no less public participation in the rule-making process in England. It is provided by the administrative authority as the only workable proposition. The Committee on Ministers' Powers in Britain was informed:

> No Minister in his senses with the fear of Parliament before his eyes would even think of making regulations without (where practicable) giving the persons who will be affected thereby (or their representatives) an opportunity of saying what they think about the proposal.[124]

In England, public participation is provided by another technique of consulting statutory advisory agencies which are supposed to reflect public opinion and express independent views. Therefore, the Tribunals and Inquiries Act, 1958 requires prior consultation with the Council on Tribunals before procedural laws are made for tribunals and enquiries.

In the US, Section 4 of the Administrative Procedure Act, 1946 provides only for opportunity to submit data, views, or arguments. It does not provide for any oral hearing, adversary or auditive. However, it is not uncommon that in the US, the statutes themselves provide for hearing over and above the minimum laid down in the Administrative Procedure Act, 1946. Unless the statute provides otherwise, the hearing is always informal resembling hearing before a legislative committee rather than before a court. The consultative practices include correspondence, consultations, conferences, gallup poll techniques, and public hearings, auditive or adversary type. Besides these, the practice of consulting advisory committees is also widely followed. For example, under the Fair Labour Standards Act, 1938, the wage orders had to originate from the industry advisory committee consisting of the employer, employee, and public representatives.

124. *See*, Garner, "Consultation in Subordinate Legislation", *Public Law* (1964) 105.

The question of "prior consultation" raises more fundamental questions of transparency, openness and accountability in the governance and functioning of democracy. It is for this reason that the Supreme Court exhorted Parliament to frame legislation along the lines of US Administrative Procedure Act, 1946, with certain well-defined exceptions, which all administrative authorities must follow before framing rules and regulations. The Supreme Court held:

> ...we would exhort Parliament to take up this issue and frame a legislation along the lines of the US Administrative Procedure Act (with certain well-defined exceptions) by which all subordinate legislation is subject to a transparent process by which due consultations with all stakeholders are held, and the rule or regulation-making power is exercised after due consideration of all stakeholders' submissions, together with an explanatory memorandum which broadly takes into account what they have said and the reasons for agreeing or disagreeing with them. Not only would such legislation reduce arbitrariness in subordinate legislation-making, but it would also conduce to openness in governance. It would also ensure the redressal, partial or otherwise, of grievances of the stakeholders concerned *prior* to the making of subordinate legislation. This would obviate, in many cases, the need for persons to approach courts to strike down subordinate legislation on the ground of such legislation being manifestly arbitrary or unreasonable.[125]

4.2.4 *Postnatal publicity*

Postnatal publicity is a necessary element in the rule-making process because the dictum that ignorance of law is no excuse is based on the justification that laws are accessible to the public.

In India, there is no general law prescribing the mode of publication of rules; therefore, the practice of publication differs from statute to statute. In some cases the statute lays down that the rules must be published in the Official Gazette, but in other cases the administrative authority is left free to choose its own mode of publication. In such cases, publication is necessary in any "recognisable" or "customary" manner. However, in *Anuradha Bhasin* v. *Union of India*, the Supreme Court held that government orders demanding compliance on part of people must be notified directly and reliably. This is regardless of whether the parent statute or the relevant rules prescribe the same or not.[126]

Where the parent statute prescribes a mode of publication, that mode must be followed. Where the parent statute is silent, rules framed by the administrative authority may prescribe the manner of publication, and such mode of publication may be sufficient if reasonable. If the rules do not prescribe the mode of publication or if the rules prescribe an unreasonable mode of publication, then the rules shall take effect only when published

125. *Cellular Operators Assn. of India* v. *TRAI*, (2016) 7 SCC 703, para. 92.
126. (2020) 3 SCC 637.

through the customary recognised official channel, namely, the Official Gazette or some other reasonable mode of publication. There may be rules and regulations which are concerned with a few individuals or are confined to a small local area. In such cases publication by other means may be sufficient. Thus, if a statutory provision requires publication of any notice for the benefit of those who are likely to be affected thereby but the language of notice is not prescribed, it is reasonable to expect that the language of the notice would be the local language and the mode of publication will be a local newspaper. Therefore, the Supreme Court in *State of Orissa* v. *Sridhar Kumar Mallik*[127] quashed the publication which had been made in a local newspaper but not in the local language. R.S. Pathak J (as he then was) held that having regard to the object with which a proclamation was required to be made in a local newspaper, the publication must have been in the local language of the area in which the newspaper circulated since the legislature attached great importance to the views of the residents to be affected by the notification. This decision marks a distinct advance over several decisions in which publication and the medium of publication have been considered merely directory. The question whether the mode, manner, and method of publication prescribed in a statute is mandatory or directory cannot be answered with reference to any fixed formula. Much would depend on the language of the statute, the purpose for which the provision was made, the intention of the legislature, inconvenience or injustice to persons resulting from whether the provision is read one way or the other, relation of a particular provision to other provisions dealing with the same subject and other considerations which may arise on facts of a particular case.[128] Hence, if the provision regarding manner and mode of publication is held to be mandatory on factors mentioned above, its non-compliance would render the rules invalid, and if the provision of publication was found to be directory, its non-compliance would not affect the validity of the rules. Likewise, if the publication is vague because of which the persons for whom the publication was intended could not properly avail the right of representation, it is bad in law.[129]

The Supreme Court in *Harla* v. *State of Rajasthan*[130] has held that a law cannot be enforced unless published. In this case during the minority of the then Maharaja of Jaipur, the Council of Ministers was appointed by the Crown representative to look after administration. The Council by a resolution enacted the Jaipur Opium Act, 1923 which was never published in any form. One Harla was prosecuted for the contravention of this law because he was in possession of opium in more quantity than permitted. The court held that the rules of natural justice demand that the laws be published before they are enforced. The same position was maintained by

127. (1985) 3 SCC 697.
128. *Raza Buland Sugar Co. Ltd.* v. *Municipal Board, Rampur*, AIR 1965 SC 895, 899.
129. *Ibid.* See also, *B.K. Srinivasan* v. *State of Karnataka*, (1987) 1 SCC 658.
130. 1951 SCC 936: AIR 1951 SC 467.

the Supreme Court in *State of Kerala* v. *P.J. Joseph*[131]. In this case, the Government of Cochin authorised the Board of Revenue to sanction extra quota of foreign liquor on payment of two per cent commission. The court was of the view that this authorisation does not have the force of law because the rule was never published.

However, if the rules framed by the authority though not published but are acted upon by it and are binding on the authority, it will not be open to the authority to contend that rules were not published. If the rules were required to be published, the authority cannot take advantage of its failure to publish them.[132]

Unless the rule-making authority has laid down a date on which the rules shall come into force, the rules generally come into force on the date of publication.[133] However, because of the special nature of service rules, the Allahabad High Court has held in *Banarasi Das Kankan* v. *U.P. Govt.*[134] that the service rules come into operation from the date they are made. Administrative agency can give retrospectivity to their rules provided the rules are not invalid on the ground of their retrospective operation.

Sometimes rule-making may be made subject to approval or permission of the competent authority or the delegating authority. In such a condition, if the rule-making is subject to "approval", rules can come into operation as soon as made and shall continue in operation until disapproved. However, if the rule-making is subject to "permission", rules do not come into operation unless permission is obtained.[135]

In England, Section 3 of the Statutory Instruments Act, 1946 provides that the rules shall not come into force unless published. Sub-clause (2) of Section 3 further provides that in case of a prosecution for the breach of any rule, it would be a good defence to plead that the rules were not made known. Section 2(1) of the Act provides the mode of publication. It lays down that unless otherwise provided, the copies of statutory instruments of general nature must be sent to the Queen's Printer to be printed, numbered, and sold to the public. However, all instruments of delegated legislation are not brought within the definition of "statutory instruments" and consequently, such delegated legislation need not be published unless so required by any other statutory provision.[136]

In the US, before the passage of the Federal Register Act, 1935, there was no provision for the publication of administrative rules and regulations. However, Section 5(1) of the Federal Register Act, 1935 now provides that all the rules which are required to be published must be published in the Federal Register. Unless it is so published, it cannot be enforced against

131. AIR 1958 SC 296. See also, *Narendra Kumar* v. *Union of India*, AIR 1960 SC 430.
132. *Bejgam Veeranna Venkata Narasimloo* v. *State of A.P.*, (1998) 1 SCC 563.
133. *State of Maharashtra* v. *Mayer Hans George*, AIR 1965 SC 722.
134. 1958 SCC OnLine All 318: AIR 1959 All 393. *See*, M.P. Jain, "Parliamentary Control of Delegated Legislation in India", *Public Law* (1964) 152.
135. *High Court of Judicature for Rajasthan* v. *P.P. Singh*, (2003) 4 SCC 239.
136. *See*, Griffith and Street, *Principles of Administrative Law* (1967) 57.

any person except the one who has actual notice of it. These provisions have been further reinforced by the Administrative Procedure Act, 1946. Section 4(*c*) defers effectivity of the rules by 30 days from the date of publication so that everyone has an opportunity of knowing them, unless the agency decides otherwise in public interest. After the publication of the rules in the Federal Register, the rules are classified, indexed, and codified under the provisions of Section 311(*a*) of the Federal Register Act, 1935. In India there is no law providing for codification and indexing of administrative rules. An attempt was made by the Law Ministry's publication branch to bring out a volume in 1960, but this practice could not be continued. This scheme of publication was carried into effect under the title of General Statutory Rules and Orders and was originally planned to be in 22 volumes, but till date about 40 volumes have been received. The difficulty remaining that the earlier volumes have become out of date and there is no scheme to update the volumes. Amongst private publications, *Current Central Legislation* is the only publication which publishes latest amendments to rules and regulations issued by the various ministries and departments of the government. It may also be noted that Rule 319 of the Lok Sabha Rules of Procedure provides that the rules required to be laid on the table of the House shall be numbered centrally and published. But these are merely mild palliatives and the disease remains largely uncured. It is suggested that the work of codification and indexing must be given to a statutory body on an All-India basis, and a separate law providing for uniformity in the publication process may be enacted.

4.3 Judicial control

In India judicial review of administrative rule-making is subject to normal rules governing the review of administrative action. Nevertheless, the principles on which the constitutionality of a statute is judged and that of subordinate legislation are different. A subordinate legislation could not enjoy the same degree of immunity as a legislative Act would.[137] This judicial review of administrative rule-making cannot be foreclosed in any manner by the enabling Act. In *State of Kerala* v. *K.M. Charia Abdulla & Company*[138], the Supreme Court held that the validity of the rules can still be challenged even in the face of such a phrase as "shall not be called in question in any court" in the enabling Act. In the same manner in *General Officer Commanding-in-Chief* v. *Subhash Chandra Yadav*[139] (*Subhash Chandra Yadav*), the Supreme Court held that an Act providing that rules made thereunder on publication in Official Gazette would be "as if enacted" in the Act, cannot take away judicial review. Furthermore, an ultra vires subordinate/delegated legislation cannot be enforced regardless

137. *State of Kerala* v. *Unni*, (2007) 2 SCC 365.
138. AIR 1965 SC 1585.
139. (1988) 2 SCC 351.

of specific plea not having been raised to strike down or declare it ultra vires.[140] Grounds of invalidity may arise on the following counts.

4.3.1 *That the enabling Act is ultra vires the Constitution*

If the enabling Act is ultra vires the Constitution which prescribes the boundaries within which the legislature can act, the rules and regulations framed thereunder would also be void. The enabling Act may violate either the implied or express limits of the Constitution.

Implied limits of the Constitution are those laid down in *Delhi Laws Act, 1912, re*[141], namely, the laying down of policy and enacting that policy into a binding rule of conduct. The legislature cannot delegate its essential power to any other agency, and if it so delegates the enabling Act will be ultra vires the Constitution. In *Delhi Laws Act*[142], *re*, the court held the later part of clause 2 invalid because it authorised the administrative agency to repeal a law which, in the opinion of the court, is an essential legislative function. In the same manner in *Hamdard Dawakhana*[143], the court held Section 3(*d*) of the Drugs and Magic Remedies (Objectionable Advertisements) Act as ultra vires the Constitution because the legislature had not provided sufficient guidelines for the exercise of administrative discretion in matters of selecting a disease to be added to the schedule. In *Mohini Jain* v. *State of Karnataka*[144] (*Mohini Jain*), the Supreme Court held that defining "capitation fee" is an essential legislative function which cannot be delegated, hence Section 2(*b*) is a case of excessive delegated legislation. In this case the Karnataka legislature had passed the Karnataka Educational Institutions (Prohibition of Capitation Fees) Act, 1984 prohibiting charging of capitation fees by private medical colleges. Section 2(*b*) of the Act defined capitation fee as "any amount, by whatever name called, paid or collected directly or indirectly in excess of the fee prescribed under Section 5". Under Section 5 of the Act, the government was authorised to prescribe fees to be charged by private medical colleges. Hence, the government issued a notification prescribing a fee of ₹60,000 from non-Karnataka and ₹25,000 from Karnataka students who did not qualify for admission on merit. Fee prescribed for students to be admitted on merit basis was ₹2000. The court held it a case of excessive delegation.

Whether a particular legislation suffers from "excessive delegation" is a question to be decided by the court with reference to certain factors which may include 1) subject-matter of the law, 2) scheme of the law, 3) provisions of the statute including Preamble, and 4) factual and circumstantial background in which the law is enacted. However, when a statute is challenged

140. *Shree Bhagwati Steel Rolling Mills* v. *CCE*, (2016) 3 SCC 643.
141. 1951 SCC 568: AIR 1951 SC 332.
142. *Ibid*.
143. AIR 1960 SC 554.
144. (1992) 3 SCC 666.

on the ground of excessive delegation, there is a presumption in favour of its constitutionality and if two interpretations are possible, one which makes the statute constitutional shall be adopted. Courts may also read down the law in order to avoid its being declared ultra vires the Constitution.[145] Applying the above indicators, the Supreme Court in *St. Johns Teachers Training Institute* v. *Regional Director, NCTE*[146] held that Regulations 5(*e*) and (*f*) which required obtaining of an NOC (No Objection Certificate) from the State by appellant is not an excessive delegation of power as sufficient guidelines have been issued to the State Governments by the National Council for Teacher Education.

To consider whether delegation of legislative power suffers from "excessive delegation", one must examine 1) scheme of the statute including its Preamble; 2) facts, circumstances, and background under which the statute was enacted; 3) history of legislation; 4) complexity of the problems which the State has to face; 5) liberal construction be given to statute, its policy and guidelines; and 6) statute, even if skeletal will be valid. However, this does not mean that court must always discover a dormant or latent legislative policy to sustain an arbitrary delegation of rule-making power to the executive.[147]

Invalidity of the rules and regulations may also arise if the enabling Act violates the express limits prescribed by the Constitution. No legislature has competence to violate the scheme of distribution of power given in the Constitution,[148] or to give its law extraterritorial applicability,[149] or violate the provision of the commerce clause, or Article 20 of the Constitution.

Another ground on which the constitutionality of the parent Act may be challenged is where the statute is well within the legislative competence, but violates the provisions of Part III of the Constitution by placing what may be called an unreasonable restriction on the exercise of fundamental rights. In *Chintaman Rao* v. *State of M.P.*[150], the court held the C.P. Regulation of Manufacturers of Bidis Act, 1948 and the rules framed thereunder as ultra vires Article 19(1)(*g*) of the Constitution which guarantees freedom of trade and profession. The impugned Act had given wide discretionary powers to the Deputy Commissioner to fix the agricultural season and prohibit the manufacture of bidis in the notified areas in that season. The Deputy Commissioner imposed a total ban on the manufacture of bidis. According to the Supreme Court, this amounted to unreasonable restriction on the exercise of the fundamental right and, hence, both the Commissioner's order and the Act are ultra vires the Constitution.

145. *St. Johns Teachers Training Institute* v. *National Council for Teacher Education*, (2003) 3 SCC 321.
146. *Ibid*, 324.
147. *Kishan Prakash Sharma* v. *Union of India*, (2001) 5 SCC 212.
148. Art. 246.
149. Art. 245.
150. 1950 SCC 695: AIR 1951 SC 118. See also, *New Manek Chowk Spg. & Wvg. Mills* v. *Ahmedabad Municipality*, AIR 1967 SC 1801.

However, while deciding the constitutional validity of any parliamentary legislation on the ground of legislative competence, courts adopt a liberal view and apply the doctrine of pith and substance for the purpose of determining whether the legislation is in respect of a particular entry in the legislative list. Courts have also held that a general word used in an entry must be construed to extend to all ancillary or subsidiary matters which can fairly and reasonably be held to be included in it.[151] Moving in the same direction, the Supreme Court observed in *Asger Ibrahim Amin* v. *LIC*[152] that the commendable objective of LIC of India (Employees) Pension Rules, 1995 being to extend the benefit to a class of people to tide over crises and vicissitudes of old age, in case of inconsistencies between the statutory provisions and avowed objective of the statute discriminating between beneficiaries within the class, the court is obliged to palliate differences between the two and reconcile them as far as possible.

4.3.2 *That the administrative legislation is ultra vires the Constitution*

It may happen that the enabling Act may not be ultra vires the Constitution, yet the rules and regulations framed thereunder may violate any provision of the Constitution. In *Narendra Kumar*[153], the Supreme Court held that even if the enabling Act is intra vires, the constitutionality of delegated legislation can still be considered because the law cannot be presumed to authorise anything unconstitutional. In *Dwarka Prasad Laxmi Narain* v. *State of U.P.*[154], Section 3(1) of the U.P. Coal Control Order issued under Section 3 of the Essential Supplies (Temporary Powers) Act, 1946 provided that no one can carry on business in coal except under a licence. Rule 3(2)(*b*) further laid down that the State Coal Controller can exempt any person from the licence requirement. The court held Rule 3(2)(*b*) as ultra vires Article 19(1)(*g*) as it places unreasonable restriction by giving arbitrary powers to the executive in granting exemptions.

In the same manner in *Himat Lal K. Shah* v. *Commr. of Police*[155], the Supreme Court held Rule 7 framed under the Bombay Police Act, 1951 as ultra vires Article 19(1)(*b*). Section 33(1) of the Bombay Police Act, 1951 had authorised the Commissioner of Police to make rules for the regulation of conduct and behaviour of assemblies and processions by prescribing the routes and time of processions. Rule 7 framed thereunder provided that no public meeting will be held without the previous permission of the Commissioner of Police. The rule was held ultra vires on the ground that the arbitrary discretion vested in the administrative agency in granting or

151. *United Provinces* v. *Atiqua Begum*, 1940 SCC OnLine FC 11: AIR 1941 FC 16. See also, *Charan Lal Sahu* v. *Union of India*, (1990) 1 SCC 613.
152. (2016) 13 SCC 797.
153. AIR 1960 SC 430.
154. AIR 1954 SC 224.
155. (1973) 1 SCC 227.

refusing permission amounts to unreasonable restriction on the exercise of the freedom of speech and expression.

Administrative rule-making may also be challenged on the ground that it is discriminatory. In *Labh Chandra Reisurana* v. *State of Bihar*[156], the Patna High Court held the rule providing for the management of Jain temples to be discriminatory and hence violative of Article 14. The impugned rule had restricted the voting right to persons who had attained the age of 21 and had made a donation of not less than ₹500 to the temple and were also living within the State for the last 10 years. In a recent case, *Kerala Samsthana Chethu Thozhilali Union*[157], the Supreme Court ruled that a rule making it compulsory for every toddy shop owner to employ one retrenched worker is arbitrary and, hence, violative of Article 14 of the Constitution. According to the court, "Take it or Leave it" condition imposed by administrative rule is arbitrary. However, a challenge on the ground of arbitrariness or unreasonableness must be such that the court might well say that the legislature never intended to give authority to make such rules.[158]

However, even in a case where the parent Act cannot be challenged before the court because of the protection of Article 31(*b*) of the Constitution on account of its placement in the 9th Schedule,[159] the rules and regulations framed thereunder can still be challenged if they violate any provision of the Constitution. This was decided by the Supreme Court in *Prag Ice & Oil Mills* v. *Union of India*[160]. In this case, the Mustard Oil (Price Control) Order, 1977 which was passed by the government under the Essential Commodities Act, 1955 was challenged on the ground that it violated Articles 14, 19 and 31 of the Constitution [Article 31 has now been omitted by the Constitution (44th Amendment) Act, 1978, Section 5]. The Act had been placed in the 9th Schedule and got the protection of Article 31(*b*) of the Constitution and, therefore, could not be challenged for any alleged inconsistency with any provision of the Constitution. The Supreme Court held that Article 31(*b*) saves only the Act and not the administrative rule-making under it. Beg CJ, as he then was, and Desai J dissented but, however, both the majority and minority upheld the constitutionality of the impugned order. However, it can still be argued that if the Act has

156. 1968 SCC OnLine Pat 52: AIR 1969 Pat 209. See also, *G. Venkatratnam* v. *Osmania Medical College*, 1967 SCC OnLine AP 52: AIR 1969 AP 35; *Rama Shankar Singh* v. *Darbhanga Medical College*, 1968 SCC OnLine Pat 29: AIR 1969 Pat 11. In these cases the rules for reserving seats for wards of government servants and for giving preference to BSc (Hons) degree in admissions were held discriminatory, and hence violative of Art. 14 of the Constitution.
157. (2006) 4 SCC 327.
158. *Cellular Operators Assn. of India* v. *TRAI*, (2016) 7 SCC 703.
159. The Supreme Court has now held that even if a statute has been put in the 9th Schedule, it can be challenged on the grounds 1) that it violates the fundamental rights of the people; and 2) that it violates the basic structure of the Constitution. *I.R. Coelho* v. *State of T.N.*, (2007) 2 SCC 1.
160. (1978) 3 SCC 459.

been placed in the protective shield of the 9th Schedule, the very purpose of the protection would be destroyed. The rule framed under the Act could still be challenged on the ground of unconstitutionality.[161]

4.3.3 *That the administrative legislation is ultra vires the enabling Act*

The challenge to the constitutionality of administrative rule-making on the ground that it is ultra vires the enabling Act can be sustained on the following counts:

(1) *That it is in excess of the power conferred by the enabling Act.*—In *Dwarka Nath* v. *MCD*[162], the Supreme Court held Rule 32 framed under the Prevention of Food Adulteration Act, 1954 as ultra vires the Act being in excess of the power conferred upon the government. The Prevention of Food Adulteration Act, 1954 authorised the Central Government under Section 23(1) to make rules for restricting the packing and labelling of any article of food with a view to preventing the public from being deceived or misled as to quantity and quality of the article. Rule 32 framed thereunder by the government provided that there shall be specified on every label name and business address of the manufacturer, batch number or code number either in Hindi or English. Action was initiated against Mohan Ghee Company for violation of Rule 32 because on ghee tins only "Mohan Ghee Laboratories, Delhi-5" was written. It was argued on behalf of Mohan Ghee Company that the requirement of address under Rule 32 is beyond the power of the enabling Act which is restricted to "quantity and quality" only. The Supreme Court agreed with the contention.

In the same manner in *T.B. Ibrahim* v. *RTA*[163], the court declared the rules framed by the administrative authority for fixing sites for the bus-stands as invalid being in excess of the power conferred by the enabling Act which authorised the agency to make rules for the control of transport vehicles.

Marching ahead in the same direction, the Supreme Court in *Ajoy Kumar Banerjee* v. *Union of India*[164], held the General Insurance (Regularisation and Revision of Pay Scales) Second Amendment Scheme, 1980 which fixed salary patterns of employees, violative of Section 16(2) of the General Insurance Business (Nationalisation)

161. See, *Vasantlal Maganbhai Sanjanwala* v. *State of Bombay*, AIR 1961 SC 4; *Latafat Ali Khan* v. *State of U.P.*, (1971) 2 SCC 355.

162. (1971) 2 SCC 314.

163. AIR 1953 SC 79. See also, *STO* v. *K.I. Abraham*, AIR 1967 SC 1823; *Durga Chand Kaushish* v. *Union of India*, 1979 SCC OnLine Del 103: AIR 1979 Del 249; *Bhandudas D. Naik* v. *Union of India*, 1978 SCC OnLine GDD 9: AIR 1979 GDD 1.

164. (1984) 3 SCC 127. See also, *K. Venkatagirigowda* v. *Bangalore University*, 1984 SCC OnLine Kar 58: AIR 1985 Kar 1.

Act, 1972. The Act had authorised the government to frame rules for the reorganisation of general insurance whereas the rules had provided for salary patterns for employees.

In *Mohini Jain*[165], the court held that the rules framed by the government under the Karnataka Educational Institutions (Prohibition of Capitation Fees) Act, 1984 are in violation of the purpose and object of the Act, hence void. In this case the statute had prohibited capitation fees whereas the rules framed thereunder prescribed a fee which could be charged by private medical colleges and which was not the tuition fee but capitation fee. The government had prescribed a fee of ₹2000 for merit students and ₹25,000 and ₹60,000 for non-merit Karnataka and non-merit, non-Karnataka students respectively. However, the Supreme Court is of the view that while deciding the validity of the rule on this ground, the delegation of power shall carry with it the power to make rules on matters which are subsidiary or ancillary to the main purpose. Thus in *TISCO Ltd.* v. *Workmen*[166], the court held that the rules relating to the creation of a quasi-judicial tribunal for deciding certain disputes are not in excess of the power conferred by Section 5 of the Coal Mines Provident Fund and Bonus Scheme Act, 1948, which authorised the government to make rules relating to bonus. Thus, courts follow the "pith and substance" rule in deciding the validity of rules on the ground of excessiveness.[167]

In a pacesetting judgment, the Supreme Court in *V. Sudeer* v. *Bar Council of India*[168] declared the Bar Council of India Training Rules, 1995 as ultra vires the enabling Act. Section 49 of the Advocates Act, 1961 as amended in 1973 provided that it shall have power to make rules for discharging its functions under the Act. The rules framed for pre-enrolment training and Bar examination, in fact, did not relate to any of its functions laid down under the Act. Quashing the rules, the Supreme Court observed that rules framed under Section 49(1) of the Act must have a statutory peg on which to hang them. If there is no statutory peg, the rule which is sought to be enacted dehors such peg will have no foothold and will become stillborn. Therefore, unless Parliament makes provision for pre-enrolment training and examination, the Bar Council of India cannot do it by rule-making power.

On the same reasoning in *Kerala Samsthana Chethu Thozhilali Union*[169], the Supreme Court held that the Kerala Abkari Shops Disposal Rules framed under the Kerala Abkari Act (1 of 1077) which provided that every toddy shop owner must employ one retrenched worker are violative of the enabling Act being beyond its policy and

165. (1992) 3 SCC 666.
166. (1972) 2 SCC 383.
167. *Supreme Court Employees' Welfare Assn.* v. *Union of India*, (1989) 4 SCC 187.
168. (1999) 3 SCC 176.
169. (2006) 4 SCC 327.

purpose.[170] Applying the same principle, the court observed that Rule 38-A made by the State under the Minor Mineral (Regulation and Development) Act, 1957, which terminated all private quarrying in sand, is against the object, scheme and, provisions of the enabling Act.[171] Because administrative rules become the part of the parent Act, so must be interpreted in a harmonious manner.[172]

The question whether the delegated legislation is in excess of the power conferred on the delegate has to be determined with reference to the specific provisions contained in the statute and also the object and purpose of the Act as can be gathered from the various provisions of the enactment. So long as the rules have a rational nexus with the object and purpose of the statute, it is not within the domain of the court to determine whether the purpose of a statute can be served better by adopting a policy different from that what has been laid down by the legislature or its delegate.[173] Thus, while determining whether the administrative authority has exceeded its power, the court does not sit as a court of appeal but merely reviews the manner in which the decision was made as the court does not have the expertise to correct the administrative decision. If a review of the administrative decision is permitted, it will be allowing the judge to substitute his own wisdom to that of the administrative authority which itself may be fallible.[174]

In the US, the role of the courts in reviewing administrative rule-making is essentially to determine whether or not the rules are within the power conferred by the enabling Act. In *AIR Reduction Company* v. *Hickel*[175], the statute provided that the "agencies of federal government" should purchase their major requirements of helium from the Secretary and gave him power to make regulations to carry out such provisions. Regulation framed thereunder was one forbidding government agencies "and their contractors" from purchasing their major helium requirements from any source but the Secretary. The court held the regulation invalid on the ground that the statute was limited to government agencies and the Secretary could not extend its reach by including government contractors.

(2) *That it is in conflict with the enabling Act.*—Administrative rule-making can also be declared invalid if it is in direct conflict with any provision of the enabling Act. In *Ram Prasad* v. *State*[176], the U.P.

170. (2006) 4 SCC 327.
171. *State of T.N.* v. *P. Krishnamurthy*, (2006) 4 SCC 517.
172. *U.P. Power Corpn. Ltd.* v. *NTPC Ltd.*, (2009) 6 SCC 235. See also, *Petroleum Natural Gas Regulatory Board* v. *Indraprastha Gas Ltd.*, (2015) 9 SCC 209.
173. *Maharashtra State Board of Secondary and Higher Secondary Education* v. *Paritosh Bhupeshkumar Sheth*, (1984) 4 SCC 27.
174. *Mansukhlal Vithaldas Chauhan* v. *State of Gujarat*, (1997) 7 SCC 622.
175. 420 F 2d 592 (DC Cir 1969).
176. 1952 SCC OnLine All 5: AIR 1952 All 843.

Panchayat Raj Act, 1947 provided in Section 49 that every case triable by the Panchayat Adalat must be tried by a Bench constituted in a manner laid down in the Act. Rule 87 framed thereunder provided that three members of the Bench would constitute a forum. This number was less than that provided under the Act. The court held the rule invalid as being in direct conflict with the enabling Act.

In *D.T.U.* v. *B.B.L. Hajelay*[177], the Delhi Corporation Act, 1957 in Section 92(1) provided that all persons drawing salary less than ₹350 p.m. will be appointed by the General Manager of the Delhi Transport Undertaking. Section 95 further provided that no person can be dismissed by any authority subordinate to the appointing authority. The General Manager framed a rule under the Act and delegated his power to the Assistant General Manager (AGM). A driver drawing salary less than ₹350 p.m. was dismissed by the AGM. He challenged the validity of the rule on the ground that it was in direct conflict with the provision of the Act. The Supreme Court declared the rule invalid and observed that the provision of the enabling Act cannot be infringed by any administrative rule or regulation. Similarly, in *Corporation Bank* v. *Saraswati Abharansala*[178], the court quashed an administrative rule which did not allow refund of excess tax deposit being in direct conflict with the parent Act which provided for refund.

Conflict with the enabling Act may also arise with reference to the "objects and purposes" of the enabling Act. Delegated legislation should promote rational and accountable policy implementation as laid down in an act.[179] Because the delegation is often effected by the use of wide formulae, it does not mean that it will authorise the making of regulations which do not relate to the "objects and purposes" of the Act. Deciding the "objects and purposes" will involve an assessment by the court not only of the provisions of the Act as a whole but also of the inferences which can be drawn from these provisions and from the surrounding circumstances in which the Act operates. A particular case of restrictive interpretation of this kind occurs when a general formula of delegation is followed by a list of specific topics on which rules may be made. Here courts will tend to limit the ambit of the general formula to matters which are ancillary to the enumerated specific powers.[180] However, if the delegated legislation is within the power or competence of the administrative authority as is evident from the parent Act, then the motive of delegated legislation for determining its validity is not material.[181]

177. (1972) 2 SCC 744.
178. (2009) 1 SCC 540.
179. *Global Energy Ltd.* v. *CERC*, (2009) 15 SCC 570.
180. See, *Hamdard Dawakhana* v. *Union of India*, AIR 1960 SC 554.
181. *State of M.P.* v. *Mahalaxmi Fabric Mills Ltd.*, 1995 Supp (1) SCC 642.

In *State of Karnataka* v. *H. Ganesh Kamath*[182], the Supreme Court struck down Rule 5(2) of the Karnataka Motor Vehicles Rules, 1963 as being inconsistent with the enabling Act. Rule 5(2) had provided that even though a person has passed the test for driving heavy motor vehicle, he cannot obtain a licence unless he has already possessed a licence for and has two years' experience in driving a medium motor vehicle, which licence again he cannot obtain unless he has previously passed the test in driving a medium motor vehicle. This rule was found to be in direct conflict with Section 7(*vii*)(*a*) of the enabling Motor Vehicles Act, 1939 which had provided that a person who passes the test in driving a heavy motor vehicle is to be deemed also to have passed the test in driving any medium motor vehicle. The highest Bench reasserted that the conferment of rule-making power by an Act does not enable the rule-making authority to make a rule which travels beyond the scope of the enabling Act or which is inconsistent therewith or repugnant thereto.

In *Kunj Behari Lal Butail* v. *State of H.P.*[183], the Supreme Court held that an administrative authority (in this case the State) cannot bring within the net of the rules what has been excluded by the Act itself. In this case, the H.P. Ceiling on Land Holdings Act, 1972 had delegated to the State Government the power to make rules "for carrying out the purpose of this Act". The Act by Section 5 had exempted "Tea Estates and land subservient thereto" from the operation of the Act. However, rules framed by the State Government had put embargo on the transfer of the land subservient to tea estates. Thus, the rules were held ultra vires the enabling Act being inconsistent and repugnant thereto.

As a general rule, substantive rights, obligations or disabilities can be created only by an Act and not by delegated legislation. Delegation of general rule-making power "for carrying out the purpose of the Act" does not confer power on administrative authority to create substantive rights, obligation or disability.[184] Such delegation may amount to Henry VIII clause and hence unconstitutional. Rule-making power is also subject to the limitation that it must promote rational and accountable framework for implementing policy of the Act.[185]

(3) *That it is in conflict with the prescribed procedure of the enabling Act.*—Sometimes the enabling Act lays down a procedure which must be followed by the administrative authority while exercising rule-making power under it. If the procedure is violated, the rules may be declared invalid. In *Banwarilal Agarwalla* v. *State of Bihar*[186], the

182. (1983) 2 SCC 402.
183. (2000) 3 SCC 40.
184. *Global Energy Ltd.* v. *Central Electricity Regulatory Commission*, (2009) 15 SCC 570.
185. *Ibid.*
186. AIR 1961 SC 849.

Mines Act, 1952 under Section 12 made it obligatory on the Central Government to consult the Mining Board constituted under the Act before making rules. The Supreme Court held that the rules framed without consulting the Mining Board were invalid being ultra vires the procedure prescribed by the enabling Act. In the same manner in *District Collector* v. *Chittor Distt. Groundnut Traders' Assn.*[187], the Central Government in exercise of its powers under Section 3 of the Essential Commodities Act, 1955 empowered State Governments to make necessary orders with the prior permission of the Central Government. The orders were however issued without the prior concurrence of the Central Government. The court held the orders ultra vires the procedure of the Act.

In determining the validity of the rules on this ground, the court looks to the spirit rather than the letter of the law. In *Raza Buland Sugar Co. Ltd.* v. *Municipal Board, Rampur*[188], the U.P. Municipalities Act, 1916 provided that the rule in the draft form must be published in the local Hindi daily. In this case the draft rules were published in an Urdu daily. The court did not accept the contention of invalidity of rules arising out of a violation of a mandatory procedure clause on the ground that what was important was the publication and not the Hindi daily. However, non-mentioning or wrong mentioning of statutory provision under which rule-making power has been exercised would not vitiate an order for which there is a source under general law or statute law.[189]

Though the principles of natural justice do not apply to legislation, but if it is the requirement of enabling Act then rules and regulations framed thereunder cannot deny the benefit of the principles of natural justice. Applying this principle in *State of T.N.* v. *P. Krishnamurthy*[190], the Supreme Court observed that the State cannot make a rule to terminate private quarrying in sand without notice and hearing because the enabling Act provides for it. Thus, the court held Rule 38-A framed by the State under the Mines and Minerals (Development and Regulation) Act, 1957 as violative of the procedure provided under the enabling Act.

(4) *That it is unreasonable, arbitrary and discriminatory.*—In India, the law is not settled whether apart from the ground of unreasonable restriction on fundamental rights, the court can invalidate an administrative rule on the ground of unreasonableness. In *Mulchand Gulabchand* v. *Mukund Shivram Bhide*[191], the Bombay High Court held the view that the statutory rules cannot be challenged on the

187. (1989) 2 SCC 58.
188. AIR 1965 SC 895.
189. *High Court of Gujarat* v. *Gujarat Kishan Mazdoor Panchayat*, (2003) 4 SCC 712.
190. (2006) 4 SCC 517.
191. 1951 SCC OnLine Bom 118: AIR 1952 Bom 296.

ground of unreasonableness as they become a part of the statute. The Supreme Court in a number of cases has also held that courts have no jurisdiction under Article 226 to go into the reasonableness of rates.[192] In *Port of Madras* v. *Aminchand Pyarelal*[193], the Supreme Court held that the scale of rates fixed by the Board cannot be declared ultra vires on the ground of unreasonableness. In the same manner in *S. Narayan Iyer* v. *Union of India*[194], the court refused to go into the question of reasonableness of telephone rates. It may be pointed out that this is taking the principle of judicial self-restraint too far. Now when Article 14 strikes at every arbitrariness in State action whether under the authority of law or in exercise of executive power, there seems to be no reason why the rates fixed by the government if found arbitrary or capricious cannot be held unreasonable. However, in *State of Assam* v. *Om Prakash Mehta*[195], the Assam High Court held Rule 24(3) framed under the Mines and Minerals (Development and Regulation) Act, 1957, which provided that if the application for renewal of lease is not disposed of within 90 days it would be deemed to have been refused, as invalid on the ground of unreasonableness. The Supreme Court in appeal though did not agree with the conclusion of the High Court, yet it never said that "unreasonableness" cannot be a ground for the invalidation of administrative rules and regulations.

Unreasonableness of administrative rule-making now can also be challenged on the ground that it violates Article 14 of the Constitution. As interpreted by the Supreme Court, Article 14 which guarantees equality before law can now be used to invalidate any law and action which is arbitrary or unreasonable. Therefore, in India, the doctrine of unreasonableness of delegated legislation has been based on a more firmer ground, *viz.* Article 14, rather than on a common-law principle like in England.[196] In *Air India* v. *Nergesh Meerza*[197], the Supreme Court quashed the service regulation framed by Air India which had provided for the termination of services of an air hostess on the first pregnancy. The court held this regulation as most unreasonable and arbitrary and interfering with the ordinary course of human nature, and hence violative of Article 14 of the Constitution.

The Supreme Court struck down the Bombay Civil Services Rules which had provided that a convicted government employee, even if he is in the appeal process, will be paid ₹1 as subsistence allowance. The court held this provision in Service Rule 151(1)(*ii*)(*b*) as "unreasonable

192. *Central Inland Water Transport Corpn.* v. *Brojo Nath Ganguly*, (1986) 3 SCC 156.
193. (1976) 3 SCC 167.
194. (1976) 3 SCC 428.
195. (1973) 1 SCC 584.
196. *See*, M.P. Jain, *Administrative Law*, Vol. XVII (ASIL 1981) 468.
197. (1981) 4 SCC 335.

and void". Chinnappa Reddy J who wrote a separate judgment remarked: "The award of subsistence allowance at the rate of rupee one per month can only be characterised as ludicrous. It is a mockery to say that subsistence allowance is awarded and to award rupee one a month." Varadarajan J stated:

> His right to get the normal subsistence allowance pending consideration of his appeal against his conviction should not depend upon the chance of his being released on bail and not being lodged in prison on conviction. Whether he is lodged in jail or released on bail, his family requires a bare minimum by way of subsistence allowance. Allowance of Re 1 is meaningless.[198]

In the same manner, the Supreme Court in *W.B. SEB* v. *Desh Bandhu Ghosh*[199] held that Regulation 34 of the W.B. Electricity Board which provided for termination of services of permanent employees by giving three months' notice or on payment of salary for the said period is totally arbitrary and, hence, violative of Article 14 of the Constitution. The Supreme Court also quashed a rule of the Haryana government which had classified persons released from military service on compassionate grounds differently from those released on any other ground for the purpose of seniority in government service on the plea that it violates Articles 14 and 16 of the Constitution.[200] In *State of Maharashtra* v. *Raj Kumar*[201], the Supreme Court similarly quashed the rule on the ground of unreasonableness as it had allowed a weightage of 10 per cent of marks to persons who had passed the SSC examination from rural areas because in the opinion of the court this had no relevance with the object of the selection of candidates having aptitude to work in rural areas. In *Indravadan H. Shah* v. *State of Gujarat*[202], the Supreme Court held Rule 6 of the Gujarat Judicial Services Recruitment Rules, 1961, providing that a Civil Judge after completing 48 years of age will not be eligible for promotion as Assistant Judge, as arbitrary and unreasonable. Similarly in *Meenakshi Malik* v. *University of Delhi*[203], a condition requiring schooling for the last two years in any school in Delhi for admission to any medical college in Delhi was held to be arbitrary

---

198. *State of Maharashtra* v. *Chandrabhan Tale*, (1983) 3 SCC 387. While both the judges agreed on the unconstitutionality of the rule, they disagreed on the juristic aspect of public employment. Varadarajan J approvingly quoted P.A. Choudhary J of the A.P. High Court who declared that public employment is a new form of property that should not be monopolised by any particular section of the people in the name of efficiency, though it cannot altogether be ignored.
199. (1985) 3 SCC 116. See also, *Central Inland Water Transport Corpn.* v. *Brojo Nath Ganguly*, (1986) 3 SCC 156.
200. *K.C. Arora* v. *State of Haryana*, (1984) 3 SCC 281. See also, *J.S. Rukmani* v. *State of T.N.*, 1984 Supp SCC 650.
201. (1982) 3 SCC 313.
202. 1986 Supp SCC 254.
203. (1989) 3 SCC 112.

and unreasonable. In *Gujarat University* v. *Rajiv Gopinath Bhatt*[204], the court quoted the rule framed by the Gujarat University, which had provided that for admission to superspeciality the first preference will be given to candidates from Gujarat University, second preference to students from other Gujarat Universities and, thereafter, seats remaining vacant will remain vacant, as unreasonable and irrational.

It may be pointed out that, unlike an administrative action, subordinate legislation cannot be challenged on the ground of violation of the principles of natural justice, therefore, this gap is filled when subordinate legislation is challenged on the ground of unreasonableness and arbitrariness under Articles 14 and 19 of the Constitution.[205] The Supreme Court again reiterated in *State of M.P.* v. *Mahalaxmi Fabric Mills Ltd.*[206] that delegated legislation is open to challenge on the ground of being arbitrary, irrational and confiscatory in nature so as to be violative of Articles 14 and 19(1)(*g*) of the Constitution.

It is important to note that the court cannot strike down an administrative rule on the ground of unreasonableness merely because the court thinks that it goes farther than is necessary, or that it does not contain provisions which in the opinion of the court would have been fair. Judges cannot substitute their wisdom with the wisdom of administrative authorities. Unless a rule is manifestly unjust, capricious, inequitable, or partial in operation, it cannot be invalidated on the ground of unreasonableness. A responsible administrative authority entrusted with the power of rule-making must ordinarily be presumed to know what is necessary, reasonable, just and fair. The validity of rules has to be judged by the generalities of the cases they cover and not by the stray instances of errors and irregularities discovered. Therefore, the test of reasonableness should be applied in the context of life's realities. These observations were made by the Supreme Court in *Maharashtra State Board of Secondary and Higher Secondary Education* v. *Paritosh Bhupeshkumar Sheth*[207], where Rule 104 of the Board which did not provide for inspection of the answer book and revaluation thereof in the presence of the student had been challenged. The net distillate of this approach is that it is not a pedantic and idealistic but a pragmatic approach which must determine the standard of reasonableness. In *G.B. Mahajan* v. *Jalgaon Municipal Council*[208], the Supreme Court further observed that the test of reasonableness as applied to administrative actions is different from the test as applied in the law of torts. In torts, the test is that of a "reasonable man" or as figuratively identified as the "man on the

204. (1996) 4 SCC 60.
205. *Indian Express Newspapers* v. *Union of India*, (1985) 1 SCC 641.
206. 1995 Supp (1) SCC 642.
207. (1984) 4 SCC 27.
208. (1991) 3 SCC 91.

Clapham Omnibus". In administrative law this is not the test because then judges can substitute their own judgment with the judgment of the administrator. Therefore, in administrative law "reasonableness" is the standard indicated by the true construction of the Act which distinguishes between what the statutory authority may or may not be authorised to do. It distinguishes between proper and improper use of power. It is often expressed by saying that the decision is unreasonable if it is one to which no reasonable authority could have come, the essence of what is now commonly called "Wednesbury unreasonableness"[209]. Therefore, an action of the administrative authority will be considered reasonable if it directs itself properly in law, considers the matter which it is bound to consider, excludes irrelevant considerations, and does not do anything so absurd that no sensible man could ever dream that it lay within the powers of the authority.

In *Khoday Distilleries Ltd.* v. *State of Karnataka*[210], the Supreme Court held that the test of reasonableness is whether it is manifestly arbitrary, such as could not be reasonably expected from the authority.

In *M.D. University* v. *Jahan Singh*[211], the Supreme Court held that even if benefit is general for everyone, it would be illegal and arbitrary because when the application is routed through the University it cannot be termed as "invitation". In this case, the executive council of the University had amended a regulation to the effect that word "invitation" would include even an offer made by a foreign university on application of a teacher and in such case, he will be entitled to increments for the period of his absence.

In a recent case, *Kanwarjit Singh Kakkar* v. *State of Punjab*[212], the Supreme Court quashed the first information report against two government doctors of Punjab for doing private practice. Government notification had provided that any private practice by a government doctor will be taken as "corruption" punishable under the Prevention of Corruption Act, 1988. The court held it as preposterous, unreasonable and arbitrary to treat private practice as "corruption". At the most, it can be a "misconduct" for which any departmental action can be taken.[213]

Reasonableness of delegated legislation must be judged having regards to various factors including effect on the person carrying on business and impossibility of the condition to be performed. If the condition is impossible to be performed, its unreasonableness shall be

209. *G.D. Mahajan* v. *Jalgaon Municipal Council*, (1991) 3 SCC 91, 110–11 based on the passage in *Associated Provincial Picture Houses Ltd.* v. *Wednesbury Corpn.*, (1948) 1 KB 223 (CA). See also, *Cellular Operators Assn. of India* v. *TRAI*, (2016) 7 SCC 703.
210. (1996) 10 SCC 304.
211. (2007) 5 SCC 77.
212. (2011) 13 SCC 158.
213. The Hindu, 1-5-2011, 12.

presumed unless State proves to the contrary. If the violation of the condition attracts penal liability, it must not be vague and must not be beyond the limits of parent Act.[214]

In the US, in the area of judicial review of administrative rule-making, the test of reasonableness plays a prominent part. The court can always see whether the authority had reasonable ground for exercising the judgment.[215] An illustration of the review power of the Supreme Court on the ground of unreasonableness is *FCC* v. *American Broadcasting Co. Inc.*[216] in which the Supreme Court invalidated regulations of the Federal Communication Commission (FCC), which prohibited broadcasting of "give-away" programmes under which prizes are distributed to home listeners for solving a problem or answering a question. The court held that it was unreasonable for the FCC to treat such programmes as "any lottery, gift, enterprise or similar scheme" which was prohibited by federal statute.[217]

In England, the rule is that administrative rules framed by any body except government departments are challengeable on the ground of unreasonableness. Rule-making by government departments is considered as an exception because Ministers are responsible to Parliament. In *Kruse* v. *Johnson*[218], Lord Russell laid down the test of unreasonableness of delegated legislation as:

(*a*) Partial or unequal operation between different classes.
(*b*) Manifestly unjust.
(*c*) Bad faith.
(*d*) Oppressiveness.
(*e*) Gross interference with the rights of the people that no justification can be found in the mind of a reasonable man.

An illustration of the exercise of the power of judicial review on the ground of unreasonableness can be found in *Arlidge* v. *Islington Corpn.*[219] in which the court invalidated a bye-law which required a landlord of a lodging-house to clean his premises at least once a year. The court observed that this bye-law imposed an absolute duty which may be difficult to perform without breaking a contract or committing a trespass for fear of criminal penalty.

In the US, administrative rule-making can also be challenged as unreasonable under the due process clause of the US Constitution. In such a challenge, the court is to see whether there is a rational relationship between the rules and the statute, or whether the rules

214. *State of Kerala* v. *Unni*, (2007) 2 SCC 365.
215. *American Trucking Associations Inc.* v. *United States*, 1953 SCC OnLine US SC 2: 97 L Ed 337: 344 US 298 (1953). See also, *Manhattan General Equipment Co.* v. *Commr.*, 1936 SCC OnLine US SC 21: 80 L Ed 528: 297 US 129 (1936).
216. 1954 SCC OnLine US SC 30: 98 L Ed 699: 347 US 284 (1953).
217. *Ibid.*
218. (1898) 2 QB 91.
219. (1909) 2 KB 127 (DC).

are reasonably approximate and calculated to carry out the purpose of the Act.

In India and England, a challenge against administrative rule-making cannot be sustained on the ground of violation of the principles of natural justice unless the primary statute provides for it. Applying this principle, the court held that Section 11(4), TRAI Act expressly provides for "consultations" by requiring "transparency" in the process of rule-making. In the opinion of the court, the term "transparency" signifies allowing all stakeholders to make their submissions to the authority and fully documenting and explaining the decision after considering all submissions. In *Cellular Operators Assn. of India* v. *TRAI*[220], the court was of the opinion that since there was no discussion in the documents of TRAI on the argument of the service providers that at times call drops take place because of the consumer himself or reasons beyond their control, show that there is no proper consultation with the service provider; hence, the conclusion that service providers are alone to be blamed for deficiency in service is not a conclusion which a reasonable person can reasonably arrive at. Therefore, it is not only sufficient that "Consultation" must take place but it is equally necessary that the product of consultation must be taken into account when the ultimate decision is taken by the administrative authority.

(5) *That it is mala fide.*—Administrative rule-making can be challenged on the ground of bad faith or ulterior purpose. The Drugs and Cosmetics Act, 1940 empowers the government to prescribe the standards of quality of drugs and cosmetics. Rule 150-A framed by the Government of India under the said Act required manufacturers of eau de cologne to add one per cent of diethyl phthalate, a poisonous substance, to render the product unpotable. The Bombay High Court held the rule invalid on the ground that the government cannot enforce its prohibition policy in the guise of prescribing standards.[221] It is the sole case in India where power of judicial review has been exercised on the ground of bad faith, and on that ground administrative legislative action has been found to be invalid. In the US, challenge on bad faith can be sustained under the due process clause of the Constitution. Similarly in England, subordinate legislation can be challenged on the ground of mala fide or bad faith. However, the allegations of mala fide or bad faith are more easily made than made out.[222]

(6) *That it encroaches upon the rights of the private citizens derived from the common law in the absence of an express authority in the enabling Act.*—Administrative rules and regulations can also be challenged on

220. (2016) 7 SCC 703.
221. *Hindustan Times*, 28-4-1972, 1, col. 4.
222. *S.P. Mittal* v. *Union of India*, (1983) 1 SCC 51.

the ground that they arbitrarily interfere with common-law rights of a private citizen. In *Sophy Kelly* v. *State of Maharashtra*[223], a regulation of the Maharashtra Education Board which provided that all Headmasters should forward all forms of candidates for SSC examination to the Board irrespective of their academic progress during the year was held ultra vires the common-law right of Headmasters to forward only forms of those students who make satisfactory progress during the year. In the same manner in *Chester* v. *Bateson*[224], a statute authorised making of regulations for public safety and successful prosecution of war. Regulation made thereunder provided that no premises can be recovered from the possession of any workman employed in the manufacture of war material, and imposed a penalty for taking legal proceedings in this behalf. The court held the regulation ultra vires the common-law right of a private citizen to move a court of law for justice.

(7) *That it conflicts with the terms of some other statute.*—In many cases it may happen that the delegated legislation conflicts with the provisions of some other statute. In England, a conflict with the statute law is a ground of invalidity of delegated legislation only where the empowering statute does not, expressly or by necessary implication, grant power to override statute law. There are many examples of statutes which have explicitly given power to override statute law and in the so-called "Henry VIII clause", power is given to amend even the parent Act or any other Act for the purpose of bringing the parent Act smoothly into operation. A classical example of this is found in Section 342(*g*)(*iv*) of the NSW Local Government Act, 1919–1969, which provides that in relation to town planning schemes "a scheme may suspend either generally or in any particular case or class of cases the operation of any provision of this or any other Act ...". As a result, Section 536(*c*) of the Act, which provides the method of computing compensation for the acquisition of land, has been suspended in some respects by a considerable number of town planning schemes.[225] In India, the conflict of delegated legislation with statute law may be a ground of invalidity even in the face of any statutory authorisation. Courts have held that the power of repeal or amendment of statute law is unconstitutional.[226]

However, in *Harishankar Bagla*[227], the court upheld the constitutionality of Section 6 of the Essential Supplies (Temporary Powers) Act, 1946 which provided, inter alia, that any order made by the government shall have effect notwithstanding anything inconsistent

223. 1966 SCC OnLine Bom 55: 1967 Mah LJ 400.
224. (1920) 1 KB 829 (DC).
225. *See*, C.K. Allen, *Law and Orders* (1965) 170.
226. See, *Delhi Laws Act, 1912, re*, 1951 SCC 568: AIR 1951 SC 332.
227. AIR 1954 SC 465.

therewith contained in any enactment, on the ground that this provision does not provide for either repeal or abrogation, but merely for bypassing the existing law to the extent of inconsistency. The same point came up for the consideration of the court in *A.V. Nachane.*[228] In this case, the Central Government framed the Life Insurance Corporation of India Class III and Class IV Employees' (Bonus and Dearness Allowance) Rules, 1981 in exercise of the powers conferred by Section 48 of the Life Insurance Corporation Act, 1956 as amended by the Life Insurance Corporation (Amendment) Ordinance, 1981. Rule 3 of these rules relates to the subject of bonus concerning Class III and Class IV employees of the Corporation. Clearly Rule 3 seeks to supersede the terms of the 1974 settlements relating to bonus. The court held that Rule 3 operating retrospectively cannot nullify the effect of the writ issued in *LIC* v. *D.J. Bahadur*[229] directing the Corporation to give effect to the terms of the 1974 settlements relating to bonus until superseded by a fresh settlement, an industrial award or relevant legislation.

It is now well settled that a rule is not only required to be made in conformity with provisions of the enabling Act but at the same time must be in conformity with the provisions of other existing law. Subordinate legislation cannot violate any plenary legislation made by the Central and State Legislature. Applying this principle, the Supreme Court in *Kerala Samsthana Chethu Thozhilali Union*[230] held that the scheme of rehabilitation of retrenched workers framed by the State by providing for "compulsory employment" for a retrenched worker by every toddy shop owner is not only violative of the enabling Act but also the provisions of the Industrial Disputes Act, 1947 which is a plenary law on the right of a workman in case a industry is closed, hence invalid because by the exercise of its rule-making power, administrative authority cannot repeal the provisions of any special law. The court further held that the impugned rule also violates the provisions of the Contract Act, 1872 and the Specific Relief Act, 1963.

(8) *Validity and the vires of the legislation, primary or delegated, has to be tested on the anvil of law-making power of the legislature.*—In a recent decision of 10 October 2003, the Supreme Court ruled that the validity of delegated legislation has to be tested on the anvil of law-making power of the legislature. If the authority has the requisite power, then irrespective of the fact whether the legislation fails in its object or not, its validity is not liable to be questioned. In this case, an NGO had challenged the notification of the government restraining the income tax authorities from proceeding against Mauritius-based

228. (1982) 1 SCC 205.
229. (1981) 1 SCC 315.
230. (2006) 4 SCC 327.

foreign international investors for being protected under the Indo-Mauritius Double Taxation Avoidance Convention. Rejecting the argument that the notification leads to "treaty shopping" and is not efficacious, the court held that the validity of a delegated legislation is to be decided not by its efficacy, but by the fact that it is within the parameters of the legislative provision delegating the power to the executive.

(9) *Effect of an ultra vires administrative legislation.*—If a subordinate legislation has been declared ultra vires by the court, it becomes null and void. It will be considered that this rule or regulation was not in existence at all. Therefore, it will neither operate as an estoppel nor can it be ratified. Thus, in *Bar Council of India* v. *Surjeet Singh*[231], the Supreme Court held that the action of the State Bar Council prescribing qualifications and conditions entitling an advocate to vote at an election is ultra vires the Advocates Act, 1961 which empowers only the Bar Council of India to make such rules and, therefore, even a ratification of such rules by the Bar Council of India cannot validate them. The same view was taken by the court in *Marathwada University* v. *Seshrao Balwant Rao Chavan*[232]. In this case, the Marathwada University Act, 1974 had empowered the executive council to appoint officers. The court held that the delegation of this power by the executive council to the Vice-Chancellor is ultra vires and the same cannot be validated by ratification of the delegant.

(10) *Waiver of the rule.*—Waiver or even relaxation of any rule by the administrative authority is not permissible unless such a power exists under the rule because it may lead to discrimination, arbitrariness and favouritism which is wholly opposed to the rule of law and constitutional values.[233]

(11) *Vagueness.*—Rules can also be challenged on the ground that they are vague. Therefore, if a rule made by the administrative authority does not lay down the date from which it will come into effect, it can be challenged on the ground of vagueness.[234]

Summarising the grounds of judicial review of delegated legislation, the Supreme Court held that it can be challenged under any of the following grounds:[235]

1. Lack of legislative competence to make the subordinate legislation.
2. Violation of fundamental rights guaranteed under the Constitution.
3. Violation of any other provision of the Constitution.
4. Failure to conform to the statute under which it is made or exceeding the limits of authority conferred by the enabling Act.

231. (1980) 4 SCC 211.
232. (1989) 3 SCC 132.
233. *State of Kerala* v. *K. Prasad*, (2007) 7 SCC 140.
234. *M.D. University* v. *Jahan Singh*, (2007) 5 SCC 77.
235. *Cellular Operators Assn. of India* v. *TRAI*, (2016) 7 SCC 703.

5. Repugnancy to the laws of the land, that is, any enactment.
6. Manifest arbitrariness/unreasonableness (to an extent where the court might well say that the legislature never intended to give authority to make such rules).

5. NEGOTIATED RULE-MAKING IN USA

Alternative Administrative Procedure Provisions of 1990 (as amended) provide for negotiated rule-making procedure. This procedure provides:

1. If the head of the administrative authority determines the need for a negotiated rule-making procedure in public interest. In reaching this decision, he will consider the following:
   (*a*) That the number of interests to be affected by the rule are limited and identifiable.
   (*b*) That the affected interests will be willing to negotiate rule-making in good faith to reach a consensus on the proposed rules.
2. After being satisfied on the above points, the authority shall appoint a negotiating committee.
   (*a*) A notice to the effect shall be published in the Federal Register that the administrative authority intends to appoint a negotiating committee to negotiate and develop the proposed rules, and nominations for the membership of the committee shall be solicited.
   (*b*) Any affected interest by the proposed rule shall nominate a member for the committee within a specified period of not less than 30 days along with submission of comments.
3. After considering the comments submitted, the authority shall determine the feasibility of appointment of the committee. Membership of the committee may be limited to 25. If the authority decides not to appoint such a committee, it shall publish the decision with reasons in the Federal Register.

   Each committee shall include at least one person representing the authority. Providing for administrative, technical and financial assistance shall be the responsibility of the authority. Subject to the approval of the committee, the administrative authority may appoint a facilitator who will chair the meetings.

   The committee shall submit a report to the authority on all the rules it has reached consensus on and also on rules on which no consensus could be reached. The committee may include any other recommendation and information it may deem necessary. After considering the report, the authority shall publish the final rules.

   The rules thus framed are subject to usual review; however, courts accord greater deference to such rules. Rules framed by this negotiating mechanism have maximum reference and acceptability.

POINTS FOR DISCUSSION

1. If law-making is taken over by the government, it may make the administration by the barrel of the secretariat pen.[236] In the backdrop of this statement, need and the norms of delegation jurisprudence may be discussed.
2. In our legal system, judicative and administrative law-making has become de facto primary and the law-making by the legislature secondary. Within the framework of the Indian Constitution, how far is this situation constitutional?
3. How far is it correct to say that the delegation of legislative power is a constitutional impropriety condoned only on the ground of expediency, but a potentially serious threat to the liberties of the people?
4. "Does any human being read through this mass of departmental legislation?" asked Lord Hewart[237]. Perhaps not; but since ignorance of law is no excuse for breaking it, administrative rules and regulations must be readily available to the public. In the light of this observation, the progress of publication of administrative rule-making and strategies for future action may be discussed.
5. Parliamentary control over delegated legislation should be a living continuity as a constitutional necessity, but extensive parliamentary control frustrates the basic object of delegating law-making power to the administration to make for economical use of parliamentary time. Strategies of parliamentary control over administrative rule-making may be discussed in the backdrop of the above observation.
6. Administrative rule-making is highly democratic because it can provide effective people's participation for better acceptance and effectivity. In the light of the experience of administrative rule-making in India, validity of this statement may be discussed. Will it be desirable to have a legislation providing for compulsory publication and consultation?
7. A critical performance audit of the Supreme Court may be made relating to the development of norms determining the constitutional validity of administrative rule-making. Will it be correct to say that judicial behaviour in this area has been residual and variegated?
8. Students may attempt to draft a Bill providing for all the problems of delegated legislation in India. Such an attempt may cover drafting, pre-publication, consultation, post-publication, compilation, laying and remedial parameters.

236. Krishna Iyer J in *Avinder Singh* v. *State of Punjab*, (1979) 1 SCC 137, 160.
237. *The New Despotism*, 96–97

SUGGESTED READINGS

1. Alan Wharm, "Judicial Control of Delegated Legislation: The Test of Reasonableness", (1973) 36 Mod L Rev 611.
2. B. Bhardwaj, "Delegated Legislation in India", 1963 SCJ (J) 26.
3. C.K. Allen, *Law and Orders: An Inquiry into the Nature and Scope of Delegated Legislation and Executive Powers in English Law* (1965).
4. C.K. Thakker, *Administrative Law* (Eastern Book Company 2012) Chaps. 4 and 5.
5. Cecil Carr, "Parliamentary Control of Delegated Legislation", 1956 Public Law 200.
6. D.C.M. Yardley, "Delegated Legislation and All that Fuss", (1965) 84 Law Notes 174.
7. D.K. Singh, *V.N. Shukla's Constitution of India* (7th Edn., 1983) 455–65.
8. E.A. Driedger, "Subordinate Legislation", (1949) 27 Can Bar Rev 550.
9. E.H. Beet, "Parliament and Delegated Legislation, 1945–53", (1955) 33 Public Administration 325.
10. Fitzgerald, "Safeguards in Delegated Legislation", (1959) 27 Can Bar Rev 550.
11. Foster, "The Delegation of Legislative Powers to Administrative Officers", (1913) 7 III LR 398.
12. Fox and Davis, "Sub-Delegated Legislation", (1955) 28 Australian LJ 486.
13. Fuchs, "Procedure in Administrative Rule-making", (1938) 52 HLR 259.
14. Garner, "Consultation in Subordinate Legislation", (1964) Public Law 105.
15. Griffith, "Delegated Legislation—Some Recent Developments", (1948) 12 Mod L Rev 297.
16. Indian Law Institute, *Delegated Legislation in India* (1964).
17. J.A.G. Griffith, "The Constitutional Significance of Delegated Legislation in England", (1950) 48 Mich L Rev 1079.
18. J.E. Kersell, *Parliamentary Supervision of Delegated Legislation: The United Kingdom, Australia, New Zealand and Canada* (1960).
19. J. Willis, "Delegatus Non Potest Delegare", (1943) 21 Can Bar Rev 257.
20. Jaffe, "An Essay on Delegation of Legislative Power", (1947) 47 Colum L Rev 359.
21. Jaffe, "The American Administrative Procedure Act", (1956) Public Law 218.
22. K.C. Wheare, "Controlling Delegated Legislation: A British Experiment", (1949) 11 Jour Pol 748.
23. M.P. Jain, *Changing Face of Administrative Law in India and Abroad* (1982) 25–29.
24. M.P. Jain, "Parliamentary Control of Delegated Legislation in India", (1964) Public Law 152.
25. Mallick, "Evaluation of Advisory Bodies", (1962) 4 JILI 511.
26. R.M. Jackson, "Judicial Review of Legislative Policy", (1955) 18 Mod L Rev 571.

27. Report from the Select Committee on Delegated Legislation, H.M.S.O., (1953) HC No. 310.
28. Report of Committee on Ministers' Powers (1932).
29. S.A. deSmith, "Sub-Delegation and Circulars", (1949) 12 Mod L Rev 37.
30. S.N. Jain, "Validity of Retrospective Delegated Legislation—The Court Develops a New Principle", (1981) 23 JILI 102.
31. S.P. Sathe, "Delegated Legislation in India" in M.J. Sethna (Ed.), Progress of Law (1962) 55.
32. Sehaj Singh Cheema, "Inseparate Powers & De Facto Offices of-Profit: The Contorted Reality of Constitutional Ideals" 9.2 NLIU LR (2020) 374.
33. Siddharth R. Gupta and Riya Khanna, "Nuances and Necessity of a "Notification" : The Law from Harla to Chatha Rice Mills" 2021 SCC OnLine Blog OpEd 35.
32. Upendra Baxi, "Development in Indian Administrative Law" in A.G. Noorani (Ed.), Public Law in India (1982) 137–40.
34. Waseem Ahmad Bhat, "Rethinking Ram Jawaya Kapur : How far the Executive can go without Legislative Authorisation?", (2020) 10 GJLDP (October) 77.

CHAPTER 5

Decision-making or Adjudicatory Power of the Administration

The term "administrative decision-making" has been used synonymously with "administrative adjudication". Today, the bulk of decisions relating to personal or property rights of the people comes not from courts but from administrative agencies exercising judicial power. From early times the administrative and judicial functions were inextricably blended in the organs of government. It was a later development that these powers were separated. Today, there is a revivalism of the past when administration has again come to acquire judicial powers. However, in the context of changed circumstances, purpose and need, it may be regarded as a new development. This new development has led to a host of controversies, and therefore, provides a fascinating pursuit for the writers of administrative law.

1. NEED FOR ADMINISTRATIVE ADJUDICATION

Administrative decision-making is a by-product of an intensive form of government and consequential socialisation of law. Vast expansion of State activity has taken place in India since 1947. Though on the day of Independence the political battle was won, but the war against poverty, illiteracy, and disease had just started. The government embarked on ambitious, massive plans of public health, education, planning, social security, transport, agriculture, industrialisation and national assistance. It was impossible to carry out these programmes and determine the legal questions involved therein with the assistance of law courts because of their highly individualistic and ritualistic approach. Therefore, if social control over this area of action was desirable, administrative decision-making was the only answer.

Another practical reason for the growth of administrative decision-making was the desire to provide a system of adjudication which was informal, cheap and quick. Litigation before a court of law is not only time consuming but is a luxury of the rich. The Supreme Court lamented on the failure of justice in *Mahabir Jute Mills* v. *Shibban Lal Saxena*[1], where after

1. (1975) 2 SCC 818.

a long-drawn-out legal battle, the case was finally decided after a period of 25 years, when most of the 400 persons who claimed justice on the ground of wrongful dismissal had died, and the new appointees in their place had completed 25 years of service. Therefore, as it became clear that the weight of social legislation would be intolerable, both for the people and the court, the burden had to be shared by the administrative adjudicatory system.

An even more important cause for the growth of administrative decision-making was the need to explore new public law standards based on moral and social principles away from the highly individualistic norms developed by courts. Employees' State Insurance Scheme in India required a new standard of medical service and treatment to which all the insured population and doctors must conform to. Town planning requires new standards of zoning, amenities, dispersal of industries, housing, and a series of similar measures. This setting up of new standards requires expertise, specialisation, and experimentation. The development of a standard for restricting traffic over a bridge with reference to load and the flow of water requires the knowledge of an engineer. Developing new standards to prevent environmental hazards arising out of industrialisation requires the knowledge of an environmentalist. Realising their limitation, the Supreme Court once said that leaving such technical matters to the decision of the court is like giving surgery to a barber and medicine to an astrologer. Therefore, the need to develop new standards and apply them has led to the growth of administrative adjudication.

Like medicine, in law also there is a growing emphasis on preventive justice rather than punitive. If it is necessary that the injury done to the person is to be remedied, it is equally necessary that the chances of injury must be eliminated. Therefore, it is necessary that any spurious drink or rotten article of food must be destroyed before being offered for public sale. This can be done only by administrative agencies exercising adjudicatory powers.

Administrative adjudication also represents a functional approach to law. In certain situations, justice lies not in disposal of the case according to law, but in fair disposition. In cases like licensing, nationalisation, fixing priorities in planning and action, the decision is to be reached not according to law as such but on the ground of policy considerations. Therefore, such matters are either unfit for courts' decision or courts, with their inherent limitations, are ill-equipped to make such decisions.

In any welfare state there may be areas of adjudication where, instead of concentrating on isolated facts in a dispute, the whole area is to be concentrated upon with sympathetic attitude coupled with an awareness of social context of the problem. The labour and capital relationship may be one of such areas where while deciding any labour dispute, the whole spectrum of industrial harmony necessary for national development is to be kept in view. Therefore, decisions in this area are to be reached not merely according to strict principles of law but on the principle of mutual give and take.

Here again administrative adjudication is the answer because courts, due to their limitations, cannot adopt this approach.

No intensive form of government can function without a decision-making system of its own. Courts are already groaning under the weight of pending cases and, as such, if the whole mass of fresh litigation arising in an intensive form of government is diverted towards them, the judicial system would virtually collapse. Therefore, in the administrative decision-making process, the government develops its own justice system which supplements the existing one.

1.1 Court of law and the administrative agency exercising adjudicatory powers

English and American views differ on the basis of distinction between a court of law and the administrative authority exercising adjudicatory powers. This difference is mainly due to the divergent constitutional structurisations in both countries and the difference in outlook. Americans put a lot of faith in judges and, therefore, in the judicialisation of the administrative process. The Englishmen, on the other hand, lay great emphasis on laymen and the informality of the administrative process.

According to the English view, the main distinction between a court of law and an administrative agency exercising adjudicatory power lies in the law and policy distinction. A court first ascertains facts and then applies law to these facts. Therefore, the function of a judge is like a slot-machine—controlled fact-finding and controlled application of law. The administrative agency exercising adjudicatory powers proceeds with controlled fact-finding and uncontrolled application of policy.

The Committee on Ministers' Powers also reached the same conclusion when it pointed out that, unlike a judicial decision which disposes of the whole matter by applying law to facts, a quasi-judicial decision is given after applying "policy" to facts.

However, this differential matrix of law and policy seems to be more apparent than real because judges today rarely act like slot-machines; they do take into consideration policy parameters also while deciding a dispute. The decision in *Maneka Gandhi* v. *Union of India*[2] would not have been possible had the court not taken into consideration the current policy and philosophy of society. On the other hand, some independent administrative agencies exercising adjudicatory powers apply law to facts in the same manner as a court. The Tax Tribunal, which is an administrative agency, applies law to facts in a highly objective manner, unconcerned with policy considerations.

"Discretion" cannot be a basis for distinction as both courts and administrative agencies—exercising adjudicatory powers use discretion for the interpretation and application of law.

2. (1978) 1 SCC 248.

According to the American view, it is the position of the person who decides which is the determining factor of difference between a court and an administrative agency exercising adjudicatory powers. In a court there are two parties and the judge sits as arbiter, detached and impartial. The institution and the presentation of a case is the responsibility of the parties. An administrative agency, on the other hand, is rarely disinterested in a case. However, even this basis of distinction is not without exception. There are independent tribunals where a presiding officer sits in the same detached manner as a judge. Election Tribunals, before their abolition, decided disputes between contesting parties in a highly detached manner. Institution and presentation was the responsibility of the parties.

"Nature of functions" is not a sufficient distinctive criterion either. It may be argued that a court exercises only judicial functions while administrative agencies exercising adjudicatory powers undertake various other administrative functions also. The President of India discharges multifarious functions and also decides disputes relating to the age of a judge under Article 217 of the Constitution. However, there are many administrative agencies like the Industrial Tribunal which exercise judicial powers only.

"Procedure" may also be a possible criterion of distinction but not without exception. There is no uniform procedure which the administrative agencies are required to follow while exercising adjudicatory powers. The procedure differs from agency to agency. Sometimes the procedure is prescribed by the statute which creates the adjudicatory authority and sometimes the agencies are left free to prescribe their own procedure, yet one common feature of these agencies is that they all follow the principles of natural justice. Courts, on the other hand, follow a uniform, fixed statutory procedure. However, in many cases administrative agencies are also vested with powers of a civil court for the purpose of summoning witnesses, examining them on oath, compelling the production of documents, etc.

Courts of law are bound by precedents, principle of res judicata, and technical rules of Evidence Act, 1872 and procedural law, but administrative tribunals are not uniformly and strictly bound by them. Furthermore, an administrative tribunal cannot decide on the constitutionality of a legislation except tribunals constituted under Articles 323-A and 323-B of the Constitution, whereas law courts (Supreme Court and High Courts) can decide this issue.

Structure and qualification may also provide possible parameters for distinction. The structure of administrative authorities exercising adjudicatory powers is not based on any uniform conventional pattern and is derived from a statute or a statutory rule. Sometimes these agencies are an integral part of the administration and sometimes autonomous. Adjudicatory powers may be given to a single individual or to a multi-member body. These agencies, besides exercising adjudicatory powers, exercise other regulatory and administrative powers. No uniform formal qualifications are prescribed for persons manning these agencies. Sometimes a legal qualification is prescribed and sometimes a technical one, but in most cases no qualification and experience is prescribed. On the other hand, the structure of courts is based on a uniform pattern and judges are required to have the necessary legal qualifications and experience; and they exercise no other functions, except judicial. However, there are administrative adjudicatory agencies which are autonomous; their members are required to have prescribed qualifications and exercise only judicial functions. For example, the Income Tax Appellate Tribunal is an autonomous body exercising only adjudicatory powers, and its members are required to have prescribed legal or technical qualifications.

One may go on and on like this without arriving at any conclusion. The only difference between a court and an administrative agency exercising adjudicatory powers seems to be the legislative classification. A court is a court because it has been classified as such; and an administrative agency exercising adjudicatory powers is an administrative agency because it has been designated as such.

2. PROBLEMS OF ADMINISTRATIVE DECISION-MAKING

Administrative justice has been a host of controversies in India. While people are not alarmed when the administration is given law-making powers, brows are certainly raised when administration is given adjudicative powers. People doubt the independence of administrators as judges and also fear their non-legal approach. Like Americans, the people of India put a lot of faith in judges.

In India, no systematic research has been done on the functioning of administrative agencies exercising adjudicatory powers and, therefore, their problems cannot be exhaustively listed. However, a few common problems with which the whole administrative adjudicatory process suffers may be discussed.

2.1 Number and complexity

Administrative agencies with adjudicatory powers have grown wild like mushrooms in the rainy season. Since 1947, these agencies have proliferated so much that an attempt even to prepare a comprehensive list seems impossible. Every statutory scheme contains its own machinery for decision-making. A large number of parallel bodies adjudicating on the same kind of dispute and giving divergent decisions is no exception. This complicates the task of administrative law in drawing uniform principles for uniform application. Therefore, the need to reorganise this formidable number into a system with fewer units cannot be overemphasised.

2.2 Bewildering variety of procedures

As the number of administrative agencies are formidable, so is their procedure. Even the best lawyer cannot say with certainty how he will proceed before a particular agency. Sometimes the procedure is laid down in the Act under which the agency is constituted. Sometimes the agency is left free to develop its own procedure. Sometimes the agency is invested with the powers of a civil court in matters of compelling attendance and production of documents. In some cases administrative and quasi-judicial bodies follow the procedure of General Clauses Act, 1897 which under Section 21 authorises such authorities to recall their own decisions if shown that such orders were obtained by fraud and misrepresentation. But in a great number of cases, the agency is required to follow only the minimum procedure of the principles of natural justice. Because the principles are not rigid and do not apply uniformly in all situations, the consequent uncertainty results at times in arbitrary actions. In the interests of justice and liberty, insistence on procedural regularity is essential. In the US and England, certainty, though limited, has been achieved by the Administrative Procedure Act, 1946 and Tribunals and Enquiries Act, 1977 respectively. In India, no such attempt has been made so far though it is overdue.

2.3 Unsystematic system of appeal

An appeal is a definite safeguard against an accident in the administration of justice. However, no uniform system of appeal has been followed in administrative adjudications. Sometimes administrative decisions are made appealable before an independent tribunal as in tax cases, and sometimes appeal is provided for before a higher administrative agency. Under Section 24 of the Medical Council Act, 1956, the decision of the Medical Council of India is appealable before the Central Government. Few Acts allow appeal on questions of law only. Section 64 of the Motor Vehicles Act, 1939 may be cited as an illustration. The period for allowing appeals also differs from agency to agency. Some Acts do not provide for any appeal and make the decision of the administrative agency final. Section 6 of the Land Acquisition Act, 1894 makes the decision of the Collector regarding public purpose final. To eliminate this ad hocism in appeals from the decisions of the administrative agencies, it is necessary that at least one appeal on questions of fact must be allowed before a higher administrative authority and another appeal on questions of law to a court of law.

Unlike American law, English Law provides the right to appeal to a law court from administrative decisions. This is done not only in the interests of justice but also with a desire to keep the judicial system unitary. On questions of facts, as a general rule, there is no appeal, but since courts recognise "no evidence" and "jurisdictional facts" as questions of law, the deficiency to a large extent is mitigated. In the US, the decision of the hearing examiner is appealable before the agency, and the decision of the agency is subject to the ordinary review powers of courts under the Constitution and the Administrative Procedure Act, 1946.

2.4 Invisibility of the decisions

Unlike courts, not all administrative agencies exercising judicial powers publish their decisions; their decisions, therefore, go beyond the pale of public criticism. In the absence of this necessary safeguard, the quality of administrative justice suffers. In some cases, even no record is prepared and justice is administered in an anti-legal fashion. It is because of this reason that the Administrative Procedure Act, 1946 insists on a formal record in all administrative adjudications. In England, the procedure is so informal that no transcript is insisted upon to save time and expense.

2.5 Unpredictability of decisions

In judicial decisions there is a certain amount of predictability. On similar facts, the decision will be the same because of the doctrine of precedent which courts in India follow. Predictability of decisions is an essential ingredient of the rule of law which insists that justice must be done through known principles. In administrative adjudication this essential element of predictability is frequently absent. Administrative agencies exercising adjudicatory powers do not follow the doctrine of precedent, hence they are not bound to follow their own decisions. This ad hocism not only makes the development of law incoherent but also violates the principles of the rule of law. Therefore, the Supreme Court's advice to such agencies is that they must be slow in overruling their own decisions.

2.6 Anonymity of decisions

In administrative adjudication, though not always, the decisions are made in a "hole-and-corner" fashion. No one knows from where the decision comes. One fine morning a person receives a communication that the President of India or the Governor, as the case may be, is pleased to take such and such decision in his case. This divided responsibility where one hears and another decides is against the concept of fair hearing.[3]

Anonymity in decision making or institutionalisation of the decisions remains an intricate problem of administrative law in India. In the US, the problem has been solved through the agency of "hearing officers". Under the provisions of the Administrative Procedure Act, 1946, a group of semi-independent hearing officers is maintained. They preside over cases not heard by agency's heads themselves. The appointment, tenure and promotion of these officers is in the hands of the Civil Service Commission to make them independent from the control of any agency. At the hearing, these hearing

3. *Gullapalli Nageswara Rao* v. *A.P. SRTC*, AIR 1959 SC 308.

officers exercise all the powers of a trial judge. They are required to make initial decisions after hearing which becomes the decision of the agency unless appealed from. The entire record of the hearing is certified by the hearing officer.

In England, the system developed after the Tribunals and Enquiries Act, 1977 does not go to the extremes of American law. There the inspectors who are the counterparts of the American hearing officers hold enquiry and hear, but do not decide. They can only make recommendations to the Minister concerned who can either accept or reject the inspectors' recommendations.

Recently a practice is developing in England where an inspector hears and decides also in many routine cases. This practice has been firmly established in Scotland.

In India, if administrative justice is to command respectability and public confidence, some such system as has been developed in the US and England is inevitable.

2.7 Combination of functions

In India, except in the case of civil servants, in all disciplinary proceedings the functions of a prosecutor and the judge are either combined in one person or in the same department. Whether it is accepted or not, in such a situation bias is inevitable.[4] In the US and England the problem has been solved, though not entirely by internal separation through the agency of hearing officers and inspectors. The Administrative Procedure Act, 1946 further provides that no official with an investigative or prosecuting function can participate in decision-making.[5]

2.8 No evidence rule

In India, the technical rules of the Evidence Act, 1872 do not apply to administrative adjudications. The gap is filled, though inadequately, by the judge-made rule of "no evidence". The Supreme Court explained the substance of this rule in *State of Haryana* v. *Rattan Singh*[6] (*Rattan Singh*). In this case, a bus of the Haryana Road Transport Corporation with Rattan Singh as conductor was taken over by a flying squad. The inspector found 11 passengers without tickets though they had paid money for it. However, the inspector did not record the statements of those persons as required under the rules. After the formality of enquiry, the services of the conductor were terminated. All the courts up to the High Court quashed the decision on the ground of insufficiency of evidence and violation of rules of

4. In *Hari Khemu Gawali* v. *Dy. Commr. of Police*, AIR 1956 SC 559, the Supreme Court held that where the functions of a prosecutor and the judge are exercised by two persons, though of the same department, there is no violation of the principles of natural justice.
5. S. 8(*b*), Administrative Procedure Act, 1946.
6. (1977) 2 SCC 491. See also, *J.D. Jain* v. *SBI*, (1982) 1 SCC 143.

natural justice as none of the 11 witnesses was examined, and the Inspector did not record the statements of witnesses as required by law. On appeal by the State, the Supreme Court reversed the decision and held that the simple point in the case was: Was there some evidence or was there no evidence—not in the technical sense governing the regular court proceedings but in a fair common-sense way as a man of understanding and worldly wisdom would accept. Viewed from this angle, the sufficiency of evidence in proof of findings of a domestic tribunal is beyond scrutiny. The evidence of the inspector is some evidence.

The end-result of the decision is that in an administrative adjudication if there is some evidence in some corner of the record, the decision is valid though it may not be any evidence at all in accordance with accepted norms of a judicial decision. *Nand Kishore Prasad* v. *State of Bihar*[7] highlights the problem. In this case, the appellant was a clerk in the District Magistrate's office. He was prosecuted before a criminal court for embezzling a certain amount, but was acquitted. Thereafter, disciplinary administrative proceedings were initiated against him and the appellant was found guilty, and hence removed from service. Upholding the decision of the administrative authority in a writ proceeding, the Supreme Court held that this was not a case of "no evidence" but of evidence which was inadequate to carry a conviction in a criminal court. In disciplinary proceedings, however, the order passed cannot be interfered with on the ground that the evidence would be insufficient in a criminal trial. It is true that this "no-evidence" rule resulting in inadequate basis for action has not earned any credibility for administrative justice.

In England, courts do not disturb the findings of fact by an administrative authority unless it is based on no evidence. *Coleen Properties Ltd.* v. *Minister of Housing and Local Govt.*[8] is an illustrative case on the point. In this case, a first-class building was included in a clearance order for undertaking a housing project. The Housing Act, 1957 provided that a first-class building cannot be so included unless it is "reasonably necessary" for the whole scheme. The inspector who gave the hearing recommended the exclusion of this building. The Minister overruled the inspector's findings and confirmed the clearance order. The court quashed the Minister's order on the ground that there was no evidence of "necessity" before the Minister. However, now a shift is visible in the approach of courts in England from the "no-evidence" rule to "sufficient-evidence or substantial-evidence" rule. Their Lordships of the House of Lords in *R.* v. *Secy. of State for Home Deptt., ex p Khawaja*[9] held that while exercising a power of judicial review, courts must see that there is "sufficient evidence" on record and thus, the "no-evidence" rule was not applied for review of administrative action.

7. (1978) 3 SCC 366.
8. (1971) 1 WLR 433 (CA).
9. 1984 AC 74: (1983) 2 WLR 321 (HL).

American law allows wide judicial review of finding of facts by administrative authorities. Courts can re-examine facts to find out whether there is substantial evidence to support administrative action. But how much evidence is substantial has been a complex question of American administrative law. Before the Administrative Procedure Act, 1946, the approach of the courts was that so much evidence as standing alone would be sufficient to support administrative action and would be substantial.[10]

After the passing of the Administrative Procedure Act, 1946, which requires in Section 10(*e*) that the determination of "substantial evidence" must be based on the whole record, two significant changes have been brought about in judicial behaviour: 1) the determination of "substantial evidence" must be made not by weighing evidence supporting the administrative action alone but after taking into consideration the evidence of the other side also; and 2) the quantum of evidence necessary to constitute "substantial" must be such that it can be accepted by any reasonable man as "substantial". Therefore, in *NLRB* v. *Universal Camera Corpn.*[11], the court struck down the action of the Board on the ground that though the action of the Board is based on some evidence, but after considering the evidence of the opposite side, no reasonable mind can accept such evidence as "substantial". In India on similar facts the decision would be the reverse.

Beyond the above area also the evidence projections of the administrative authorities are uncertain. However, the Supreme Court in *Bareilly Electricity Supply Co. Ltd.* v. *Workmen*[12] while deciding a bonus dispute laid down the broad evidence projections of administrative authorities exercising adjudicatory powers. The Supreme Court observed that administrative tribunals are not bound by the strict rules of evidence and procedure. They follow the principles of natural justice. But this does not mean that they can act on something which is not evidence at all. On the other hand, what it means is that no material can be relied upon to establish contested facts which are not spoken of by persons who are competent to speak about them and are not subjected to cross-examination by the party against whom they are sought to be used. If a balance sheet is produced, it does not itself become proof of the entries therein. If the entries are challenged, then every entry must be proved by producing books. If a letter or other document is produced to establish a fact, then either the writer must appear or an affidavit must be filed. Even if all the technicalities of the Evidence Act, 1872 are not applicable, it is inconceivable that the tribunal can act on what is not evidence but hearsay, further, the tribunal cannot base its awards on copies of documents the originals of which, though in existence, are not produced and proved either by affidavits or witnesses who have executed them, if they are alive and can be produced. Again, if

10. *Interstate Commerce Commission* v. *Union Pacific Railroad Company*, 1912 SCC OnLine US SC 24: 56 L Ed 308: 222 US 541 (1912).
11. 190 F 2d 429 (2nd Cir 1951).
12. (1971) 2 SCC 617.

the party wants an inspection, it is incumbent on the tribunal to permit inspection so far as it is relevant to the enquiry. The applicability of these principles are well recognised and admit no doubt.[13]

It must be borne in mind that the remarks of the Supreme Court relate to an independent tribunal, therefore, no other administrative authority exercising adjudicatory powers is bound by it.

In England, generally the legal rules of evidence are not followed by tribunals. Therefore, a tribunal may take into consideration an unauthenticated document without calling the author to prove it. In the US also, in cases of non-regulatory agencies, the same informality in matters of evidence persists.[14]

In order to create confidence among people in administrative justice, a code prescribing a minimum procedure for administrative agencies exercising adjudicatory powers must be adopted. Till this is done, judicial review must be enlarged by using the test of reasonableness of administrative findings of fact and law.

2.9 Official perspective

In administrative justice, official perspective is inherent. In any disciplinary proceeding, the presumption is of guilt rather than innocence. The actions are taken on the basis of expediency and various other extra-legal considerations. This projection of official perspective does more damage where the administrative agency is not required to follow the standard rules of evidence and procedure. Though no research has been undertaken in this aspect of administrative justice, but it is certain that official perspective does infest administrative adjudication.

2.10 Official bias

Official or departmental bias is one of the most baffling problems of administrative law. In the opinion of the Committee on Ministers' Powers, bias arising from strong and sincere conviction as to public policy may operate as a more serious disqualification than pecuniary interest. Therefore, the Committee suggested that in such cases where the Minister would approach the issue with a desire that the decision should go one way rather than another, Parliament should provide that the matter should be judged by an independent tribunal.[15] However, the problem of departmental bias is something which is inherent in administrative process itself. Realising this the Appeal Court in *Franklin* v. *Minister of Town and Country Planning*[16] held that the mere desire of the Minister that the issue be decided in a

13. *Bareilly Electricity Supply Co. Ltd.* v. *Workmen*, (1971) 2 SCC 617, 629.
14. *Richardson* v. *Perales*, 1971 SCC OnLine US SC 93: 28 L Ed 2d 842: 402 US 389 (1971).
15. Report of the Committee on Ministers' Powers, 78.
16. 1948 AC 87 (HL). In 1957, the Frank Committee also made a similar recommendation, 5.

particular way will not vitiate administrative action unless bad faith or improper purpose is proved. In India, the Supreme Court quashed the decision of the Andhra Pradesh government nationalising road transport, among other grounds, on the ground of departmental bias because the Secretary of Transport who had initiated the scheme also heard the objections.[17] Realising the inevitability of departmental bias in the administrative process, the Supreme Court, however, quickly added a caveat to its approach and held in *Gullapalli Nageswara Rao* v. *State of A.P.*[18] that if the Minister concerned hears the objections, the decision would be valid because he is a formal head of the department. In the US and England, the problem has been minimised to a great measure through internal separation wherein hearing officers are inducted to conduct hearings. For detailed treatment of this problem, see the Chapter "Practice and Procedure of Administrative Adjudication: Rules of Natural Justice" in this book.

2.11 Plea bargaining

Plea bargaining means the bargaining of "plea of guilt" with lesser charges and punishment. It is very common that a poor employee is bullied by an overbearing superior to accept the charge against him on the promise that a lesser punishment will be awarded. Plea bargaining, besides being immoral, violates the accepted canons of justice. It does the most damage where people are poor and illiterate.

It is for this reason plea bargaining as is being used in the US is not available in India. It is still considered unethical that any person after committing a crime, if he admits it, can get away with a flee-bite punishment. In India, a limited compounding of offences is allowed under Section 320 of the Criminal Procedure Code, 1973 (CrPC). Beyond this provision, no negotiated settlement of crimes until recently was allowed in India. This was made clear by the Supreme Court while disposing a criminal appeal in which the High Court had reduced the imprisonment punishment of eight years to imprisonment already undergone on the ground that the accused agreed not to challenge the legality of the lower court's decision in his case.[19] With the amendment of the CrPC, now plea bargaining has become a part of criminal justice system in India. However, it is too early to comment on its efficacy.[20]

2.12 Political interference

Instrumentalities of administrative justice are, by their very nature, subject to some manner of political interference, though this cannot be said

17. *Gullapalli Nageswara Rao* v. *A.P. SRTC*, AIR 1959 SC 308.
18. AIR 1959 SC 1376.
19. *State of U.P.* v. *Chandrika*, (1999) 8 SCC 638.
20. Code of Criminal Procedure (Amendment) Act, 2005, S. 265-A onwards.

with certainty about every tribunal. No statistics are available to prove the quantum of political interference, but a strong conviction persists among people that administrative justice is polluted by political interference. It was this conviction which made people raise a hue and cry against the government's proposal for establishing service tribunals to decide service disputes of government servants during the Emergency of 1975–77. Some system must, therefore, be devised to invest administrative agencies exercising adjudicatory powers with a reasonable degree of freedom, responsibility, and security of tenure.

2.13 Off-the-record consultation

Section 5(*c*) of the Administrative Procedure Act, 1946 provides that no administrative authority exercising adjudicatory powers is to consult any person or party upon any fact in issue except upon notice and opportunity for all parties to participate. This is done to avoid off-the-record consultations by the authority in a manner that may prejudice the case of the other party. In England, a standard rule has developed which applies to all enquiries; if the Minister differs from the findings of fact by the inspector, or receives any new evidence, or takes into consideration any new issue after the close of the hearing, he must bring it to the notice of the other party and must reopen the enquiry if so demanded by the other party. This limitation on off-the-record consultation will now avoid such problems as were involved in *Errington* v. *Ministry of Health*[21].

In India, there is no law to eliminate the dangers inherent in off-the-record consultation by an administrative authority. The principles of natural justice only demand that the authority must not base its decision on any evidence which is not brought to the notice of the other party. Since in India, there is no legal requirement for the preparation of a "record" in the sense in which it is insisted upon in the US, off-the-record consultation which may prejudice the mind of the authority is endemic.

2.14 Reasoned decisions

In the US, the right to reasoned decision arises from the provisions of the Administrative Procedure Act, 1946 and also from the due process clause of the Constitution. In England, the provisions of the Tribunals and Enquiries Act, 1977 require an agency to give reasons only when demanded.

In India apart from the requirement, if any, of the statute establishing the administrative agency, there is no requirement for the administrative authority to give reasons apart from the principles of natural justice. Earlier view was that administrative authorities exercising adjudicatory powers need not give reasons in every case.[22] However, now speaking order is

21. (1935) 1 KB 249 (CA).
22. (1977) 1 SCC 472.

insisted upon except in exceptional situations. Reasons are necessary concomitants of transparency and good-governance. Reasons develop faith of people in administrative justice and make it possible for a court to review an administrative action.[23]

2.15 Legal representation and cross-examination

Apart from the requirement of a specific statute, there is no general requirement of the principles of natural justice that the administrative agency should always allow legal representation and cross-examination in every case. Detailed discussion on the subject has been made in the chapter on natural justice, in this book. In the US, the requirement of legal representation and cross-examination is insisted upon by the due process clause and the Administrative Procedure Act, 1946. In England, the administrative procedure being more informal, this requirement is not insisted upon in every case.

From the above discussion it appears that the one problem with which administrative justice in India is confronted is the problem of organisation and procedure of the administrative agencies exercising adjudicatory powers. If there is merit in a flexible procedure, there is also the danger that informality may not develop an anti-legal posture. Therefore, the need for a minimum procedure code cannot be overemphasised. This will combine the elements of flexibility and certainty in the realm of administrative justice.

2.16 Administrative versus judicial action

Sometimes it happens that a person is proceeded against both in the department and in a court of law. In such a situation, what impact will a judicial decision have on administrative adjudicatory process? The Indian Supreme Court held that merely because an accused is acquitted by a court of law, the power of the authority to continue the departmental enquiry and action is not taken away, nor is its discretion in any manner fettered, as in a judicial proceeding the standard of proof differs much from that in an administrative proceeding. While in departmental proceedings, the standard of proof is one of preponderance of possibilities; in a criminal case, the charge has to be proved beyond reasonable doubt. Furthermore, both the proceedings operate in distinct and different jurisdiction areas. In departmental proceedings, factors operating on the mind of the authority may be many, such as enforcement of discipline or to investigate the level of integrity of the delinquent and other staff. This proposition was laid down by the highest Bench in *Corpn. of the City of Nagpur* v. *Ramchandra*[24]. In this case, an employee had been suspended pending enquiry on the charge

23. For details *see*, Chap. 7, "Practice and Procedure of Administrative Adjudication: Rules of Natural Justice" of this book, p. 187.
24. (1981) 2 SCC 714.

of swindling the money deposited with the Corporation as fine by the people. A criminal case was also filed in which he was acquitted. It was held that departmental action could still be taken.

Elaborating the law further, the Supreme Court in *M. Paul Anthony* v. *Bharat Gold Mines Ltd.*[25] concluded:

(1) Both the proceedings can proceed separately or simultaneously.
(2) If both the proceedings are based on identical facts and the charge in criminal proceeding is of a grave nature, which involves complicated questions of law and fact, it is desirable that departmental proceedings may be stayed till the conclusion of the criminal case.
(3) Whether the nature of charge in a criminal case is grave and involves complicated questions of law and fact would depend on the basis of evidence collected during investigation and reflected in the charge-sheet.
(4) Factors mentioned in 2 and 3 above cannot be considered in isolation to stay departmental proceedings, but due regard has to be paid to the fact that departmental proceedings cannot be unduly delayed. Departmental proceedings if stayed due to pendency of a criminal case can be revised so as to conclude them at an early date. The purpose is that if the employee is found not guilty, his honour may be vindicated and in case he is found guilty, the administration may get rid of him at an early date.

POINTS FOR DISCUSSION

1. Administrative decision-making is a by-product of an intensive form of government and consequential socialisation of law. Against this backdrop, need-parameters of administrative adjudication may be discussed. Is it correct to say that the strategy of administrative adjudication was developed not as a result of public necessity but for governmental convenience and expediency?
2. Today in the 21st century we appear to be losing ourselves in a labyrinth of administrative adjudication through which even the most expert guide could not be relied on to conduct us. In this background, the formidable problem of a bewildering variety of administrative procedures may be discussed. Discussion may aim at evolving certain basic principles on which a uniform administrative procedure code may be drafted, relevant to the Indian context.
3. In India, the process of establishing administrative adjudicatory agencies has not developed as a system. Therefore, in order to maintain some degree of coherence and surveillance over these agencies, is it necessary to establish a standing agency? After discussing the constitution and working of the Council on tribunals in England and

25. (1999) 3 SCC 679.

the Administrative Conference in the US, students should be able to develop a working hypothesis for the establishment of some such institution in India also.

4. Administrative justice in India has been through a host of controversies. However, official perspective, departmental bias, plea bargaining and political interference are some of such controversies which are making the administrative adjudicatory process irrelevant. Students may discuss the technique of internal separation through the medium of the Hearing Officer in the US and Hearing Inspectors in England as a means of finding an adequate answer to these problems. How and to what extent may this strategy be employed in India?
5. Can an enquiry be instituted against an authority exercising adjudicatory powers? In the light of the answer to this question, students may discuss the concept of "fairness" in the exercise of quasi-judicial functions.

SUGGESTED READINGS

1. Byse, "The Federal Administrative Procedure Act", (1958–59) 1 JILI 89.
2. C.K. Thakker, *Administrative Law* (Eastern Book Company 2012) Chap. 7.
3. E.C.S. Wade, "Administration under the Law", (1957) 73 LQR 470.
4. G. Ganz, *Administrative Procedures* (Sweet and Maxwell 1974) Chap. IV.
5. H.W.R. Wade, *Towards Administrative Justice* (University of Michigan Press 1963).
6. Henry J. Friendly, *The Federal Administrative Agencies: The Need for Better Definition of Standards* (Harvard University Press 1962).
7. Jaffe, "The American Administrative Procedure Act", 1956 Public Law 218.
8. Levin, "Hearing Procedure in Three Indian Administrative Agencies", (1962) 4 JILI 205.
9. M.P. Jain, "Tasks before the Administrative Reforms Commission: Reform of Indian Administrative Law", (1966) 2 Banaras LJ 100.
10. Michael Adler, "The Rise and fall of Administrative Justice - A Cautionary Tale", 8(2) Socio-Legal Rev. 28 (2012).
11. R.M. Jackson, *The Machinery of Justice in England* (6th Edn.) Chap. VI.
12. Report on Reform of Judicial Administration, Vol. II (1958) 671–95.
13. Robson, *Justice and Administrative Law* (3rd Edn. Greenwood Press 1951).
14. S.N. Jain, "Problems of Administrative Justice in India", 1971 Law and Commonwealth 640.
15. V.G. Ramchandran, "Administrative Justice", 1971 Law and Commonwealth 633.
16. V.S. Chauhan, "Reasoned Decision: A Principle of Natural Justice", 37 JILI (1995) 92
17. Wade, "Anglo-American Administrative Law", (1966) 82 LQR 226.

Chapter 6

Tribunalisation of Justice

(Executive—Centric Justice)

The decision-making or adjudicatory functions of the administration are exercised in such a variety of ways that it is difficult to bring them under any bibliographical control. However, the most popular modes of adjudication through tribunals may be discussed in this chapter.

The history of tribunalisation of justice in India dates back to 1941 when, in order to provide specialised and speedy administrative justice, Income Tax Appellate Tribunal was established in India. This tribunal soon acquired reputation of fairness in the administration of justice. After Independence, need was being felt to establish tribunals for determining administrative disputes with flexibility and speed. Today tribunalisation may also be a globalisation of trade and WTO Agreement imperative which demands justice which is open, fair and speedy.

Administrative tribunals could be classified into four categories:

(1) Tribunals setup outside main stream judicial system and decide disputes between government and private individuals.

(2) Tribunals setup within judicial framework and decide disputes between citizens like Rent, Motor Vehicle and Industrial Tribunals.

(3) Tribunals established to decide disputes between private individuals but established outside the main stream judicial system. The Company Law Board (CLB) 1988, 1991 falls within this unique category. Functions discharged by the High Court in this area were transferred to four branches of the CLB.

(4) Tribunals constituted under Articles 323-A and 323-B of the Constitution to decide disputes between government and the citizens. (*See* Chap. 14).

Validity of the third category tribunals was upheld by the Supreme Court in *Union of India* v. *Delhi High Court Bar Assn.*[1], in 2002. Encouraged by the development, the government established more tribunals within the areas of company law, tax law and intellectual property, and the jurisdiction of

1. (2002) 4 SCC 275.

the High Courts was taken away in these areas. This created a real conflict between constitutional judiciary and Parliament in which the executive always tried to subdue and tame the judiciary by curtailing its jurisdiction either overtly or covertly.

It was against this backdrop that in *L. Chandra Kumar*[2] the court asserted the power of judicial review and superintendence over tribunals by holding that excluding the jurisdiction of the High Court violates the basic structure of the Constitution. The court did not declare Articles 323-A and 323-B as unconstitutional, but invalidated those provisions of law which excluded the jurisdiction of the constitutional court under Articles 226, 227 and 32 of the Constitution.

Moving in the same direction, Parliament in 2002 amended the Companies Act, 1956 and established the National Company Law Tribunal with 62 members and the National Company Law Appellate Tribunal with 3 members to exercise jurisdiction under the law which took away the jurisdiction of the High Courts under Articles 226 and 227 of the Constitution. Constitutional validity of these tribunals was challenged in *Union of India* v. *Madras Bar Assn.*[3] The Madras High Court struck down certain provisions of the Act, but upheld the validity of National Company Law Tribunal. The matter then came before the Supreme Court. In the meantime, the government issued an ordinance and the National Taxation Tribunal was created. Constitutional validity of the law was again challenged in various High Courts which were also transferred to the Supreme Court.

After hearing the matter for three days, the matter was referred to a larger Bench of five judges. The larger Bench considered the three questions referred to it:

1. Does Parliament has competence to vest essential judicial functions in a tribunal outside its authority?
2. What is the constitutional limit to the transfer of such power to the tribunal?
3. Whether creation of independent tribunals violates the separation of powers and independence of the judiciary?

The Supreme Court missed an opportunity and did not decide on the role of tribunals in the overall constitutional justice delivery system. It only focused on the qualifications, tenure, conditions of service and the manner of appointment of judges of the tribunals. However, the court de-linked tribunals created under Article 323-B and other tribunals. Therefore, if the judges of the tribunals have the same qualifications, tenure, conditions of service and independent manner of appointment, then only tribunals can be a substitute for the judicial justice. Nevertheless, the jurisdiction of the constitutional courts cannot be taken away being the basic structure of

2. *L. Chandra Kumar* v. *Union of India*, (1997) 3 SCC 261.
3. (2010) 11 SCC 1.

the Constitution. On the same reasoning in *Madras Bar Assn.* v. *Union of India*[4], the National Tax Tribunal was held unconstitutional.

In *Shamnad Basheer* v. *Union of India*[5], the Division Bench of the Madras High Court struck down the main provisions relating to the Intellectual Property Appellate Board (IPAB) established under the Trade Marks Act, 1999 as unconstitutional on the ground that an officer of the executive cannot act in a judicial capacity.

1. LEGITIMACY OF TRIBUNALS IN THE OVERALL JUSTICE DELIVERY SYSTEM

People have a right under Article 21 of the Constitution to a specialised, quality and speedy justice. However, it is a fact that our existing judicial system cannot deliver due to inherent delays, technicalities of procedure, by labyrinth of appeals and unaffordable cost. Therefore, need for the administrative tribunals cannot be over emphasised. The core question is how to organise tribunals in a manner that does not violate the integrity of the constitutional judicial system which forms the basic structure of the Constitution. Tribunals thus may be organised as a part of the Civil and Criminal Court System under the canopy of the Supreme Court of India as have been organised in the UK under the Tribunals, Courts and Enforcement Act, 2007.

2. STATUTORY TRIBUNALS

Intensive form of government is responsible for entrusting the administration with adjudicatory powers. For the exercise of this power, a tribunal is a very efficacious instrumentality, which from a functional point of view is somewhere between a court and the government department exercising adjudicatory power. The dictionary meaning of the word "tribunal" is "seat of a judge" and, if used in this sense, it is a wide expression which includes within it "court" also. But in administrative law, this term "tribunal" is used in a special sense and refers to adjudicatory bodies outside the sphere of ordinary courts of the land. Under the Constitution in Articles 136, 226 and 227, the terms "court" and "tribunal" have been used to mean two different things.[6] Therefore, a tribunal may possess some but not all trappings of a court.[7] A body in order to be designated as a "tribunal" must be one which is administrative in character, but is invested with judicial powers to adjudicate on questions of law or fact affecting the rights of citizens in a judicial manner.

4. (2014) 10 SCC 1.
5. 2015 SCC OnLine Mad 299: (2015) 2 LW 941.
6. *Harinagar Sugar Mills Ltd.* v. *Shyam Sunder Jhunjhunwala*, AIR 1961 SC 1669.
7. *Associated Cement Companies Ltd.* v. *P.N. Sharma*, AIR 1965 SC 1595.

In *Kihoto Hollohan* v. *Zachillhu*[8], the Supreme Court referred to its earlier decisions[9] and observed that in order to determine whether an authority exercising adjudicatory powers is a tribunal or not, the test is whether

(1) there is a *lis*—an affirmation by one party and denial by the other;
(2) the dispute involved decision on the rights and obligations of parties; and
(3) the authority is called upon to decide it.

From a functional point of view, an administrative tribunal is neither exclusively a judicial body nor exclusively an administrative body but is somewhere between the two. However, generally an administrative tribunal shall have the following characteristics:[10]

(1) An administrative tribunal is the creation of a statute and thus has statutory origin.
(2) It has some trappings of a court but not all.
(3) An administrative tribunal is entrusted with the judicial powers of a State and, thus, performs judicial and quasi-judicial functions, as distinguished from pure administrative or executive functions, and is bound to act judicially.
(4) Even with regard to procedural matters, an administrative tribunal possesses powers of a court to summon witnesses, to administer oath and to compel production of documents, etc.
(5) An administrative tribunal is not bound by strict rules of evidence and procedure.
(6) The decisions of most of the tribunals are in fact judicial rather than administrative inasmuch as they have to record findings of facts objectively and then apply law to them without regard to executive policy. Though the discretion is conferred on them, it is to be exercised objectively and judicially.
(7) Most of the tribunals are not concerned exclusively with cases in which the government is a party; they also decide disputes between two parties; for example the Election Tribunal, Rent Tribunal, Industrial Tribunal, etc. On the other hand, the Income Tax Appellate Tribunal always decides disputes between the government and the assessees.
(8) Administrative tribunals are independent and they are not subject to any administrative interference in the discharge of their judicial or quasi-judicial functions.
(9) The prerogative writs of certiorari and prohibition are available against the decisions of administrative tribunals.

---

8. 1992 Supp (2) SCC 651.
9. *Harinagar Sugar Mills Ltd.* v. *Shyam Sunder Jhunjhunwala*, AIR 1961 SC 1669; *Associated Cement Companies Ltd.* v. *P.N. Sharma*, AIR 1965 SC 1595.
10. "Frank's Report", 1957 Cmnd 218, para. 40 quoted in C.K. Thakker, *Administrative Law* (Eastern Book Company 1992) 231.

In the Indian context, the term "tribunal" may be used in four different senses. *Firstly*, all administrative bodies exercising quasi-judicial functions, whether as part and parcel of the department or otherwise, may be termed as "tribunals". The only distinguishing feature of these bodies as against other bodies exercising administrative powers is that these bodies have to follow the rules of natural justice while rendering decisions. *Secondly*, all those administrative adjudicatory bodies may be regarded as tribunals which are outside the control of the department involved in the dispute and, hence, decide disputes like a judge free from any departmental bias. The Income Tax Appellate Tribunal may be covered in this category as it is under the control of the Ministry of Law, and not Ministry of Finance, hence it can decide matters impartially. *Thirdly*, the term "tribunal" as used in Article 136 of the Constitution has a special meaning. With reference to its special leave jurisdiction, the Supreme Court held that the authority must exercise "inherent judicial powers of the State".[11] The court would not hear an appeal merely from an administrative body, which in its decision-making process is required to follow the principles of natural justice, if it is not discharging the inherent judicial powers of the State. Thus, the test to identify a tribunal is not its control, composition or procedure but its functions. Consequently, even departmental bodies may be classified as "tribunals".[12] *Fourthly*, the term "tribunal" is also used for those tribunals which are constituted and established under Articles 323-A and 323-B of the Indian Constitution, such as administrative service tribunals. These tribunals have a constitutional origin and enjoy the powers and status of a High Court in matters within their jurisdiction and are amenable to the jurisdiction of the Supreme Court and the High Courts under Articles 32, 136 and 226 of the Constitution.

Much research has not been undertaken in India on administrative tribunals, however, the Indian Law Institute, New Delhi has done some pioneering work. It has listed 43 tribunals functioning under various Central enactments. It has also identified 25 bodies which have been held to be tribunals under Article 136 of the Constitution.[13]

Articles 323-A and 323-B of the Constitution indicate that we are at the threshold of a new era of tribunals. No exhaustive list of tribunals can be prepared as they appear under various names. However, the following authorities have been held to be tribunals within the meaning of Article 227 of the Constitution:

11. *Associated Cement Companies Ltd.* v. *P.N. Sharma*, AIR 1965 SC 1595.
12. Custodian General of Evacuee Property; the Central Government exercising powers under S. 111(3) of the Companies Act, 1956; the Central Board of Revenue exercising appellate powers under S. 190 of the Sea Customs Act, 1878; and also the Central Government exercising powers under S. 191 of the Sea Customs Act, 1878 have been held to be tribunals. *See*, S.N. Jain, *Administrative Tribunals in India: Existing and Proposed* (Indian Law Institute 1977).
13. *Ibid.*

(1) Industrial Tribunals established under the Industrial Disputes Act, 1947.
(2) Railway Rates Tribunals established under the Railways Act, 1890.
(3) Income Tax Appellate Tribunal established under the Income Tax Act, 1961.
(4) Employees' Insurance Court established under the Employees' State Insurance Act, 1948.
(5) Court of Survey established under the Merchant Shipping Act, 1958.
(6) Copyright Board established under the Copyright Act, 1958.
(7) Unlawful Activities Tribunal established under the Unlawful Activities (Prevention) Act, 1967.
(8) The Press and Registration Appellate Board established under the Press and Registration of Books Act, 1867.
(9) Foreigners' tribunal established under the Foreigners Act, 1946.
(10) Compensation tribunals established under the various Zamindari Abolition Acts, Slum Clearance and Planning Laws, Air Corporations (Transfer of Undertakings and Repeal) Act, 1994, Life Insurance Corporation Act, 1956, etc.
(11) Claims' Tribunals established under the Motor Vehicles Act, 1988.
(12) Rent Control Authority.
(13) Excise Appellate Authority.
(14) Commissioner for religious endowments.
(15) Panchayat court.
(16) Custodian, Evacuee Property.
(17) Payment of Wages Authority.
(18) Statutory arbitrator.
(19) Speaker exercising powers under paragraph 6(1) of the 10th Schedule of the Constitution.

On the other hand, the following authorities are not tribunals under Article 227 of the Constitution:[14]

(1) Domestic tribunal.
(2) Conciliation officer.
(3) Military tribunal.
(4) Private arbitrator.
(5) Legislative Assembly.
(6) Registrar acting as taxing officer.
(7) Customs officer.
(8) Zonal Manager of Life Insurance Corporation of India.
(9) Advisory Board under preventive detention laws.
(10) State Government exercising power to make a reference under the Industrial Disputes Act, 1947.

14. C.K. Thakker, *Administrative Law* (Eastern Book Company 1992) 227.

In India these tribunals do not follow any uniform procedure. The procedure is sometimes laid down in the statute, and sometimes the tribunal is left free to develop its own procedure. The procedure for the Copyright Board is given in the Copyright Act, 1957, while the Tax Appellate Tribunal is left free to decide its own procedure. However, as a matter of general practice, the tribunals exercise the powers of a civil court relating to examination, discovery, inspection, production of documents, compelling attendance of witnesses and issuing commissions. In the absence of statutory requirements, the tribunals follow the principles of natural justice. Their proceedings are considered as judicial proceedings for the purposes of Sections 193, 195 and 226 of the Penal Code, 1860 (IPC), and they are deemed to be civil courts for the purposes of Sections 480 and 482, CrPC. In the interests of flexibility and adaptability, the technical rules of the Evidence Act, 1872 do not apply to tribunals. However, the rules of procedure of the tribunals should not violate the requirements of fair procedure and they must conduct themselves with openness, fairness and impartiality. To this end in view, tribunals are required to give reasons for their decisions. This is necessary not only for a sound system of judicial review but also in the interest of discipline for the tribunal and public confidence.[15] The principle of res judicata in its technical sense does not apply to tribunals.[16] Tribunals are bound by the law declared by the Supreme Court,[17] and the tribunals working under the territorial jurisdiction of a High Court are bound by the law laid down by that High Court.[18] Tribunals are subject to the writ jurisdiction of the Supreme Court and the High Courts. By the Constitution (42nd Amendment) Act, 1976, Articles 323-A and 323-B had been added to the Constitution which authorised the government to establish special tribunals to perform a substitutional role to the High Court. Under this provision, administrative service tribunals had been established as a substitute to the High Court in service matters of government servants. These tribunals thus, were not under the jurisdiction of High Courts under Articles 226 and 227 of the Constitution. In a significant judgment in 1997, the Supreme Court declared Articles 323-A and 323-B as unconstitutional insofar as they took away the jurisdiction of the High Courts and, thus, these tribunals have been brought under the jurisdiction of High Courts. Jurisdiction of High Courts under Article 226/227 cannot be excluded expressly or impliedly by any legislation or even by any constitutional amendment as being the basic structure of the Constitution.[19]

As the tribunals are under the supervisory jurisdiction of High Courts, various High Courts have laid down a few rules regarding the functioning

15. *S.N. Mukherjee* v. *Union of India*, (1990) 4 SCC 594.
16. *India General Navigation and Railway Co.* v. *Workmen*, AIR 1960 SC 1286.
17. Art. 141 of the Indian Constitution.
18. *Jain Exports (P) Ltd.* v. *Union of India*, (1988) 3 SCC 579; See also, *Kollidam Aaru Pathukappu Nala Sangam* v. *Union of India*, 2014 SCC OnLine Mad 4928.
19. *L. Chandra Kumar* v. *Union of India*, (1997) 3 SCC 261.

of these tribunals. In *Mallappa Murigeppa Sajjan* v. *State*[20], the Karnataka High Court held that the government cannot suspend the working of a tribunal. The tribunal in this case had been constituted under the Karnataka Land Reforms Act, 1961. It had official and non-official members. Non-official members were drawn from the Congress (I) Party. When the Congress (U) government came to power, it issued an order directing the suspension of the working of the tribunal until further orders. Non-official members challenged this order as mala fide. Allowing the appeal, the court held that because the Act has not given the government a power of superintendence over the tribunal, the government could not directly impinge on the judicial functioning of the tribunal which falls under the supervisory jurisdiction of the High Court under Article 227 of the Constitution.

In *P. Satyanarayana* v. *Land Reforms Tribunal*[21], the Andhra Pradesh High Court ruled that in the absence of any statutory provisions, a tribunal cannot review its own decisions. However, it can recall its orders obtained through fraud in exercise of its inherent powers. In *G. Rajalakshmi* v. *Appellate Authority*[22], the question before the court was: If the tribunal fails to consider the objections filed before it, can the appellate tribunal consider the merits of the case as the original authority? The Andhra Pradesh High Court answering the question in the negative held that the proper course in such a situation would be to remand the case to the original tribunal.

When out of several charges only a few could be proved and the rest were found either irrelevant or non-existent, can a person be held guilty by a quasi-judicial body? The Supreme Court held that the order can be sustained if the exclusion of irrelevant and non-existent grounds could not have affected the ultimate decisions.[23]

It is not possible to discuss all the statutory tribunals functioning in India in various spheres. Hence, as an illustrative measure, the details of the Income Tax Appellate Tribunal may be noted. This tribunal functions under the Income Tax Act, 1961 as a second appellate authority to hear appeals in cases relating to income tax, wealth tax, and estate duty. The tribunal functions under the control of the Ministry of Law to ensure its independence. It consists of as many judicial and accountant members as the Central Government may deem fit to appoint. Any person may be appointed as a judicial member who has held a civil judicial post for at least 10 years, or who has been a member of the Central Legal Service for at least three years, or has been an advocate of not less than 10 years' standing. Ten years' practice as a Chartered Accountant, or service as Assistant Commissioner for at least three years is the prescribed qualification for an accountant member. The members hold office till the age of 60 and enjoy the status of a full-time civil servant. Ordinarily, the judicial member is appointed by the Central

20. 1979 SCC OnLine Kar 262: AIR 1980 Kar 53.
21. 1979 SCC OnLine AP 194: AIR 1980 AP 149.
22. 1979 SCC OnLine AP 189: AIR 1980 AP 100.
23. *Sawarn Singh* v. *State of Punjab*, (1976) 2 SCC 868.

Government as the President of the tribunal. Members of the tribunal may be empowered to sit singly or in Benches. Ordinarily, the Bench consists of one judicial member and one accountant member. A special Bench consisting of three or more members may also be constituted by the President. The decisions are given by majority and in case of equal division, the case is referred to one or more other members. The proceedings of the tribunal are not open to the public and its decisions are not published. Appeals to the tribunal may be filed by the assessee and the Income Tax Officer acting on the directions of the Commissioner against an order of the Assistant Appellate Commissioner. The tribunal is free to prescribe its own procedure and, therefore, the Income Tax (Appellate Tribunal) Rules, 1963 have been passed to regulate the procedure. The hearing before the tribunal is oral, and it exercises the powers of a civil court relating to examination, discovery, inspection, production of documents, compelling attendance of witnesses and issuing orders for formation of commissions. The decisions of the tribunal are final on questions of fact.[24] But a reference may be made to the High Court or the Supreme Court on questions of law. The decision of the High Court on a reference is appealable before the Supreme Court if the High Court certifies it as a fit case for appeal. The Law Commission and the Direct Taxes Administration Committee have reviewed the functioning of the tribunal and made various recommendations regarding appointment of its members, appeal and procedure to improve its functioning.[25] The fact that in 1963–64 the Income Tax Department lost 88 per cent of the appeals brought by it before the tribunal indicates the independent and impartial manner in which the tribunal discharges its functions.[26]

If statutory tribunals are to develop in India as a system for the administration of justice and not as mere administrative expedients, it is necessary that their functioning be properly supervised. With this end in view, in England, a council on tribunals was constituted under the Tribunals and Inquiries Act, 1958. The membership of this committee is 16. Except five legal members, the rest are lay persons. This constitution introduces the elements of public opinion and flexibility in the functioning of the Council. Parliamentary Commissioner (Ombudsman) is also an ex officio member. Except Parliamentary Commissioner, all the members are appointed by the Lord Chancellor and the Secretary of State for Scotland, acting jointly. The Council has only advisory jurisdiction. Its main function is to deal with the problems of tribunals and enquiries, and for this purpose it is in constant negotiation with the government regarding new proposals for legislation, rules of procedure, organisational problems, quality of members, individual complaints, etc. Therefore, right from the proposal stage to the final establishment of a tribunal, the Council is in the picture to help

24. *Karam Chand Thapar & Bros. (P) Ltd.* v. *CIT*, (1972) 4 SCC 124.
25. *See*, Law Commission of India Report on Income Tax Act, 1922 (25th Report 1958) 48 and the Report of the Direct Taxes Administrative Committee (1958–59) 81–86.
26. *Sampath Iyengar Souvenir*, 103 (published on the occasion of Silver Jubilee of the Tribunal).

administrative justice to develop as an organised system. The Council is empowered to receive complaints against the functioning of tribunals and enquiries. After investigation, it can publish its views to create public opinion for reform in the system.

To supervise the working of administrative agencies exercising adjudicatory powers in the US, the Congress passed a legislation in 1964 for the establishment of an administrative conference, which came into existence in 1968. Its present membership is 83. The Conference has three components: Chairman, Council and General Assembly. The Chairman is appointed by the President for a period of five years. The Council consists of 10 members appointed by the President for three-year terms. The members of the General Assembly are chosen by different federal agencies. A few members of the public are also chosen by the Chairman with the approval of the Council for a term of two years. The Conference is entirely a recommendatory body, and its main function is to put forward recommendations to improve the efficiency, adequacy and fairness of the legal procedure of federal administrative agencies exercising adjudicatory and rule-making powers. More recent recommendations of the Conference have dealt with procedural refinement, *i.e.* recruitment and status of hearing examiners, summary decisions, discovery, sovereign immunity, etc.

In India, there is an undeniable need for such an agency which could supervise the functioning of decision-making and rule-making administrative agencies. Such an agency would help in the development of administrative justice as a system.

In 2021 Parliament passed the Tribunal Reforms Bill. It provides for uniform pay and rules for the Search-cum-Selection Committee for tribunals, and also makes provisions for the removal of tribunal members. It empowers the Central Government to remove any Chairman or member from office on the recommendation of the Search-cum-Selection Committee on the grounds:

1. insolvency,
2. conviction for an offence which involves moral turpitude,
3. physical or mental incapacity,
4. conflict of interest, and
5. abuse of power in a manner as to render his continuance in office prejudicial to public interest.

In the Search-cum-Selection Committee for State tribunals, the Bill brings in the Chief Secretary of the State and the Chairman of the Public Service Commission with a voting right, and Secretary or Principal Secretary of the State's General Administrative Department with no voting right. The Chief Justice of the High Court will be the Chairman of the Committee without any casting vote.

Empowered by this law, the Central Government has dissolved eight tribunals on the ground of delay in justice delivery and disproportionate budgetary constraints. Pending cases have been transferred to High Courts and civil courts for faster disposal.

The fact remains that this law instead of making tribunals as an effective instrument for justice delivery system along with the courts has brought tribunals under the jurisdiction of the executive control. This development in the tribunalisation of justice in India for providing speedy and specialised justice along with courts of law raises serious concerns. Independence and judicialization of the process of the administrative tribunals will be essential for imposing rule of law on the administration.

3. DOMESTIC TRIBUNALS

The term "domestic tribunal" refers to those administrative agencies which are designed to regulate professional conduct and to enforce discipline among the members by exercising investigatory and adjudicatory powers. Such agencies may be contractual or statutory. Contractual domestic tribunals are those which exercise jurisdiction arising not from any statute but from an agreement between the parties. An agency constituted by a private club to decide disputes between its members is a contractual domestic tribunal. Such a tribunal is not subject to the writ jurisdiction of the court, but in certain situations remedy by way of injunction, declaration or damages may be available.

Statutory domestic tribunals are those which derive power and authority from a statute and exercise regulatory and disciplinary jurisdiction over its members. Such agencies have been established under the Advocates Act, 1961; Chartered Accountants Act, 1949; Medical Councils Act, 1945 and Press Council Act, 1965. The list is merely illustrative and not exhaustive. Such tribunals are free to develop their procedure, but in every case they are bound to follow the principles of natural justice. The decisions of statutory domestic tribunals are subject to the writ jurisdiction of the Supreme Court and High Courts in the same manner as any other statutory tribunals. However, the scope of judicial review in case of domestic tribunals is highly limited because the essential function of a domestic tribunal is discipline among its members. This seems to be the thrust of the Supreme Court decision in *Rattan Singh*[27]. In this case, Rattan Singh who was a conductor of the Haryana Road Transport Corporation was dismissed. On the Palwal route, his bus was taken over by the flying squad. The inspector found 11 passengers without tickets though they had paid the fare. An enquiry was held on the report of the inspector and the services of the conductor were terminated. A suit for declaring that the services were illegally terminated was filed by the conductor. The court granted the declaration, and on appeal the High Court sustained the decision on the grounds:

27. *State of Haryana* v. *Rattan Singh*, (1977) 2 SCC 491.

(1) that none of the 11 witnesses were examined by the domestic tribunal;
(2) that the inspector did not record the statement of the 11 passengers which was necessary as per the rules.

On appeal, the Supreme Court disagreed with the High Court and observed that the simple point involved in the case was, was there any evidence or was there no evidence—not in the technical sense governing regular court proceedings, but in a fair common-sense way as a man of understanding and worldly wisdom would accept. Viewed from this angle, sufficiency of evidence in proof of findings by a domestic tribunal is beyond scrutiny.

As an illustrative measure, the constitution and the functioning of the domestic adjudicatory authority constituted under the Advocates Act, 1961 to regulate and enforce discipline in the legal profession may be noted. The Advocates Act, 1961 makes provisions for the creation of a Bar Council at the State level and a Bar Council of India at the Centre. The State Bar Council is empowered by Section 35 of the Act to enforce discipline in the legal profession. The task of deciding cases of professional misconduct is entrusted to a disciplinary committee. The State Bar Council, either on its own initiative or on an application by any other person, can refer the matter of alleged professional misconduct by a lawyer to the disciplinary committee. For the conduct of business before it, the committee exercises the power of a civil court relating to examination, discovery, inspection, production of documents, compelling attendance of witnesses and issuing commissions. Its proceedings are deemed to be judicial proceedings within the meaning of Sections 193 and 228, IPC. The committee is also deemed to be a civil court within the meaning of Sections 482 and 485, CrPC. It has the power to either reprimand or suspend or remove the name of a lawyer from its rolls. The decisions of the committee are appealable before the Bar Council of India within a period of 60 days from the date of the order. From the orders of the Bar Council of India, a further appeal lies to the Supreme Court under Section 38 of the Act.

Besides tribunals, there exists a whole multitude of administrative officers and agencies exercising adjudicatory powers in varied forms. No systematic research has so far been undertaken in India regarding the manner of functioning of these officers and agencies. Therefore, this still remains a dark and dismal patch in the administrative law in India.[28]

With the introduction of the new economic policy, liberalisation, privatisation and globalisation of economy, a huge domestic and global regulatory

---

28. For detailed study *see,* S.N. Jain, *Administrative Tribunals in India* (Indian Law Institute 1977); Balram K. Gupta, "Administrative Tribunals and Judicial Review: A Comment on Forty-second Amendment" in Rajeev Dhavan and Alice Jacob (Eds.), *Indian Constitution: Trends and Issues* (N.M. Tripathi 1978) 401; Jain and Jain, *Principles of Administrative Law* (3rd Edn. N.M. Tripathi 1979) 162, Chap. 5; S.P. Sathe, "Forty-Fourth Constitutional Amendment", (23 October 1976) 11 Economic and Political Weekly, No. 43 ; U. Baxi, "Constitutional Changes: An Analysis of the Swaran Singh Committee Report", (1976) 2 SCC J-17; I.P. Massey, "Constitution Amended" (11-12-1976) Secular Democracy Journal 13.

space has been created which is being filled by administrative tribunals and regulatory agencies exercising adjudicatory powers. However, there exists no consistent pattern or policy in their constitution, powers and functions. Much depends on administrative convenience. At times, these are not independent and impartial forums and, hence, cannot render objective and fair decisions consistent with the recognised principles of adjudication.

Right to adjudication by an independent and impartial forum is a fundamental right covered under Article 14 of the Constitution. Therefore, wherever access to enforce such right before courts is denied or restricted by creating an alternative forum for adjudication, such law can be challenged if it violates the right to adjudication by an independent and impartial forum.

The Supreme Court in *Union of India* v. *Madras Bar Assn.*[29] made valuable recommendations for the better working of administrative tribunals and regulatory agencies exercising adjudicatory powers. In this case, constitution of National Company Law Tribunal (NCLT) and National Company Law Appellate Tribunal (NCLAT) was in challenge. After laying down that the enabling power of the legislature under Articles 323-A and 323-B to establish tribunals is plenary, the Supreme Court made the following valuable recommendations to make these forums true vehicles of justice, necessary to give meaning to the fundamental right to adjudication by an independent forum.

(1) The tribunals must be independent of civil services.
(2) The tribunals should not become post-retirement havens for civil servants.
(3) Independence of the tribunals must be ensured.
(4) Members of the tribunals should be independent persons and not serving civil servants.
(5) Even technical members must not be civil servants.
(6) Continued existence of the tribunals must not be dependent on the will of the government.
(7) The tribunals must not depend on government for infrastructural facilities or personnel.
(8) The tribunals should resemble more the court and not bureaucratic boards.
(9) There should be a separation between administrative and adjudicatory functions of the regulatory agency.
(10) Members of the tribunals should not retain lien in any government department.
(11) The tribunals must be headed by judicial persons and not technical persons.
(12) High Court jurisdiction may be supplemented but cannot be supplanted.

29. (2010) 11 SCC 1.

If these recommendations are sincerely operationalised, the tribunals will be able to replace law courts, a purpose for which these are created.

4. TRIBUNALISATION OF JUSTICE IN THE UK (ONE SYSTEM ONE SERVICE)

British Constitution is unwritten, unitary and based on the principles of supremacy of Parliament and rule of law. Therefore, the power of Parliament to create tribunals and vest them with vast judicial power cannot be contested.

In spite of Dicey's opposition to tribunals in 19th century as violation of rule of law, tribunals in England had started arriving. However, after World War II due to crises, opinion was building up against administrative justice which led to the appointment of Frank Committee. On the recommendation of this Committee, the Tribunals and Inquiries Act, 1958 (modified in 1991) was passed with the purpose of streamlining the administrative justice delivery system. However, tribunals were not integrated with the unified judicial system and continued as a separate executive system for delivering administrative justice.

Therefore, questions continued to be raised for streamlining the administrative justice delivery system to enforce independence, impartiality, transparency and speed into the system which is now also a requirement of the European Convention on Human Rights. It was for this purpose that Sir Andrew Leggatt Commission was appointed in 2003 and on its recommendations, Parliament passed the Tribunals, Courts and Enforcement Act, 2007.

Under this Act, two-tier tribunal system was established and integrated with the judicial system.

I. First tier tribunals (seven chambers)
   1. Social Entitlement
   2. Immigration and Asylum
   3. Health
   4. Education and Social Care
   5. War Pensions and Armed Forces Compensation
   6. Tax General Regulatory
   7. Land Property and Housing

II. Upper tribunals (four chambers)
   1. Administrative Appeals
   2. Immigration and Asylum
   3. Tax and Chancery
   4. Land

In 2011, tribunal services were joined with the court services to form Her Majesty Court and Tribunal Services. This service operates within a Framework Agreement between Lord Chancellor, Lord Chief Justice and Senior President of Tribunal. They support both tribunals and courts.

4.1 Elements: Administrative justice delivery system

(1) Appointments

(a) Tribunal judges are appointed in the same manner as High Court judges on the recommendation of the Judicial Appointments Commission.

(b) Non-legal members are also appointed in the same manner except that advice of professional bodies is obtained. (Now there is move away from experts and lay persons as members on the Tribunal.)

(2) Status of Office of Tribunal Judiciary

(a) Legal members of tribunals are designated as "judges".

(b) Upper tribunal has the status of the High Court.

(c) Senior President of the upper tribunal acts as the head of the entire tribunal judiciary. It gives them a collective voice.

(d) Presidents of the Chambers are High Court judges or Court of Appeal judges.

(3) Evidence and procedure

(a) Tribunals are generally not bound by the technical law of evidence.

(b) Besides evidence, judges are free to draw on their cumulative knowledge and experience.

(c) Procedure is less formal and less adversarial. However, principles of natural justice cannot be ignored. They follow the case management of courts. Tribunals may ask parties to negotiate and settle the matter. Oral hearing is allowed with the permission of the tribunal, which is allowed if it is the only effective way of participating in the proceeding and would enhance quality of the decision.

(d) There is move towards using ADR (Alternative Dispute Resolution) in matters heard by tribunals.

(4) Speaking decisions

(a) Act is silent on the point. However, some tribunals give reasons as a matter of course while others do not give reasons as a policy. Nevertheless, reasons become necessary in view of appeal provisions.

(5) Legal representation

(a) Tribunals generally follow the principle of reducing legal representation to cases where it would enhance the quality of decision. Therefore, legal representation may be allowed in cases of

(i) complexity of law and facts,

(ii) need for skilled advocacy,

(iii) disability and lack of relevant skills on the part of complainant,

(iv) use of expert witness, and

(v) where presence of lawyer would increase winnability chances.

(6) Appeals
(a) First appeal from the first tier tribunal lies to the upper tribunal with the leave of the first or upper tribunal.
(b) Second appeal would lie before the Court of Appeal if
(i) certified by the upper tribunal or Court of Appeal;
(ii) it is matter of public importance; and
(iii) there is an error of law on the face of the record.
(c) Tribunals can review their own decisions.
(7) Support and oversight of administrative justice through tribunals is provided by:
(a) Unified Tribunals Service,
(b) Tribunal Procedure Committee, and
(c) Administrative Justice and Tribunals Council.

Today, administrative justice delivery system in the UK stands side by side concurrently with the ordinary civil and criminal jurisdiction integrated within the existing national judicial system.

Today, the demand for a system of administrative justice delivery mechanism which is capable of providing quality, quantity and speedy justice cannot be over emphasised due to socialisation of law, increase in the level of awareness of the people, developments of science and technology and the imperatives of new economic liberalisation and globalisation. Any system which can meet the expectations must be efficient, effective, transparent, independent, impartial and integrated with the unified judicial system of the country.

Thus, tribunals in the UK have been established like courts of law under the financial and administrative control of the Lord Chancellor and not the Ministry and stand side by side with the civil and criminal courts under the canopy of national judiciary headed by the Lord Chancellor. This has also taken care of the Dicey's objections to the growth of administrative law in the UK. The viability of establishing tribunals as a system along with civil and criminal court system in India rather than as an ad hoc executive project is worth exploring.

5. CAN ENQUIRY BE INSTITUTED AGAINST PERSON EXERCISING QUASI-JUDICIAL POWERS?

Recently in *Union of India* v. *K.K. Dhawan*[30], the Supreme Court has answered this question in the affirmative. In this case, an Income Tax Officer exercising quasi-judicial powers, while deciding the case, acted with undue haste to give benefit to the assessee. Departmental enquiry was instituted against him. Holding the departmental action valid, the court held that when an officer in exercise of judicial or quasi-judicial powers acts

30. (1993) 2 SCC 56. In this case, court explained its earlier decision in *Union of India* v. *R.K. Desai*, (1993) 2 SCC 49 observing that in that case enquiry officer did not find anything against the officer.

negligently or recklessly or in order to confer undue favour on a person, he is not acting as a judge and, hence, can be subjected to disciplinary action. Such action can be taken in the following cases:

(1) Where the officer has acted in a manner as would reflect on his reputation for integrity or good faith or devotion to duty.
(2) If there is a prima facie case to show recklessness or misconduct in the discharge of duties.
(3) If he has acted in a manner unbecoming of a government servant.
(4) If he has acted negligently or omitted the prescribed conditions which are necessary for the exercise of statutory powers.
(5) If he has acted in a manner to unduly favour a party.
(6) If he has been actuated by corrupt motives, however small the bribe may be.

POINTS FOR DISCUSSION

1. Need of establishing tribunals as a system along with civil and criminal courts rather than an ad hoc executive project may be discussed.
2. "All disputes be decided by courts unless special considerations make tribunal a prefered destination." This proposition may be discussed.
3. Why should tribunals be the part of administration?
4. Do you think that bringing tribunals more close to courts in terms of independence and process will impose rule of law on the administration?
5. Do you think that it will be reasonable to impose judicial norms on the tribunals and yet expect them to deliver justice in an informal manner?

SUGGESTED READINGS

1. Alok Kumar, "Administrative Adjudication : A Comparative Understanding With Special Reference to Tribunals", 1 SML L Rev 105 (2018).
2. C.K. Thakker, *Administrative Law* (Eastern Book Company 2012) Chap. 7.
3. D.H. Hene, "Domestic Tribunals in Great Britain", (1955) 11 British Journal of Administrative Law 24.
4. G.W. Keeton, *Trial by Tribunal: A Study of the Development and Functioning of the Tribunal of Inquiry* (Museum Press 1960).
5. Garner, "The Council on Tribunals", 1965 Public Law 321.
6. Hanuman Prasad, "A Comparative Approach to the Problem of Tribunals in India and in England", (1980) 12 Lawyer 129.
7. Hari Sharan Saxena, "Notes and Comments: Tribunals and Natural Justice Principles", 38 JILI (1996) 348.

8. J.A. Farmer, *Tribunals and Government* (Weidenfeld and Nicolson 1974).
9. J.A.G. Griffith, "Tribunals and Inquiries", (1959) 22 MLR 125.
10. P. Leelakrishnan, "Reviewing Decisions of Administrative Tribunal: Paternalistic Approach of the Indian Supreme Court and Need for Institutional Reforms", 54 JILI (2012) 1.
11. Peter Cane, *Administrative Tribunals and Adjudication* (Hart Publication 2009).
12. Peter Cane, "Judicial Review in Age of Tribunals", (2009) PL 479.
13. Pratik Datta, "Towards a Tribunal Services Agency", (2015) 8 NUJS L Rev 181.
14. R.S.W. Pollard, *Administrative Tribunals at Work: A Symposium* (Stevens 1950).
15. "Report of the Committee on Administrative Tribunals and Enquiries (The Franks Committee)", (1957) Cmnd 218.
16. S.N. Jain, *Administrative Tribunals in India: Existing and Proposed* (Indian Law Institute, New Delhi 1977).
17. Schwartz, "Memorandum to the Committee on Administrative Tribunals and Enquiries", (1957) 35 CBR 743.
18. Simon, "Administrative Tribunals and the Rule of Law", (1954) I British Journal of Administrative Law 1–19.
19. Wraith and Hutchesson, *Administrative Tribunals* (1973).

CHAPTER 7

Practice and Procedure of Administrative Adjudication: Rules of Natural Justice

Any skeptic may argue that the expression "natural justice" is misleading because there is nothing "natural" about "justice" which is a matter of perception and even otherwise. There is very little justice in nature which is based on the principle "survival of the fittest", *i.e.* strong will prevail over the weak. Nevertheless, "natural" about justice is that it refers to certain pre-existing, immutable, universal principles which when observed bring fairness and reasonableness in administrative adjudicatory process, making it possible even for the weak to prevail over the strong.

Principles of natural justice which are judge-made rules and still continue to be a classical example of judicial activism were developed by the courts to prevent accidents in the exercise of outsourced power of adjudication entrusted to the administrative authorities.

In India there is no statute laying down the minimum procedure which administrative agencies must follow while exercising decision-making powers. There is, therefore, a bewildering variety of administrative procedure. Sometimes the statute under which the administrative agency exercises power lays down the procedure which the administrative agency must follow,[1] but at times the administrative agency is left free to devise its own procedure.[2] However, courts have always insisted that the administrative agencies must follow a minimum of fair procedure. This minimum fair procedure refers to the principles of natural justice.

1. PRINCIPLES OF NATURAL JUSTICE

Rules of natural justice have developed with the growth of civilisation, and the content thereof is often considered as a proper measure of the level of civilisation and rule of law prevailing in the community.[3] In order to protect himself against the excesses of organised power, man has always appealed to someone beyond his own creation. Such someone could only be God and

1. S. 5(A), Land Acquisition Act, 1894.
2. S. 33, Indian Medical Council Act, 1956.
3. *K.I. Shephard* v. *Union of India*, (1987) 4 SCC 431, 448, *per* R.N. Misra J.

His laws, divine law or natural law, to which all temporal laws and actions must conform. This is the origin of the concept of natural justice. However, natural justice is not justice of the nature where the lion devours the lamb and the tiger feeds upon the antelope. Natural justice is of the "higher law of nature" or "natural law" where the lion and lamb lie down together and the tiger frisks with the antelope.[4] Thus, natural justice implies fairness, reasonableness, equity and equality. Natural justice is a concept of common law, and it is the common-law world counterpart of the American "due process" and civil law "proportionality". Natural justice represents higher procedural principles developed by judges which every administrative agency must follow when taking any decision adversely affecting the rights of a private individual.

Natural justice is another name for common-sense justice and is based on the natural sense of man of what is right and what is wrong[5]. Natural justice is not an articulation of any saint or sage. Natural law has inherent rationality which is in conformity with natural justice and may lead to all right conclusions. Application of the principles of natural justice can improve the quality of administrative decision, enforce rule of law and accountability in the administration and show respect for human dignity. Thus, the basis of all positive law is natural justice. Rules of natural justice are not codified canons. They are principles ingrained in the conscience of man. Justice is based substantially on natural ideals and values which are universal. Natural justice is not circumscribed by linguistic technicalities and grammatical niceties or logical prevarication. It supplies the omission of a formulated law. It is the substance of justice which has to determine its form. What particular form of natural justice should be implied and what its extent should be in a given case must depend to a great extent on the facts and circumstances of that case and the framework of the statute under which an action is taken.[6] The expressions "natural justice" and "legal justice" do not present a watertight classification. It is the substance of justice which is to be secured by both, and whenever legal justice fails to achieve this purpose, natural justice is called in aid of legal justice.[7]

1.1 Early instances

For centuries courts have recognised breach of natural justice as a ground of judicial review of an administrative action. The earliest instance is *Bonham's case*[8] (1610) where the court quashed the decision of the administrative authority on the ground that law which provided that authority

4. *Union of India* v. *Tulsiram Patel*, (1985) 3 SCC 398, 464. See also, *Ravi S. Naik* v. *Union of India*, 1994 Supp (2) SCC 641; *Maharashtra State Financial Corpn.* v. *Suvarna Board Mills*, (1994) 5 SCC 566.
5. See generally, *Dharampal Satyapal Ltd.* v. *CCE*, (2015) 8 SCC 519.
6. See, *Canara Bank* v. *Debasis Das*, (2003) 4 SCC 557.
7. *Ibid*, 570.
8. (1610) 8 Co Rep 107: 77 ER 638.

can impose fine in exercise of its discretion and can keep half of the fine imposed for its own use violates the principle of natural justice (bias) which militates against impartiality of the authority in deciding the amount of fine. In the *Bagg's case*[9] (1615) the court applied the principle of fair hearing in a situation where a person was disenfranchised without hearing. In *Bentley's case*[10] (1748) the court applied the principles of natural justice in a case where Cambridge University cancelled the degree of the petitioner without hearing. In *Cooper* v. *Wandsworth Board of Works*[11] (1863), the court quashed the decision of the Board to pull down the house of the plaintiff without hearing on the ground that he did not give statutory prior notice before undertaking construction even though the law did not provide for hearing. The court observed that no one can be deprived of his property without hearing even where the law did not provide for such a hearing. The court emphasised that in such cases common law of "fairness" will fill the deficiency of statutory law. In *Board of Education* v. *Rice*[12] (1911), the court observed that it is implied in every decision of the Board that it must first ascertain law and facts in good faith and listen fairly to both sides because it is the duty of every one under common law who decides anything. After these initial promising beginnings, except for a period where the court lost its track due to administrative and quasi-judicial controversy, courts always enforce common law concept of "fairness" against every one who is under a duty to decide anything even though the statutory law did not provide for it.

During the period of Reformation, the forces of secularism repudiating the formulae, characteristic of medieval thought with universal application, now concentrated on individual phenomenon, and indulged in a more specialised type of enquiry into specific problems. Side by side with the particularisation, a need was equally felt for evolving a new and secularised type of universalism known as the "Enlightenment". Man in relation to his environment (nature) had certain basic problems which differed in degree and dimension. A systematic pattern of ideas and values had to be evolved out of the doctrine of natural law for universal application and acceptance. This juristic humanitarianism with its universal approach led to the development of the principles of natural justice. Thus, dogmatic approach to problems of the Dark Ages gave way to a more particularised approach to problems during Reformation and to a more specialised enquiry into a specific problem. This led to individualisation of justice. In the course of time, systematic patterns developed out of this particularisation led to the development of general principles for universal application, which came to be known as the principles of natural justice. Earliest expression of "natural justice" could be found in philosophical expressions of Roman jurists (*jus*

9. (1615) 11 Co Rep 95b: 77 ER 1271.
10. *R.* v. *Chancellor of Cambridge, ex p Bentley*, (1748) 2 Ld Raym 1334.
11. (1863) 14 CBNS 180: (1863) 143 ER 414.
12. 1911 AC 179 (HL).

naturale) and signified rules and principles for the conduct of man, which were independent of enacted law or customs and could be discovered by the rational intelligence of man and would grow out of and conform to his nature—which meant the whole mental, moral and physical constitution of man.[13] The basis of the principles of natural justice is rule of law. The observance of these principles is demanded by our sense of justice to which the total system of governance must conform.

Natural justice has meant many things to many writers, lawyers and systems of law. It is used interchangeably with divine law, *jus gentium*, the common law of England, "due process" of the US, "dharma" of India, and "proportionality" of the civil-law system. Its roots can also be traced to African customary law where there is a yorba saying, "Wicked and inequitous is he who decides a case upon a testimony of only one party to it." It is a concept of changing content. However, this does not mean that at a given time, no fixed principles of natural justice can be identified. The principles of natural justice through various decisions of courts can be easily ascertained, though their application in a given situation may depend on multifarious factors. For fairness itself, it is a flexible, pragmatic and relative concept, not a rigid, ritualistic or sophisticated abstraction. It is not a bull in a china shop or a bee in one's bonnet.[14] Often the concept of natural justice is criticised as being an unruly horse. Replying to the criticism, Lord Denning said, "with a good man in the saddle, the unruly horse can be kept under control. It can jump over obstacles. It can leap fences put up by fictions and come down on the other side of justice"[15]. Natural justice contents yield to change with exigencies of different situations and, therefore, do not apply in the same manner to situations which are not alike. They are neither cast in a rigid mould nor can they be put in a legal straitjacket. They are not immutable and can be adapted, modified, and excluded by statute, rules or the Constitution; except where such exclusion is not charged with the vice of unreasonableness and consequential voidness.[16]

Indeed, natural justice is a pervasive facet of secular law where a spiritual touch enlivens legislation, administration and adjudication to make fairness a creed of life. It has many colours and shades, many forms and shapes, and save where valid law excludes it, applies when people are adversely affected by acts of any administrative authority. It is the bane of a healthy government, recognised from earliest times and not a mystic testament of a judge-made law. Indeed, from the legendary days of Adam and *Kautilya's*

---

13. *Black's Law Dictionary* cited in *Union of India* v. *Tulsiram Patel*, (1985) 3 SCC 398, 463–65.
14. Krishna Iyer J in *Mohinder Singh Gill* v. *Chief Election Commr.*, (1978) 1 SCC 405, 434. See also, *Dharampal Satyapal Ltd.* v. *CCE*, (2015) 8 SCC 519.
15. *Enderby Town Football Club Ltd.* v. *Football Assn. Ltd.*, 1971 Ch 591, 606: (1970) 3 WLR 1021 (CA).
16. *Satyavir Singh* v. *Union of India*, (1985) 4 SCC 252. See also, *Ravi S. Naik* v. *Union of India*, 1994 Supp (2) SCC 641; *Jamaat-E-Islami Hind* v. *Union of India*, (1995) 1 SCC 428; *Shiv Sagar Tiwari* v. *Union of India*, (1997) 1 SCC 444.

Arthashastra, the rule of law has had this stamp of natural justice which makes it social justice.

The principles of natural justice have enriched law and constitutions the world over. Though the Indian Constitution does not use the expression natural justice, the concept of natural justice divested of all its metaphysical and theological trappings pervades the whole scheme of the Constitution. The concept of social and economic justice, in the Preamble of the Constitution, conceptually speaking, is the concept of fairness in social and economic activities of society, which is the basis of the principles of natural justice. Article 311 contains all the principles of natural justice without using the expression as such. The duty to act fairly is part of fair procedure, envisaged under Articles 14 and 21 of the Constitution. Every activity of a public authority or those under public duty or obligation must be informed by reason and guided by public interest.[17] Exercise of jurisdiction by courts in India, in this behalf, is not something extra-constitutional. Now the principles of natural justice are firmly grounded in Articles 14 and 21 of the Constitution. With the introduction of the concept of substantive and procedural due process in Article 21 of the Constitution, all that fairness which is included in the principles of natural justice can be read into Article 21 when a person is deprived of his life and personal liberty. In other areas, it is Article 14 which now incorporates the principles of natural justice. Article 14 now applies not only to discriminatory class legislation but also to arbitrary or discriminatory State action. Because violation of natural justice results in arbitrariness, therefore, violation of natural justice is violation of the equality clause of Article 14. This all suggests that now the principles of natural justice are grounded in the Constitution.[18] Therefore, the principles of natural justice cannot be wholly disregarded by law because this would violate the fundamental rights guaranteed by Articles 14 and 21 of the Constitution. It was for this reason that the Supreme Court barely saved Section 314 of the Bombay Municipal Corporation Act, 1888 which empowered the Commissioner to get illegal constructions and structures removed or demolished without notice by holding that Section 314 does not contain a command, and only gives a discretion to the Commissioner which must be reasonably exercised.[19] In *State of U.P.* v. *Vijay Kumar Tripathi*[20], the Supreme Court further held that the principles of natural justice must be read into the provision of a law. Such a course is necessary where the rule excludes, either expressly or by necessary implication, the application of the principles of natural justice. In the same manner in *Saij Gram Panchayat* v. *State of Gujarat*[21], where the government had transferred Panchayat area

17. *LIC* v. *Consumer Education and Research Centre*, (1995) 5 SCC 482, 500.
18. *Satyavir Singh* v. *Union of India*, (1985) 4 SCC 252. See also, *State of Maharashtra* v. *Kamal Sukumar Durgule*, (1985) 1 SCC 234; *Dev Dutta* v. *Union of India*, (2008) 8 SCC 725.
19. *Olga Tellis* v. *Bombay Municipal Corpn.*, (1985) 3 SCC 545.
20. 1995 Supp (1) SCC 552.
21. (1999) 2 SCC 366. See also, *Piara Singh* v. *State of Punjab*, (2000) 5 SCC 765.

as a notified area, the court held that though the law did not provide for hearing before transfer of land, yet denial of such opportunity is not in consonance with the scheme of law governing our society. The validity of the law that excludes the principles of natural justice becomes suspect. The principles of natural justice are not violated where the opportunity of being heard was afforded but not utilised.[22]

In *H.L. Trehan* v. *Union of India*[23] (*H.L. Trehan*), the Supreme Court made it absolutely explicit that even when the authority has statutory power to take action without hearing, it would be arbitrary to take action without hearing and, thus, violative of Article 14 of the Constitution. In the same manner in *D.K. Yadav* v. *J.M.A. Industries Ltd.*[24], the Supreme Court further held that even where statutory standing orders empowered the management to terminate the services of an employee, who overstayed the leave period, without hearing, the termination of services would be violative of Article 21 of the Constitution, as such a procedure established by law which deprives a person of his livelihood cannot be said to be just, fair and reasonable under Article 21 of the Constitution.

Moving with the same strides, the Supreme Court in *SBI* v. *K.P. Narayanan Kutty*[25], following its earlier decision,[26] held that the principles of natural justice have to be read into the relevant service rule [R. 50(3)(*ii*), State Bank of India (Supervisory Staff) Service Rules]. In this case, the enquiry officer had found certain charges against an officer of the Bank as partly proved. The disciplinary authority holding that charges were proved, in fact fully proved, passed the order of dismissal which was challenged. It was contended that Rule 50(3)(*ii*) of the State Bank of India (Supervisory Staff) Service Rules does not provide for any notice and hearing, hence the action cannot be challenged on the ground of violation of the principles of natural justice. The Supreme Court held that the principles of natural justice must be read into the service rules and the officer must be given an opportunity to persuade the disciplinary authority to accept the favourable conclusion of the enquiry officer. In the same manner, in *Industrial Infrastructure Development Corpn. (Gwalior) M.P. Ltd.* v. *CIT*[27], the court opined that where the law requires that an authority must make enquiry or when the authority is required to act according to rules and regulations, the action of the authority shall require application of the principles of natural justice.

Situations in which principles of natural justice are attracted.—Principles of natural justice are attracted whenever a person suffers a civil consequence, or a prejudice is caused to him by any administrative action. Civil

22. *Nagar Palika, Nataur* v. *U.P. Public Services Tribunal*, (1998) 2 SCC 400.
23. (1989) 1 SCC 764.
24. (1993) 3 SCC 259.
25. (2003) 2 SCC 449.
26. *Punjab National Bank* v. *Kunj Behari Misra*, (1998) 7 SCC 84.
27. (2018) 4 SCC 494; see also, *K.S.B. Ali* v. *State of A.P.*, (2018) 11 SCC 277.

consequences means infraction of personal or property rights, violation of civil liberties, material deprivation or sufferance of non-pecuniary damages. Loss of legitimate expectation may also attract the principles of natural justice. Thus, where a person cannot justify his claim on the basis of any law but suffer a prejudice or adverse consequences, he is entitled to the benefit of the principles of natural justice. Therefore, in comprehensive connotation, every administrative action that causes a prejudice, or harm, or adverse consequences in his civil life, inflicts civil consequences. In *Tejshree Ghag* v. *Prakash Parashuram Patil*[28], the Supreme Court exemplified that where an employee is transferred to a non-equivalent post resulting in loss of pay, he suffers a civil consequence as his status and salary are adversely affected, hence the principles of natural justice are attracted. In the same manner when on the basis of noting on file, a High Court has passed adverse remarks against a Chief Minister that allotment of land had his blessings, the Supreme Court expunged the remarks because principles of natural justice had been violated.[29] In *Dev Dutta* v. *Union of India*[30] (*Dev Dutta*), the Supreme Court held that though office rule provides for communication of an "adverse entry" in the confidential report, yet even "good entry" is also to be communicated if it eliminates a person from promotion. Natural justice which is a facet of Article 14 of the Constitution overrides all contrary rules.[31] In conclusion, it is now settled that mere breach of the principles of natural justice is not sufficient for judicial intervention unless such breach also entails avoidable prejudice caused to the person. Nevertheless, the applicability of the principles of natural justice is not dependent on any statutory provisions. Wherever a prejudice is caused the principles are necessarily attracted.[32]

Thus in any event when civil consequences ensue, there is hardly any distinction between an administrative order and a quasi-judicial order,[33] and principles of natural justice are attracted in both the situations. In other words, principles of natural justice are attracted where there is some right which is likely to be affected by any act of the administration, including a legitimate expectation.[34]

For some three or four hundred years, Anglo-American courts have actively applied two principles of natural justice. However, this reduction of the concept of natural justice to only two principles should not be allowed to obscure the fact that natural justice goes to "the very kernel of the problem of administrative justice"[35]. These two principles are:

28. (2007) 6 SCC 220.
29. *State of Maharashtra* v. *Public Concern for Governance Trust*, (2007) 3 SCC 587.
30. (2008) 8 SCC 725.
31. *Ibid.*
32. *SEBI* v. *Akshya Infrastructure (P) Ltd.*, (2014) 11 SCC 112. See also, *Dharampal Satyapal Ltd.* v. *CCE*, (2015) 8 SCC 519.
33. *Rajesh Kumar* v. *CIT*, (2007) 2 SCC 181.
34. *Ashoka Smokeless Coal India (P) Ltd.* v. *Union of India*, (2007) 2 SCC 640.
35. H.W.R. Wade, *Administrative Law* (1967) 154.

(1) *Nemo in propria causa judex, esse debet.*—No one should be made a judge in his own cause, or the rule against bias.
(2) *Audi alteram partem.*—Hear the other party, or the rule of fair hearing, or the rule that no one should be condemned unheard.

To these two principles now transparency and good-governance may be added as a new dimension which includes the duty to pass a speaking order.[36]

These principles will now be discussed in detail because they provide the foundation on which the whole superstructure of judicial control of administrative action is based.

1.2 Rule against bias

"Bias" means an operative prejudice, whether conscious or unconscious, in relation to a party or issue. Such operative prejudice may be the result of a preconceived opinion or a predisposition or a predetermination to decide a case in a particular manner, so much so that it does not leave the mind open. In other words, "bias" may be generally defined as partiality or preference which is not founded on reason and is actuated by self-interest—whether pecuniary or personal.[37] Therefore, the rule against bias strikes against those factors which may improperly influence a judge in arriving at a decision in any particular case. The requirement of this principle is that the judge must be impartial and must decide the case objectively on the basis of the evidence on record. The dictionary meaning of the word "bias" also suggests "anything which tends or may be regarded as tending to cause such a person to decide a case otherwise on evidence must be held to be biased". In other words, a predisposition to decide for or against one party without regard to the merit of the case is "bias". Therefore, if a person, for whatever reason, cannot take an objective decision on the basis of evidence on record, he shall be said to be biased. A person cannot take an objective decision in a case in which he has an interest, for, as human psychology tells us, very rarely can people take decisions against their own interests. Therefore the maxim that a person cannot be made a judge in his own cause. The Supreme Court in *Crawford Bayley & Co.* v. *Union of India*[38] restated that the doctrine of rule against bias comes into play if it is shown that the officer concerned has a personal connection or personal interest or has personally acted in the matter concerned and/or has already taken a decision one way or the other which he may be interested in supporting. This rule of disqualification is applied not only to avoid the possibility of a partial decision but also to ensure public confidence in the impartiality of the administrative adjudicatory process because not only must "no man

36. *Haryana Financial Corpn.* v. *Kailash Chandra Ahuja*, (2008) 9 SCC 31. See also, *Dharampal Satyapal Ltd.* v. *CCE*, (2015) 8 SCC 519.
37. *G.N. Nayak* v. *Goa University*, (2002) 2 SCC 712.
38. (2006) 6 SCC 25.

be a judge in his own cause" but also "justice should not only be done but should manifestly and undoubtedly be seen to be done"[39]. The minimal requirement of natural justice is that the authority must be composed of impartial persons acting fairly, without prejudice and bias. In this manner impartiality, objectivity and public confidence provide the foundation on which the superstructure of the rule against bias is built. A decision which is a result of bias is a nullity and the trial is "coram non judice"[40]. Inference of bias, therefore, can be drawn only on the basis of factual matrix and not merely on the basis of insinuations, conjectures and surmises.[41] Bias cannot be presumed, it must be proved from facts of the case.[42]

The principle *nemo judex in causa sua* will not apply where the authority has no personal *lis* with the person concerned. Therefore, where cases of malpractice and pilferage by consumers of electricity were decided by the Electricity Board itself, the Supreme Court held that it is not a violation of the rule against bias. Such cases are similar to income tax and sales tax cases.[43]

In the same manner, every kind of preference is not sufficient to vitiate an administrative action. If a preference is rational and unaccompanied by considerations of personal interest, pecuniary or otherwise, it would not vitiate a decision. Therefore, if a senior officer expresses appreciation of the work of a junior in the confidential report, it would not amount to bias nor would it preclude the officer from being part of the Departmental Promotion Committee to consider such junior officer along with others for promotion.[44]

Bias manifests itself variously and may affect a decision in a variety of ways. However, mere passing of an ex parte order by the administrative authority which is adverse to the party does not constitute a bias unless other adequate and substantial evidence are brought on record.[45]

1.2.1 *Personal bias*

Personal bias arises from a certain relationship equation between the deciding authority and the parties which incline him unfavourably or otherwise on the side of one of the parties before him. Such equation may develop out of varied forms of personal or professional hostility or friendship. However, no exhaustive list is possible.[46]

---

39. *Per* Lord Hewart CJ in *R.* v. *Sussex Justices, ex p McCarthy*, (1924) 1 KB 256, 259.
40. *Ranjit Thakur* v. *Union of India*, (1987) 4 SCC 611.
41. *M. Sankaranarayanan* v. *State of Karnataka*, (1993) 1 SCC 54. See also, *Crawford Bayley & Co.* v. *Union of India*, (2006) 6 SCC 25.
42. *D.C. Aggarwal* v. *SBI*, (2006) 5 SCC 153.
43. *Hyderabad Vanaspathi Ltd.* v. *A.P. SEB*, (1998) 4 SCC 470.
44. *G.N. Nayak* v. *Goa University*, (2002) 2 SCC 712.
45. *Manish S. Pardasani* v. *State Excise*, (2019) 2 SCC 660.
46. *Meenglas Tea Estate* v. *Workmen*, AIR 1963 SC 1719. The Supreme Court held that the Manager cannot conduct an enquiry against a worker arising from the allegation that he had beaten the Manager. In *D.K. Khanna* v. *Union of India*, 1972 SCC OnLine HP 22: AIR 1973

Mineral Development Corpn. Ltd. v. *State of Bihar*[47] is a typical case of personal bias. In this case, the petitioners were granted mining licence for 99 years in 1947. But in 1953, the Secretary of the Revenue Board sent a notice to the petitioners to show cause within 15 days why the licence should not be cancelled for violations of Sections 10, 12 and 14 of the Mining Act, 1952. The petitioners submitted a written reply denying the allegations. Two years later, the government issued a notification cancelling the licence. The action of the government was challenged on the ground of personal bias. The facts relevant to personal bias before the court were

(1) that Raja Kamakhya Narain Singh, the owner of the Mineral Development Corporation Ltd., had opposed the Minister in the General Election of 1952; and
(2) that the Minister had filed a criminal case under Section 500 of the Penal Code, 1860 against the petitioner which was transferred by the Bihar High Court to Delhi on the ground of political rivalry between the parties.

The court quashed the order of the government, among other grounds, on the ground of personal bias.[48]

Similarly, in *S.P. Kapoor* v. *State of H.P.*[49] (*S.P. Kapoor*), the Supreme Court quashed the selection list prepared by the Departmental Promotion Committee which had considered the confidential reports of candidates prepared by an officer who himself was a candidate for promotion. Again, in *Baidyanath Mahapatra* v. *State of Orissa*[50], the Supreme Court quashed the order of the tribunal confirming premature retirement on the ground that the Chairman of the tribunal was also a member of the review committee which had recommended premature retirement. However, in *M.V. Thimmaiah* v. *UPSC*[51], the Supreme Court cautioned that as a plea of mala fide, favouritism and colourable exercise of power is generally raised by interested party, the court should not draw conclusions unless allegations are substantiated beyond doubt.

Real likelihood of bias/reasonable suspicion of bias.—However, in order to challenge an administrative action successfully on the ground of

HP 30, the High Court quashed the selection of the candidate where his son-in-law was the member of the selection committee.

47. AIR 1960 SC 468.
48. Other typical cases of personal bias are:
(1) *Meenglas Tea Estate* v. *Workmen*, AIR 1963 SC 1719, Manager conducts enquiry against workman who is alleged to have assaulted him.
(2) *Ramjag Singh* v. *State of Bihar*, 1957 SCC OnLine Pat 218: AIR 1958 Pat 7, Gram Panchayat sits as an appellate court against its own conviction.
(3) *A.K. Kraipak* v. *Union of India*, (1969) 2 SCC 262, candidate for selection is himself a member of the selection board.
49. (1981) 4 SCC 716.
50. (1989) 4 SCC 664. See also, *Rattan Lal Sharma* v. *Hari Ram (Co-Education) Higher Secondary School*, (1993) 4 SCC 10. A witness was also a member of the enquiry committee.
51. (2008) 2 SCC 119.

personal bias, it is essential to prove that there is a "reasonable suspicion of bias"[52] or a "real likelihood of bias". The "reasonable suspicion" test looks mainly to outward appearance, and the "real likelihood" test focuses on the court's own evaluation of possibilities. However, in practice, the tests have much in common with one another and in the vast majority of cases, they will lead to the same result. In this area of bias the real question is not whether a person was biased. It is difficult to prove the state of mind of a person. Therefore, what the courts see is whether there is reasonable ground for believing that the deciding officer was likely to have been biased. In deciding the question of bias, judges have to take into consideration the human possibilities and the ordinary course of human conduct.[53] But, there must be real likelihood of bias and not mere suspicion of bias before the proceedings can be quashed on the ground that the person conducting the proceedings is disqualified by bias. The apprehension must be judged from a healthy, reasonable and average point of view and not on mere apprehension and vague suspicion of whimsical, capricious and unreasonable people.[54] In the same manner passing of an ex parte interim stay order shall not by itself amount to real likelihood of bias unless founded on substantial material.[55] Therefore, in *Jiwan K. Lohia* v. *Durga Dutt Lohia*[56], upholding the decision of the High Court while removing an arbitrator appointed by the court on the ground of bias, the Supreme Court observed that with regard to bias the test to be applied is not whether in fact bias has affected the judgment but whether a litigant could reasonably apprehend that a bias attributable might have operated against him in the final decision. The test of bias is whether a reasonable man, in possession of relevant information, would have thought that the bias was likely and whether the person concerned "was likely to be disposed to decide the matter only in a particular way".

Therefore, the real test of "real likelihood of bias" is whether a reasonable man, in possession of relevant information, would have thought that bias was likely and whether the authority concerned was likely to be disposed to decide the matter in a particular way. What is relevant is the reasonableness of the apprehension in that regard in the mind of the party. Hence the proper approach in case of bias for the court is not to look into his own mind and ask "Am I biased?", but to look into the mind of the party before it.[57] The court must look at the impression which would be given to the other party. Therefore, the test is not what actually happened but the substantial possibility of that which appeared to have happened.

52. *Metropolitan Properties Co. (FGC) Ltd.* v. *Lannon*, (1969) 1 QB 577: (1968) 3 WLR 694 (CA).
53. *S.N. Jodhawat* v. *University of Jodhpur*, ILR (1981) 31 Raj 137. See also, *G.N. Nayak* v. *Goa University*, (2002) 2 SCC 712.
54. *B.B. Rajwanshi* v. *State of U.P.*, (1988) 2 SCC 415.
55. *Manish S. Pardasani* v. *State Excise*, (2019) 2 SCC 660.
56. (1992) 1 SCC 56.
57. *Ranjit Thakur* v. *Union of India*, (1987) 4 SCC 611.

Even if the deciding officer was as impartial as could be, nevertheless if right-minded persons would think that, in the circumstances, there was a real likelihood of bias, the deciding officer is disqualified. Therefore, the court would not enquire whether there was bias in fact if reasonable people might think that there was a bias. The reason is plain enough, writes Lord Denning, "Justice must be rooted in confidence; and confidence is destroyed when right-minded people go away thinking: 'The judge was biased'."[58] It was on this ground that in *Metropolitan Properties Co. (FGC) Ltd.* v. *Lannon*[59], the court held that Lannon was disqualified from sitting as Chairman of a Rent Assessment Committee because his father was a tenant who had a case pending against that Company, even though it was acknowledged that there was no actual bias and no want of good faith on the part of Lannon. However, if the bias of a person is inconsequential, the administrative action is not vitiated. In *Ramanand Prasad Singh* v. *Union of India*[60], the Supreme Court held that participation in the selection committee as a member where his brother was a candidate but was not selected is inconsequential bias on which the whole select list cannot be quashed. In the same manner in *Jasvinder Singh* v. *State of J&K*[61], the Supreme Court held that in the absence of any specific allegation of bias against the selection board or any member thereof, awarding of higher percentage of marks to those who got lower marks in a written examination would not vitiate selection, especially, when there were only a few negligible instances and there was no conscious effort to bring some candidates within the selection zone. In *Federation of Railway Officers Assn.* v. *Union of India*[62], the court further held that allegation of bias on imaginary basis cannot be sustained. In this case, a study group had recommended for formation of new railway zones after considering all factors relevant to the efficient functioning of Railway, none of which was irrelevant. The Association had challenged it on the ground that the report was prepared under pressure from a Minister to suit his whims.

No uniform cut and dried formula can be laid down to determine real likelihood of bias. Each case is to be determined on the basis of its facts and circumstance. Therefore, if on the basis of facts and surrounding circumstances necessary conclusion is that there is a real danger of bias and not merely an apprehension of bias, administrative action shall stand vitiated. It is an inward looking criteria. In *Charanjit Singh* v. *Harinder Sharma*[63], the court held that there is a real likelihood of bias when in a small place there is a relationship between selectees and members of the selection committee. Therefore, in order to sustain people's confidence in

58. Lord Denning, *The Discipline of Law* (1982) 87.
59. (1969) 1 QB 577: (1968) 3 WLR 694 (CA).
60. (1996) 4 SCC 64.
61. (2003) 2 SCC 132.
62. (2003) 4 SCC 289.
63. (2002) 9 SCC 732.

the administrative justice, it is desirable that even the slightest apprehension of bias be removed because it would be the worst day for administrative justice if a person leaves the chamber of an administrative authority feeling that the authority was biased. It is for this reason that the Supreme Court in *D.C. Aggarwal* v. *SBI*[64] directed that the interview committee, in which certain members were those who had been impleaded as respondents in a litigation by the appellant, be reconstituted and the case of his promotion be considered afresh. However, when the reconstituted committee again rejected his claim for promotion on the ground of poor performance, the court held that there is no presumption of bias and it cannot be presumed that all top ranking officers would conspire to deny appellant his right. Frustration of departmental enquiries on mere technical grounds has not found favour with the courts. Therefore courts in India and England have developed the doctrine of de facto prejudice, wherein if there is violation of a rule which is directory, the element of de facto prejudice must be shown. It will not be permissible to challenge administrative action merely on the basis of apprehension of prejudice. In *Union of India* v. *Alok Kumar*[65], the court did not quash departmental enquiry merely on the ground that enquiry officer was a retired railway officer. A few cases in this connection may be noted by way of illustrations.

1.2.1.1 *Manak Lal* v. *Prem Chand Singhvi*[66]

In order to decide a complaint for professional misconduct filed by Dr Prem Chand against Manak Lal, an advocate of the Rajasthan High Court, the High Court appointed a tribunal consisting of a senior advocate, once Advocate General of Rajasthan, as Chairman. The decision of the tribunal was challenged on the ground of personal bias arising from the fact that the Chairman had represented Dr Prem Chand in an earlier case. The Supreme Court refused to quash the action holding that the Chairman had no personal contact with his client and did not remember that he appeared on his behalf, and that, therefore, there seemed to be no "real likelihood of bias". However, the high professional standards led the court to quash the action in the final analysis on the ground that justice should not only be done but must appear to have been done.

1.2.1.2 *State of U.P.* v. *Mohd. Nooh*[67]

In this case, a Deputy Superintendent of Police was appointed to conduct a departmental enquiry against a police constable. In order to contradict the testimony of a witness, the presiding officer offered himself as witness. The

64. (2006) 5 SCC 153.
65. (2010) 5 SCC 349.
66. AIR 1957 SC 425.
67. AIR 1958 SC 86.

Supreme Court quashed the administrative action on the ground that when the presiding officer himself becomes a witness, there is certainly a "real likelihood of bias" against the constable.

1.2.1.3 *A.K. Kraipak* v. *Union of India*[68] *(Kraipak)*

In this case, Naqishbund, who was the Acting Chief Conservator of Forests, was a member of the selection board and also a candidate for selection to the All-India cadre of the Forest Service. Though he did not take part in the deliberations of the board when his name was considered and approved, the Supreme Court held that there was a real likelihood of bias, for the mere presence of the candidate on the selection board may adversely influence the judgment of the other member.

1.2.1.4 *J. Mohapatra and Company* v. *State of Orissa*[69] *(J. Mohapatra)*

In this case, the State of Orissa had constituted an assessment committee in order to recommend and select books of various authors and publishers on various school subjects. Some of the persons whose books were in the selection list were members of the assessment committee. The meeting of the committee was held. In this meeting when the books were being assessed, an individual member would withdraw when his book was taken up for consideration. However, that member participated in deliberations when books of other members were considered. The result was that the books of members of the assessment committee were accorded approval. The action of the government was challenged on the ground of bias. Quashing the action, the Supreme Court held that when some members whose books were in the list for selection were members of the assessment committee, there is every likelihood of bias. Actual bias is not material, but the possibility of such bias in all such cases. Therefore, the court concluded that withdrawal of persons is not sufficient because the element of *quid pro quo* with other members cannot be eliminated. It may be pointed out that the doctrine of necessity does not apply in this case.

1.2.1.5 *Ganga Bai Charities* v. *CIT*[70]

In this case, a lawyer while acting as special counsel for the Income Tax Department had given his opinion that the assessee trust was not entitled to tax exemption. Later on he was elevated as a judge of the High Court and seven years later heard and decided the same point, in a reference, against the trust. None of the parties brought this aspect before the judge

68. (1969) 2 SCC 262.
69. (1984) 4 SCC 103.
70. (1992) 3 SCC 690.

during hearing. On appeal, the Supreme Court rightly held that there was no real likelihood of bias as opinion had been given seven years ago and the judge may not have remembered the routine opinion given as a busy lawyer after a long lapse of time. However in *Fakruddin* v. *Consolidation Training Institute*[71], the Supreme Court held that when a judge who was formerly the lawyer of the client whose case he decides even after objection, there is a real likelihood of bias. In *R. Balakrishna Pillai* v. *State of Kerala*[72], moving away from its earlier perception, the Supreme Court held that where one of the judges was the opposing advocate in an enquiry commission proceeding against the appellant, it cannot be presumed that the judge is biased. The court observed that though the state of mind of the person who entertains an apprehension of bias is relevant, but that is not all. Apprehension must appear to the court as genuine, reasonable and justifiable.

A plea of bias can be raised against a judge also and in this connection, reference may be made to *Sheonandan Paswan* v. *State of Bihar*[73]. In this case, the Supreme Court held that withdrawal of criminal cases against the former Chief Minister of Bihar, Jagannath Misra, was valid. After the judgment was delivered, Baharul Islam J who was one of the judges who decided the case resigned only 46 days before his retirement to accept the Congress Party nomination for election and become a Minister. In a review petition, it was alleged that Islam J was biased when he held the withdrawal of criminal cases against Misra, who also belonged to the Congress Party, as valid. Though the petition was dismissed for technical reasons, yet fact remains that judicial bias is a justiciable issue.

However, it may be noted that if a party willingly and with full knowledge of the facts submits to the jurisdiction of an administrative body then it cannot, on being unsuccessful, raise the plea of bias.[74] An objection on the ground of bias must be taken immediately. Where a committee considered the inter se seniority of two batches of recruits—one of them contending that the wife of the head of the committee being also one of the recruits, seniority should not have been determined by the committee. The Supreme Court rejected the plea on the ground that such objection should have been taken at the time of constitution of the committee itself.[75]

1.2.1.6 *Tata Cellular* v. *Union of India*[76]

In this case, the tender for operating the Cellular Mobile Telephone Service in four metropolitan cities filed by the son of one of the members of the Tender Evaluation Committee had been accepted. This was challenged on the basis of personal bias. Applying the principle of necessity, as

71. (1995) 4 SCC 538.
72. (2000) 7 SCC 129.
73. (1983) 1 SCC 438.
74. *G. Sarana* v. *University of Lucknow*, (1976) 3 SCC 585.
75. *U.D. Lama* v. *State of Sikkim*, (1997) 1 SCC 111.
76. (1994) 6 SCC 651.

the involvement of the Director General of the Telecommunications and Telecom Authority was necessary in view of Section 3(6) of the Telegraph Act, 1885, the court held that the involvement of his father as a member of the Tender Evaluation Committee did not vitiate the selection on the ground of bias. It may be noted in this case that the Tender Evaluation Committee was only a recommendatory body and selection was based on merit through the normal procedure. Therefore, it is necessary to ascertain what role that person played in the decision-making against whom bias is alleged.

1.2.1.7 *G.N. Nayak* v. *Goa University*[77]

In this case, a senior officer expressed appreciation of the work of a junior officer in his confidential report. He was also a member of the Departmental Promotion Committee to consider such junior officer along with others for promotion. The committee recommended this junior officer for promotion which was challenged on the ground of personal bias actuated by an element of personal interest. The Supreme Court held that unless preference is unreasonable and is based on self-interest, it will not vitiate an administrative decision.

1.2.1.8 *Ghanshyam Upadhyay* v. *State of U.P.*[78]

In this case, there was a Commission of Inquiry against police encounter and prayer was made in the petition for replacing the Commission of Inquiry constituted by the State Government with an independent Special Investigation Team constituted by the Supreme Court only on the basis of a newspaper report alleging bias and conflict of interest. The plea was rejected and the Supreme Court held that the allegations of bias made against the members of the Commission merely on the basis of newspaper reports and nothing more are liable to be rejected outright as a newspaper item without any further proof is of no evidentiary value. The manner in which allegations of bias and conflict of interest were made against members of the Commission who were high dignitaries merely on the basis of a newspaper report was also disapproved.

1.2.1.9 *Manish S. Pardasani* v. *State Excise*[79]

In this case, the Supreme Court observed that real likelihood of bias is not established in the absence of adequate and substantial material. Passing of ex parte interim stay/adverse orders does not by itself amount to bias. The plea of "bias" has to be founded on substantial material qua the officer

77. (2002) 2 SCC 712.
78. (2020) 16 SCC 811.
79. (2019) 2 SCC 660.

concerned who acts in a quasi-judicial capacity and if the *lis* can be decided on other legal grounds, such plea should not be entertained. Further, every adverse order passed against a litigant is injurious to a losing party; however, that does not give him a right to attack the adverse order by attributing bias against the authority/court.

1.2.1.10 *Padma* v. *Hiralal Motilal Desarda*[80]

S was a Director in the Special Planning Authority, *viz.* the City and Industrial Development Corporation (CIDCO). The Authority allotted plots to three associations comprising family members or relatives of *S*. The Supreme Court quashed the allotments on the ground of bias holding that in such circumstances *S* ought to have, at least, very specifically informed CIDCO of his relationship with the associations, and CIDCO while dealing with them should be consciously aware of that fact.

1.2.1.11 *Mohd. Yunus Khan* v. *State of U.P.*[81] *(Yunus Khan)*

Disciplinary proceedings started against a constable for being late for parade. Authority which initiated proceedings also became a witness, accepted enquiry report and also imposed punishment of dismissal. It was held that the administrative action is in flagrant violation of rule against bias.

1.2.2 *Pecuniary bias*

Judicial approach is unanimous and decisive on the point that any financial interest, howsoever small it may be, would vitiate administrative action. The disqualification will not be avoided by non-participation of the biased member in the proceedings if he was present when the decision was reached.[82]

In *R.* v. *Hendon Rural Distt. Council, ex p Chorley*[83], the court in England quashed the decision of the Planning Commission where one of the members was an estate agent who was acting for the applicant to whom the permission was granted.

In *N.B. Jeejeebhoy* v. *Asstt. Collector*[84], the Chief Justice reconstituted the Bench when it was found that one of the members of the Bench was a member of the cooperative society for which the land had been acquired. The Madras High Court also quashed the decision of the Collector who in his capacity as the Chairman of the Regional Transport Authority had granted a permit in favour of a cooperative society of which he was also

80. (2002) 7 SCC 564.
81. (2010) 10 SCC 539.
82. *R.* v. *Hendon Rural Distt. Council, ex p Chorley*, (1933) 2 KB 696 (DC).
83. (1933) 2 KB 696 (DC).
84. AIR 1965 SC 1096.

the Chairman.[85] Similarly, the Andhra Pradesh High Court also quashed the order of the Regional Transport Authority where one of its members had issued a permit in his own favour.[86] The Supreme Court also in *J. Mohapatra*[87] quashed the decision of the Textbooks' Selection Committee because some of its members were also authors of the books which were considered for selection.

Reference may also be made to *R.* v. *Bow Street Metropolitan Stipendiary Magistrate, ex p Pinochet Ugarte* (*No.* 2)[88]. In this case, a petition was brought by Augusto Pinochet for reconsideration of the decision of the appellate committee which heard his appeal on the ground of bias. Pinochet was the dictator of Chile from 1973 to 1990. He is alleged to have committed crime against humanity including torture, murders and hostage taking, etc. He came to England in 1998 for medical treatment. Immediately thereafter, Garzon J of Spain issued an international warrant of his arrest, exercising jurisdiction under the principle of "universal jurisdiction" of international law for committing crime against humanity. Pursuant to the warrant, the Magistrate in England issued an arrest warrant for his arrest under the provisions of Extradition Act, 1989. Pinochet was arrested, however, the warrant was quashed by the Divisional Court of Queen's Bench Division, but at the same time court certified this case as a fit case for appeal on the ground of scope of immunity of a former Head of State in the UK. On appeal, the House of Lords vacated the decision of the Divisional Court. It is against this decision that this petition was brought for reconsideration of the decision on the ground that Lord Hoffmann, who was the member of the appellate committee, was biased. In order to prove bias, the petitioner raised three major points before the committee: 1) that the appellate committee allowed Amnesty International, which tries to secure the observance of human rights of the people world over and had criticised the crime against humanity committed during the Pinochet era in Chile, to become intervener in the case; 2) that Lord Hoffmann was the Director of the Amnesty International Charity; and 3) that the wife of Lord Hoffmann is also associated with the organisation in administrative capacity. On these facts, it was contended that though Lord Hoffmann may not be actually biased, but there is a real likelihood or danger of bias.

Laying down the law, the House of Lords opined that the rule against bias has two very similar but not identical implications:

(1) If a judge has financial or proprietary interest in the case, or is a party to the suit, he is automatically disqualified to act as a judge without investigation of a "real likelihood of bias" or "suspicion of bias" unless he makes a voluntary disclosure.

---

85. *Visakapatnam Coop. Motor Transport Ltd.* v. *G. Bangaruraju*, 1953 SCC OnLine Mad 20: AIR 1953 Mad 709.
86. 1955 SCC OnLine AP 113: AIR 1957 AP 739.
87. (1984) 4 SCC 103.
88. (2000) 1 AC 119: (1999) 2 WLR 272 (HL).

(2) If a judge has no financial or proprietary interest and is also not a party to case, but his conduct or behaviour give rise to a suspicion of bias, then there is no automatic disqualification unless a "real likelihood" is proved.

On this basis, the House of Lords ruled that this case falls in the first category and set aside the order.

In this age of free market economy where investment in shares is very common, should every hearing authority having slightest financial interest in the matter rescue himself? Considered opinion is that it would serve no public interest if the deciding officer rescues himself where he has no substantial pecuniary interest. Better option seems to be that deciding officer should disclose his interest to the parties and if the parties have no objection, he may hear the case.

1.2.3 *Subject-matter bias*

Those cases fall within this category where the deciding officer is directly, or otherwise, involved in the subject-matter of the case. Here again mere involvement would not vitiate the administrative action unless there is a real likelihood of bias.

In *R.* v. *Deal Justices, ex p Curling*[89], the Magistrate was not declared disqualified to try a case of cruelty to an animal on the ground that he was a member of the Royal Society for the Prevention of Cruelty to Animals, as this did not prove a real likelihood of bias.

Similarly, in *Murlidhar* v. *Kadam Singh*[90], the court refused to quash the decision of the Election Tribunal on the ground that the wife of the Chairman was a member of the Congress Party whose candidate the petitioner defeated. In the same manner, in *Sub-Committee on Judicial Accountability* v. *Union of India*[91] (*Judicial Accountability*), the court did not allow the challenge of bias against the Speaker for his actions under the Judges (Inquiry) Act, 1968 on the basis that he was affiliated to a particular political party. The court also sustained its decision on the ground of "necessity", as no other person could take a decision under the Act.

However, in *Gullapalli Nageswara Rao* v. *A.P. SRTC*[92] (*Nageswara Rao*), the Supreme Court quashed the decision of the Andhra Pradesh government, nationalising road transport, on the ground that the Secretary of the Transport Department who gave the hearing was interested in the subject-matter. It may be mentioned that in the US and England, predisposition in favour of a policy in the public interest is not considered as legal bias vitiating administrative action.

---

89. (1881) 45 LT 439 (DC).
90. 1954 SCC OnLine MP 103: AIR 1954 MB 111.
91. (1991) 4 SCC 699.
92. AIR 1959 SC 308.

1.2.4 *Departmental bias/institutional bias*

The problem of departmental bias is something which is inherent in the administrative process, and if not effectively checked, it may negate the very concept of fairness in administrative proceedings.

The question of departmental bias was considered by the Supreme Court in *Nageswara Rao*[93]. In this case, the petitioner challenged the order of the government nationalising road transport. One of the grounds for challenge was that the Secretary of the Transport Department who gave the hearing was biased, being the person who initiated the scheme and also being the head of the department, whose responsibility was to execute it. The court quashed the order on the ground that, under the circumstances, the Secretary was biased and, hence, no fair hearing could be expected.

Thereafter, the Act was amended and the function of hearing the objection was given over to the Minister concerned. The decision of the government was again challenged by *G. Nageswara Rao*[94] on the ground of departmental bias because the Minister was the head of the department concerned which initiated the scheme and was also ultimately responsible for its execution. However, on this occasion the Supreme Court rejected the challenge on the ground that the Minister was not a part of the department in the same manner as the Secretary was. The reasoning of the court is not very convincing perhaps because, as observed earlier, departmental bias is something which is inherent in the administrative process. In the US and England, the problem of departmental bias has been solved, to some extent, with the institution of hearing officers and inspectors.

The problem of departmental bias also arises in a different context—when the functions of a judge and prosecutor are combined in the same department. It is not uncommon to find that the same department which initiates a matter also decides it, therefore, at times, departmental fraternity and loyalty militates against the concept of fair hearing.

This problem came up before the Supreme Court in *Hari Khemu Gawali* v. *Dy. Commr. of Police*[95]. In this case, an externment order was challenged on the ground that since the police department which initiated the proceedings and the department which heard and decided the case were the same, the element of departmental bias vitiated administrative action. The court rejected the challenge on the ground that so long as the two functions (initiation and decision) were discharged by two separate officers, though they were affiliated to the same department, there was no bias.

The decision of the court may be correct in the ideal perspective, but it may not always prove wise in practice. It may be suggested that the technique of internal separation which is being followed in the US and England

---

93. *Ibid.*
94. *Gullapalli Nageswara Rao* v. *State of A.P.*, AIR 1959 SC 1376 [known as *Gullapalli case (II)*]. See also, *Prakash Chandra Sahu* v. *Orissa RTC*, 1979 SCC OnLine Ori 161: AIR 1980 Ori 122.
95. AIR 1956 SC 559.

can be profitably used in India if a certain amount of confidence is to be developed in the minds of the people in administrative decision-making.

In *Krishna Bus Service (P) Ltd.* v. *State of Haryana*[96], the Supreme Court, however, quashed the notification of the government which had conferred powers of a Deputy Superintendent of Police on the General Manager, Haryana Roadways in matters of inspection of vehicles on the ground of departmental bias. In this case, private bus operators had alleged that the General Manager of Haryana Roadways who was a rival in business in the State could not be expected to discharge his duties in a fair and reasonable manner and would be too lenient in inspecting the vehicles belonging to his own department. The reason for quashing the notification according to the Supreme Court was the conflict between the duty and the interest of the department and the consequential erosion of public confidence in administrative justice.

However, where there is no such conflict between duty and interest of the department, concept of institutional bias cannot be narrowly construed in view of compelling institutional constraints. Moving in this direction, the Supreme Court in *South Indian Cashew Factories Workers' Union* v. *Kerala State Cashew Development Corpn. Ltd.*[97] held that where findings of the enquiry officer were based on evidence and were not perverse, the mere fact that the enquiry was conducted by an officer of the management would not vitiate the enquiry. In this case, an enquiry had been conducted by the Assistant Personnel Manager of the Corporation. The Union raised an industrial dispute in which the Labour Court set aside the enquiry on the ground of institutional bias, as the enquiry officer was part of the institution and had also made certain unwarranted remarks against the employee. The Supreme Court, in appeal, rightly held that in the absence of any special individual bias attributable to a particular officer, presumption of institutional bias cannot be sustained merely on the ground that the enquiry officer is a part of the management.

1.2.5 *Policy notion bias*

Bias arising out of preconceived policy notions is a very delicate problem of administrative law. On one hand, no judge as a human being is expected to sit as a blank sheet of paper and on the other, preconceived policy notions may vitiate a fair trial.

A classic case bringing this problem to the forefront is *Franklin* v. *Minister of Town and Country Planning*[98] (*Franklin*), also known as the Stevenage case. In this case, the appellant challenged the Stevenage New Town Designation Order, 1946 on the ground that no fair hearing was

96. (1985) 3 SCC 711. See also, *Institute of Chartered Accountants of India* v. *L.K. Ratna*, (1986) 4 SCC 537.
97. (2006) 5 SCC 201.
98. 1948 AC 87 (HL).

given because the Minister had entertained bias in his determination which was clear from his speech at Stevenage when he said, "I want to carry out a daring exercise in town planning (jeers, catcalls, boos). It is no good your jeering! It is going to be done." Though the court did not accept the challenge on the technical ground that the Minister in confirming the report was not performing any quasi-judicial function, but the problem still remains that the bias arising from strong policy convictions may operate as a more serious threat to fair action than any other single factor.

This point came up for consideration before the Supreme Court in *T. Govindaraja Mudaliar* v. *State of T.N.*[99] The government decided in principle to nationalise road transport and appointed a committee to frame the scheme. The Home Secretary was made a member of this committee. Later on, the scheme of nationalisation was finalised, published and objections were heard by the Home Secretary. It was contended that the hearing was vitiated by the rule against bias because the Secretary had already made up his mind on the question of nationalisation, as he was a member of the committee which took this policy decision. The court rejected the challenge on the ground that the Secretary as a member of the committee did not finally determine any issue as to foreclose his mind. He simply helped the government in framing the scheme. Similarly, in *J.Y. Kondala Rao* v. *A.P. SRTC*[100], the court did not quash the order of the Minister, who had heard the objections of private operators, nationalising road transport on the ground that the same Minister had presided over a meeting only a few days earlier in which nationalisation was favoured. The court rejected the contention on the ground that the decision of the committee was not "final and irrevocable" but merely a policy decision.

A trend that has grown in almost all jurisdictions is that policy bias is not considered as bias which vitiates an administrative action. In *Bajaj Hindustan Ltd.* v. *Sir Shadi Lal Enterprises Ltd.*[101], court did not allow a challenge to an administrative action on the ground of policy bias.

1.2.6 *Preconceived notion bias*

This type of bias is also called as "unconscious bias". All persons exercising adjudicatory powers are humans with human prejudices, no matter some persons are more humans than others. This may include "class bias" and "personality" bias. Every person is a product of a class and inherits some characteristics of that class which may also reflect in his decision-making process. In the same manner, every person's personality is a combination of his biological and social heredity which determine his values and attitudes in a way that may condition his decision-making process. The problem of

---

99. (1973) 1 SCC 336. See also, *J.Y. Kondala Rao* v. *A.P. SRTC*, AIR 1961 SC 82; *(Dr.) K.S. Rao* v. *State of Hyderabad*, 1957 SCC OnLine AP 7: AIR 1957 AP 414.
100. AIR 1961 SC 82.
101. (2011) 1 SCC 640.

unconscious bias is such which is inherent in any adjudication and cannot be eliminated unless detected by some overt action of the authority, and if so detected can vitiate an administrative hearing if it has a direct relation with the decision. This may include a situation where the deciding officer openly expresses his prejudice.

The problem of bias arising from preconceived notions may have to be disposed of as an inherent limitation of the administrative process. It is useless to accuse a public officer of bias merely because he is predisposed in favour of some policy in the public interest. Lord Devlin once said, "The judge who is confident that he has no prejudices (or bias) at all is almost certain to be a bad judge. Prejudice cannot be exorcised, but like a weakness of the flesh it can be subdued. But it has first to be detected."

1.2.7 *Bias on account of obstinacy*

The Supreme Court[102] has discovered a new category of bias arising from thoroughly unreasonable obstinacy. Obstinacy implies unreasonable and unwavering persistence, and the deciding officer would not take "no" for an answer. This new category of bias was discovered in a situation where a judge of the Calcutta High Court upheld his own judgment while sitting in appeal against his own judgment. Of course, a direct violation of the rule that no judge can sit in appeal against his own judgment is not possible, therefore, this rule can only be violated indirectly. In this case, in a fresh writ petition, the judge validated his own order in an earlier writ petition which had been overruled by the Division Bench. What applies to judicial process can be applied to administrative process as well.

1.2.7.1 *Doctrine of necessity*

Bias would not disqualify an officer from taking an action if no other person is competent to act in his place. This exception is based on the doctrine of necessity. The law permits certain things to be done as a matter of necessity which it would otherwise not countenance on the touchstone of judicial propriety. The doctrine of necessity makes it imperative for the authority to decide, and considerations of judicial propriety must yield. It can be invoked in cases of bias where there is no authority to decide the issue. If the doctrine of necessity is not allowed full play in certain unavoidable situations, it would impede the course of justice itself and the defaulting party would benefit from it. If the choice is between either to allow a biased person to act or stifle the action altogether, the choice must fall in favour of the former as it is the only way to promote decision-making. Therefore, the court held that bias would not vitiate the action of the Speaker in impeachment proceedings[103] and that of the Chief Election Commissioner

102. *The Tribune* 18-5-1998, 11.
103. *Sub-Committee on Judicial Accountability* v. *Union of India*, (1991) 4 SCC 699.

in election matters.[104] The rule against bias causes curious problems in contempt cases. In *Vinay Chandra Mishra*[105], *re*, the court ruled that in case of *facie curiae* (contempt in the face of the court) the rule against bias does not apply. Court can punish for contempt on the spot. However, in order to bring an element of fairness in contempt cases, Allahabad High Court has made a rule that the judge will place the matter before the Chief Justice who would then allot it to any judge for hearing.

If choice is between hearing by a "biased person or no hearings", which will benefit defaulting party, the rule of necessity will accept hearing even by a biased person. In *Ashok Kumar Yadav* v. *State of Haryana*[106] selections made by the Public Service Commission were challenged on the ground of personal bias because many selected candidates were near relatives of the members of the Commission. Court did not quash selections on the ground of "necessity". In a reference made by the President in 2009 under Article 143 of the Constitution to seek the opinion of the court—whether Chairman and the members of the Public Service Commission were disqualified when their relatives appeared for interview before them on account of bias?—the court advised in the negative based on the necessity rule.

However, where any alternative is possible, the rule of necessity will not apply. In *Amar Nath Chowdhury* v. *Braithwaite & Co. Ltd.*[107], on the ground of misconduct, disciplinary authority has dismissed a person from service. He went in appeal before the Board of Directors where the Chairman-cum-Managing Director was the same person who was also the Chairman of the disciplinary authority and who did not rescue himself, which was an alternative. Court held that the rule of necessity can not be applied to save the action.

In the US, the disqualification arising out of bias arises from the due process clause of the US Constitution. Therefore, an administrative action can be challenged in the US on all those counts of bias on which it can be challenged in India and England. Recent trends in the judicial behaviour of the US Supreme Court also indicate that where the administrative authority prejudged the issue, the action will be vitiated.[108]

In 1993, the US Supreme Court made a "recusal policy" which provided that it would not serve any public purpose if judges rescue themselves as an abundant caution in every slight financial or personal involvement. In 2003, Scalia J did not rescue himself when it was pointed out that he had gone for duck hunting with the Vice-President, Dick Cheney, who was a respondent in the case. Scalia J replied, "If it is reasonable to think that a Supreme Court judge can be bought so cheap, the nation is in deeper trouble than I had imagined."

---

104. *Election Commission of India* v. *Subramaniam Swamy*, (1996) 4 SCC 104.
105. (1995) 2 SCC 584.
106. (1985) 4 SCC 417. See also, *Supreme Court of India* v. *Subhash Chandra Agrawal*, (2011) 1 SCC 496.
107. (2002) 2 SCC 290.
108. *American Cyanamid Company* v. *Federal Trade Commission*, 363 F 2d 757 (6th Cir 1966).

However, the term "bias" must be confined to its proper place. If bias arising out of preconceived notions means the total absence of preconceptions in the mind of the judge, then no one has ever had a fair trial, and no one ever will.[109] Therefore, unless the strength of the preconceived notions is such that it has the capacity of foreclosing the mind of the judge, administrative action would not be vitiated.

1.3 "Audi alteram partem" or the rule of fair hearing

This is the second long arm of natural justice which protects the "little man" from arbitrary administrative actions whenever his right to person or property is jeopardised. Thus, one of the objectives of giving a hearing in application of the principles of natural justice is to see that an illegal action or decision does not take place. Any wrong order may adversely affect a person, and it is essentially for this reason that a reasonable opportunity may have to be granted before passing an administrative order.[110] The principle of *audi alteram partem* is the basic concept of the principles of natural justice. The omnipotency inherent in the doctrine is that no one should be condemned unheard. In the field of administrative action, this principle has been applied to ensure fair play and justice to affected persons. However, the doctrine is not the cure to all ills in the process. Its application depends upon the factual matrix to improve administrative efficiency, expediency and to mete out justice. The procedure adopted must be just and fair.[111] The expression *audi alteram partem* simply implies that a person must be given an opportunity to defend himself. This principle is a *sine qua non* of every civilised society. Corollary deduced from this rule is *qui aliquid statuerit parte inaudita altera, aequum licet dixerit, haud aequum facerit* (he who shall decide anything without the other side having been heard, although he may have said what is right, will not have done what is right). The same principle was expressed by Lord Hewart when he said, "It is not merely of some importance, but is of fundamental importance that justice should not only be done, but should manifestly and undoubtedly be seem to be done."[112] As has been frequently observed, the benefit of this rule was given to Adam and Eve even by God before they were punished for disobeying His command. This signifies that even if the authority already knows every thing and the person has nothing more to tell, even then this rule of natural justice is attracted, unless application of this rule would be a mere empty formality. Administrative difficulty in giving notice and hearing to a person cannot provide any justification for depriving the person of an opportunity of being heard.[113] Furthermore, observance of the rules of natural justice

109. *Linahan, re*, 138 F 2d 650, 652 (2nd Cir 1943) *per* Frank J.
110. *BALCO Employees' Union* v. *Union of India*, (2002) 2 SCC 333.
111. *Sarat Kumar Dash* v. *Biswajit Patnaik*, 1995 Supp (1) SCC 434.
112. *R.* v. *Sussex Justices, ex p McCarthy*, (1924) 1 KB 256, 259: 1923 All ER Rep 233.
113. *Bhagwant Singh* v. *Commr. of Police*, (1985) 2 SCC 537.

has no relevance to the fatness of the stake, but is essentially related to the demands of a given situation.[114] The whole course of decisions beginning with *R.* v. *University of Cambridge*[115] (also known as the *Dr Bentley case*), in which the Court of King's Bench held that the University of Cambridge could not cancel the degree of a great but rebellious scholar without giving him an opportunity of defending himself, firmly establishes that although there may not be a statutory requirement that both parties shall be heard, yet the justice of the common law will supply the omission of the legislature. In the same manner even if the legislature specifically authorises an administrative action without hearing, then, except in cases of recognised exceptions, the law would be violative of the principles of fair hearing, now also read into Articles 14 and 21 of the Indian Constitution.[116] The court thus held that though the rules permit award of censure entry without notice and hearing, yet the principles of natural justice should be read into such rules and no censure entry can be awarded without any notice and hearing.[117] However, refusal to participate in an enquiry without a valid reason cannot be pleaded as violation of natural justice at a later stage.[118]

Administrative agencies in India are not bound by the technical rules of procedure of law courts; this accentuates the need to follow the minimum procedure of fair hearing. Courts, from case to case, have in their decisions developed a fine code of administrative procedure, which applies to every administrative decision-making but in a pragmatically flexible manner.[119]

In *Krishna Mohan Medical College and Hospital* v. *Union of India*[120], the Supreme Court observed that reasonable opportunity of hearing which is synonymous to "fair hearing", it is no longer res integra, is an important ingredient of *audi alteram partem* rule and embraces almost every facet of fair procedure. The rule of "fair hearing" requires that the affected party should be given an opportunity to meet the case against him effectively and the right to fair hearing takes within its fold a just decision supplemented by reasons and rationale. Reasonable opportunity of hearing or right to "fair hearing" casts a steadfast and sacrosanct obligation on the adjudicator to ensure fairness in procedure and action, so much so that any remiss or dereliction in connection therewith would be at the pain of invalidation of the decision eventually taken. Every executive authority empowered to take an administrative action having the potential of visiting any person with civil consequences must take care to ensure that justice is not only done but also manifestly appears to have been done.

114. *Jain Exports (P) Ltd.* v. *Union of India*, (1988) 3 SCC 579.
115. (1723) 1 Str 757: 93 ER 698.
116. *Olga Tellis* v. *Bombay Municipal Corpn.*, (1985) 3 SCC 545. See also, *D.K. Yadav* v. *J.M.A. Industries Ltd.*, (1993) 3 SCC 259.
117. *State of U.P.* v. *Vijay Kumar Tripathi*, 1995 Supp (1) SCC 552. See also, *Saij Gram Panchayat* v. *State of Gujarat*, (1999) 2 SCC 366; *Piara Singh* v. *State of Punjab*, (2000) 5 SCC 765.
118. *Bank of India* v. *Apurba Kumar Saha*, (1994) 2 SCC 615.
119. *Dharampal Satyapal Ltd.* v. *CCE*, (2015) 8 SCC 519. See also, *Kanachur Islamic Education Trust* v. *Union of India*, (2017) 15 SCC 702.
120. (2017) 15 SCC 719.

In *State of Haryana* v. *Northern Indian Glass Industries Ltd.*[121], the Supreme Court noted that *audi alteram partem* rule is not applicable where the conduct of the affected party itself is vitiated by fraud, malpractice and misfeasance; where conclusion of the decision-making authority regarding such conduct is tallying with the report of the subordinate authority; and where legal position of the affected parties is already well known.

In *State Bank of Patiala* v. *S.K. Sharma*[122], the Supreme Court rightly observed that where an enquiry is not convened by any statutory provision and the only obligation of the administrative authority is to observe the principles of natural justice, the court/tribunal should make a distinction between a total violation of the rule of fair hearing and violation of a facet of that rule. In other words, a distinction must be made between "no opportunity" or "no adequate opportunity". In case of the former, the order passed would undoubtedly be invalid and the authority may be asked to conduct proceedings afresh according to the rule of fair hearing. But in the latter case, the effect of violation of a facet of the rule of fair hearing has to be examined from the standpoint of prejudice. In other words, the court/tribunal has to see whether in the totality of circumstances the person has suffered a prejudice. If the answer is in the affirmative, the action shall be invalid. The sole purpose of the rule of fair hearing is to avoid failure of justice. It is this purpose which should be a guide in applying the rule of fair hearing to varying situations that may arise. There may be situations where the interest of the State or public interest may call for curtailing the rule of fair hearing. In such circumstances, the court may have to balance public/State interest with the requirement of natural justice and arrive at an appropriate decision.

In *Vipulbhai Mansingbhai Chaudhary* v. *State of Gujarat*[123], the Supreme Court held that where an order passed in exercise of a power conferred by a statute is set aside on the ground that such an order was passed in breach of the principles of natural justice, the power could once again be exercised by complying with the principles of natural justice. Any statutory power can "be exercised from time to time as occasion requires". Such a principle is recognised by Section 14, General Clauses Act, 1897. Power conferred on the courts to adjudicate the rights and obligations of the parties is an exception to the principle. The doctrines of res judicata and double jeopardy prohibit the repeated invocation of the jurisdiction of the civil courts or repeated attempts to prosecute a person on the same set of facts constituting an offence. In a case where the flaw in the order appealed against consists of in the non-observance of certain procedure or in not giving effect

121. (2015) 15 SCC 588.
122. (1996) 3 SCC 364. See also, *Jamaat-E-Islami Hind* v. *Union of India*, (1995) 1 SCC 428, it was held that the requirement of natural justice in a case of this kind (organisation had been declared as illegal organisation) had to be tailored to safeguard public interest which must always weigh over every lesser interest.
123. (2017) 13 SCC 51.

to the maxim "audi alteram partem", it is open to the officer concerned to start the procedure once again with a view to follow the rules of procedure and the principles of natural justice.

Byles J in *Cooper* v. *Wandsworth Board of Works*[124] (*Cooper*) observed:

> The laws of God and man both give the party an opportunity to make his defence, if he has any. I remember to have heard it observed by a very learned man, upon such an occasion, that even God Himself did not pass sentence upon Adam, before he was called upon to make his defence. 'Adam' (says God), 'Where art thou? Hast thou not eaten of the tree, whereof I commanded thee that thou shouldest not eat?' And the same question was put to Eve also.

A civil right adversely affected is the core for the invocation of this rule. But what is a civil consequence?

> ... bypassing verbal booby-traps? 'Civil consequences' undoubtedly cover infraction of not merely property or personal rights but of civil liberties, material deprivations and non-pecuniary damages. In its comprehensive connotation, everything that affects a citizen in his civil life inflicts a civil consequence.[125]

To this may be added the infraction of some legitimate expectations also, of which it would not be fair to deprive a person.[126] "Legitimate expectations" though cannot defeat or invalidate a legislation but may vitiate an administrative action. Therefore, when persons enjoy certain benefits or advantages under a policy of a government, even though they may not have a legal right, yet they cannot be deprived of their legitimate expectations by changing the policy without following the principles of fair hearing.[127] However, denial of legitimate expectations can be justified by overriding public interest. Relief in such cases would be limited only to cases where it amounts to a denial of a right, or where the action is arbitrary, unreasonable and not in public interest.[128]

(For detailed discussion on the doctrine of legitimate expectation, *see* Chapter 8 of this book.)

Therefore, no order involving adverse civil consequences can be passed against any person without giving him an opportunity to be heard against the passing of such order, and this rule of natural justice applicable to quasi-judicial and administrative proceedings would also a fortiori apply to judicial proceedings, such as a petition for winding up of a company. No system of law designed to promote justice through fair play in action can permit the court to make a winding-up order which has the effect of

124. (1863) 14 CBNS 180: (1863) 143 ER 414. See also, *Krishen Mohan Medical College and Hospital* v. *Union of India*, (2017) 15 SCC 719.
125. *Mohinder Singh Gill* v. *Chief Election Commr.*, (1978) 1 SCC 405, 440.
126. *Per* Denning MR in *Schmidt* v. *Secy. of State for Home Affairs*, (1969) 2 WLR 337: (1969) 2 Ch 149 (CA).
127. *Navjyoti Coop. Group Housing Society* v. *Union of India*, (1992) 4 SCC 477. See also, *Scheduled Caste and Weaker Section Welfare Assn.* v. *State of Karnataka*, (1991) 2 SCC 604.
128. *Union of India* v. *Hindustan Development Corpn.*, (1993) 3 SCC 499. See also, *Madras City Wine Merchants' Assn.* v. *State of T.N.*, (1994) 5 SCC 509.

bringing about termination of services of workers without giving them an opportunity of being heard against the making of such order. It would be violative of the basic principles of fair procedure, and in the absence of any express provisions in the Companies Act, 1956 forbidding workers from appearing at the hearing of the winding-up petition and participating in it, the workers must be held entitled to appear and be heard in the winding-up petition.[129] In the same manner, in *Jt. Council of Bus Syndicate* v. *Union of India*[130], the Supreme Court held that before increasing the insurance tariff on operators of buses, taxis and goods vehicles, parties affected by this escalation should be given an opportunity of hearing, whether required by the statute or not.[131] In *Piara Singh* v. *State of Punjab*[132], the Supreme Court held that before setting aside an auction sale on the ground of defective proclamation, the authority ought to give notice and hearing to the highest bidder as his right would be adversely affected. This extension of the reach of the principles of natural justice would certainly go a long way in providing protection to a vulnerable section of our society.

Before the decision of the Highest Bench in *S.L. Kapoor* v. *Jagmohan*[133] (*Jagmohan*), the rule was that the principles of natural justice shall apply only where an administrative action has caused some "prejudice" to a person, meaning thereby that he must have suffered some "civil consequences". Therefore, the person had to show something extra in order to prove "prejudice" or "civil consequence". This approach had stultified the growth of administrative law within an area of highly-practical significance. It is gratifying that in *Jagmohan* the court took a bold step in holding that a separate showing of prejudice caused is not necessary. The non-observance of natural justice is in itself a prejudice caused. Hence, merely because the facts are admitted or are indisputable, it does not follow that the principles of natural justice need not be observed.

1.3.1 *Duty to act judicially or the duty to act fairly*[134]

Law is clear on the point that in cases classified as "quasi-judicial", there is a "duty to act judicially", *i.e.* to follow the principles of natural justice in full, but in cases which are classified as "administrative" there is only a "duty to act fairly", which simply means that the administrative authority must act justly and fairly and not arbitrarily or capriciously.

Though after the epoch-making decision of the Supreme Court in *Kraipak*[135], the dividing line between quasi-judicial and administrative

129. *National Textile Workers' Union* v. *P.R. Ramakrishnan*, (1983) 1 SCC 228 *per* Bhagwati J.
130. 1992 Supp (2) SCC 125.
131. *Ibid.*
132. (2000) 5 SCC 765.
133. (1980) 4 SCC 379. See also, *A.R. Antulay* v. *R.S. Nayak*, (1988) 2 SCC 602.
134. For detailed discussion *see*, C.K. Thakker, "From Duty to Act Judicially to Duty to Act Fairly", (2003) 4 SCC J-1.
135. (1969) 2 SCC 262.

functions of the administration has become thin but is still not completely obliterated. There still exists a vast area of administrative and executive functions of the administration, wherein a person does not claim a right but still has legitimate expectations of receiving a benefit or a privilege. It is in this area that though there is no duty of the administration to act judicially, but certainly there is a duty to act fairly. Lord Pearson stated this position in *Pearlberg* v. *Varty*[136] thus:

> But where some person or body is entrusted by Parliament with administrative or executive functions, there is no presumption that compliance with the principles of natural justice is required, although, as 'Parliament is not to be presumed to act unfairly', the Courts may be able in suitable cases (perhaps always) to imply an obligation to act with fairness.[137]

In India, this position was taken by the Supreme Court in various cases starting from *Keshav Mills Co. Ltd.* v. *Union of India*[138] (*Keshav Mills Co. Ltd.*). In this case, the government, on the basis of a report of an enquiry committee, had taken over the management of the Mill Company, which had been closed down without supplying the copy of the report to the management and affording an opportunity of hearing. The takeover was challenged on the ground of violation of the principles of natural justice. The Supreme Court though did not interfere with the order on the ground that no prejudice was caused to the Mill Company, yet observed:

> The only essential point that has to be kept in mind in all cases ... that the administrative authority concerned should act fairly, impartially and reasonably.[139]

Following the same line of reasoning, the Supreme Court in *M.S. Nally Bharat Engg. Co. Ltd.* v. *State of Bihar*[140] held that "fairness" is the basic principle of good administration. In this case, the government had transferred the case of a workman from one Labour Court to another without any notice and hearing to the employer. The court set aside the order on the ground of lack of fairness.

The basic purpose behind developing the "fairness doctrine" within the area of "administrative or executive" functions of the administration, wherein the principles of natural justice are not attracted, is to reconcile "fairness to the individual" with the "flexibility of administrative action". It is an attempt at over-judicialisation of the administrative process. Therefore, where an administrative authority is not exercising quasi-judicial powers and as such there is no duty to act judicially because the principles of natural justice are not attracted in such cases, court may still insist on a "duty to act fairly". As both the doctrines operate in different areas of administrative action, so there is no chance of any conflict. C.K. Thakker rightly concludes:

136. (1972) 1 WLR 534 (HL).
137. *Ibid*, (WLR) 547.
138. (1973) 1 SCC 380. See also, *Dharampal Satyapal Ltd.* v. *CCE*, (2015) 8 SCC 519.
139. *Ibid*, 381.
140. (1990) 2 SCC 48.

> ... 'acting fairly' is an additional weapon in the armoury of the Court. It is not intended to be substituted for another much more powerful weapon 'acting judicially'. Where, however, the former 'acting judicially' cannot be wielded, the Court will try to reach injustice by taking resort to the latter less powerful weapon 'acting fairly'.[141]

The right to fair hearing is a code of procedure and, hence, covers every stage through which an administrative adjudication passes, starting from notice to final determination. The fluctuating content of the rule of fair hearing produced by the irreconcilable mass of court decisions has tempted some writers to say that the *audi alteram partem* rule has ceased to exist.[142] However, Lord Reid has condemned this view as "tainted by the perennial fallacy that because something cannot be cut and dried or nicely weighed or measured therefore it does not exist". Impossibility of laying down a universally valid test to cover an infinite variety of circumstances that may exist is not unnatural also. Detailed requirement of *audi alteram partem* range is a continuum from notice to the final determination.

1.3.2 *Right to notice*

The term "notice" originated from the Latin word "notitia" which means "being known". In its popular sense it is equivalent to information, intelligence or knowledge. In legal sense, it embraces a knowledge of circumstances that ought to induce suspicion or belief, as well as direct information of that fact.

Notice embodies rule of fairness and must precede an adverse order. It should be clear and precise so as to give the party adequate information of the case he has to meet. Time given should be adequate for a person so that he could prepare an effective defence. Denial of notice and an opportunity to respond make the administrative decision completely vitiated.[143]

If requirement of notice is a statutory requirement then notice must be given in a manner provided by law. Therefore, recently the Supreme Court held that if a cheque has been dishonoured, proper notice as required under the Negotiable Instrument Act, 1881 must be given either by post or courier, personal information to the drawer will not suffice.[144]

Notice is the starting point of any hearing. Unless a person knows the formulation of subjects and issues involved in the case, he cannot defend himself. It is not enough that the notice in a case be given, but it must be adequate also. The adequacy of notice is a relative term and must be decided with reference to each case. But generally, a notice in order to be adequate must contain the following:

141. C.K. Thakker, "From Duty to Act Judicially to Duty to Act Fairly", (2003) 4 SCC J-1, 11.
142. *See*, Benjafield and Whitmore, *Principles Of Australian Administrative Law* (1971) 145. See also, *Ridge* v. *Baldwin*, 1964 AC 40, 64: (1963) 2 WLR 935 (HL).
143. *Canara Bank* v. *Debasis Das*, (2003) 4 SCC 557.
144. *The Hindu* 20-12-2007, 6.

(1) Time, place and nature of hearing.
(2) Legal authority under which hearing is to be held.
(3) Statement of specific charges which the person has to meet.
(4) Particular penalty or action which is proposed to be awarded/taken.[145]

In *State of U.P.* v. *Vam Organic Chemicals Ltd.*[146], the Supreme Court stressed that before any "notice" is issued, there must exist sufficient reasons for a proposed action for which notice is to be issued. Therefore, reasons are a precondition for issuing any notice, and these must be contained in notice. In this case, a person was granted recognition certificate for dealing in certain items. Thereafter, government decided to delete certain items from the certificate. Court held that sufficient reasons are a precondition before notice is issued and should form part of the notice. The court further emphasised that even if it is a "rectification of a mistake", notice must be given where a person would suffer a serious prejudice. Rectification cannot divest a vested right.

The test of adequacy of notice will be whether it gives sufficient information and material so as to enable the person concerned to put up an effective defence. Therefore, the contents of notice, persons who are entitled to notice, and the time of giving notice are important matters to ascertain any violation of the principles of natural justice. Sufficient time should also be given to comply with the requirement of a notice. Thus, when only 24 hours were given to demolish a structure allegedly in a dilapidated condition, the court held that the notice was not proper.[147] In the same manner where the notice contained only one charge, the person cannot be punished for any other charge for which notice was not given.[148]

In *Joseph Vilangandan* v. *Executive Engineer*[149], the court held that the notice given was inadequate. The facts of this case were that when the appellant did not start the contract work within time, he received a letter from the Executive Engineer in which the relevant sentence was, "You are, therefore, requested to show cause within seven days from the receipt of this notice why the work may not be arranged otherwise at your risk and loss through other agencies after debarring you as defaulter." The reply contained a statement that the delay was caused by the conduct of the respondent. Thereafter, the contract was cancelled and the appellant was debarred from all future contracts under the PWD. Quashing the order, the Supreme Court held that the words "debarring you as defaulter" did not give adequate notice to the appellant of the fact that he would be debarred from "all future contracts" with the PWD. In the same manner in *Appropriate Authority* v. *Vijay Kumar Sharma*[150], the Supreme Court

145. *Gorkha Security Services* v. *Govt. (NCT of Delhi)*, (2014) 9 SCC 105.
146. (2010) 6 SCC 222.
147. *State of J&K* v. *Haji Wali Mohammed*, (1972) 2 SCC 402.
148. *Govindsingh Ramsinghbhai* v. C. *Subbarav*, 1969 SCC OnLine Guj 6: AIR 1971 Guj 131.
149. (1978) 3 SCC 36.
150. (2001) 10 SCC 739.

held that if material, on the basis of which compulsory purchase of property by the Income Tax Department was made, was not disclosed in the show-cause notice, and the venue of hearing was changed without giving reasonable time to transferor to reach the venue, there is a violation of the principles of natural justice.

The requirement of notice under Section 105-B of the Bombay Municipal Corporation Act, 1888 to an allottee of municipal premises for eviction need not be given to all persons living with the allottee.[151] In the same manner, the principles of natural justice are not violated if notice is not given to all the members of a society proposing amalgamation of the society.[152] However, when a dealership agreement is modified[153] or a telephone is disconnected, notice becomes necessary.[154]

If notice is to be given to a large class of persons who are educated, it may be given by publishing it in a newspaper. In such a case, individual notice is not the requirement of natural justice. In *Shiv Sagar Tiwari* v. *Union of India*[155], the court held that the notice published in newspapers to enable the out-of-turn allottees of government quarters in Delhi to represent themselves before the Supreme Court against the proposed cancellation of allotments is sufficient and adequate notice.

However, the requirement of notice will not be insisted upon as a mere technical formality when the party concerned clearly knows the case against it, and is not thereby prejudiced in any manner in putting up an effective defence. Therefore, in *Keshav Mills Co. Ltd.*[156], the court did not quash the order of the government taking over the mill for a period of five years on the technical ground that the appellants were not issued notice before this action was taken, as, at an earlier stage, a full-scale hearing had already been given and there was nothing more which the appellants wanted to know. In the same manner in *Maharashtra State Financial Corpn.* v. *Suvarna Board Mills*[157], the court held that a notice calling upon the party to repay dues within 15 days failing which the factory would be taken over is sufficient for taking over the factory and no fresh notice is required. In the same manner no fresh notice is required for pulling down an unauthorised structure when notice for removing such structure has already been given.[158] Similarly, in *State of Karnataka* v. *Mangalore University Non-Teaching Employees' Assn.*[159], the court held that where no prejudice is

151. *Ajit Baburao Sawant* v. *BEST Undertaking*, 1984 SCC OnLine Bom 254: AIR 1985 Bom 362.
152. *Daman Singh* v. *State of Punjab*, (1985) 2 SCC 670.
153. *Sub-Divisional Controller of Food & Supplies* v. *Amulya Ratan Sadhu*, 1985 SCC OnLine Cal 34: AIR 1985 Cal 281.
154. *Union of India* v. *Narayanbhai Keshavlal Patel*, 1984 SCC OnLine Guj 121: AIR 1985 Guj 31.
155. (1997) 1 SCC 444.
156. (1973) 1 SCC 380.
157. (1994) 5 SCC 566.
158. *Cantonment Board* v. *Mohanlal*, (1996) 2 SCC 23.
159. (2002) 3 SCC 302.

caused to the person on account of non-affording of an opportunity to make representation, violation of the principles of natural justice cannot be insisted upon. In this case, house rent and city compensatory allowance were given to the employees at a higher rate. At a later date, the government wanted to recover excess payment. The Vice-Chancellor espoused the cause of the employees although unsuccessfully. In these circumstances, the court was of the view that action taken for the recovery of excess payment without notice and affording an opportunity to make representation did not vitiate the action. Maintaining the same tenor, the court did not quash the order of the Election Commission of India issued without any notice to the other party on the ground that such order did not cause any "prejudice" to the petitioner political party and was merely temporary in nature. In this case the Election Commission of India had issued an order to the All India Anna Dravida Munnetra Kazhagam (AIADMK) political party in power to cover "two leaves" painted on government buses at government cost because it was likely to be confused with the symbol of the AIADMK party. The order had been contested on the ground that it was issued without any notice of hearing. It was emphasised that courts of law should not take a strait jacket approach to the violations of the principles of natural justice rather a practical, reasonable and contextual approach is necessary to meet the ends of justice.[160] Thus, while deciding on "prejudice or injustice" caused, court must act with broad vision and look for substance and not mere technicalities.[161]

In the same manner when certain tax benefits were given under a notification which was nullified by a later legislation with retrospective effect, no new notice was necessary to recover the amount which had become refundable as in such a situation it would be a useless formality as no prejudice would be caused to the party.[162]

However, in *Union of India* v. *Narendra Singh*[163], the Supreme Court made it amply clear that even if a mistake in the decision-making process is to be corrected, which has adverse consequences for a person, he must be given notice. In this case, an erroneous promotion had been cancelled without following the process of law. An opportunity of hearing may not be given if mistake or error is apparent on the face of the record.

Article 21 of the Constitution requires that a detenu must be furnished with the grounds of detention and if the grounds are vague, the detention order may be quashed by the court.[164] In other areas of administrative action, a notice has been held to be vague if it does not specify the action

160. *All India Anna Dravida Munnetra Kazhagam* v. *Election Commr.*, 2014 SCC OnLine Mad 761: (2014) 2 CTC 742.
161. *State* v. *N.S. Gnaneswaran*, (2013) 3 SCC 594.
162. See *R.C. Tobacco (P) Ltd.* v. *Union of India*, (2005) 7 SCC 725; *Dharampal Satyapal Ltd.* v. *CCE*, (2015) 8 SCC 519.
163. (2008) 2 SCC 750.
164. *State of Bombay* v. *Atma Ram Sridhar Vaidya*, 1951 SCC 43: AIR 1951 SC 157.

proposed to be taken,[165] or the property proposed to be acquired,[166] or the grounds on which licence is to be cancelled.[167] Requirement of notice, mandated by statute, can be waived if it is solely for the benefit of the individual concerned.[168] If the notice issued by the administrative authority has been quashed on any ground by the court, the administrative authority can issue notice again and for this permission of the court is not necessary. This is based on the principle that "any statutory power can be exercised from time to time as the occasion requires"[169].

1.3.2.1 *Consequences of non-issue of notice*

The principles emerging from case-law are:[170]

(1) Non-issuance of notice or mistake in the issue of notice, or defective service of notice does not affect the jurisdiction of the authority if, otherwise, a reasonable opportunity of being heard has been given.
(2) Issuance of notice as prescribed by law constitutes a part of reasonable opportunity of being heard.
(3) If prejudice has been caused by non-issuance or invalid service of notice, the proceedings would be vitiated. But, irregular service of notice would not render the proceedings invalid, more so if the person by his conduct has rendered service impracticable or impossible or is otherwise aware of the proceedings/notice either actually or constructively.
(4) In case of non-issuance of notice, or defective service, which violates the principles of natural justice, an administrative authority may decide the case *de novo* with proper notice. Violation of the principles of natural justice vitiates order but not the proceeding.
(5) A show-cause notice if contains unspecified, vague or unintelligible allegations would imply a denial of proper opportunity of being heard.[171]

1.3.3 *Right to know the evidence against him*

Every person before an administrative authority exercising adjudicatory powers has the right to know the evidence to be used against him. This principle was firmly established in *Dhakeswari Cotton Mills Ltd.* v. *CIT*[172]

165. *Abdul Latif Nomani* v. *Commr.*, 1966 SCC OnLine All 303: AIR 1968 All 44.
166. *Tulsa Singh* v. *State of Haryana*, 1972 SCC OnLine P&H 312: AIR 1973 Punj 263.
167. *Mulkh Raj Kishore Kumar & Co.* v. *State of Punjab*, 1971 SCC OnLine P&H 401: AIR 1973 P&H 62.
168. *Collector of Customs* v. *Universal Synthetics*, (2001) 10 SCC 190.
169. S. 14, General Clauses Act, 1897. See also, *Vipulbhai Mansingbhai Chaudhary* v. *State of Gujarat*, (2017) 13 SCC 51.
170. *CST* v. *Subhash & Company*, (2003) 3 SCC 454. See also, *Prabin Ram Phukan* v. *State of Assam*, (2015) 3 SCC 605; *Rajasthan Housing Board* v. *New Pink City Nirman Sahkari Samiti Ltd.*, (2015) 7 SCC 601.
171. *CCE* v. *Brindavan Beverages (P) Ltd.*, (2007) 5 SCC 388.
172. AIR 1955 SC 65.

(*Dhakeswari Cotton Mills Ltd.*) In this case, the Appellate Income Tax Tribunal did not disclose the information supplied to it by the department. The Supreme Court held that the assessee was not given a fair hearing. However, the supply of adverse material, unless the law otherwise provides, in original form is not necessary. It is sufficient if the summary of the contents of the material is supplied, provided it is not misleading. A person may be allowed to inspect the file and take notes. Whatever mode is used, the fundamental remains the same that nothing should be used against the person which has not been brought to his notice.

1.3.4 *Right to present case and evidence/oral hearing*

The adjudicatory authority should afford a reasonable opportunity to the party to present his case. This can be done through writing or orally at the discretion of the authority, unless the statute under which the authority is functioning directs otherwise.

The requirements of natural justice are met only if an opportunity to represent is given in view of the proposed action. The demands of natural justice are not met even if the very person proceeded against has been furnished information on which the action is based, if it is furnished in a casual way or for some other purposes. This does not mean that the opportunity need be a "double opportunity", that is, one opportunity on the factual allegations and another on the proposed penalty. But both may be rolled into one.[173]

Courts are unanimous on the point that oral hearing is not an integral part of fair hearing unless the circumstances are so exceptional that without an oral hearing a person cannot put up an effective defence. Therefore, where complex legal and technical questions are involved, or where the stakes are very high, oral hearing shall become a part of fair hearing.[174] Thus in the absence of a statutory requirement for oral hearing, courts will decide the matter taking into consideration the facts and circumstances of every case.[175] In *RBI* v. *Sahara India Financial Corpn. Ltd.*[176], Reserve Bank of India issued a show-cause notice to the Corporation and after examining the reply restrained it from accepting deposits. The Supreme Court held that because by this decision the whole business of the Corporation is adversely affected, therefore, personal hearing ought to have been given.

---

173. *S.L. Kapoor* v. *Jagmohan*, (1980) 4 SCC 379.
174. *State of U.P.* v. *Dharmander Prasad Singh*, (1989) 2 SCC 505.
175. In *Ram Chandra Tripathi* v. *U.P. Public Services Tribunal*, (1994) 5 SCC 180, the court held that de-confirmation of an employee in view of the High Court injunction does not warrant hearing. In *Director of School Education* v. *O. Karuppa Thevan*, 1994 Supp (2) SCC 666, the court held that hearing in case of transfer of an employee is not necessary. In *State Bank of Patiala* v. *Mahendra Kumar Singhal*, 1994 Supp (2) SCC 463, the court held that in the absence of any rule to the contrary, personal hearing in departmental appeal is not necessary.
176. (2008) 7 SCC 135.

In *Union of India* v. *Jyoti Prakash Mitter*[177], the court refused to quash the order of the President of India in a dispute relating to the age of a High Court judge on the ground that the President did not grant an oral hearing even on request. The court was of the view that when the person has been given an opportunity to submit his case in writing, there is no violation of the principles of natural justice if an oral hearing is not given. However, in *Southern Painters* v. *Fertilizers & Chemicals Travancore Ltd.*[178], the Supreme Court held that deletion of name from the approved list of contractors warrants hearing.[179] Though the same is the law in England[180], but in practice oral hearing is the rule. In the US, the right to oral hearing flows from the Administrative Procedure Act, 1946.

The administrative authority must further provide full opportunity to present evidence—testimonial or documentary. In *Dhakeswari Cotton Mills Ltd*[181], the Supreme Court quashed the decision of the administrative authority on the ground that not allowing the assessee to produce material evidence violates the rule of fair hearing. Again in *R.B. Shreeram Durga Prasad* v. *Settlement Commission (IT & WT)*[182] (*R.B. Shreeram Durga Prasad*), where the Commissioner only allowed the assessee an opportunity to make submissions on objections of the Commissioner of Income Tax regarding settlement of assessment, the Supreme Court held that mere opportunity to make submissions is not enough. Clear opportunity must be given to demonstrate that the reporting authority was not justified in making objections. However, it does not mean that a person can be allowed to unnecessarily prolong and confuse the administrative proceedings by adducing irrelevant evidence. The question of relevancy of evidence is, therefore, a justiciable issue.

The opportunity to present evidence raises another question as to what extent the authority should help the party in presenting his evidence. This point came up for consideration of the Supreme Court in *Nehru Motor Transport Coop. Society Ltd.* v. *State of Rajasthan*[183]. In this case, an enquiry was held under the Motor Vehicles Act, 1939 for nationalisation of road transport. The witnesses whose names were filed by the objectors did not appear even in response to the summons issued by the administrative authority. The authority refused to issue any coercive process. The Supreme Court refused to quash the order of nationalisation holding that the authority is not bound to use its coercive process when the statements of the material witnesses were already on the file. If the statements of the witnesses are not on file, whether the denial of a coercive process would amount to a violation of the rule of fair hearing still remains to be decided.

177. (1971) 1 SCC 396.
178. 1994 Supp (2) SCC 699.
179. See also, *Bhagwan Shukla* v. *Union of India*, (1994) 6 SCC 154.
180. *Local Govt. Board* v. *Arlidge*, 1915 AC 120 (HL).
181. AIR 1955 SC 65.
182. (1989) 1 SCC 628.
183. AIR 1963 SC 1098.

In *A.K. Roy* v. *Union of India*[184] (*A.K. Roy*), the Supreme Court held that if the detenu desires to examine any witnesses, he shall have to keep them present at the appointed time and no obligation can be cast on the advisory board to summon them. The board can also limit the time within which the detenu must complete his evidence.

1.3.5 *Right to rebut adverse evidence*

The right to rebut adverse evidence presupposes that the person has been informed about the evidence against him. In *Dhakeswari Cotton Mills Ltd.*[185], the court quashed the order of the Tax Tribunal where the information supplied by the department against the assessee was not disclosed to him. This does not, however, necessitate the supply of adverse material in original in all cases. It is sufficient if the summary of the contents of the adverse material is made available, provided it is not misleading.[186]

It is not enough that the party should know the adverse material on file but it is further necessary that he must have an opportunity to rebut the evidence. Rebuttal can be done either orally or in writing at the discretion of the administrative authority provided the statute does not provide otherwise.

The opportunity to rebut evidence necessarily involves the consideration of two factors: cross-examination and legal representation.

1.3.5.1 *Cross-examination*

Cross-examination is a most powerful weapon to elicit and establish the truth. However, courts do not insist on cross-examination in administrative adjudication unless the circumstances are such that in the absence of it a person cannot put up an effective defence. The right to cross-examination as an ingredient of fair hearing was considered by the Supreme Court in *State of J&K* v. *Bakshi Gulam Mohammad*[187]. In this case, an enquiry was instituted against Bakshi Gulam Mohammad, former Chief Minister of Jammu and Kashmir State, under the Jammu and Kashmir Commission of Inquiry Act, 1962. The request of Bakshi Gulam Mohammad to cross-examine witnesses who had filed affidavits against him was denied. The decision of the Commission was challenged before the Supreme Court and one of the grounds of challenge was that the denial of the opportunity to cross-examine witnesses violates the rule of fair hearing. The Supreme Court disallowed the challenge on the ground that the evidence of the witnesses was in the form of affidavits and the copies had been made available to the party.

184. (1982) 1 SCC 271.
185. AIR 1955 SC 65.
186. *City Corner* v. *Collector*, (1976) 1 SCC 124.
187. AIR 1967 SC 122. See also, *Gurbachan Singh* v. *State of Bombay*, AIR 1952 SC 221.

The Supreme Court reiterated this position in *Kanungo & Co.* v. *Collector of Customs*[188]. In this case, the business premises of the appellant were searched and 390 watches were confiscated. The order was challenged on the ground that the appellant was not allowed to cross-examine the persons who gave information to the authorities. The court came to the conclusion that the principles of natural justice do not require that in matters of seizure of goods under the Sea Customs Act, 1878, the person should be allowed to cross-examine the informants. In the same manner in *Surjeet Singh Chhabra* v. *Union of India*[189], the court held that in case of confiscation under the Foreign Exchange Regulation Act, 1973, failure to afford an opportunity to cross-examine a Panch witness is not violative of the principles of natural justice. In *State of Kerala* v. *K.T. Shaduli Grocery Dealer*[190], the court held that the denial of the dealer's request by the sales tax authorities to cross-examine the third party before making the best-judgment assessment, is a denial of fair-hearing.[191] The same principle was reiterated by the Supreme Court in *Town Area Committee* v. *Jagdish Prasad*[192]. In this case, the department submitted the charge-sheet, got an explanation and thereafter straightaway passed the dismissal order. The court quashed the order holding that the rule of fair hearing includes an opportunity to cross examine the witnesses and to lead evidence. However, in externment proceedings[193] and proceedings before customs authorities to determine whether goods were smuggled or not, the right of cross-examination was held not to be a part of natural justice.[194] On the grounds of practicability also, an opportunity of cross-examination may be disallowed. Therefore, the Supreme Court rejected the contention of the appellants that they were not allowed to cross-examine girl students on the ground that if it was allowed, no girl would come forward to give evidence and, further, that it would not be possible for the college authorities to protect girl students outside the college precincts.[195] Thus in the absence of a statutory requirement about legal representation, courts will have to decide the matter taking into consideration the facts and circumstances of each case. In the same manner in *State of Maharashtra* v. *Salem Hasan Khan*[196], the Supreme Court held that in the case of a bad charactered person while passing an externment order, an evidence need not be discussed as it may give rise to a fresh spate of violence against witnesses.

Where the witnesses have orally deposed, the refusal to allow cross-examination would certainly amount to violation of the principles of natural

188. (1973) 2 SCC 438.
189. (1997) 1 SCC 508.
190. (1977) 2 SCC 777.
191. See also, *Ram Bharosey Agarwal* v. *Har Swarup Maheshwari*, (1976) 3 SCC 435.
192. (1979) 1 SCC 60.
193. *Gurbachan Singh* v. *State of Bombay*, AIR 1952 SC 221.
194. *Kanungo & Co.* v. *Collector of Customs*, (1973) 2 SCC 438.
195. *Hira Nath Mishra* v. *Rajendra Medical College*, (1973) 1 SCC 805. In this case, male students had entered quite naked in a Girls' Hostel late at night and misbehaved with them.
196. (1989) 2 SCC 316.

justice.[197] In *S.C. Girotra* v. *United Commercial Bank*[198], the Bank got certain reports prepared on which the charges were based. These reports were certified by the Bank Officers who were examined by the enquiry officer. On the basis of the report, an employee was dismissed. The court held that there was a violation of the principles of natural justice as the employee was not allowed to cross-examine the officers who deposed orally before the enquiry officer. In the area of labour relations and disciplinary proceedings against civil servants also, the right to cross-examination is included in the rule of fair hearing.[199] In the US, the right to cross-examination is included in the due process clause and also in the Administrative Procedure Act, 1946. In England, the law is the same as in India and courts are engaged in working out the details of the right to cross-examination.[200]

Regarding the right to the detenu of cross-examination before the advisory board, the Supreme Court did not find it an integral and inseparable part of the principles of natural justice. The court reasoned that *firstly* the question before the board is not whether the detenu is guilty of any charge but whether there is a sufficient cause for his detention and, *secondly*, the witnesses would be most reluctant to testify and often it may harm public interest to disclose their identity. The court did not agree with the contention that there can be no effective hearing without the right of cross-examination.[201] Thus, once again an important component of fairness in a situation of total eclipse of freedom was lost in a great confusion of rhetoric.

1.3.5.2 *Legal representation*

Normally, representation through a lawyer in any administrative proceeding is not considered an indispensable part of the rule of natural justice, as oral hearing is not included in the minima of fair hearing.[202] This denial of legal representation is justified on the ground that lawyers tend to complicate matters, prolong the proceedings, and destroy the essential informality of the proceedings. It is further justified on the ground that representation through a lawyer of choice would give an edge to the rich over the poor who cannot afford a good lawyer. No research has so far been made to test the truth of these assertions, but the fact remains that unless some kind of legal aid is provided by the agency itself, the denial of legal representation, to use the words of Prof. Allen, would be a "mistaken kindness" to the poor people.

To what extent legal representation would be allowed in administrative proceedings depends on the provisions of the statute. Factory laws do not

197. *Meenglas Tea Estate* v. *Workmen*, AIR 1963 SC 1719.
198. 1995 Supp (3) SCC 212.
199. *Central Bank of India Ltd.* v. *Karunamoy Banerjee*, AIR 1968 SC 266.
200. *R.* v. *Gaming Board of Great Britain, ex p Benaim*, (1970) 2 QB 417: (1970) 2 WLR 1009 (CA).
201. *A.K. Roy* v. *Union of India*, (1982) 1 SCC 271.
202. *N. Kalindi* v. *Tata Locomotive & Engg. Co. Ltd.*, AIR 1960 SC 914.

permit legal representation, Industrial Disputes Acts allow it with the permission of the tribunal and some statutes like the Income Tax Act, 1961 permit legal representation as a matter of right.

Right to legal representation through a lawyer or agent of choice may be restricted by a standing order also. In *Crescent Dyes and Chemicals Ltd.* v. *Ram Naresh Tripathi*[203], the Supreme Court held that where a standing order restricted the right of representation to any employee of the factory only, it would not be considered as a denial of natural justice as to vitiate an administrative enquiry.

However, courts in India have held that in situations where the person is illiterate,[204] or the matter is complicated and technical,[205] or expert evidence is on record,[206] or a question of law is involved,[207] or the person is facing a trained prosecutor,[208] some professional assistance must be given to the party to make his right to defend himself meaningful.

It is relevant to note at this stage that the Supreme Court in *M.H. Hoskot* v. *State of Maharashtra*[209], while importing the concept of "fair procedure" in Article 21 of the Constitution, held that the right to personal liberty implies provision by the State of free legal service to a prisoner who is indigent or otherwise disabled from securing legal assistance where the ends of justice call for such service.

In *Khatri* (2) v. *State of Bihar*[210], the Supreme Court further ruled that the State is constitutionally bound to provide legal aid to the poor or indigent accused not only at the stage of trial but at the time of remand also. Such right cannot be denied on the ground of financial constraints or administrative inability or that the accused did not ask for it. The Supreme Court emphasised that it is the duty of the presiding officer to inform the accused of such right.

In the same manner in *Nandini Satpathy* v. *P.L. Dani*[211], the court held that the accused must be allowed legal representation during custodial interrogation, and the police must wait for a reasonable time for the arrival of a lawyer. However, the court, which took the right step, did not take a long stride in holding that the State must provide a lawyer if the accused is indigent. The observation of the court could well be inducted in the administration. In the area of criminal justice the Criminal Procedure Code, 1973 now provides for legal aid to the accused.

---

203. (1993) 2 SCC 115.
204. *James Bushi* v. *Collector of Ganjam*, 1959 SCC OnLine Ori 61: AIR 1959 Ori 152.
205. *Nitya Ranjan Bohidar* v. *State*, 1961 SCC OnLine Ori 40: AIR 1962 Ori 78.
206. *Harishchandra Pathak* v. *Registrar, Coop. Societies*, 1965 SCC OnLine MP 86: (1966) 12 FLR 141.
207. *Jagmohandas Jagjivandas Mody* v. *State of Bombay*, 1961 SCC OnLine Guj 20: AIR 1962 Guj 197; *Krishna Chandra Tandon* v. *Union of India*, (1974) 4 SCC 374.
208. *C.L. Subramaniam* v. *Collector of Customs*, (1972) 3 SCC 542.
209. (1978) 3 SCC 544.
210. (1981) 1 SCC 627.
211. (1978) 2 SCC 424.

Legal assistance in preventive detention cases poses a curious problem because, on the one hand, preventive detention laws disallow legal representation and on the other, they seek to detain people for unproved crimes. However, it is gratifying to note that in this highly-sensitive area, judicial behaviour has shown some remarkable signs of improvement. In *Nand Lal Bajaj* v. *State of Punjab*[212], the court allowed legal representation to the detainee through a lawyer, even when Section 11 of the Prevention of Black Marketing and Maintenance of Supplies of Essential Commodities Act, 1980 and Section 8(*e*) of the Conservation of Foreign Exchange and Prevention of Smuggling Activities Act, 1974 (COFEPOSA) denied legal representation in express terms because the State had been represented through a lawyer. The Supreme Court observed that even when the law does not allow legal representation to the detenu, he is entitled to make such a request, and the advisory board is bound to consider this request on merit and is not precluded to allow such assistance when it allows the State to be represented through a lawyer. Maintaining the same tenor, the court in *A.K. Roy*[213], while deciding the constitutionality of the National Security Act, 1980, held that if the Act disallows legal representation to a detenu, the State also cannot take the help of a lawyer. In its eagerness to protect the interest of the detenu, the court in *Phillippa Anne Duke* v. *State of T.N.*[214] and *Devji Vallabhbhai Tandel* v. *Administrator*[215] conferred upon him the right to appear through his friend who in truth and substance is not a legal practitioner, and is also not a comrade-in-profession of the detenu for which he is detained. Therefore, even in the face of constitutional and statutory denial of legal representation to a detenu, he is entitled to a common-law right of representation through a "friend"[216].

However, even this right is not unlimited and can be reasonably regulated by law. In *Railway Protection Force* v. *K. Raghuram Babu*[217], the Supreme Court opined that the common-law right of representation by a "friend" can be regulated by law. In this case, a standing order rule had provided that a person can take the assistance of a "friend" who is an employee of the Force. This implies that assistance cannot be taken from a friend who is not a member of the Force. Court emphasised that ordinarily, in a departmental or domestic enquiry, no person has a right to be represented by a lawyer unless law provides for it or a person has suffered serious prejudice, as such proceedings are not suits or criminal trials.

In the US, a person has a right to legal representation which is guaranteed by the combined effect of the "due process" clause of the Constitution and Section 6(*a*) of the Administrative Procedure Act, 1946.

---

212. (1981) 4 SCC 327.
213. (1982) 1 SCC 271.
214. (1982) 2 SCC 389.
215. (1982) 2 SCC 222.
216. *Ibid*, AIR 1238.
217. (2008) 4 SCC 406.

In England, ordinarily, the right to be represented by a lawyer is not included in the principles of fair hearing. But where there is a right to appear in person, or a technical matter of law and fact is involved, the denial of legal representation is considered as an antithesis of fair hearing.[218] The Franks Committee has also recommended that the right of legal representation should not be curtailed save in exceptional circumstances.

1.3.6 *No evidence should be taken at the back of other party*

That ex parte evidence taken in the absence of the other party violates the principles of fair hearing was discussed by the court in *Errington* v. *Ministry of Health*[219] (*Errington*). The facts were that in 1933, Jarrow Corporation passed a clearance order for the demolition of certain buildings found unfit for human habitation and submitted the same for the confirmation of the Minister of Health. An enquiry was held and the owners of the building were given a hearing. Thereafter some officials of the Ministry again visited the place and collected evidence, but the owners were not informed about the visit. The clearance order was confirmed by the Minister after taking into account the facts thus collected. On challenge the clearance order was quashed by the court, and one of the grounds for so deciding was that the ex parte statements taken in the absence of the other party, without affording an opportunity to rebut, is against the recognised principles of natural justice.

This decision does not imply that administrative agencies cannot obtain information in the manner they consider best. The main thrust of *Errington*[220] is that whatever information is obtained by the administrative authority must be disclosed to the other party and an opportunity to rebut it must be provided.

The same approach was followed by the court in *Ceylon University* v. *Fernando*[221], where the Privy Council upheld the order of the University under circumstances where the evidence of witnesses was taken at the back of the student charged with misconduct, but he was informed of their statements.

The Indian Supreme Court reiterated this position in *Hira Nath Mishra* v. *Rajendra Medical College*[222]. In this case, 36 girl students of a medical college filed a report with the Principal regarding misbehaviour of the boys in the girls' hostel. The enquiry committee appointed by the Principal recorded the statements of the girls, but in the absence of the appellants. The appellants were also identified by the girls through photographs. The committee found the appellants guilty and consequently an expulsion order

218. *R.* v. *Assessment Committee of St. Mary Abbotts, Kensington*, (1891) 1 QB 378 (CA); *Pett* v. *Greyhound Racing Assn.* Ltd., (1969) 1 QB 125: (1968) 2 WLR 1471 (CA).
219. (1935) 1 KB 249 (CA).
220. (1935) 1 KB 249 (CA).
221. (1960) 1 WLR 223 (PC).
222. (1973) 1 SCC 805.

was served on them. The order of expulsion was challenged before the Supreme Court, and one of the grounds of challenge was that the evidence was taken behind their backs. The court rejected the contention holding that the girls would not have ventured to make the statements in the presence of the appellants except at a great risk of retaliation and harassment. In this case, whatever evidence was collected behind the backs of the appellants was brought to their notice and they were provided with an opportunity to rebut the evidence. Every case has to be decided on its own merit. In *Shantidevi Kamaleshkumar Yadav* v. *State of Maharashtra*[223], the court remanded the case back where Caste Scrutiny Committee, after completing the hearing, recorded the statement of the *tahsildar* without giving notice to the other party.

Therefore, any administrative agency may inform its mind in any manner it thinks best. It may take official notice of certain things and may make off-the-record consultation, but fairness demands that the party must be apprised of all these matters if these form the basis of the agency's decision. In the US, Section 5(*c*) of the Administrative Procedure Act, 1946 provides that no officer is to consult any person or party upon any fact in issue except upon notice and opportunity for all parties to participate. Section 7(*d*) further provides that where an agency decision rests on official notice of a material fact not appearing in evidence on the record, any party on timely request shall be afforded an opportunity to show to the contrary. A somewhat similar solution has been adopted in England in the case of ministerial enquiries.[224] But, there is nothing to prevent an administrator from collecting information before the hearing, and he is not compelled to disclose it.[225] Equally, there is no compulsion to disclose information which is obtained after the hearing.[226] The rationale behind this formulation is that to make an administrator solely dependent on evidence adduced by trial procedures would destroy the value of the administrative process.

1.3.7 *Report of the enquiry to be shown to the other party*

In no administrative proceeding it is necessary that everything must be done by the same officer alone. He is permitted to take help from his subordinates. If it is not so, the administration would come to a grinding halt because today the administration is ubiquitous and impinges freely and deeply on every aspect of an individual's life.

In very many cases, especially in disciplinary matters, it happens that the enquiry is entrusted to someone else and on the report being submitted, action is taken by the competent authority. Under these circumstances, a

223. (2008) 9 SCC 718.
224. Statutory Instrument 1962, No. 1424, para. 9. *See also*, Griffith, "The Council and the Chalkpit", (1961) 39 Public Administration 369.
225. *B. Johnson and Co. (Builders) Ltd.* v. *Minister of Health*, (1947) 2 All ER 395 (CA).
226. *See*, De Smith, *Judicial Control of Administrative Action* (1968) 194–95.

very obvious question of mega importance arises: "[W]hether the copy of the report of the inquiry officer be supplied to the charged employee before a final decision is taken by the competent authority?"

Keeping in view the importance of this question and its wide ramifications, Thakker J in *Union of India* v. *E. Bashyan*[227] did not venture to pronounce a final judgment on it, but rather thought it proper to refer this question to a larger Bench. This was a special leave petition by the Union of India from the judgment and order dated 12 November 1987 of the Central Administrative Tribunal, New Bombay, wherein this question had been answered in the affirmative, holding that the failure to supply the enquiry report to the delinquent before the disciplinary authority takes a final decision would constitute a violation of Article 311(2) of the Constitution and also of the principles of natural justice.

This question is important from the constitutional and administrative laws' points of view. One of the cardinal principles of administrative law is that any action which has civil consequences for any person cannot be taken without complying with the principles of natural justice. Therefore, the administrative law question in disciplinary matters has always been: "[W]hether failure to supply the copy of the report of the inquiry to the delinquent employee before the final decision is taken by the competent authority would violate the principles of natural justice?"

In the same manner, the constitutional question in such a situation will be: "[W]hether failure to supply a copy of the report of the inquiry to the delinquent would violate the provisions of Article 311(2) of the Constitution of India?" Article 311(2) of the Constitution provides that no government employee can be dismissed or removed or reduced in rank without giving him a reasonable opportunity of being heard in respect of charges framed against him. Therefore, it has always been a perplexing question: "[W]hether failure to supply the report of the inquiry officer to the charged government employee before a final decision is taken would amount to failure to provide a 'reasonable opportunity' as required under Article 311(2)?" Another constitutional question that can be asked in such a situation can also be: "[W]hether any final action which is taken by the authority on the basis of the report of the inquiry without first supplying a copy of it to the delinquent would be arbitrary and, hence, violative of Article 14 of the Constitution, which enshrines the great harmonising and rationalising principle?"[228]

At the very outset, it must be made clear that the question of supplying a copy of the report of the enquiry to the delinquent government employee before a final action is taken in his case on the basis of the report is not

227. (1988) 2 SCC 196.

228. *Satyavir Singh* v. *Union of India*, (1985) 4 SCC 252. The Supreme Court opined that Art. 14 applies not only to discriminatory class legislation but also to arbitrary or discriminatory State action. Violation of the principles of natural justice results in arbitrariness grounded in Art. 14 of the Constitution.

the same thing as a second opportunity against the punishment, which has been abolished by the Constitution (42nd Amendment) Act, 1976.[229] After this amendment, a second show-cause notice as regards the measure of penalty before its imposition is no more necessary. However, the issue of supplying a copy of the enquiry report to the delinquent employee before the authority takes a final decision on the guilt is altogether a different matter and is not covered under the purview of Section 44 of the 42nd Amendment, which only prohibits a second show-cause notice against the proposed punishment. A "second show-cause notice" refers to a situation where the disciplinary authority has already taken a decision on the guilt and proposed punishment. However, the issue of supplying a copy of the report of the enquiry officer refers to a situation where the authority has yet to take a decision on the guilt and the consequential punishment on the basis of the report of the enquiry officer. Therefore, in this context, the issue of the "second show-cause notice" is post-decisional, and that of supplying the report of the enquiry officer is predecisional.

Audi alteram partem or the rule of fair hearing, Thakker J rightly observed:

> It needs to be highlighted that serving a copy of the Enquiry Report on the delinquent to enable him to point out anomalies, if any, therein before the axe falls and before finding about guilt is recorded by the Disciplinary Authority is altogether a different matter from serving a second show cause notice to enable the delinquent [to represent] in the context of the measure of the penalty to be imposed.[230]

After reaching this basic conclusion that the "second show-cause notice" is different from serving a "copy of the inquiry report", the only question that remains to be answered is: "[W]hether failure to serve a copy of the inquiry report on the delinquent so as to enable him to point out anomalies, if any, therein before the final decision is reached violates the 'reasonable opportunity' clause of Article 311(2), in case of government employees, and the principles of natural justice for other employees?"

It is important to note that until recently there was no precedent or law which made it obligatory, in all cases, for the disciplinary authority to serve a copy of the enquiry report on the delinquent before a final action on the basis of the report is reached. However, it was for the first time on 6 November 1987 that a Full Bench of the Central Administrative Tribunal, speaking through K. Madhava Reddy J, Chairman, held that supplying a copy of the enquiry report to the delinquent before recording a finding against him is obligatory, and, failure to do so would vitiate the enquiry.[231] Before this decision, this question had not been answered squarely by any court in India.

---

229. *See*, S. 44 of the Constitution (42nd Amendment) Act, 1976.
230. *Union of India* v. *E. Bashyan*, (1988) 2 SCC 196, 198.
231. *Premnath K. Sharma* v. *Union of India*, (1988) 6 ATC 904. Decision was given on 6-11-1987.

About a quarter of a century ago, in 1964, a similar question had also come before the Supreme Court in *Union of India* v. *H.C. Goel*[232], though in a different context. In this case, the Enquiry Officer had found the charged employee not guilty of the charge of making an offer of a bribe to his superior officer. The Union Public Service Commission had also endorsed the conclusions of the Enquiry Officer. Nevertheless, the disciplinary authority, rejecting the report of the Enquiry Officer, found the delinquent officer guilty and punished him. This action was challenged on the ground that the decision of the disciplinary authority was not based on evidence and hence void. The highest Bench, while quashing the administrative action enunciated, the following propositions:

(1) The enquiry officer holds the enquiry against the delinquent as a delegate of the government.

(2) The object of the enquiry by an enquiry officer is to enable the government to hold an investigation into the charges framed against the delinquent, so that the government can, in due course, consider the evidence adduced and decide whether the said charges are proved or not.

(3) The findings on the merit recorded by the enquiry officer are intended merely to supply appropriate material for consideration of the government. Neither the findings nor the recommendations are binding on the disciplinary authority as was held in *A.N. D'Silva* v. *Union of India*[233].

(4) The enquiry report (along with the evidence recorded by the enquiry officer) constitutes the material on which the government has ultimately to act. That is the only purpose of the enquiry and the report which the enquiry officer makes as a result thereof.[234]

From the above propositions it becomes clear that the enquiry officer as a delegate of the disciplinary authority investigates the matter, collects evidence, and makes his recommendations on the basis thereon. Therefore, when the disciplinary authority holds the delinquent guilty, contrary to the material and the recommendation of the enquiry officer in his report, then the authority certainly is acting on "no evidence" before it and, hence, its decision holding the delinquent guilty is not legal. The decision of the highest Bench in this case, therefore, is a pointer to the fact that if the disciplinary authority disagrees with the "not guilty" report of the enquiry officer and decides to hold the delinquent "guilty", the report of the enquiry officer must be supplied to the "delinquent to give him an opportunity to address the mind of the disciplinary authority who alone can find him guilty". Nevertheless, in spite of this pointer, the court did not clearly lay down the

232. AIR 1964 SC 364.
233. AIR 1962 SC 1130.
234. See also, *Union of India* v. *E. Bashyan*, (1988) 2 SCC 196. Thakker J also enunciated these propositions, 198.

principle that the failure to supply a copy of the enquiry report to the delinquent before a final action is taken violates the principles of natural justice and the provisions of "reasonable opportunity" of Article 311(2).

In 1964, the highest Bench missed yet another opportunity of squarely answering this important question. In *Suresh Koshy George* v. *University of Kerala*[235], instead of answering the question, the Supreme Court raised another question: Whether the denial to furnish a copy of the report when demanded would amount to violation of the principles of natural justice? In this case, the Vice-Chancellor had instituted an enquiry into the charge of use of unfair means by a student and, on the basis of the report, the University had expelled him. This action was challenged on the ground that a copy of the report was not supplied. The court held that since a copy of the report was not specifically asked for by the student, there was no breach of the principles of natural justice.

The same question was once again posed to the Supreme Court in *Keshav Mills Co. Ltd.*[236] In this case, the appellant company after doing business for 30 years suddenly had to be closed down because of fall in production. As a result, 1200 persons became unemployed. The Government of India appointed a commission to enquire into the affairs of the company under Section 15 of the Industries (Development and Regulation) Act, 1951. On the basis of the report of the enquiry commission, the government passed an order, under Section 18-A of the Act, authorising the Gujarat State Textile Corporation to take over the Mill for a period of five years. This decision was challenged before the Supreme Court, and one of the grounds of challenge was that the report of the enquiry commission was not furnished. The court held that it was not possible to lay down any general principle on the question as to whether the report of an investigating body or an inspector appointed by an administrative authority should be made available to the person concerned before the authority reaches a decision upon that report. The answer to this question must always depend on the facts and circumstances of each case. It is not at all unlikely that there may be certain cases where, unless the report is given to the party, the party concerned cannot make any effective representation about the action taken on the basis of that report. Whether the report should be furnished or not must, therefore, depend on the circumstances of every individual case. Therefore, if the non-disclosure of a report causes any prejudice in any manner to a party, it must be disclosed, otherwise non-disclosure would amount to a violation of the principles of natural justice.

Maintaining the same line of approach, in *Bishnu Ram Borah* v. *Parag Saikia*[237], the highest Bench again reiterated that refusal to give a copy of

---

235. AIR 1969 SC 198.
236. (1973) 1 SCC 380.
237. (1984) 2 SCC 488; see also, *Chingleput Bottlers* v. *Majestic Bottling Company*, (1984) 3 SCC 258. Also see, *Central Board of Excise & Customs* v. *K.S. Mahalingam*, (1986) 3 SCC 35.

the report before a final decision is reached would not be such as to amount to denial of the principles of natural justice in all cases for the obvious reason that the rules of natural justice must necessarily vary with the nature of the right and the attendant circumstances. In *Plantation Division A&N Islands* v. *Munnu Barrick*[238], the Supreme Court once again emphasised the "prejudice doctrine" which makes it obligatory on the part of a workman to show that he had been prejudiced by reason of non-supply of enquiry report. Therefore, the principles of natural justice must be seen in circumstantial flexibility. An administrative action can be quashed only if non-observance of the principles of natural justice has caused serious prejudice to the complainant.[239]

The same position was maintained in *Haryana Financial Corpn.* v. *Kailash Chandra Ahuja*[240]. In this case after the conclusion of an enquiry, a show-cause notice was issued as to why he should not be dismissed from service. The report given was considered and an oral hearing was also provided and, thereafter, a dismissal order was passed. The dismissal order had been challenged on the ground that report of the enquiry was not given to him. Court held that non-supply of the enquiry report would not ipso facto result in proceedings being declared void, unless some serious prejudice is caused. Hence in every case, the question to be answered is: What difference non-supply of an enquiry report would make?

Those who hold the view that it must be obligatory in all cases for the disciplinary authority to supply a copy of the enquiry report to the delinquent before a final decision is reached argue that there may be errors and omissions, misstatements, and lack of evidence in the report of the enquiry officer which will affect the mind of the disciplinary authority. Therefore, if no opportunity is given to the delinquent to make a representation on the basis of the report, it would be a clear violation of the principles of natural justice. This is the line of reasoning which found favour with Thakker J also when he observed:

> The Disciplinary Authority builds his final conclusion on the basis of his own assessment of evidence taking into account the reasoning articulated in the Enquiry Officer's report and the recommendations made therein. If the report is not made available to the delinquent, this crucial material which enters into the consideration of the Disciplinary Authority never comes to be known to the delinquent and he gets no opportunity whatsoever to have a say in regard to this critical material at any point of time till the Disciplinary Authority holds him guilty or condemns him.[241] [He further goes on to say:] There can be glaring errors and omissions in the report. Or it may have been based on no evidence or rendered in disregard of or by overlooking evidence. Even so, the delinquent will have no opportunity to point out to the Disciplinary Authority about such

238. (2005) 2 SCC 237.
239. *P.D. Agrawal* v. *SBI*, (2006) 8 SCC 776.
240. (2008) 9 SCC 31.
241. *Union of India* v. *E. Bashyan*, (1988) 2 SCC 196, 198.

> errors and omissions and disabuse the mind of the Disciplinary Authority before the axe falls on him and he is punished.[242]

Thakker J, after finding a similarity between the report of the enquiry officer in disciplinary proceedings and the report of the Commissioner appointed by the court for taking accounts in a partnership suit, comments:

> It would be a startling proposition to propound that the court can accept or reject the report of the Commissioner with or without modification, without even showing the same to the parties or without hearing the parties in the context of the report.[243]

Those who hold the view that it must not be obligatory on the part of the disciplinary authority to supply a copy of the enquiry report to the delinquent before a final decision argue that the only virtue of the principles of natural justice is that they are not rigid like the principles of law and, hence, can be moulded to suit the requirement of fairness in an individual case. Therefore, it would not be proper to hold that in every case, non-supply of a copy of the enquiry report would amount to violation of the principles of natural justice. It is also argued that the second show-cause notice compulsory under Article 311 was abolished in 1976 only to avoid long delays in prosecution of delinquent employees which had led to a further deterioration in public service discipline. Thus, it is in the public interest that the disciplinary proceedings must be brought to a final termination as quickly as possible. They further argue that the administrative process which developed due to the inadequacies of the judicial process would lose its vitality and viability if any attempt is made to overjudicialise it.

It was perhaps this reasoning which led the House of Lords to suggest in *Local Govt. Board* v. *Arlidge*[244] (*Arlidge*) that the report of an inspector need not be shown if it is not tendered as a piece of evidence. In this case the Hampstead Borough Council had passed a closing order in respect of a dwelling house which was considered unfit for human habitation. On an appeal by Arlidge to the Local Government Board, the Minister appointed an inspector to hold an enquiry, and on the basis of the inspector's report, confirmed the closing order. This order was challenged before the court, and one of the grounds of challenge was that the report of the enquiry was not shown to the petitioner before the authority took the final action on the basis of that report. Denying the challenge, Their Lordships of the House of Lords held that the report of the inspector was merely a step in statutory procedure for enabling the administrative authority to arrive at a conclusion and, therefore, the report need not be shown. This is still the law in England, though as a matter of practice the report is usually shown to the other party. However, *Kanda* v. *Govt. of Malaya*[245] is a pointer in

---

242. *Ibid.*
243. *Ibid*, para. 4.
244. 1915 AC 120 (HL).
245. 1962 AC 322: (1962) 2 WLR 1153 (PC).

a different direction. In this case, Inspector Kanda had been dismissed by the Government of Malaya on the basis of an enquiry report which he had never seen. He brought an action for a declaration that his dismissal was void. Quashing the dismissal, Their Lordships of the Privy Council held, "....Their Lordships do not think it was correct to let the adjudicating officer have the report of inquiry unless the accused also had it so as to be able to correct or contradict the statements in it to his prejudice." Visible trend is that English Law now is also moving towards "prejudice" principle.

The report of the enquiry officer in relation to a decision thereupon by the disciplinary authority may take any of the following broad shapes:

(1) The enquiry report may indict the delinquent and the disciplinary authority may exonerate him.
(2) The enquiry report may exonerate the delinquent and the disciplinary authority may indict him.
(3) The enquiry report may indict the delinquent and the disciplinary authority may also indict him.
(4) The enquiry report may exonerate the delinquent and the disciplinary authority may also exonerate him.

In the first and fourth situations, supply of the enquiry report would be unnecessary. In the second case if the report of the enquiry is not supplied to the delinquent along with the comments of the disciplinary authority, it would violate the principle of fairness because in its absence the decision of the disciplinary authority would be based on "no evidence". Similarly, in the third situation, it will be in the interest of fairness if a copy of the report is supplied to the delinquent before a final decision is taken in his case. This will all the more be necessary in situations where enquiry has been held for the imposition of any major penalty. The report may contain errors, omissions, misstatements, or it may be based on "no evidence" or "insufficient evidence". In this situation, unless the delinquent is given an opportunity to clear the matter, any decision of holding him guilty would be against the principles of natural justice and the requirement of "reasonable opportunity" under Article 311(2). In this behalf, it is gratifying to note that the rules relating to disciplinary proceedings against civil servants working in the Central Public Works Department require that if a major penalty like dismissal, removal or reduction in rank is to be imposed on the delinquent, he must be given a show-cause notice along with the copy of the report to enable him to make a representation to the disciplinary authority.[246]

But in *Kailash Chander Asthana* v. *State of U.P.*[247], a Bench of three judges of the Supreme Court held that after the 42nd Amendment of Article 311, a copy of the enquiry report need not be shown to the delinquent government servant. Curiously enough, in *Union of India* v. *Mohd.*

246. Indian Law Institute, *Disciplinary Proceedings Against Government Servants: A Case-Study* (N.M. Tripathi 1962) 80.
247. (1988) 3 SCC 600.

Ramzan Khan[248] (*Mohd. Ramzan Khan*), again a Bench of three judges of the Supreme Court held the opposite by holding that non-furnishing of the enquiry report would amount to denial of the principles of natural justice. This could happen because the earlier decision of the coordinate Bench was not cited before it. Therefore, in *Electronic Corpn. of India* v. *B. Karunakar*[249], when the same question came before the court, the matter was referred to a larger Bench.

It may be pointed out that the rule laid down in *Mohd. Ramzan Khan* will not apply if the disciplinary authority itself is the hearing officer. There will not be a violation of Article 14 also, as both the cases come under different classifications.[250]

The larger Bench to which this question of mega importance was referred answered it in the affirmative. The court held that the delinquent employee has a right to a copy of the enquiry report before the disciplinary authority takes a decision on the question of his guilt. The court further emphasised that this rule extends to all establishments—government, non-government, public or private. Failure of the employee to ask for the report would not amount to waiver. Rules/standing orders denying this first-stage right will be invalid.[251] Thus, the court tilted the scales in favour of the claims of individual justice against the claims of discipline in public services. However, keeping in view the basic fact that the principles of natural justice are not rigid like the rules of law, the court modifying its stand in *S.K. Singh* v. *Central Bank of India*[252] held that there would be no automatic invalidation of administrative orders if the report was not shown. It must be shown by the party what prejudice has been caused to him when the report of the enquiry officer was not shown to him. This has brought an element of fairness back into the law on this point.

1.3.8 *Reasoned decisions or speaking orders*

"Reason" is an essential requirement of the rule of law. It provides a link between fact and decision, guard against non-application of mind, arbitrariness, and maintain public confidence in judicial and administrative authorities. Reasons also serve a wider principle that justice must not only be done, it must also appear to be done.

In India, in the absence of any particular statutory requirement, there is no general requirement for administrative agencies to give reasons for their decisions. However, if the statute under which the agency is functioning requires reasoned decisions, courts consider it mandatory for the administrative agency to give reasons, which should not be merely "rubber-stamp"

---

248. (1991) 1 SCC 588.
249. (1992) 1 SCC 709.
250. *Union of India* v. *Mohd. Ramzan Khan*, (1991) 1 SCC 588.
251. *ECIL* v. *B. Karunakar*, (1993) 4 SCC 727.
252. (1996) 6 SCC 415.

reasons but a brief, clear statement, providing the link between the material on which certain conclusions are based and the actual conclusion.[253] In *M.J. Sivani* v. *State of Karnataka*[254], the court reiterated that when the rules direct recording of reasons, it is a *sine qua non* and a condition precedent for a valid order. Appropriate brief reasons, though not like a judgment, are necessary for a valid order. Normally, they must be communicated to the affected party so that he may have an opportunity to have them tested in the appropriate forum. An administrative order itself may contain reasons, or the file may disclose reasons to arrive at the decision showing application of mind to the facts in issue.

If reasons are given, court can determine the relevance of reasons. In case reasons given are wrong, it may vitiate an administrative action. In *Global Energy Ltd.* v. *Central Electricity Regulatory Commission*[255], the court opined that when reason given for disqualification from seeking licence is that the applicant is involved in legal proceedings which may adversely affect the interest of electricity sector or consumer, court can vitiate an action because of recording of a wrong reason.

In cases where the statute does not provide for reasoned decisions, courts in India are still in the process of developing workable parameters between the claims of individual justice and administrative flexibility.

1.3.8.1 *Reasons may be mandated by the Constitution*

In case of legislative silence, a reasoned decision may be a constitutional requirement. In *Anumathi Sadhukhan* v. *A.K. Chatterjee*[256], the Calcutta High Court allowed the challenge to the validity of law which did not require a speaking order on the ground of unreasonable restriction on the exercise of fundamental rights. In this case, clauses 9 and 13 of the West Bengal Rice Mills Control Order, 1949—which had authorised the refusal to issue or renew a licence, or for suspension or cancellation of a licence already issued "without assigning any reasons"—were held as imposing unreasonable restrictions on the petitioner's right to trade and business guaranteed under Article 19(1)(*g*) of the Constitution, hence unconstitutional. The Madras[257] and Andhra Pradesh High Courts[258] also reiterated the same proposition and held that a law which does not require a reasoned decision constitutes an unreasonable restriction on the fundamental rights guaranteed under Article 19, clauses (2) to (6). There is no decision of the

253. *Gurdial Singh Fijji* v. *State of Punjab*, (1979) 2 SCC 368. See also, *Union of India* v. *Mohan Lal Capoor*, (1973) 2 SCC 836.
254. (1995) 6 SCC 289.
255. (2009) 15 SCC 570.
256. 1951 SCC OnLine Cal 57: AIR 1951 Cal 90.
257. *P. Narasimha* v. *District Magistrate, Cuddapah*, 1952 SCC OnLine Mad 181: AIR 1953 Mad 476.
258. *V.K. Balarama Chetty* v. *State*, 1957 SCC OnLine AP 76: AIR 1958 AP 93. See also, *Dundoo Balakrishnamurthy* v. *Municipal Commr.*, 1961 SCC OnLine AP 65: AIR 1961 AP 489, where this proposition was neither allowed nor denied.

Supreme Court on this point. However, in *Kishan Chand Arora* v. *Commr. of Police*[259] (*Kishan Chand Arora*), the Supreme Court with a majority of 3:2 negatived the proposition by holding that the Commissioner was exercising administrative and not quasi-judicial functions and, therefore, was not obliged to give reasons. In this case, the question before the court was whether Section 39 of the Calcutta Police Act, 1866, which authorised the Commissioner of Police to refuse a licence at his discretion to any eating or entertainment house, imposed an unreasonable restriction on the fundamental right guaranteed under Article 19(1)(*g*) of the Constitution. It may be pointed out that since the distinction between administrative and quasi-judicial functions has become blurred,[260] *Kishan Chand Arora* cannot be accepted as a proposition negativing the requirement of "reasons" as a constitutional mandate.

Reasons are the link between the order and the mind of the maker. "Reasoned decisions" also involve a question of "procedural fairness". A law which allows any administrative authority to take a decision affecting the rights of the people without assigning any reason cannot be accepted as laying down a procedure which is fair, just and reasonable and, hence, would be violative of Articles 14 and 21 of the Constitution.[261] The requirement of "reasons" may also be implied from the principles of natural justice.[262] In *Sunil Batra* v. *Delhi Admn.*[263], the Supreme Court read in Section 56 of the Prisons Act, 1894 an implied duty on the Jail Superintendent to give reasons for putting fetters on a prisoner.

It may be emphasised that the implied requirement of "reasons" is the foundation on which the whole scheme of judicial review under the Indian Constitution is based. Articles 32, 136, 226 and 227 provide for judicial review of administrative actions. The decisions of administrative agencies unaccompanied by reasons will have the effect of whittling down the efficacy of these constitutional provisions. If an administrative authority is allowed to keep its errors off the record by not writing reasons, the whole concept of judicial review would be meaningless.

1.3.8.2 *Reasons may be mandated by law*

If reasons are mandated by law, it is considered as mandatory. There is a plethora of laws which mandate reasons for an administrative action. For example, Section 31 of the Arbitration and Conciliation Act, 1996 mandates reasons by the arbitrator for an award. If reasons are not given when mandated by law, it would vitiate an administrative action.

259. AIR 1961 SC 705.
260. *A.K. Kraipak* v. *Union of India*, (1969) 2 SCC 262; *State of Mysore* v. *J.V. Bhat*, (1975) 1 SCC 110.
261. *Maneka Gandhi* v. *Union of India*, (1978) 1 SCC 248; *Govt. Branch Press* v. *D.B. Belliappa*, (1979) 1 SCC 477.
262. *Siemens Engg. & Mfg. Co. of India Ltd.* v. *Union of India*, (1976) 2 SCC 981.
263. (1978) 4 SCC 494.

1.3.8.3 *Reasons may be mandated by the principles of natural justice*

Reasons may be mandated by the principles of natural justice when an authority's action causes serious prejudice. This situation may arise where law is silent, but a person has suffered a serious personal or proprietary prejudice. Therefore, judicial, quasi-judicial and even administrative decisions must be supported by reasons as a requirement of a higher law, even if statutory law is silent. It will serve a wider principle of administrative law that it is not enough that justice be done but it must also be seen to be done.[264] In *Dev Dutta*[265], the Supreme Court opined that besides two known principles of natural justice, the third principle is transparency and good-governance; which mandate a duty to give reasons when a person suffers a prejudice, even in the face of contrary instructions. In this case, a person was not promoted even though he had a "good" entry in his confidential record because others had better entries. However, this "good" entry had not been communicated to him as office instruction provided that only adverse entry is to be communicated. Court held that even a good entry is to be communicated if a person suffers prejudice. Transparency and good-governance, as a facet of fairness, demand a duty to give reasons by the authority which gave entry. If reasons are not given, it would make an action arbitrary violative of Article 14 of the Constitution, which is a constitutional habitat of the principles of natural justice. Thus, even in the face of legislative silence "reasons" may be mandated by the principles of natural justice. In all disciplinary matters reasons are mandatory.

1.3.8.4 *Reasons may be mandated by the nature of functions which an administrative authority exercises*

Though the principles of natural justice as a rule of fairness apply to administrative and quasi-judicial functions, no matter with varying degree, yet if the authority is exercising quasi-judicial functions, or where there is a provision of appeal or revision against the decision of the authority, it must give reasons for its decisions. In *Mahabir Prasad Santosh Kumar* v. *State of U.P.*[266], court emphasised that if a quasi-judicial order is subject to appeal or revision, authority must give reasons even though not mandated by the statute. Similar are the observations of the court in *S.N. Mukherjee* v. *Union of India*[267] when it opined that unless giving of the reasons has been barred by law, either expressly or by necessary implication in public interest, authority exercising quasi-judicial powers, which is subject to appeal or revision by the higher administrative authority, must give reasons for the decision as without reasons appellate or revisional powers cannot be exercised.

264. *Karanti Associates (P) Ltd.* v. *Masood Ahmed Khan*, (2010) 9 SCC 496.
265. (2008) 8 SCC 725.
266. (1970) 1 SCC 764.
267. (1990) 4 SCC 594.

Recognising the efficacy of reasons as a deterrent against misuse of power by an administrative authority court in *Bhagat Ram Patanga* v. *State of Punjab*[268], the Supreme Court pointed out that even if no appeal or revision is provided, an administrative authority exercising quasi-judicial powers must give reasons for its decision.

While exercising the appellate or revisional powers, higher administrative authority may adopt any of the three options:

(1) It may confirm the order of the lower forum.
(2) It may reverse the order of the lower forum.
(3) It may vary the order of the lower forum.

In exercise of second and third option, law is certain that appellate administrative authority must give reasons for its decision.[269] However, courts were changing position where first option was exercised and appellate authority has confirmed the decision of the lower forum and reasons already existed as given by the lower forum.[270] In the interest of fairness, court has finally held in *Divl. Forest Officer* v. *Madhusudhan Rao*[271] that no doubt an appellate or revisional authority is not required to give detailed reasons for agreeing or confirming the order of the lower forum, but in the interest of justice, some brief reasons should be indicated even in an order affirming the decision of the lower forum. It will guard against non-application of mind.

In this behalf, the Supreme Court gave a bit of advice to the administrative authorities exercising quasi-judicial powers. The court observed:

> If courts of law are to be replaced by [the] administrative authorities and tribunals, as indeed, in some kinds of cases, with the proliferation of Administrative Law, they may have to be so replaced, it is essential that administrative authorities and tribunals should accord fair and proper hearing to the persons sought to be affected by their orders and give sufficiently clear and explicit reasons in support of the orders made by them. Then alone administrative authorities and tribunals exercising quasi-judicial function will be able to justify their existence and carry credibility with the people by inspiring confidence in the adjudicatory process.[272]

The same opinion was reiterated by Bhagwati J in *Maneka Gandhi* v. *Union of India*[273] (*Maneka Gandhi*) when he observed that the Central Government was wholly unjustified in withholding the reasons for impounding the passport of the petitioner, and in this way not only a

268. (1972) 2 SCC 170.
269. *Harinagar Sugar Mills Ltd.* v. *Shyam Sunder Jhunjhunwala*, AIR 1961 SC 1669; *State of Gujarat* v. *Patil Raghav Natha*, (1969) 2 SCC 187; *CIT* v. *Walchand & Co. (P) Ltd.*, AIR 1967 SC 1435.
270. *M.P. Industries Ltd.* v. *Union of India*, AIR 1966 SC 671. See also, *Rangnath* v. *Daulatrao*, (1975) 1 SCC 686; *Tara Chand Khatri* v. *MCD*, (1977) 1 SCC 472.
271. (2008) 3 SCC 469. See also, *Rani Lakshmi Bai Kshetriya Gramin Bank* v. *Jagdish Sharan Varshney*, (2009) 4 SCC 240.
272. *Siemens Engg. & Mfg. Co. of India Ltd.* v. *Union of India*, (1976) 2 SCC 981.
273. (1978) 1 SCC 248.

breach of statutory duty was committed but it also amounted to denial of an opportunity of hearing to the petitioner.

Reasons are required to be recorded when it affects the public interest. When the only obvious remedy available to the aggrieved person against the award is judicial review under Article 226 of the Constitution and if reasons are not given, it will be difficult for the High Court to exercise its powers. The reasons would indicate as to how the mind of the arbitrator was applied to the facts of the case.[274] In the same manner, in matters of granting exemption by the State, requirement of recording reasons is implicit even in the absence of express statutory provisions to give an administrative decision a non-arbitrary look.[275] Keeping in view the basic principle of administrative law that every State action must satisfy the rule of non-arbitrariness, the Supreme Court in *Kishan Lal* v. *Union of India*[276] held that while disposing an application made under Section 220(2-A) for reduction in interest imposed on account of default in payment of tax, it must be disposed of by a speaking order by the Central Board of Direct Taxes.

In disciplinary matters where full-scale hearing is given to the person, and a detailed report giving full facts and reasons is prepared by the enquiry officer, perhaps, the writing of reasons by the disciplinary authority when it fully agrees with the report will be a mere duplication of the process. The highest Bench also observed in *Tara Chand Khatri* v. *MCD*[277] that it would be laying down the proposition a little too broadly to say that even an order of concurrence must be supported by reasons. However, where the disciplinary authority disagrees with the report of the enquiry officer, it must state its reasons. In this case, an assistant teacher had been dismissed on the ground of moral turpitude. An enquiry was conducted in which the charge was fully established. The Assistant Education Commissioner confirmed the report without giving reasons. On appeal, the Commissioner of Education also upheld the dismissal by "an elaborate order". The petition challenging the dismissal order was dismissed by the Delhi High Court. In the special leave appeal under Article 136 the main contention was that the order of dismissal was bad, as the Assistant Education Commissioner, while confirming the report of the enquiry officer, did not give reasons.

It may be noted that, even in cases where reasons are to be given, the reasons must not always be in writing and supplied to the parties immediately. An oral pronouncement of reasons in the presence of parties, and their subsequent recording on file to the knowledge of the parties, will be sufficient compliance with the requirement.[278] If reasons are given, their adequacy is

274. *Star Enterprises* v. *City and Industrial Development Corpn. of Maharashtra Ltd.*, (1990) 3 SCC 280.
275. *T.R. Thandur* v. *Union of India*, (1996) 3 SCC 690.
276. (1998) 2 SCC 392. Delhi High Court had held that reasons are not necessary.
277. (1977) 1 SCC 472.
278. *Maharashtra SRTC* v. *Balwant Regular Motor Service*, AIR 1969 SC 329.

a justiciable issue. Courts do not prescribe any particular form or scale of reasons.[279] The nature and elaboration of reasons shall, therefore, depend on the fact situation of every case.[280] However, the reasons should reveal a rational nexus between the facts considered and the conclusions reached.[281] Mere mechanical or rubber stamp and uniform reasons given would not satisfy the requirement.[282] The reasons must show that the authority has applied its mind to the case[283], and must be given in such a manner that the appellate court may be in a position to canvass the correctness of the reasons given by it.[284] The reasons must also be intelligible, sufficient to sustain the decision, and must deal with all the substantial points. Mere fact that the proceedings were treated confidential does not dispense with the requirement of recording reasons.[285] The validity of an administrative action must be judged by the reasons recorded therein and not in the light of subsequent explanation or affidavit.[286] Therefore, it is not permissible for the authority to support the order by reasons not contained in the record.

The variegated and residual judicial behaviour in such an important area as "reasoned decisions" does not undermine the efficacy of "reasons" in any way, but merely indicates the difficulty of evolving a single inflexible rule that can be reasonably applied to all the varied fact situations of every case.[287] It is worthwhile to recollect that India is a party to the recommendations of the 1959 Delhi Congress of the International Commission of Jurists which suggested:

> It will further the Rule of Law if the executive is required to formulate its reasons when reaching its decisions of a judicial or administrative character and affecting the rights of individuals and at the request of a party concerned to communicate them to him.[288]

Thus, in order to maintain and uphold the rule of law, it is necessary that in all administrative and quasi-judicial actions, the requirement of a "reasoned decision" must be implied unless expressly excluded.[289]

---

279. *M.P. Industries Ltd.* v. *Union of India*, AIR 1966 SC 671.
280. *Ibid.*
281. *Union of India* v. *Mohan Lal Capoor*, (1973) 2 SCC 836.
282. *Ibid.*
283. *A. Vedachala Mudaliar* v. *State of Madras*, 1951 SCC OnLine Mad 215: AIR 1952 Mad 276.
284. *Mannarghat Union Motor Services Ltd.* v. *RTA*, 1951 SCC OnLine Mad 244: AIR 1953 Mad 59.
285. *Harinagar Sugar Mills Ltd.* v. *Shyam Sunder Jhunjhunwala*, AIR 1961 SC 1669.
286. *Mohinder Singh Gill* v. *Chief Election Commr.*, (1978) 1 SCC 405. See also, *Union of India* v. *E.G. Nambudiri*, (1991) 3 SCC 38.
287. *Poyser & Mills' Arbitration, re*, (1964) 2 QB 467: (1963) 2 WLR 1309.
288. "The Rule of Law in a Free Society", A Report on the International Congress of Jurists (New Delhi 1959) 8.
289. *See*, M.P. Singh, "Duty to Give Reasons for Quasi-Judicial and Administrative Decisions", (1979) 21 JILI 45. However, such an express exclusion would be unconstitutional where the violation of fundamental rights is involved.

In *Chairman and Managing Director, United Commercial Bank* v. *P.C. Kakkar*[290], wherein the High Court had reduced the punishment awarded by the administrative authority without giving reasons, the Supreme Court held that mere expression that the punishment is "shockingly disproportionate" would not meet the requirement of law; the court must give reasons because reasons substitute subjectivity by objectivity. Therefore, the "right to reasons" is an indispensable part of a sound judicial system and one of the statutory requirements of natural justice. However, keeping in view the twin claims of individual justice and administrative flexibility, the better proposition seems to be that the administrative agencies must give reasons when demanded; because in certain situations, giving of the reasons may do more injustice than not giving them.

Duty to assign reasons even in the absence of a statutory provision as a requirement of the principles of natural justice, when administrative actions carries civil or evil consequences, is a judge-made law. There is still a controversy whether "reasons" comprise a third pillar of natural justice. One view suggests that giving of reasons is a matter of legislative policy which should be left to the decision of the legislature. However, there are those who hold the view that reasons are implicit in every administrative action having civil consequences as a requirement of the principles of natural justice, and the exceptions, if any, would be required to be provided for either expressly or by necessary implications as arising out of the "useless formality" and "no-prejudice" doctrines.[291] Better view appears to be that good administration implies reasons where a person legitimately expects to be treated fairly.

Nevertheless, reasons may be withheld where public interest so requires, or where it would frustrate the procedure or produce more harm than benefit, or where a person has not suffered any prejudice.

The Supreme Court in *Dev Dutta*[292] emphasised that now transparency and good-governance have been added as a new dimension to natural justice which includes the duty to give reasons.

In England, Section 12(1) of the Tribunals and Inquiries Act, 1958 imposes a duty to give reasons only where the party requests for them on or before the giving or notification of the decision. But many tribunals give reasons as a matter of course without waiting for such requests. This clause however admits certain exceptions. In some cases of rule-making actions based on hearing, reasons may not be given. Reasons may also be refused by any individual tribunal if in its opinion it may cause injustice. For example, the Mental Health Tribunal, which determines the question whether a mental patient should be forcibly confined, does not give reasons in the interests of the patient. The Lord Chancellor also has the power under the Tribunals and Inquiries Act, 1958 to direct by order that in certain classes

290. (2003) 4 SCC 364.
291. *Rajesh Kumar* v. *CIT*, (2007) 2 SCC 181.
292. (2008) 8 SCC 725.

of decisions, the authority shall not give reasons if in its opinion it is unnecessary or impracticable.[293]

It may be noted that the Committee on Ministers' Powers (1932) made a strong plea that the principles of natural justice must be so extended as to include reasoned decisions. Therefore, there is now a clear trend towards transparency which requires that administrative authorities must give reasons for their decisions.[294] However, reasons may be withheld in public interest and other justifiable reasons.

In the US, Section 8(*b*) of the Administrative Procedure Act, 1946 requires administrative agencies to give reasons for their decisions. The right to reasoned decisions also arises from the due process clause of the Constitution. A decision unaccompanied by reason may not be considered a "due" decision. Furthermore, due process also includes a right to have a written record which must consist of evidence, arguments, reasons, and all the papers filed in the case.

The principles on the recording of reasons have been summarised by the Supreme Court in *Kranti Associates (P) Ltd.* v. *Masood Ahmed Khan*[295] as follows:

(*a*) In India the judicial trend has always been to record reasons, even in administrative decisions, if such decisions affect anyone prejudicially.
(*b*) A quasi-judicial authority must record reasons in support of its conclusions.
(*c*) Insistence on recording of reasons is meant to serve the wider principle of justice that justice must not only be done it must also appear to be done as well.
(*d*) Recording of reasons also operates as a valid restraint on any possible arbitrary exercise of judicial and quasi-judicial or even administrative power.
(*e*) Reasons reassure that discretion has been exercised by the decision-maker on relevant grounds and by disregarding extraneous considerations.
(*f*) Reasons have virtually become as indispensable a component of a decision-making process as observing principles of natural justice by judicial, quasi-judicial and even by administrative bodies.
(*g*) Reasons facilitate the process of judicial review by superior courts.
(*h*) The ongoing judicial trend in all countries committed to rule of law and constitutional governance is in favour of reasoned decisions based on relevant facts. This is virtually the lifeblood of judicial decision-making justifying the principle that reason is the soul of justice.
(*i*) Judicial or even quasi-judicial opinions these days can be as different as the judges and authorities who deliver them. All these decisions serve one common purpose which is to demonstrate by reason that the relevant factors have been objectively considered. This is important for sustaining the litigants' faith in the justice delivery system.

293. S. 12(4), Tribunals and Inquiries Act, 1958.
294. See, *R.* v. *Higher Education Funding Council, ex p Institute of Dental Surgery*, (1994) 1 WLR 242 (DC).
295. (2010) 9 SCC 496, 510, para. 47.

(*j*) Insistence on reason is a requirement for both judicial accountability and transparency.

(*k*) If a judge or a quasi-judicial authority is not candid enough about his/her decision-making process then it is impossible to know whether the person deciding is faithful to the doctrine of precedent or to principles of incrementalism.

(*l*) Reasons in support of decisions must be cogent, clear and succinct. A pretence of reasons or "rubber-stamp reasons" is not to be equated with a valid decision-making process.

(*m*) It cannot be doubted that transparency is the sine qua non of restraint on abuse of judicial powers. Transparency in decision-making not only makes the judges and decision-makers less prone to errors but also makes them subject to broader scrutiny.[296]

(*n*) Since the requirement to record reasons emanates from the broad doctrine of fairness in decision-making, the said requirement is now virtually a component of human rights and was considered part of Strasbourg Jurisprudence[297], wherein the Court referred to Article 6 of the European Convention of Human Rights which requires, "adequate and intelligent reasons must be given for judicial decisions".

(*o*) In all common law jurisdictions judgments play a vital role in setting up precedents for the future. Therefore, for development of law, requirement of giving reasons for the decision is of the essence and is virtually a part of "due process".

1.3.9 *Institutional decision or one who decides must hear*

The expression "one who decides must hear", which is popular in common-law jurisdiction, is known by the term "institutional or anonymous decisions" in American law. Unlike law courts, the decision in many administrative proceedings is not the decision of one man from start to finish. Often one person hears and another decides. The divided responsibility may work contrary to the concept of fair hearing.

This problem was raised before the House of Lords in *Arlidge*[298]. In this case, the Hampstead Borough Council made a closing order in respect of a dwelling house. Hearing was given by the inspector but the actual decision confirming the closing order came from the Local Government Board. The decision was challenged on the ground that it was a denial of natural justice insofar as the person who actually decided the case did not hear. The challenge was rejected on the ground that government departments are not expected to conduct their business like a court of law and, therefore, could act according to their routine, taking the assistance of their subordinates. This still remains the position of law in England even after the Tribunals and Inquiries Act, 1977 because the inspector who holds the

296. *See*, David Shapiro, "Defence of Judicial Candor", (1987) 100 Harv L Rev 731–37.

297. See, *Ruiz Torija* v. *Spain*, (1994) 19 EHRR 553; *Anya* v. *University of Oxford*, 2001 EWCA Civ 405: 2001 ICR 847 (CA).

298. 1915 AC 120 (HL).

enquiry cannot take any decision, but is only entitled to make a recommendation to the Minister.

In the US, the concept of "one who decides must hear" was discussed by the *Morgan* v. *United States*[299] (*Morgan*). In this case, the statute authorised the Secretary of Agriculture to make an order fixing the maximum rates for dealings in stockyards of Kansas City. The hearing in this case was given by a subordinate officer, and the final decision regarding rates came from the Secretary. It may be noted that there was evidence on file showing that the Secretary did not personally consider the case and appraise the evidence. Under these circumstances, the US Supreme Court, quashing the order of the Secretary, observed that when an official is vested by law with the power to decide, he has the duty to exercise real deciding function in which evidence is received and weighed by the trier of facts. That duty cannot be performed by one who has not considered the evidence or the arguments. It is not an impersonal obligation. It is a duty akin to that of a judge. The one who decides must hear.[300]

The momentum which this case generated in administrative procedure led the draftsmen of the Administrative Procedure Act, 1946 to make provisions for eliminating the separation between hearing and decision-making within the agency. The Administrative Procedure Act, 1946 requires a positive decision from the person or the body that actually receives the evidence. Those cases which are heard by the examiners are initially decided by them. Therefore, unlike inspectors in England, the examiners in the US exercise powers analogous to that exercised by a trial judge.

In India, *Nageswara Rao*[301] is a case where an administrative action was challenged on the ground that the one who decided did not hear. In this case, the petitioners challenged the order of the government confirming the scheme of road nationalisation. The Secretary of the Transport Department gave the hearing, but the final decision came from the Chief Minister. The Supreme Court held that this divided responsibility was against the concept of fair hearing because if one who decides does not hear the party, he gets no opportunity of clearing doubts in his mind by reasoned arguments. However, in *G. Nageswara Rao* v. *State of A.P.* (*II*)[302] [*Gullapalli* (*II*)], where the Minister gave hearing and the Chief Minister decided the case, the Supreme Court held that there was no violation of the principles of natural justice.

In the same manner when hearing was required to be given by the Central Government but was actually given by the Joint Secretary and ultimately order was passed by the Deputy Secretary, the Supreme Court held that it is a clear case of an institutional hearing and hence not violative of

299. 80 L Ed 1288: 298 US 468 (1935).
300. *Local Govt. Board* v. *Arlidge*, 1915 AC 120 (HL).
301. AIR 1959 SC 308.
302. AIR 1959 SC 1376.

the principles of natural justice.[303] Whatever may be the merit of this rule, the fact remains that in view of the complexity of modern administration, a literal application of this rule will cause a spoke to be put in the wheels of administration, bringing it to a grinding halt. This, again, is not the correct import of *Morgan*[304] on which the Supreme Court based its decision in *Gullapalli (II)*[305]. The real thrust of *Morgan*[306] is that the person or authority charged with the responsibility of taking a decision may take help from subordinates, but he must personally consider and appraise the evidence and independently come to a decision. Demanding something more than this would amount to breaking a quixotic lance against something deeply ingrained in the administrative process.

1.3.10 *Rule against dictation*

Any administrative authority invested with the power of decision-making must exercise this power in exercise of its own judgment. The decision must be actually of the one who decides. Therefore, if a decision is taken at the direction of any outside agency, there is a violation of fair hearing. In *Mahadayal Premchandra* v. *CTO*[307], the Supreme Court quashed the decision of the Commercial Tax Officer imposing tax on the petitioner on directions from his superior officer even when he himself was of the opinion that the petitioner was not liable to tax. In the same manner, in *Orient Paper Mills Ltd.* v. *Union of India*[308], the Supreme Court quashed the order of the Deputy Superintendent levying excise duty passed on the directions of the Collector.

1.3.11 *Financial incapacity to attend the enquiry*

This new break in the concept of natural justice has special relevance in developing countries. If the circumstances are such that due to financial incapacity a person is unable to attend enquiry proceedings and, thus, does not have the opportunity to adduce and rebut evidence, it may amount to a denial of fair hearing. In *Ghanshyam Das Srivastava* v. *State of M.P.*[309], the Supreme Court held that when due to non-payment of even suspension allowance for a long period, the employee could not attend the departmental enquiry held away from his home, the ex parte order of the government violated the fundamentals of fair hearing. In the same manner if due to

303. *Kalinga Mining Corpn.* v. *Union of India*, (2013) 5 SCC 252.
304. 80 L Ed 1288: 298 US 468 (1935)
305. AIR 1959 SC 1376.
306. 80 L Ed 1288: 298 US 468 (1935).
307. AIR 1958 SC 667. See also, *Commr. of Police* v. *Gordhandas Bhanji*, 1951 SCC 1088: AIR 1952 SC 16; *Rambharosa Singh* v. *State of Bihar*, 1953 SCC OnLine Pat 46: AIR 1953 Pat 370; *Purtabpore Co. Ltd.* v. *Cane Commr. of Bihar*, (1969) 1 SCC 308.
308. (1970) 3 SCC 76.
309. (1973) 1 SCC 656.

financial incapacity of a person defence witnesses could not be examined, then any decision by an administrative authority shall violate the principles of fair hearing. In *Mumtaz Hussain Ansari* v. *State of U.P.*[310], the appellant, a District Superintendent of Police at Pilibhit, had been charged on various counts including wilful absence from duty. Before the tribunal, he wanted eight witnesses to be examined in his defence. The tribunal asked him to deposit ₹900 for the allowance to be paid to the witnesses. The appellant could not deposit the amount and, hence, witnesses were not examined. The Supreme Court ruled that if the appellant was under suspension for a long time and, hence, could not deposit the amount due to his financial incapacity, the failure not to summon defence witnesses at the government's expense was a violation of the principles of natural justice, unless it was decided by the authority that the evidence of such witnesses was not material.

1.3.12 *Decision post-haste*

Fundamentals of fair hearing demand that the administrative authority must not rush to make decisions. In *City Corner* v. *Collector*[311], the appellant applied for a licence under the Places of Public Resort Act, 1888 for conducting games of skill and dance. The licence was granted to him on 10 October 1974. Thereafter, the appellant spent about ₹27,000 and put up a temporary structure. On 21 January 1975, the Additional District Magistrate asked him to show cause as to why the licence should not be revoked because the Superintendent of Police and two other local associations had objected to the grant of licence. On 25 January 1975, the notice reached the appellant and on 27 January 1975, he wrote back for the supply of original adverse material because the summary supplied was misleading. Without caring to wait for a reply, the licence was revoked on 28 January 1975. The Supreme Court held that the order passed post-haste without supplying copies of adverse material, or intimating that the summary of documents already supplied was sufficient, offends the principles of natural justice. In the same manner, in *S.P. Kapoor*[312], the Supreme Court quashed the action of the government taken in haste. In this case, the Departmental Promotion Committee was constituted the very next day of the finalisation of the seniority list of the candidates, who were continuing on ad hoc promotion for about six years. At the time of constitution of the committee, one of its members (Secretary to the department concerned) was on leave for a short period and, therefore, the person officiating (Principal Secretary to the Chief Minister) was included in his place as a committee member. Selections were made and the orders of appointment were also issued on the very date of the constitution of the committee. The Supreme Court

310. (1984) 3 SCC 295.
311. (1976) 1 SCC 124.
312. (1981) 4 SCC 716.

held that the way the whole thing was completed in haste gives rise to the suspicion that some high-up was interested in pushing through the matter hastily and, hence, the matter requires to be considered afresh.

1.4 Should the third party to dispute be heard

Essence of any fair adjudication is that the parties to the dispute must be heard. However, should a third party to a dispute also be entitled to a hearing, particularly, if the decision is likely to adversely affect his interest? This was the question before the Supreme Court in *Antonio S.C. Pereira* v. *Ricardina Noronha*[313], a case under Goa, Daman and Diu Administration of the Evacuee Property Act, 1962. In this case, question of title to the property was pending before the civil court, but in the meantime an application was filed before the Custodian, Evacuee Property for declaring property as non-evacuee and for restoration of the property. The Custodian ultimately allowed the petition, but without hearing the person who was contesting the title suit of the property before the civil court. The question before the Supreme Court was whether a "third person" to the dispute before the Custodian should have been heard? Answering the question in affirmative, the court observed that even if law does not provide for it, a third person must be heard in the same dispute if he is likely to suffer substantial injury by the decision.

1.5 Off-the-record consultation

It is imperative that administrative authorities exercising adjudicatory powers should not consult any person or party about any fact in issue without giving notice and opportunity to the other party to participate.[314] In England, this rule applies to all enquiries. In India, in the absence of any statutory rule, the Supreme Court in *State of Kerala* v. *Zoom Developers (P) Ltd.*[315] rightly held that off-the-record advice or opinion, which was taken into consideration without bringing it to the notice of the other party to rebut, violates the principles of fair hearing.

1.6 Fact-finding enquiry/pre-hearing

Though pre-hearing does not decide anything as it is merely a fact-finding exercise which may give rise to a full hearing later on, yet because it may have serious implications for future hearing, or for a person's reputation as a professional or public man, or for goodwill of a business because of the publicity it generates, principles of natural justice are attracted. Even though ultimately it may find nothing worth enquiring, but prejudice

313. (2006) 7 SCC 740.
314. *See*, S. 5(2), Administrative Procedure Act, 1946.
315. (2009) 4 SCC 563.

already caused from the fact that the person was under scanner cannot be remedied.

2. POST-DECISIONAL HEARING

The idea of post-decisional hearing has been developed to maintain a balance between administrative efficiency and fairness to the individual. This harmonising tool was developed by the Supreme Court in *Maneka Gandhi*[316]. In this case, the passport dated 1 June 1976 of the petitioner, a journalist, was impounded "in the public interest" by an order dated 2 July 1977, and the government having declined to furnish her the reasons for its decision.[317] She filed a petition before the Supreme Court under Article 32 challenging the validity of the impoundment order. The government also did not give her any pre-decisional notice and hearing. One of the contentions of the government, relevant for our purposes, was that the rule of *audi alteram partem* must be held to be excluded because it may have frustrated the very purpose of impounding the passport. Rejecting the contention, the court rightly held that though the impoundment of the passport was an administrative action, yet the rule of fair hearing was attracted by necessary implication, and it would not be fair to exclude the application of this cardinal rule on the ground of administrative convenience. However, the court did not outright quash the order and allowed the return of the passport because of the special socio-political factors attending the case. On the contrary, the technique of post-decisional hearing was developed in order to balance these factors against the clear requirements of law, justice and fairness. The court stressed that a fair opportunity of being heard following immediately the order impounding the passport would satisfy the mandate of natural justice. The concept of post-decisional hearing in situations where pre-decisional hearing is required either expressly or by necessary implication is itself based on wrong hypothesis that administrative efficiency and fairness to the individual are discrete values. One cannot expect that a post-decisional hearing would be anything more than a mere empty formalistic ritual.

The same technique of validating void administrative decision by post-decisional hearing was adopted in *Swadeshi Cotton Mills* v. *Union of India*[318] (*Swadeshi Cotton Mills*). The court validated the order of the government for taking over the management of the company, which had been passed in violation of the *audi alteram partem* rule and which was found to have been attracted by necessary implication, as the government had agreed to give a post-decisional hearing. However, doubts were expressed over the

316. (1978) 1 SCC 248.

317. The government, however, filed an affidavit in the court stating that her passport was impounded because her presence was required before the Shah Commission which was inquiring into the 1975 Emergency excesses.

318. (1981) 1 SCC 664.

majority decision in this case which led Koshal J to refer this matter for the decision of a larger Bench, when he was confronted with the same problem in *Tea Trading Corpn. of India Ltd.* v. *Pashok Tea Co. Ltd.*[319] (*Pashok Tea Co. Ltd.*).

Besides this, *K.I. Shephard* v. *Union of India*[320] also reflects the thought process of the highest Bench on this important issue. In this case, in terms of the scheme drawn under Section 45 of the Banking Regulation Act, 1949, three erstwhile banks had been amalgamated. Pursuant to the scheme, certain employees of the amalgamated banks were excluded from employment and their services were not taken over. Some excluded employees filed writs before the High Court under Article 226 for relief. The Single Judge granted partial relief by proposing post-decisional hearing. On appeal, the Division Bench dismissed the writ petitions. Some of the excluded employees then filed writ petitions directly before the Supreme Court. Allowing the writs, the court held that post-decisional hearing in this case would not do justice, especially, where the normal rule of fair hearing should apply. The court pointed out that there is no justification to throw a person out of employment and then give him an opportunity of representation, when the requirement is that he should have an opportunity as a condition precedent to the action. The court observed that it is a common experience that once a decision is taken, there is a tendency to uphold it and the representation may not yield any fruitful result. Therefore, even in cases of emergent situations, pre-decisional hearing is necessary which may not be an elaborate one, especially in cases where the action has grave consequences such as loss of livelihood.

Justifying the idea of post-decisional hearing, Professor de Smith writes:

> Can the absence of a hearing before a decision is made be adequately compensated for by a hearing ex post facto? A prior hearing may be better than a subsequent hearing, but a subsequent hearing is better than no hearing at all; and in some cases the courts have held that statutory provisions for an administrative appeal or even full judicial review on merits is sufficient to negative the existence of any implied duty to hear before the original decision is made. The approach may be acceptable where the original decision does not cause serious detriment to the person affected, or where there is also a paramount need for prompt action, or where it is impracticable to afford antecedent hearings.[321]

In substance, it is the "necessity for speed" which justifies post-decisional hearing at a later stage. In emergent situations, the principles of natural justice are excluded and, therefore, if the court comes to the conclusion that in a given situation these rules are applicable, there seems to be no reason as to why their observance should not be insisted upon at the pre-

319. (1981) 4 SCC 113.
320. (1987) 4 SCC 431.
321. Stanley A. De Smith, *Judicial Review of Administrative Action* (3rd Edn., Stevens 1973) 170.

decisional stage. Following this line of reasoning, the Supreme Court in *H.L. Trehan*[322] observed:

> In our opinion, the post-decisional opportunity of hearing does not subserve the rules of natural justice. The authority who embarks upon a post-decisional hearing will naturally proceed with a closed mind and there is hardly any chance of getting a proper consideration of the representation at such a post-decisional opportunity.

Thus, in every case where the pre-decisional hearing is warranted, post-decisional hearing will not validate the action except in very exceptional circumstances.[323] Such exceptional circumstances may include deprivation of liberty, livelihood and property, unless dire public interest demands otherwise. Thus, a balance between the interest of the affected individual and public interest has to be maintained. Fact remains that at times "to do a great right, it is permissible sometimes to do a little wrong"[324]. Recent trend of judicial decision appears to restrict its application to exceptional situations, which require immediate action in public interest.[325]

In the US, "due process" implies fair hearing with promptitude. Therefore, pre-decisional hearing is a rule and post decisional hearing is an exception. Generally, pre-decisional hearing is insisted upon when administrative action impairs liberty and property interests, and post-decisional hearing is allowed in case of violation of dire public interest in situations of emergency and impracticability.

The courts have developed three-part balancing test to determine when pre-decisional or post-decisional hearing is mandated. These include 1) public interest involved; 2) risks involved in allowing pre-decisional hearing, and values of the Constitution involved; and 3) government's financial and administrative implications.[326] This balancing test has been further refined by including 1) important government and general public interest; 2) need for prompt action; and 3) quality of control over force of the government.[327] Court have rightly insisted on adequate compensation if an action is found contrary to law, or status ante cannot be restored.[328] Post-decisional hearing is thus not a violation of the principles of natural justice, but a modification of it in special circumstances.

---

322. (1989) 1 SCC 764, 770, para. 12.
323. See, *Bari Doab Bank Ltd.* v. *Union of India*, (1997) 6 SCC 417. Government passed the order of moratorium under the Banking Regulations Act, 1949 on the petitioner-Bank—held, petitioners are not entitled to pre-decisional hearing before passing the order, as post-decisional hearing at the stage of filing objections to the draft scheme would be sufficient.
324. *Charan Lal Sahu* v. *Union of India*, (1990) 1 SCC 613.
325. Soli Sorabjee, "Obliging Government to Control itself: Recent Developments in Indian Administrative Law", (1994) Public Law 39.
326. *F. David Mathew* v. *Geroge H. Eldrige*, 1976 SCC OnLine US SC 22: 47 L Ed 2d 18: 424 US 319 (1976).
327. *Fuentes* v. *L. Shevin Parham*, 1972 SCC OnLine US SC 137: 32 L Ed 2d 556: 407 US 67 (1972).
328. *Reich* v. *Collins*, 1994 SCC OnLine US SC 98: 130 L Ed 2d 454: 513 US 106 (1994).

Elaborating the law further, the Supreme Court in *Canara Bank* v. *V.K. Awasthy*[329] further emphasised that in judging the legal validity of post-decisional hearing, legal formulations cannot be divorced from the fact situation of the case, as the purpose of natural justice is to prohibit accidents in administrative justice. In this case, no pre-decisional hearing had been given, however, the appellate authority granted personal hearing, even though it was not required, under law before confirming the dismissal order of an officer of the Bank. Under these circumstances, in the absence of any specific prejudice shown by the officer, the court came to the conclusion that post-decisional hearing can obliterate the procedural deficiency of pre-decisional hearing, but because the delinquent Bank officer had the opportunity to meet the stand of the Bank, hence, there was no violation of the principles of natural justice. However, where pre-decisional hearing is warranted by law, post-decisional hearing is not proper, especially, where authority has already made up its mind and the result is a foregone conclusion.[330]

3. EXCEPTIONS TO THE RULE OF NATURAL JUSTICE

The word "exception" in the context of natural justice is really a misnomer, because in these exclusionary cases, the rule of *audi alteram partem* is held inapplicable not by way of an exception to "fair play in action", but because nothing unfair can be inferred by not affording an opportunity to present or meet a case.[331] Such situations where nothing unfair can be inferred by not affording a fair hearing must be few and exceptional in every civilised society. Principles of natural justice are ultimately weighed in the balance of fairness and, hence, the courts have been circumspect in extending these principles to situations where it would cause more injustice rather than justice.[332] For example, a party would forfeit its right to hearing if undue advantage obtained is protracting the proceedings somehow and nullifying the objectives.[333] Thus, where a teacher of the Navodaya Vidyalaya was dismissed on gross moral turpitude without giving exhaustive hearing per Central Civil Services (Classification, Control and Appeal) Rules rules, the court held the termination valid on the ground that fairness cannot be made counter-productive.[334]

Application of the principles of natural justice can be excluded either expressly or by necessary implication, subject to the provisions of Articles 14 and 21 of the Constitution. Therefore, where the Ordinance provided for hearing before taking over non-government schools, but the Bihar Non-Government Secondary Schools (Taking-over of Management

329. (2005) 6 SCC 321.
330. *Shekhar Ghosh* v. *Union of India*, (2007) 1 SCC 331.
331. *Maneka Gandhi* v. *Union of India*, (1978) 1 SCC 248.
332. *Karnataka Public Service Commission* v. *B.M. Vijay Shankar*, (1992) 2 SCC 206.
333. *Ram Krishna Verma* v. *State of U.P.*, (1992) 2 SCC 620.
334. *Avinash Nagra* v. *Navodaya Vidyalaya Samiti*, (1997) 2 SCC 534.

and Control) Act, 1981 following the Ordinance deliberately omitted it, the Supreme Court held that by implication the legislature excluded the rule of hearing.[335] Therefore, if the statute, expressly or by necessary implication, precludes the rules of natural justice, it will not suffer invalidation on the ground of arbitrariness, unless a person suffers adverse civil consequences. In such situation, fair hearing will be read into the law.[336] Other exclusionary situations may include the following.

3.1 Exclusion in emergency

In such exceptional cases of emergency where prompt action, preventive or remedial, is needed, the requirement of notice and hearing may be obviated. Therefore, if the right to be heard will paralyse the process, law will exclude it. It has been said that no army can be commanded by a debating society, but it is also true that the House of Commons did debate, during the days of debacle and disaster, agony and crisis of World War II, the life and death aspect of the Supreme Command by the then British Prime Minister to the distress of all friends and to the delight of all foes. Hence, if to condemn unheard is wrong, it is wrong except where it is overborne by dire social necessity.[337] Therefore, in situations where a dangerous building is to be demolished,[338] or a company has to be wound up to save depositors,[339] or there is an imminent danger to peace,[340] or a trade dangerous to society is to be prohibited,[341] dire social necessity requires exclusion of the elaborate process of fair hearing. In the same manner, where power theft was detected by officials, immediate disconnection of supply is not violative of the principles of natural justice.[342]

Even in a situation of emergency where precious rights of people are involved, post-decisional hearing has relevance to administrative and judicial gentlemanliness.[343] Otherwise, some pre-decisional hearing, no matter in a rudimentary form, must be given depending on the fact situation of every case.

However, the administrative determination of an emergency situation calling for the exclusion of rules of natural justice is not final. Courts may review the determination of such a situation. In *Swadeshi Cotton Mills*[344],

335. *Rash Lal Yadav* v. *State of Bihar*, (1994) 5 SCC 267.
336. *Automotive Tyre Manufacturers Assn.* v. *Designated Authority*, (2011) 2 SCC 258.
337. Extract from the judgment of Krishna Iyer J in *Mohinder Singh Gill* v. *Chief Election Commr.*, (1978) 1 SCC 405, 432. See also, *Liversidge* v. *Anderson*, 1942 AC 206 (HL).
338. *Nathubhai Dhulaji* v. *Municipal Corpn.*, 1957 SCC OnLine Bom 264: AIR 1959 Bom 332.
339. *Joseph Kuruvilla Vellukunnel* v. *RBI*, AIR 1962 SC 1371.
340. *Babulal Parate* v. *State of Maharashtra*, AIR 1961 SC 884.
341. *Cooverjee* v. *Excise Commr.*, AIR 1954 SC 220.
342. *Hyderabad Vanaspathi Ltd.* v. *A.P. SEB*, (1998) 4 SCC 470.
343. *Maneka Gandhi* v. *Union of India*, (1978) 1 SCC 248. See also, *Mohinder Singh Gill* v. *Chief Election Commr.*, (1978) 1 SCC 405, 432.
344. (1981) 1 SCC 664. See also, *Tea Trading Corpn. of India Ltd.* v. *Pashok Tea Co. Ltd.*, (1981) 4 SCC 113. Mention may be made of *S.L. Kapoor* v. *Jagmohan*, (1980) 4 SCC 379, where it

the court held that the word "immediate" in Section 18-AA of the Industries (Development and Regulation) Act, 1951 cannot stand in the way of the application of the rules of natural justice.

Under Section 18-A of the Industries (Development and Regulation) Act, 1951, the Central Government can take over an industry after investigation, but under Section 18-AA(1) the government can take over without any notice and hearing on the ground that production has been or is likely to be affected and, hence, immediate action is necessary. The question was whether Section 18-AA(1) excludes the principles of natural justice. The government took the plea that since Section 18-AA(1) relates to emergent situations, therefore, the principles of natural justice are excluded. Furthermore, it was also argued that since Section 18-A provides for hearing and Section 18-AA(1) does not so provide, consequently Parliament has excluded hearing therein. Rejecting these arguments, the court held that even in emergent situations the competing claims of "hurry and hearing" are to be reconciled, no matter the application of the *audi alteram partem* rule at the pre-decisional stage may be "a short measure of fair hearing adjusted, attuned and tailored to the exigency of the situation".[345]

The fact is that the principles of natural justice cannot be used to paralyse the exercise of administrative power when need of promptitude and urgency demand prompt action. Upholding the validity of a Standing Order which had authorised the administration to dismiss any employee in exceptional situations, after recording reasons, the Supreme Court held that where an employee is involved in a serious act of indiscipline which is likely to affect the functioning of the institution, prompt action, which involves an element of deterrence to save the situation from worsening, is necessary; principles of natural justice may not apply in the larger interest of society.[346]

In the same manner the principles of natural justice may not be attracted in situations where concerns of national security are involved. National security is a matter of State policy and must be left to the State to be decided on justiciable facts. In such matters a person cannot insist on strict observance of the principles of natural justice. Therefore, the court may, after satisfying itself that it is a case involving matters of national security, exclude the principles of natural justice even without assigning any reason.[347]

---

was held that even in emergent situations where swift action is necessary to avert disaster, minimal natural justice is not excluded.

345. *See also*, M.P. Jain, *Changing Face of Administrative Law in India and Abroad* (1982) 23–24. Also see, *K.I. Shephard* v. *Union of India*, (1987) 4 SCC 431. Highest Bench ruled that even in emergent situations, pre-decisional hearing is necessary which may not be an elaborate one especially when the action has grave civil consequences.

346. *Ajit Kumar Nag* v. *Indian Oil Corpn. Ltd.*, (2005) 7 SCC 764.

347. *Digi Cable Network (India) (P) Ltd.* v. *Union of India*, (2019) 4 SCC 451.

Natural justice is pragmatically flexible and is amenable to capsulation under compulsive pressure of circumstances.[348] It is in this context that the Supreme Court observed:

> The principles of natural justice must be confined within their proper limits and not allowed to run wild. The concept of natural justice is a magnificent thoroughbred on which this nation gallops forward towards its proclaimed and destined goal of 'Justice, social, economic and political'. This thoroughbred must not be allowed to turn into a wild and unruly horse, careering off where it lists, unsaddling its rider, and bursting into fields where the sign *no pasaran* is put up.[349]

3.2 Exclusion in cases of confidentiality

In *Malak Singh* v. *State of P&H*[350], the Supreme Court held that the maintenance of surveillance register by the police is a confidential document. Neither the person whose name is entered in the register nor any other member of the public can have access to it. Furthermore, the court observed that the observance of the principles of natural justice in such a situation may defeat the very purpose of surveillance, and there is every possibility of the ends of justice being defeated instead of being served. The same principle was followed in *S.P. Gupta* v. *Union of India*[351], where the Supreme Court held that no opportunity of being heard can be given to an Additional Judge of a High Court before his name is dropped from being confirmed. It may be pointed out that in a country like India, surveillance may provide a very serious constraint on the liberty of the people, therefore, the maintenance of the surveillance register cannot be so utterly administrative and non-judicial that it is difficult to conceive the application of the rules of natural justice.

3.3 Exclusion in case of purely administrative matters

A student of the university was removed from the rolls for unsatisfactory academic performance without being given any pre-decisional hearing. The Supreme Court in *Jawaharlal Nehru University* v. *B.S. Narwal*[352] held that the very nature of academic adjudication appears to negate any right of an opportunity to be heard. Therefore, if the competent academic authorities examine and assess the work of a student over a period of time and declare it to be unsatisfactory, the rules of natural justice may be excluded. In the same manner, in *Karnataka Public Service Commission* v. *B.M.*

348. *Mohinder Singh Gill* v. *Chief Election Commr.*, (1978) 1 SCC 405, 436.
349. *Satyavir Singh* v. *Union of India*, (1985) 4 SCC 252, 265, para. 34.
350. (1981) 1 SCC 420. Generally, the court is inclined against confidentiality and would prefer an open government. See, *S.P. Gupta* v. *Union of India*, 1981 Supp SCC 87.
351. 1981 Supp SCC 87.
352. (1980) 4 SCC 480.

Vijay Shankar[353], when the Commission cancelled the examination of the candidate—because in violation of rules, the candidate wrote his roll number on every page of the answer-sheet—the Supreme Court held that the principles of natural justice were not attracted. The court observed that the rule of hearing be strictly construed in academic discipline and if this was ignored, it would not only be against the public interest but would also erode the social sense of fairness. However, this exclusion would not apply in case of disciplinary matters, or where the academic body performs non-academic functions. Granting sanction of prosecution is a purely administrative function, therefore, the principles of natural justice are not attracted.[354] In the same manner, cancellation of a bid for failure to execute lease deed and to deposit security amount, held, would not attract the principles of natural justice.[355] However, even in situations where there is a complete non-application of mind, or where an action is based on no evidence or is mala fide, the court gives relief even in administrative actions by quashing the action. Thus, in *Somesh Tiwari* v. *Union of India*[356], where an employee was transferred even when an anonymous complaint against him was found false, the court held that the transfer was mala fide.

3.4 Exclusion based on impracticability

In *R. Radhakrishen* v. *Osmania University*[357], where the entire MBA entrance examination was cancelled by the university because of mass copying, the court held that notice and hearing to all candidates is not possible in such a situation, which had assumed national proportions. Thus, the court sanctified the exclusion of the rules of natural justice on the ground of administrative impracticability. Moving in the same direction, the Supreme Court once again in *Union of India* v. *O. Chakradhar*[358] held that in cancellation of a panel, select, reserve, waiting, merit or rank lists, individual hearing to candidates is not necessary where the mischief in conducting selection was so widespread and all-pervasive, affecting the result, that it was difficult to identify the persons unlawfully benefited or deprived of selection. Thus, even the consequent termination of service does not attract the principles of natural justice. Anyone who analyses judicial behaviour in this area may be tempted to conclude that "fairness" and "administrative convenience" have been taken by the court as discrete values, and this underlines not only the basic fallacy in judicial behaviour, but also exposes the administration's indolence and inertia. It may be recalled that when Japanese bombs cascaded upon Pearl Harbour on 7 December 1941,

353. (1992) 2 SCC 206.
354. *Supdt. of Police (CBI)* v. *Deepak Chowdhary*, (1995) 6 SCC 225.
355. *State of Karnataka* v. *Suveen Kumar Shetty*, (2002) 3 SCC 426.
356. (2009) 2 SCC 592.
357. 1974 SCC OnLine AP 190: AIR 1974 AP 283. See also, *Bihar School Examination Board* v. *Subhas Chandra Sinha*, (1970) 1 SCC 648.
358. (2002) 3 SCC 146.

plunging the US into a global struggle for existence during World War II, orders were passed for the relocation of thousands of persons of Japanese ancestry on the West Coast in relocation camps. Stone J, in his powerful dissent, was not prepared to accept that the inconvenience and administrative difficulty of holding individual loyalty hearings for the 1,12,000 persons involved could justify the governmental action.[359] The Supreme Court expressed the same sentiment in *W.B. Electricity Regulatory Commission* v. *CESC Ltd.*[360], when it opined that when a statute confers a right which is in conformity with the principles of natural justice, the same cannot be negativated by a court on an imaginary ground that there is a likelihood of an unmanageable hearing before the authority, or practical inconvenience. In this case, the W.B. Electricity Regulatory Commission had contended that though Electricity Regulatory Commissions Act, 1998 requires consumers' hearing before fixing tariff, yet giving hearing to 17 lakh electricity consumers would be a practical impossibility and inconvenience. Rejecting the contention, the court observed that the Act does not give individual rights to every consumer and the same is regulated by Regulations and, therefore, the question of indiscriminate hearing does not arise.

3.5 Exclusion in cases of interim preventive action

If the action of the administrative authority is a suspension order in the nature of a preventive action and not a final order, the application of the principles of natural justice may be excluded. In *Abhay KumarYadav* v. *K. Srinivasan*[361], an institution passed an order debarring a student from entering the premises of the institution and attending classes till the pendency of a criminal case against him for stabbing a co-student. This order was challenged on the ground of denial of natural justice. The Delhi High Court rejecting the contention held that such an order could be compared with an order of suspension pending enquiry, which is preventive in nature, in order to maintain campus peace and, hence, the principles of natural justice shall not apply. Therefore, natural justice may be excluded if its effect would be to stultify the action sought to be taken, or would defeat and paralyse the administration of law. The Supreme Court in *Maneka Gandhi*[362] observed:

> Where an obligation to give notice and opportunity to be heard would obstruct the taking of prompt action, especially action of a preventive or remedial nature... right to prior notice and opportunity of hearing arises only by implication...

359. *Kiyoshi Hirabayashi* v. *United States*, 1943 SCC OnLine US SC 142: 87 L Ed 1774: 320 US 81 (1943).
360. (2002) 8 SCC 715.
361. 1981 SCC OnLine Del 102: AIR 1981 Del 381. *See also*, M.P. Jain, "Administrative Law", (1981) 17 ASIL 481–82.
362. (1978) 1 SCC 248.

3.6 Exclusion in cases of legislative action

Legislative action, plenary or subordinate, is not subject to the rules of natural justice because these rules lay down a policy without reference to a particular individual. On the same logic, principles of natural justice can also be excluded by a provision of the Constitution also. The Indian Constitution excludes the principles of natural justice in Articles 22, 31(A), (B), (C) and 311(2) as a matter of policy. Nevertheless, if the legislative exclusion is arbitrary, unreasonable and unfair, courts may quash such a provision under Articles 14 and 21 of the Constitution. In *Laxmi Khandsari* v. *State of U.P.*[363], the Supreme Court held that the notification of the Uttar Pradesh Government Sugarcane (Control) Order, 1966 directing that no power-crusher of a khandsari unit in a reserved area of a sugar mill will work during the period from 9 October to 1 December 1980 is legislative in character and, hence, the principles of natural justice are not attracted. In this context, the court mentioned the analogy of price fixing.[364] This order had been challenged on the ground that the petitioners' valuable rights were infringed upon without any notice and hearing. In the same manner, the court held in *J.R. Vohra* v. *India Export House (P) Ltd.*[365] (*J.R. Vohra*) that Sections 21 and 37 of the Delhi Rent Control Act, 1958 dealing with the termination of limited tenancies do not violate the principles of natural justice. The court observed that if a limited tenancy has been validly created then at the expiry of the period, a warrant of possession can be issued without any notice or hearing to the tenant. In *Panipat Woollen and General Mills Co. Ltd.* v. *Union of India*[366], the court further held that where a decision is left to the legislature itself under an Act, the question of affording an opportunity of hearing to affected persons before taking a decision does not arise. In this case, the legislature had itself fixed the criteria and on the basis of that criteria, it had also identified persons and undertakings to which the law applied. Therefore, it was natural to suppose that the legislature is not expected to give a notice and afford a hearing while laying down a general rule. The same trend in judicial thinking is visible in *Union of India* v. *Cynamide India Ltd.*[367], when the Supreme Court held that no principles of natural justice had been violated when the government issued a notification fixing prices of certain drugs. The court reasoned that since the notification flowed from a legislative act and not an administrative one, so the principles of natural justice would not apply. *L.N.M. Institute of Economic Development and Social Change* v. *State of Bihar*[368] is a high benchmark in this direction. In this case, the Bihar Legislative Assembly

363. (1981) 2 SCC 600.
364. *Saraswati Industrial Syndicate Ltd.* v. *Union of India*, (1974) 2 SCC 630. *See also*, M.P. Jain, "Administrative Law", (1981) 17 ASIL 470.
365. (1985) 1 SCC 712.
366. (1986) 4 SCC 368.
367. (1987) 2 SCC 720.
368. (1988) 2 SCC 433.

passed a statute for taking over a private Institute named after its former Chief Minister. The Act also provided for termination of the services of its employees. In pursuance of these provisions, the government terminated the services of the employees of the Institute. Justifying the action, the court held that where there is a legislative direction for termination of services of employees of an institute which is taken over by the government, compliance with the principles of natural justice may not be read into such a direction, and if terminations are effected without giving employees concerned an opportunity of being heard, no exception can be taken of the same. The same principle was followed by the court in *Charan Lal Sahu* v. *Union of India*[369] (*Charan Lal Sahu*), also known as the *Bhopal Gas Disaster case*, where the constitutionality of the Bhopal Gas Leak Disaster (Processing of Claims) Act, 1985 was involved. The Supreme Court held, "For legislation by Parliament no principle of natural justice is attracted, provided such legislation is within the competence of the legislature." The same principle applies in case of subordinate legislation. Hence for fixing tax, fee and charges, principles of natural justice are not attracted. However, in case of modification, representation made must be considered.[370] Similarly, where seniority rules were relaxed with retrospective effect for reserved category candidates, the court held that no hearing was necessary to those who were adversely affected as it was a rule-making function.[371] To sum up, in case of a legislative act of the legislature, no question of application of the rule of natural justice arises. However, in case of subordinate legislation, legislature may provide for observance of the principles of natural justice, and in that case, its violation would vitiate administrative legislative action. This legal aspect was exemplified by the Supreme Court in *State of Punjab* v. *Tehal Singh*[372]. In this case, the Punjab Panchayati Raj Act, 1994 did not provide for any opportunity of notice and hearing to the residents before any area falling under a particular Gram Sabha is excluded and included in another Gram Sabha. The court held that residents of that area who have been excluded and included in a different Gram Sabha cannot make a complaint regarding denial of the rules of natural justice. Thus, where the legislature in its wisdom has not chosen to provide for any opportunity for observance of the principles of natural justice, its observance cannot be insisted upon. It need not be overemphasised that this trend increases the possibilities of legislative arbitrariness. Therefore, there seems to be no reason to exempt legislative actions from natural justice in areas where law is based on adjudicative facts. Similarly, in *Suresh Chandra Nanhorya* v.

369. (1990) 1 SCC 613. See also, *Madras City Wine Merchants' Assn.* v. *State of T.N.*, (1994) 5 SCC 509.
370. *Visakhapatnam Port Trust* v. *Ram Bahadur Thakur (P) Ltd.*, (1997) 4 SCC 582.
371. *M. Venkateswarlu* v. *State of A.P.*, (1996) 5 SCC 167.
372. (2002) 2 SCC 7. See also, *Laxmi Narain & Sons* v. *State of Haryana*, (2001) 10 SCC 370, court held that in case of issuing a notification to amend the schedule to the Act, principles of natural justice are not attracted.

Rajendra Rajak[373], the Supreme Court emphasised that principles of natural justice will always be read into legislative silence where an administrative action violates the fundamental rights of an individual. Thus, legislative silence cannot always be treated as denial of the benefit of natural justice unless strong implications exist.

Principles of natural justice do not supplant law but supplement law, therefore, unless language of the law leaves no other option, exclusion cannot be inferred. Principles of natural justice are integral to good governance, so the burden of proof lies on one who alleges exclusion. Exclusion would depend on 1) the language of the statute; 2) the scheme of statutory provisions; 3) the nature of the power conferred; 4) the purpose of the law; and 5) the effect of exclusion.

The principles of natural justice have been given a constitutional status in the US by the 5th and 14th Amendments. These amendments provide that no person shall be deprived of "life, liberty or property without the due process of law". This constitutional guarantee has been consistently interpreted as meaning, generally, that the rights of a citizen shall not be interfered with unless he has been given a hearing in an objective manner. The recent approach of courts is that hearing under the "due process" clause must be given whenever a decision is based on "adjudicative facts", *i.e.* facts which pertain to the parties, their business and activities. Hearing may be avoided only where emergency action is necessary.

In England, the history of the application of the principles of natural justice up to the mid-1960s reveals two opposite viewpoints. According to one point of view, in the absence of any statutory requirement of hearing, a hearing will be implied by courts whenever any decision affects the rights of subjects. This aspect is clearly reflected in *Cooper*[374]. In this case, the Metropolis Management Act, 1855 provided that a person who intended to build a house should give seven days' notice to the District Board, failing which the Board could demolish the house. Cooper built a house without giving the required notice and, consequently, his house was demolished without giving him a hearing. The court held that Cooper could maintain an action for trespass because no valid decision could be reached in breach of the principles of natural justice. This principle of applying the rules of natural justice by implication has been followed in a multitude of cases dealing with 1) interference with property rights,[375] 2) deprivation of membership of professional or other non-statutory bodies,[376] 3) dismissal from office,[377] 4) imposition of penalties,[378] and 5) deprivation of advantages.[379] The other viewpoint was based on a restrictive attitude towards certiorari

373. (2006) 7 SCC 800.
374. (1863) 14 CBNS 180: (1863) 143 ER 414.
375. *Errington* v. *Ministry of Health*, (1935) 1 KB 249 (CA).
376. *General Medical Council* v. *Spackman*, 1943 AC 627 (HL).
377. *Hogg* v. *Scott*, 1947 KB 759.
378. *R.* v. *North, ex p Oakey*, (1927) 1 KB 491 (CA).
379. *R.* v. *Boycott, ex p Keasley*, (1939) 2 KB 651 (DC).

and prohibition which were generally used to compel the observance of the principles of natural justice in situations where there was no express statutory requirement for hearing. The holders of this view advocated "freedom of action" for the administration. Therefore, in *Franklin*[380] when the House of Lords had to consider whether the Minister was subject to the rules of natural justice in designating the site of a new township, it decided that the Minister was acting executively and not judicially, hence, was not subject to the rules of natural justice. Following the same line of reasoning, the Privy Council held in *Nakkuda Ali* v. *Jayaratne*[381] that in the absence of any express statutory requirement for hearing, the rules of natural justice are not attracted, even when the power to cancel a licence is coupled with the fact that "reasonable grounds" must exist for the exercise of the power.

Fortunately, in 1963, Cooper's formulation was reasserted in *Ridge* v. *Baldwin*[382] (*Ridge*). The appellant in this case was the Chief Constable of Brighton, England who had been dismissed from service by the area Watch Committee in exercise of its powers under the Municipal Corporations Act, 1882, on the ground of negligence in the discharge of duties. The Act did not require any hearing before dismissal. A declaratory judgment was sought on the ground of violation of the rules of natural justice. The declaration was refused both by the court of first instance and the Court of Appeal on the strength of Nakhuda Ali's holding. However, by a majority of 4:1, the House of Lords decided that there is no point in labelling functions as quasi-judicial and administrative because even the administrative or executive functions are subject to the rules of natural justice. *Ridge* brought new liberality in approach to the question of the application of the rules of natural justice and judicial review. Formerly the presumption had been that there was no obligation to give a hearing unless the statute expressly provided for it; now the presumption is that there is always such an obligation unless the statute clearly excludes it, notwithstanding the vesting of a power in subjective terms.[383] Nevertheless, it does not mean that the rules of natural justice shall be applied in every administrative action to the same extent. In situations where policy considerations are paramount, the requirement of natural justice would be minimal and at times would probably vanish altogether.

3.7 Where no right of the person is infringed

Where no right has been conferred on a person by any statute nor any such right arises from the common law, the principles of natural justice are not applicable. This can be illustrated by the decision of the Supreme Court in

380. 1948 AC 87 (HL).
381. 1951 AC 66 (PC).
382. 1964 AC 40: (1963) 2 WLR 935 (HL).
383. Nettheim, "The Privy Council, Natural Justice and Certiorari", (1967) 2 Fed L Rev 215.

J.R. Vohra[384]. The Delhi Rent Control Act, 1958 makes provisions for the creation of limited tenancies. Sections 21 and 37 of the Act provide for the termination of limited tenancies. The combined effect of these sections is that after the expiry of the term, a limited tenancy can be terminated and a warrant of possession can be issued by the authority to the landlord without any notice of hearing to the tenant. Upholding the validity of a warrant of possession without complying with the principles of natural justice, the Supreme Court held that after the expiry of the period of any limited tenancy, a person has no right to stay in possession and, hence, no right of his is prejudicially affected which may warrant the application of the principles of natural justice. In the same manner, the court in *Andhra Steel Corpn. Ltd.* v. *A.P. SEB*[385] held that a concession can be withdrawn at any time without affording any opportunity of hearing to affected persons, except when the law requires otherwise, or the authority is bound by promissory estoppel. In this case, the Electricity Board had withdrawn the concession in electricity rate without any notice and hearing to the appellant. Therefore, where an order of extension was cancelled before it became operational,[386] or the order of stepping up salary was withdrawn before the person was actually paid,[387] or the services of the probationer were terminated without any charge,[388] the principles of natural justice are not attracted.

However, in *East Coast Railway* v. *Mahadev Appa Rao*[389], the Supreme Court was of the view that—while no candidate has a right to a post for which he appeared for the examination or even if found a place in the select list—the State cannot cancel the examination and the select list in an arbitrary manner, without application of mind, and for mala fide reasons. In this case after the typing test, a select list was cancelled because some candidates complained that the typewriters were defective and the authority did not make any investigation into the matter.

3.8 Exclusion in case of statutory exception or necessity

Disqualification on the ground of bias against a person will not be applicable if he is the only person competent or authorised to decide that matter or take that action. If this exception is not allowed, there would be no other means for deciding that matter, and the whole administration would come to a grinding halt. But the necessity must be genuine and real. Therefore, the doctrine of necessity cannot be invoked where the members of the textbook selection committee were themselves the authors of books because

384. (1985) 1 SCC 712.
385. (1991) 3 SCC 263.
386. *State of U.P.* v. *Girish Bihari*, (1997) 4 SCC 362.
387. *Calcutta Municipal Corpn.* v. *Sujit Baran Mukherjee*, (1997) 11 SCC 463.
388. *High Court of Judicature at Patna* v. *M.M.P. Sinha*, (1997) 10 SCC 409. See also, *Om Prakash Mann* v. *Director of Education*, (2006) 7 SCC 558.
389. (2010) 7 SCC 676.

the constitution of the selection committee could have been changed very easily by the government.[390]

Charan Lal Sahu[391] is a classical example of the application of this exception. In this case, the constitutional validity of the Bhopal Gas Leak Disaster (Processing of Claims) Act, 1985, which had authorised the Central Government to represent all the victims in matters of compensation award, had been challenged on the ground that because the Central Government owned 22 per cent share in the Union Carbide Company and as such it was a joint tortfeasor and, thus, there was a conflict between the interests of the government and the victims. Negativating the contention, the court observed that even if the argument was correct, the doctrine of necessity would be applicable to the situation because if the government did not represent the whole class of gas victims, no other sovereign body could so represent and, thus, the principles of natural justice were not attracted.

In the same manner, in *Judicial Accountability*[392], the Supreme Court did not allow the contention of mala fide against the Speaker of the Lok Sabha on the ground of his affiliation to the Congress Party because under the Judges (Inquiry) Act, 1968, only the Speaker has the statutory authority to take all actions.[393]

It was on the basis of this principle alone that judges of the Court of Appeal were held competent to decide the question whether they were subject to payment of tax because they were bound to act ex necessitate.[394] In a reference case under Article 317(1) of the Constitution in 2009, the Supreme Court opined that the members of the Public Service Commission are not disqualified when their relatives appear for interview on the ground of "necessity".[395] However, this rule is applicable only in the absence of any other alternative.[396] If substitution is possible, this rule will have no application.

3.9 Exclusion in case of contractual arrangement

In *State of Gujarat* v. *Meghji Pethraj Shah Charitable Trust*[397], the Supreme Court held that the principles of natural justice are not attracted in case of termination of an arrangement in any contractual field. Termination of an arrangement or agreement is neither a quasi-judicial nor an administrative act so the duty to act judicially is not attracted.

---

390. *J. Mohapatra and Company* v. *State of Orissa*, (1984) 4 SCC 103.
391. (1990) 1 SCC 613.
392. (1991) 4 SCC 699.
393. *See*, the heading "Doctrine of necessity" at p. 208 of this chapter.
394. *Judges* v. *Attorney General for Saskatchewan*, (1937) 53 TLR 464 (PC).
395. *Reference under Article 317(1) of the Constitution of India, re*, (2009) 1 SCC 337. See also, *Ashok Kumar Yadav* v. *State of Haryana*, (1985) 4 SCC 417.
396. *Amar Nath Chowdhury* v. *Braithwaite & Co. Ltd*, (2002) 2 SCC 290.
397. (1994) 3 SCC 552.

3.10 Exclusion in case of government policy decision

In *BALCO Employees' Union* v. *Union of India*[398], the Supreme Court was of the view that in taking of a policy decision in economic matters at length, the principles of natural justice have no role to play. In this case, employees had challenged the government's policy decision regarding disinvestment in Public Sector Undertakings. The court held that even though workers may have interest in the decision, but unless the policy decision to disinvest is capricious, arbitrary, illegal or uninformed, and is not contrary to law, the decision cannot be challenged on the grounds of violation of the principles of natural justice. Therefore, if in exercise of executive powers the government takes any policy decision, the principles of natural justice can be excluded because it will be impossible and impracticable to give formal hearing to all those who may be affected whenever a policy decision is taken, and at times it will be against public interest to do so. However, it may be noted that to consult an association or union before a policy decision is taken, as a good administrative practice, is different from a right of the association or union to be consulted before taking a policy decision.[399] Non-consultation would not be fatal to policy decision.

3.11 "Useless formality" theory

"Useless formality" theory is yet another exception to the application of the principles of natural justice. Where on the admitted or undisputed facts, only one conclusion is possible, and under law only one penalty is permissible, the court may not insist on the observance of the principles of natural justice because it would be futile to order its observance.[400] Therefore, where the result would not be different and is demonstrable beyond doubt, an order of compliance with the principles of natural justice will not be justified.[401] However, where facts are disputed, no unilateral administrative decision by a authority without hearing the other party can be saved by applying the "unless formality" theory.[402] The Supreme Court applied this theory in *Dharmarathmakara Raibahadur Arcot Ramaswamy Mudaliar Educational Institution* v. *Educational Appellate Tribunal*[403]. In this case, a lecturer who had been granted leave for doing MPhil, in violation of leave condition, had joined a PhD course. She was given notice and after considering her reply, wherein she had admitted joining the PhD course, her services were terminated. She challenged the termination order before the Education Tribunal on the ground that the provisions of the Karnataka Private Educational Institutions (Discipline and Control) Act, 1975, which

398. (2002) 2 SCC 333.
399. *Indian Airlines Officers' Assn.* v. *Indian Airlines Ltd.*, (2007) 10 SCC 684.
400. *S.L. Kapoor* v. *Jagmohan*, (1980) 4 SCC 379, 395.
401. *R.* v. *Eailing Magistrate's Court, ex p Fannaran*, (1996) 8 Admn LR 351, 358 (Lord Straughton).
402. *Prakash Ratan Sinha* v. *State of Bihar*, (2009) 14 SCC 690.
403. (1999) 7 SCC 332.

under Sections 6 to 8 had provided for a statutory enquiry before termination of services of any teacher, were not complied with. The tribunal and, subsequently, the High Court in appeal held the termination invalid for failure to comply with the statutory requirements of the Act. However, allowing the appeal, the Supreme Court held that an opportunity to show cause was not necessary where facts were undisputed, and the affected person could not put forth any valid defence even when an opportunity was given by the court. The court observed that giving an opportunity of hearing is a check and balance concept that no one's rights be taken away without hearing, where the statute so requires, but this is not necessary when one admits one's violations. Thus, in cases where a grant of opportunity in terms of the principles of natural justice does not improve the situation, "useless formality" theory is pressed into service.[404]

Similarly in *Karnataka SRTC* v. *S.G. Kotturappa*[405], the court opined that where the respondent had committed repeated acts of misconduct and had also accepted minor punishment, he is not entitled to the benefit of the principles of natural justice as it would be a mere formality, that too, in the case of misconduct by a daily wager. The Supreme Court remarked:

> The question as to what extent, principles of natural justice are required to be complied with would depend upon the fact situation obtaining in each case. The principles of natural justice cannot be applied in vacuum. They cannot be put in any straitjacket formula. The principles of natural justice are furthermore not required to be complied with when it will lead to an empty formality.[406]

Moving further, in *Punjab National Bank* v. *Manjeet Singh*[407], the court held that in view of the binding nature of the award, the court will not insist on compliance with the principles of natural justice, as it would be a mere empty formality unless factual position or legal implications under the award is disputed. In this case, an award had been passed by an Industrial Tribunal to which banks, Employees' Union, and bank associations were parties. This award was challenged on the ground that every one in the constituency was not heard and, therefore, no unilateral decision can be taken by banks without giving notice and a hearing to the employees.

Another situation where it may be futile to comply with the principles of natural justice would be where an administrative action is *per se* illegal, as an ineligible candidate has been considered for appointment. It has been settled that the principles of natural justice may not be applied unless prejudice is caused, and there is no prejudice if an ineligible candidate is considered for appointment.[408] Therefore, in such a situation, compliance with the principles of natural justice would be a futile formality. Similarly, it would be a mere empty formality if the principles of natural justice were insisted

404. *Canara Bank* v. *Debasis Das*, (2003) 4 SCC 557.
405. (2005) 3 SCC 409.
406. (2005) 3 SCC 409, 411.
407. (2006) 8 SCC 647.
408. *Ashok Kumar Sonkar* v. *Union of India*, (2007) 4 SCC 54.

upon in a situation where the report of the expert was obtained, but was not considered by the administrative authority.[409] In *Bihar SEB* v. *Pulak Enterprises*[410], the Supreme Court held that where fixing of a surcharge is just arithmetical and based on a given formula, no purpose will be served by applying the rule of fair hearing.

In the same manner, in *Biecco Lawrie Ltd.* v. *State of W.B.*[411], the court held that where an employee unequivocally accepted that his bad behaviour is due to his mental sickness and on previous occasion also, he was dismissed due to his bad behaviour, but on request was given another chance, "useless formality" theory will be attracted. Following the same line of reasoning in *Dharampal Satyapal Ltd.* v. *CCE*[412], the Supreme Court opined that in situations where a fair hearing would make no difference in the sense that it would not change the ultimate conclusion reached, there is no legal duty to hold a hearing as in such a situation no prejudice will be caused to the person concerned. In this case the appellant had been granted certain benefits under a notification which was later nullified by Section 154 of the 2003 Act with retrospective effect. As a consequence the amount which the appellant had received became refundable. Here the quantification of the amount to be refunded was not in dispute. The court held that in such situation hearing would be an empty formality as the appellant had not suffered any prejudice.

However, "useless formality" theory has still not been able to firmly establish itself in administrative law because there exists a strong opinion which suggests that this theory is wrong, as a court cannot prejudge any issue.[413]

3.12 Exclusion in case of waiver

If a person who has a right to hearing declines the offer of hearing given to him by the administrative authority, he shall be deemed to have waived his right to hearing and on that account cannot claim judicial review. However, waiver cannot be presumed if the person did not insist on hearing or if the waiver is ill-informed or if the exceptional circumstances are such which make the enquiry improper without hearing.

4. EFFECT OF BREACH OF THE RULES OF NATURAL JUSTICE: ACTION VOID OR VOIDABLE

Courts are unanimous that a decision rendered in violation of the rule against bias is merely voidable and not void. The aggrieved party may thus

409. *Noble Synthetics Ltd.* v. *CCE*, (2005) 3 SCC 674.
410. (2009) 5 SCC 641.
411. (2009) 10 SCC 32.
412. (2015) 8 SCC 519. See also, *R.C. Tobacco (P) Ltd.* v. *Union of India*, (2005) 7 SCC 725.
413. See, *Indian Drugs and Pharmaceuticals Ltd.* v. *Punjab Drug Manufacturers Assn.*, (1999) 6 SCC 247.

waive his right to avoid the decision; as where timely objection is not made even though there is full knowledge of the bias and the right to object to it.[414]

However, there is fundamental disagreement amongst courts and jurists as to the effect of a breach of the rule of fair hearing on any decision. Prof. H.W.R. Wade is of the view that breaches of the rules of natural justice must have the effect of producing void decisions where the authority has acted ultra vires and and where there is an error of law.[415] But D.M. Gordon argues that procedural breaches can never render a decision void as jurisdictional error. At first Prof. de Smith appeared to have agreed with him, but later on he changed his stance.[416] Courts' decisions are also available on both sides.[417] A full-scale examination of the problem came in *Ridge*[418]. The House of Lords was divided. Lord Reid and Lord Hodson considered the decision of the Watch Committee which terminated the services of the constable as void because the rule of fair hearing had been violated.[419] But Lord Evershed and Lord Devlin considered it merely voidable.[420] Later a decision confirmed this uncertainty.[421] The Privy Council in *Durayappah* v. *Fernando*[422] was of the view that denial of natural justice makes a decision voidable and not void. It is rather unfortunate that the law on this point of practical significance is in a state of utter confusion.[423]

In India, the Supreme Court in *Nawabkhan Abbaskhan* v. *State of Gujarat*[424] (*Nawabkhan*) categorically held that an order which infringes a fundamental freedom, passed in violation of the *audi alteram partem* rule, is a nullity.[425] The appellant in this case had been prosecuted and convicted for disobeying an externment order which was later held invalid for want of hearing. The Supreme Court emphasised that an externment order passed in violation of the rules of natural justice is of no effect, and its violation is no offence because such a determination is a jurisdictional error going to the very roots of a determination.

---

414. *Metropolitan Properties Co. (FGC) Ltd.* v. *Lannon*, (1969) 1 QB 577: (1968) 3 WLR 694 (CA).
415. Wade, *Administrative Law* (1967) 188; "Unlawful Administrative Action: Void or Voidable?", (1967) 83 LQR 499. *See also*, Akehurst, "Void or Voidable?—Natural Justice and Unnatural Meanings", (1968) 31 Mod L Rev 2.
416. De Smith, *Judicial Review of Administrative Action* (1959) 294. He has changed his stance in 1968 Edn., 222.
417. See, *R.* v. *North, ex p Oakey*, (1927) 1 KB 491 (CA); *White* v. *Kuzych*, 1951 AC 585.
418. 1964 AC 40: (1963) 2 WLR 935 (HL).
419. *Ibid*, AC 80.
420. *Ibid*, AC 86. Lord Morris can be counted on both sides.
421. *Leary* v. *National Union of Vehicle Builders*, 1971 Ch 34: (1970) 3 WLR 434. There is a dicta that a decision in violation of natural justice is void. *R.* v. *Aston University Senate, ex p Roffey*, (1969) 2 QB 538: (1969) 2 WLR 1418 (DC). Decision in violation of natural justice was held voidable.
422. (1967) 2 AC 337: (1967) 3 WLR 289 (PC).
423. See, *Boddington* v. *British Transport Police*, (1999) 2 AC 143: (1998) 2 WLR 639 (HL); *R* v. *Bassetlaw District Council, ex p Oxby*, (CA), *The Times* 18-12-1997.
424. (1974) 2 SCC 121.
425. *Ibid*, 133.

However, the decision of the Supreme Court in *Maneka Gandhi*[426] created doubts about the efficacy of this proposition. In this case, the passport authority had impounded thc passport of the appellant without giving any notice and hearing. The court, however, concluded that the impounding of the passport attracts the rules of natural justice and their violation is a fatal flaw which could make the order void. But, taking note of the assurance of the government that the appellant would be provided with a post-decisional hearing, the court declined to interfere with the impoundment order. The effect of this decision is that an order passed in violation of the rules of natural justice is not void or non est and, hence, can be validated by a post-decisional hearing. The same was the conclusion of the Supreme Court in *Swadeshi Cotton Mills*[427]. In this case, the Government of India, in exercise of its powers under Section 18-AA(1)(*a*) of the Industries (Development and Regulation) Act, 1951, passed the order for taking over the management of the company by the National Textile Corporation. This order had been passed without compliance with the principles of natural justice. The court speaking through Sarkaria and Desai JJ, though held that a quasi-judicial or administrative decision rendered in violation of the *audi alteram partem rule*, whenever it can be read as an implied requirement of the law, is null and void, yet it refrained from striking down the impugned order on the assurance of the Solicitor General that a post-decisional hearing would be given. The operational principle laid down by the court is that an order passed in violation of the rules of natural justice is not such a nullity, non est and stillborn which cannot be revived by a post-decisional hearing. It is certainly contrary to the holding of the court in *Nawabkhan*[428].

Once again the Supreme Court in *Pashok Tea Co. Ltd.*[429] was called upon to pronounce on the effect of a breach of the rules of natural justice. In this case, in pursuance of the two orders passed by the Central Government under clause (*a*) of sub-section (1) of Section 16-E of the Tea Act, 1953, the Tea Trading Corporation of India took over the management of the two estates owned by the Pashok Tea Company. The orders were challenged before the Calcutta High Court in two writ petitions which were allowed. An appeal to the Division Bench also failed. Hence, the appeal before the Supreme Court. It may be noted that clause (*a*) of sub-section (1) of Section 16-E of the Tea Act, 1953 is basically the same as Section 18-AA of the Industries (Development and Regulation) Act,1951, which had been found to contain the rules of natural justice by necessary implication in *Swadeshi Cotton Mills*[430]. The orders in the instant case had been passed without giving any hearing. On the strength of the observation of the Supreme Court, it was contended by the government that even if it

426. (1978) 1 SCC 248.
427. (1981) 1 SCC 664.
428. (1974) 2 SCC 121.
429. (1981) 4 SCC 113.
430. (1981) 1 SCC 664.

be held that the impugned orders could be passed only after the company had been given a fair opportunity to be heard, the attributes of a nullity attaching to the two orders make them only voidable and not non est, and that their "voidability" would also vanish if the opportunity is given ex post facto. This contention was seriously challenged on the ground that if a pre-decisional hearing is required to be given either expressly or by necessary implication as part of the rule of natural justice, failure to give it would make the order non est or stillborn which cannot be revived by any post-decisional hearing.[431] It is only where pre-decisional hearing cannot be read into the statute because of the necessity of an emergent action that the post-decisional hearing is required to be given. Thus, in view of the doubts expressed on the majority view in *Swadeshi Cotton Mills*[432], Koshal J thought that this important question of law may be properly determined by a larger Bench.

However, a decision of the Supreme Court in *A.R. Antulay* v. *R.S. Nayak*[433], favoured the proposition that any action in violation of the principles of natural justice is a nullity. One of the questions for the consideration of the Supreme Court was: "[W]hether the Supreme Court's direction dated 16 February 1984 given suo motu, directing the withdrawal of a criminal case against A.R. Antulay, a former Chief Minister of the State of Maharashtra, from a special judge and its transfer thereof to the High Court without affording an opportunity to him, was void and, hence, liable to be set aside?" Answering the question in the affirmative, the court held that an action in violation of the principles of natural justice is a nullity and the trial "coram non judice".

Following the same line of reasoning, the Supreme Court in *R.B. Shreeram Durga Prasad*[434] held that the decision of the Settlement Commission of denying the composite assessment without hearing renders the action as completely void and of no value.

Similarly in *Yunus Khan*[435], the court held that if there is a violation of the principles of natural justice at the initial stage which render proceedings null and void, such proceedings cannot be validated at the appellate stage even if fairness of that appellate authority is beyond dispute. In this case, in

---

431. Bhagwati J, while writing a foreword to K.N. Goyal J's, *Administrative Law* (in Hindi) (1981), also mentioned that

> it is clear law that if prior hearing is required to be given as a part of the rule of natural justice, failure to give it would indubitably invalidate the exercise of the power and it cannot be saved by post-decisional hearing. It is only where the necessity for prior hearing cannot be read into the statute because to do so would be to defeat the object and purpose of the exercise of the power, that post-decisional hearing is required to be given and if that is not done, the exercise of the power would be vitiated.

432. (1981) 1 SCC 664.
433. (1988) 2 SCC 602.
434. (1989) 1 SCC 628. See also, *Ravi S. Naik* v. *Union of India*, 1994 Supp (2) SCC 641. The Supreme Court held that order passed in violation of the principles of natural justice is ultra vires and, hence, suffers from jurisdictional error.
435. (2010) 10 SCC 539.

a disciplinary proceeding, authority which initiated proceedings was also a witness, accepted enquiry report and imposed punishment. The Supreme Court held the proceedings as void. However, even when an action is void, it is valid until it is declared void by a court and cannot be ignored.[436]

Nevertheless, it may be pointed out that whenever an order is struck down as invalid, being violative of the principles of natural justice, there is no final decision on the case and, therefore, proceedings are left open. All that is done is that the order assailed by virtue of its inherent defect is vacated, but the proceedings are not terminated.[437] The administrative authority may start the proceedings de novo.

In *Vipulbhai Mansingbhai Chaudhary* v. *State of Gujarat*[438], the Supreme Court held that where an order passed in exercise of a power conferred by a statute is set aside on the ground that such an order was passed in breach of the principles of natural justice, the power could once again be exercised by complying with the principles of natural justice. Any statutory power can "be exercised from time to time as occasion requires". Such a principle is recognised by Section 14 of the General Clauses Act, 1897. Power conferred on the courts to adjudicate the rights and obligations of the parties is an exception to the principle. The doctrines of res judicata and double jeopardy prohibit the repeated invocation of the jurisdiction of the civil courts or repeated attempts to prosecute a person on the same set of facts constituting an office. Where an order passed in exercise of a power conferred by a statute is set aside on the ground that such an order was passed in breach of the principles of natural justice, the power can once again be exercised by complying with the principles of natural justice. In a case where the flaw in the order appealed against consists of in the non-observance of certain procedure or in not giving effect to the maxim "audi alteram partem", it is open to the officer concerned to start the procedure once again with a view to follow the rules of procedure and the principles of natural justice.

Those who suggest that a decision in breach of the *audi alteram partem* rule is merely voidable simply try to emphasise the fluctuating contents of the rule and the administrative inconvenience, which would be caused if the decision is considered as void. It may be pointed out that courts should not worry about administrative inconvenience because the administration can well look after its own convenience. Furthermore, in situations of denial of fair hearing at the pre-decisional stage, a post-decisional hearing cannot serve any purpose, as in all probability it will be nothing more than a shallow public relations exercise. If the rules of natural justice are sacrificed for the sake of administrative convenience, it would be like throwing the baby with the bathwater. Fact remains that there is no such thing as technical

436. *Krishnadevi Malchand Kamathia* v. *Bombay Environmental Action Group*, (2011) 3 SCC 363.

437. *CST* v. *Subhash & Company*, (2003) 3 SCC 454. See also, *Bharati Reddy* v. *State of Karnataka*, (2018) 6 SCC 162.

438. (2017) 13 SCC 51.

violation of the principles of natural justice. There are no percentages in it. The core issue is "prejudice caused". If prejudice caused is real, it is a void decision. In the ultimate analysis, it is the "pragmatic realism" which must be the controlling factor.

5. CAN BREACH OF NATURAL JUSTICE AT THE INITIAL STAGE BE CURED AT THE ADMINISTRATIVE APPEAL STAGE?

If proper hearing was not given at the initial stage of the hearing, can this defect be cured by giving hearing at the appellate stage of the same administrative hearing? Difficulty arises from the fact that if an administrative decision in violation of natural justice is void, an appeal from a void decision cannot cure invalidity. On the other hand it may be argued that an appeal is different from judicial review and therefore, it can rehear the case and thus invalidity can be cured. In *Leary* v. *National Union of Vehicle Builders*[439], the court held:

> If the rules and the law combine to give the member the right to a fair trial and the right of appeal, why should he be told that he ought to be satisfied with an unjust trial and a fair appeal? ... As a general rule ... I hold that a failure of natural justice in the trial body cannot be cured by a sufficiency of natural justice in an appellate body.

However, in *Calvin* v. *Carr*[440], the Privy Council sounded a different note when it held that there may be a situation where the defect at the initial stage may be cured at the appeal stage. Nevertheless, much will depend on the fact-situation of each case. If the defect is flagrant and consequences severe, then even a perfect appeal cannot produce just result. A distinction is to be drawn between a domestic and a statutory hearing. For example, where in a disciplinary proceeding a student was not given hearing but at the final appeal stage he was heard, the defect can be cured. If enquiry is statutory and consequences are severe, appeal hearing would not cure the defect of denial of natural justice at the initial stage.

POINTS FOR DISCUSSION

1. The principles of natural justice are not precise rules of unchaining contents; their scope will vary according to the context. Even where the rules of natural justice are prima facie applicable, they may be partly or wholly excluded by clear statutory language or necessary implication. Therefore, the whole concept of natural justice has acquired a kaleidoscopic unpredictability. Against this backdrop, the suitability and efficacy of the principles of natural justice in providing a minimum standard Administrative Procedure Code may

439. 1971 Ch 34: (1970) 3 WLR 434.
440. 1980 AC 574: (1979) 2 WLR 755 (PC).

be discussed. Is it a good substitute for a codified Administrative Procedure Code?

2. The rule against bias has two main aspects: *Firstly*, that an administrator exercising adjudicatory powers must not have any direct personal or proprietary interest in the outcome of the proceedings. *Secondly*, there must be a "real likelihood" of bias. The first rule is very strict but the second is uncertain and vague. How should the test of disqualification for likelihood of bias be formulated? Students may discuss the following formulations:
   (*a*) "Real likelihood" of bias means "a reasonable suspicion" of bias.
   (*b*) "Real likelihood" of bias means "actual bias".
3. Legal representation and cross-examination are not essential to fair hearing, and natural justice does not require that reasons for decisions should be given.[441] Students may discuss these formulations with special reference to the constitutional requirements of Articles 19 and 21. Students may also attempt to identify the legal basis in the absence of legislative silence on the grounds of which legal representation, cross-examination, and reasoned decisions may be made a mandatory procedural requirement for administrative agencies, exercising adjudicatory powers.
4. One of the fundamental principles of administrative law is that the violation of the principles of natural justice vitiates an administrative action which may be quashed by a court of law. Against the background of this formulation, students may discuss whether an administrative action in violation of the principles of natural justice is void or voidable. The discussion must include elaboration and reconciliation of the principles of law laid down in *Nawabkhan*[442], *Maneka Gandhi*[443], and other recent decisions.
5. In situations where due to some emergent nature of the action, pre-decisional hearing cannot be provided, no matter if it is attracted in that situation, ex post facto or post-decisional hearing may be required. The whole concept of post-decisional hearing may be discussed with special reference to India.
6. The word "exception" in the context of natural justice is a misnomer because in certain situations, the principles of natural justice are inapplicable not by way of an exception but because nothing unfair can be inferred by not applying these principles. In this context, students may be asked to identify areas in which the application of the rules of natural justice may be excluded. Can the exclusionary rules be challenged on the ground of unreasonableness in a court of law?

441. *Pett* v. *Greyhound Racing Assn. Ltd.* (No. 2), (1970) 1 QB 46: (1969) 2 WLR 1228; *R.* v. *Gaming Board of Great Britain, ex p Benaim*, (1970) 2 QB 417: (1970) 2 WLR 1009 (CA).
442. (1974) 2 SCC 121.
443. (1978) 1 SCC 248.

7. When a Minister acting in a representative and responsible capacity decides a matter, why should a court interfere?
8. No one complains about violation of the principles of fair hearing when a decision goes in his favour. Therefore, why should the courts bother about fair hearing?

SUGGESTED READINGS

1. A.L. Goodhart, " 'Ridge v. Baldwin': Administration and Natural Justice", (1964) 80 LQR 105.
2. Alice Jacob, "Requirement to Findings of Fact in Administrative Determinations—Judicial Experience in India and United States", (1966) 8 JILI 54.
3. Ayushi Sutaria, "Is Right to Oral Hearing a Mandatory Requirement of Natural Justice? A Case-Law Analysis", 1.2 CALQ (2013) 85
4. C.K. Thakker, *Administrative Law* (Eastern Book Company 2012) Chap. VI.
5. C.K. Thakker, "From Duty to Act Judicially to Duty to Act Fairly", (2003) 4 SCC J-1.
6. D.G. Benjafield and H. Whitmore, "The House of Lords and Natural Justice", (1963) Australian Law Journal 140.
7. G.H.L. Fridman, "Natural Justice", (1963) Law Journal 716.
8. G.J. Webber, "Natural Justice in Recent English Case Law", (1964) Current Legal Problems 17.
9. G.W. Keeton, "Natural Justice in English Law", (1955) 8 Current Legal Problems 24.
10. H.W.R. Wade, "Bias—A Question of Appearance or Reality", (1969) 85 LQR 23.
11. H.W.R. Wade, "The Twilight of Natural Justice", (1951) 67 LQR 103.
12. H.W.R. Wade, "Unlawful Administrative Action: Void or Voidable?" (1967) 83 LQR 499: (1968) 84 LQR 95.
13. Lord Denning, *The Discipline of Law* (1982) 83–87.
14. M.B. Akehurst, "Void or Voidable?—Natural Justice and Unnatural Meanings", (1968) 31 Mod Law Rev 2, 138.
15. M.P. Jain, Changing Face of Administrative Law in India and Abroad (1982) Lecture I, "Judicial Creativity".
16. M.P. Singh, "Administrative Action in Violation of Natural Justice Affecting Fundamental Rights: Void or Voidable?" (1979) 2 SCC J-1.
17. M.P. Singh, "Duty to Give Reasons for Quasi-Judicial and Administrative Decisions", (1979) 21 JILI 45.
18. Nathanson, "The Right to Fair Hearing in India, English and American Administrative Law", (1958–59) 1 JILI 423.
19. Nettheim, "The Privy Council, Natural Justice and Certiorari", (1967) 2 Fed L Rev 215.
20. P. Brett, "The Rebirth of Natural Justice", (1964) 6 Malaya LR 100.

21. P. Leelakrishnan* and Mini S., "Procedural Fairness in Administrative Decision-Making : Approach of the Supreme Court in a Decade", 59 JILI (2017) 335.
22. Paul Craig, "Perspectives on Process: Common Law, Statutory and Political" (2010) PL 275.
23. Paul Jackson, *Natural Justice* (1974).
24. S.A. de Smith, "The Right to a Hearing in English Administrative Law", (1955) 68 Harv L Rev 509.
25. S. Mohan, "Canalised Natural Justice", (1980) 12 Lawyer 163.
26. S.N. Jain, "Administrative Law Aspects of 'Maneka Gandhi' ", (1979) 21 JILI 382.
27. S.N. Jain, "Is an Individual Bound by an Illegal Executive Order? Distinction between 'Void' and 'Voidable' Order", (1974) 16 JILI 322.
28. Sanjayan Rajasingham, "Reforming the Rule Against Bias in Administrative Law", 3.3 CALQ (2017) 28.
29. Tanya Tekriwal and Shilpi, "Recusal of Judges - A Step Towards Impartial Adjudication", 9.2 NLIU LR (2020) 481.
30. Timothy Endicott, *Administrative Law* (Oxford University Press) Chaps. 4, 5, 6.
31. Upendra Baxi, "Development in Indian Administrative Law" in A.G. Noorani (Ed.), *Public Law in India* 156–63.
32. V.S. Deshpande, "Speaking Order", AIR 1969 (J) 147.
33. V.S. Deshpande, "The One Who Decides Must Hear", (1959–60) 2 JILI 423.

Chapter 8

Judicial Review of Administrative Actions: Principles

The system of judicial review of administrative actions has been inherited from Britain. It is on this foundation that the Indian courts have built the superstructure of control mechanism. The whole law of judicial review of administrative actions has been developed by judges on case-to-case basis. Consequently, a thicket of technicality and inconsistency surrounds it.

The core rationale for judicial review of administrative action may include:

1. to enforce constitutionalism by keeping the administrative authorities within their legal limits;
2. to enforce rule of law on the administration;
3. to protect the rights and entitlements of people against arbitrary exercise of power of the administration;
4. to enforce accountability under the law on the administration.

All this is to be achieved within the overarching principles of comity, contextuality, proportionality, subsidiarity and judicial self-restraint.

However, the present trend of judicial decisions is to widen the scope of judicial review of administrative actions and to restrict the immunity from judicial review to a class of cases, which relate to deployment of troops and entering into international treaties, etc.[1]

Judicial review may take four shapes:

(1) *Legislative review*: Here the court reviews the constitutionality of law passed by the legislature or rules framed by the administrative authorities.

(2) *Judicial review*: Here the court reviews the decisions of lower courts and its own decisions.

(3) *Constitutional review*: In this case court reviews the constitutionality of a constitutional amendment.

(4) *Administrative action review*: In this case court reviews the constitutionality of administrative action and also examines its fairness, reasonableness and justness.

---

1. *Indian Railway Construction Co. Ltd.* v. *Ajay Kumar*, (2003) 4 SCC 579.

In this chapter we are concerned primarily with the fourth type of judicial review. The scope of judicial review of an administrative action is very limited. Unless the court comes to a conclusion that the decision-maker has not understood the law correctly that regulates his decision-making power or when it is found that the decision of the decision-maker is vitiated by irrationality and that too on the principle of "Wednesbury unreasonableness" or unless it is found that there has been a procedural impropriety in the decision-making process, it would not be permissible for the High Court to interfere in the decision-making process. It is not permissible for the court to examine the validity of the decision but the court can examine only the correctness of the decision-making process. It could thus be seen that interference by the High Court would be warranted only when the decision impugned is vitiated by an apparent error of law, *i.e.* when the error is apparent on the face of the record and is self-evident. Or when the decision impugned is so arbitrary and capricious that no reasonable person would have ever arrived at. The test is not what the court considers reasonable or unreasonable but a decision which the court thinks that no reasonable person could have taken. Not only must this but such a decision have led to manifest injustice.[2]

In the exercise of judicial review, the court is not concerned with correctness of findings of fact on the basis of which orders are made so long as they are reasonable and supported by evidence. The court does not sit as appellate authority and supplant "the feel of the expert" by its own review. However, scope of judicial review certainly extends to the decision-making process to ascertain whether all relevant factors have been taken into consideration and correspondingly no irrelevant consideration has crept in the decision-making process. Further held, discretionary powers conferred on administrative authorities cannot be unfettered or unguided and must be exercised within legal limits.[3]

1. JURISDICTION OF THE SUPREME COURT

1.1 Under Articles 32 and 136

In any democratic society, primary control on government is by the people but experiences has proved the weakness of this control, especially where majority of the people are disempowered, hence auxiliary control becomes imperative and this auxiliary control is the "judiciary with a power of judicial review". Judicial review is alternative to force. It is based on general principles of rule of law, separation of power, federalism and fundamental rights.

India has a hierarchical judicial system in which the Indian Supreme Court is the Apex Court. It is the final interpreter of law and the ultimate

2. *Municipal Council, Neemuch* v. *Mahadeo Real Estate*, (2019) 10 SCC 738.
3. *Manomoy Ganguly* v. *Union of India*, (2018) 18 SCC 83.

court of appeal in all civil, criminal and constitutional matters. It is also the final protector of people's fundamental rights.

Judicial review is thus not only an integral part of the Constitution but also a basic structure of the Constitution, which cannot be abolished or whittled down even by an amendment of the Constitution.[4] In any democratic society, judicial review is the soul of the system because without it democracy and the rule of law cannot be maintained.[5] Thus, extraordinary jurisdiction of the court under Articles 32 or 136 of the Constitution cannot be taken away by legislation or the principle of election or estoppel or even by amending the Constitution.[6]

Thus in India, there are no "no-go" areas for the judiciary, and there is no limit on its power of judicial review except self-restraint. However, this does not mean that judicial power is without limits. Bold lines of the Constitution bind the judiciary in the same manner as they bind other organs of the State.

The Supreme Court is invested with the power of judicial review under Article 32. Article 32(1) guarantees the right to move the Supreme Court for the enforcement of fundamental rights, and Article 32(2) invests the Supreme Court with the power to issue directions, orders or writs for the enforcement of these rights. The right to move the Supreme Court for the enforcement of any fundamental right is itself a fundamental right, and the court has no power to refuse in its discretion the grant of an appropriate remedy, if the violation of any fundamental right is proved.[7] Therefore, it is not only the right and power but also the duty of the Supreme Court to protect and safeguard the fundamental rights of the people.[8] Where no fundamental right of a person is violated, court can decline jurisdiction. It is for this reason that in *Federation of Bar Associations* v. *Union of India*[9], the court declined relief in a public interest litigation (PIL) petition for the establishment of High Court Benches at other places in Karnataka.

The nature and purpose of judicial review is not the review of the decision of the administrative authority but of the decision-making process. Therefore, the Supreme Court cannot assume appellate jurisdiction and reappreciate the primary or perceptive facts found by the fact-finding authority.[10] The right of seeking judicial review depends on the facts of each individual case, however, there cannot be a review of an abstract proposition of law.[11]

---

4. *Kesavananda Bharati* v. *State of Kerala*, (1973) 4 SCC 225.
5. *Minerva Mills Ltd.* v. *Union of India*, (1980) 3 SCC 625.
6. *Prashant Ramachandra Deshpande* v. *Maruti Balaram Haibatti*, 1995 Supp (2) SCC 539.
7. N. *Masthan Sahib* v. *Chief Commr., Pondicherry*, AIR 1962 SC 797, 804. See also, *Fertiliser Corpn. Kamgar Union* v. *Union of India*, (1981) 1 SCC 568, 574–75.
8. C.K. Thakker, *Administrative Law* (Eastern Book Company 1992).
9. (2000) 6 SCC 715.
10. *Excise and Taxation Officer-cum-Assessing Authority* v. *Gopi Nath & Sons*, 1992 Supp (2) SCC 312. See also, *Apparel Export Promotion Council* v. *A.K. Chopra*, (1999) 1 SCC 759; *Union of India* v. *Lt. Gen. Rajendra Singh Kadyan*, (2000) 6 SCC 698.
11. *Sarojini Ramaswami* v. *Union of India*, (1992) 4 SCC 506.

Though the jurisdiction of the Supreme Court under Article 32 is confined to the enforcement of fundamental rights, yet if there is a clear abuse of process of the court, a petition is maintainable even if no violation of any fundamental right is involved. Thus, when a person manipulated facts in order to get a decree by a court to defeat the ends of justice, in such a situation a petition under Article 32 is maintainable.[12] While exercising jurisdiction the court will not go into questions of policy of the State, which is required to be dealt with by the legislature. On this basis, the court declined jurisdiction where the personal laws of Hindus, Muslims and Christians were challenged as violative of the fundamental rights of women.[13] The court also cannot issue direction which would result in an amendment of an existing government policy.[14] Existence of an alternative remedy does not affect the jurisdiction of the writ court, but it would be a good ground for not entertaining the petition.[15]

The judgment of the court operates in rem, hence, no new parties can reagitate a concluded issue on fresh grounds. Where the Supreme Court under Article 136 held that special duty allowance payable to Central Government employees in North-Eastern region will not be admissible to employees belonging to the region, a subsequent writ by the local employees on new ground will not be maintainable.[16] In the same manner, a final judgment/order passed by the Supreme Court, after even exhausting the remedy of review under Article 137 of the Constitution, cannot be assailed under Article 32 of the Constitution by an aggrieved person, whether he was a party to the case or not.[17] Although the right to move the Supreme Court for the enforcement of fundamental right is itself a fundamental right, yet as regards the issuance of writs against judicial orders of the Supreme Court it cannot be allowed. It has been firmly established that the court can grant compensation for established breach of fundamental rights and abuse of power, while exercising jurisdiction under Article 32 of the Constitution.[18] For this purpose, the court can enforce fundamental rights even against private bodies or individuals. The court can exercise jurisdiction suo motu or on the basis of a PIL in the absence of any personal approach by the victim.[19] In order to enforce the concept of accountability, the court can also award exemplary damages for oppressive, arbitrary and unconstitutional action of government servants, while exercising jurisdiction under Article 32 of the Constitution.[20] The State has a right to change

12. *Jhumman Singh* v. *CBI*, (1995) 3 SCC 420.
13. *Ahmedabad Women Action Group (AWAG)* v. *Union of India*, (1997) 3 SCC 573.
14. *Madhav Institute of Technology and Science* v. *Rajendra Singh*, (2000) 6 SCC 608.
15. *State of Bihar* v. *Jain Plastics and Chemicals Ltd.*, (2002) 1 SCC 216.
16. *Sadhan Kumar Goswami* v. *Union of India*, (1997) 2 SCC 225.
17. *Rupa Ashok Hurra* v. *Ashok Hurra*, (2002) 4 SCC 388.
18. *D.K. Basu* v. *State of W.B.*, (1997) 1 SCC 416; *Thirath Ram Saini* v. *State of Punjab*, (1997) 11 SCC 623.
19. *Bodhisattwa Gautam* v. *Subhra Chakraborty*, (1996) 1 SCC 490.
20. *Common Cause (Petrol pumps matter)* v. *Union of India*, (1996) 6 SCC 593.

its policy from time to time in public interest under the changing circumstances and, therefore, generally the court would not interfere unless the change of policy is arbitrary or violative of law and the Constitution.[21]

Creation and abolition of a post is within the competence of the executive, and a court cannot interfere unless bad faith is proved.[22] While exercising the power of judicial review, an assessment is based on "implication" and not on the "aims and object" of the action. Fundamental freedoms cannot be sacrificed or compromised in the name of expediency, unless compelling public interest reasons are there. If an interference is justified on principle, court would look into proportionality of the measures of the administration. Where majoritarian impulses determine action which impinges upon individual autonomy and freedom, court apply deeper first scrutiny. There is always a presumption of constitutionality, courts avoid interpretations which render the action unconstitutional. If an action is within administrative competence, courts generally uphold it irrespective of its own views unless the action is patently arbitrary.[23] Generally, courts do not interfere in "policy" matters of the legislature, but executive policy is put to a more exacting scrutiny. Court may interfere if an administrative policy is unconstitutional, or beyond the provision of an Act or regulation, or is ultra vires the authority of an administrative instrumentality, or is contrary to statutory policy or larger public policy. Executive orders cannot be termed as "policy decisions", hence courts can interfere.[24] End of law is "justice", therefore, court can pass an order to do complete justice in the case under Article 142 of the Constitution.[25]

In fiscal matters, courts allow a wider space to administration and do not apply strict scrutiny. However, where fundamental rights of the people are also involved, this space is strictly monitored. In *State of A.P.* v. *P. Laxmi Devi*[26], court allowed such space to the administration. In this case, Stamp Act, 1899 as amended in 1998 provided that in case of low valuation of property, the registration officer may increase the valuation. A person shall have to deposit 50 per cent of duty on increased value before making a reference to the Collector. It was provided to ensure prompt realisation of duty. Reversing the judgment of the High Court, the Supreme Court held that in fiscal matters greater latitude be given to the government and court should not do strict scrutiny.

Petitions under Article 32 may also be a review petition or a recall petition. Review petition is decided after hearing the parties, but court may grant recall without hearing all the affected parties. In such a case,

21. *State of Punjab* v. *Ram Lubhaya Bagga*, (1998) 4 SCC 117.
22. *State of Haryana* v. *Navneet Verma*, (2008) 2 SCC 65.
23. *Karnataka Bank Ltd.* v. *State of A.P.*, (2008) 2 SCC 254.
24. *DDA* v. *Joint Action Committee*, (2008) 2 SCC 672.
25. *Shantidevi Kamaleshkumar Yadav* v. *State of Maharashtra*, (2008) 9 SCC 718.
26. (2008) 4 SCC 720.

recall will be in violation of the principles of natural justice and hence, untenable.[27]

Article 136, which is in the nature of a residuary reserve power of judicial review in the area of public law, lays down that the Supreme Court may, in its discretion, grant special leave to appeal from any judgment, decree, determination, sentence or order in any cause or matter passed or made by any court or tribunal. Thus, Article 136 does not confer a right of appeal on any party, but confers a discretionary power on the Supreme Court to interfere in suitable cases to advance the cause of justice.[28] Even in cases where special leave is granted, the discretionary power vested in the court continues to remain with the court, even at the stage when the appeal comes for hearing. The power under Article 136 of the Constitution, on the one hand, is an exceptional power to be exercised sparingly—with caution and care to remedy extraordinary situations of gross failure of justice—while on the other, it is an overriding power whereunder the court may generously step in to impart justice and remedy injustice.[29] In exercise of its discretion, court may grant special leave to appeal against the decision even of a Sessions Court or the court of a sub-judge. This is another matter that today "special leave" has become "ordinary second appeal".

Since the court has the power to grant special leave to appeal against the decisions of administrative tribunals and other agencies, it is now regarded as an important mode of judicial review of administrative adjudicatory actions.

Article 136 also refers to tribunals, a term which necessarily refers to a statutory body having the power to affect the rights of the people and the duty to act judicially. A "tribunal" for the purpose of Article 136 must have some trappings of a law court which include

(1) that the proceedings before it must start on an application in the nature of a plaint;
(2) that it possesses the powers of a civil court in matters compelling attendance of witnesses, discovery and inspection;
(3) that it allows cross-examination and legal representation;
(4) that it decides on the basis of evidence and according to law; and
(5) that its members are qualified to be judges.[30]

On the basis of these, the Supreme Court found that the conciliation officer acting under the U.P. Industrial Disputes Act, 1947 is not a tribunal as he does not enjoy the powers of a civil court.[31] In the same manner, an arbitrator appointed under the Industrial Disputes Act, 1947 is not considered to be a tribunal, as he is appointed by the parties and is not invested with

27. *Asit Kumar Kar* v. *State of W.B.*, (2009) 2 SCC 703; see also, *All Bengal Excise Licencees' Assn.* v. *Raghabendra Singh*, (2007) 11 SCC 374.
28. *Mathai* v. *George*, (2010) 4 SCC 358.
29. *Ashok Nagar Welfare Assn.* v. *R.K. Sharma*, (2002) 1 SCC 749.
30. *Bharat Bank Ltd.* v. *Employees*, 1956 SCC OnLine Cal 18: AIR 1950 SC 188.
31. *Jaswant Sugar Mills Ltd.* v. *Lakshmi Chand*, AIR 1963 SC 677.

inherent judicial power of the State.[32] But on the other hand, an Industrial Tribunal, Election Commission, Railway Rates Tribunal, Labour Appellate Tribunal, Income Tax Appellate Tribunal, Custodian General of Evacuee Property, Authority under the Payment of Wages Act, 1936, and the Central Government acting under Section 111(3) of the Companies Act, 1956 and under Section 30 of the Mines and Minerals (Development and Regulation) Act, 1957 have been held to be "tribunals" within the meaning of Article 136. Administrative service tribunals constituted under the Administrative Tribunals Act, 1985 are also covered within the jurisdiction of the Supreme Court under Article 136.

The power to grant special leave to appeal is discretionary and, therefore, cannot be defined exhaustively. Courts will exercise this power in exceptional circumstances to prevent the miscarriage of justice.[33] The term "exceptional circumstances" cannot be defined by any set formula. However, the court may exercise its power in cases where there has been an illegality or irregularity of procedure or violation of the principles of natural justice resulting in gross miscarriage of justice.[34] In the same manner, the Supreme Court may decline jurisdiction where the conduct of the petitioner is objectionable,[35] or where an appeal involves a matter of purely academic interest and is of no practical value[36] or is frivolous,[37] or where there is unreasonable delay in filing petitions.[38]

Normally, in exercise of its powers under Article 136, the Supreme Court does not re-examine the questions of fact unless the decision of the authority is patently perverse and manifestly unjust.[39] In *Variety Emporium* v. *V.R.M. Mohd. Ibrahim Naina*[40], though the Supreme Court reiterated that concurrent finding of facts by courts below shall not be lightly interfered, yet added that this does not mean that injustice must be perpetuated because it has been committed by the lower courts. Therefore, if the concurrent decision is manifestly unjust, it is not only the right but also the duty of the Supreme Court to do justice. In the same manner, the court would not grant leave to appeal if other remedies of appeal and revision are available. But it is not a rule without exception.[41] "Finality clause" in a statute excluding judicial review would not be a bar for the exercise of this jurisdiction by the Supreme Court.[42] The court would not permit the

32. *Engg. Mazdoor Sabha* v. *Hind Cycles Ltd.*, AIR 1963 SC 874.
33. *Pritam Singh* v. *State*, 1950 SCC 189: AIR 1950 SC 169.
34. *State of U.P.* v. *Ram Manorath*, (1972) 3 SCC 215.
35. *State of Maharashtra* v. *Ramdas Shrinivas Nayak*, (1982) 2 SCC 463.
36. *CED* v. *Ratna Kumari Kumbhat*, 1993 Supp (1) SCC 420.
37. *State of Punjab* v. *Bir Singh*, 1992 Supp (2) SCC 103.
38. *Union of India* v. *Om Prakash Agarwal*, 1992 Supp (2) SCC 129.
39. *Gian Singh* v. *State of Punjab*, (1974) 4 SCC 305. See also, *Nadodi Jayaraman* v. *State of T.N.*, 1992 Supp (3) SCC 161; *Hindustan Development Corpn. Ltd.* v. *State of Rajasthan*, 1995 Supp (2) SCC 752.
40. (1985) 1 SCC 251.
41. *Ram Saran Das & Bros.* v. *CTO*, AIR 1962 SC 1326.
42. *Dhakeswari Cotton Mills Ltd.* v. *CIT*, AIR 1955 SC 65.

plea of jurisdiction of the tribunal to be raised before it for the first time,[43] but where a question of law is involved the court may allow it.[44] In *Ujagar Singh* v. *State (Delhi Admn.)*[45], popularly known as the *Vidya Jain murder case*, the Supreme Court, rejecting the application of the special leave to appeal under Article 136, observed that it is time to realise that the jurisdiction of the court to grant special leave to appeal can be invoked in very exceptional circumstances. A question of law of general public importance, or a decision which shocks the conscience of the court are some of the prime requisites for the grant of special leave. Substantial question of law must be discernible from the pleadings. If pleadings are contemptuous, irrelevant and incoherent and do not disclose any question of law, much less a substantial question of law, a special leave petition (SLP) is liable to be dismissed in limine.[46] An SLP may also be granted where against the impugned order no appeal or revision lies.[47]

Special leave to appeal can be granted under Article 136 only against any judgment or decree of any court or tribunal. If the authority is neither a court nor a tribunal, no leave to appeal can be granted. In *Manju Varma* v. *State of U.P.*[48], a question before the court was: Whether an order passed by the Chief Justice of the Allahabad High Court on administrative side to transfer a case from the Lucknow Bench to Allahabad Bench of the High Court was a decision of a "court or tribunal"? The court held that the decision of the Chief Justice is at best can be said to be a decision of a "tribunal". The court clarified that the expression "tribunal" as used under Article 136 does not mean something as a "court", but includes, within its ambit, all adjudicating bodies, provided they are constituted by the State and are invested with the judicial functions, except those established under any law relating to armed forces. Granting special leave in the case, the court observed that powers under Article 136 can be exercised provided two conditions are present: 1) the proposed appeal must be against a judicial or quasi-judicial order; and 2) the decision must be of a court or tribunal.

In order to render justice to the deprived and disempowered sections of society, the Supreme Court in *State of Karnataka* v. *Appa Balu Ingale*[49] held that the power of judicial review under Articles 32, 136, 226 can be exercised to supplement changing social needs, values and felt necessities of the time, having regard to social inequalities, inequities and imbalances the law intended to remove. However, the jurisdiction of the court cannot be invoked lightly. If the amount involved in the appeal is meagre, the petition may not be admitted.[50]

43. *Remington Rand of India Ltd.* v. *Thiru R. Jambulingam*, (1975) 3 SCC 254.
44. *Alembic Chemical Works Co. Ltd.* v. *Workmen*, AIR 1961 SC 647.
45. (1979) 4 SCC 530.
46. *Charanjit Singh* v. *R.C. Jain*, (2003) 1 SCC 758.
47. *Usha K. Pillai* v. *Raj K. Srinivas*, (1993) 3 SCC 208.
48. (2005) 1 SCC 73.
49. 1995 Supp (4) SCC 469 (*per* K. Ramaswamy J).
50. *Collector of Customs* v. *Madras Rubber Factory*, (1995) 5 SCC 439; *Eicher Goodearth Ltd.* v. *CCE*, (1995) 5 SCC 443.

Though the principle of res judicata applies to writ proceedings, but the Supreme Court held that non-filing of appeals before the Supreme Court by the State in similar matters in the past would not itself bar the jurisdiction of the court under Article 136 of the Constitution.[51] In the same manner if an SLP has been dismissed in limine,[52] or without laying any law, the principle of res judicata will not apply.[53] However, a respondent will not be permitted to reopen the question which had been decided by the Supreme Court by dismissing the SLP filed earlier.[54]

Generally, no new plea can be directly taken in an SLP, but the failure to take plea of non-maintainability of suit before the civil court can be directly taken before the Supreme Court because any order or decree passed by any court without jurisdiction is non est in law.[55]

In order to prevent the abuse of court's jurisdiction under Article 136, the court held that if it is satisfied that the respondent abused the process of law and misused the legal system by deceit, falsehood or sharp practice, the court besides granting any other relief may also impose exemplary cost.[56]

It is for the Supreme Court to decide whether to entertain an appeal or not. When the point of law raised in appeal is of general public importance, appeal cannot be dismissed in limine on the preliminary issue of maintainability on the ground that no appeal was preferred against the earlier decisions of the High Court.[57] Thus, a new plea involving a question of law not taken before the forum below can be raised before the Supreme Court.[58] Nevertheless, a new plea of res judicata will not be allowed to be raised before the court, if not taken before a forum below because res judicata is a mixed question of law and fact.[59]

The court also has the power to recall its judgment either on a review petition or suo motu. The court recalled its judgment in *S. Jamaldeen* v. *High Court of Madras*[60] suo motu because it had decided the question of inter se seniority of direct and regularised recruits to the Tamil Nadu Judicial Service without giving notice to the High Court and the Public Service Commission.

Keeping in view the congestion of cases before it, the Supreme Court itself has suggested to the government to curtail its jurisdiction of special leave to appeal under Article 136. But because Article 136 is also a lawyer's paradise, the move always faced strong opposition from the Bar.[61] In

51. *State of Bihar* v. *Ramdeo Yadav*, (1996) 3 SCC 493.
52. *Yogendra Narayan Chowdhury* v. *Union of India*, (1996) 7 SCC 1.
53. *Kirloskar Bros. Ltd.* v. *ESI Corpn.*, (1996) 2 SCC 682.
54. *State of Gujarat* v. *Bhaterdevi Ramnivas Sanwalram*, (2002) 7 SCC 500.
55. *P.M.A. Metropolitan* v. *Moran Mar Marthoma*, 1995 Supp (4) SCC 286.
56. *MCD* v. *Kamla Devi*, (1996) 8 SCC 285.
57. *STO* v. *Shree Durga Oil Mills*, (1998) 1 SCC 572.
58. *Grasim Industries Ltd.* v. *Collector of Customs*, (2002) 4 SCC 297.
59. *Madhukar D. Shende* v. *Tarabai Aba Shedage*, (2002) 2 SCC 85.
60. (1998) 2 SCC 705 recalled for rehearing in (1998) 2 SCC 705.
61. *Indian Express* 14-4-1979 reports:
Supreme Court plea not accepted by the Government

February 2016, a PIL has been filed before the Supreme Court for creation of regional court of appeals to transfer the appellate jurisdiction of the Supreme Court to court of appeals. Thus, the Supreme Court of India would confine itself with writ jurisdiction only. The decision of the court will have far reaching consequences for the justice delivery system in India.

1.2 Jurisdiction of the High Courts under Articles 226 and 227

Article 226 empowers the High Courts to issue directions, orders or writs for the enforcement of fundamental rights and for any other purpose also. Thus, the power of judicial review of the High Courts is wider than that of the Supreme Court. The words "for any other purpose" enable the High Courts to exercise their power of judicial review for the enforcement of ordinary legal rights which are not fundamental rights. The jurisdiction

---

(Express News Service: New Delhi, April 13)

The Government has not accepted the Supreme Court's request to fetter its powers to grant special leave of appeal from any judgment on any matter.

The request was meant to decrease the number of cases pending before the Supreme Court. And it would have necessitated an amendment to Art. 136 of the Constitution.

Special leave to appeal is determined by Art. 136 and it is unrestricted in scope. The discretion lies entirely with the Supreme Court.

The extraordinary power conferred by Art. 136 cannot be taken away by any legislation short of a constitutional amendment.

The Government, which came to power in the wake of the Emergency, does not want to give a remote impression of putting any restriction on the Supreme Court's powers or privileges.

On the other hand, the Supreme Court's predicament is that the cases for the special leave to appeal are piling up. They now average nearly 1000 a month as against a mere 100 a few years ago.

Lord Scarman, former Chairman of the British Law Commission and now a member of the court of appeal who was recently in India, reportedly told the Supreme Court judges that the way they have increased the hearings, the system would collapse under its own weight.

The Government feels that the Supreme Court has itself to blame for the spurt in cases of special leave to appeal. Over the period, the Government believes that the Supreme Court has unnecessarily stretched the scope of Art. 136 and has admitted such cases as it should not have.

A Law Ministry spokesman points out how the Supreme Court used to take care till the early sixties to admit only those cases which related either to the interpretation of the Constitution or to the relationship between two States.

Now in the name of "social justice", according to the Law Ministry spokesman, Art. 136 has been stretched beyond recognition, so much so the Supreme Court grants special leave to appeal even in ordinary criminal cases.

No doubt the power of the Supreme Court to grant special leave to appeal from the decision of any court or tribunal save military tribunals is not subject to any constitutional limitation. It is, however, presumed that the cases admitted will not be many and the power conferred will be used sparingly.

According to the Supreme Court sources, the court has imposed certain limitations on its own powers. When the Supreme Court reaches the conclusion that a person has been dealt with arbitrarily, or a court or tribunal has not given a fair deal to a litigant, then it gives special leave to appeal.

It is pointed out that the Supreme Court does not assume a jurisdiction which is not warranted by the provisions of the Constitution, nor provides a relief which has been omitted in the Constitution. Similarly, the court does not grant special leave on grounds which would not sustain the appeal itself.

of the High Court under Article 226 for the enforcement of fundamental rights is mandatory, whereas for the enforcement of ordinary legal rights it is discretionary.[62] The power of judicial review of the High Court under Article 226 is constitutional and, therefore, no measure of finality given by the legislature to any action or decision can take away this power.[63] A High Court is bound to follow the technical procedure of the English Law in the matter of issuing a writ, hence a petition will not be thrown out because a proper writ has not been prayed for.[64] A High Court can issue a writ to a person or authority having its location or residence within the territorial jurisdiction of the court, or if the cause of action either wholly or partly arises within its territorial jurisdiction. Therefore, a High Court can issue a writ even when the person or authority is located outside its territorial jurisdiction.

However, mere location of head office of a company within the territorial jurisdiction of a High Court will not automatically confer jurisdiction on that High Court if no part of cause of action arises in its jurisdiction. Thus, in *Kalyan Banerjee* v. *Mohd. Iqbal*[65], the Supreme Court held that where an employee was appointed in Jharkhand and his services were terminated there which did not require the sanction of the head office, which was in West Bengal, then the West Bengal High Court will not have any jurisdiction simply because the head office of the company was located there.

The power of the High Court under Article 226 is discretionary,[66] and the power cannot be exercised as a court of appeal.[67] The jurisdiction is supervisory in nature. It can strike down an impugned rule and direct the authorities to reframe it, but cannot itself frame it.[68] The power of judicial review under Article 226 is not directed against the decision but is confined to the decision-making process.[69] A High Court would generally not reappreciate evidences, or enter into determination of questions which demand an elaborate examination of evidence, or interfere in the punishment imposed unless the administrative determination is mala fide, or made in contravention of the principles of natural justice, or prompted by extraneous consideration, or is in violation of any constitutional provision, or is such that shocks the conscience of the court.[70] Nevertheless, if the court finds that an administrative order has been passed without following the principles of natural justice, the case may be remanded back. The High

62. *Manjula Manjari Dei* v. *Director of Public Instruction*, 1952 SCC OnLine Ori 18: AIR 1952 Ori 344. See also, *Kailash Chander Sharma* v. *State of Haryana*, 1989 Supp (2) SCC 696.
63. *Kihoto Hollohan* v. *Zachillhu*, 1992 Supp (2) SCC 651.
64. *Kanu Sanyal* v. *Distt. Magistrate, Darjeeling*, (1973) 2 SCC 674.
65. 1981 Supp SCC 65.
66. *State of Maharashtra* v. *Manubhai Pragaji Vashi*, (1995) 5 SCC 730.
67. *State of U.P.* v. *S.K.M. Inter College*, 1995 Supp (2) SCC 535.
68. *Swapan Kumar Choudhary* v. *Tapas Chakravorty*, (1995) 4 SCC 478.
69. *Excise and Taxation Officer-cum-Assessing Authority* v. *Gopi Nath & Sons*, 1992 Supp (2) SCC 312; *HUDA* v. *Roochira Ceramics*, (1996) 6 SCC 584.
70. *B.C. Chaturvedi* v. *Union of India*, (1995) 6 SCC 749.

Court has no power to decide the case itself.[71] High Court, being a court of plenary jurisdiction, has inherent power to do "complete justice" between the parties similar to the Supreme Court's power under Article 142 of the Constitution.[72] Unless the facts and circumstances of the case clearly justify the laches or delay, a writ petitioner would not be entitled to relief against anybody, including the State.[73] The Constitution places no limitations or fetters on the power of the High Court except self-imposed limitation, therefore, the arms of the court are long enough to reach injustice wherever it is found. It is for this reason that the distinction between public law and private law is being obliterated, and a person can enforce a legal right founded upon a contract or a statute or instrument having the force of law.[74] While dismissing a petition in limine or summary dismissal, the High Court must record reasons so that in appeal the Supreme Court is not denied the opportunity of testing and weighing those reasons.[75] Thus, summary dismissal without reason by short order would be unsustainable, as failure to give reasons would amount to denial of justice.[76]

Court-martial proceedings under the Army Act, 1950 are subject to review by the High Court under Article 226 of the Constitution. However, court-martial is not subject to superintendence of the High Court under Article 227. Proceedings of a properly constituted court-martial, if conducted in accordance with the rules, are beyond the scope of judicial review. Where evidence was sufficient, subject-matter was within jurisdiction, prescribed procedure was followed and the punishment awarded was within power, the court held that the conviction and the sentence passed by court-martial cannot be disturbed. The court further held that mere want of proper and adequate pre-trial investigation would not, in the absence of prejudice caused to the accused or violation of a mandatory provision, vitiate the court-martial proceedings.[77]

In the same manner, in election cases where a High Court exercises original jurisdiction, its jurisdiction is neither appellate nor review. Therefore, the court in such cases can go into the error of fact touching the merit of decision. The court would exercise the expanded power of judicial review.[78]

Where the facts justify filing of petition either under Article 226 or 227, but the petition is filed under both the articles, the court treats the petition under Article 226 so as not to deprive the party of the right to appeal.[79]

71. *Indian Oil Corpn.* v. *Lala Bhairo Prasad Saraf & Sons*, (2019) 9 SCC 505.
72. *Income Tax Appellate Tribunal* v. *CIT*, (1996) 7 SCC 454.
73. *State of Maharashtra* v. *Digambar*, (1995) 4 SCC 683; *State of J&K* v. *Ashok Kumar Gupta*, (1996) 2 SCC 82.
74. *Air India Statutory Corpn.* v. *United Labour Union*, (1997) 9 SCC 377.
75. *Llewellyn Furtado* v. *State of Goa*, (1997) 7 SCC 533.
76. *Vishnu Dev Sharma* v. *State of U.P.*, (2008) 3 SCC 172.
77. *Union of India* v. *Major A. Hussain*, (1998) 1 SCC 537.
78. *Uttamrao Shivdas Jankar* v. *Ranjitsinh Vijaysinh Mohite Patil*, (2009) 13 SCC 131.
79. *Sushilabai Laxminarayan Mudliyar* v. *Nihalchand Waghajibhai Shaha*, 1993 Supp (1) SCC 11.

Under Article 226 there is nothing that precludes the court from reviewing its own decisions because such power is inherent in every court of plenary jurisdiction. This is necessary to prevent miscarriage or to correct grave errors committed by it. However, this power is to be exercised only when there is error apparent on record or when there is discovery of new matter or evidence which even after exercise of due diligence was not within the knowledge of the person seeking or review or could not be produced by him at the time the earlier order was made or on any such analogous grounds. In the same manner court has power to recall its own decisions on similar grounds.[80]

Administrative decisions are subject to judicial review under Article 226 of the Constitution only on grounds of perversity, patent illegality, irrationality, want of power to take the decision and procedural irregularity. Except on these grounds, administrative decisions are not interfered with in exercise of the extraordinary power of judicial review. A decision is vitiated by irrationality if the decision is so outrageous that it is in defiance of all logic; when no person acting reasonably could possibly have taken the decision, having regard to the materials on record. A decision may sometimes be set aside and quashed under Article 226 on the ground of illegality. This is when there is an apparent error of law on the face of the decision which goes to the root of the decision and/or in other words, an apparent error but for which the decision would have been otherwise. Judicial review under Article 226 is directed not against the decision, but the decision-making process. A patent illegality and/or error apparent on the face of the decision which goes to the root of the decision may vitiate the decision-making process.[81]

The expanding horizons of jurisprudence regarding exercise of executive power as per rule of law and as per public trust doctrine led to lowering of the threshold of tolerance for what is unfair, unreasonable and arbitrary. Judicial review is wide enough to strike at and annul any State action that is arbitrary, unguided, whimsical, unfair and discriminatory. Government and so also all public bodies are trustees of the power vested in them. Discharge of the trust reposed in them in the best possible manner is their primary duty. The power to engage, employ or recruit servants, agents, advisors and representatives must, like any other power, be exercised in a fair, reasonable, non-discriminatory and objective manner.[82]

In *Maharashtra Chess Assn.* v. *Union of India*[83], the Supreme Court held that while the powers the High Court may exercise under its writ jurisdiction are not subject to strict legal principles, two clear principles emerge with respect to when a High Court's writ jurisdiction may be engaged. *First*, the decision of the High Court to entertain or not entertain a particular

80. *State of Rajasthan* v. *Surendra Mohnot*, (2014) 14 SCC 77.
81. *Sarvepalli Ramaiah* v. *District Collector, Chittoor*, (2019) 4 SCC 500.
82. *State of Punjab* v. *Brijeshwar Singh Chahal*, (2016) 6 SCC 1.
83. (2020) 13 SCC 285.

action under its writ jurisdiction is fundamentally discretionary. *Secondly*, limitations placed on the court's decision to exercise or refuse to exercise its writ jurisdiction are self-imposed. It is a well-settled principle that the writ jurisdiction of a High Court cannot be completely excluded by statute. If a High Court is tasked with being the final recourse to upholding the rule of law within its territorial jurisdiction, it must necessarily have the power to examine any case before it and make a determination of whether or not its writ jurisdiction is engaged. Judicial review under Article 226 is an intrinsic feature of the basic structure of the Constitution.

Article 227 invests High Courts with the power of superintendence over administrative agencies exercising adjudicatory powers. The nature of this power is both administrative and judicial.

Article 227 though confers the right of superintendence over all courts and tribunals throughout the territories in relation to which a High Court exercises jurisdiction, but no corresponding right is conferred upon a litigant to invoke the jurisdiction under this article as a matter of right. In fact, the power of superintendence casts a duty upon a High Court to keep the inferior courts and tribunals within the limits of their authority and make sure that they do not cross the limits, ensuring the performance of duty by such courts and tribunals in accordance with law. Only wrong decision may not be the ground for the exercise of jurisdiction under Article 227 unless the wrong is referable to a grave dereliction of duty and flagrant abuse of power by the subordinate courts and tribunals, resulting in grave injustice to any party.[84]

Jurisdiction of the High Court under Article 227 is revisional and not appellate, hence it is limited and restrictive in nature. For this reason, it does not confer an unlimited authority to correct all wrong orders made within the jurisdiction of the courts and tribunals below. Jurisdiction under Article 227, thus, may be exercised for want of jurisdiction, errors of law, perverse findings, gross violation of the principles of natural justice, and where finding of fact is based on no evidence resulting in manifest injustice.[85]

The Constitution (42nd Amendment) Act, 1976 denuded this power of the High Courts by deleting the word "tribunal" in Article 227, but the Constitution (44th Amendment) Act, 1978 restored this power.

The Supreme Court observed that Article 227 does not invest the High Courts with unlimited right to interfere with the administrative adjudicatory process. This power is to be exercised to prevent grave miscarriage of justice or flagrant violation of law.[86] The power of superintendence of the High Court under Article 227 is not confined to administrative superintendence only, such power includes the power of judicial review also. As regards administrative actions, the High Court can interfere in cases

84. *Ouseph Mathai* v. *M. Abdul Khadir*, (2002) 1 SCC 319.
85. *Essen Deinki* v. *Rajiv Kumar*, (2002) 8 SCC 400.
86. *D.N. Banerji* v. *P.R. Mukherjee*, AIR 1953 SC 58.

of erroneous assumption of jurisdiction or acting beyond its jurisdiction, refusal to exercise jurisdiction, an error of law apparent on the face of the record, arbitrary or capricious exercise of authority or discretion, a patent error in procedure, arriving at a finding which is perverse or based on no material, or resulting in manifest injustice. As regards subordinate court, its findings of fact can be reviewed if based on no evidence or upon manifest misreading of evidence or if its conclusions are perverse.[87]

The jurisdiction under Articles 226 and 227 are separate and independent. Challenge to judicial orders of subordinate courts could lie by way of statutory appeal or revision or under Article 227 and not by way of writ under Article 226 or 32 of the Constitution. While appellate or revisional jurisdiction is regulated by the statutes, power of superintendence under Article 227 is constitutional.[88] The power of judicial superintendence over inferior courts and tribunals, which is intended to keep them within bounds, is not limited by technical rules which govern the exercise of power under Article 226. Thus, the power under Article 226 can be exercised only on an application, but power under Article 227 can be exercised either on an application or suo motu. In the same proceeding, the court can quash an order under Article 227 and also issue further directions, like making further inquiries after taking evidence, which is not available in the proceedings under Article 226. The power under Article 227 may be exercised even in cases where no appeal or revision lies to the High Court.[89] However, where any alternative remedy is available to the person, the court may not exercise this power.[90]

In the same manner, power under Article 227 cannot be exercised by the High Court to influence the lower judiciary in exercise of its judicial powers. Therefore, a High Court cannot give general directions to lower courts—regarding dispensing with personal attendance and personal examination of an accused by the court—which are inconsistent with the provisions of the Criminal Procedure Code, 1973.[91]

The term "tribunal" in reference to Article 227 is to be interpreted in the same manner as in Article 136. Any authority created by law with the power to adjudicate upon the rights of the parties, and invested with the trappings of a law court shall be considered as tribunal. But this will not include a tribunal constituted by or under any law relating to the armed forces. The power of superintendence of the High Court under Article 227 extends not only to quash the decision of a tribunal but also to give directions regarding the disposal of the case. The power under Article 227 may be exercised by the High Court either on petition from an aggrieved person

87. *Achutananda Baidya* v. *Prafullya Kumar Gayen*, (1997) 5 SCC 76.
88. *Radhey Shyam* v. *Chhabi Naik*, (2015) 5 SCC 423.
89. *Ram Roop* v. *Bishwa Nath*, 1958 SCC OnLine All 38: AIR 1958 All 456. See also, *Waryam Singh* v. *Amarnath*, AIR 1954 SC 215.
90. *Ibid.*
91. *TGN Kumar* v. *State of Kerala*, (2011) 2 SCC 772.

or suo motu.[92] The 42nd Amendment had added Articles 323-A and 323-B to the Constitution, which had authorised Parliament to establish special courts to perform substitutional role of the High Courts. In 1985, the Administrative Tribunals Act was passed by Parliament and service tribunals were established to determine service matters of government servants. The jurisdiction of High Courts over these tribunals under Articles 226 and 227 had been taken away, as these tribunals had been given substitutional role of the High Courts. However, now the Supreme Court in *L. Chandra Kumar* v. *Union of India*[93] has restored the power of the High Courts under Articles 226 and 227 of the Constitution by declaring Articles 323-A(2) and 323-B(*d*) of the Constitution as unconstitutional. The court held that the power of judicial review of the High Courts under Articles 226 and 227 is a basic feature of the Constitution which cannot be abridged or ousted.

Before leaving the area of public law review, it is pertinent to note that in the US, in the federal jurisdiction, the use of writs as means of controlling administrative action has been abandoned. The decision of the Supreme Court in *Degge* v. *Hitchcock*[94] has confined the writ of certiorari to judicial decisions only. Writs have been replaced by injunction, declaratory action, and a combination of the two. The prophesy of Lord Denning, written in 1949, that just as the pick and shovel are no longer suitable for the winning of coal, so are the procedures of mandamus, certiorari and action on a case not suitable for the winning of freedom in the new age, has thus proved true.[95] Perhaps Lord Denning's prophesy was founded on the technicalities with which these writs suffered.

Judicial control over administrative action is also exercised extensively by remanding the case to the administrative authority, instead of merely quashing it as is done in India. It has a definite advantage because besides removing the cause of grievance, the decision largely remains the decision of the administrative authority. However, in the US, writs still hold the ground, though slowly the ground is slipping under their feet. Civil practice law and rules of the New York State, Administrative Review Act of Illinois State, and Model State Administrative Procedure Act, 1946 provide for a simple and less technical form of judicial review of administrative actions.

In principles and modes, public law review in England is more or less the same as in India. Where on the one side, prerogative writs are being stripped of their technicalities, on the other an increasing use is being made of the private law remedies of injunction and declaratory actions to control administrative actions.

Judicial review of an administrative or a legislative action is a basic feature of the Constitution, which cannot be taken away even by amending the Constitution, as by amending the Constitution the basic features of

92. *State of Orissa* v. *Murlidhar Jena*, AIR 1963 SC 404.
93. (1997) 3 SCC 261.
94. 1913 SCC OnLine US SC 174: 57 L Ed 1135: 229 US 162 (1913).
95. Denning, *Freedom Under Law* 126.

the Constitution cannot be abrogated. Therefore, the doctrine of immunity from judicial review has been restricted only to a few class of cases, *i.e.* deployment of troops, foreign affairs and national security. In these areas, courts regard themselves as ill-equipped to investigate beyond an initial decision whether the claim of a government is bona fide. Thus, even in such a non-justiciable area, judicial review is not entirely excluded. In justiciable area of judicial review, it is not the review of administrative action but of the process of action. Administrative authority may be compelled to exercise power, but not to exercise it in a particular manner. There may be various options available to the administration, court will not impose the option which it thinks is the best option. It is for the administration to select an option which it considers best in public interest. One can classify grounds of judicial review of administrative action into three categories—illegality, irrationality and procedural impropriety. The courts will be slow to interfere with any administrative action if it does not fall in any of these three categories. The administrative authority must not transgress the limits, substantive or procedural, set by the law and must act reasonably. The authority must act properly within law, apply its mind to matters which it is bound to consider, and exclude all that is not relevant, and there should not be anything so absurd in the decision that no sensible person could even dream that it lay within the powers of the authority. This is what is termed as "Wednesbury test of reasonableness". Over and above, this authority must act in good faith. All these factors are not selectively exclusive, they may overlap.[96]

While exercising writ jurisdiction, the court acts not only as a court of law but also as a court of equity. Therefore, if there is a clear error or omission on the part of the court to consider a justifiable claim, it can be subject to review. In the same manner even contractual disputes involving public law elements are amenable to writ jurisdiction. Thus, where a party supplied sugar to the Food Corporation of India (FCI) in terms of a statutory order under Essential Commodities Act, 1955, and there was no factual dispute also, the Supreme Court held that a writ petition is maintainable for securing payment arbitrarily withheld.[97]

In *63 Moons Technologies Ltd.* v. *Union of India*[98], the Supreme Court held that an administrative order cannot be justified before the court on additional grounds not contained in the original order. When a statutory functionary makes an order based on certain grounds, its validity must be judged by the reasons so mentioned and cannot be supplemented by fresh reasons in the shape of affidavit or otherwise. Otherwise, an order bad in the beginning may, by the time it comes to court on account of a challenge, get validated by additional grounds later brought out.

96. See, *Indian Railway Construction Co. Ltd.* v. *Ajay Kumar*, (2003) 4 SCC 579.
97. *Food Corporation of India* v. *SEIL Ltd.*, (2008) 3 SCC 440.
98. (2019) 18 SCC 401.

1.2.1 *Judicial review of administrative policy*

Norms of judicial review of an administrative policy are more exacting and intrusive than the legislative policy. In case of an administrative policy, there is more need for scrutiny and balancing. Courts are very reluctant to strike down a legislation unless there is a clear violation of constitutional provisions. A court is not concerned with wisdom of the legislature but only with its legislative competence, and it will uphold the policy irrespective of its own views.[99] However, an administrative policy laid down by its rule-making power, or in exercise of its executive powers, can be reviewed if

(1) it is unconstitutional;
(2) it is beyond the powers of the parent Act or regulation;
(3) the delegate has acted beyond the power of delegation;
(4) it is contrary to statutory policy or a larger policy.[100]

Executive decisions cannot be termed as policy decisions, and there is also no presumption of its constitutionality. Courts will apply the doctrine of Wednesbury unreasonableness and the doctrine of proportionality in judging the validity of an administrative policy.

The court in the exercise of judicial review will interpret policy decisions as they exist rather than to expand their scope.[101] It is for the State to determine what should be the policy for grant/refusal of concessional power at different points of time and not for the court.[102]

In *State of H.P.* v. *Rajesh Chander Sood*[103], the Supreme Court held that financial viability and sustainability of the government-controlled corporate bodies and whether, when and how such bodies require to be wound up are policy matters of the government. Likewise, conditions of service, where and how much wages to be paid, as also post-retiral benefits payable to employees of such corporate bodies are also policy matters of the government.

In *Union of India* v. *M. Selvakumar*[104], the Supreme Court observed that horizontal reservation and relaxation for physically handicapped category candidates for Civil Services Examination is a matter of governmental policy and not within the domain of courts to embark upon enquiry into the same. Courts can only interfere where policy framed is absolutely capricious and not informed by reasons or totally arbitrary offending Article 14 of the Constitution.

In *Digi Cable Network (India) (P) Ltd.* v. *Union of India*[105], the Supreme Court held that national security is a matter of policy. Courts cannot decide

99. *Karnataka Bank Ltd.* v. *State of A.P.*, (2008) 2 SCC 254.
100. *DDA* v. *Joint Action Committee*, (2008) 2 SCC 672.
101. *Union of India* v. *Om Dutt Sharma*, (2020) 2 SCC 133.
102. *Kothari Industrial Corpn. Ltd.* v. *T.N. Electricity Board*, (2016) 4 SCC 134.
103. (2016) 10 SCC 77: (2016) 2 SCC (L&S) 730.
104. (2017) 3 SCC 504.
105. (2019) 4 SCC 451.

whether something is in the interest of the State or not. It should be left to the executive. In situations involving national security, a party cannot insist on strict observance with the principles of natural justice. Under such situations, it is the duty of courts to read into and provide for statutory exclusion, if not expressly provided in rules governing the field. However, depending upon facts of a particular case, it will be open for the court to satisfy itself whether there were justifiable facts. It can call for files and see whether it is a case involving interest of national security. Once the State is of stand that the issue involves national security, the court shall not disclose reasons to the affected party.

In *Essar Steel Ltd.* v. *Union of India*[106], the Supreme Court noted that policy regarding economic/commercial matters should not be interfered with unless it is demonstrated that it has been enacted in an arbitrary, unreasonable or mala fide manner, or that it offends the provisions of the Constitution.

In *Union of India* v. *Lt. Col. P.K. Choudhary*[107], the Supreme Court noted that Command tenure being a policy matter, the scope of judicial review is extremely limited.

1.2.2 *Compliance with the court orders*

In India, the compliance jurisprudence is not so developed. There is no systematic study about the impact of and compliance with court orders. It is rightly said that the real trouble of the litigant begins after the court has granted him a decree. Contempt proceedings are too much for a poor litigant who has already suffered financially and physically in a long-drawn-out expensive litigation. However, at present, the law does not provide any alternative. Therefore, the need for the development of a system for judicial feedback on impact and compliance cannot be overemphasised.

For the satisfaction of a common man who has no strings to pull, the Supreme Court has clearly indicated that if the government does not obey its orders, in suitable cases, the officer concerned may be imprisoned and the government property may be attached. In *Union of India* v. *Satish Chandra Sharma*[108], Krishna Iyer J observed:

> We are in no mood to condone wilful procrastination nor suffer wanton stagnation in [a]dministration as a ground for default in obeying court orders. The law does not respect lazy bosses nor 'cheeky' evaders.

Nevertheless, behaving in a pragmatic manner and taking into consideration the paper-logged procedure, millions of babus and miles of red tape in governmental functioning, the court stressed that contempt power must be used sparingly if it is convinced that there has been wilful defiance or

106. (2016) 11 SCC 1.
107. (2016) 4 SCC 236.
108. (1980) 2 SCC 144.

disobedience.[109] Court has now developed the concept of "continuous mandamus" to monitor compliance of its directions.

2. PUBLIC LAW REVIEW

2.1 Constituency of public law review: Against whom a writ can be issued

Under the provisions of Articles 32 and 226 of the Indian Constitution, the Supreme Court and the High Courts have the power to issue writs in the nature of habeas corpus, mandamus, certiorari, prohibition and quo warranto. The jurisdiction of the Supreme Court is limited only to the enforcement of fundamental rights, while the High Courts can issue writs not only for the enforcement of fundamental rights but also for other purposes.

Authorities amenable to the writ jurisdiction of the Supreme Court.—The main purpose of Article 32 is to protect an individual against the infringement of his fundamental rights. The threat to fundamental rights may arise from the following sources:

(1) Government and Parliament of India, governments and legislatures of States and local governments.
(2) Government departmental undertakings.
(3) Agencies incorporated by statutes.
(4) Agencies registered under statutes; for example, Companies Act, 1956 and Societies Registration Act, 1860.
(5) Courts.
(6) Private individuals and bodies.

Judicial opinion is clear that the authorities falling under the first three categories are amenable to the writ jurisdiction of the Supreme Court and are included within the definition of "State" in Article 12.[110]

Agencies falling under the fourth category (incorporated public or private companies, government companies, registered societies) may be included within the term "State" and, therefore, are amenable to the writ jurisdiction of the Supreme Court, if such authorities are instrumentalities or agencies of the government.[111]

Courts of law are not mentioned as such in Article 12, but they may pose a threat to the fundamental rights of the people in exercise of their

109. *Union of India* v. *Satish Chandra Sharma*, (1980) 2 SCC 144, 150–51. P.D. Desai J, Chief Justice of the H.P. High Court, ordered the government to pay compensation with interest at the residence of the appellant who was unpaid for a decade for acquisition of his property due to governmental inertia and callousness. [*Indian Express*, Chandigarh 11-5-1984].

110. *Rajasthan SEB* v. *Mohan Lal*, AIR 1967 SC 1857; *Sukhdev Singh* v. *Bhagatram Sardar Singh Raghuvanshi*, (1975) 1 SCC 421.

111. *Ramana Dayaram Shetty* v. *International Airport Authority of India*, (1979) 3 SCC 489. For details read under the heading "Authorities amenable to the writ jurisdiction of the High Court" in this chapter.

administrative powers. In *Prem Chand Garg* v. *Excise Commr.*[112], the Supreme Court struck down certain rules framed by it as violative of fundamental rights.

Some of the fundamental rights given under Articles 15(2), 17, 23(1) and 24 can be claimed against private individuals also. The judicial opinion is that these rights, though belong to private individuals, cannot be enforced by private individuals. Therefore, as the law stands today, such private individuals and bodies are not amenable to the jurisdiction of the Supreme Court, no matter they violate fundamental rights.[113] There seems to be no valid reason for this kind of a judicial exclusion.

The approach of the court in the area of fundamental rights must not be whether the authority is "State" within the meaning of Article 12. The correct approach should be that every authority or person who poses a threat to a fundamental right should be amenable to the jurisdiction of the court. Therefore, not the "type of agency" but the "threat to the fundamental rights" must be the determining factor for the issue of writs under Article 32.

Authorities amenable to the writ jurisdiction of High Courts.—The High Courts have a wider power to issue writs against "any person or authority" for the enforcement of fundamental rights and any other legal right. As regards the "person and authority" against whom such writs can be issued, the law seems to be in a thicket of inconsistencies. There is no controversy about the writs of habeas corpus and quo warranto which can be issued against private individuals and public officers respectively. Therefore, the discussion will mainly concentrate on writs of certiorari, prohibition and mandamus.

It is gratifying to note that the area for the operation of these writs has been extended, and rightly so, to cover various administrative agencies exercising multifarious functions. The Supreme Court clarified that the term "authority" used in Article 226 of the Constitution has a wider and liberal meaning unlike the use of the term in Article 12. Article 12 is relevant only for the enforcement of fundamental rights under Article 32. Article 226 confers powers on the High Courts to issue writs for the enforcement of fundamental rights and also for "any other purpose"[114]. This has widened the scope of judicial review by widening the reach of Article 226 and that of mandamus.

There is no dispute that all constitutional and administrative authorities are amenable to the jurisdiction of the courts. Therefore, a writ can be issued against public acts of the President of India, Governors, Union and State Governments, Ministers, government officers and departments,

112. AIR 1963 SC 996.
113. Writ of habeas corpus being the exception.
114. *U.P. State Coop. Land Development Bank Ltd.* v. *Chandra Bhan Dubey*, (1999) 1 SCC 741. See also, *Andi Mukta Sadguru Shree Muktajee Vandas Swami Suvarna Jayanti Mahotsav Smarak Trust* v. *V.R. Rudani*, (1989) 2 SCC 691.

and other bodies given in the Constitution, *i.e.* Union Public Service Commission, Election Tribunal, Finance Commission, Water Dispute Authority and Attorney General of India.[115]

The combined effect of *Constitution of India, re*[116], and *State of Punjab* v. *Satyapal*[117], is that a writ can be issued in appropriate cases, where there is a violation of the Constitution or any law, to Parliament and State legislatures.

State of M.P. v. *Babu Lal*[118] has established the law beyond doubt that a writ of certiorari can be issued against a court to correct the record if the court has usurped jurisdiction. In this case, a civil suit, collusive in nature, was filed by Babulal against one Baddiya, a member of the Scheduled Tribe who was prohibited under a law of Madhya Pradesh to transfer land to a non-tribal except with the prior permission of the competent authority, for mutation in revenue record as owner of land. The court decreed the suit on the basis of a compromise deed filed by the parties transferring the rights in favour of the plaintiff. The government filed a writ before the High Court which was dismissed with an advice that the government could go in for declaration. On appeal, the Supreme Court issued the writ of certiorari. The writ can also be issued to any judge quashing an action taken in an administrative capacity.[119]

The opinion of the courts is also decisive that writs can be issued to statutory bodies irrespective of their functions and "profit" orientations. Therefore, writs can be issued to bodies like the Life Insurance Corporation of India (LIC), NSC, University, Dock Labour Board, State Transport Corporation, Warehousing Corporation, Steel Authority of India (SAIL), etc.[120]

The law relating to the amenability of registered agencies, *i.e.* companies registered under the Companies Act, 1956 and societies registered under the Societies Registration Act, 1860, is still in a developing stage and has not reached the stage of maturity.

---

115. See, *Madhav Rao Jivaji Rao Scindia* v. *Union of India*, (1971) 1 SCC 85; *K.A. Mathialagan* v. *Governor of T.N.*, 1972 SCC OnLine Mad 242: AIR 1973 Mad 198; *Shivji Nathubhai* v. *Union of India*, AIR 1960 SC 606; *Kokku Venkataramaiah* v. *State of A.P.*, 1959 SCC OnLine AP 122: AIR 1960 AP 420; *Deo Dutt Sharma* v. *Zahoor Ahmed Zaid*, 1959 SCC OnLine Raj 65: AIR 1960 Raj 25; *Gullapalli Nageswara Rao* v. *A.P. SRTC*, AIR 1959 SC 308; *Mira Chatterjee* v. *Public Service Commission*, 1958 SCC OnLine Cal 161: AIR 1958 Cal 345; *Mohinder Singh Gill* v. *Chief Election Commr.*, (1978) 1 SCC 405, 432; *Mayer Simon Parur* v. *Advocate General of Kerala*, 1974 SCC OnLine Ker 45: AIR 1975 Ker 57.

116. *Powers, Privileges and Immunities of State Legislatures, re*, AIR 1965 SC 745.

117. AIR 1969 SC 903.

118. (1977) 2 SCC 435.

119. See, *K. Prabhakaran Nair* v. *State of Kerala*, 1969 SCC OnLine Ker 42: AIR 1970 Ker 27; *Pradyat Kumar Bose* v. *Chief Justice of Calcutta High Court*, AIR 1956 SC 285 (Supreme Court did not express any final opinion).

120. *LIC* v. *Sunil Kumar Mukherjee*, AIR 1964 SC 847; *Mafatlal Narandas Barot* v. *J.D. Rathod*, AIR 1966 SC 1364; *Narendra Narian Misra* v. *Gorakhpur University*, 1974 SCC OnLine All 341: AIR 1975 All 290; *Hira Nath Mishra* v. *Rajendra Medical College*, (1973) 1 SCC 805; *Bihar State Harijan Kalyan Parishad* v. *Union of India*, (1985) 2 SCC 644.

However, some High Courts have taken the view that not only government companies but private companies also are amenable to the writ jurisdiction because their bye-laws have the force of law. Standing orders made by the companies under the Industrial Employment (Standing Orders) Act, 1946 were considered as having the force of law.[121] The Kerala High Court also issued a writ against the Cashew Corporation of India, a government company, on the ground that it was performing a statutory function, under the Imports and Exports Control Act, 1947 and Import Control Order, 1955, of controlling import and export of cashew nuts.[122] Similarly, various High Courts have issued writs against societies registered under the Societies Registration Act, 1860 on the ground that their bye-laws have statutory force.[123] However, the view of the Supreme Court in *Coop. Central Bank Ltd.* v. *Industrial Tribunal*[124] does not favour this approach.

An authority may also be constituted under the executive powers of government. Such authorities, though do not owe their origin to any statute, are controlled and regulated by the government. The Calcutta High Court was of the view that such agencies are amenable to the writ jurisdiction of the High Court and so issued a writ against the State Medical Faculty, an unincorporated or non-statutory body, solely established by the government, in exercise of its executive powers.[125] However, the High Courts of Manipur and Madhya Pradesh reached a different conclusion because in their opinion such bodies cannot be classified as public authorities.[126] As regards the amenability of private institutions and private persons to the writ jurisdiction of the High Courts, the trend of judicial decisions is wholesome. The courts have broken new ground in order to redress the injury caused to a private individual. The Supreme Court has taken the view that a writ can be issued against a private college affiliated to a university on the ground that the university rules which are applied to the college, especially in disciplinary matters of the staff, have the force of law.[127] In the same manner, students can invoke the writ jurisdiction of the High Courts

121. *Borhan Kumar* v. *Indian Oil Corpn.*, 1970 SCC OnLine Pat 42: AIR 1971 Pat 174; *Prafulla Chandra Sarma* v. *Oil India Ltd.*, 1970 SCC OnLine Gau 30: AIR 1971 Assam & Ngld 19; *Abani Bhusan Biswas* v. *Hindustan Cables Ltd.*, 1967 SCC OnLine Cal 69: AIR 1968 Cal 124.
122. *K.L. Mathew* v. *Union of India*, 1973 SCC OnLine Ker 65: AIR 1974 Ker 4.
123. *Dukhooram Gupta* v. *Coop. Agricultural Assn. Ltd.*, 1961 SCC OnLine MP 5. AIR 1961 MP 289; *Madan Mohan Sen Gupta* v. *State of W.B.*, 1965 SCC OnLine Cal 31: AIR 1966 Cal 23; *Ramswarup Gupta* v. *M.P. State Coop. Mktg. Federation Ltd.*, 1976 SCC OnLine MP 17: AIR 1976 MP 152; *Harbhajan Singh* v. *State of Punjab*, 1971 SCC OnLine P&H 298: AIR 1973 P&H 31; *Nayagarh Coop. Central Bank Ltd.* v. *Narayan Rath*, (1977) 3 SCC 576; *Amir Jamia* v. *Desh Arath Raj*, 1968 SCC OnLine Del 187: ILR 1969 Del 202.
124. (1969) 2 SCC 43.
125. *Bijoy Ranjan* v. *B.C. Das Gupta*, 1952 SCC OnLine Cal 13: AIR 1953 Cal 289.
126. *Sathkhosei Thangoo* v. *Dictt. Soldiers' Sailors' and Airmen's Board*, 1967 SCC OnLine Mani 27: AIR 1968 Mani 68; *S.K. Kalani & Co.* v. *Iron and Steel Controller*, 1968 SCC OnLine MP 59: AIR 1969 MP 25.
127. *Prabhakar Ramakrishna Jodh* v. *A.L. Pande*, (1965) 2 SCR 713; *Vaish Degree College* v. *Lakshmi Narain*, (1976) 2 SCC 58.

against a private college for the violation of any university rule which has a force of law.[128] In *Raj Soni* v. *Air Officer Incharge Admn.*[129], the Supreme Court further held that a private body—even if it is not a State under Article 12, but if governed by a statute—is bound to provide the benefit under the statute and, hence, the benefit of writ would be available. In the case above, the Supreme Court issued a writ against an Air Force School which was unaided, but recognised and the Delhi Education Act, 1973 and Rules that governed it.

The Supreme Court in *Ramana Dayaram Shetty* v. *International Airport Authority of India*[130] (*R.D. Shetty*) has rightly extended its reach in matters of issuing writs by liberalising the test which brings an administrative authority within the gravitational orbit of the term "State" in Article 12 of the Constitution. The core question in writ jurisdiction in India has always been whether an administrative authority is included in the category of "other authorities" as contemplated by Article 12 within the definition of the term "State". In *Rajasthan SEB* v. *Mohan Lal*[131], the court held that a constitutional or a statutory authority would be within the meaning of the expression "other authorities" if it has been invested with the statutory power to issue binding directions to third parties, the disobedience of which would entail penal consequences, or if it has the sovereign power to make rules and regulations having the force of law. This test was followed in *Sukhdev Singh* v. *Bhagatram Sardar Singh Raghuvanshi*[132]. However, in this case, Mathew J enunciated a broader test, namely, whether the administrative authority is an instrumentality or agency of the government: if it is, it would fall within the meaning of the expression "other authorities" and would be "State". This test of "governmental instrumentality or agency" was found to be most satisfactory by the Supreme Court in *R.D. Shetty*[133]. In this case, one of the questions involved was whether the International Airports Authority constituted under the International Airports Authority Act, 1971 is "State" within the meaning of that expression in Article 12. It is no denying the fact that the question of determining whether an administrative authority is acting as an instrumentality or agency of the government is a highly complex question. However, Bhagwati J attempted to particularise certain relevant factors which may provide an answer to the above question, though such factors may not be exhaustive. He observed that a finding of extensive and unusual financial assistance plus an unusual degree of control over the management and policies might lead one

128. *Kumkum Khanna* v. *Jessus and Mary College*, 1975 SCC OnLine Del 136: AIR 1976 Del 35. See also, *Ghanashyam Misra* v. *Orissa Assn. of Sanskrit Learning and Culture*, 1969 SCC OnLine Ori 71: AIR 1971 Ori 212; *Harekrashna Mahtab* v. *Chief Minister of Orissa*, 1970 SCC OnLine Ori 35: AIR 1971 Ori 175; *Radha Kumari Singh* v. *Mahanth Mahadevanand Mahila Mahavidyalaya*, 1976 SCC OnLine Pat 25: AIR 1976 Pat 378.
129. (1990) 3 SCC 261.
130. (1979) 3 SCC 489.
131. AIR 1967 SC 1857.
132. (1975) 1 SCC 421.
133. (1979) 3 SCC 489.

to characterise an operation as State action. Moreover, the existence of deep and pervasive State control may afford an indication that the corporation is a State agency or instrumentality. It may also be a relevant factor to consider whether the administrative authority enjoys monopoly status, which is State conferred or State protected, for there can be little doubt that this type of monopoly status would tie the authority to the State. Again, if the functions of the authority are of public importance and closely related to governmental functions, it would be a relevant factor in classifying the authority as an instrumentality or agency of the government. However, it does not mean that an agency, which is otherwise a private entity, would be an instrumentality of the government by reason of carrying the functions of public importance. But the public nature of functions, if impregnated with governmental character, or tied or entwined with government, or fortified by some other additional factor, may render the authority an instrumentality or agency of the government. Specifically, if a department of government is transferred to an administrative authority, it would be a strong factor supportive of this inference. The court will have to consider the cumulative effect of these various factors and arrive at its decision on the basis of a particularised enquiry into the facts and circumstances of each case. It is not enough to examine seriatim each of the factors upon which an administrative authority is claimed to be an instrumentality or agency of the government, and to dismiss each individually as being insufficient to support a finding to that effect. It is the aggregate or cumulative effect of all the relevant factors that is controlling.[134] Therefore, in order to decide whether an administrative authority is subject to the writ issuing jurisdiction of the court, the test is not the establishment of the authority by a statute, or its incorporation under the Companies Act, 1956 or Societies Registration Act, 1860, but its relationship with the government.

Picking up the same thread, the Supreme Court in *Som Prakash Rekhi* v. *Union of India*[135] held that the Bharat Petroleum Corporation, a government company registered under the Companies Act,1956 is "State" within the meaning of Article 12 of the Constitution. By the Burmah Shell (Acquisition of Undertakings in India) Act, 1976, the government had acquired the undertakings in India of the Burmah Shell Oil Storage and Distribution Company and handed them over to Bharat Petroleum Corporation Ltd., a government company formed for this purpose. A writ petition was filed by an employee of the Burmah Shell Company, who had retired and was entitled to get pension from the Bharat Petroleum Corporation, for the restoration of cut in his pension. A preliminary objection was taken against the writ that no writ could lie against Bharat Petroleum Ltd.—since it being a company registered under the Companies Act, 1956, was not "State" within the meaning of Article 12 of the Constitution. Overruling the objection, the Supreme Court held that the true test for classifying a body as

134. *Ramana Dayaram Shetty* v. *International Airport Authority of India*, (1979) 3 SCC 489.
135. (1981) 1 SCC 449.

"State" within the meaning of Article 12 is not whether it is created by a statute or under a statute but whether, besides discharging the functions or doing business as a proxy of the State, there is an element of ability to affect legal relations by virtue of power vested in it by law.[136] While dealing with the various forms of public enterprise such as government departments, statutory corporations and government companies, the court observed that merely because a company or other legal person had functional and jural individuality for certain purposes and areas of law, it did not follow that for the effective enforcement of fundamental rights, "[w]e should not scan the real character of the entity". If it was found that it was not "a mere agent or surrogate of the State" and was in fact owned or controlled by the State and "in effect an incarnation of State", why should it not be included within Article 12 of the Constitution. In the instant case, on the basis of the extensive control exercised by the government through the Acquisition Act, 1976, the court ruled that unlike an ordinary company Bharat Petroleum Ltd. was a limb of government, an agency of the State, a vicarious creature of statute working on the wheels of the Acquisition Act, 1976.

Applying the same "instrumentality or agency" test in *Ajay Hasia* v. *Khalid Mujib Sehravardi*[137], the Supreme Court held that the Regional Engineering College, Srinagar, established and administered by a society registered under the Jammu and Kashmir Registration of Societies Act, 1898, is "State" within the meaning of Article 12. In this case, the validity of admission procedure of the college had been challenged. The court observed that the composition of society was dominated by the representatives of the Central and State Governments; the rules to be made by the society had to be approved by the Central Government, and the accounts of the society were required to be submitted for government approval and scrutiny. In view of such control mechanism of the government, the engineering college was held to be an "other authority" within the meaning of Article 12 of the Constitution.

Against the backdrop of these cases, now it has been consistently held that government companies and cooperative societies are "State" within the meaning of Article 12 of the Constitution. Therefore, now bodies such as the FCI,[138] Oil and Natural Gas Commission,[139] Bihar State Electricity Board,[140] U.P. State Warehousing Corporation,[141] Panchayat,[142] Cooperative Society,[143] Central Inland Water Transport

136. (1981) 1 SCC 449, 452.
137. (1981) 1 SCC 722.
138. *State of Punjab* v. *Raja Ram*, (1981) 2 SCC 66.
139. *K.C. Joshi* v. *Union of India*, (1985) 3 SCC 153.
140. *Surya Narain Yadav* v. *Bihar SEB*, (1985) 3 SCC 38.
141. *U.P. Warehousing Corpn.* v. *Vijay Narayan Vajpayee*, (1980) 3 SCC 459.
142. *State of Gujarat* v. *Raman Lal Keshav Lal*, (1980) 4 SCC 653.
143. *Chhotelal Pannalal Nagar* v. *District Magistrate, Indore*, 1977 SCC OnLine MP 43: AIR 1978 MP 191. See also, *Tekraj Vasandi* v. *Union of India*, (1988) 1 SCC 236. The Supreme Court held that a registered society will be treated as "State" if either government business has been undertaken by it or it is performing a public obligation of the State.

Corporation,[144] LIC,[145] Industrial Finance Corporation,[146] Road Transport Corporation,[147] Railway Board,[148] Reserve Bank of India,[149] nationalised banks,[150] State Finance Corporation,[151] Bharat Petroleum Corporation,[152] Industrial Statistical Institute,[153] SAIL,[154] Project and Equipment Corporation of India,[155] Hindustan Steel Limited,[156] Indian Council of Agricultural Research,[157] Modern Bakery,[158] a school run by a public trust receiving full or substantial amount of expenses by way of grant from government,[159] and G.B. Pant University of Agriculture and Technology[160] have been brought within the writ jurisdiction of the courts. The FCI is an instrumentality of State because one expects a fair and impartial deal from it.[161] But applying the same "instrumentality and agency test", the court held that the Institute of Constitutional and Parliamentary Studies, New Delhi is not "State" for the purposes of writ jurisdiction.[162]

Even though the courts in India have greatly extended the meaning of the term "State" in order to extend their long arms, nevertheless, the question still to be decided is whether a public corporation owned by private individuals can be considered as "State". This question was debated before the Supreme Court in *M.C. Mehta* v. *Union of India*[163] (*M.C. Mehta*). In this case, the point for discussion was whether Shriram Fertiliser and Chemicals Ltd., Delhi, a public company owned by Delhi Cloth Mills Ltd., is "State" within the meaning of Article 12 of the Constitution. It was contended that Shriram Company is "State" because it is carrying on an industry, vital to the public interest with a potential to affect the life and health of the people under the active control of the government. Furthermore, it is carrying on an industry which, according to the declared policy of the government, was ultimately intended to be carried out by the government itself. It was also

144. *Central Inland Water Transport Corpn.* v. *Brojo Nath Ganguly*, (1986) 3 SCC 156.
145. *LIC* v. *Manubhai D. Shah*, (1992) 3 SCC 637.
146. *Sukhdev Singh* v. *Bhagatram Sardar Singh Raghuvanshi*, (1975) 1 SCC 421.
147. *Mysore SRTC* v. *Devraj Urs*, (1976) 2 SCC 862.
148. *Railway Board* v. *Observer Publications (P) Ltd.*, (1972) 2 SCC 266.
149. *RBI* v. *N.C. Paliwal*, (1976) 4 SCC 838.
150. *K.I. Shephard* v. *Union of India*, (1987) 4 SCC 431.
151. *Gujarat State Financial Corpn.* v. *Lotus Hotels (P) Ltd.*, (1983) 3 SCC 379.
152. *M.S. Desai & Co.* v. *Hindustan Petroleum Corpn. Ltd.*, 1986 SCC OnLine Guj 73: AIR 1987 Guj 19.
153. *B.S. Minhas* v. *Indian Statistical Institute*, (1983) 4 SCC 582.
154. *Bihar State Harijan Kalyan Parishad* v. *Union of India*, (1985) 2 SCC 644.
155. *A.L. Kalra* v. *Project and Equipment Corpn. of India Ltd.*, (1984) 3 SCC 316.
156. *Workmen* v. *Hindustan Steel Ltd.*, 1984 Supp SCC 554.
157. *P.K. Ramachandra Iyer* v. *Union of India*, (1984) 2 SCC 141; *S.M. Ilyas* v. *Indian Council of Agricultural Research*, (1993) 1 SCC 182.
158. *Gujarat Electricity Board* v. *Kantilal Rajabhai Patel*, 1988 SCC OnLine Guj 7: AIR 1988 Guj 261.
159. *Manmohan Singh Jaitla* v. *UT of Chandigarh*, 1984 Supp SCC 540.
160. *Combined Entrance Examination* v. *Osiris Das*, (1992) 3 SCC 543.
161. *Workers' Union* v. *Food Corporation of India*, (1996) 9 SCC 439.
162. *Tekraj Vasandi* v. *Union of India*, (1988) 1 SCC 236.
163. (1987) 1 SCC 395.

pointed out that a sizeable financial aid comes from the government. Taking aid of the US State action doctrine, it was also argued that a private activity if supported, controlled or regulated by State may get so intertwined with governmental activity as to be termed as "State action", and it would then be subject to the same constitutional restraints as the State. The Supreme Court though discussed these arguments in detail—leading to an inescapable conclusion that the corporate device will not be allowed to be used as a barrier for ousting the constitutional control of fundamental rights—yet it missed a unique opportunity of deciding the question squarely, which had a direct bearing on the expansion of human rights jurisprudence and social conscientiousness with reference to corporate structure in India.

However, following the same liberal trend, the Supreme Court in *Unni Krishnan, J.P.* v. *State of A.P.*[164] observed that the term "authority" used in Article 226 must receive a liberal meaning unlike the term in Article 12 because Article 12 is relevant only for the enforcement of fundamental rights under Article 32, but Article 226 confers powers on the High Court not only for the enforcement of fundamental rights but for non-fundamental rights also. Therefore, the term "authority" as used in Article 226 must not be confined only to statutory authorities and instrumentalities of the State. It may cover any other person or body performing public duty. Applying the test of "public duty", the Supreme Court held that a private medical or engineering college comes within the writ jurisdiction of the court, irrespective of the question of aid and affiliation. Therefore, where "public interest element" is present, a writ is maintainable. The Supreme Court thus allowed a writ against a non-aided private educational institution where its employees were seeking parity in scale with employees of government institutions.[165]

In *Pradeep Kumar Biswas* v. *Indian Institute of Chemical Biology*[166], the Supreme Court once again got the opportunity to define the scope of word "State" in Article 12 of the Constitution, which determines the reach of writ jurisdiction of the constitutional courts. In this case, the appellant had filed a writ petition against Indian Institute of Chemical Biology, Calcutta, a unit of Council of Scientific and Industrial Research (CSIR), for quashing his termination order before the Calcutta High Court which was rejected on the ground that the CSIR is not a "State", as decided by the Supreme Court way back in 1975 in *Sabhajit Tewary* v. *Union of India*[167] (*Sabhajit Tewary*), and, hence, not under the writ jurisdiction of the court. The appellant approached the Supreme Court where a two-judge Bench decided that the decision in *Sabhajit Tewary* deserves reconsideration. Therefore, the matter was referred to the Constitution Bench.

164. (1993) 1 SCC 645.
165. *K. Krishnamacharyulu* v. *Sri Venkateswara Hindu College of Engg.*, (1997) 3 SCC 571.
166. (2002) 5 SCC 111.
167. (1975) 1 SCC 485.

Overruling *Sabhajit Tewary* ruling, the Constitution Bench held that the CSIR is "State" within the meaning of the term in Article 12 and, hence, within the writ jurisdiction of the court. The majority of the Bench opined that the definition of the term "State" in Article 12 of the Constitution is inclusive and not exhaustive and, hence, represents "great generalities of the Constitution" the contents of which are to be supplied by the court from time to time. The majority further held that bodies created for the purpose of promoting the educational and economic interests of the people are covered within the scope of "other authorities" in Article 12 of the Constitution. The test applied in this case was: Whether the authority is financially, functionally and administratively dominated or under the control of the government?

Such a control must be particular to the authority and must be pervasive. If it is found then an authority or a body is a "State" within the meaning of Article 12. Amplifying the reason for the need to expand the meaning of the term "State", the court observed that with the widening of the concept of equality under Articles 14 and 16 of the Constitution by judicial interpretation, courts sought to curb arbitrary exercise of power against individuals by "centres of power", and for this reason there is a need for corresponding expansion in judicial definition of the term "State", to bring all such powers within the writ jurisdiction of the Supreme Court and the High Courts. Therefore, a body, whether created by a statute or under a statute, if set up in the national interest to further the economic welfare of society, a function which is fundamental in the governance of the country, falls within the definition of the term "State" being an "other authority". The court indicated that powers vested in the Prime Minister as ex officio President of the society proves the dominant role played by the government in the affairs of the CSIR.

In another case, *Mysore Paper Mills Ltd.* v. *Officers' Assn.*[168], the court held that a government company—where 97 per cent of its shares are held by the government or financial institutions under the control of the government, its directors being nominee of the government, and entrusted with public duties—is "State" within Article 12 of the Constitution, being the agency and instrumentality of the State as these facts show a pervasive State control over the day-to-day functioning of the company. Applying the test, the court concluded that the Mysore Paper Mills Ltd., a government company, registered under the Companies Act, 1956, is "State" and, hence, under the writ jurisdiction of the court. On the same analogy, nationalised banks were held to be "State"[169].

Within the area of public law review, an interesting question which came before the court was whether a society, though not sponsored by the government, but taken over by the government under the Co-operative Societies

168. (2002) 2 SCC 167.
169. *Bank of India* v. *O.P. Swarnakar*, (2003) 2 SCC 721.

Act, 1912, is "State" in order to be within the jurisdictional reach of the writ jurisdiction. The matter is pending before the Constitution Bench of the Supreme Court.[170]

It is no denying the fact that though the extension of the court's writ jurisdiction to companies and societies would make them more responsible and responsive, yet if it in any manner hampers the corporate management viability, it may adversely affect the economic grounds and accountability. It is for this reason that the Supreme Court has left the question open whether the Air India Corporation is a State and, therefore, bound by constitutional reservations under Article 16(4) of the Constitution.[171]

Though the trends in judicial behaviour as discussed above are welcome, the whole approach has been halting and variegated. The trend of the Indian courts to take shelter behind technicalities of law makes the growth of law stultifying. The primary purpose of jurisdiction of the High Courts as laid down under Article 226(1) is to protect the "little man" from any injury of a substantial nature, or from substantial failure of justice, besides enforcing his fundamental rights. Therefore, instead of being obsessed with the status of "person or authority", the court must exercise its power for the protection of the "little man". A threat of injustice may arise not only from the constitutional or statutory agencies but also from private persons and bodies commanding vast economic and political powers. It is gratifying that the Supreme Court in *Bodhisattwa Gautam* v. *Subhra Chakraborty*[172] held that the court can enforce fundamental rights even against private bodies or individuals and also award compensation for violation of fundamental rights. The court may exercise its jurisdiction suo motu or on the basis of a PIL in the absence of personal approach by the victim.

Reach of the public law review is directly proportionate to the reach of the writ jurisdiction of the courts. It is for this reason that judiciary has always tried to expand the writ jurisdiction. However, in a very intensely contested case, *Zee Telefilms Ltd.* v. *Union of India*[173], where stakes were very high, the main question before the Constitution Bench of the Supreme Court was whether the Board of Control for Cricket in India (BCCI), a society registered under the Societies Registration Act, 1860 and recognised by the government to promote the game of cricket, is State within the expression "other authorities" under Article 12 of the Constitution and, hence, subject to the writ jurisdiction of the court? After analysing the entire case law, the Supreme Court with a majority of 3:2 answered the question in the negative by holding that the BCCI is not under the writ jurisdiction of the court. Facts established in this case showed that the BCCI is not a creature

170. See, *P. Vijaya Rajan* v. *State of T.N.*, 1992 Supp (2) SCC 104.
171. *Air India* v. *B.R. Age*, (1995) 6 SCC 359. See also, *Calcutta State Transport Corpn.* v. *CIT*, (1996) 8 SCC 758. Whether STC is an "authority" under Art. 12, question was left open.
172. (1996) 1 SCC 490. This case came before the Supreme Court in an SLP petition under Art. 136.
173. (2005) 4 SCC 649.

of the statute; no part of its share capital is held by the government; there is no State control; Board's monopoly status in the game is not State conferred or protected; the Board is autonomous; and is not created by a transfer of a government owned corporation. Keeping these fact in view, the court held that the BCCI is not "State" within the meaning of "other authorities" in Article 12 of the Constitution. The court observed that today, State is distancing itself from commercial activities and, therefore, there seems to be no need to further expand the scope of "other authorities" under Article 12 by judicial interpretation. The court concluded:

> It should also be borne in mind that...in a democracy there is a dividing line between a State enterprise and a non-State enterprise, which is distinct and the judiciary should not be an instrument to erase the said dividing line unless, of course, the circumstances of the day require it to do so.[174]

The minority in this case, speaking through Sinha J, emphasised on functional and purposive approach rather than the "agency and instrumentality" test followed by the majority. The minority emphasised that when the body acts as a public authority and has a public duty to perform; when it is bound to protect human rights; when it regulates a profession or vocation of a citizen which is, otherwise, a fundamental right under a statute or its own rule; when it regulates the rights of a citizen contained in Article 19(1)(*a*) of the Constitution available to the general public and the viewers of the game in particular; when it exercises de facto or de jure monopoly; when the State outsources its legislative power in its favour; and when it has a positive obligation of a public nature, it is "State" within the meaning of Article 12 of the Constitution and, hence, under the writ jurisdiction of the court. If the State is withdrawing, due to new economic policy imperatives, it is all the more important for the court to fill the gap so that a corporate device may not be used as a barrier for ousting the constitutional vigilance of fundamental rights.

2.2 Writ can be issued against a private entity exercising public function

It is gratifying that realising the new economic policy imperatives the Supreme Court in *BCCI* v. *Cricket Assn. of Bihar*[175] has now finally held that a private entity exercising public functions, though may not be a "State" within the meaning of Article 12 of the Constitution, yet it will be within the writ jurisdiction of High Courts under Article 226 of the Constitution. This case arose out of two writ petitions filed in public interest by the Cricket Association of Bihar before the Bombay High Court for the relief of directing the BCCI to recall its order for directing an enquiry into the allegation of betting and spot-fixing.

---

174. (2005) 4 SCC 649, 653. See also, *A.C. Muthiah* v. *BCCI*, (2011) 6 SCC 617.
175. (2015) 3 SCC 251.

In this case two questions came for consideration before the Supreme Court in appeal.

(1) Whether BCCI is "State" within the meaning of Article 12 of the Constitution?

(2) Whether BCCI is within the writ jurisdiction of High Courts under Article 226 of the Constitution?

Answering the first question in the negative, the Supreme Court opined that BCCI is a private entity and is not subject to any organisational, administrative or financial control of the State, hence cannot be included within the definition of "State" under Article 12 of the Constitution.

The Supreme Court answered the second question in the affirmative and opined that BCCI is under the writ jurisdiction of High Courts under Article 226, even though it is not a "State" under Article 12 of the Constitution. The rationale behind the decision is that when a private entity is performing a "public function" it will be under the gravitational object of the writ jurisdiction of High Courts. The Government of India allows BCCI to select a team which represents India. This also is a visible trend in almost all jurisdictions. In *R. (ProLife Alliance)* v. *British Broadcasting Corpn.*[176], the Court of Appeal held BBC (non-statutory corporation) as fully reviewable entity for its discriminatory action in allocating talk time for various political parties.[177] The Human Rights Act, 1998 (UK) applies to "public authorities" and Section 6 defines "public authorities" to include any body which has functions of a "public nature", may be statutory or non-statutory. Moving in the same direction the Supreme Court held that a writ is maintainable against a private body if it is exercising public function. Defining "public function", the court opined that public function is that which is similar or closely related to those performed by the State in exercise of its sovereign functions.[178]

In *Marwari Balika Vidyalaya* v. *Asha Srivastava*[179], the Supreme Court held that a writ petition against private unaided school is maintainable. The words "any person or authority" used in Article 226 cannot be confined only to statutory authorities and instrumentalities of State but may cover any other person or body performing public duty.

However, in *N. Sankaranarayanan* v. *T.N. Housing Board*[180], the court observed that writ petition for mandamus concerning private property dispute is not maintainable against State and its authorities. Furthermore, no writ can be issued against private individuals in property disputes.

In *Kelvin Jute Co. Ltd.* v. *Krishna Kumar Agarwala*[181], it was noted that private trust dealing with provident fund exempted under Section 17 of

176. (2002) 3 WLR 1080 (CA).
177. *R. (ProLife Alliance)* v. *British Broadcasting Corpn.*, (2002) 3 WLR 1080 (CA).
178. *Rajbir Surajbhan Singh* v. *Institute of Banking Personnel Selection*, (2019) 14 SCC 219.
179. (2020) 14 SCC 449.
180. (2020) 14 SCC 457.
181. (2016) 14 SCC 326.

the 1952 Act is performing public function/duty/acting as instrumentality/agency of "State", hence, is amenable to writ jurisdiction.

In *Ramakrishna Mission* v. *Kago Kunya*[182], the Supreme Court clarified that a private body can be held to be amenable when it performs public functions which are normally expected to be performed by the State or its authorities. Before an organisation can be held to discharge a public function, the function must be of a character that is closely related to functions which are performed by the State in its sovereign capacity.

Judicial review of a private entity discharging public function is the same: Whether such entity is "State" within the meaning of Article 12 of the Constitution or not? The principles and extent of application of judicial review will also be the same. Rules and regulations framed by such entity will be subject to same tests and standards as would apply to similar provisions emanating from a statute or the general executive power of the State. This case will go a long way in protecting the rights of the people against powerful private entities performing public functions.

2.3 Can a writ be issued against State/public authority exercising private law functions?

Elaborating on this aspect of law, the Supreme Court opined that private law remedies are not enforceable through writ, even though the authority is "State" within Article 12 of the Constitution. Private law is that part of the legal system which regulates relationship between private individuals, such as law of contract or tort. Therefore, even if the authority is subject to the writ jurisdiction of the High Court, writ cannot be issued if the action is within the domain of private law, such as contractual and commercial actions. Thus, even if a body performing public duty is amenable to writ jurisdiction, all its decisions are not subject to judicial review. Only those decisions which have public element therein can be judicially reviewed under the writ jurisdiction.[183] "Public element" would certainly include if the administrative action is violative of law or fundamental rights guaranteed by the Constitution.[184]

It may be emphasised that in this age of globalisation and liberalisation of economy, public law and private law distinction seems arbitrary. If an entity is performing in public space, no matter under public law or private law, if violates public interest, it must be brought under the controlling power of the constitutional judiciary. This will improve the functioning of public actors performing under private law in public space. It is for this reason now that courts are turning private law liabilities of public authorities into public law remedies being "abuse of public power". Initiative of the Supreme Court in creating the category of "constitutional tort" is a step

182. (2019) 16 SCC 303.
183. *K.K. Saksena* v. *International Commission on Irrigation Drainage*, (2015) 4 SCC 670.
184. *Noble Resources Ltd.* v. *State of Orissa*, (2006) 10 SCC 236.

in that direction. Fact remains that arbitrary acts of the State cannot be excluded from the ambit of judicial review merely on the ground that it is a "contractual matter".[185]

2.4 Locus standi to challenge administrative action

After discussing the subject "against whom a writ may lie", a legitimate question arises as to who can challenge an administrative action? This brings us to the problem of standing of a person necessary to entitle him to sue the administrative agencies. The development in this area has been a patchwork of case-law. It has not yet been fully realised that no one will spend his money and time in challenging an action unless he has some interest in it; why then should he be discouraged?

In case of a writ of habeas corpus, any person can file the writ to secure the release of a person in illegal detention, public or private. In the early days of 1979, a lawyer of the Supreme Court filed a writ to secure the release of undertrials in various jails in Bihar.[186]

A writ of quo warranto also can be filed by any person to challenge the appointment of a person to a public office, whether or not he has a personal interest in it. This is allowed perhaps on the ground that everyone has an interest that public money must not be wasted on invalid appointments. In the same manner, filing of a writ petition in public interest is also an exception to the general rule of locus standi.[187]

The general rule governing the writs of mandamus and certiorari is that it is only the person whose rights have been infringed who can apply for the writ. However, it is not necessary that it must be only his personal right which is adversely affected. He may challenge an action even when he has a right common with others. Therefore, a taxpayer shall have standing to prevent a misapplication or misappropriation of public funds by an authority,[188] and an ordinary citizen shall have standing to challenge an election held contrary to the provisions of law.[189] In the same manner, in case of a breach or abuse of a statutory duty, anybody who is adversely affected can file a petition for writ, no matter if he does not have an enforceable right.[190]

However, a mere interest would not entitle a person to a writ unless he can show that his interest is more than that of an ordinary member. It is on this count that the Supreme Court refused to grant the writs in *Maganbhai Ishwarbhai Patel* v. *Union of India*[191], where the petitioners sought to restrain the government from giving effect to a Kutch Tribunal

185. *State of U.P.* v. *Ashok Kumar Nigam*, (2013) 3 SCC 372.
186. *Hussainara Khatoon (I)* v. *State of Bihar*, (1980) 1 SCC 81, 91, 93, 98, 108, 115.
187. *Ghulam Qadir* v. *Special Tribunal*, (2002) 1 SCC 33.
188. *Kalyan Singh* v. *State of U.P.*, AIR 1962 SC 1183.
189. *T. Venkateswara Rao* v. *State of A.P.*, 1957 SCC OnLine AP 279: AIR 1958 AP 458.
190. *K.N. Guruswamy* v. *State of Mysore*, AIR 1954 SC 592.
191. (1970) 3 SCC 400. See also, 12, *I.C. Bose Road Tenants' Assn.* v. *Collector of Howrah*, 1977 SCC OnLine Cal 221: AIR 1977 Cal 437.

award by handing over certain territory in the Rann of Kutch to Pakistan. The court found that no petitioner had any clear interest in the action of the government, because neither did anyone live there nor did they have any property there. On the other hand, a member of the public who has a right to worship in a particular temple shall have locus standi to challenge the misapplication or misappropriation of temple property and the appointment of trustees.[192]

In case of juristic persons such as companies, normally, the juristic person must vindicate its own rights. However, the trend of judicial decisions is that even a shareholder can sue for the infringement of a juristic person's right if he can show that his personal rights are directly and substantially affected adversely by the action.[193]

It is gratifying to note that the courts have started realising the public purpose which public law review serves in any intensive form of society. The essential purpose of public law review is not so much the enforcement of rights as the control of administrative action. Therefore, whosoever challenges an administrative action which is patently bad, the courts ought not to raise objection in reviewing such action on the technical ground of locus standi.

In another case, the International Airports Authority invited tenders from "registered second-class hoteliers" for running a second-class restaurant and two snack bars at the International Airport, Bombay. It was stipulated that "the acceptance of tender will rest with the Director ... who reserves for himself the right to reject all or any of the tenders received without assigning any reason". In this case, the highest tender was accepted but the snag was that the tenderer was not a "registered second-class hotelier". A writ was filed by a person who had not filed any tender, challenging the award of the contract to a person who was not a registered second-class hotelier. An objection was raised regarding maintainability of the proceedings on the ground of locus standi. The contention of the petitioner was that he was in the same position as the successful tenderer because if an essential condition could be ignored in the tenderer's case, it could be ignored in his case also. The petitioner argued that he did not fill a tender because of the prescribed requisite qualification. He could have applied had he known that the condition of eligibility was indeed flexible. This resulted in violation of the right to equality. The Supreme Court though did not disturb the contract in exercise of its discretion but accepted the plea on standing.[194]

These liberal trends in judicial behaviour are certainly welcome, but one is not to forget the warning given by Prof. de Smith that in a developed

192. *Nabaghan Naik* v. *Sadananda Das*, 1971 SCC OnLine Ori 29: AIR 1972 Ori 188.
193. *Dwarkadas Shrinivas* v. *Sholapur Spg. and Wvg. Co.*, AIR 1954 SC 119; *Rustom Cavasjee Cooper (Banks Nationalisation)* v. *Union of India*, (1970) 1 SCC 248; *Bennett Coleman & Company* v. *Union of India*, (1972) 2 SCC 788.
194. *Ramana Dayaram Shetty* v. *International Airport Authority of India*, (1979) 3 SCC 489.

legal system, the professional litigant and the meddlesome interloper, who invoke the jurisdiction of the court in matters that do not concern them, must be discouraged.[195] Therefore, V.S. Deshpande J rightly observed that a petitioner will have standing to sustain a public action only if he fulfils one of the two following qualifications: 1) he must either convince the court that the direction of law has such a real public significance that it involves a public right and an injury to the public interest; or 2) establish that he has a sufficient interest of his own over and above the general interest of other members of the public in bringing the action.[196] This thinking is clearly reflected in the judicial behaviour where the Rajasthan High Court came to the conclusion that an advocate had no locus standi to challenge the action of the President establishing a Bench of the High Court at Jaipur on the ground that the Chief Justice had not been consulted,[197] but on the other hand, various High Courts have held that a person has a right to challenge the constitutional validity of the caretaker government of Mr Charan Singh at the Centre.[198] Though no particularisation of relevant factors determining locus standi in all situations can be exhaustive in view of the increasing assumption of new tasks by the government and the various administrative agencies, yet the need for maintaining a proper balance between private right and public defence cannot be overemphasised.

The technical doctrine of "locus standi" is being gradually widened to give it a "social" content in conformity with the letter and spirit of the Indian Constitution.[199] In *Fertiliser Corpn. Kamgar Union* v. *Union of India*[200] (*Fertiliser Corpn. Kamgar Union*), Krishna Iyer J prepared a real case for a broad-based application of the principle of locus standi necessary to challenge administrative actions. He made the following points:

(1) If the tone of public life in the country were sufficiently honest and fairminded, formal norms to control administration may not be needed. But when "corruption permeates the entire fabric of the government", legality is the first casualty, for then the State power "is exercised on grounds unrelated to its nominal purposes".

(2) In such a climate, civil remedies for administrative wrongdoings depend upon the action of an individual citizen. An individual must at his own expense challenge the vast panoply of State power by a civil action in a court at a great financial cost to himself.

195. De Smith, *Judicial Review of Administrative Action*, 362–63. See also, *Jasbhai Motibhai Desai* v. *Roshan Kumar, Haji Bashir Ahmed*, (1976) 1 SCC 671. The Supreme Court held that a meddlesome interloper has no locus standi but a stranger may have one where exceptional circumstances involving a grave miscarriage of justice have an adverse effect on public interest.

196. "Standing and Justiciability", (1971) 13 JILI 153, 178.

197. *Ram Rakh Vyas* v. *Union of India*, 1977 SCC OnLine Raj 25: AIR 1977 Raj 243.

198. Writs were filed in the High Courts of Calcutta, Tamil Nadu and other High Courts.

199. *Fertiliser Corpn. Kamgar Union* v. *Union of India*, (1981) 1 SCC 568.

200. (1981) 1 SCC 568.

(3) A pragmatic approach to social justice compels us to interpret constitutional provisions (including Articles 32 and 226) liberally with a view to see that effective policing of the corridors of power is carried out by courts until other ombudsman arrangements are made. Court's function, of course, is limited to testing whether an administrative action has been fair and free from the taint of unreasonableness and has substantially complied with the procedural norms set for it by the rules of public administration, and that the action of the administration is not mala fide.
(4) Locus standi must be liberalised to meet the challenges of the times. *Ubi jus ibi remedium* must be enlarged to embrace all interests of public-minded citizens or organisations with serious concern for conservation of public resources and the direction and correction of public power so as to promote justice in all its facets.
(5) The restrictive rules of standing are antithesis to a healthy system of administrative law. If a plaintiff with a good case is turned away, merely because he is not sufficiently affected personally, that means that some government agency is left free to violate law, and that is contrary to the public interest. Litigants are unlikely to spend their time and money unless they have some real interest at stake. In the rare cases where they wish to sue merely out of public spirit, why should they be discouraged? Effective access to justice is the most basic human requirement—the "most basic human right"—of a system which purports to guarantee legal rights.
(6) The PIL is part of the process of participative justice, and "standing" in civil litigation of that pattern must have liberal reception at the judicial doorsteps. It has been conclusively proved that the liberalised standing rules had caused no significant increase in the number of actions brought, arguing that parties will not litigate at considerable personal cost unless they have a real interest in the matter.
(7) If a citizen is no more than a wayfarer or officious intervener without any interest or concern beyond what belongs to any one of the 660 million people of this country, the doors of the court will not be ajar for him. But, if he belongs to an organisation which has special interest in the subject-matter, or has some concern deeper than that of a busybody, "he cannot be told off at the gates, although whether the issue raised by him is justifiable may still remain to be considered".
(8) Justiciability of the issues and standing to agitate them are two different things.

There is no dispute that the orthodox rule of interpretation regarding locus standi of a person to reach the court had undergone a sea change with the development of constitutional law in India, and the constitutional courts have been adopting a liberal approach in dealing with the cases or dislodging the claim of a litigant merely on hypertechnical grounds. If a person approaching the court can satisfy that the impugned action is likely to affect his right, which is shown to be having some source in some statutory provision, the petition filed by such person cannot be rejected on the ground of his not having locus standi. In other words, if a person is found to be not merely a stranger having no right whatsoever to any post or property, he cannot be non-suited on the ground of his not having locus standi.[201]

In order to make writ jurisdiction more people centric by extending its long arms, the Supreme Court maintained that a person in the same trade has a right to file a writ for the cancellation of a licence granted to another person in violation of the provisions of the applicable law and the rules, because it will have an impact on his trade and he will suffer civil consequences. In *Sai Chalchitra* v. *Commr.*[202], the appellant who was running a cinema had filed a writ petition against the grant of a licence to another person, in violation of law, for opening a video parlour. The High Court declined the writ on the ground of locus standi because the appellant had not suffered any damage and no legal right of his was violated. By allowing locus standi, the Supreme Court is trying to provide extended protection to the rights of the people, while infusing administration with a culture of fairness also.

2.5 Standing in the PIL

The first building blocks for the expanding concept of locus standi were provided by those Supreme Court decisions which indicated that the expression "aggrieved persons" to whom standing may be given is an elastic concept, the meaning of which would vary from circumstance to circumstance and from statute to statute, and that while in private law its ambit was narrow, in regard to professional conduct and morality it had to be taken as having a wide import.[203] In order to have a coherent view of the standing in a PIL, the following situational responses of the courts in India may be noted.

2.5.1 *Expression "standing" to include notional injury*

The concept of "direct personal injury" has been expanded to include a "notional injury" within the area of public law litigation. Therefore, the court held that a ratepayer has standing to control deliberations of the corporation meetings which may involve a waste of time and money because it is his money which will be wasted.[204] In the same manner, it was held that a taxpayer has locus standi to challenge the decision of a municipality

201. *Ghulam Qadir* v. *Special Tribunal*, (2002) 1 SCC 33.
202. (2005) 3 SCC 683.
203. *Jasbhai Motibhai Desai* v. *Roshan Kumar, Haji Bashir Ahmed*, (1976) 1 SCC 671; *Bar Council of Maharashtra* v. *M.V. Dabholkar*, (1975) 2 SCC 702.
204. *Narendra Nath Chakravorty* v. *Corpn. of Calcutta*, 1959 SCC OnLine Cal 97: AIR 1960 Cal 102.

for erecting even a privately donated statue because the statue would have to be maintained out of taxpayers' money.[205] Elaborating the same idea, the Orissa High Court in *Nabaghan Naik* v. *Sadananda Das*[206] held that the members of the general public who worship or who have the right to worship the deity have a sufficient interest to challenge the appointment of trustees and mismanagement of the temple's affairs.

2.5.2 *"Public duties" standing*

Public duties are owned by the State to the people at large and, therefore, every citizen has a right to enforce the performance of such duties for the benefit of all. In *Municipal Council, Ratlam* v. *Vardichan*[207], the Supreme Court allowed "standing" to an ordinary citizen to initiate action against the municipality which failed to discharge its public duties, such as maintenance of roads and providing sanitary facilities. In the area of criminal law also, where it is the duty of the State to prosecute a criminal because a crime is considered to be an offence against society, the court allowed a private party to initiate and pursue a criminal case in a situation where the State has not prosecuted the offender for reasons which do not bear on public interest, but are prompted by private influence, mala fides and other extraneous considerations.[208]

2.5.3 *"Class" standing*

Courts have recognised the right of a member of a "class" to initiate action in a case where the whole class is likely to be affected by an action. In *Sunil Batra* (2) v. *Delhi Admn.*[209] [*Sunil Batra (II)*], the Supreme Court granted standing to Sunil Batra as one of the prisoners to challenge the lodging of the prisoners in unsatisfactory and inhuman prison conditions. The court also recognised his right to move the court in regard to the alleged torture of another prisoner. Similarly, the court recognised the right of members of a union to move the court on a matter which may affect their jobs. This was firmly established in *Fertiliser Corpn. Kamgar Union*[210] that the members of the union had the right to challenge the corporation decision for sale of the chemical plant at Sindri. Therefore, if a person belongs to an organisation which has a special interest in the subject-matter and has some deeper concern than that of a busybody, he cannot be refused the court's access. Walking forward with the same stride, the technical doc

205. *R. Vardarajan* v. *Salem Municipal Council*, 1971 SCC OnLine Mad 22: AIR 1973 Mad 55.
206. 1971 SCC OnLine Ori 29: AIR 1972 Ori 188.
207. (1980) 4 SCC 162; *K. Ramadas Shenoy* v. *Town Municipal Council, Udipi*, (1974) 2 SCC 506. V.D. Misra J, Chief Justice of the Himachal Pradesh High Court, recently admitted a writ of a citizen against the Simla Municipality for the enforcement of its ordinary duty of keeping the city clean. [*Indian Express* 5-5-1983].
208. *P.S.R. Sadhanantham* v. *Arunachalam*, (1980) 3 SCC 141.
209. (1980) 3 SCC 488.
210. (1981) 1 SCC 568.

trine of locus standi was given "social content" in conformity with the letters and the spirit of the Constitution. In a major judgment[211] supporting the workers' rights, the highest Bench ruled that workers have locus standi to be heard in a winding-up proceeding of a company. According to the Companies Act, 1956, only the creditors and contributaries are entitled to be heard in a winding-up proceeding. The workmen have no locus standi except when their dues are unpaid, but that would be only in their capacity as creditors. Bringing out the concept of "locus standi" from the thickets of the 19th century laissez faire doctrine into the fresh breeze of the directive principles of state policy, which enjoin on the government to secure workers' participation in the management of the undertakings, Bhagwati J, who wrote the main judgment, said that the concept of company has undergone radical transformation and the traditional view that a company is a property of the shareholders is now an exploded myth in view of the new social values. It is not only the shareholders, who have supplied capital, who are interested in the enterprise, which is being run by the company, but the workers who supply labour are also equally, if not more, interested because what is produced by the enterprise is the result of labour as well as capital. Capital is only one of the factors of production, and it cannot confer on the owner exclusive domain over all other factors. While the owner invests only part of his money in the company and bears only a limited financial risk and otherwise contributes nothing to the production, the workers contribute a major share of the product. The workers invest their "sweat and toil" and in fact "their life itself". Reddy J said the same thing when he began his judgment quoting Shakespeare, "You take my life when you do take the means whereby I live." In this manner, the workers' locus standi to participate in winding-up proceedings of the company which adversely affect their very "livelihood" is also implied in the principles of natural justice. Thus, developing horizons of the technical doctrine of "locus standi" would go a long way in the direction of the implementation of the new social values aimed at improving the quality of life in this country.[212]

The same approach has been developed further to cover a person who, though a member of the class to which the victim belongs, is not himself likely to be affected by the action. It is on this ground that any person can be allowed standing to file a petition of quo warranto to challenge the appointment to a public office.

2.5.4 *"Public concern" standing*

Under this category, a person acquires standing not because he belongs to a class or has any special interest or has suffered personal injury, but because

211. *National Textile Workers' Union* v. *P.R. Ramakrishnan*, (1983) 1 SCC 228:. For details *see*, Upendra Baxi, "Pre-Marxist Socialism and the Supreme Court of India", (1983) 4 SCC J-3.
212. According to a survey conducted in the US, India ranks 85th on the graph of "quality of life" out of 110 countries. The US comes fourth. First three positions go to Scandinavian countries. [*Indian Express*, Chandigarh 7-12-1982].

being a responsible citizen he feels concerned on a matter of public concern. It is on this ground that the Consumer Education and Research Centre, Ahmedabad was allowed access to the court for challenging a Gujarat government notification winding up the Machhu Commission, inquiring into the Morvi Dam disaster of 11 August 1979 in which 1826 persons lost their lives and an estimated damage of 100 crores was caused in the Morvi town of Rajkot district. The government had appointed a one-man commission of B.K. Mehta J.[213] The decision to wind up the enquiry commission was found by the court not only unreasonable but mala fide also. Similarly, the Citizens For Democracy (CFD) was allowed to intervene in *Sunil Batra* (2)[214]; Hindustani Andolan was allowed to intervene in *R.K. Garg* v. *Union of India*[215], (also known as the *Special Bearer Bonds case*); the People's Union for Civil Liberties (PUCL) was allowed to intervene in *A.K. Roy* v. *Union of India*[216], (also known as the *National Security Ordinance case*); the Free Legal Aid Committee, Jamshedpur was allowed to initiate action for improving prison conditions;[217] the Free Legal Aid Committee, Hazaribagh was allowed to initiate proceedings for the release of illegally detained prisoners, who were in detention for almost two or three decades;[218] the Delhi units of two civil rights organisations—the PUCL and the CFD—were allowed to file a joint writ petition for the release of the report of the National Police Commission;[219] a Delhi-based citizens' group was allowed to initiate proceedings on inequities of specific pension rules; the members of the Chipko Movement were allowed to initiate action for the illegal felling of trees in forests; Bandhua Mukti Morcha was allowed standing to seek release of bonded labourers in the stone quarries of Faridabad district;[220] the People's Union for Democratic Rights was allowed to seek relief on behalf of the labourers working on the Salal Hydro-Electric Project against exploitation and denial of the benefit of labour laws by contractors;[221] and Lok Vidayan Sanghatana was allowed standing to petition for staying the telecast of the serial Honi Anhoni, on the ground that it spreads superstition and obscurity.[222]

Under this category, not only groups and organisations have been allowed standing but individuals have also been granted access to courts.

---

213. *Consumer Education & Research Centre* v. *State of Gujarat*, (1981) 22 GLR 712. The Centre has also been allowed standing in matters relating to tariff increase by the Gujarat State Electricity Board, Gujarat Road Transport Corporation and Indian Airlines to excise refunds claimed by manufacturers on grounds of wrongful levy and to low cost insurance policy floated by the Life Insurance Corporation.
214. (1980) 3 SCC 488.
215. (1981) 4 SCC 675.
216. (1982) 1 SCC 271.
217. Writ Petition No. 53 of 1980 (SC).
218. *Veena Sethi* v. *State of Bihar*, (1982) 2 SCC 583.
219. *Indian Express* 19-7-1982.
220. *Bandhua Mukti Morcha* v. *Union of India*, (1984) 3 SCC 161.
221. *Salal Hydro-Electric Project* v. *State of J&K*, (1984) 3 SCC 538.
222. *See*, R.V. Pillai, "T.V. Censorship and Law", *Tribune* 29-8-1988, 4.

Two Professors of law from Delhi University were allowed to initiate proceedings for investigation into the functioning of a Women's Protective Home in Agra, though neither of these Professors nor any of their friends or relatives were affected by the sub-human conditions in the Home.[223] Similarly, the court allowed journalists to move petitions in the Supreme Court. One petition concerned the bulldozing of Bombay pavement dwellings at the height of the monsoon season. The other petition was based on a series of investigative reports on Naxalite prisoners in Tamil Nadu.[224] The writ petition filed by C.K. Daphtary, former Attorney General of India, against senior officers of the Delhi Telephones and the Government of India for excessive billing by the telephone authorities, which is a common feature, is noteworthy. His plea to the Delhi High Court to treat his petition as a social action litigation (SAL) and to afford relief, which would benefit all the subscribers, was promptly accepted.[225] *New India Assurance Co.* v. *Kamla*[226] is again a pointer in the right direction. In this case, three journalists in order to highlight the inhuman traffic in women purchased Kamla from the flesh trade market in Morena in Madhya Pradesh and filed a writ in the Supreme Court praying for various reliefs, so that this inhuman treatment to women may be mitigated. Acceptance of this writ by the Supreme Court and the direction to the State Government for investigation clearly show that any "public-minded citizen" can approach the court with grievances of the poor and the illiterate, the silent majority. It is against this backdrop that the efforts of the public-spirited citizens who filed a writ in the Supreme Court to attract the attention of the government in order to secure relief to alleviate the sufferings of the labourers engaged in the construction of ASIAD 1982 complex may be appreciated.[227] The court also allowed standing to an employee of the Border Roads Organisation (BRO) to file a writ petition against the Union of India for seeking action against drunken army men who indiscriminately shot and killed at least five workers of the BRO on Independence Day in 1982. The incident was reported by the *Indian Express* on 26 October 1982. It was alleged that the army authorities were hushing up the matter.[228] Standing has also been allowed to individuals seeking investigation into cases of prison torture and human sacrifice.[229] In the same manner, the University College of Law Students' Legal Aid Society, Dharwar was allowed standing for challenging the levy of capitation fees for professional course admissions at the cost of meritorious students.[230] Standing was also granted to the General

223. *Upendra Baxi* v. *State of U.P.*, (1983) 2 SCC 308.
224. *Indian Express* 13-8-1981.
225. *Indian Express* 18-10-1981.
226. (2001) 4 SCC 342. *See also*, *Coomi Kapoor* v. *State of M.P.*, WP (Cri) No. 2229 of 1981 (SC).
227. *People's Union for Democratic Rights* v. *Union of India*, (1982) 3 SCC 235.
228. *Indian Express*, Chandigarh 3-12-1982.
229. *Indian Express* 9-11-1982.
230. *Indian Express* 2-3-1983.

Secretary, Public Interest Law Service Society, Cochin who sought a ban on the sale and distribution of all the drugs recommended to be banned by the Drugs Consultative Committee.[231] Sheela Barse, a journalist, was allowed standing to seek relief against the torture of women in police lock-ups in Maharashtra.[232] Maintaining the same tenor, the highest Bench ruled in *D.S. Nakara* v. *Union of India*[233] that any member of public having sufficient interest can maintain an action for judicial redress for public injury arising from the breach of public duty, or from violation of some provision of the Constitution or law, and seek enforcement of public duty and observance of such constitutional or legal provision. Hence, standing was allowed to the petitioner for enforcing the rights available to a large number of old and infirm retirees. In this case, on 25 May 1979, pension rules for government servants were liberalised, but benefit was given only to those who retired on or after that. A petition was filed on behalf of all the pensioners who had been denied benefit and thus suffered prejudice. The time is fast approaching when the court would allow access to its aid to consider the plight of workers dying of sclerosis in Mandsaur, adivasis losing limbs while collecting metal on a firing range in Madhya Pradesh, and landless labourers or brick-kiln workers or tribals in a forest.[234]

Maintaining the thrust forward, a parent of a student of Medical College, Shimla was allowed standing for banning ragging in the college.[235] Neerja Chaudhary, a journalist, was allowed standing to compel the government to rehabilitate the released bonded labourers.[236] Similarly in *D.C. Wadhwa* v. *State of Bihar*[237], the court held that every citizen has a right to question the law made by the executive usurping legislative functions which is a fraud on the Constitution. In this case, the petitioner, a professor in the Gokhale Institute of Politics and Economics, had found, on the basis of his research, that the practice of repromulgation of ordinances by the Bihar government was a colourable exercise of power. The high benchmark is *Ramesh* v. *Union of India*[238] (*Ramesh*), where the court allowed standing to a citizen to file a petition for maintenance of communal harmony even though no provision of the Constitution was violated. In this case, a petition had been filed by a person for restraining the government from telecasting the serial Tamas which according to him breeds communal hatred.

231. *Indian Express* 11-4-1983.
232. *Sheela Barse* v. *State of Maharashtra*, (1983) 2 SCC 96. The court issued detailed directions to the government for the protection of women in police lock-up. See also, *Kadra Pahadiya* v. *State of Bihar*, (1983) 2 SCC 104. In this case, a researcher and social scientist sought relief for three young boys belonging to a backward tribe who were languishing in jails for eight years without trial, kept in leg-irons and forced to work outside the jail.
233. (1983) 1 SCC 305.
234. *Indian Express* 17-4-1980, 14-8-1980, 29-9-1980, 13-7-1981, 15-7-1981, 27-5-1981, 29-5-1981 and 5-11-1982.
235. *State of H.P.* v. *Parent of a Student of Medical College*, (1985) 3 SCC 169.
236. *Neeraja Chaudhary* v. *State of M.P.*, (1984) 3 SCC 243.
237. (1987) 1 SCC 378.
238. (1988) 1 SCC 668.

The liberal theory in the PIL is that the judge would not ask the petitioner how he was affected and what was his personal injury or loss. The major outcome of these cases would be a widening of the power of the citizen to move the courts even when his own rights are not violated. In *S.P. Gupta* v. *Union of India*[239], popularly known as the *Judge's case*, the court discussed the rationale behind this expansion of the rule of locus standi. In this case, the petitioners were generally lawyers practising in High Courts and the Supreme Court who felt that the independence of the judiciary in India has been threatened by certain governmental action relating to 1) the issuance of a circular by the Union Law Minister on 18 March 1981; 2) the practice of granting short-term extensions to Additional Judges on the expiry of their initial term; and 3) the transfer of judges from one High Court to another. One of the very important issues involved in this case was the standing of the lawyer-petitioners to have access to the court in this matter of public importance, *i.e.* independence of the judiciary. Granting them standing, the court observed that the profession of lawyers is an integral part of the judicial system and, therefore, the lawyers have sufficient interest to maintain an action for the preservation of the independence of the judiciary, which is a basic feature of the Constitution.[240] Thus, though the rule of locus standi was liberalised, it does not mean that it is without any limitation. The court was quick to add that the petitioner must not be a mere wayfarer or officious intervener or bystander or meddlesome interloper.[241] He must be acting bona fide and must have sufficient interest before he can be accorded standing. "Sufficient interest" would have to be determined by the court in each individual case.[242] One such situation where the petitioner shall be deemed as not having "sufficient interest" would be where though the administrative action or inaction causes public injury and also specific injury to an individual or a group, yet the latter does not want to maintain any action for reasons not actuated by poverty, illiteracy or fear. This would be something like thrusting a relief on someone who does not want it.[243] Furthermore, the individual who moves the court in matters of public interest must be acting bona fide with a view to vindicate the cause of justice,[244] so if he is acting for personal gains or private profit, or out of political motivation or other oblique considerations, the court would not allow itself to be activated at the instance of such person.[245]

The main thrust of the court's ruling in this case is that any individual acting bona fide and having sufficient interest can have access to the court

239. 1981 Supp SCC 87.
240. 1981 Supp SCC 87, 214–15, *per* Bhagwati J.
241. *Ibid*, SCC 220.
242. *Ibid*, SCC 214.
243. *Ibid*, SCC 264.
244. *Ibid*, SCC 211.
245. 1981 Supp SCC 87, 214–15, 702, *per* Desai J. See also, *Janata Dal* v. *H.S. Chowdhary*, (1992) 4 SCC 305. Court observed that court should not allow its process to be abused by politicians.

for the purpose of redressing public injury; enforcing public duty; protecting social, collective, diffused rights and interests; or vindicating public interest.[246] This desired liberalisation of the rule of locus standi would not only make the administration more responsible and responsive to the people, but would also make it possible for the courts to effectively police the corridors of power and prevent violations of law.[247] Among the many justifications provided by Bhagwati J for this liberal approach to the rule of locus standi, the following are important from the present perspective. First, the rule of law will be "substantially impaired" if "no one can have standing to maintain an action for judicial redress in case of public wrong or public injury". It is "absolutely essential that the rule of law must wean people away from lawlessness on streets and win them for the court of law". If the breach of public duties was "allowed" to go unredressed by courts on the ground of standing, it would "promote disrespect for the rule of law". It will also lead to corruption and encourage inefficiency. It might also create possibilities of the "political machinery" itself becoming a participant in the misuse or abuse of power. Finally, the newly emergent social and economic rights require a new kind of enforcement.[248] Besides controlling administrative wrongs and illegalities which may otherwise remain unchecked, it may also ensure "interest representation" and "people's participation" in the administrative process.[249] If only the "directly injured" has the right to move the court, it would sometimes lead to anomalous situations. When forests are denuded, the court will hear only the forest official, who may be in collusion with the vandals; or when protected species are shot, it will entertain only complaints from wardens, who may be conspiring with the poachers.

However, this liberal approach will not apply in cases where conviction and sentence of a regular criminal court are challenged through a PIL. This was ruled by the Supreme Court in *Simranjit Singh Mann* v. *Union of India*[250], wherein a Akali Dal (M) leader had challenged the conviction and sentence of the two accused in the General Vaidya murder case on the ground that he has an interest in the future of the two convicts and also in upholding the rule of law. The Supreme Court observed that the petitioner being a total stranger to the prosecution has no locus standi to maintain the petition. Similarly, in *Karamjeet Singh* v. *Union of India*[251], the court refused standing where the petitioner had filed a PIL petition as a "next friend" of the same two convicts in the General Vaidya murder case whom he claimed were under a disability due to their intense obsession based on religious beliefs.

246. *Ibid*, SCC 214–15.
247. 1981 Supp SCC 87, 211 16, 702, *per* Desai J.
248. *See*, note 62 of Upendra Baxi, "Taking Suffering Seriously: Social Action Litigation in the Supreme Court of India", Mimeographed 1991–92. See also, *Iqbal M. Chagla* v. *P. Shivshankar*, 1981 Supp SCC 87.
249. *See*, S.N. Jain, "Locus Standi and Public Interest Litigation", Mimeographed 20.
250. (1992) 4 SCC 653.
251. (1992) 4 SCC 666.

However, some may be tempted to comment that this new constitutionalism is an "unseemly trend", and besides providing an unreasonable constraint on administrative efficiency and celerity, would also open a floodgate of litigation.[252] If what is happening in some foreign countries, where the liberal rule of standing in PIL has come to stay, can be any indicator, then the fallacy can be easily established. Litigation, especially in India, is not such an enjoyable process that everyone would litigate for a lark. This fact is proved statistically also. In the Supreme Court, 35,000 cases were filed in 1985 and in comparison to this only, 200 PIL petitions were filed. What is important to note is that if 35,000 cases benefited 35,000 persons, perhaps 200 PIL petitions may have benefited millions.[253] The trend of liberalising standing in PIL opens up a new era of unique judicial role perception and performance in India. The nature of the judicial process is not purely adjudicatory, nor is it functionally that of an umpire. The dynamics of the judicial process has a new "enforcement" dimension which includes "rights mobilisation" without which the rights and interests of the poor and illiterate, the silent majority, would become sterile.

Besides judicial activism in the area of locus standi, standing can be bestowed by statute also. The legislature by passing the Bhopal Gas Leak Disaster (Processing of Claims) Act, 1985 conferred standing on the Central Government to represent on behalf of the gas victims before the Supreme Court for the settlement of compensation claims.

These liberal trends in law relating to locus standi reached a culmination point in *Ramesh* v. *Union of India*[254]. In this case, a writ was filed regarding the telecast of serial Tamas which depicted communal violence after the partition of India in 1947. It was a public interest writ, wherein the attention of the court had been drawn to the public and national interest which the serial was likely to jeopardise by developing communal hatred. Rejecting the preliminary objection as to locus standi of the petitioner, the Supreme Court held that the writ is maintainable even though no provision of the Constitution is violated, including Articles 21 and 25. The Supreme Court further observed that the petitioner can file the petition and draw the attention of the court to ensure that the communal atmosphere is kept clean and unpolluted.

In the US, the question of locus standi is a by-product of the "cases and controversies" clause of the US Constitution. Unless a person has a direct personal interest in the action, it will not be a situation of "case and controversy". However, today the trend is towards the expansion of horizons of standing.[255]

---

252. M.J. Antony, "Court as Watchdog of Citizens' Rights", *Indian Express* 13-8-1981. See, *Indian Express*, Editorial 17-11-1982.
253. *Indian Express* 27-10-1986, 6.
254. (1988) 1 SCC 668.
255. *Assn. of Data Processing Service Organisations* v. *Camp*, 1970 SCC OnLine US SC 53: 25 L Ed 2d 184: 397 US 150 (1970).

The courts are moving away from "economic injury concept" to "non-economic value concept". A taxpayer is deemed to have sufficient interest to challenge the unconstitutionality of the exercise of power by Congress if it violates the taxing and spending clauses of the Constitution. Tremendous development is taking place regarding consumers' standing to challenge an administrative action, and a consumer is now allowed to challenge an administrative action if it affects the price or quality of product and services.

In *Reade* v. *Ewing*[256], the court allowed a challenge by a consumer against the order of the administrative authority allowing a vitamin content to be supplied from a synthetic source on the ground that it affects the quality of the product which the person consumes. In the same manner, in *Citizens Committee for Hudson Valley* v. *Volpe*[257], the court allowed a challenge by citizens against the decision of the authority which had the effect of destroying the scenic river area by the construction of a highway.

A big stride was taken by the court in *Office of Communication* v. *Federal Communication Centre*[258], in which the Supreme Court accepted the standing of the representatives of television viewers as sufficient to challenge the action of the authority renewing the television operation licence on the ground that the station discriminated against blacks in its programmes and, thus, denied the viewer of a fair programme required by law.

In England, too, the development of standing law is a patchwork of case-law. Public interest actions, like the interest of a taxpayer, were enforced in the name of Attorney General who lent his name to the private individual. However, now the courts have started allowing challenge in the name of the individual taxpayer.[259] In the case of prerogative writs, the law is liberal and any person can point out the excess or abuse of jurisdiction by any administrative authority. Therefore, the court accepted the standing of a member of the public to enforce the law against gambling houses.[260] In this case, the Police Commissioner had circulated a confidential note that on account of shortage of police force, vigilance over gambling houses shall cease.

In January 1978, the new rules of court were brought into force in England. In respect of all remedies, Order 53, Rule 3(5) lays down one simple test of locus standi. The test is that the applicant must have "a sufficient interest in the matter to which the application relates". What is the test of "sufficient interest"? The courts have developed the test in *R.* v. *Metropolitan Police Commr., ex p Blackburn*[261] and *Attorney General, ex rel McWhirter* v. *Independent Broadcasting Authority*[262] as:

256. 205 F 2d 630 (1953).
257. 425 F 2d 97 (2nd Cir 1970).
258. 359 F 2d 994 (DC Cir 1966).
259. *Prescott* v. *Birmingham Corpn.*, 1955 Ch 210: (1954) 3 WLR 990 (CA).
260. *R.* v. *Metropolitan Police Commr., ex p Blackburn*, (1968) 2 QB 118: (1968) 2 WLR 893 (CA).
261. (1968) 2 QB 118: (1968) 2 WLR 893 (CA).
262. 1973 QB 629: (1973) 2 WLR 344 (CA).

> The court will not listen to a busybody who is interfering in things which do not concern him, but it will listen to an ordinary citizen who comes asking that the law should be declared and enforced, even though he is only one of a hundred, or one of a thousand, or one of a million, who are affected by it.

Thus, through this *actio popularis*, an ordinary citizen can enforce the law in England for the benefit of all—as against public authorities in respect of their statutory duties.[263]

2.6 Laches or unreasonable delay

Though the writ-issuing power of the Supreme Court and the High Courts for the enforcement of fundamental rights is mandatory, however, the court may refuse remedy if there is an unreasonable delay in invoking the jurisdiction of the court. Unlike limitation, there is no fixed period for laches. Every case will be determined on its own merit. Without reference to the limitation law, the court must see whether there is any explanation for the delay in filing the petition.[264]

As regards the power of the High Court to issue writs for any other purpose, if the period of limitation as laid down in the Limitation Act, 1963 has expired, the High Court will decline jurisdiction. The rationale is that if the relief cannot be claimed in the ordinary manner because the limitation period has expired, the same will not be granted by the High Court in exercise of its extraordinary power.[265] However, the High Court is not bound by the limitation law in the sense that a petition even if within limitation may still be refused on the ground of unreasonable delay[266] because the extraordinary remedy is discretionary.

Applying these principles, the Supreme Court held in *Arun Kumar Chatterjee* v. *South Eastern Railway*[267] that when the appellant had made a representation against the seniority list to the administration in 1967, which was replied in 1973, there is no inordinate delay in filing the petition in view of the fact that the railway administration was itself guilty of the delay. Likewise, a delay of four years was ignored by the Karnataka High Court in view of the serious adverse consequences to the petitioner.[268] But, on the other hand, an unexplained delay of two years after the completion of acquisition process was found fatal for the maintainability of the writ petition.[269] Again, even a delay of a few days was considered as fatal because it upset the admission of others.[270] From these decisions it appears that "laches or delay" is a matter of discretion with the court,

263. Lord Denning, *The Discipline of Law* (1982) 133.
264. *Tilokchand Motichand* v. *H.B. Munshi*, (1969) 1 SCC 110, *per* Hidayatullah CJ.
265. *Durga Prashad* v. *Controller of Imports and Exports*, (1969) 1 SCC 185.
266. *Kamini Kumar Das Choudhury* v. *State of W.B.*, (1972) 2 SCC 420.
267. (1985) 2 SCC 451.
268. *Mohd. Ismail* v. *State of Karnataka*, 1984 SCC OnLine Kar 148: AIR 1985 Kar 123.
269. *Keshav Pal* v. *State of Bihar*, 1984 SCC OnLine Pat 229: AIR 1985 Pat 70.
270. *Krishna Kumar Roy* v. *State of U.P.*, 1980 SCC OnLine All 810: AIR 1981 All 287.

which must be exercised judiciously and reasonably on the basis of the fact situation of every case. The Supreme Court in *P.S. Sadasivaswamy* v. *State of T.N.*[271] also observed that it would be a sound and wise exercise of discretion for the courts to refuse to exercise their extraordinary powers under Article 226 in the case of persons who do not approach it expeditiously for relief, and who stand by and allow things to happen and then approach the court to put forward State claims and try to unsettle settled matters. Therefore, in *M.S. Mudhol* v. *S.D. Halegkar*[272], the Supreme Court ruled that the challenge to the appointment of principal after a period of nine years on the ground that he did not fulfil the requisite qualification, cannot be allowed. Similarly in *LIC* v. *Jyotish Chandra Biswas*[273], the court did not allow petition filed after a lapse of six years against dismissal from service for long absence from duty.

For the application of the doctrine of laches, no distinction is made between petitions for the enforcement of fundamental rights and for other purposes.[274] Unfortunately, the courts do not take into consideration the time taken in pursuing non-legal remedies for the application of this doctrine.[275] Therefore, if a person who has been denied licence proceeds with the matter through his political representative, for example, an MLA or MP, instead of rushing through the expensive and dilatory judicial process, the time, thus, consumed will not be considered an excusable delay. It is difficult to reconcile this judicial behaviour with the norms of functioning of an intensive form of democratic society.

Can laches extinguish fundamental rights? Following *Tilokchand Motichand* v. *H.B. Munshi*[276] and *Rabindranath Bose* v. *Union of India*[277], the Supreme Court in *R.S. Makashi* v. *I.M. Menon*[278] reiterated the same principle that laches applies to writ petitions under Articles 32 and 226 for the enforcement of fundamental rights and, hence, would extinguish fundamental rights. In this case, the bone of contention was the seniority between two groups of government employees. The cause of action arose in 1968, but the writ under Article 226 was filed after eight years. The petitioners claimed violation of their fundamental right. Unfortunately this decision of the Supreme Court, which was a three-judge Bench decision, did not even refer to a five-judge Bench decision in *Ramchandra Shankar Deodhar* v. *State of Maharashtra*[279], in which, speaking for the majority,

271. (1975) 1 SCC 152. *See also*, C.K. Thakker, *Administrative Law* (Eastern Book Company 1992) 395–400.
272. (1993) 3 SCC 591.
273. (2000) 6 SCC 562.
274. *Trilokchand Motichand* v. *H.B. Munshi*, (1969) 1 SCC 110; *Ramchandra Shankar Deodhar* v. *State of Maharashtra*, (1974) 1 SCC 317.
275. *Gandhinagar Motor Transport Society* v. *V. Kasbekar*, 1953 SCC OnLine Bom 64: AIR 1954 Bom 202. For criticism *see*, Seervai, *Constitutional Law* (1976) 843.
276. (1969) 1 SCC 110.
277. (1970) 1 SCC 84.
278. (1982) 1 SCC 379.
279. (1974) 1 SCC 317.

Bhagwati J said that the claim for the enforcement of fundamental right of equal opportunity under Article 16 is itself a fundamental right guaranteed under Article 32 and the Supreme Court, which has been assigned the role of a sentinel on the *qui vive* for the protection of fundamental rights, cannot easily allow itself to be persuaded to refuse relief solely on the jejune ground of laches, delay or the like.[280] Moving in the same direction the court allowed a writ petition of persons displaced due to acquisition of land for a steel plant, for seeking employment in the plant after 38 years of acquisition of land and 33 years after the setting up of the plant, in view of the nature of the problem and the decision taken by the government just about four years ago to provide employment to the displaced persons.[281]

In *Jawahar Lal Sazawal* v. *State of J&K*[282], the Supreme Court was of the view that a writ petition filed before the High Court on 1982 and coming for hearing after 16 long years is not barred by laches due to special circumstances of the case. In this case, a writ had been filed in the High Court in 1972 by permanent government servants, serving in government industrial undertaking subsequent to privatisation, for a declaration that they still continue to be government servants was dismissed as premature. The company granted them wages at a rate admissible to government servants till 1979. In 1980, it denied them parity. Such order was challenged in 1981 before the Supreme Court which relegated the petitioners to the remedy under Article 226. A writ accordingly was filed before the High Court in 1982 which came up for hearing after 16 years. In the same manner, where the petitioner was an illiterate widow with meagre resources who had been deprived by the Railways her gangman husband's arrears of family pension, the court held that the petition was admissible despite delay.[283] Sufficient cause for condoning delay or laches was also found by the court when the lawyer withheld papers and did not inform the client of an adverse decision in a writ petition.[284] Similarly, in *Virender Chaudhary* v. *Bharat Petroleum Corpn.*[285], the Supreme Court did not allow a challenge to a grant of licence of liquefied petroleum gas (LPG) dealership to a rival in business after a delay of one-and-a-half years keeping in view the huge investment involved and the employees engaged. The doctrine of laches is an equity doctrine and can be applied in a flexible manner to suit the requirement of each case for justice. A question of delay or laches is a question which must be considered by the writ court. Where jurisdiction is exercised by the High Court, it cannot be assailed under Article 136, more so when the order is legally sustainable.[286]

280. *Ibid*, SCC 325–27.
281. *Butu Prasad Kumbhar* v. *SAIL*, 1995 Supp (2) SCC 225.
282. (2002) 3 SCC 219.
283. *S.K. Mastan Bee* v. *South Central Rly.*, (2003) 1 SCC 184.
284. *Devendra Swamy* v. *Karnataka SRTC*, (2002) 9 SCC 644.
285. (2009) 1 SCC 297.
286. *Dayal Singh* v. *Union of India*, (2003) 2 SCC 593.

2.7 Alternative remedy

The law is that the Supreme Court and High Courts cannot refuse relief under Articles 32 and 226 on the ground of alternative remedy if the person complains of violation of his fundamental rights. But, if the person invokes the jurisdiction of the High Court for any other purpose, in exercise of its discretion, the High Court may refuse relief. The law was laid down with sufficient clarity by the Supreme Court in *A.V. Venkateswaran* v. *Ramchand Sobhraj Wadhwani*[287]. In this case, the petitioners had imported Sheaffer pens with gold plating from Australia. The customs authorities charged a higher rate of duty than was fixed for ordinary pens. This action was challenged in a writ proceeding. The main contention before the court was that the petitioner had not exhausted the alternative remedy of review by the Central Government before coming to the court. The court observed that the rule of exhaustion of an alternative remedy is not one that bars the jurisdiction of the court, but it is a rule which courts have laid down for the exercise of their discretion.[288] Even in the face of an alternative remedy, the discretion lies with the High Court to entertain the petition. No inflexible rules can be laid down for the exercise of discretion in this regard. Even then the broad policy behind the doctrine is that the writ jurisdiction is not meant to short-circuit or circumvent statutory procedures. It is only where statutory remedies are entirely ill-suited to meet the demands of extraordinary situations, as for instance, where the very vires of the statute is in question, or where private or public wrongs are so inextricably mixed up, and the prevention of public injury and the vindication of public justice require that recourse may be had to an extraordinary remedy. However, even then the court must have good and sufficient reasons to bypass the alternative remedy provided by statute.[289] Therefore, if the alternative remedy is either not adequate,[290] or was lost for no fault of the person,[291] or is illusory,[292] or involves delay,[293] the High Court may grant relief. Leaving aside these cases, in all cases of absence of jurisdiction and abuse of jurisdiction, the court may exercise jurisdiction even when alternative remedies are available.[294] In the same manner, where there is a violation of fundamental rights, the Supreme Court in exercise of its jurisdiction under Article 32 and the High Court under Article 226 will issue writs, and an alternative remedy will not be considered a bar because it is the duty of the Supreme Court

287. AIR 1961 SC 1506.
288. *State of U.P.* v. *Indian Hume Pipe Co. Ltd.*, (1977) 2 SCC 724.
289. *CCE* v. *Dunlop India Ltd.*, (1985) 1 SCC 260, *per* O. Chinnappa Reddy J.
290. *Himmatlal Harilal Mehta* v. *State of M.P.*, AIR 1954 SC 403; *Ganpat Roy* v. *ADM*, (1985) 2 SCC 307.
291. *Zila Parishad* v. *Kundan Sugar Mills*, AIR 1968 SC 98.
292. *Bhartia Electric Steel Co. Ltd.* v. *CTO*, 1956 SCC OnLine Cal 18: AIR 1956 Cal 299; *Ram & Shyam Co.* v. *State of Haryana*, (1985) 3 SCC 267.
293. *Bhagirath Singh* v. *State of Punjab*, 1964 SCC OnLine Puj 248: AIR 1965 Punj 170.
294. *Baburam Prakash Chandra Maheshwari* v. *Antarim Zila Parishad*, AIR 1969 SC 556.

and the High Court to issue appropriate writs for the enforcement of fundamental rights.[295]

It may be pointed out that the 42nd Amendment had absolutely barred the jurisdiction of the High Courts in all cases where alternative remedy was provided for by or under any other law, except in cases of the enforcement of fundamental rights. Clause (3) inserted in Article 226 had provided that no petition for the redress of any injury referred to in sub-clause (*b*) or (*c*) of clause (1) shall be entertained if any other remedy for such redress is provided for by or under any other law for the time being in force. However, this amendment has now been repealed by the 44th Amendment.

Parallel remedies in respect of same matter at the same time, ordinarily, are not permissible, but extraordinary situations or circumstances may warrant a different approach where court's orders are violated or thwarted with impunity. In such cases, an alternative remedy will not bar the jurisdiction of writ courts.[296] However, in a writ petition filed during the pendency of an appeal before the statutory authority, an alternative remedy will be a bar to the exercise of jurisdiction.[297] In the same manner, where the remedy by way of an appeal and revision was available, a High Court cannot assume jurisdiction.[298] Normally, in a dispute relating to terms of private contract, the proper course would be arbitration or institution of a suit and not the writ petition.[299]

Though the existence of an alternative remedy does not oust the jurisdiction of writ courts, yet it would be a good ground for not entertaining the petition.[300] Where a statute provided service tribunals for adjudicating disputes of government servants, the said tribunal cannot be bypassed by filing a writ petition on the ground that the tribunal lacks power to pass an interim order.[301] In *Sadhana Lodh* v. *National Insurance Co. Ltd.*[302], the Supreme Court further held that a writ petition by an insurer challenging the award of a tribunal is not maintainable in the face of the fact that an alternative remedy by filing an appeal before the High Court under the Motor Vehicles Act, 1988 was available to the insurer.

From the above discussion, it becomes clear that the rule of exclusion of writ jurisdiction when an alternative remedy is available is a rule of discretion and not one of compulsion. In at least four contingencies, the court may still exercise writ jurisdiction in spite of the availability of an alternative remedy. Such contingencies include following situations:

295. *Himmatlal Harilal Mehta* v. *State of M.P.*, AIR 1954 SC 403. *See also*, C.K. Thakker, *Administrative Law* (Eastern Book Company 1992) 400–05.
296. *Awadh Bihari Yadav* v. *State of Bihar*, (1995) 6 SCC 31.
297. *Bombay Metropolitan Region Development Authority* v. *Gokak Patel Volkart Ltd.*, (1995) 1 SCC 642.
298. *Swetambar Sthanakwasi Jain Samiti* v. *Sri R.J.I. College*, (1996) 3 SCC 11.
299. *State of U.P.* v. *Bridge & Roof Co. (India) Ltd.*, (1996) 6 SCC 22.
300. *State of Bihar* v. *Jain Plastics and Chemicals Ltd.*, (2002) 1 SCC 216.
301. *Minor Irrigation & Rural Engg. Services* v. *Sahngoo Ram Arya*, (2002) 5 SCC 521.
302. (2003) 3 SCC 524.

(1) Where writ seeks the enforcement of fundamental rights.
(2) Where there is a failure of the principles of natural justice.
(3) Where orders or proceedings are wholly without jurisdiction.
(4) Where the vires of the law is challenged.

Applying these principles, the Supreme Court in *Harbanslal Sahnia* v. *Indian Oil Corpn. Ltd.*[303] held that where the petitioner's dealership, which was their bread and butter, was terminated on irrelevant and non-existence cause, an alternative remedy by way of arbitration would not oust the jurisdiction of the writ court.

In *Balkrishna Ram* v. *Union of India*[304], the Supreme Court noted that the principle that the High Court should not exercise its extraordinary writ jurisdiction when efficacious alternative remedy is available is a rule of prudence and not rule of law. The existence of such remedy does not mean that jurisdiction of the High Court is ousted. The rule of alternative remedy is a rule of discretion and not rule of jurisdiction. Merely because the court may not exercise its jurisdiction is no ground to hold that it has no jurisdiction. In relation to orders passed by the Armed Forces Tribunal (AFT), the High Court would be justified in exercising its writ jurisdiction because of some glaring illegality committed by AFT. Besides, alternative remedy must also be efficacious. To expect a Non-Commissioned Officer (NCO) or Junior Commissioned Officer (JCO) to approach the Supreme Court in every case may not be justified because it is extremely difficult and beyond monetary reach of ordinary litigant to approach the Supreme Court. Thus, exercise of writ jurisdiction against orders of AFT is within the discretion of the High Court and there cannot be a blanket ban on exercise of such jurisdiction.

In the US, except in cases of lack of jurisdiction, exhaustion of an alternative remedy is invariably insisted upon.[305] But in a federal jurisdiction, the rule is rigorously followed even in cases of lack of jurisdiction.[306] In England, there is no requirement for the exhaustion of alternative remedies if the action is unlawful.[307]

2.8 Res judicata

In order to provide flexibilities to the administrative process, though the principle analogous to res judicata does not apply to administrative jurisdiction,[308] yet this principle has been firmly grounded in the area of public law review as a matter of public policy. If a petition has been heard and dismissed, the same petition on the same ground cannot be filed in the

303. (2003) 2 SCC 107.
304. (2020) 2 SCC 442.
305. *Ward* v. *Keenan*, 70 A 2d 77: 3 NJ 298 (1949).
306. *Myers* v. *Bethlehem Shipbuilding Corpn.*, 82 L Ed 638: 303 US 41 (1938).
307. *Cooper* v. *Wilson*, (1937) 2 KB 309 (CA).
308. *Ganpat Roy* v. *ADM*, (1985) 2 SCC 307.

same court again. The principle of res judicata also applies in cases for the enforcement of fundamental rights. A person is free to reach the High Court or the Supreme Court for the enforcement of his fundamental rights. If such person has made a choice of the forum and his petition has been heard and dismissed or accepted, he cannot agitate the same matter before another court in a writ proceeding.[309] But if the petition has been dismissed otherwise than on merits, the person may file a fresh writ in another forum. Therefore, if the petition under Article 136 has been dismissed in limine by the Supreme Court by a non-speaking order, it will not preclude the party from seeking the same relief under Article 226 from the High Court on identical grounds.[310] In the same manner, contentions raised in an earlier SLP, which was dismissed, could not be raised in a subsequent appeal before the Supreme Court between the same parties.[311] The principle of res judicata, however, does not apply in the case of habeas corpus petitions; if a habeas corpus petition has been dismissed on merits by the High Court, it can again be filed in the Supreme Court.[312]

Res judicata shall apply even if a petition has been dismissed without giving notice to the other party.[313] Summary dismissal of a petition without recording reasons does not attract res judicata and a fresh petition on the same ground can be entertained.[314] Similarly, if a petition has been dismissed as withdrawn, res judicata shall not apply.[315] The principle of res judicata shall also not apply if the court incidentally records findings on issues not raised before it.[316] Findings given in a petition at one stage and later held to be final, a challenge to such finding at a later stage of the same petition will be barred by res judicata.[317]

The question of the applicability of constructive res judicata to writs was considered by the Supreme Court in *State of U.P.* v. *Nawab Hussain*[318]. In that case, a Sub-Inspector of Police challenged his dismissal by the Deputy Inspector-General of Police (DIG) on the ground that he was not given a fair hearing. The High Court, however, dismissed his petition. He filed a suit thereafter, and raised an additional plea that he was appointed by the Inspector-General of Police so cannot be dismissed by the DIG, who is a subordinate officer. The Supreme Court held that the additional plea is barred by constructive res judicata.

However, raising the question of constitutionality of a provision of law stands on different footing than raising a matter on a bare question of

309. *Daryao* v. *State of U.P.*, AIR 1961 SC 1457.
310. *Indian Oil Corpn. Ltd.* v. *State of Bihar*, (1986) 4 SCC 146.
311. *P. Lal* v. *Union of India*, (2003) 3 SCC 393.
312. *Niranjan Singh* v. *State of M.P.*, (1972) 2 SCC 542.
313. *Virudhunagar Steel Rolling Mills Ltd.* v. *State of Madras*, AIR 1968 SC 1196.
314. *Workmen* v. *Cochin Port Trust*, (1978) 3 SCC 119.
315. *Ahmedabad Mfg. & Calico Printing Co. Ltd.* v. *Workmen*, (1981) 2 SCC 663.
316. *Madhvi Amma Bhawani Amma* v. *Kunjikutty Pillai Meenakshi Pillai*, (2000) 6 SCC 301.
317. *M.C. Mehta* v. *Kamal Nath*, (2002) 3 SCC 653.
318. (1977) 2 SCC 806.

law, or mixed question of law and fact, or on fact. There is a presumption always in favour of the constitutionality of law. Onus is heavy on the person challenging it. When a person enters a court for relief and does not challenge the constitutionality of law governing the matters directly and substantially in issue, it only means and implies that he goes by the presumption of constitutionality. He cannot on this instance be deemed to have raised the question of constitutionality and, therefore, the question of constitutionality shall not be deemed to have been decided against him alongwith all matters which were directly and substantially in issue. Therefore, if the question of constitutionality is raised in another writ proceeding, the principle of constructive res judicata shall not be attracted.[319] Summary disposal of writ petition by the High Court does not constitute res judicata. Further, where a recurring liability has been held to be ultra vires the power, earlier summary disposal of the case would not operate as res judicata.[320] In the same manner, once an order passed on merit by the Supreme Court exercising the power under Article 136 has become final, no writ petition under Article 132 on the selfsame issue is maintainable.[321]

Thus, it can be concluded that the principles of res judicata and constructive res judicata apply to writs also as they apply in case of civil suits. Therefore, if a dispute has already been decided by a competent court which has become final, any petition under Articles 32 or 226 will be barred.[322]

Moving in the same direction, the Supreme Court in *U.P. SRTC* v. *State of U.P.*[323] held that once it has decided in two earlier decisions that the draft scheme of nationalisation of certain road routes under Section 100(4) of the Motor Vehicles Act, 1988 has not lapsed, it is not open to the High Court to reopen the matter again in a writ proceeding and hold contrary to the decision of the Supreme Court. This decision, thus, concludes the controversy that reopening of the same issue by the High Court or any court or tribunal and recording a contrary finding is a clear violation of the principle of res judicata, which has now been firmly established in writ jurisdiction itself, as a matter of public policy.

The principle of res judicata applies to the PIL also in the same manner as it applies to other litigation. Thus, if a matter has been completely and effectively adjudicated upon in an individual writ petition, court will not entertain a PIL on the same matter.[324]

2.9 No dismissal of petition without a speaking order

In the immediate past, a tendency was growing amongst High Courts to dismiss petitions under Articles 226 and 227 in limine without a speaking

319. *Nand Kishore* v. *State of Punjab*, (1995) 6 SCC 614.
320. *Union of India* v. *Ranchi Municipal Corpn.*, (1996) 7 SCC 542.
321. *Babu Singh Bains* v. *Union of India*, (1996) 6 SCC 565.
322. *Direct Recruit Class II Engg. Officers' Assn.* v. *State of Maharashtra*, (1990) 2 SCC 715.
323. (2005) 1 SCC 444.
324. *Joydeep Mukharjee* v. *State of W.B.*, (2011) 2 SCC 706.

order. Deprecating this practice, the Supreme Court in *Arun* v. *IG of Police*[325] observed that High Courts should not dismiss petitions in limine without a speaking order just by the use of a laconic word "rejected" or "dismissed" because a speaking order would help the Supreme Court in understanding the thought process of the High Court, which in turn would facilitate a quick and satisfactory disposal of SLPs. No matter this practice will certainly inspire public confidence in judicial administration, but it has started giving rise to accumulation of cases before High Courts. High Courts now feel it convenient to admit a petition rather than writing reasons for dismissal. This will not apply to the Supreme Court which can dismiss a petition in limine without recording reasons because being the highest court, there is no appeal thereafter.[326] Recording of reasons is not only necessary for appeal, but is also necessary for generating public confidence and, hence, the need to record reasons can never be obviated. In a recent decision, the court held that failure to give reasons amounts to denial of public law review and justice, hence, any summary dismissal without reasons by short order is unsustainable.[327]

2.10 High Court must be approached first

There is a growing tendency to file petitions before the Supreme Court even in a case where it could have been filed before the High Court. Discouraging this tendency, the Supreme Court held in *P.N. Kumar* v. *MCD*[328] that in cases where writ can be filed before the High Court, parties should not approach the Supreme Court.

2.11 Power to grant remedial assistance is implicit in public law review

Under Article 32(1) of the Constitution, the court has the power to devise any procedure appropriate for the purpose of enforcing the fundamental rights under Article 32(2). The power of the court is, thus, not only injunctive in ambit to prevent the violation of fundamental rights, but is also remedial in scope to provide relief in case of breach of these rights. Thus, the court has implicit power to grant remedial assistance by way of compensation in such cases. However, this does not mean that in every case of breach of fundamental right, compensation can be awarded because Article 32 cannot be used as a substitute for the ordinary civil court process of compensation. An award of compensation must be confined to exceptional cases of gross and patent violations of fundamental rights. Such

325. (1986) 3 SCC 696.
326. *D.C. Saxena* v. *Chief Justice of India*, (1996) 5 SCC 216, *per* K. Ramaswamy J (N.P. Singh and Bharucha JJ, concurring).
327. *Vishnu Dev Sharma* v. *State of U.P.*, (2008) 3 SCC 172.
328. (1987) 4 SCC 609.

exceptional cases, though may not be defined with any exactitude, yet may include situations where either the fundamental rights of a large section of a society are involved, or the affected persons are not expected to pursue action in a civil court due to their socio-economic disadvantage. The same principle shall apply to High Courts also.[329]

Compensation granted by the Supreme Court and the High Court is in addition to the private law remedy for tortious action and punishment to wrongdoer under criminal law. An award of compensation in writ proceedings may be adjusted against damages awarded in civil suit. The old doctrine of relegating the aggrieved to the remedies available in civil law limits the role of the constitutional courts too much, as the protector and custodian of the indefeasible rights of citizens.[330]

2.12 Greater good of greater number

In a pace-setting decision, the Supreme Court held in *Sadhuram Bansal* v. *Pulin Behari Sarkar*[331] that in certain situations social justice must prevail over the technical rules. Thus, jurisprudence has shifted away from technical rules to the recognition of human beings as human beings because without this approach any science of law would become jejune. In this case, a residential complex which had been occupied by tenants had been sold by the owner to an outsider even when the persons who were actually living thereon were prepared to purchase even at a higher price. The court held that as between two parties if a deal is made with one party without serious detriment to the other, then the court would lean in favour of the weaker section of society. Thus, social justice as a recognition of the greater good of greater number, without the deprivation of any right of anybody, was established as a principle of public law review. It is with this spirit that writ jurisdiction was used for enforcing contractual obligations against the government.[332]

2.13 Compulsion of administrative expediency and the constraints of public law review

Today the government in any welfare state is the regulator and dispenser of special services and provider of a large number of benefits, including jobs, contracts, licences, quotas and various other benefits. In such a society, public law review of administrative action assumes a delicate position in view of the demands of administrative expediency and flexibility. The judicial behaviour in the immediate past has been lax, and the courts have

329. *M.C. Mehta* v. *Union of India*, (1987) 1 SCC 395.
330. *D.K. Basu* v. *State of W.B.*, (1997) 1 SCC 416; *Thirath Ram Saini* v. *State of Punjab*, (1997) 11 SCC 623.
331. (1984) 3 SCC 410. See also, *National Textile Workers' Union* v. *P.R. Ramakrishnan*, (1983) 3 SCC 105.
332. *M.S. Desai & Co.* v. *Hindustan Petroleum Corpn. Ltd.*, 1986 SCC OnLine Guj 73.

not confined their invigilation of administrative decisions to situations of arbitrariness and mala fide. It was for this reason that the highest Bench deprecated the practice of passing ex parte prohibitory orders just by mere asking even at the cost of public interest.[333]

In *R.D. Shetty*[334], Bhagwati J reiterated a well-settled rule of administrative law that an executive authority must be rigorously held to the standards by which it professes its action to be judged, and it must scrupulously observe those standards on pain of invalidation of an act in violation of them. Government actions must be informed with reasons and should be free from arbitrariness. It was a case where the International Airports Authority had given the contract, in exercise of its discretion, to a contractor who did not fulfil the prescribed qualification laid down for the tenderers. The court, though did not interfere with the decision of the authority on the ground of expediency, yet clearly laid down that the discretion of the government in giving contracts is not unlimited in that the government cannot give or withhold largesse in its arbitrary discretion. The government is still a government when it acts in the matters of granting largesse and it cannot act arbitrarily.

In *T.N. Education Deptt. Ministerial & General Subordinate Services Assn.* v. *State of T.N.*[335], the court refused to interfere in the administrative functioning of the State in the absence of arbitrariness or mala fides. The court held:

> All life, including administrative life, involves experiment, trial and error, but within the leading strings of fundamental rights, and, absent unconstitutional 'excesses', judicial correction is not right.[336] ...the court cannot substitute its wisdom for Government's, save to see that unreasonable perversity, mala fide manipulation, indefensible arbitrariness and like infirmities do not defile the equation for integration.[337]

This was a case where district board schools and government schools—and their services—were integrated. The basis of ratio for promotion and fixing of common seniority was assailed by the government wing as arbitrary, mala fide and capricious, but the court held, punctuated by the above remarks, that it was rational enough to warrant its non-interference.

In *State of Kerala* v. *T.P. Roshana*[338], Krishna Iyer J rightly observed that any incisive study of the exercise of the writ power in India may reveal that it limits its action to quashing or nullifying orders, but stops short of reconstruction whereby a valid scheme may replace a void project. This seems to be the most pragmatic approach in the area of public law review keeping in view the dictates of administrative expediency and flexibility.

333. *State of Rajasthan* v. *Swaika Properties*, (1985) 3 SCC 217.
334. (1979) 3 SCC 489.
335. (1980) 3 SCC 97.
336. *Ibid*, SCC 99, para. 7.
337. *Ibid*, SCC 100, para. 8.
338. (1979) 1 SCC 572.

Fact remains that in spite of all these problems, judiciary still remains the most dispassionate and trust worthy custodian that the system can afford to translate constitutional abstracts into constitutional commands and to represent public consciousness, public reason and constitutional vision.

2.14 Court does not sit as an appellate court while exercising power of review

The basic principle of judicial review is that it is only the decision-making process and not the merits of the decision which is reviewable unless the decision or action of the administrative authority is vitiated by arbitrariness, unfairness, illegality, irrationality, or when the decision is such that no reasonable person on proper application of mind could take such a decision. However, the court would not substitute its own opinion for that of experts.

In *Karpagam Faculty of Medical Sciences & Research* v. *Union of India*[339], the Supreme Court of India held that constitutional courts cannot sit over decisions of expert bodies as a court of appeal. Courts should show deference and consideration to recommendations of Expert Committee in absence of any allegations pertaining to malice or arbitrariness in decision-making.[340] In academic matters, unless there is a clear violation of statutory provisions, regulations or notification issued, the court should not interfere since those issues fall within the domain of experts.[341]

It is a settled law that fixing of pay scale should be left to an expert body like the Pay Commission or other similar body; however, in *Yashwant Sinha* v. *CBI*[342], the court held that debate and expert opinion is envisaged as part of the decision-making process. Final decision always vests with competent authority. If every different opinion were to be treated as requiring compliance prior to execution of a contract, that would defeat the very purpose of debate in the decision-making process.

In *Tata Cellular* v. *Union of India*[343], the Supreme Court observed that judicial review is concerned with reviewing not the merits of the decision but the decision-making process itself. It is thus different from an appeal. While hearing an appeal, the court is concerned with the merits of the decision, but in judicial review the court is basically concerned with the decision-making process because, even otherwise, the court is hardly equipped to review the merits of the decision. The court rightly remarked that it is not the function of the court to act as a superboard, or with the zeal of a pedantic schoolmaster, substituting its judgment for that of the administrator.

339. (2017) 16 SCC 568.
340. *UPSC* v. *M. Sathiya Priya*, (2018) 15 SCC 796.
341. *Karpagam Faculty of Medical Sciences & Research* v. *Union of India*, (2017) 16 SCC 568; *UPSC* v. *M. Sathiya Priya*, (2018) 15 SCC 796.
342. (2020) 2 SCC 338.
343. (1994) 6 SCC 651.

Following the same principle, the Supreme Court in *United Commercial Bank* v. *P.C. Kakkar*[344] held that court should not interfere with administrator's decision unless it is illogical, or suffers from procedural impropriety, or was shocking to the conscience of the court in the sense that it was in defiance of logic or moral standards (Wednesbury principle). The court would not go into the correctness of the choice made by the administrator and will not substitute its decision to that of the administrator. The scope of judicial review is limited to the deficiency of the decision-making process and not the decision.

The duty of the court in exercising the power of judicial review is thus to confine itself to the following questions:[345]

(1) Whether a decision-making authority exceeded its powers?
(2) Whether the authority has committed an error of law?
(3) Whether the authority has committed a breach of the principles of natural justice?
(4) Whether the authority has reached a decision which no reasonable person would have reached?
(5) Whether the authority has abused its powers?

The power of judicial review is not directed against the decision but is confined to the decision-making process.[346] Therefore, courts generally do not appreciate evidences, or enter into determination of questions, which demand elaborate examination of evidences, or interfere in the punishment imposed unless the administrative decision is mala fide, or made in contravention of the principles of natural justice or in violation of any constitutional provision, or is such which shocks the conscience of the court.[347]

Thus, the judicial review of administrative actions can be exercised on the following grounds:

(1) *Illegality*: This means that the decision-maker must correctly understand the law that regulates his decision-making power and must give effect to it.
(2) *Irrationality*: This means that the decision is so outrageous in its defiance of logic or accepted moral standards that no sensible person could have arrived at such a decision.
(3) *Procedural impropriety*: This means that the procedure for taking an administrative decision and action must be fair, reasonable and just.
(4) *Proportionality*: This means that in any administrative decision and action, the end and means relationship must be rational.
(5) *Unreasonableness*: This means that either the facts do not warrant the conclusion reached by the authority or the decision is partial and unequal in its operation.

344. (2003) 4 SCC 364.
345. (1994) 6 SCC 651, 676.
346. *HUDA* v. *Roochira Ceramics*, (1996) 6 SCC 584.
347. *B.C. Chaturvedi* v. *Union of India*, (1995) 6 SCC 749.

Thus, the modern trend in the area of judicial review is towards judicial restraint.[348] Against this backdrop, the policy decision of the government is not the subject of judicial review unless it is unreasonable or against public interest.[349]

2.15 Allied principles of judicial review

1. *Principle of comity.*—Even in the face of doctrine of separation of powers if all the organs of the State do not function in a spirit of mutuality and coordination, public good cannot be served in any constitutional democracy. This principle requires that all authorities of State must support the functions of each other necessary to enable authorities to discharge their functions in a responsible manner as per the norms and values of the Constitution. Each organ of State and authority must show respect to the other in a manner as not to disable the other from discharging its functions which under law it is expected to undertake in a responsible manner. Thus, the most vexing question of judicial review has been: How to control the actions of the administrative authorities and impose rule of law without damaging their capacity to do their work effectively which under the law they are mandated to do? The principle of comity thus validates balancing of constitutionalism with pragmatism.

2. *Principle of subsidiarity.*—This principle signifies that the public functions and powers must be exercised at a level where it can be undertaken more appropriately in a responsible manner. For the exercise of the power of judicial review it may be a principle of judicial self-restraint and justiciability. Political questions can be better decided by the political branches of the State. All policy matters can be better decided by the legislative branch of the State. Matters judicial in nature can be better decided by the judiciary. The principle behind the doctrine is that government functions can be better exercised if assigned at a level nearer to the lifeline of the people. This will ensure better effectiveness, efficiency and accountability. In this manner subsidiarity as a principle of allocating power must guide the courts in exercising power of judicial review of administrative action.

3. *Principle of contextuality.*—"In law context is everything" is the most fundamental principle of administrative law. In many situations generality of law falter before the specifics of life. Therefore, unless law takes into account the context in which it is to be applied, it cannot do justice and cannot fulfil its role as an instrument of social engineering in society. Consequently, the validity of an administrative action should be judged against the backdrop of context which may include:

(*a*) The nature of authority to which powers have been delegated. If the administrative authority is a representative and responsible body, it

348. *Tata Cellular* v. *Union of India*, (1994) 6 SCC 651, 677–78.
349. *State of U.P.* v. *U.P. University Colleges Pensioners' Assn.*, (1994) 2 SCC 729.

can be trusted for the exercise of discretionary powers and court in such a case may not apply strict scrutiny test.

(*b*) Nature and extent of powers exercised.

(*c*) Procedure and process which the administrative authority follows.

(*d*) Express and implied limits within which the authority is to exercise powers.

(*e*) Impact on the constituency of people to which the action applies.

(*f*) Danger and cost to the administrative framework and processes.

The principle of contextual pragmatism makes administrative law complex but enhances its justice delivery potentialities.

4. *Principles of proportionality.*—It is a civil law doctrine which is now creeping into common-law jurisdiction replacing Wednesbury doctrine of unreasonableness. In the application of the doctrine court examines whether burden imposed by law is too burdensome to be disproportionate. Court will exercise the power of judicial review to examine whether there is a proportion/balance between the limitation on the right and the legitimate end sought to be achieved. Thus, "proportionality" is a three-step check applied by the court while reviewing any law or administrative action.

(*a*) *Means check*: that the means adopted by the administrative authority are within its power and are least burdensome besides being rationally connected to the end.

(*b*) *End check*: that end to be achieved is legitimate and within the power of the authority.

(*c*) *Proportion or balance check*: that there is a balance between means and ends. Balancing is a difficult task as ground realities and value priorities cannot be ignored.

2.16 Administrative policy decisions

Unless government's policy decisions are contrary to any statutory or constitutional provision, court shall not interfere with it. It is not for the courts, opined the Supreme Court, to consider the relative merit of the policy and to strike it down merely on the ground that another policy would have been fairer and better. It is the prerogative of the administration. The administration has, while taking decision, right to "trial and error" as long as both trial and error are bona fide and within the limits of authority. For testing the correctness of a policy, appropriate forum is Parliament and not the courts. Therefore, the courts are very circumspect in conducting an enquiry into policy statements of the government and most reluctant to impugn the judgment of the experts unless there is an illegality in it.[350]

Applying the same principle, the court in *Aruna Roy* v. *Union of India*[351] held that it is for Parliament to take a decision on a national education

350. *BALCO Employees' Union* v. *Union of India*, (2002) 2 SCC 333.

351. (2002) 7 SCC 368.

policy one way or the other, court cannot take a decision on the good or bad points of an educational policy. Court can intervene in the implementation of policy only if it is against any statute or the Constitution.

Applying the same principle in *Directorate of Film Festivals* v. *Gaurav Ashwin Jain*[352], the court held that if the government adopts different policies to different situations to produce different results or objective, it is not discriminatory. Thus, the exclusion of judicial review in policy matters is not total but is restricted to situations where there is a violation of fundamental rights, or of any provision of the Constitution, or the basic structure of the Constitution, or of any statutory provision, or where the policy is manifestly arbitrary. Court cannot interfere with a policy either on the ground that it is erroneous or on the ground that a better, fairer or wiser alternative was available. Legality of the policy, and not the wisdom or soundness of the policy, is the subject of judicial review.[353]

Though court cannot make a policy for the government, yet it can bring to its notice issues of concerns involving public interest where situation so demands. In *Mohd. Abdul Kadir* v. *DG of Police*[354], the policy matter involved was regularisation of ad hoc employees working for a long period without increment and retiral benefit. The court did not pass regularisation orders, however, brought to the notice of the government the need for justice in such a case.

However, in *Mansukhbhai Dhamjibhai Patel* v. *State of Gujarat*[355], the Supreme Court held that Gujarat State Government Policy for regrant of land already acquired under the Land Acquisition Act, 1894 is in violation of settled law as consistently held by the Supreme Court for violation of the principles enshrined in Article 14 of the Constitution.

In conclusion the Supreme Court opined that where policy is contrary to law or is in violation of constitutional provisions, or is arbitrary or irrational, the same may be struck down by the court in exercise of its power of judicial review. Applying this principle the court held that Kramonnati Scheme which had granted benefit of two higher pay scales to all government servants first after completing 12 years of service and second after completing another 12 years of service but denied this benefit to teachers is discriminatory violating Articles 14 and 16 of the Constitution. Moving further the court held that fixation of 1 August 2003 as date for granting benefit, without any justiciable basis, is arbitrary since many employees have completed 24 years of service in 1999.[356]

Courts can interfere only where policy framed is absolutely capricious, not informed by reasons or is mala fide or totally arbitrary offending

352. (2007) 4 SCC 737. See also, *BALCO Employees' Union* v. *Union of India*, (2002) 2 SCC 333.
353. *Ibid.*
354. (2009) 6 SCC 611.
355. (2018) 2 SCC 642.
356. *State of M.P.* v. *Mala Banerjee*, (2015) 7 SCC 698. See also, *Federation of Railway Officers Assn.* v. *Union of India*, (2003) 4 SCC 289.

Article 14 or any other provisions of the Constitution.[357] The Supreme Court reiterated the same principle of judicial review in *Union of India* v. *M. Selvakumar*[358]. In this case, the challenge before the court was on the ground that since attempts for physically handicapped candidates belonging to General category was increased from 4 to 7 for the Civil Services Examination, there should be a proximate increase in attempts to be taken by physically handicapped candidates belonging to the OBC category. The Supreme Court held that the horizontal reservations and relaxation for physically handicapped category candidates for Civil Services Examination is a matter of governmental policy and it is not in the domain of the court to enquire as to whether a particular policy is wise and acceptable or whether a better policy could be evolved. The court can only interfere if the policy framed is absolutely capricious and non-informed by reasons or totally arbitrary offending the requirement of Article 14 of the Constitution.

An administrative policy is not a no-go area for the court, however, courts have acted with self-restraint in order to balance majoritarian impulse with individual rights by applying the proportionality principle. Nevertheless, courts put administrative policy to a more rigorous scrutiny than the legislative policy.

In this manner, it is the legality of the policy and not the wisdom or advisability or soundness of policy which is the subject-matter of judicial review.

2.17 Curative petitions

In innovating and developing constitutional jurisprudence, the role of the Supreme Court has always been unique. One such example can be the innovation of the concept of curative petition. It was observed that a tendency is growing to challenge under Article 32 of the Constitution final judgments or orders of the court after dismissal of review petitions. The reason for such an unhealthy and unconstitutional practice was the absence of a forum where the petitioners could seek relief. The Constitution Bench in *Rupa Ashok Hurra* v. *Ashok Hurra*[359] (*Rupa Ashok Hurra*) struck a balance between the finality or certainty of the judgments or orders of the Supreme Court, as a court of last resort, and setting right miscarriage of justice complained of by holding that a petition under Article 32 would not be maintainable to challenge or quash the final order contained in the judgment or order of the Supreme Court. However, if there is an apparent miscarriage of justice, a petitioner can approach the court through a curative petition. The petitioner will be entitled to relief *ex debito justitiae* if

357. *Essar Steel Ltd.* v. *Union of India*, (2016) 11 SCC 1.

358. (2017) 3 SCC 504. See also, *Mansukhbhai Dhamjibhai Patel* v. *State of Gujarat*, (2018) 2 SCC 642.

359. (2002) 4 SCC 388; *Naresh Kumar* v. *Union of India*, (2004) 4 SCC 540; *Sidram S. Patil* v. *Gurunath Shivappa Patil*, (2005) 2 SCC 358.

he is able to establish 1) violation of the principles of natural justice in that he was not a party to the dispute, but the judgment or order affected his interests, or even when he was a party to the dispute the matter proceeded as if he had the notice, though he was not served with the notice of the proceedings; 2) that the judge in the proceedings failed to disclose his connection with the subject-matter or the parties, giving scope for an apprehension of bias, and the judgment had adversely affected the petitioner; or 3) an abuse of court process.

Explaining the scope of curative petitions in *Sanjay Singh* v. *U.P. Public Service Commission*[360], the Supreme Court clarified that the decision of *Rupa Ashok Hurra* does not lay down that the ratio decidendi of any earlier decision cannot be re-examined or differed in another case. In this case, the petitioner did not seek to upset the order of the Supreme Court given in *U.P. Public Services Commission* v. *Subhash Chandra Dixit*[361], he simply wanted the court to re-examine the decision regarding scaling of marks in written examination which required reconsideration. The court held that it is a case neither for review under Article 137 of the Constitution nor for setting aside any previous order of the Supreme Court, hence a writ is maintainable. Explaining the matter further, the court observed that where any violation of fundamental right is involved in a petition under Article 32, it cannot be dismissed merely because it seeks to distinguish or challenge the ratio of an earlier judgment. Any curative petition must be certified by a Senior Advocate and circulated to the Bench of three seniormost judges of the Supreme Court and the judge who passed the orders. The petition will be heard if the majority agrees to hear it. Exemplary costs may be imposed if the petition is found to be vexatious.

2.18 Continuous mandamus

Another innovation within the area of judicial review is the concept of continuous mandamus. This concept was developed by the Supreme Court so that it could oversee the implementation of its directions to the administrative authorities, which at times is necessary—especially, where fundamental rights of the people are involved because contempt proceedings are technical and time-consuming. In *Prakash Singh* v. *Union of India*[362], the Supreme Court gave detailed directions to the Central and State Governments to take time-bound measures to insulate police machinery from political or executive interference to make police force more efficient and effective, necessary to strengthen and preserve the rule of law and to protect the human rights of the people. The directions were not operationalised by all within the time prescribed on the ground that the directions were merely recommendatory. The Supreme Court clarified that

360. (2007) 3 SCC 720.
361. (2003) 12 SCC 701.
362. (2006) 8 SCC 1.

it can give binding directions under Article 32 read with Article 142 of the Constitution and thus, mandamus issued in the case was continuous. This innovation would infuse an element of responsibility and fairness in the administration. Certainly, constitutional adjudication is different from any other adjudication. There is a moral dimension to every major constitutional issue. The language of the text is not necessarily a controlling factor. The Constitution works because of its generalities and creativity of the judges who interpret it. The court observed that fundamental rights of the people are not only to be protected by the State, they should be facilitated by it. The basic purpose of this innovation is to monitor the progress of court directive implementation, so that the court can keep a watch, ensuring continuance of investigation and compliance.

2.19 Finality of administrative action

The subject of administrative finality is extremely complex with intricate ramifications because courts very often shift their positions. The grasp of general principles may be simple, yet their application to a particular situation demands flexibility and subtlety.

Students of administrative law fear not so much the fact of the growing powers of administration as that of the powers assuming a finality. Generally, a clause is inserted in the statute by which the actions of an administrative authority is made final. Such a clause may be given various names, *i.e.* finality clause, private clause, exclusion clause, ouster clause, conclusive clause.

2.19.1 *Modes of conferring finality*

No specific generalisation is possible as to the manner in which administrative actions are made final. However, there may be five usual modes of conferring finality on any administrative action:

(1) Sometimes, the finality clause in a statute may make the administrative action final by expressly barring the jurisdiction of the court. For example, Section 2 of the Foreigners Act, 1946 provides that the administrative actions taken under this Act "shall not be called in question in any legal proceeding before any court of law".
(2) Sometimes, the finality clause does not expressly bar the jurisdiction of the court, but otherwise makes the administrative action final. For example, Section 17(2) of the Industrial Disputes Act, 1947 provides that "the actions of the administrative authority shall be final".
(3) Sometimes, the statute neither expressly bars the jurisdiction of courts nor confers finality on the administrative action, yet the finality of the administrative action may be inferred by necessary implication. Such an inference may be drawn when the statute is a self-contained code

which gives a right and also provides a machinery for the vindication of such right.

(4) Inference of finality may also be drawn if the power of the authority to take certain action is rendered in subjective terms. For example, if the authority is "satisfied" or the action is "desirable" or if it appears "necessary", "expedient", etc., to that authority that such action should be taken. However, leaving aside emergency situations, courts have indicated that the authority's own declaration about the "satisfaction", "necessity" or "expediency" is not conclusive.[363]

(5) Yet there may be another category of finality clause. An Act may provide a certain time-limit within which an administrative action can be challenged in court and after the lapse of that period, the action becomes final. Housing Acts in England contain a proviso that a person aggrieved by the order may question its validity within six weeks and unless it is so challenged, the "order shall not be questioned in any legal proceedings whatsoever". In such cases, the court has asserted that the statutory period for judicial review cannot be a rule of absolute limitation, but it is certainly a rule of discretion and in appropriate cases, the court can interfere even after the lapse of six weeks.[364]

2.19.2 *Finality clause and the power of judicial review*

The question of conferring finality on administrative actions in India can be conveniently studied under the following headings:

(1) Constitutional modes of judicial review and administrative finality.
(2) Non-constitutional modes of judicial review and administrative finality.

Constitutional modes of judicial review and administrative finality.—No finality clause contained in any statute and expressed in any language can bar the judicial review available under Articles 32, 226, 337 and 136 of the Constitution. In *Deokinandan Prasad* v. *State of Bihar*[365], the Supreme Court held that Section 23 of the Pension Act, 1871, which provided that suits relating to matters mentioned therein cannot be entertained in any court, does not bar the constitutional modes of judicial review. In the same manner, the Andhra Pradesh High Court quashed Section 6(*a*) of the A.P.

363. *Earl Fitzwilliam's Wentworth Estates Co. Ltd.* v. *Minister of Town and Country Planning*, (1951) 2 KB 284 (CA).

364. *Ashbridge Investments Ltd.* v. *Minister of Housing and Local Govt.*, (1965) 1 WLR 1320 (CA). This overrules *Smith* v. *East Elloe Rural District Council*, 1956 AC 736: (1956) 2 WLR 888 (HL) where it was held that after six weeks, order becomes conclusive.

365. (1971) 2 SCC 330. See also, *Durga Shankar Mehta* v. *Raghuraj Singh*, AIR 1954 SC 520, wherein the Supreme Court held that S. 105 of the Representation of the People Act, 1951 which made every order of the Election Tribunal final and conclusive does not bar constitutional modes of judicial review.

Preventive Detention Act, 1970, which provided that the order of detention would not be invalidated on the ground that it contained some vague and irrelevant grounds, as violative of Article 22(5) of the Constitution.[366]

Even in cases where the Constitution itself makes the action of an administrative authority final, the constitutional modes of judicial review cannot be barred by any necessary implication. In *Union of India* v. *Jyoti Prakash Mitter*[367], the Supreme Court held that even in the face of Article 217(3) of the Constitution which makes the order of the President final, in cases of dispute relating to the age of a judge, the constitutional mode of judicial review is not barred.

Sticking to the same kind of judicial behaviour, the Supreme Court again held in *Indira Nehru Gandhi* v. *Raj Narain*[368] that clause (4) of Article 329-A, inserted by the Constitution (39th Amendment) Act, 1975, which frees the disputed election of the Prime Minister and the Speaker from the restraints of all election laws, does not bar the constitutional modes of judicial review. In *Satyavir Singh* v. *Union of India*[369] also the Supreme Court held that Article 311(3) of the Constitution which makes the decision of the government on question whether it is impracticable to hold an enquiry against a government servant before a disciplinary action as final, is not so final that the court cannot do anything. Therefore, even in the face of finality clause of Article 311(3), court can still consider whether the power has been properly exercised. Similarly, the Supreme Court, while upholding the validity of the Constitution (52nd Amendment) Act, 1985, popularly known as the anti-defection law, held that clause (7), which has taken away the power of judicial review of the courts by making the actions taken by the Speaker under the Act as final, shall not take away the writ jurisdiction of the High Courts and the Supreme Court.[370] Clause (7) provided that "no court shall have jurisdiction in respect of any matter connected with the disqualification of any member of a House under the Tenth Schedule notwithstanding anything in the Constitution".

Non-constitutional modes of judicial review and administrative finality.—The non-constitutional mode of judicial review is exercised by the civil courts. Section 9 of the Civil Procedure Code, 1908 (CPC), lays down that courts shall have jurisdiction to try all suits of a civil nature excepting suits of which their cognizance is barred either expressly or by necessary implication.

The approach of the court in cases of express exclusion of the jurisdiction of the civil courts has been to strictly interpret the clause and if the words are clear and the statute is a self-contained code, to refrain from

366. ILR 1972 AP 1025.
367. (1971) 1 SCC 396. See also, *Election Commission* v. *Saka Venkata Subba Rao*, AIR 1953 SC 210.
368. 1975 Supp SCC 1.
369. (1985) 4 SCC 252.
370. *Kihoto Hollohan* v. *Zachillhu*, 1992 Supp (2) SCC 651.

exercising jurisdiction. In *Firm of Illuri Subbayya Chetty & Sons* v. *State of A.P.*[371], the Supreme Court held that Section 18-A of the Madras General Sales Tax Act, 1939, which provided that no suit can be instituted in any civil court to set aside or modify the assessment made under the Act, does bar the jurisdiction of the civil court. In this case, a suit had been filed in a civil court on the ground that the administrative authority instead of taxing sale has taxed purchases also. However, in *Provincial Govt. of Madras* v. *J.S. Basappa*[372], Hidayatullah J took a contrary view on more or less similar facts, and held that the word "final" means final for the purpose of the Act only. But this view of the court was soon reversed in *State of Kerala* v. *N. Ramaswami Iyer & Sons*[373], and the Supreme Court held that the finality clause contained in Kerala Sales Tax Act, 1963 bars the jurisdiction of the civil courts in entertaining any suit for the recovery of excess tax collected by the sales tax authority.

Judicial behaviour became still more explicit in *Ram Singh* v. *Gram Panchayat Mehal Kalan*[374], when the Supreme Court held that Section 13 of the Punjab Village Common Lands (Regulation) Act, 1961, which barred the jurisdiction of the civil court in question whether a property is for common purpose of the village, is final and the civil court cannot interfere with the decision of the Collector on this point. The Supreme Court further emphasised that when the jurisdiction of the civil court is expressly excluded, the plaintiff cannot be allowed to circumvent that provision by means of clever drafting of pleadings.

The implied exclusion of the jurisdiction of the civil courts may be inferred if the statute containing finality clause is a self-contained code. The inference of implied exclusion may also be drawn when the action is left to the subjective satisfaction of the administrative authority by using such words as "if satisfied" or "if in the opinion of the administrative authority it is just and proper". In view of such an implied exclusion, if the civil courts decline jurisdiction, it may be a case of self-limitation and not inherent lack of power. However, if the statute creates a new right and also provides a machinery for the vindication of such right, the jurisdiction of the civil court shall be deemed to have been barred by necessary implication. Generally speaking, the broad guiding considerations in such situations are: whenever a right not pre-existing at common law is created by a statute, and whether the statute itself provides a machinery for the enforcement of that right; then even in the absence of an exclusionary provision, the civil court's jurisdiction is impliedly barred. If, however, a pre-existing right in common law is recognised by the statute and a new statutory remedy for its enforcement is provided, without expressly excluding the

371. AIR 1964 SC 322. See also, *Secy. of State* v. *Mask & Co.*, 1940 SCC OnLine PC 10: AIR 1940 PC 105.
372. AIR 1964 SC 1873.
373. AIR 1966 SC 1738. See also, *Kamala Mills Ltd.* v. *State of Bombay*, AIR 1965 SC 1942.
374. (1986) 4 SCC 364; See also, *Anwar* v. *ADJ, Bulandshahr*, (1986) 4 SCC 21.

jurisdiction of the civil court, then both the common-law and statutory remedies might become concurrent leaving open an element of election to the plaintiff.[375] In *Premier Automobiles Ltd.* v. *Kamlekar Shantaram Wadke*[376], the Supreme Court held that the jurisdiction is impliedly barred as the Industrial Disputes Act, 1947 is a self-contained code. The facts of this case were that in Premier Automobiles Ltd., there were two unions: the Sabha Union and the Association Union. There were some employees who were not members of either. On 31 December 1966, under the incentive scheme, an agreement was entered into between the Sabha Union and the company which applied to its members and others who opted for it. Later on, because of the increase in the membership of the Association Union, the company entered into a fresh agreement with it overruling the Sabha agreement; hence the dispute. The court below and the High Court granted the request for injunction, restraining the company from giving effect to the later agreement, on the ground that it is a dispute which arises under the common law and the law of contract, as it relates to the conditions of service. On appeal, the Supreme Court held that the jurisdiction of the civil court is impliedly barred, as the Industrial Disputes Act, 1947 is a self-contained code and the subject-matter could form an industrial dispute where the remedy lies under the Industrial Disputes Act, 1947.

The same stand was taken by the Supreme Court in *Upadhyaya Hargovind Devshanker* v. *Dhirendrasinh Virbhadrasinhji Solanki*[377]. The Representation of the People Act, 1951 as amended by the Amendment Act, 1966 is a self-contained code. Under Section 80-A of the Act, election petitions are to be decided by any Single Judge of the High Court as designated by the Chief Justice. The decision of the Single Judge has been made appealable to the Supreme Court. There is no provision for appeal against interlocutory orders. Therefore, in view of the fact that the Representation of the People Act, 1951 is a self-contained code, the Supreme Court held that no appeal shall lie to the Division Bench against the decision of the Single Judge, where such appeal is available under the Letters Patent provisions and no other judge of the High Court can hear the election petition except the one designated by the Chief Justice.

However, the law relating to administrative finality as discussed above does not cover the cases of ultra vires acts of the administrative authority, or the unconstitutionality of law under which the authority exercises power. The finality clause does not bar the jurisdiction of the courts if an action is ultra vires the powers of the administrative authority. In *Munni*

---

375. *Raja Ram Kumar Bhargava* v. *Union of India*, (1988) 1 SCC 681.

376. (1976) 1 SCC 496.

377. (1988) 2 SCC 1. See also, *Chhotalal Jivabhai Patel* v. *Vadilal Lallubhai Mehta*, (1971) 12 GLR 850; *Kadiravan* v. *B. Thirumalaikumar*, ILR (1970) 2 Mad 183; *Laxmi Narayan Nayak* v. *Ramratan Chaturvedi*, 1985 SCC OnLine MP 156: AIR 1986 MP 165 overruled. *Siaram* v. *Nathuram*, 1967 SCC OnLine All 107: 1968 All LJ 576; *Ramdhan* v. *Bhanwar Lal*, 1983 SCC OnLine Raj 32: AIR 1985 Raj 185, upheld.

Devi v. *Gokal Chand*[378], the Supreme Court held that the U.P. (Temporary Control of Rent and Eviction) Act, 1947, which gives power to the District Magistrate to allot a vacant shop and also makes the decision of the District Magistrate final, does not bar the jurisdiction of the court in cases where the authority commits a jurisdictional error and allots a shop which is not vacant. Therefore, not only in the cases of substantive ultra vires but in cases of procedural ultra vires also, the finality clause is not final. In *Pabbojan Tea Co. Ltd.* v. *Commr.*[379], the Supreme Court held that the finality clause as laid down under Section 24 of the Minimum Wages Act, 1941 does not bar jurisdiction of the civil courts, if the authority has violated the mandatory procedure of hearing before fixing the minimum wages for the tea plant workers. Similarly, in *Shiv Kumar Chadha* v. *MCD*[380], the Supreme Court held Section 347-E of the Delhi Municipal Corporation Act, 1957, which bars the jurisdiction of the civil court in cases of demolition of unauthorised structures, does not oust the court's jurisdiction to go into the question whether the order was a nullity being vitiated by a jurisdictional error.

In the same manner, it is also not the implication of the finality clause that void laws be enforced without a remedy. This view was expressed by the Supreme Court in *Dhulabhai* v. *State of M.P.*[381] (*Dhulabhai*). In this case, certain notifications issued by the government under the Madhya Bharat Sales Tax Act, 1950 were declared ultra vires Article 301 of the Constitution. Thereafter, a suit was filed for the recovery of tax charged under these unconstitutional notifications. Section 17 of the Act contained a finality clause which provided that the orders made under the Act shall not be called in question in any court. The Supreme Court, upholding the maintainability of the civil suit in the face of the finality clause, held that it is not the implication of the finality clause that void laws be enforced without any remedy.

Reiterating the propositions laid down in *Dhulabhai* by Hidayatullah CJ, the Supreme Court in *Mohd. Baquir El-Edroos* v. *State of Gujarat*[382] held that Section 2(1)(*e*) of the Explanation of the Bombay Personal Inams Abolition Act, 1952, which provides that if any question arises whether any grant is an inam, such question shall be referred to the State Government and the decision of the State Government shall be final, cannot exclude the jurisdiction of the civil court. Explaining the reasons, the court observed that the Act does not give any detail about the reference and to the enquiry

---

378. (1969) 2 SCC 879.
379. AIR 1968 SC 271.
380. (1993) 3 SCC 161. See also, *Kihoto Hollohan* v. *Zachillhu*, 1992 Supp (2) SCC 651. Court held that the finality clause under the anti-defection law does not bar judicial review of actions falling outside the jurisdiction of the authority.
381. AIR 1969 SC 78. See also, *K.S. Venkataraman & Co. (P) Ltd.* v. *State of Madras*, AIR 1966 SC 1089 in which *Raleigh Investment Co. Ltd.* v. *Governor General in Council*, 1947 SCC OnLine FC 7: AIR 1947 PC 78 was overruled.
382. (1981) 4 SCC 383.

by the government, and no appeal has been provided for, hence it cannot be said that the case of the plaintiff has been considered by the government in the same way as it would have been considered if the case had been filed before a civil court. Accepting the first proposition of *Dhulabhai,* the court further held that where a statute gives a finality to the orders of the special tribunal, the civil court's jurisdiction shall be excluded "if there is adequate remedy to do what the civil courts would normally do in a suit"[383]. The highest Bench also found that the second proposition of *Dhulabhai,* which provides that "where there is an express bar to the jurisdiction of the court", "an examination of the scheme of the particular Act to find out the adequacy or the sufficiency of the remedies provided may be relevant", is not attracted in the instant case because the Act does not lay down the detailed procedure to be followed by the State Government, and there is no detailed procedure for appeal and revision also. Therefore, the court concluded that the "finality clause" in Section 2(1)(*e*) does not bar the jurisdiction of the civil court.

The declaration by the President of India under Articles 341 and 342 of the Constitution, with respect to the lists of Scheduled Castes and Scheduled Tribes in relation to a State, was held by the court to be conclusive subject to the amendment by Parliament. Thus, by necessary implication, the jurisdiction of the civil court to take cognizance and give a declaration stands prohibited.[384]

Exclusion of the civil court's jurisdiction cannot be readily inferred on ground of availability of remedy and the forum under special acts, when the action in question is taken without complying with the provisions of the Act. Where the high-power transmission line was taken over the property of the respondent without his consent, it was argued that the civil court's jurisdiction is barred as a statutory remedy under the Electricity Act, 1910 is available. The court held that laying transmission line without the consent of the respondent and without any approved scheme cannot be treated in accordance with the provisions of the Act and, hence, the jurisdiction of the civil court is not barred.[385] The finality clause providing for the exclusion of court's jurisdiction cannot be provided by the rules framed by the administrative authority. Where the rules framed under the Electricity (Supply) Act, 1948 provided for the exclusion of the jurisdiction of the court, it was accepted that this cannot bar the jurisdiction of the civil court to entertain a suit and consider the validity of the orders passed by the Board against consumers.[386]

383. M.P Jain, "Judicial Response to Privative Clauses in India", (1980) 22 JILI, 6–10. *See also,* M.P. Jain, "Administrative Law", (1981) 17 ASIL 517–18.
384. *State of T.N.* v. *A. Gurusamy,* (1997) 3 SCC 542.
385. *M.P. Electricity Board* v. *Vijaya Timber Co.,* (1997) 1 SCC 68.
386. *Hyderabad Vanaspathi Ltd.* v. *A.P. SEB,* (1998) 4 SCC 470.

2.20 Comparative study: The position regarding ouster or finality

In England where Parliament is supreme and can exclude judicial review of any administrative action, the attitude of courts in the 19th century was to accept the finality clause as final. In *Institute of Patent Agents* v. *Joseph Lockwood*[387], the House of Lords interpreted the finality clause "as contained in this Act" to mean that the jurisdiction of the court is barred. However, as courts jealously guard their jurisdiction, the Lockwood doctrine was overruled in *Minister of Health* v. *R., ex p Yaffe*[388]. Interpreting a finality clause couched in similar language, the court held that it can still scrutinise whether the subordinate legislation conflicts with the parent Act, or whether the procedural requirements have been complied with. The tool which the court may wield to get around the finality clause is the interpretation of the clause in such a manner as not to exclude the power of the court where it is so possible without offending the canons of interpretation.

This judicial behaviour in the face of parliamentary sovereignty created controversy in England, resulting in the inclusion of this question in the terms of reference of the Franks Committee. This Committee recommended that in cases involving jurisdictional facts and in cases where appeal on the point of law is not provided, the power of judicial review should not be excluded. On this recommendation, Section 11(1) was inserted in the Tribunals and Inquiries Act, 1958 which provided that any finality clause in any statute passed before 1958 shall not exclude judicial review.

Therefore, in England, there cannot be finality in cases of ultra vires actions of the administrative authority. *Anisminic Ltd.* v. *Foreign Compensation Commission*[389] (*Anisminic*) is a pace-setter for judicial behaviour in this direction. In this case, following the Suez crisis, the Egyptian government took over British companies and signed a treaty in which the Egyptian government made available a certain amount of money to the British government for distribution amongst the companies. The names of the companies were given in the treaty and included the name of the appellant-company. This amount was made over to the Foreign Compensation Commission constituted under the Foreign Compensation Act, 1950. Section 4 of the Act contained a finality clause to the effect that the decisions of the Commission shall not be called in question in any court. The claim of Anisminic Ltd. was rejected on the ground that they had transferred their interest to an Egyptian company. Under the Act, the Commission had no power to decide the question of entitlement to compensation. The court held that since the Commission had committed an error of jurisdiction in determining an issue which was outside its jurisdiction, the jurisdiction of the court was not barred. As the distinction

387. 1894 AC 347 (HL).
388. 1931 AC 347 (HL).
389. (1969) 2 AC 147: (1969) 2 WLR 163 (HL). The principle laid down in this case was followed in *S.E. Asia Fire Bricks* v. *Non-Metallic Mineral Products Mfg. Employees Union*, 1981 AC 363 (PC).

between an error of jurisdiction and an error within jurisdiction is not very clear, the decision in *Anisminic*[390] makes the judicial review broad-based even in the face of a clear finality clause. Therefore, even if the constitutionality of an Act of Parliament cannot be questioned by courts, the courts can still enquire as to what Parliament intended in passing the impugned provision, or whether there was any abuse of power conferred by Parliament, or whether the rules of natural justice were observed by the authority, or whether the authority acted within or in excess of jurisdiction.[391]

Another technique of giving finality to an administrative action used in England was to confer power on administrative authorities in "subjective terms". For example, the use of words like "when they are satisfied" or "as they deem it fit and proper", etc. gave the administrative authority absolute discretion in the exercise of their power. This technique was used in England to meet the conditions created by wars. However, even in the face of absolute subjective discretion conferred by Parliament on administrative authorities, courts consistently held that the discretionary powers must be exercised judiciously, and that if the power is exercised in bad faith then courts will exercise the power of judicial review.[392] Thus, even in England where Parliament is supreme, "finality" is not absolutely final.

Under the French Constitution, Parliament is supreme. Courts have no power to declare the law of Parliament unconstitutional in the popular sense, though constitutional council exercises pre-promulgation review. It may follow, therefore, that the finality clause in any French statute would oust the jurisdiction of the court. However, it is heartening to note that French courts have never accepted this position, and there is no instance in French legal history of a successful exclusion of judicial review, though it still remains a theoretical possibility. In Lamotte (17 February 1950), power was given to an administrative officer to requisition and bring into cultivation any farmland which is abandoned or uncultivated for more than two years. The statute contained a finality clause to the effect that the action of the administrator cannot be the object of any administrative or judicial proceedings. The Conseil d'Etat held that this does not bar judicial review in cases of excess of jurisdiction.[393]

There is no denying the fact that in the area of administrative finality, courts hold a very delicate balance between power and liberty in a modern form of government. Therefore, a trend in judicial behaviour which regards "finality" and "judicial review" as complementary and not contradictory is a welcome sign.

In the US, the right to judicial review, which is grounded both in "due process" and the constitutional position of judicial power, cannot be taken

390. (1969) 2 AC 147: (1969) 2 WLR 163 (HL).
391. *See*, C.K. Thakker, *Administrative Law* (Eastern Book Company 1992) 259.
392. *Robinson* v. *Minister of Town and Country Planning*, 1947 KB 702 (CA). *See also*, C.K. Thakker, *Administrative Law* (Eastern Book Company 1992) 260.
393. Quoted in Brown and Garner, *French Administrative Law* (1967).

away by any "finality" clause in the statute. The basis of this proposition is that the Congress cannot override the fundamental principle of the constitution of separation of power, and so it cannot divest courts of their inherent power to review the actions of administrative authorities which are illegal, arbitrary or unreasonable, and which impair personal or property rights.

The decision of the US Supreme Court in *Breen* v. *Selective Service Local Board No. 16 Bridgeport Connecticut*[394] (*Breen*) is a pointer in this direction. Though judicial review outside the constitutional structurisation can be regulated by the Congress,[395] yet to interpret the finality clause literally may mean the creation of serious constitutional problems. In *Breen*, the petitioner, who was an undergraduate student and, thus, entitled to deferment, was classified as "available for military service". The statute contained a finality clause which prohibited judicial review of "classification" after the registrant responds negatively to an induction order. The Supreme Court held that the statute cannot be interpreted literally as a bar to pre-induction review. Therefore, the denial of judicial review in the US in the face of finality clause constitutes judicial self-limitation and not the lack of power. The US Supreme Court rightly stated in *Barlow* v. *Collins*[396] that "preclusion of judicial review of administrative actions ... is not lightly to be interfered with".

2.21 Illegal orders cannot be repeated

In *Jaipur Development Authority* v. *Mahesh Sharma*[397], the Supreme Court emphasised that neither can illegal or ultra vires administrative orders be repeated by administrative authority on the plea of equality nor can such orders be legalised.

2.22 Administrative review or revision

Unless a statute confers such powers, administrative authorities cannot review or revise their orders. In *Kalabharati Advertising* v. *H.V. Narichania*[398], the Supreme Court held that administrative authorities cannot review their decisions in the garb of clarification. Order once passed cannot even be modified or corrected. This is necessary in the interest of finality of administrative actions.

394. 1970 SCC OnLine US SC 17: 24 L Ed 2d 653: 396 US 460 (1970). See also, *Shaughnessy* v. *Pedreiro*, 1955 SCC OnLine US SC 38: 99 L Ed 868: 349 US 48 (1955).
395. S. 12, Administrative Procedure Act, 1946. It states, "Except so far as (1) statutes preclude judicial review, or (2) agency action is by law committed to agency discretion, the power of judicial review has been retained."
396. 1970 SCC OnLine US SC 54: 25 L Ed 2d 192: 397 US 159, 166 (1970).
397. (2010) 9 SCC 782.
398. (2010) 9 SCC 437.

3. VIOLATION OF PROCEDURAL NORMS

To what extent an administrative action in violation of a prescribed norm of procedure will be invalid is a complex question. The Supreme Court had the opportunity of examining this question in *State Bank of Patiala* v. *S.K. Sharma*[399]. In this case, an order was passed imposing punishment on an employee after an enquiry in violation of a procedural norm laid down in Rule 68(*b*)(*iii*) of Bank Officers' Service Regulation, which provided that the copies of the statement of witnesses must be provided to the employee at least three days before the enquiry. In this case, though the employee had been given an opportunity to examine the file and take notes, but copies of the statements of witnesses had not been provided as such. Upholding the validity of the administrative action, the Supreme Court discussed in detail the legal consequences of the violation of a procedural norm. The court held:

(1) An order passed imposing punishment on an employee consequent upon a disciplinary or departmental enquiry in violation of the rules or regulations or statutory provisions governing such enquiries should not be set aside automatically. The court or tribunal should enquire whether (*a*) the provision violated is of substantive nature, or (*b*) whether it is procedural in character.

(2) In case of violation of a procedural provision, the position is that procedural provisions are generally meant for affording a reasonable and adequate opportunity to the delinquent employee. They are generally conceived in his interest. Violation of any and every procedural provision cannot be said to automatically vitiate an enquiry held or order passed. Except in cases falling under "no notice, no opportunity and no hearing" categories, the complaint of violation of procedural provision should be examined from the point of view of prejudice, *viz.* whether such violation has prejudiced the delinquent employee in defending himself properly and effectively. If it is found that he has been so prejudiced, appropriate orders have to be made to repair and remedy the prejudice, including setting aside the enquiry and/or the order of punishment. If no prejudice is established to have resulted therefrom, it is obvious, no interference is called for. In this connection, it may be remembered that there may be certain procedural provisions which are of a fundamental character, and whose violation is by itself a proof of prejudice. The court cannot insist on proof of prejudice in such cases. For example, where there is an express provision providing that after the evidence of the employer or government is over, the employee shall be given an opportunity to produce evidences in his defence and if, in a given case, the delinquent employee has not been afforded that opportunity, even when requested, the prejudice is self-evident. No proof of prejudice is required in such a case.

399. (1996) 3 SCC 364.

(3) The whole question can also be looked from the point of view whether the procedural provision is directory or mandatory. In the case of a procedural provision which is directory and not mandatory in character, the complaint of violation has to be examined from the standpoint of substantial compliance. An order passed in violation of such a provision can be set aside only where such violation has occasioned prejudice to the delinquent employee.

In case the violation of a procedural provision is of mandatory character, it has to be ascertained whether the provision is conceived in the interest of the person proceeded against or in public interest. If it is in the interest of the person, then it must be seen whether the delinquent employee has waived the said requirement, either expressly or by his conduct. If he is found to have waived it, then the order of punishment cannot be set aside on violation of that provision. If, on the other hand, it is found that the delinquent employee has not waived it, or the provision could not be waived by him because it is conceived in the public interest, then the court shall make appropriate directions, including the setting aside of the order of punishment.

(4) Where the enquiry is not governed by any specific rule or regulation and the authority is simply to follow the principles of natural justice, then a distinction must be made between "no opportunity" and "no adequate opportunity". In case of "no opportunity", order would undoubtedly be invalid and the authority may be asked to take proceedings afresh according to law. In case of "no adequate opportunity", the effect of violation must be examined from the standpoint of prejudice caused to the delinquent employee. If prejudice has been caused, court may pass necessary order including the quashing of the order of punishment.

(5) There may be situations where the interest of the State or public interest may call for the curtailing of the rule of fair hearing. In such situations, the court will have to balance public or State interest with the requirement of fair hearing and arrive at an appropriate decision.

(6) The test of prejudice or substantial compliance shall not apply in case of violation of a substantive provision of law. For example, provisions regarding the constitution of the enquiry committee must be strictly complied with, and violation of such a provision would render the administrative order invalid.

These principles shall not apply in cases where bias is alleged.

4. DOCTRINE OF LEGITIMATE EXPECTATION

The doctrine of legitimate expectation belongs to the domain of public law and is intended to give relief to the people when they are not able to justify their claims on the basis of law, in the strict sense of the term, though they had suffered a civil consequence because their legitimate expectation had been violated. It is something between a "right" and "no right" and is different from anticipation, desire and hope. The term "legitimate expectation" was first used by Lord Denning in 1969 and from that time it has assumed the position of a significant doctrine of public law in almost all jurisdictions.[400]

In India, the Supreme Court has developed this doctrine in order to check the arbitrary exercise of power by the administrative authorities. In private law, a person can approach the court only when his right based on statute or contract is violated, but this rule of locus standi is relaxed in public law to allow standing even when a legitimate expectation from a public authority is not fulfilled. Therefore, this doctrine provides a central space between "no claim" and a "legal claim", wherein a public authority can be made accountable on the ground of an expectation which is legitimate. For example, if the government has made a scheme for providing drinking water in villages in certain area but later on changed it, so as to exclude certain villages from the purview of the scheme, then in such a case, what is violated is the legitimate expectation of the people in the excluded villages for tap water, and the government can be held responsible if the exclusion is not fair and reasonable. Thus, this doctrine becomes a part of the principles of natural justice, and no one can be deprived of his legitimate expectations without following the principles of natural justice.

The doctrine of legitimate expectation is not applicable against statute. The doctrine flows from established practice which is regular, consistent, predictable and certain conduct, process or activity of the decision-making authority. Expectation should be legitimate, *i.e.* reasonable, logical and valid. The doctrine can be invoked where a person has dealing, transactions or negotiations with or has legal relationship with the State Authority. It is not applicable where legislative enactment operates.[401]

Mere disappointment of expectation, sans any legal or vested right, cannot be a ground for invoking the doctrine.[402]

In *Kerala State Beverages (M&M) Corpn. Ltd.* v. *P.P. Suresh*[403], the Supreme Court observed that for a legitimate expectation to arise, the decisions of the administrative authority must affect the person by depriving him of some benefit or advantage which

(*i*) he had in the past been permitted by the decision-maker to enjoy and which he can legitimately expect to be permitted to continue to do until there has been communicated to him some rational ground for withdrawing it on which he has been given an opportunity to comment; or

400. *See*, R. Clerk, "In Pursuit of Fair Justice", AIR 1996 (J) 11.
401. *State of U.P.* v. *United Bank of India*, (2016) 2 SCC 757.
402. *State of Kerala* v. *Kerala Rare Earth & Minerals Ltd.*, (2016) 6 SCC 323.
403. (2019) 9 SCC 710.

(*ii*) he has received assurance from the decision-maker that they will not be withdrawn without giving him first an opportunity of advancing reasons for contending that they should not be withdrawn.

The procedural part of legitimate expectation relates to a representation that a hearing or other appropriate procedure will be afforded before the decision is made. The substantive part of the principle is that if a representation is made that a benefit of a substantive nature will be granted or if the person is already in receipt of the benefit, that it will be continued and not be substantially varied, then the same could be enforced. An expectation entertained by a person may not be found to be legitimate due to the existence of some countervailing consideration of policy or law. Administrative policies may change with changing circumstances, including changes in the political complexion of governments. The liberty to make such changes is something that is inherent in our constitutional form of government. The decision-makers' freedom to change the policy in public interest cannot be fettered by applying the principle of substantive legitimate expectation. So long as the government does not act in an arbitrary or an unreasonable manner, the change in policy does not call for interference by judicial review on the ground of a legitimate expectation of an individual or a group of individuals being defeated.

In case of a complaint that an administrative authority has reneged from a promise without giving an opportunity of hearing which was the past practice, a claim of legitimate expectation can be raised. In other words, if the policy or practice was to give an opportunity before the benefit is withdrawn, the non-compliance of such a practice would result in defeating the legitimate expectation of an individual or a group of individuals. There can be situations where the very claim made can be with regard to an opportunity not being given before withdrawing a promise which results in defeating the "legitimate expectation".

The principle of procedural legitimate expectation would apply to cases where a promise is made and is withdrawn without affording an opportunity to the person affected. The imminent requirement of fairness in administrative action is to give an opportunity to the person who is deprived of a past benefit. There is an exception to the said rule. If an announcement is made by the government of a policy conferring benefit on a large number of people, but subsequently, due to overriding public interest, the benefits that were announced earlier are withdrawn, it is not expedient to provide individual opportunities to such an innominate number of persons. In other words, in such cases, an opportunity to each individual to explain the circumstances of his case need not be given. In cases involving an interest based on legitimate expectation, the court will not interfere on grounds of procedural fairness and natural justice, if the deciding authority has been allotted a full range of choice and the decision is taken fairly and objectively.

Like the bulk of the administrative law, the doctrine of legitimate expectation is also a fine example of judicial creativity. Nevertheless, it is not extra legal and extra-constitutional. A natural habitat for this doctrine can be found in Article 14 of the Constitution, which abhors arbitrariness and insists on fairness in all administrative dealings. It is now firmly established that the protection of Article 14 is available not only in case of arbitrary "class legislation", but also in case of arbitrary "State action". Thus, the doctrine is being hailed as a fine principle of administrative jurisprudence for reconciling power with liberty.[404]

The doctrine has negative and positive contents both. If applied negatively, an administrative authority can be prohibited from violating the legitimate expectations of the people, and if applied in a positive manner, an administrative authority can be compelled to fulfil the legitimate expectations of the people. This is based on the principle that public power is a trust which must be exercised in the best interest of its beneficiaries—the people.

4.1 Development in England

As mentioned earlier, though the term "legitimate expectation" was first used by Lord Denning in *Schmidt* v. *Secy. of State for Home Affairs*[405], wherein the government had cut short the period already allowed to an alien to enter and stay in England; the court held that the person had legitimate expectation to stay in England which cannot be violated without following a procedure which is fair and reasonable. In this manner, Lord Denning used the term "legitimate expectation" as an alternative expression to the word "right".

However, it was in *Breen* v. *Amalgamated Engg. Union*[406] (now *Amalgamated Engineering and Foundry Workers' Union*) that the doctrine of legitimate expectation found its legitimate place. In this case, the district committee of a trade union had refused to endorse a member's election as shop steward. The court held that if a person claims a privilege, he can be turned away without hearing, but here a person has something more than a mere privilege—a legitimate expectation that his election would be approved unless there are relevant reasons for not doing so, therefore, the natural justice principles are attracted to the case in order to ensure fairness.

In the same manner, in *McInnes* v. *Onslow Fane*[407], also the doctrine of legitimate expectation found fine exposition. In the case of the British Boxing Board of Control, a domestic tribunal had rejected an application for entrance licence without hearing. The court speaking through

404. *Food Corporation of India* v. *Kamdhenu Cattle Feed Industries*, (1993) 1 SCC 71.

405. (1969) 2 WLR 337: (1969) 2 Ch 149 (CA).

406. (1971) 2 QB 175: (1971) 2 WLR 742 (CA); see also, *Padfield* v. *Minister of Agriculture Fisheries and Food*, 1968 AC 997: (1968) 2 WLR 924 (HL). The House of Lords held that dairy farmers have legitimate expectation that their complaint would be referred to a committee for investigation.

407. (1978) 1 WLR 1520.

Megarry VC made a distinction between application, forfeiture and legitimate expectation situations in licence cases. On the one extreme, are the application cases where a person has no right to the grant of his application, while on the other are forfeiture cases, in which a person's existing right is violated, and therefore he is clearly entitled to the benefit of the principles of natural justice. In between these extreme situations lies a third situation of legitimate expectation cases. This situation may cover cases of renewal of licences. In this situation, a person can legitimately expect that his licence will be renewed and if his licence is not renewed, he has a right to know what makes him unsuitable now when he was suitable earlier—the principles of natural justice.

The Privy Council in *Attorney General of Hong Kong* v. *Ng Yuen Shiu*[408], while quashing the removal order passed by the Hong Kong Immigration Authority without notice and hearing also, held that there is a violation of the legitimate expectation of the immigrant based on announcement of the authority that while examining the cases of illegal immigration, each case would be decided on its own merit and, therefore, a removal order cannot be passed without a fair hearing.

Invoking the doctrine of legitimate expectation, the House of Lords in *Council of Civil Services Union* v. *Minister of Civil Service*[409] (*CCSU*) held that legitimate expectations may arise from an expression or promise made by the authority, or from an established past practice which cannot be violated without good reasons. In this case, the administrative authority had withdrawn a long-standing practice by a mere oral instruction.[410]

In a sense, the doctrine of legitimate expectation imposes a duty on the authority to act fairly and is not restricted to situations where expectationer is to be consulted or be given an opportunity to make representation. This was held by the court in *R.* v. *Secy. of State for Home Deptt., ex p Ruddock*[411]. In this case, violating the established criteria for the issuance of interception order, the Home Department had issued warrant for the interception of telephone calls of the applicant. Though the court did not grant relief as nothing unfair or improper was found, yet the duty to act fairly where legitimate expectations are involved was firmly established.

In the same manner, in *R.* v. *Secy. of State for Home Deptt., ex p Asif Mahmood Khan*[412], the court held that if the authority had made a statement that a certain criterion or procedure would be followed, the people can legitimately expect that it would be followed in the decision-making process of the authority and, therefore, the authority is under an obliga-

408. (1983) 2 AC 629: (1983) 2 WLR 735 (PC).
409. 1985 AC 374: (1984) 3 WLR 1174 (HL).
410. In this case, the staff at the Communication Headquarters had a long standing to belong to National Trade Unions, and thus an established practice of alteration in terms and conditions of service only through consultation. In this case, though the relief was denied on the ground of national security, but the doctrine of legitimate expectation was firmly rooted.
411. (1987) 1 WLR 1482 (QBD).
412. (1984) 1 WLR 1337 (CA).

tion to follow that criterion or procedure. In this case, in violation of the provisions of the circular regarding entry of adopted children in England, the authority had refused entry to the adopted child of Mr Khan. The court quashed the order of the authority as it was on considerations of policies which were not in existence when the circular had been issued.

In *R.* v. *Secy. of State for Transport, ex p Greater London Council*[413], the doctrine was applied in tax cases. The court held that a taxpayer had legitimate expectations to make representation that he should not pay tax at the maximum rate.

Though the doctrine as evolved in England is still in an evolutionary stage, yet one thing is certain that it is an equity doctrine and, therefore, the benefit of the doctrine cannot be claimed as a matter of course. It is a flexible doctrine which can be moulded to suit the requirements of each individual case. The court did not apply the doctrine where applicant's own conduct was unlawful or claim was unworthy. In *Cinnamond* v. *British Airports Authority*[414], the court upheld the decision of the authority to prohibit the entry of taxi drivers into the airport because of their own past conduct which invited fines. In *Lloyd* v. *McMahon*[415], the House of Lords further held that the doctrine does not include within its ambit a right to oral hearing. Courts have also not protected expectations by judicial review when nothing unfair was found on the part of the authority or legitimate public interest demanded otherwise.[416] The doctrine, however, has been applied to statutory as well as non-statutory authorities.[417]

Evolving the doctrine further, courts in England support the opinion that the claim of legitimate expectation must not always fail against legal incapacity. Therefore, on the grounds of equity, recourse to legitimate expectation can be taken even when the expectation is based on representation which is beyond the powers of the authority. In such a situation, the court balances individual interest against public interest.[418]

4.2 Development in India

The capacity of the Supreme Court to import legal doctrines and to plant them in a different soil and climate and to make them flourish and bear fruits is tremendous. The importation of the doctrine of legitimate expectation is recent. The first reference to the doctrine is found in *State of Kerala* v. *K.G. Madhavan Pillai*[419]. In this case, the government had issued

413. 1986 QB 556: (1985) 3 WLR 574.
414. (1980) 1 WLR 582 (CA).
415. 1987 AC 625: (1987) 2 WLR 821 (HL).
416. *Breen* v. *Selective Service Local Board No. 16 Bridgeport Connecticut*, 1970 SCC OnLine US SC 17: 24 L Ed 2d 653: 396 US 460 (1970). See also, *Shaughnessy* v. *Pedreiro*, 1955 SCC OnLine US SC 38: 99 L Ed 868: 349 US 48 (1955).
417. *See*, R. Clerk, "In Pursuit of Fair Justice", AIR 1996 (J) 11
418. *Stretch* v. *United Kingdom*, (2004) 38 EHRR 12; *Rowland* v. *Environment Agency*, 2005 Ch 1: (2004) 3 WLR 249 (CA).
419. (1988) 4 SCC 669.

a sanction to the respondents to open a new unaided school and to upgrade the existing ones. However, after 15 days a direction was issued to keep the sanction in abeyance. This order was challenged on the ground of violation of the principles of natural justice. The court held that the sanction order created legitimate expectation in the respondents which was violated by the second order without following the principles of natural justice, which is sufficient to vitiate an administrative order.[420] The doctrine was further applied in *Scheduled Caste and Weaker Section Welfare Assn.* v. *State of Karnataka*[421]. In this case, the government had issued a notification notifying areas where slum clearance scheme will be introduced. However, the notification was subsequently amended and certain areas notified earlier were left out. The court held that the earlier notification had raised legitimate expectation in the people living in an area which had been left out in a subsequent notification and, hence, legitimate expectations cannot be denied without a fair hearing. Thus, where a person has legitimate expectation to be treated in a particular way which falls short of an enforceable right, the administrative authority cannot deny him his legitimate expectations without a fair hearing. Legitimate expectation of fair hearing may arise by a promise or an established practice.[422]

The same principle was followed by the Supreme Court in *Navjyoti Coop. Group Housing Society* v. *Union of India*[423]. In this case, the development authority, without notice and hearing, had changed the order of priority for the allotment of land to cooperative societies from "serial number of registration" to the "date of approval of list of members". Quashing the order on the ground of violation of legitimate expectation, the court held that where persons have been enjoying certain benefits or advantage under an old government policy, they derive a legitimate expectation, even though they may not have any legal right under private law in regard to its continuance. However, before changing that policy affecting adversely that benefit or advantage, the aggrieved persons are entitled to a fair hearing.

The concept of legitimate expectation has now gained importance in administrative law as a component of natural justice, non-arbitrariness and the rule of law.[424] It aims at checking the growing abuse of administrative power as a supplement to the principles of natural justice, unreasonableness, fiduciary duty of administrative authorities and in future, perhaps, the principle of proportionality.[425]

---

420. It is curious to note that in this case doctrine was invoked by the government to deny respondents a legal standing. However, court held that respondents not only have locus standi but are also entitled to the benefit of the principles of natural justice.
421. (1991) 2 SCC 604.
422. See also, *State of H.P.* v. *Kailash Chand Mahajan*, 1992 Supp (2) SCC 351.
423. (1992) 4 SCC 477.
424. *Food Corporation of India* v. *Kamdhenu Cattle Feed Industries*, (1993) 1 SCC 71, 76.
425. *Union of India* v. *Hindustan Development Corpn.*, (1993) 3 SCC 499.

The court in *Union of India* v. *Hindustan Development Corpn.*[426] got the opportunity of laying down the meaning and scope of this doctrine. Explaining the meaning of the doctrine and the legitimacy of the doctrine when it arises, the court held:

> Time is a three-fold present: the present as we experience it, the past as a present memory and future as a present expectation. For legal purposes, the expectation cannot be the same as anticipation. It is different from a wish, a desire or a hope nor can it amount to a claim or demand on the ground of a right. However earnest and sincere a wish, a desire or a hope may be and however confidently one may look to them to be fulfilled, they by themselves cannot amount to an assertable expectation and a mere disappointment does not attract legal consequences. A pious hope even leading to a moral obligation cannot amount to a legitimate expectation. The legitimacy of an expectation can be inferred only if it is founded on the sanction of law or custom or an established procedure followed in regular and natural sequence. Again it is distinguishable from a genuine expectation. Such expectation should be justifiably legitimate and protectable. Every such legitimate expectation does not by itself fructify into a right and, therefore, it does not amount to a right in the conventional sense.[427]

In this case, in the absence of any fixed procedure for fixing price and quantity for the supply of foodgrains, the government adopted a dual pricing system (lower price for big suppliers and higher price for small suppliers) in the public interest in order to break the cartel. The court held that there is no denial of legitimate expectation, as it is not based on any law, custom or past practice. The court said that it is not possible to give an exhaustive list wherein legitimate expectations arise, but by and large they arise in promotion cases, though not guaranteed as a statutory right, in cases of contracts, distribution of largess by the government and in somewhat similar situations.

Explaining the same principle further, the Supreme Court in *Jitendra Kumar* v. *State of Haryana*[428] held that government has a right to review the decisions taken by the previous establishment and, hence, it can suspend the process of recruitment started by previous government because of allegations of irregularities, and this cannot be challenged on the ground of violation of legitimate expectation because legitimate expectation is different from mere anticipation, desire and hope.

Demarcating the scope of the doctrine, the court held that legitimate expectation gives sufficient locus standi to the applicant for judicial review. The doctrine is to be confined mostly to a right of fair hearing before a decision, which results in negativating a promise or withdrawing an undertaking, is taken. Though the denial of legitimate expectation is a ground for challenging an administrative action, but the court will not interfere unless the denial is arbitrary, unreasonable, not in the public interest, and

426. *Union of India* v. *Hindustan Development Corpn.*, (1993) 3 SCC 499.
427. *Ibid*, 540.
428. (2008) 2 SCC 161.

inconsistent with the principles of natural justice, or where denial is in violation of a right. However, it does not mean that an administrative body cannot change its policy, so denial of legitimate expectation can be justified only by showing some overriding public interest.[429] The court further held that unless the fair hearing is not a pre-condition for the exercise of power, the doctrine has no role to play, and the court should not interfere with the exercise of discretion by the administrative authority. The court must allow full choice to the authority which the legislature is presumed to have intended. Thus, the extent of judicial review of administrative action is very limited. The doctrine of legitimate expectation is "not the key which unlocks the treasury of natural justice and it ought not to unlock the gates which shuts the court out of review on the merits". The court should exercise self-restraint and restrict the claim of denial of legitimate expectation to the legal limitations.[430]

The doctrine of legitimate expectation confers upon person a right to fairness which is enforceable in case of its denial. But whether an expectation is legitimate or not is a question of fact which has to be determined not according to claimant's perception but in the larger public interest. Thus, in *UT of Chandigarh* v. *Dilbagh Singh*[431], the court held that selectees are not entitled to an opportunity of hearing before cancellation of the list even though they have legitimate expectations, but they have no indefeasible right to be appointed in absence of any rule to that effect. On the other hand, in *U.P. Awas Evam Vikas Parishad* v. *Gyan Devi*[432], the court held that the local body which has the right to lead evidence under Section 20(2) of the Land Acquisition Act, 1894 for the purpose of determining compensation can legitimately expect to receive notice about the pendency of the proceedings and its right to lead evidence, and if this legitimate expectation is denied the court can intervene. Again in *M.P. Oil Extraction* v. *State of M.P.*[433], the Supreme Court held that selected industries with which an agreement has been entered into by the government can legitimately expect that the renewal clause should be given effect to in usual manner and according to past practice; unless there is any special reason not to adhere to such practice, the denial of legitimate expectation would vitiate an administrative action.

In *National Buildings Construction Corpn.* v. *S. Raghunathan*[434], the Supreme Court brought in the concept of "detriment" in legitimate

429. See also, *P.T.R. Exports (Madras) (P) Ltd.* v. *Union of India*, (1996) 5 SCC 268. Court will interfere only if the change of policy is mala fide and there is an abuse of power which the applicant must prove.

430. *Union of India* v. *Hindustan Development Corpn.*, (1993) 3 SCC 499.

431. (1993) 1 SCC 154. See also, *Supreme Court Advocates-on-Record Assn.* v. *Union of India*, (1993) 4 SCC 441 (*per* Verma, Dayal, Roy, Anand and Bharucha JJ), 478. Opined that doctrine applicable in selecting appointees to Supreme Court to make them non-arbitrary.

432. (1995) 2 SCC 326.

433. (1997) 7 SCC 592.

434. (1998) 7 SCC 66. See also, *Sethi Auto Service Station* v. *DDA*, (2009) 1 SCC 180.

expectation theory and held that enforcement of any legitimate expectation required 1) reliance on representation, and 2) resultant detriment. The court further observed that though the government has the power to change its policy in public interest, yet the court can look into the question of proportionality of change of policy and can see whether legitimate expectation has been properly balanced against the need for change. However, court's discretion must not transgress Wednesbury principle. Court cannot judge the merit of the policy. Therefore, unless the change of policy is so outrageous that no sensible person, who had applied his mind to the question to be decided, could have arrived at it, court will not interfere because flexibility necessarily inherent in this principle must not be sacrificed on the altar of legal certainty. Therefore, legitimate expectation has no role to play where administrative action is in furtherance of a public policy, or is in public interest, unless it amounts to an abuse of power. In this case, persons working on deputation in Iraq were given 125 per cent of basic pay as foreign allowance. After revision of pay scales by the Fourth Pay Commission, this allowance was withdrawn. The court rejected the contention of violation of legitimate expectation on the ground that peculiar situation prevailing in Iraq justified the change in policy. Thus, unless the change of policy is clearly irrational or perverse, court will not interfere.

Similarly the court rejected the contention of legitimate expectation in *State of Bihar* v. *S.A. Hassan*[435]. In this case, government had taken over the management of a private medical college. Employees initially continued on an ad hoc basis but were regularised later on. There was no material on record to show that erstwhile management was liable for pension or any pensionary benefits in relation to its employees. Under these circumstances, court rejected the claim of employees to count their past services towards retiral benefits being legitimate expectations. Dealing with the applicability of the doctrine, the Supreme Court in *Chanchal Goyal* v. *State of Rajasthan*[436] further held that if service of a person has been terminated in terms of his original appointment order, this does not provide legitimate expectation against termination. In this case, appellant had been appointed, temporarily, for a period of six months or till the availability of a candidate selected by the Public Service Commission. Service rules prohibited continuance of a temporary appointment beyond one year without the approval of the Public Service Commission. In such circumstance, the court held, mere continuance in service by virtue of successive extension orders does not imply waiver of the condition attached to the original order, and hence does not provide a ground for legitimate expectation.

However, where a person has been given interim licence for any trade or business, the court held, he has legitimate expectation that the criteria

435. (2002) 3 SCC 566.
436. (2003) 3 SCC 485.

which were already followed would be continued while granting final licence.[437]

Elaborating the law further in *Punjab Communications Ltd.* v. *Union of India*[438], the Supreme Court observed that legitimate expectations may be procedural and substantive both. The procedural part of it relates to a representation that a hearing or other appropriate procedure will be afforded before any change in decision is made. The substantive part of the principle relates to the representation that a benefit of a substantive nature will be granted or will be continued. Procedural legitimate expectation cannot be withdrawn without giving a person some opportunity of advancing reason for contending that it should not be withdrawn. In the same manner, substantive expectation cannot be withdrawn unless some rational grounds for withdrawing it has been communicated to the person and on which he has been given an opportunity to comment. The principle of legitimate expectation in the substantive sense that the decision-making authority can normally be compelled to give effect to his representation, unless overriding public interest demands otherwise, has become the part of Indian law, no matter it has still not been accepted in many jurisdictions.[439] On the other hand, European courts go a step further and try to balance legitimate interest with the demand of public interest.

The doctrine of legitimate expectation supplements the doctrine of locus standi by providing sufficient standing to any one who cannot point to the existence of a substantive right to obtain the leave of the court for judicial review. Thus, legitimate expectations give applicant sufficient locus standi for judicial review. Relief is mostly confined to the right of fair hearing before a decision to withdraw a promise or undertaking is taken. It does not give the right to claim a relief from an administrative authority as no crystallised right is involved. In *Bannari Amman Sugars Ltd.* v. *CTO*[440], since the State had not indicated reasons justifying withdrawal of benefit, court insisted that appellants be given an opportunity of hearing to present their side of the picture. Any overriding public interest would justify denial of any legitimate expectation.

It is an equity doctrine, therefore, a person's own conduct may disentitle him to the benefit of this doctrine. This was demonstrated by the Supreme Court in *Raj Kumar* v. *Union of India*[441]. In this case, on a wrong interpretation of law, Border Security Force (BSF) personnel were permitted to resign before attaining the age of superannuation. Their resignations were accepted and their retiral benefits were also released. However, later realising their mistake, the BSF asked them to rejoin. Nevertheless, all did not join. Those who did not join demanded the benefits not given to them

437. *Global Energy Ltd.* v. *Central Electricity Regulatory Commission*, (2009) 15 SCC 570.
438. (1999) 4 SCC 727.
439. *Canada Assistance Plan, re*, (1991) 83 DLR (4th) 297.
440. (2005) 1 SCC 625.
441. (2006) 1 SCC 737. See also, *MRF Ltd.* v. *CST*, (2006) 8 SCC 702.

on the ground of violation of legitimate expectation. The Supreme Court observed that who did not join are not entitled to any equity because of their own conduct.

Legitimate expectation is not a legal right was once again exemplified by the Supreme Court in *Ram Pravesh Singh* v. *State of Bihar*[442]. Bihar government, Bihar Electricity Board, and Rural Electrification Corporation had organised a cooperative society to implement a rural electrification scheme. However, later on due to financial reasons decided to merge the Society with the Electricity Board. Though the assets and liabilities of the Society were taken over by the Board, employees were not absorbed. This was challenged by the employees on the ground that their legitimate expectation to be absorbed in the service of the Board has been violated. Rejecting the claim, the court held legitimate expectation is not a legal right, it is an expectation of a benefit, relief or remedy that may ordinarily flow from a promise or an established practice. Explaining the meaning of established practice, the court observed that the term established practice refers to a regular, consistent, predictable and certain conduct. Any expectation which is based on sporadic, casual or random acts, or which is unreasonable, illogical or invalid cannot be a legitimate expectation. Applying the same principle in *Confederation of Ex-Servicemen Assns.* v. *Union of India*[443], the Supreme Court did not accept the petition of the Confederation for free and full medical facilities to ex-serviceman. In this case, government had framed a scheme to provide free medical aid to ex-servicemen, provided they paid "one time contribution". This was a policy change from total free medical aid. This change of policy was challenged on the ground of violation of legitimate expectation that total free medical aid would continue. Rejecting the plea, the Supreme Court observed that the doctrine has no application because neither there is any promise nor any consistent past practice which is being withdrawn. In short, a person is said to have a legitimate expectation of a particular treatment if any representation or promise is made by an authority, either expressly or impliedly, or if the regular and consistent practice of the authority gives room for such expectation in the normal course. It may only entitle an expectant 1) to an opportunity to show cause before the expectation is dashed; 2) to an explanation as to the cause of denial; or 3) to a direction, requiring the authority to follow the promised procedure or established practice. A change of policy in public interest, conduct of the expectant, or any other valid or bona fide reason given by the administrative authority may be sufficient to negate the legitimate expectation. A total stranger, unconnected with the authority or a person, who has no previous dealings with the authority, or who has not entered into negotiation for any transaction with the authority cannot

442. (2006) 8 SCC 381. See also, *Bannari Amman Sugars Ltd.* v. *CTO*, (2005) 1 SCC 625.
443. (2005) 13 SCC 265.

invoke the doctrine merely on the ground that the authority has a general obligation to act fairly.[444]

In *Indibly Creative (P) Ltd.* v. *State of W.B.*[445], the Supreme Court noted that a film which receives certification from the Censor Board raises legitimate expectation in the producer for its exhibition. In pursuance of such expectation the producer enters into contracts with theatre owners and makes other arrangements. If State, through the police, power without statutory authority compels theatre owners to refrain from screening such film, that would be destructive of legitimate expectation of the producer.

Bottom line is that legitimate expectation must always yield to larger public interest exemplifying the proposition, the Supreme Court held in *P. Suseela* v. *UGC*[446] that even if the appellants had legitimate expectations to be exempted from qualifying the National Eligibility Test (NET) on the basis of MPhil/PhD degrees for appointment as lecturers/assistant professors in institutions governed by the UGC Act under its past policy, their expectations must yield to larger public interest, which in the instant case was to have highly qualified persons in institutions of higher learning and for which the past policy of granting NET exemption was withdrawn and NET was made compulsory for all future appointments. This change of policy was for obvious reason that some institutions may grant MPhil/PhD degrees without following rigorous academic standards of excellence.

Can legitimate expectation be postponed by the administrative authority for an indefinite period on the ground of any future proposed plan or change of policy, which has not yet come into existence? This doctrine of legitimate expectation was the main contention before the Supreme Court in *T. Vijayalakshmi* v. *Town Planning Member*[447]. Appellants in this case were owners of agricultural land who were entitled by law to use the same for residential purposes. They filed an application for the approval of a building plan before the Planning Authority. Their application was rejected on the ground that the land in question would form part of Valley Zone within the proposed comprehensive development plan, which will come into operation in near future. Upholding the contention of the appellants, the court observed that the doctrine of legitimate expectation would have a role to play in a case of this nature. Therefore, an administrative authority cannot postpone decision on any important right for an indefinite period. It must take a decision within a statutory time limit, if any, or within the reasonable time. The rights of the parties must be decided on the basis of existing law and cannot be postponed, much less taken away, on ground of any proposed future law or change of policy.

The doctrine of legitimate expectation shares space with the principle of promissory estoppel. If, thus, the principle of promissory estoppel would

444. *Ram Pravesh Singh* v. *State of Bihar*, (2006) 8 SCC 381.
445. (2020) 12 SCC 436.
446. (2015) 8 SCC 129.
447. (2006) 8 SCC 502.

apply, there may not be any reason as to why the doctrine of legitimate expectation would not.[448] However, this doctrine cannot be applied in the face of exercise of legislative power.

In *Lalaram* v. *Jaipur Development Authority*[449], the Supreme Court noted that the government stands on the same footing as a private individual so far as the obligation in law is concerned and the former is equally bound as the latter, and it is difficult to see on what principle, could a government, committed to the rule of law, claim immunity from the doctrine of promissory estoppel.

Before extending benefits to its subjects by laying down any policy, the government must ponder over the pros and cons thereof and its capacity to accord the same as it would be unfair and immoral on its part thereafter not to act as per its promise. The equitable notion of exacting fairness in governmental dealings requires that there is no unfettered discretion in public law and that a sovereign authority possessing powers is required to use them for public good. And that the duty to act fairly and to adopt a procedure which is "fair play in action", also raises a reasonable or legitimate expectation in every citizen to be treated fairly in his dealings with the State and its instrumentalities.

This obligation as a part of good administration is obligated by the requirement of non-arbitrariness in a State action, which, as a corollary, makes it incumbent on the State to consider and give due weight to the reasonable or legitimate expectations of the persons, likely to be affected by the decision, so much so that any failure to do so would proclaim unfairness in the exercise of power, thus vitiating the decision by its abuse or lack of bona fides. The besieged decision would then be exposed to the challenge on the ground of arbitrariness. Mere reasonable or legitimate expectation of a citizen may not by itself be a distinct enforceable right in all circumstances, but the failure to consider and give due weight to it may render the decision arbitrary. Thus, the requirement of due consideration of legitimate expectation formed a part of the principle of non-arbitrariness, a necessary concomitant of the rule of law. The doctrine of legitimate expectation is founded on the principle of reasonableness and fairness and arises out of the principles of natural justice and can be invoked as a substantive and enforceable right.

It cannot be overemphasised that the concept of legitimate expectation has now emerged as an important doctrine. It is stated that it is the latest recruit to a long list of concepts fashioned by the court to review an administrative action.[450] It operates in public domain, and in appropriate cases, constitutes a substantive and enforceable right.[451] As a doctrine it takes its

448. *Southern Petrochemical Industries Co. Ltd.* v. *Electricity Inspector & ETIO*, (2007) 5 SCC 447.

449. (2016) 11 SCC 31.

450. *Union of India* v. *Hindustan Development Corpn.*, (1993) 3 SCC 499.

451. *M.P. Oil Extraction* v. *State of M.P.*, (1997) 7 SCC 592.

place beside such principles as rules of natural justice, rule of law, non-arbitrariness, reasonableness, fairness, promissory estoppel, fiduciary duty and, perhaps, proportionality to check the abuse of the exercise of administrative power.[452] The principle at the root of the doctrine is the rule of law which requires regularity, predictability and certainty in governments' dealing with the public.[453] An expectation could be based on an express promise, or representation, or policy, or by an established past action or settled conduct which is not illegal. It could be a representation to the individual or generally to a class of persons. Whether an expectation exists is a question of law, but clear statutory words override any expectation, however founded. However, as an equity doctrine it is not rigid and operates in areas of manifest injustice. It enforces a certain standard of public morality in all public dealings. However, considerations of public interest would outweigh its application. It would immensely benefit those who are likely to be denied relief on the ground that they have no statutory right to claim relief.

The doctrine has been evolved to ensure regularity, predictability and certainty in government dealing with the public and, thus, shares space with the doctrine of "public trust". It is now considered to be a part of the principles of natural justice. Therefore, if by reason of the existing state of affairs, a party is given to understand that the other party shall not take away the benefit without complying with the principles of natural justice, the doctrine of legitimate expectation shall be applicable.[454]

Like in England, courts in India support the opinion that in certain situations recourse to the doctrine of legitimate expectation can be taken even when the expectation is based on unlawful representation, which is beyond the power of the authority. In such situation, court would balance public interest against individual interest.[455]

Nevertheless, in a recent decision, the Supreme Court, speaking through Pasayat J, held that a government Minister's promise cannot be enforced on the ground of legitimate expectation. In this case, a Law House claimed that it had printed 500 sets of North Eastern Regional Local Acts and Rules worth ₹1 crore on the assurance by the Minister that the government would place an order to purchase them. However, later the Minister did nothing except circulating a note. High Court, accepting the plea of legitimate expectation, directed the government to purchase the law books as promised by the Minister. Reversing the order of the High Court, the Supreme Court held that where a promise is made which cannot be supported by any consideration, the promisee cannot bring an action on the basis of that promise. The doctrine can be applied only if a decision is not arbitrary or unreasonable and is taken in public interest. The court further

452. *Food Corporation of India* v. *Kamdhenu Cattle Feed Industries*, (1993) 1 SCC 71.
453. *Chanchal Goyal* v. *State of Rajasthan*, (2003) 3 SCC 485.
454. *Southern Petrochemical Industries Co. Ltd.* v. *Electricity Inspector & ETIO*, (2007) 5 SCC 447.
455. *Ashoka Smokeless Coal India (P) Ltd.* v. *Union of India*, (2007) 2 SCC 640.

explained that if promise is a question of policy, even then a court cannot interfere unless it is irrational, perverse, or one which no reasonable man could have made. A claim based merely on legitimate expectation without anything more cannot ipso facto give a right. It is on the same logic that the manifestos of political parties do not attract the doctrine of legitimate expectation.[456] In the same manner in a process of recruitment, which was started by the previous government and was suspended by the present government, there is no violation of legitimate expectation which is different from "anticipation"[457].

A recourse to legitimate expectation cannot be taken when it is based on unlawful representation which is beyond the powers of the authority. However, in a situation where a local authority granted a lease to the applicant for 22 years, which was beyond the power of the authority and, hence, the authority refused to review it on the same ground, the court held that the local authority cannot take advantage of its own fault and awarded damages on the ground that the action did not go against public interest nor did it prejudice the duties of the authority. Therefore, there is a strong judicial opinion that legitimate expectation must not always fail against legal incapacity, unless strong public interest or prejudice to a statutory duty is proved.[458]

The fact remains that legitimate expectation is somewhere between a "Right" and "No Right". However, moral obligation can not amount to "Legitimate Expectation". Moral obligation is also not a wish, desire or hope, hence cannot be demanded as legitimate expectation. It can be enforced only when founded on law, custom or established practice followed in regular and natural sequence. Exemplifying it, the Supreme Court held that the State Government providing funds for paying pension for eight years shall not constitute as legitimate expectation as an enforceable right.[459]

Explaining the law further, the court observed that legitimate expectation may be substantive and procedural. Substantive legitimate expectation may arise if a person is deprived of some benefit or advantage which he has been permitted to enjoy and which he can legitimately expect to continue until withdrawn on some reasonable ground. There arises a substantive legitimate expectation which can be enforced against the authority. In the same manner, procedural legitimate expectation arises where the representation relates to a hearing before the benefit is withdrawn. Breach of such promise shall also confer an enforceable right. However, in public interest, the authority may change its policy and deprive a person of

456. *The Hindu* 19-4-2008, 13; *State of Arunachal Pradesh* v. *Nezone Law House*, (2008) 5 SCC 609. See also, *State of Bihar* v. *Bihar State 'Plus-2' Lecturers Associations*, (2008) 7 SCC 231.

457. *Jitendra Kumar* v. *State of Haryana*, (2008) 2 SCC 161.

458. *Stretch* v. *United Kingdom*, (2004) 38 EHRR 12. See also, *Rowland* v. *Environment Agency*, 2005 Ch 1: (2004) 3 WLR 249 (CA).

459. *State of Bihar* v. *Sachindra Narayan*, (2019) 3 SCC 803.

his legitimate expectation. Thus, freedom of action of the authority which is inherent in any constitutional governance cannot be fettered by taking recourse to the principle of legitimate expectation, unless the change is unfair, unreasonable and arbitrary.

Applying this principle, the Supreme Court held in *Kerala State Beverages (M&M) Corpn. Ltd.* v. *P.P. Suresh*[460] that assurance given to the respondents that they would be considered for appointment in the future does not give rise to any substantive legitimate expectation which may be enforceable. The court gave due deference to the decision of the State to change its policy keeping in view the large number of unemployment in the State. The court also did not accept the challenge of violation of procedural legitimate expectation because it was shown that due opportunity of being heard was given to the workers.

The Supreme Court has now finally settled the following principles in relation to the doctrine of legitimate expectation.[461]

(1) The doctrine is founded on the principle of reasonableness and fairness and also on public interest in executive policy or law. It is also a necessary concomitant of non-arbitrariness, rule of law and Principles of natural justice.

(2) The doctrine cannot be used to fetter changes in administrative policy in public interest.

(3) Legitimate expectation is different from anticipation which cannot amount to an assertable expectation.

(4) Legitimate expectation should be justifiable, legitimate and protectable.

(5) This doctrine can be invoked as a substantive and enforceable right.

(6) Doctrine of legitimate expectation cannot be invoked if it has the effect of jeopardising public interest for private benefit.

(7) Doctrine of legitimate expectation shares space with promissory estoppel and the principles of natural justice.

(8) Legitimate expectation can be inferred only if it is founded on sanction of law or custom or established procedure following in a regular and natural sequence; hence, moral obligation cannot amount to legitimate expectation. Legitimate expectation is also not a wish or desire or hope and hence cannot be enforced as a right.

(9) The doctrine of legitimate expectation is not applicable against a statute. It can be invoked where a person has a legal relationship with the administrative authority.

(10) Legitimate expectation may be substantive and procedural both. Substantive expectation may arise where a person is being deprived of some benefit or advantage which that person has been permitted

460. (2019) 9 SCC 710; see also, *Lalaram* v. *Jaipur Development Authority*, (2016) 11 SCC 31.

461. *Monnet Ispat & Energy Ltd.* v. *Union of India*, (2012) 11 SCC 1. See also, *Union of India* v. *Shri Hanuman Industries*, (2015) 6 SCC 600.

to enjoy and which he can legitimately expect to continue until withdrawn on some legitimate ground. Procedural expectation arises when an assurance is given that the benefit or advantage will not be withdrawn without giving him an opportunity to be heard. However, the court will not quash an administrative action on the ground of violation of procedural expectation if it is not expedient to provide hearing and the decision has been taken fairly and objectively.

(11) Mere reasonable or legitimate expectation may not be by itself a distinct enforceable right in all circumstances but the failure to consider and give due weight to it may render the decision arbitrary.

5. DOCTRINE OF PUBLIC ACCOUNTABILITY

The doctrine of public accountability is one of the most important emerging facet of administrative law in recent times. The basic purpose of the emergence of the doctrine is to check the growing misuse of power by the administration and to provide speedy relief to the victims of such exercise of power. The doctrine is based on the premise that the power in the hands of administrative authorities is a public trust which must be exercised in the best interest of the people. Therefore, the trustee (public servant) who enriches himself by corrupt means holds the property acquired by him as a constructive trustee.

The celebrated decision of the Privy Council in *Attorney General of Hong Kong* v. *Reid*[462] (*Reid*) has greatly widened the scope of this principle of jurisprudence in public law adjudication. Lord Templeman observed that engaging in bribery is an evil practice, which threatens the foundations of any civilised society, and that any benefit obtained by a fiduciary through the breach of duty belongs in equity to the beneficiary (the State); this is the basic norm subject to which all legal principles require to be interpreted. The Privy Council further observed that when bribe is accepted by a fiduciary (public servant) in breach of his duty, then he holds that bribe in trust for the person to whom the duty was owed. If the property representing the bribe decreases in value, the fiduciary (public servant) must pay the difference between that value and the initial amount of the bribe because he should not have accepted the bribe and incurred the risk of loss. If the property increases in value, the fiduciary is not entitled to any surplus in excess of the initial value of the bribe because he is not allowed by any means to make a profit out of a breach of a duty.

It was further held that a gift accepted by a person in fiduciary position as an incentive for breach of duty constituted a bribe and, although in law it belonged to the fiduciary, in equity he not only becomes a debtor for the amount of the bribe to the person to whom the duty was owed but he also

462. (1993) 3 WLR 1143 (PC).

holds the bribe and any property acquired therewith on constructive trust for that person.

In this pace-setting case the respondent, Reid, who was a Crown prosecutor in Hong Kong, took bribes as an inducement to suppress certain criminal prosecutions and with those monies acquired properties in New Zealand in his name, in the name of wife and his solicitor. The administration of Hong Kong claimed these properties on the ground that owners thereof are constructive trustees for the Crown. The Privy Council upheld the claim.

The Privy Council observed that if the theory of constructive trust is not applied and properties attached when available, the danger is that properties may be sold and the proceeds whisked away to some "numbered bank account".

It was further observed that one can understand the immorality of the bankers who maintained numbered bank accounts, but it is difficult to understand the amorality of the governments and their laws which sanction such practices—in effect encouraging them. The law laid down in this case equally applies to a situation even when fiduciary relationship does not exist.

The concept of constructive trust and equity to enforce public accountability as laid down in *Reid*[463] was followed by the Supreme Court in *Attorney General for India* v. *Amratlal Prajivandas*[464]. In this case, the court was dealing with the challenge to the validity of the "illegally-acquired properties" in clause (*c*) of Section 3(1) of the Smugglers and Foreign Exchange Manipulators (Forfeiture of Property) Act, 1976 (SAFEMA). The Act provided for the forfeiture of properties earned by smuggling or other illegal activities, whether standing in the name of the offender or in the name of other parties. The court upheld the validity of the Act.

The Supreme Court in *DDA* v. *Skipper Construction Co. (P) Ltd.*[465] not only further followed the above principle but enlarged its scope by stating that even if there was no fiduciary relationship, or no holder of public office was involved, yet if it is found that someone has acquired properties by defrauding the people, and if it is found that the persons defrauded should be restored to the position in which they would have been but for the said fraud, the court can make necessary orders. This is what equity means and in India, the courts are not only courts of law but also courts of equity. The court further held that all such properties must be immediately attached. The burden of proof to prove that the attached properties were not acquired with the aid of monies or properties received in the course of corrupt deals shall lie on the holder of such properties.[466]

463. (1994) 1 AC 324: (1993) 3 WLR 1143 (PC).
464. (1994) 5 SCC 54.
465. (1996) 4 SCC 622 .
466. *Ibid*, AIR 642.

The court further observed that a law like the SAFEMA has become an absolute necessity, if the canker of corruption is not to prove the death-knell of this nation; and suggested that Parliament act in this matter if they really mean business.[467]

In this case, Skipper—a private limited company—had purchased a plot of land in an auction from the Delhi Development Authority (DDA), but did not deposit the bid amount. When the DDA proposed to cancel the allotment, Skipper obtained a stay from the High Court. Meanwhile, it started selling the space in the proposed building. Thus, prospective buyers of space were cheated to the tune of about ₹14 crores. This was done in violation of the Supreme Court order.

Further elaborating the doctrine of public accountability, the court applied the theory of "lifting the corporate veil" in order to fix the accountability on persons who are the actual operators. The court observed that the concept of corporate entity was evolved to encourage and promote trade and commerce, but not to commit illegality or defraud people. In such cases, the court would look at the reality behind the corporate veil so as to do justice between the parties.[468] The court further held that in order to compensate those who are defrauded or cheated, the court can pass necessary orders under Article 142 of the Constitution. The absence of a statutory law like the SAFEMA will not inhibit the Supreme Court while making appropriate orders under Article 142.

Though the court certainly put the right foot forward, but did not take a long stride. It missed the opportunity of providing to the doctrine of public accountability its due reach. The court did not express any opinion on the question whether the misdeeds of public servants, which are not only beyond their authority but done with mala fide intent, would bind them personally or the State/corporation will be vicariously liable. It cannot be overemphasised that if the doctrine of accountability is to be given its full sweep, the concept of State/corporation liability be shifted to officer's liability in appropriate cases. This will have an inhibiting effect on the temptation of the public servants to misuse power for personal gains.

In order to strengthen the public accountability further in *State of Bihar* v. *Subhash Singh*[469], the court held that the head of a department is ultimately responsible and accountable unless there are special circumstances absolving him of the accountability. The Supreme Court observed that no matter if there is a hierarchical responsibility for decision-making, yet the head of the department or designated officer is ultimately responsible and accountable for the result of the action done or decision taken. Despite this, if there is any special circumstance absolving him of the accountability, or if someone else is responsible for the action, he needs to bring it to the notice of the court. The controlling officer holds each of them responsible

467. *DDA* v. *Skipper Construction Co. (P) Ltd.*, (1996) 4 SCC 622.
468. *Ibid.*
469. (1997) 4 SCC 430.

at the pain of disciplinary action. The object thereby is to ensure compliance with the rule of law.[470]

The concept of public liability has been further strengthened by the court by strictly applying the contempt law. Recently, many senior public servants were sent to jail for deliberately violating court orders. The court has also imposed cost personally against the erring officer, after due notice and hearing, for delay in the discharge of duties.[471] In the same manner, where the public servant has caused a loss to the public exchequer, the court has allowed the government to recover such loss personally from the erring officer.[472]

It is now established law that the writ courts, while exercising jurisdiction under Articles 32 and 226 of the Constitution, can award compensating and exemplary cost for the violation of a person's fundamental rights and the abuse of power by the State.[473] In *Nilabati Behera* v. *State of Orissa*[474] (*Nilabati Behera*), the court held that a claim in public law for compensation for violation of human rights and abuse of power is an acknowledged remedy for the enforcement and protection of such rights. Thus, every individual has an enforceable right to compensation when he is a victim of violation of his fundamental rights and abuse of power. In such a situation, the court observed that leaving the victim to the remedies available in civil law limits the role of constitutional courts as protectors and guarantors of fundamental rights of the citizens. Thus courts are under an obligation to make the State or its servants accountable to the people by compensating them for the violation of their fundamental rights.

The principle of accountability through compensation was further reinforced by two more principles evolved by the Supreme Court. In *Nilabati Behera*[475], the court laid down that the concept of sovereign immunity is not applicable to the case of violation of the right to life and personal liberty guaranteed by Article 21 of the Constitution. In *M.C. Mehta*[476], the court further held that if the harm is caused due to handling of hazardous material, the liability of the State or its instrumentality will be absolutely strict under the rule of *Rylands* v. *Fletcher*[477], and such a liability will not admit even the recognised exception of the rule such as an act of God. The compensation, thus, provided under the public law is in addition to the private law remedy for tortious action and punishment to the wrongdoer under criminal law. Following the principle, the court awarded a compensation of ₹ 10,000 to the legal heirs of each of the deceased who died in a fire, in

470. (1997) 4 SCC 430
471. *State of Bihar* v. *Subhash Singh*, (1997) 4 SCC 430.
472. *State of Kerala* v. *Thressia*, 1995 Supp (2) SCC 449.
473. See, *Rudul Sah* v. *State of Bihar*, (1983) 4 SCC 141; *D.K. Basu* v. *State of W.B.*, (1997) 1 SCC 416.
474. (1993) 2 SCC 746.
475. *Ibid.*
476. (1987) 1 SCC 395.
477. (1868) LR 3 HL 330 (HL).

a *jhuggi* colony, caused due to illegal and unauthorised electricity connections given by the employees of the Delhi Electricity Supply Undertaking.[478] The scope of public accountability has been further strengthened by developing such principles as "pollutor must pay" in case of environmental pollution,[479] and that every administrative authority shall be accountable for the proper and efficient discharge of its statutory duty.[480]

The establishment of Central Human Rights Commission and States Human Rights Commissions under the Human Rights Protection Act, 1993 is also a step in the direction of making the State accountable for the violation of human rights of the people. These Commissions exercise jurisdiction suo motu or on a complaint and provide justice in an informal manner to the victim of violations of human rights and abuse of power.

At this point, a few cases decided by the Supreme Court may be noted:

(1) For abusing the process of court, the public officer was held responsible and liable to pay costs from his own pocket.[481]

(2) For adopting casual approach by which the land could not be purchased by the authority and instead purchased by private builder, the officer was held personally liable.[482]

(3) For irregularities committed in auction of land resulting in loss to the public,[483] the official was held responsible for the loss.

(4) For oppressive, arbitrary and unconstitutional actions of public servants, it was held that exemplary damages can be awarded.[484]

(5) For abuse of power, while exercising discretionary power in granting State largesse in an arbitrary, unjust, unfair and mala fide manner, public servant can be held personally liable.[485]

(6) For abuse of power for extraneous reasons in acceptance of tender, all public officers concerned, including Minister, shall be liable to punishment.[486]

(7) For granting illegal promotion with retrospective effect which resulted in frittering away huge public funds, it was held that erring officers shall be personally liable.[487]

(8) For misuse of public power, not only the Minister but also the official working under him will be personally liable.[488] Thus, a departmental head is vicariously responsible for the actions of his subordinates,

478. *H.C. Srivastava* v. *Union of India*, (1996) 8 SCC 80.
479. *Indian Council for Enviro-Legal Action* v. *Union of India*, (1996) 3 SCC 212.
480. *Municipal Council, Ratlam* v. *Vardichan*, (1980) 4 SCC 162. Court held that lack of funds will not be defence for the enforcement of statutory duty.
481. *State of Kerala* v. *Thressia*, 1995 Supp (2) SCC 449.
482. *State of Maharashtra* v. *Pandurang K. Pangare*, 1995 Supp (2) SCC 119.
483. *DDA* v. *Skipper Construction Co. (P) Ltd.*, (1996) 4 SCC 622.
484. *Common Cause (Petrol pumps matter)* v. *Union of India*, (1996) 6 SCC 593.
485. *Ibid.* See also, *Shivsagar Tiwari* v. *Union of India*, (1996) 6 SCC 558.
486. *Dutta Associates (P) Ltd.* v. *Indo Mercantiles (P) Ltd.*, (1997) 1 SCC 53.
487. *H.R. Ramachandraiah* v. *State of Karnataka*, (1997) 3 SCC 639.
488. *Jaipur Development Authority* v. *Daulat Mal Jain*, (1997) 1 SCC 35.

> although in actual fact he is not responsible for their use of power which he must, of necessity, delegate to them.[489]

The Central Bureau of Investigation (CBI) is the prime instrumentality within the area of enforcing accountability. It is under the control of the executive so it was functioning in a manner which left much to be desired, especially in enforcing accountability in high places. The Supreme Court in a pace-setting judgment separated the CBI from the executive by vesting its superintendence in the Central Vigilance Commission (CVC) and directed a fixed tenure, of at least two years, for its Director except in extraordinary circumstances. It also held that the CBI would no longer need government concurrence to investigate corruption cases against government officers of Joint Secretary level and above. Taking note of the inertia, the court directed that the CVC be given statutory status and its superintendence over the functioning of the CBI. In order to ensure independence of the Commission, the court further directed that the selection for the post of Commissioner would be made by a committee comprising the Prime Minister, Home Minister and the leader of the Opposition from a panel of outstanding civil servants and others with impeccable integrity. Recommendation for the appointment of the CBI Director will be made by a committee headed by the Vigilance Commissioner with the Home Secretary and Secretary (personnel) as members. The court further said that the CBI Director shall have full freedom to allocate work and constitute investigation teams, and the post of the Director of the Enforcement Directorate shall be upgraded to that of Additional Secretary/Special Secretary of the government. The court further recommended the constitution of a body on the lines of Director of Prosecution in the UK for prosecution of cases. The judges said that till the appointment of this body, special counsel shall be appointed for the conduct of important trials on the recommendation of the Attorney General. The court directed the preparation of a panel of competent lawyers to act as prosecuting attorneys in cases of significance. Every prosecution which resulted in a discharge or acquittal of the accused must be reviewed and responsibility should be fixed of dereliction of duty, if any. The court asked the Central Government to ask the States to set up similar mechanisms. With all these directions, the Supreme Court entertained the belief that the investigative agencies shall function better now and the principle of accountability shall be better served.[490]

Moving swiftly in the direction of accountability, the Supreme Court in another pace-setting judgment held that Members of Parliament (MPs) and Members of Legislative Assemblies (MLAs) are public servants under the Prevention of Corruption Act, 1988. The court observed that there is no doubt that these persons hold an office and are authorised to carry out public duty. The court clarified that these persons also cannot claim exemption

489. *State of Punjab* v. *G.S. Gill*, (1997) 6 SCC 129.
490. *The Tribune* 18-12-1997, 1.

from prosecution under Article 105(2) of the Constitution regarding the protection of privileges as MPs and MLAs. As for any offence committed outside Parliament or legislature, the court held that Article 105(2) could not be interpreted as a charter of freedom of speech and also freedom for corruption. The object of Article 105(2) is to ensure independence to legislators in parliamentary democracy, but it cannot put a Member above law. This immunity cannot cover corruption and bribery. Though there is no authority prescribed under the Prevention of Corruption Act, 1988, the court observed, yet prosecution can be launched with the permission of the Speaker of the Lok Sabha or the Chairman of the Rajya Sabha, as the case may be.[491] Thus, by redefining the role of the State, rewriting the rules, codes and manuals, relaying decision-making, fixing accountability at all levels, and providing for transparency in administration, the court is simply trying to make government function better in the interest of the people by swinging public opinion.

Before parting with the subject of public accountability, one is impelled to reproduce classical observations of the Supreme Court which require serious consideration by every thinking individual. The Supreme Court observed:

> Some persons in the upper strata (which means the rich and the influential class of the society) have made the 'property career' the sole aim of their life. The means have become irrelevant—in a land where its greatest son born in this century said 'means are more important than the ends'. A sense of bravado prevails; every thing can be managed; every authority and every institution can be managed. All it takes is to 'tackle' or 'manage' it in an appropriate manner. They have developed an utter disregard for law—nay, a contempt for it; the feeling that law is meant for lesser mortals and not for them. The courts in the country have been trying to combat this trend, with some success as the recent events show. But how many matters can we handle. How many more of such matters are still there? The real question is how to swing the polity into action, a polity which has become indolent and soft in its vitals? Can the courts alone do it? Even so, to what extent, in the prevailing state of affairs? Not that we wish to launch upon a diatribe against anyone in particular but Judges of this Court are also permitted, we presume, to ask in anguish, 'what have we made of our country in less than fifty years?' Where has the respect and regard for law gone? And who is responsible for it?[492]

A similar note was struck by the Supreme Court in *UT of Chandigarh* v. *Kuldeep Singh*[493] when it observed:

> Every public servant is a trustee of the society and in all facets of public administration, every public servant has to exhibit honesty, integrity, sincerity and faithfulness in implementation of the political, social, economic and constitutional

491. *The Tribune* 18-4-1998, 1 (*JMM Bribery case*). However, in another decision court held that the officers of government companies or public sector undertakings are not entitled to protection of sanction before prosecution under S. 197 CrPC.

492. *DDA* v. *Skipper Construction Co. (P) Ltd.*, (1996) 4 SCC 622, 645–46.

493. (1997) 9 SCC 199.

> policies to integrate the nation, to achieve excellence and efficiency in the public administration. A public servant entrusted with duty and power to implement constitutional policy... should exhibit transparency in implementation and should be accountable for due effectuation of constitutional goals.

In *State of Punjab* v. *G.S. Gill*[494], the Supreme Court further observed:

> Many of the functions which the modern State undertakes are designed to make opportunities more nearly equal for everybody and to protect weaker individuals from the rapacity of the strong. In these days of fallen rectitude and honesty in the performance of public duty and the bureaucracy is too willing to sabotage public policy and constitutional philosophy. Judiciary/Tribunals should be astute in the declaration of law or in its solemn [power of] judicial review or dispensation of justice to issue directions or mandamus against the law, constitutional comments or public policy.

In *Vineet Narain* v. *Union of India*[495], the Supreme Court went on to emphasise that when it comes to corruption, as it exists at different levels, it proves to be both powerful and stubborn to stall any real or superficial moves in that direction. In other words, the politico-bureaucratic wall proves to be impregnable against all possible onslaughts against corruption. The judicial response has been slow and varied, but that is the only response available at the moment. There is no premium on honesty. Every thing is a matter of manipulation. Being a soft state, every thing is circumvented and manipulated. In the name of elimination of corruption, we see shadow boxing.

It was against this conceptual backdrop that the Supreme Court decided *P.V. Narasimha Rao* v. *State*[496] (popularly known as *Jharkhand Mukti Morcha bribery case*). In 1991 elections, Congress remained 14 members short of a clear majority in Parliament. On 28 July 1993, government faced a no confidence motion which was defeated by 265 to 251. Thereafter, a first information report (FIR) was filed with the CBI alleging conspiracy of taking and receiving bribe by the members of the Jharkhand Mukti Morcha (JMM) and others for voting against the motion. It was for quashing the FIR that a petition was filed with the Delhi High Court which was dismissed. Thus, the appeal before the Supreme Court which was heard by a Constitution Bench. The Constitution Bench with a majority of 3:2 held that Article 105 of the Constitution confers immunity on the Members of Parliament for freedom of speech and the right to give vote in Parliament.

Therefore, those MPs who received bribes and voted in Parliament cannot be prosecuted. However, those MPs who gave bribes or did not vote can be subjected to criminal proceedings. The court further held that an MP is a public servant and, therefore, can be proceeded against under the Prevention of Corruption Act, 1988 and the Penal Code, 1860. This decision

494. (1997) 6 SCC 129, 137.
495. (1998) 1 SCC 226.
496. (1998) 4 SCC 626. Special CBI Court has in Oct. 2000 awarded three years' rigorous imprisonment to Narasimha Rao, Former Prime Minister, and Buta Singh, Former Minister.

of the court generated a lot of controversy. It was argued that Article 105 of the Constitution does not protect corruption. The purpose of immunity is to preserve legislative independence, but taking bribe is no part of any legislative process. The court failed to follow its own wisdom reflected in its earlier decisions,[497] aimed at rooting out corruption in high places. It is certain that the object of immunity is to ensure independence of a MP for a healthy functioning, and protecting him against crime will be repugnant to any healthy functioning. The object of Article 105 of the Constitution is not to create a superman immune from law of crimes.

Another classical case decided by the Supreme Court on public accountability was *Common Cause (Petrol pumps matter)* v. *Union of India*[498] (known as the *Capt. Satish Sharma case*). This case was the result of a PIL petition which brought to the notice of the court arbitrary allotment of petrol outlets by the concerned Minister. The court cancelled all allotments and also imposed exemplary damages of ₹50 lakhs for misfeasance of a public servant. In a review petition, reversing its decision, the court held that imposing exemplary damages is a concept of tort, where it can be awarded for misfeasance if the plaintiff has suffered due to any arbitrary administrative action. Further because in a PIL petition there is a no plaintiff whose interest is adversely affected, no damages can be awarded. The court further observed that merely because a person is elected and inducted as a Minister in the government, he cannot be said to be holding a trust on behalf of the people and, hence, cannot be said to have committed the criminal breach of trust. The Supreme Court explained that the idea that a person on being elected by the people and on becoming a Minister holds a sacred trust on behalf of the people is a philosophical concept and reflects the image of virtue in its highest conceivable perfection, hence, this philosophy cannot be employed for the determination of the offence of criminal breach of trust. The court cautioned that if the Ministers of government work under threat of being proceeded in a court of law, or under constant fear of exemplary damages being awarded against them, they will develop a defensive attitude which will not be in the interest of the administration. This case also generated a lot of controversy and it was felt as if a good cause was lost in the abstraction of pure logic, and the court failed to catch the bull by its horns. Fact remains that law is not pure logic but experience.

After importing the principle of "public trust" in exercise of administrative power, the court focused its attention on government litigation because, today, government has become the biggest litigant in India. Unfortunately, there is no accountability in the government for violating the spirit of

497. See also, *Gill* v. *R.*, 1948 SCC OnLine PC 10: (1947–48) 75 IA 41. Privy Council held that if a judge accepts bribe, he is not acting in exercise of any public duty and, hence, there is no immunity; *K. Satwant Singh* v. *State of Punjab*, AIR 1960 SC 266. A Constitution Bench of the Supreme Court held that some offences like accepting bribe cannot be committed by a public servant while acting in discharge of his office, as official status only furnishes an opportunity.

498. (1996) 6 SCC 593.

Section 80 of the CPC, which aims at infusing fairness in the administration by curtailing its litigative tendency. Section 80, which provides for two months notice to the government before filing any suit or proceeding against it, aims at providing sufficient time to rethink the whole matter and take suitable action in the case before entering into contestation. However, the fact is that in a majority of cases either the notice is not replied or if replied, it is vague and evasive. Certainly, no effort is made to settle the matter outside the court. This defeats not only the purpose of law but also puts heavy cost on the public exchequer, besides adding to the misery of the litigants. Therefore, in *Salem Advocate Bar Assn.* (2) v. *Union of India*[499], court issued directions that whenever a statute requires service of notice as a condition precedent for filing suit, the government will nominate, within three months, an officer who shall be made responsible to ensure that replies to the notice under Section 80 of the CPC are sent within stipulated time, after due application of mind. The court emphasised that if a reply is not sent within time, or is vague or evasive, and has been sent without proper application of mind, the court must award heavy cost which must be recovered by the government from the officer concerned, besides taking appropriate disciplinary action against the delinquent officer. The Supreme Court also directed the courts that the cost awarded in such matter should not be nominal but real cost which may be calculated after taking into consideration 1) cost of time spent by the successful party; 2) cost of transportation and lodging; 3) court, lawyer and typing fee etc.; and 4) any other incidental cost. These directives will certainly make administration responsive besides reducing the heavy burden on the public exchequer and the misery of the people.

6. DOCTRINE OF PROPORTIONALITY

With the growth of administrative law, there was a need to control the possible abuse of discretionary powers by the administration. For this purpose, courts have evolved various principles like illegality, irrationality, procedural impropriety and proportionality. The last is the latest entrant in administrative law. Through the use of this doctrine, court would not allow administration to use a sledgehammer to crack a nut where a paring knife would suffice. Thus, it is a principle where courts would examine priorities and processes of the administration for reaching or recalling a decision. However, courts have always tried to temper this doctrine with the doctrine of "flexibility"[500].

The doctrine of proportionality was developed in the 19th century in Europe and originated in Prussia. In the EU jurisdictions, courts evaluate the necessity, suitability, utility and desirability of an administrative action. However, the courts do not sit as a appellate authority or super

499. (2005) 6 SCC 344.
500. *Coimbatore District Central Coop. Bank* v. *Employees Assn.*, (2007) 4 SCC 669.

legislature and show deference to administrative and legislative authorities. Nevertheless, while applying the proportionality test, courts apply more exacting and intrusive parameters than the Wednesbury test of unreasonableness.

The doctrine which was originally developed to control the police power of the State, now applies to 1) administrative discretionary action, 2) constitutionality of law where fundamental rights are involved, and 3) quantum of punishment. While applying the doctrine, court examines the following:

(1) Did the action pursue a legitimate aim?
(2) Were the measures employed to achieve the aim suitable?
(3) Could the aim have been achieved by less restrictive or onerous alternatives?
(4) Is the restriction or derogation justified in the overall interest of a democratic society and human dignity?

The application of the doctrine of proportionality in administrative law is a debatable issue and has not been fully and finally settled. Proportionality means that action should not be more drastic than it ought to be for obtaining the desired result. It covers some common ground with reasonableness. Proportionality is a course of action which could have been reasonably followed and should not be excessive or severe, etc. Proportionality can be described as a principle where the court is

> concerned with the way in which the administrator has ordered his priorities; the very essence of decision-making consists, surely, in the attribution of relative importance to the factors in the case,... . This is precisely what proportionality is about.[501]

If elaborated further, it is the "preparedness to hold that a decision which overrides a fundamental right without sufficient objective justification will, as a matter of law, necessarily be disproportionate to the aims in view.... The deployment of proportionality sets in focus the true nature of the exercise; the elaboration of a rule about permissible priorities"[502]. The doctrine of proportionality used in fundamental rights' context involves a balancing test and the necessity test. The "balancing test" means scrutiny of excessive and onerous penalties, or infringements of rights or interests, and a manifest imbalance of relevant considerations. The "necessity test" means that the infringement of fundamental rights in question must be by the least restrictive alternative.[503]

---

501. *See*, J. Laws, "Is the High Court the Guardian of Fundamental Constitutional Rights?", 1993 PL 59 quoted in *Union of India* v. *G. Ganayutham*, (1997) 7 SCC 463, 473.
502. *Coimbatore District Central Coop. Bank* v. *Employees Assn.*, (2007) 4 SCC 474.
503. *Ibid*. De Smith, Woolf and Jowell, *Judicial Review of Administrative Action* (5th Edn. Sweet & Maxwell 1995) 601–05. See also, *Coimbatore District Central Coop. Bank* v. *Employees Assn.*, (2007) 4 SCC 669.

6.1 Development in England

While judging the validity of an administrative action or statutory discretion, normally, the Wednesbury test is applied. According to this test, the court would consider whether irrelevant matters had been taken into consideration, or whether relevant matters had not been taken into consideration, or whether the action is bona fide. The court would also consider whether the decision was absurd or perverse. The court would not, however, go into the correctness of choice made by the administrator amongst the various alternatives open to him. Nor the court would substitute its decision to that of the administrator. The decision of the administrator must be within the four corners of law and not one which no sensible person could have reasonably arrived at. Besides these, the decision should be bona fide. The decision could be one of many choices open to the authority, but it is for that authority to decide upon the choice and the court does not substitute its own view.[504]

In a further development in 1985, Lord Diplock in *CCSU*[505] summarised the principles of judicial review of administrative action as illegality, procedural impropriety and irrationality. He further said that the doctrine of proportionality as a principle of judicial review may become later available in the same manner as is available in several Member States of the European Economic Community. Illegality means that no authority should act beyond its powers. Therefore, excess of jurisdiction is the basis of judicial review on ground of illegality. Irrationality is the Wednesbury test of unreasonableness. It applies to actions which are so outrageous in defiance of logic or accepted moral standards that no sensible person, who had applied his mind to the question to be decided, could have arrived at. Procedural impropriety refers to what may be called procedural ultra vires. Adoption of "proportionality" as a ground of judicial review was left for the future. However, the Wednesbury test of reasonableness is not the standard of "the man on the Clapham Omnibus". It is the standard indicated by a true construction of the act which distinguishes between what is authorised and what is not. These are called CCSU standards of judicial review.[506]

The next decision came in 1991 by the House of Lords in *R.* v. *Secy. of State for Home Deptt., ex p Brind*[507] (*Brind*), where it was again reiterated that the doctrine of proportionality cannot become a part of administrative law in England unless the European Convention of Human Rights and fundamental freedoms are incorporated by Parliament into domestic law. In this case, Lord Bridge explained the two judgments which the court can

504. *Associated Provincial Picture Houses Ltd.* v. *Wednesbury Corpn.*, (1948) 1 KB 223 (CA). In this case, a person had challenged the local authority order that allowed performance on Sunday, but disallowed children below the age of 15 to be admitted to performance.
505. 1985 AC 374: (1984) 3 WLR 1174 (HL).
506. *Ibid.*
507. (1991) 1 AC 696: (1991) 2 WLR 588 (HL).

make while exercising power of judicial review of an administrative action: 1) Primary judgment as to whether the particular competing public interest justifies the particular restriction. 2) Secondary judgment as to whether a reasonable administrative officer, on material before him, could reasonably make the primary judgment. It was held that the court would make only the secondary judgment, and the primary judgment would be made by the administrative officer whom Parliament has entrusted the discretion.

The same principle was restated in 1996 in *R.* v. *Ministry of Defence, ex p Smith*[508] (*Smith*). Lord Bingham explained that in the case appellants' rights as human beings are in issue which are justiciable, the court can thrust itself into the position of the primary decision-maker.[509]

With the incorporation of the European Human Rights Convention into domestic law of England in 1998, when Parliament passed the Human Rights Act, 1998, reluctance on the part of the English courts in applying the doctrine for determining the validity of an administrative action has now changed, and the courts are making use of the doctrine in administrative law where human rights of the people are violated. However, because of the concept of parliamentary sovereignty, court merely issue a "declaration of incompatibility", while reviewing a law, if an interpretation compatible to the law of Parliament is not possible. This gives an opportunity to Parliament to rethink the whole issue afresh.

6.2 Development in India

In India, fundamental rights form a part of the Indian Constitution, therefore, courts have always used the doctrine of proportionality in judging the reasonableness of a restriction on the exercise of fundamental rights. The law is clear on the point that while deciding the reasonableness of the restriction on fundamental rights, the nature of the right alleged to have been infringed, the underlying purpose of the restriction imposed, the extent and urgency of the evil sought to be remedied thereby, disproportion of the imposition, prevailing conditions at the time should all enter into judicial verdict.[510] Thus, while exercising the power of judicial review, court performs the primary role in Brind's sense of evaluating if a particular competing public interest justifies the particular restriction under law. This situation arises when the court is deciding on the constitutionality of a law imposing unreasonable restriction on the exercise of fundamental rights.

However, whether the courts dealing with executive or administrative action or discretion exercised under statutory powers, where fundamental rights are not involved, could apply the principle of "proportionality" and take up primary role is still not certain. In 1997, while deciding *Union of*

---

508. 1996 QB 517: (1996) 2 WLR 305 (CA).
509. *Ibid*, QB 556.
510. *Laxmi Khandsari* v. *State of U.P.*, (1981) 2 SCC 600; *D.K. Trivedi & Sons* v. *State of Gujarat*, 1986 Supp SCC 20; *State of A.P.* v. *McDowell & Co.*, (1996) 3 SCC 709.

India v. *G. Ganayutham*[511], the court left this question open because it was not necessary for the decision in the case, as the party had not pleaded the violation of fundamental rights. In this case, 50 per cent of respondent's pension and 50 per cent of gratuity had been withheld on proof of his misconduct. One of the grounds taken by the respondent was that the penalty was excessive. The Central Administrative Tribunal came to the conclusion that the punishment awarded was "too severe", that the lapse was procedural, there was no collusion between the respondent and any party, that the officer had otherwise done excellent work and, therefore, it was a fit case where the withholding of pension of 50 per cent had to be restricted for a period of 10 years, instead of on a permanent basis. Allowing the appeal, the Supreme Court held that in such cases the judicial review is restricted to secondary judgment,[512] and thus, the review court cannot substitute its own views of the punishment. The power of judicial review is limited to illegality, procedural impropriety and irrationality meaning, thereby, that no sensible person, who weighed the pros and cons, could have arrived at, or that the punishment is outrageous in defiance of any logic or standard of morality. Therefore, as neither the Wednesbury[513] nor CCSU tests[514] had been satisfied, the order of the tribunal was set aside. It was emphasised by the court that unless the court or tribunal opines in its secondary role, that the administrator was, on the material before him, irrational according to the Wednesbury or CCSU norms, the punishment cannot be quashed. Even then, the matter was remitted back to the appropriate authority for reconsideration. It is only in a very rare situation in order to shorten litigation that the court may substitute its own view on punishment. Such a rare situation may include a case where punishment awarded is such which shocks the conscience of the court or tribunal.[515] A similar view was taken in *Indian Oil Corpn. Ltd.* v. *Ashok Kumar Arora*[516], when the court held that in matters of punishment it will not intervene unless the punishment is wholly disproportionate.

It may be noted that the Supreme Court had applied the doctrine of proportionality while quashing the punishment of dismissal from service and sentence of imprisonment awarded by the court-martial under the Army Act, 1950.[517]

However, while quashing the punishment on the ground that it was "strikingly disproportionate", the court observed:

511. (1997) 7 SCC 463. See also, *State of A.P.* v. *McDowell & Co.*, (1996) 3 SCC 709. Held:

> It is one thing to say that a restriction imposed upon fundamental right can be struck down if it is disproportionate, excessive or unreasonable and quite another thing to say if it thinks it unreasonable, unnecessary or unwarranted.

512. *R.* v. *Secy. of State for Home Deptt., ex p Brind*, (1991) 1 AC 696: (1991) 2 WLR 588 (HL).
513. *Associated Provincial Picture Houses Ltd.* v. *Wednesbury Corpn.*, (1948) 1 KB 223 (CA).
514. 1985 AC 374: (1984) 3 WLR 1174: (1984) 3 All ER 935 (HL).
515. *B.C. Chaturvedi* v. *Union of India*, (1995) 6 SCC 749.
516. (1997) 3 SCC 72.
517. *Ranjit Thakur* v. *Union of India*, (1987) 4 SCC 611.

> ....The question of the choice and quantum of punishment is within the jurisdiction and discretion of the court-martial. But the sentence has to suit the offence and the offender. It should not be vindictive or unduly harsh. It should not be so disproportionate to the offence as to shock the conscience and amount in itself to conclusive evidence of bias. The doctrine of proportionality, as part of the concept of judicial review, would ensure that even on an aspect which is, otherwise, within the exclusive province of the court-martial, if the decision of the court even as to sentence is an outrageous defiance of logic, then the sentence would not be immune from correction. Irrationality and perversity are recognised grounds of judicial review.[518]

It is pertinent to note that though this case applied the doctrine of proportionality but in fact the court confined itself to the description of irrationality as laid down in *CCSU*[519], namely, that it should be in outrageous defiance of logic.

It is a cardinal principle of criminal jurisprudence that the punishment imposed should not be disproportionate to the gravity of the offence proved. However, while dealing with a disciplinary matter of a government servant, the Supreme Court in *State of Orissa* v. *Bidyabhushan Mohapatra*[520] held that if the High Court is satisfied that some but not all the findings of the tribunal were unassailable, then it had no jurisdiction to direct the disciplinary authority to review the penalty.

> If the order may be supported on any finding as to substantial misdemeanour for which the punishment can lawfully be imposed, it is not for the Court to consider whether that ground alone would have weighed with the authority in dismissing the public servant.[521]

The jurisdiction of the High Court under Article 226 of the Constitution, according to the Supreme Court, is highly limited. It can only go into the questions of illegality, irrationality and procedural impropriety, therefore, it is not within the power of the court to substitute a decision taken by a competent authority simply because the decision sought to be substituted is a better one.[522] Thus, it is clear that while deciding the proportionality of a punishment or penalty, the CCSU rules are to be followed.[523] Therefore, unless the punishment is so outrageous and in defiance of logic that no sensible person could have arrived at it, the court would not interfere.

In cases of adjudication under the Industrial Disputes Act, 1947, the principle of proportionality fully applies by virtue of Section 11-A of the Act. The Industrial Court as well as the High Court, on a perusal of the charges and the punishment imposed, can always reduce the punishment if it is

518. *Ibid*, 620.
519. 1985 AC 374: (1984) 3 WLR 1174 (HL).
520. AIR 1963 SC 779.
521. *Ibid*.
522. *Dwarkadas Marfatia and Sons* v. *Port of Bombay*, (1989) 3 SCC 293. See also, *State of A.P.* v. *McDowell & Co.*, (1996) 3 SCC 709.
523. *Council of Civil Services Union* v. *Minister of Civil Service*, 1985 AC 374: (1984) 3 WLR 1174 (HL).

disproportionate to the gravity of the charge held proved. The rule of proportionality shares ground with the rule against arbitrariness. Therefore, in the absence of any statutory provision if a major penalty has been imposed for a minor lapse, it would be clearly arbitrary falling within the inhibition of Article 14.[524]

The rule of proportionality is fully applicable in constitutional adjudication where the court has to decide on the reasonableness of a restriction on the exercise of fundamental rights. However, its application in the field of administrative law is still in an evolving stage. For the present, the doctrine is not available in administrative law in the sense that the court cannot go into the question of choice made and priority fixed by the administrator, the court can only see if, given the material before the administrative officer, he has acted as a reasonable man. In an action for review of an administrative action, the court cannot act as a court of appeal. Even in cases where the validity of a restriction imposed on the fundamental right is involved, the court must exercise self-restraint and allow greater margin of appreciation to the administrator and the legislature in certain cases.[525]

In order to fine-tune the balance between individual rights and societal needs, courts have always used this doctrine with a judicious mix of the principle of "flexibility". Courts take into consideration factual matrix of the case while applying this doctrine. In *Allahabad Jal Sansthan* v. *Daya Shankar Rai*[526], the Supreme Court opined that while protecting interest of the workman, interest of the employer and the societal needs must be taken into consideration because complete detriment of the employer would only lead towards skewing investment away from labour intensive market, thus strangling economic development. In the same manner, in *Hombe Gowda Educational Trust* v. *State of Karnataka*[527], the Supreme Court observed that though dismissal causes grave hardship but grave misconduct should not go unpunished. Thus, courts are now more willing to provide more space to employers in labour relations in the interest of societal concerns.

In *Canara Bank* v. *V.K. Awasthy*[528], while explaining the applicability of the doctrine, the court observed that in situations where no fundamental freedoms are involved, the court will only play a secondary role, while primary judgment will remain with the administrative authorities. However, in situations where fundamental freedoms are directly and substantially involved, the court will exercise primary judgment. Regarding application of the doctrine of proportionality to determine quantum of punishment, the Supreme Court was of the view that it cannot be a routine matter. If departmental proceedings establish charges of failure to discharge duties

524. See, *National Remote Sensing Agency* v. *G. Reddappa*, 1991 SCC OnLine AP 17: (1991) 1 AP LJ 243.
525. *Union of India* v. *G. Ganayutham*, (1997) 7 SCC 463.
526. (2005) 5 SCC 124.
527. (2006) 1 SCC 430.
528. (2005) 6 SCC 321.

with honesty, integrity and diligence, the scope of judicial review is highly limited to situations of illegality and irrationality only.

Same position was taken by the court in *State of Meghalaya* v. *Mecken Singh N. Marak*[529]. In this case, a police officer lost his service revolver and government cash while travelling in public transport in violation of the rule, which mandated travel in private transport. After enquiry, he was dismissed. The High Court quashed his dismissal on the ground of proportionality for the punishment being too harsh. Overruling the decision, the Supreme Court laid down that while applying the proportionality rule, the court must take into consideration the mental makeup of employee, nature of duty, job requirement and honesty, and should not lightly interfere with the decision of the administrative authority, meaning; thereby, that court should not exercise primary judgment. In *Ambedkar Institute of Hotel Management, Nutrition and Catering Technology* v. *Vaibhav Singh Chauhan*[530], where a student was disqualified as per the rules for using unfair means in the examination, the Supreme Court maintained that courts should not lightly interfere in the question of quantum of punishment unless there is violation of any rule or the principles of natural justice. Primary judgment in disciplinary matters must not be generally and lightly made by the courts.

In *Kerala State Beverages (M&M) Corpn. Ltd.* v. *P.P. Suresh*[531], it was held that an administrative action to balance competing interests of similarly situated sections of society and in public interest is proportionate.

While discussing the constitutionality of the Aadhaar Act, 2016 (a social security legislation), the Supreme Court considered in detail if this Act meets the test of proportionality between legitimate aim of the State which in this case was proper identification of the person for providing welfare measures and the right to privacy inherent in Article 21 of the Constitution (right to personal liberty. The court identified four components of the principle of proportionality:

1. *Legitimate purpose*: The measure restricting a legitimate expectation must have a legitimate purpose.
2. *Reasonable connection*: The measure selected to achieve the legitimate purpose must be reasonable and fair.
3. *Necessity*: The measure selected must be least restrictive but equally effective alternative.
4. *Proper Balance*: The measure selected must not have a disproportionate impact on the rights of the person.[532]

Summing up the current position of the application of the doctrine of proportionality in administrative law in England and India, the Supreme Court was of the view:

529. (2008) 7 SCC 580.
530. (2009) 1 SCC 59.
531. (2019) 9 SCC 710.
532. *K.S. Puttaswamy (Aadhaar-5J.)* v. *Union of India*, (2019) 1 SCC 1.

(1) With the growth of administrative law, there is a need to control the possible abuse of discretionary powers exercised by the administration. For this purpose, courts have developed various principles. The proportionality principle is the latest induction. It is a principle where court review the process, method or manner in which authorities have ordered their priorities or recalled a decision.[533]

(2) The doctrine of proportionality includes "balancing" and "necessity" tests. "Balancing test" permits scrutiny of punishments on infringement of rights, interests, and a manifest imbalance of relevant considerations. The "necessity test" requires infringement of fundamental rights to least restrictive alternative.[534]

(3) To judge the validity of any administrative order or statutory discretion, normally, the Wednesbury test is to be applied to find out if the decision was illegal or suffered from procedural improprieties, or was one which no sensible decision-maker, could, on material before him and within the framework of the law, have arrived at. The court would consider whether relevant matters had not been taken into account, or whether irrelevant matters had been taken into account, or whether the action was not bona fide. The court would also consider whether the decision was absurd or perverse. The court would not, however, go into the correctness of the choices made by the administrator amongst the various alternatives open to him. Nor the court would substitute its decision to that of the administrator. This is the Wednesbury test.[535]

(4) The court would not interfere with the administrator's decision unless it was illegal or suffered from procedural impropriety or was irrational—in the sense that it was in outrageous defiance of logic or moral standards. The possibility of other tests, including proportionality, being brought into English administrative law in future is not ruled out. These are CCSU principles.[536]

(5) (*a*) As per *R.* v. *Secy. of State for Home Deptt., ex p Bugdaycay*[537], *Brind*[538] and *Smith*[539] before European Convention on Human Rights was incorporated into English Law, the English courts merely exercised secondary judgment to find out if the decision-maker could have, on the material before him, arrived at the primary judgment in the manner it has been done.

533. *Coimbatore District Central Coop. Bank* v. *Employees' Assn.*, (2007) 4 SCC 669.

534. *Ibid.* See also, *Union of India* v. *Unicorn Industries*, (2019) 10 SCC 575 and *K.S. Puttaswamy (Aadhaar-5J.)* v. *Union of India*, (2019) 1 SCC 1.

535. *Associated Provincial Picture Houses Ltd.* v. *Wednesbury Corpn.*, (1948) 1 KB 223 (CA).

536. *Council of Civil Services Union* v. *Minister of Civil Service*, 1985 AC 374: (1984) 3 WLR 1174 (HL).

537. 1987 AC 514: (1987) 2 WLR 606 (HL).

538. (1991) 1 AC 696: (1991) 2 WLR 588 (HL).

539. 1996 QB 517: (1996) 2 WLR 305 (CA).

(b) Now when the European Convention on Human Rights has been incorporated in English Law, making available the principle of proportionality, the English courts will render primary judgment on the validity of administrative action to find out if the restriction is disproportionate or excessive, or is not based upon fair balancing of fundamental freedoms, and the need for the restriction thereupon. In view of the concept of parliamentary supremacy, though courts have no jurisdiction to declare the law invalid, hence, they issue a "declaration of incompatibility" asking Parliament to rethink and remedy the situation. Thus, English courts, after the passing of the Human Rights Act,1998, have started making use of this doctrine in administrative law.

(6) (a) The position in India, in administrative law, is that where no fundamental freedoms as aforesaid are involved, courts/ tribunals will only play a secondary role, while the primary judgment as to reasonableness will remain with the executive or administrative authority. The secondary judgment of the court is to be based on Wednesbury and CCSU principles to find out if the executive or administrative authority has reasonably arrived at his decision as a primary authority.

(b) Whether in a case of administrative or executive action, affecting fundamental freedoms, the courts in India will apply the principle of "proportionality" and assume the primary role is left open to be decided in appropriate cases. It will then be necessary to decide whether the courts will have a primary role only if the freedoms under Articles 19 and 21, etc., are involved and not for Article 14.[540]

(c) Jurisdiction of the court to interfere with the quantum of punishment is limited to very exceptional circumstances. In the opinion of the court, "verbal abuse" may entail punishment of dismissal from service.[541] Court applies the doctrine of proportionality in a limited manner.

(7) In the present context, the doctrine of proportionality is gaining ground at the cost of Wednesbury unreasonableness to make the scrutiny of administrative actions more exacting and intrusive.[542]

(8) The proportionality test, though gaining ground, has not completely replaced the Wednesbury test of unreasonableness. Both tests are coexisting under English and Indian laws. The proportionality test is applied when there is a violation of fundamental rights, and the Wednesbury test is applied when there is violation of ordinary rights.[543]

---

540. *Union of India* v. *G. Ganayutham*, (1997) 7 SCC 463, 478–79, *per* Jagannadha Rao J.

541. *P.D. Agrawal* v. *SBI*, (2006) 8 SCC 776.

542. *State of U.P.* v. *Sheo Shanker Lal Srivastava*, (2006) 3 SCC 276.

543. *All India Railway Recruitment Board* v. *K. Shyam Kumar*, (2010) 6 SCC 614.

7. JUDICIAL REVIEW OF ADMINISTRATIVE ACTIONS: GROUNDS

Judicial review is central in dealing with the malignancy in the exercise of administrative power. Outsourcing of legislative and adjudicatory powers to administrative authorities, as an imperative of modern system of governance, has brought the law of judicial review of administrative actions in prime focus. Law dealing with judicial review of administrative actions is largely judge-induced and judge-led, consequently, thickets of technicalities and inconsistencies surround it. Any one who surveys the spectrum of judicial review finds that the fundamentals on which courts base their decisions include the rule of law, administrative efficiency, fairness, and accountability. These fundamentals are necessary for making administrative actions "people-centric". Courts have generally exhibited a sense of self-restraint where judicially manageable standards do not exist for judicial intervention.[544] However, "self-restraint" is not the absence or lack of power of judicial review. Courts have not hesitated, in exceptional situations, even to review policy matters and subjective satisfaction of the executive.

Judicial review is the basic feature of the Indian Constitution and, therefore, cannot be abrogated even by an amendment of the Constitution. However, in view of the new economic policy of liberalisation, privatisation and globalisation, courts are allowing wider flexibilities to the administration. Trend of judicial decisions indicate that unless an administrative action is violative of the Constitution or law, or is arbitrary or mala fide, courts do not interfere with administrative decisions. Fact remains that without a good system of judicial review, any society would collapse under its own weight making "development" counter-productive.

Generally, judicial review of any administrative action can be exercised on four grounds: 1) illegality, 2) irrationality, 3) procedural impropriety, and 4) proportionality. These grounds of judicial review were developed by Lord Diplock in *CCSU*[545]. Though these grounds of judicial review are not exhaustive and cannot be put in watertight compartments, yet these provide sufficient base for the courts to exercise their review jurisdiction over administrative actions in the interest of efficiency, fairness and accountability.

7.1 Illegality

This ground of judicial review is based on the principle that administrative authorities must correctly understand the law and its limits before any action is taken. Therefore, if the authority lacks jurisdiction, or fails to exercise jurisdiction, or abuses jurisdiction, or exceeds jurisdiction, it shall

544. *Essar Oil Ltd.* v. *Halar Utkarsh Samiti*, (2004) 2 SCC 392; *N.D. Jayal* v. *Union of India*, (2004) 9 SCC 362; *Hira Tikkoo* v. *UT, Chandigarh*, (2004) 6 SCC 765; *State of Karnataka* v. *Praveen Bhai Thogadia*, (2004) 4 SCC 684; *E.V. Chinnaiah* v. *State of A.P.*, (2005) 1 SCC 394.
545. 1985 AC 374: (1984) 3 WLR 1174 (HL) (CCSU Rules).

be deemed that the authority has acted "illegally". Court may quash an administrative action on the ground of illegality in following situations.

7.1.1 *Lack of jurisdiction*

Court may review an administrative action on the ground that the authority exercised jurisdiction which did not belong to it. This review power may be exercised inter alia on the following grounds:

(1) That the law under which an administrative authority is constituted and exercising jurisdiction is itself unconstitutional.
(2) That the authority is not properly constituted as required by law.
(3) That the authority has wrongly decided a jurisdictional fact and, thereby, assumed jurisdiction which did not belong to it.
(4) That some of the essential preliminary proceedings or conditions have been disregarded which were conditions precedent for the exercise of jurisdiction, such as:
    (*a*) non-formation of necessary opinion before assuming jurisdiction,
    (*b*) non-issue of statutory notice, or
    (*c*) non-institution of proceedings within specified time.
(5) That the authority is incompetent to assume jurisdiction in respect of subject-matter, area and parties.

7.1.2 *Excess of jurisdiction*

This covers a situation wherein though an authority initially had the jurisdiction but exceeded it and, hence, its actions become illegal. This may happen under the following situations:

(1) Continue to exercise jurisdiction despite occurrence of an event ousting jurisdiction.
(2) Entertaining matters outside its jurisdiction.

7.1.3 *Abuse of jurisdiction*

All administrative powers must be exercised fairly, in good faith, for the purpose it is given, therefore, if powers are abused it will be a ground for judicial review. In the following situations, an abuse of power may arise:

(1) Malfeasance in office. It is a tort doctrine imported into administrative law. The Supreme Court in *LDA* v. *M.K. Gupta*[546] held that where the Minister allotted petrol outlets from his discretionary quota in arbitrary, mala fide, and unjust manner, it is misfeasance in office subject to judicial review of the court.
(2) An error apparent on the face of the record which may be a result of misinterpretation or misapplication of law.

546. (1994) 1 SCC 243.

(3) Consideration of extraneous material.
(4) Non-consideration of relevant material.
(5) Colourable exercise of power or misdirection in law. Administrative power cannot be used for the purpose it was not given. Therefore, achieving an unauthorised purpose will be a colourable exercise of power subject to judicial review.
(6) Mala fide exercise of power or bad faith or malice.

No public authority can act in bad faith or with corrupt motives. If any administrative authority has acted in a mala fide manner, it will be subject to the review jurisdiction of the court. In case of mixed considerations, courts try to find out the dominant purpose which impelled administrative action. Power is exercised maliciously when an action is motivated by personal animosity towards one who is affected by it. It is considered as fraud on power. Mala fide as a ground of judicial review is not available against legislative action. Even if executive may have ulterior motives in moving a legislation, but such malice cannot be transferred to the legislature or an administrative authority exercising rule-making powers.

"Mala fide" is an open textured expression. In *R.S. Garg* v. *State of U.P.*[547], the Supreme Court explaining the reach of this expression held that where authority had made up its mind from the very beginning to promote the respondent, as approval of the Chief Minister was obtained earlier than the creation of post, and the order of promotion was issued in haste, it goes to prove that the action of the authority smacks of mala fide.

7.1.4 *Failure to exercise jurisdiction*

If any administrative authority has been given power by law, no matter discretionary, the authority must exercise it in one way or the other. Public power is not a personal power, it is a public trust and, therefore, must be exercised in public interest. Failure or denial to exercise jurisdiction will be an illegality. Failure to exercise power may arise

(1) where an authority has sub-delegated its powers without the authority of law; or
(2) where it is exercising its power under dictation or transcription; or
(3) where it has fettered its powers by self-imposed restrictions unwarranted by law; or
(4) where it declines jurisdiction which belongs to it under law; or
(5) where there is non-application of mind by the authority and is acting in a perfunctory or mechanical manner, ignoring conditions precedent.

547. (2006) 6 SCC 430.

7.2 Irrationality (Wednesbury test)

Irrationality as a ground of judicial review was developed by the court in *Associated Provincial Picture House Ltd.* v. *Wednesbury Corpn.*[548], later came to be known as "Wednesbury test" to determine "irrationality" of an administrative action. A decision of the administrative authority shall be considered as irrational

(1) if it is without the authority of law,
(2) if it is based on no evidence,
(3) if it is based on irrelevant and extraneous consideration, and
(4) if it is so outrageous in its defiance to logic or accepted norms of moral standard that no sensible person, on the given facts and circumstances, could arrive at such a decision. In other words, it is so absurd that no sensible person could ever dream that it lay within the power of the administrative authority. It is the use of the doctrine in a substantive sense. Therefore, if the decision of the authority is so capricious, perverse, arbitrary, unreasonable and manifestly unjust that no sensible person can come to that conclusion, court would quash it. However, the standard of rationality of administrative action is not to be judged by the standard of "any person" (man in a Clapham Omnibus). It is a standard indicated by true construction of law, proper or improper use of power, and perversity of the decision which no sensible man can arrive at. In applying this test, court would not apply "strict scrutiny" and would not judge adequacy or sufficiency of the material unless fundamental rights are violated, and would not substitute its judgment with the judgment of the administrator unless the decision is perverse; or
(5) it is so unreasonable that it may be described as done in bad faith.

Irrationality in umbrella sense may include 1) taking into consideration irrelevant material; 2) ignoring relevant considerations; 3) using power for improper purpose; and 4) exercising power in a mala fide manner. However, when used in "substantive sense", it may mean that an administrative action is so irrational that no public authority could take it.

The principle of irrationality shares space with the rule of law, reasonableness and non-arbitrariness. If the action of the administrative authority violates any of these principles, court can quash such action as violative of Articles 14, 19 or 21 of the Constitution. Reasonableness, besides being a constitutional requirement, may also arise from a statutory mandate. Thus, where a statute provides, "if authority has reason to believe", courts have held these words to limit administrative discretion to the extent that the exercise of power must be objective and not subjective. Where there is no express requirement of "reasonableness", courts have implied this requirement in every administrative action because no administrative action

548. (1948) 1 KB 223 (CA).

should be irrational, arbitrary and subjective. Therefore, if law allows an administrative authority to take action "as it may deem fit", courts have interpreted these words to mean "as it may reasonably deem fit". It is necessary to infuse every administrative action with "fairness" necessary to build a rule of law society.

7.3 Procedural impropriety

Procedure of a decision is as important as the decision itself because if "procedure" is not fair, decision cannot be trustworthy. Therefore, courts have insisted on a "fair procedure" requirement in every administrative action. Requirement of a "fair procedure" may arise in the following ways:

(1) As a constitutional mandate where fundamental rights of the people are violated;

(2) As a statutory mandate. If a statute lays down any procedure which administrative authority must follow before taking action, it must be faithfully followed and any violation of the procedural norm would vitiate an administrative action.

(3) As an implied requirement where statute is silent about procedure.

Where statute is silent, courts have insisted that administrative authorities must follow the principles of natural justice which provide fair minimum administrative procedure which every administrative authority must follow, while taking a decision which has civil or evil consequences. These rules of natural justice which guarantee "fair play in action" include:

(1) *Rule against Bias.*—No one should be made judge in his own cause.

(2) *Rule of fair hearing.*—No one should be condemned unheard.[549]

7.4 Proportionality[550]

Proportionality means that the administrative action should not be more drastic than it ought to be for obtaining desired result. This implies that canon should not be used to shoot a sparrow. Thus, this doctrine tries to balance means with ends. Proportionality shares space with "reasonableness" and courts, while exercising the power of review, see "is it a course of action that could have been reasonably followed". The courts in India have been following this doctrine for a long time, but English courts have started using this doctrine in administrative law after the passing of the Human Rights Act, 1998.

This doctrine is being applied in the following situations:

(1) Where an administrative action invades fundamental rights, courts make strict scrutiny of the administrative action and go into the

549. For detailed discussion on the principles of natural justice refer to Chap. 7 of this book.

550. For detailed discussion of the doctrine of proportionality, see, the heading "Doctrine of Proportionality" in this chapter, p. 378.

question of correctness of the choices made by the authority. The court would also balance adverse effects on the right and the object sought to be achieved.

(2) Where a question of quantum of punishment imposed by the administrative authority is involved, the court would not make strict scrutiny. Courts follow the principle that though quantum of punishment is within the jurisdiction of the administrative authority, but arbitrariness must be avoided. This principle may be termed as "deference principle" where court show respect to the choice made by the administrative authority except when the choice is manifestly disproportionate.

While reviewing an administrative action on the ground of proportionality, courts generally examine:

(1) Whether the relative merits of different objectives or interests have been appropriately weighed and fairly balanced?
(2) Whether the action under review was, in the circumstances, excessively restrictive or inflicted an unnecessary burden?

Elaborating on the scope of judicial review of administrative action, on grounds mentioned above, the court observed that it is limited to consideration of the legality of decision-making process and not legality of the decision per se. Mere possibility of another view cannot be a ground for interference. Therefore, courts will not interfere unless the decision suffers from illegality, irrationality, procedural impropriety and proportionality deficiency. Mere assertion of these grounds is not sufficient, each ground must be proved by evidence on record. Asserting the power of judicial review, the court emphasised that the doctrine of immunity from judicial review is restricted to cases or class of cases which relate to deployment of troops and entering into international treaties, etc. In policy matters and where subjective satisfaction of the authority is involved, courts will not interfere unless the decision is totally perverse and violates any provisions of the Constitution.[551] The extent of, depth and intensity of judicial review depends on the subject-matter of judicial review.[552]

Aristotle once said that the generalities of law faulter before the specifics of life, thus, courts, while exercising their power of review, always try to balance generalities with specifics in order to meet the ends of justice.

By creatively exercising the power of judicial review of administrative action, courts in India have progressively eliminated all "no-go" areas of the administration. Today, there exists no limitation on the power of judicial review of the courts except self-restraint. This has thrown new challenges and opportunities before the court, as it can now do justice in any manner of case to any manner of people.

551. *Assn. of Registration Plates* v. *Union of India*, (2005) 1 SCC 679.
552. *State of W.B.* v. *Debasish Mukherjee*, (2011) 14 SCC 187.

Even the prerogative power of the President and the Governor to grant pardon under Articles 72 and 161 is not immune from judicial review. Court can review this power on the following grounds: 1) if the power has been exercised without the advice of the government; 2) if there is an excess of jurisdiction; 3) if there is non-application of mind; 4) if the order is mala fide; or 5) if the order is based on extraneous considerations.[553]

8. INVENTING NEW GROUNDS OF JUDICIAL REVIEW

The grounds of judicial review mentioned above cannot be exhaustive because constitutional courts exercising their powers of judicial review in an activist manner may invent new grounds for improving political and administrative culture necessary for improving governance outcomes for the people. Needless to say that judicial activism is not merely interpreting the law and the Constitution but imaginatively and creatively sharing the values and passion of the Constitution also for transformation of the society.

Thus, the new norm of judicial review of administrative action is to promote good governance and to enforce rule of law on the administration so that the administration acts efficiently and honestly to promote public good. To achieve these objectives the court has always invented new grounds of judicial review. This has expanded radically the power of judicial review to include diverse forms of "public" power in response to the changing architecture of the administration. Therefore, scope and intensity of judicial review has increased. However, the courts do not substitute their judgment with that of the administration unless there is some specific fault. Courts generally do not interfere in "policy" matters formulated by experts. In the same manner courts hesitate to interfere in "discretionary" powers which are given to the administration to respond appropriately to the needs of a particular situation unless it is exercised with oblique and/or extraneous purposes or upon extraneous considerations, or arbitrarily without applying its mind to the relevant considerations, or where it is guided by irrelevant considerations not necessary to achieve the object.[554]

8.1 Constitutional morality

"Constitutional morality" as a tool of constitutional interpretation implies enforcing the provisions of the Constitution and its values. It signifies commitment to constitutional principles and values generally reflected in the Preamble of the Constitution. These values must reflect in every aspect

553. *Narayan Dutt* v. *State of Punjab*, (2011) 4 SCC 353. See also, *S.R. Tewari* v. *Union of India*, (2013) 6 SCC 602; *High Court of Judicature of Patna* v. *Shyam Deo Singh*, (2014) 4 SCC 773.

554. *Center for Public Interest Litigation* v. *Union of India*, (2016) 6 SCC 408; see also, *Mangalam Organics Ltd.* v. *Union of India*, (2017) 7 SCC 221.

of governance of the country. One finds the echo of the term in the final speech of Dr Ambedkar on 4 November 1948, when the Draft Constitution was being approved. The Constitution of India uses this term only at two places—Articles 25 and 26 (religious freedom). Most important advocate of constitutional morality is Ronald Dworkin who emphasised moral reading of the Constitution by fusing moral philosophy with the legal philosophy. The tool of constitutional morality is generally used to determine the constitutionality of social, public or popular concepts of morality. The classical use of this concept as a tool of constitutional interpretation was seen in the historic *Sabarimala case*[555], where the Supreme Court held unconstitutional the practice of exclusion of women from entering the temple of Lord Ayyappa during menstruation period. The Supreme Court used this doctrine in *NCT Delhi* v. *Union of India*[556] to define the power of Lt. Governor in the democratic framework of the Indian Constitution. The court opined that constitutional morality is not just the form or procedure of the Constitution but provides an enabling framework that allows societies the possibilities of self-renewal. In the *Navtej Singh Johar* v. *Union of India*[557], the Supreme Court while deciding the constitutionality of Section 377 IPC, 1860 (criminalisation of homosexuality) observed that constitutional morality cannot be sacrificed at the altar of social morality.

However, the use of the tool of constitutional morality to interpret the Constitution is being criticised as "judicial overreach". It allows subjective interpretation of the Constitution by the judiciary. The use of the concept of constitutional morality as a ground of judicial review is certainly a step forward to fill "constitutional silence" in order to fully harness the transformative capacity of the Constitution necessary to transform a "semi-feudal society" into a "modern industrial society". One can hope that this transformative tool of interpretation will be used with full force within the area of administrative law also.

POINTS FOR DISCUSSION

1. The efforts of courts in developing a rational law of locus standi has been an exercise in futility because no one would waste his time and money in challenging an administrative action in which he has no interest. However, it is equally true that in any developed legal system, professional litigants and meddlesome interlopers need discouragement. How is the dilemma to be solved in the best interests of individual justice and administrative viability? Discussion on the subject should aim at evolving workable principles of locus standi to sustain public actions.

555. *Indian Young Lawyers Assn. (Sabarimala Temple–5J.)* v. *State of Kerala*, (2019) 11 SCC 1.
556. (2018) 8 SCC 501.
557. (2018) 10 SCC 1.

2. The basis of the SAL is the gradual liberalisation of the technical rule of locus standi. This gradual unfolding and its possible limits may be discussed.
3. The system of judicial review of administrative actions has been inherited from England. It is on this foundation that the Indian courts have built the superstructure of control mechanism. In this background, the students may discuss historically the development of principles and instrumentalities of judicial review in England.
4. The constituency of public law review in India still remains undermined. The reason seems to be that the "type of agency" and not the "rights of the person" is the focal point of attention by courts. What possible parameters can be developed to redetermine the constituency of public law review so as to cover every possible violation of public and private right through an administrative action?
5. Sometimes it is suggested that keeping in view the norms of functioning of an intensive form of government in a democratic society, if a person first proceeds through his political representative, instead of rushing through the expensive and dilatory judicial process, the time, thus, consumed in seeking a negotiated relief against any administrative action must be considered as an excusable delay by the courts. Is it a sound suggestion keeping in view the socio-political realities in India?
6. If class actions, as provided in the CPC, are encouraged and other grievance mechanisms like the institution of ombudsman is strengthened, the SAL jurisdiction of the court may not be as necessary as it seems today. Students may discuss the validity of this statement.
7. The doctrine of legitimate expectation is the latest recruit to a long list of concepts fashioned by the courts to check the abuse of the exercise of administrative powers. It imposes morality in all public dealings. In the light of this statement, this doctrine may be discussed, keeping in view its impact on the flexibility of administrative action.
8. Public accountability is a concept developed to make administration responsive and responsible. This doctrine may be discussed as developed in India through case law with a special emphasis on the concept of administrative powers as public trust.
9. The doctrine of proportionality is fully established as a constitutional law concept, but its application in administrative law is still being debated. Desirability of applying this doctrine in administrative law may be discussed keeping in view its various claims and counter-claims.
10. In certain situations, curtailing the right to procedural due process becomes necessary in public interest. Such situations may be discussed in order to develop some norms necessary for balancing public interest with the requirement of fair hearing.

11. What is the proper purpose of judicial review? Is it supervision of the exercise of power by the administration or justice to the petitioner?
12. Do you think that judicial review will be unnecessary if the legislature develops better methods for scrutinising administrative rule-making, administrative policies, programmes and their execution?
13. Administrative decisions may be reviewed by the court on the ground of unreasonableness. Do you think that judicial reasonableness will always be better than the reasonableness of the Parliament or the executive?
14. Judges must exercise the power of judicial review in a manner that does not show disrespect to the other organs of the State. Do you think that this can be a good principle of judicial review?
15. While exercising powers of judicial review on grounds of rule of law or constitutional morality, the court may determine its own jurisdiction and powers. Do you think that it is an antithesis of the principle of representative and responsible government in a constitutional liberal democracy?
16. Legitimacy and constitutional foundations in a libral democracy may be discussed. Do judges while exercising power of judicial review play a political role?

SUGGESTED READINGS

1. A.K. Sikri, "Proportionality as a Tool for Advancing Rule of Law", (2019) 3 SCC J-1.
2. A.T. Markose, "Legal Interest Required to Challenge the Validity of Administrative Action: A Preliminary Survey", (1959) 1 JILI 273.
3. Albert, "Standing to Challenge an Administrative Action: An Inadequate Surrogate for Claims for Relief", (1973–74) 83 Yale LJ 425.
4. Anand Byrareddy, "Proportionality Vis-à-Vis Irrationality in Administrative Law", (2008) 7 SCC J-29.
5. Ashish Chugh, "Is the Supreme Court Disproportionately Applying the Proportionality Principle?" (2004) 8 SCC J-33.
6. Australian Law Reform Commission Paper No. 4, "Access to the Courts—Standing: Public Interest Suit", and Working Paper No. 7, under the same title (1977).
7. B.K. Nehru, *Thoughts on Our Present Discontents* (Allied Publishers, 1986) Introduction to B.K. Nehru by M. Hidyatullah.
8. C.K. Thakker, *Administrative Law* (Eastern Book Company 1992) 372–403.
9. D.S. Broder, *Changing of the Guard: Power and Leadership in America* (Penguin Books 1981).
10. Davis, "The Liberalized Law of Standing", (1970) 37 U Chi L Rev 450.
11. Denning, *The Discipline of Law* (1979) Part III.
12. Dotan, "Why Administrators Should be Bound by their Policies", (1997) 17 Oxford Journal of Legal Studies 23.

13. H.M. Seervai, "Article 32 of the Constitution and Limitation", 71 Bom LR (J) 45.
14. J. Minattur, "Private Discrimination: Is it Constitutional?", (1973) Journal of Constitutional and Parliamentary Studies 77.
15. Jayanta Chakraborty, "Doctrine of Legitimate Expectation-A Comparative Study of UK, USA & India", (2018) 5.1 IJLPP 21.
16. K.E. Scott, "Standing in the Supreme Court: A Functional Analysis", (1973) 86 Harv L Rev 645.
17. Lord Denning, *The Discipline of Law* (1982) 106–09.
18. M. Hidayatullah, "Highways and Bye-lanes of Justice", (1984) 2 SCC J-1.
19. M.M. Blecher, "Is the Class Action Doing the Job?" (1973) 55 Fed Rules Decisions 365.
20. M.P. Jain, *Changing Face of Administrative Law in India and Abroad* (Indian Law Institute 1982).
21. M.P. Jain, "Justice Bhagwati and Indian Administrative Law", (1980) The Banaras Law Journal 47.
22. P.N. Bhagwati J talks to Dina Vakil , "How the Supreme Court enforces Citizens' Rights", Indian Express, Sunday Magazine 31-1-1982.
23. P. Leelakrishnan, "Reviewing Decisions of Administrative Tribunal: Paternalistic Approach of the Indian Supreme Court and Need for Institutional Reforms", 54 JILI (2012) 1.
24. Peter Cane, "The Function of Standing Rules in Administrative Law", (1980) Public Law 303.
25. Rabie and Eckard: "Locus Standi: The Administrator's Shield and the Environmentalists' Shackle", (1976) 9 Comp and Int Law J of S.A. 41.
26. S.N. Jain, *Locus Standi and Public Interest Litigation* (Mimeographed).
27. S. Rangarajan, "Some Thoughts on Legal Research", paper presented in conference on the reforms of the Indian legal system, 4–6 February 1982, organised by the Indian Law Institute (Mimeographed) 6–7.
28. Seervai, *Constitutional Law of India* (1979) 2026–29.
29. Sudhish Pai, "Is Wednesbury on the Terminal Decline?" (2008) 2 SCC J-15.
30 Syed Shah Mohammed,"Judicial Review of Administrative Action", Quadri, (2001) 6 SCC J-1.
31. Tarun Krishnakumar, "The Wednesbury Principles : Formulation, Evolution and Demise?", 1.1 CALQ (2013) 3.
32. Thio Li-ann, "1. Administrative and Constitutional Law", (2003) 4 SALAnnRev 1.
33. Upendra Baxi, *Crises of the Indian Legal System* (Vikas 1982).
34. Upendra Baxi, "Developments in Indian Administrative Law" in A.G. Noorani (Ed.), *Public Law in India* (Vikas 1982).
35. Upendra Baxi, "On How Not to Judge the Judges", a paper presented to a seminar on Judicial Process and Social Change (Andhra University, Waltair and the Indian Law Institute, Delhi 1980, Mimeographed).

36. Upendra Baxi, "Pre-Marxist Socialism and the Supreme Court of India", (1984) 4 SCC J-3.
37. Upendra Baxi, *The Indian Supreme Court and Politics* (Eastern Book Co. 1980).
38. V.S. Deshpande, "Judicial Review, Expansion and Self-restraint", (1973) 15 JILI 531.
39. V.S. Deshpande, "Standing and Justiciability", (1971) 13 JILI 153.
40. V. Sudhish Pai, "Is Wednesbury on the Terminal Decline?", (2008) 2 SCC J-15.
41. W. Simon, "Class Actions—Useful Tool or Engine of Destruction?" (1973) 55 Fed Rules Decisions 375.

Chapter 9

Judicial Review of Administrative Action: Modes

1. PUBLIC LAW REVIEW

Though the remarkable feature of judicial review is that it gives power to the court to create its own powers and invent its one role yet the basic purpose of judicial review is to enforce constitutionalism and to guard against majoritarianism. Thus, an important aspect of public law review is not only the enforcement of private rights but to keep the administrative and quasi-administrative machinery within proper control. This aspect of public law review was rightly stressed by the Supreme Court in *S.L. Kapoor* v. *Jagmohan*[1]. In this case, two non-official members of the New Delhi Municipal Committee had filed a petition before the Supreme Court under Article 136 against the governmental action of superseding the Municipal Committee without complying with the principles of natural justice. During the pendency of the case, the term of office of the petitioners had expired. It was argued that since the petition has become infructuous, the court has no power to continue with the appeal. Rejecting the contention, the Supreme Court held that since the petition involves an issue of public importance, the court can still decide the issue even in the face of loss of standing of the petitioners.

It is no denying the fact that today due to the intensive form of government, there is a tremendous increase in the functions of the administration as a facilitator, regulator and provider. Therefore, if these new-found powers are properly exercised, these may lead to real socio-economic growth, and if abused these may lead to a totalitarian state.[2] Against this backdrop, the prime function of judicial review is to check the abuse of administrative powers and to enforce accountability on the operators of these powers.

The Supreme Court and High Courts exercise the power of public law review through writs of certiorari, prohibition, mandamus, quo warranto, and habeas corpus, and through the exercise of power under Articles 136

1. (1980) 4 SCC 379.
2. Lord Denning, *Freedom under the Law* (Stevens 1949) 126 quoted in C.K. Thakker, *Administrative Law* (Eastern Book Company 1992) 374.

and 227 of the Constitution. These modes of public law review may now be discussed in detail.

1.1 Writ of certiorari

"Certiorari" is a Latin word, being the passive form of the word "certiorare" meaning to "inform". It was essentially a royal demand for information. The King, wishing to be certified of some matter, ordered that the necessary information be provided for him. In the beginning, certiorari was never used to call for the record of proceedings of an Act or ordinance for quashing these. The proper remedy in such cases was declaration and mandamus. However, with the passage of time the scope of certiorari has undergone a change.[3] "Certiorari" may be defined as a judicial order operating in personam and made in the original legal proceedings, directed by the Supreme Court or a High Court to any constitutional, statutory or non-statutory body or person, requiring the records of any action to be certified by the court and dealt with according to law.

It is a remedy operating in personam, therefore, a writ can be issued even where an authority has become functus officio, to the keeper of the records.

As has been discussed earlier in this chapter, the constituency within which certiorari can be operative has been tremendously enlarged because it is corrective in nature. A writ can now be issued against constitutional bodies (legislature, executive and judiciary or their officers), statutory bodies (like corporations and other authorities created under a statute), non-statutory bodies (like companies and cooperative societies), and private bodies and persons.

The requirement that certiorari can be issued only when the action is judicial or quasi-judicial is no more valid. Certiorari can be issued to quash actions which are administrative in nature. In *A.K. Kraipak* v. *Union of India*[4], the writ of certiorari was issued to quash the action of a selection board.

1.1.1 *Grounds for the issue of a writ of certiorari*

Certiorari can be issued on any of the following grounds.

1.1.1.1 *Lack of jurisdiction*

Lack of jurisdiction refers to such situations where an authority has no jurisdiction at all to take action. Such situations may arise

(1) if the authority is improperly constituted;

(2) if the authority commits an error in its decision on jurisdictional facts and, thereby, assumes jurisdiction which never belonged to it;

3. *Prabodh Verma* v. *State of U.P.*, (1984) 4 SCC 251.
4. (1969) 2 SCC 262.

(3) if the authority is incompetent to take action in respect of a locality, party or subject-matter;
(4) if the law which gives jurisdiction is itself unconstitutional; and
(5) if preliminary essentials have been disregarded, *i.e.* omission to serve notice as required by law.

It may be noted that when an authority has jurisdiction to determine a matter, it does not lose it by coming to a wrong conclusion on law or fact.

1.1.1.1.1 Notable instances

(1) *Rafiq Khan* v. *State of U.P.*[5]—Section 85 of the U.P. Panchayat Raj Act, 1947 gave power to the Sub-Divisional Magistrate (SDM) to either quash the entire order of the Panchayat Adalat or to cancel its jurisdiction. The SDM had no power to modify the order in any manner. The court issued the writ of certiorari to quash the decision of the SDM where he had modified the conviction passed by the Panchayat Adalat by quashing the conviction of the accused for one offence and maintaining it in respect of the other offence.
(2) *Budh Prakash Jai Prakash* v. *STO*[6].—This case illustrates lack of jurisdiction where the subject-matter was outside the scope of the extent of jurisdiction of an authority. In this case, the Sales Tax Officer, exercising powers under the U.P. Sales Tax Act, 1948, imposed tax on forward contracts irrespective of the place where the delivery took place. The court issued the writ of certiorari on the ground that the subject-matter was outside the jurisdiction of the authority.
(3) *Nalini Ranjan Guha* v. *Annada Shankar Roy*[7]—This case illustrates lack of jurisdiction where an agency committed an error on jurisdictional facts. The jurisdiction of the Compensation Commissioner under the War Injuries Ordinance, 1941 depended on the existence or otherwise of the war injury. Therefore, as the Commissioner was wrong in his findings as regards the injury, a writ of certiorari was issued by the High Court to quash it.

Certiorari may also be issued to quash the decision of an authority declining jurisdiction where it legally belongs to it.[8]

1.1.1.2 *Excess of jurisdiction*

Excess of jurisdiction refers to cases where an authority has jurisdiction but it exceeds its permitted limits.

---

5. 1953 SCC OnLine All 212: AIR 1954 All 3. See also, *Chetkar Jha* v. *Vishwanath Prasad Verma*, (1970) 2 SCC 217.
6. 1982 SCC OnLine All 53: AIR 1952 All 764.
7. 1951 SCC OnLine Cal 324: AIR 1952 Cal 112.
8. *Latif Gani Bidi Manufacturers* v. *Abdul Rashid Sheikh Mohammad Khan*, 1962 SCC OnLine Bom 71: AIR 1964 Bom 89.

J.K. Chaudhuri v. *R.K. Datta Gupta*[9] is illustrative of this aspect. In this case, the governing body of a college affiliated to the Gauhati University dismissed its Principal, Datta Gupta, on the ground of misconduct. The executive committee of the Gauhati University, after hearing representations, ordered reinstatement. The court issued certiorari to quash the decision on the ground of excess of jurisdiction, because the jurisdiction of the university under Section 21(9) of the Gauhati University Act, 1947 was confined to teachers and did not extend to a case where the person holds the office of principal also.

1.1.1.3 *Abuse of jurisdiction*

Certiorari will also lie to quash an action where an authority has jurisdiction but has abused it. An authority shall be deemed to have abused its jurisdiction when it exercises its power for an improper purpose, or on extraneous considerations, or in bad faith, or leaves out a relevant consideration, or does not exercise the power by itself but at the instance and discretion of someone else. All these factors have been discussed in detail in Chapter 3 of this book under the heading "Administrative Discretion" at page 62.

1.1.1.4 *Violation of the principles of natural justice*

Principles of natural justice have been discussed in detail in Chapter 7 of this book. These principles include the following:

(1) *Rule against bias.*—Bias may include
  (*a*) personal bias,
  (*b*) pecuniary bias,
  (*c*) subject-matter bias,
  (*d*) departmental bias, and
  (*e*) preconceived notion bias.

(2) *Rule of audi alteram partem.*—This right to fair hearing may include
  (*a*) the right to know adverse evidence,
  (*b*) the right to present a case,
  (*c*) the right to rebut evidence,
  (*d*) the right to cross-examination and legal representation, and
  (*e*) the right to reasoned decisions, etc.

If an administrative agency violates any of the above rules in a case where they must be observed, the decision of the agency may be quashed by the court through the writ of certiorari.

9. AIR 1958 SC 722.

1.1.1.4.1 Notable instances

(1) *State of Punjab* v. *K.R. Erry*[10].—In this case, the pension benefits of an Assistant Engineer, Public Works Department, were reduced based on an adverse confidential report without giving him a hearing. The court issued certiorari to quash the decision on the ground of violation of the principles of natural justice.

(2) *Sirsi Municipality* v. *Cecelia Kom Francis Tellis*[11].—In this case, a hospital worker was dismissed for alleged negligence, which resulted in the death of a patient in the maternity ward of the municipal hospital, without providing him a hearing. The court quashed the decision on the ground of violation of the principles of natural justice.

(3) *Daud Ahmad* v. *District Magistrate, Allahabad*[12].—In this case, the District Magistrate (DM) requisitioned property in the personal possession of the owner for a judge without giving any hearing. Section 3 of the U.P. (Temporary) Accommodation Requisition Act, 1947 provided that an accommodation in personal possession cannot be requisitioned unless the DM is of the opinion that an alternative accommodation exists. The court came to the conclusion that the owner should have been given an opportunity to be heard before arriving at the conclusion, and issued the writ of certiorari to quash the action.

1.1.1.5 *Error of law apparent on the face of the record*

It is well settled that certiorari will be issued to quash decisions which though made within jurisdiction reveal on the "face of the record" an error of law.[13]

The "record" for this purpose shall include

(1) documents in which the determination is recorded,
(2) documents which indicate the proceedings and pleadings,
(3) reports, the extracts of which are included in the record, and
(4) documents which are mentioned in the formal order to be the basis of the decision.

The term "error apparent on the face of the record" cannot be defined with exactitude. The real difficulty is not so much with the statement of principles as it is in its application to the facts of a particular case.[14] Except in a rare case, it is possible to argue on both sides.[15]

Whether or not an error is an error of law, and an error which is apparent on the face of the record, must always depend on the facts and

10. (1973) 1 SCC 120.
11. (1973) 1 SCC 409.
12. (1972) 1 SCC 655.
13. *G. Veerappa Pillai* v. *Raman & Raman Ltd.*, (1952) 1 SCC 334.
14. *Hari Vishnu Kamath* v. *Syed. Ahmad Ishaque*, AIR 1955 SC 233.
15. *Ujjam Bai* v. *State of U.P.*, AIR 1962 SC 1621.

circumstances of each case and on the nature and scope of the legal provision, which is alleged to have been misconstrued or contravened.[16]

"Error apparent on the face of the record" shall include not a mere error but a manifest error based on clear ignorance or disregard of the law,[17] or on a wrong proposition of the law,[18] or on clear inconsistency between facts, and the law and the decision.[19] An error of law apparent on the record is an insult to the legal system which the courts cannot overlook. It may also include cases of abuse of jurisdiction. For this purpose where the decision is based on "no evidence", it will be considered as a question of law.

In *Sangram Singh* v. *Election Tribunal*[20], the Election Tribunal construed Section 9 of the Civil Procedure Code, 1908 (CPC) to mean that if a person fails to appear before it without good cause, he can be debarred from taking part in subsequent proceedings. The court quashed the decision of the tribunal on the ground of an error of law, apparent on the face of the record.

1.1.1.6 *Fraud*

If a decision of the agency has been obtained by fraud, or a fraud operates to take away jurisdiction or bestows jurisdiction or results in denial of justice, the decision may be quashed by issuing a certiorari. There is no Indian case on the point.

As discussed earlier, it is a discretionary remedy and the High Court can refuse it on the ground of acquiescence, laches, available alternative remedy and no benefit to the party.

It is well-settled law that certiorari cannot be issued to disturb a finding of fact unless it is based on no evidence, or purely on surmises and conjectures, or which is manifestly against the basic principles of natural justice. In that case, the finding of fact shall be deemed to suffer from an error of law.[21] The court has also emphasised that the purpose of certiorari is not only negative (to quash an action) but it contains affirmative action also. In *Gujarat Steel Tubes Ltd.* v. *Mazdoor Sabha*[22], the Supreme Court held that while quashing the order of dismissal, the court can also order reinstatement and the payment of back wages. The court made it clear that while the extraordinary remedy is of Anglo-Saxon vintage, it is not a carbon copy of the English process. Judicial power is not restricted where glaring injustice demands affirmative action.

---

16. *Syed Yakoob* v. *K.S. Radhakrishnan*, AIR 1964 SC 477.
17. *Chetkar Jha* v. *Vishwanath Prasad Verma*, (1970) 2 SCC 217.
18. *Nanagram* v. *Ghinsilal*, 1951 SCC OnLine Raj 27: AIR 1952 Raj 107.
19. *R.* v. *Westminster Compensation Appeal Tribunal and Sell, ex p Road Haulage Executive*, (1953) 1 All ER 687. See also, *Agarwal & Co.* v. *CIT*, (1970) 2 SCC 48.
20. AIR 1955 SC 425.
21. *Mukunda Bore* v. *Bangshidhar Buragohain*, (1980) 4 SCC 336.
22. (1980) 2 SCC 593. For a different approach see, *U.P. Warehousing Corpn.* v. *Vijay Narayan Vajpayee*, (1980) 3 SCC 459.

1.2 Writ of prohibition

Prohibition is a judicial order issued by the Supreme Court or a High Court to any constitutional, statutory or non-statutory agency to prevent these agencies from continuing their proceedings in excess or abuse of their jurisdiction, or in violation of the principles of natural justice, or in contravention of the law of the land.

Before the writ of prohibition can be issued, there must be something to be done. It is a writ of right and a court cannot refuse it in cases of excess of jurisdiction, or where jurisdiction is being exercised in violation of the law of the land.[23]

Law relating to injunctions in the Specific Relief Act, 1963 to some extent, but not entirely, cover the same ground. But due to limitations imposed on the grant of injunction, most of the field of prohibition remains uncovered.

Prohibition has also much in common with certiorari, both in scope and the rules by which it is governed. But there is one fundamental difference between the two. Prohibition is issued at a stage when proceedings are in progress to forbid the authority from continuing the proceedings. Certiorari is issued at a stage when proceedings have terminated and the authority has given a final decision to quash the decision. Sometimes these two writs may overlap. If an agency gives a decision which does not finally dispose of the matter, certiorari will lie to quash the decision and prohibition will lie to forbid the agency from further continuing the proceedings. The usual practice is to pray for prohibition and alternatively certiorari because it may happen that pending proceedings for prohibition the agency may hand over its final decision.

1.2.1 *Grounds for the issue of prohibition*

Prohibition can be issued on the same grounds on which certiorari can be issued except in case of an error of law apparent on the face of the record. The grounds for the issue of prohibition are:

(1) lack of excess of jurisdiction,[24]
(2) violation of the principles of natural justice,
(3) infringement of fundamental rights,
(4) fraud, and
(5) contravention of the law of the land.

All the grounds except the last have been discussed in detail earlier. Therefore, the expression "contravention of the law of the land" requires elucidation.

The definition of prohibition given in *Halsbury's Laws of England* states that an order of prohibition forbids an agency to continue proceedings in

23. *Isha Beevi* v. *Tax Recovery Officer*, (1976) 1 SCC 70.
24. *CCE* v. *National Tobacco Co. of India Ltd.*, (1972) 2 SCC 560.

contravention of the law of the land. This would prima facie mean that erroneous interpretation of law, especially statute law, which forms the bulk of law in operation is included in the grounds for the issue of prohibition. In India, this is not of much significance because it refers to an era in England where certain agencies were not subject to the writ of certiorari to whom prohibition was issued for every error regarding the law of the land.

In India, prohibition is issued to protect the individual from arbitrary administrative actions. In *T.M. Munusamappa & Sons* v. *Custodian, Evacuee Property*[25], the Custodian, after accepting the petitioners as tenants of the evacuee property and after accepting rent for five months, purported to proceed against them as if they were in permissive possession. Prohibition was issued to forbid him from proceeding further.

Prohibition is a writ of right, hence the existence of an alternative remedy is an irrelevant consideration when the complaint is that the inferior tribunal is exceeding its jurisdiction, or is assuming jurisdiction not vested in it by law because it would amount to forcing a person to first suffer and submit to the jurisdiction of the authority, which is illegal, and then take advantage of the alternative remedy before approaching the court.[26]

It is an efficacious and speedy remedy where a person does not desire any other relief except to stop the administrative agency. An alternative remedy does not bar the issue of this writ.[27] The fact that something must be left to be done is necessary, for the issue of the writ is not a rule of disability. It can be issued even when the agency has reached a decision to stop the authority from enforcing its decision. It can be issued even in cases where an authority has not kept any record.

1.3 Writ of mandamus

Mandamus is a judicial remedy issued in the form of an order from the Supreme Court or a High Court to any constitutional, statutory or a non-statutory agency to do or forbear from doing some specific act, which that agency is obliged to do or refrain from doing under the law, and which is in the nature of a public duty or a statutory duty.

In *Hari Krishna Mandir Trust* v. *State of Maharashtra*[28], the Supreme Court noted that mandamus is issued in case public authority fails to exercise power or discretion or exercises the same mala fide or erroneously. Mandamus is to enforce a legal duty. It must be shown that such duty exists towards the applicant. Once the same is established, the High Court is duty-bound to issue the writ of mandamus.

25. 1951 SCC OnLine Mad 288: AIR 1952 Mad 789.
26. *Sri Lakshmindra Theertha Swamiar of Sri Shirur Mutt* v. *Hindu Religious Endowments*, 1951 SCC OnLine Mad 384: AIR 1952 Mad 613.
27. *Bengal Immunity Co. Ltd.* v. *State of Bihar*, AIR 1955 SC 661.
28. (2020) 9 SCC 356.

It is considered as a residuary remedy of public law. It is a general remedy whenever justice has been denied to any person.[29] English writers trace the development of this writ from the Norman conquest; however, it was only in the early part of the 18th century that the writ came to be frequently used in public law to compel the performance of public duties.

1.3.1 *Conditions for the grant of mandamus*

(1) *There must be a public or common-law duty.*—Until recently, the law was that mandamus would lie only to enforce a duty which is public in nature. Therefore, a duty private in nature and arising out of a contract was not enforceable through this writ. It was on this basis that in *ITC* v. *State of Madras*[30] the court refused to issue mandamus where the petitioners wanted the government to fulfil its obligation arising out of a contract. However, in *Gujarat State Financial Corpn.* v. *Lotus Hotels (P) Ltd.*[31], the Supreme Court issued the writ of mandamus for the specific performance of a contract to advance money. In this case, the Gujarat Financial Corporation, a government instrumentality, had sanctioned a loan of ₹30 lakhs to Lotus Hotel for the construction, but later refused to pay the amount.

A public duty is one which is created either by a statute, rules or regulations having the force of law, the Constitution, or by some rule of common law.[32]

The public duty enforceable through mandamus must also be an absolute duty. Absolute is one which is mandatory and not discretionary. Therefore in *Manjula Manjari Dei* v. *Director of Public Instruction*[33], the court refused to issue mandamus against the Director of Public Instruction compelling him to include the petitioner's textbook in the list of approved books because it was a matter at the complete discretion of the authority. There is a shift in judicial perception and mandamus can be issued even if performance of duty by the State is discretionary. However, if an authority is under law obliged to exercise discretion, mandamus would lie to exercise it in one way or the other.[34] Mandamus would also lie if the public authority invested with discretionary powers abuses the power or exceeds it, or acts mala fide. Mandamus, thus, is issued to compel performance of public duties which may be administrative, ministerial or statutory in nature. A statutory duty may be either directory or mandatory. A

29. *R.* v. *Barker*, (1762) 3 Burr 1265, 1267: 97 ER 823.
30. 1953 SCC OnLine Mad 240: ILR 1954 Mad 754.
31. (1983) 3 SCC 379.
32. *Commr of Police* v. *Gordhandas Bhanji*, 1951 SCC 1088: AIR 1952 SC 16.
33. 1952 SCC OnLine Ori 18: AIR 1952 Ori 344. See also, *Vijay Mehta* v. *State of Rajasthan*, 1979 SCC OnLine Raj 60: AIR 1980 Raj 207.
34. *Alcock, Ashdown & Co. Ltd.* v. *Chief Revenue Authority*, 1923 SCC OnLine PC 30: (1922–23) 50 IA 227.

statutory duty, if intended to be mandatory in character, is indicated by the use of the words "shall" or "must", but this is not conclusive as "shall" and "must" have, sometimes, been interpreted as "may". Therefore, what is determinative of the nature of duty, whether it is obligatory, mandatory or directory, is the scheme of the statute in which the duty has been set out. Even if the duty is not set out clearly and specifically in the statute, it may be implied as correlative to a right. If in the performance of this duty, the authority, in whom the discretion is vested under the statute, does not act independently and passes an order under the instructions and orders of another authority, the court may issue mandamus to that authority to exercise its own discretion.[35] A writ of mandamus along with suitable directions can be issued by the court for the protection and enforcement of fundamental rights.[36] Mandamus cannot be issued to enforce administrative directions which do not have the force of law, hence it is discretionary that the authority accept it or reject it.[37] But where the administrative instructions are binding, mandamus would lie to enforce them.[38]

Mandamus would also lie to compel an authority to refund the amount of fee it has collected under law which has been declared ultra vires by the competent court.[39]

The expression "public duty" does not imply that the person or body whose duty it is must be a public official or an official body. Therefore, mandamus would lie against a company constituted under a statute for the purpose of compelling it to fulfil its public responsibilities.[40] A writ can be issued against a private individual also for the enforcement of public duties. Thus, in *Rohtas Industries Ltd.* v. *Staff Union*[41], a writ was issued against the award of an arbitrator appointed under Section 10(1) of the Industrial Disputes Act, 1947.

(2) *There must be a specific demand and refusal.*—Before mandamus can be granted, there must be a specific demand for the fulfilment of a duty and also a specific refusal by the authority. Therefore, in *Naubat Rai* v. *Union of India*[42], the court refused mandamus because the petitioner who was illegally dismissed from the military farm never applied to the authority for reinstatement.

However, the specific demand for the performance of a duty may not be necessary where it appears that the demand would be

35. *Mansukhlal Vithaldas Chauhan* v. *State of Gujarat*, (1997) 7 SCC 622.
36. *Vishaka* v. *State of Rajasthan*, (1997) 6 SCC 241. Court issued mandamus with directions to protect women against sexual harassment at workplace.
37. *G.J. Fernandez* v. *State of Mysore*, AIR 1967 SC 1753.
38. *Jagjit Singh* v. *State of Punjab*, (1978) 2 SCC 196.
39. *Shiv Shankar Dal Mills* v. *State of Haryana*, (1980) 2 SCC 437.
40. *Praga Tools Corpn.* v. *C.A. Imanuel*, (1969) 1 SCC 585.
41. (1976) 2 SCC 82. See also, *Sarvaraya Sugars Ltd.* v. *A.P. Civil Supplies Corpn. Ltd.*, 1981 SCC OnLine AP 61: AIR 1981 AP 402.
42. AIR 1953 Punj 137.

unavailing, or where the respondent by his own conduct has made the demand impossible, or where the duty sought to be enforced is of a public nature and no one is specially empowered to demand performance, or where the duty is imperatively required by law of a ministerial officer, or where a person has by inadvertence omitted to do some act which he was under a duty to do and the time within which he can do it has expired.[43]

However, express demand and refusal are not necessary. Demand and refusal can be inferred from the circumstances also. Therefore, in *Venugopalan* v. *Commr., Vijayawada Municipality*[44], the court inferred demand and refusal from the situation in which the petitioner filed a suit for injunction restraining the Municipality from holding elections and the suit was contested by the Municipality.

(3) *There must be a clear right to enforce the duty.*—Mandamus will not be issued unless there is, in the applicant, a right to compel the performance of some duty cast on the authority. Therefore, in *S.P. Manocha* v. *State of M.P.*[45], the court refused to issue mandamus to the college to admit the petitioner because the petitioner could not establish a clear right to admission in the college. In the same manner, the court did not grant mandamus for payment of interest on delayed refund under the Customs Act, 1962 as the claim was not backed by a statutory right at the relevant time.[46]

The right to enforce a duty must subsist till the date of the petition. If the right has been lawfully terminated before filing the petition, mandamus cannot be issued.[47]

The right to enforce the duty must belong to the petitioner. Therefore, a shareholder cannot enforce the right of the company, which is itself a legal person capable of enforcing its own rights, unless the petitioner can show that in the infringement of the company's rights his own personal rights have been adversely affected.[48]

However, this does not mean that a person can never enforce a public right which does not specifically belong to any individual. Mandamus can be issued on the petition of a taxpayer to restrain a municipality from misallocation or misappropriation of public funds. In *K.N. Guruswamy* v. *State of Mysore*[49], the court held that in the case of lack of power and abuse of power by the administrative authority, anybody who is affected by the action, though he may not have a substantive, enforceable right, can claim mandamus.

43. *Guru Charan* v. *Belonia Vidyapith*, AIR 1955 Tri 33.
44. 1956 SCC OnLine AP 201: AIR 1957 AP 833.
45. 1972 SCC OnLine MP 59: AIR 1973 MP 84; see, *Shabi Construction Company* v. *City & Industrial Development Corpn.*, (1995) 4 SCC 301.
46. *Union of India* v. *Orient Enterprises*, (1998) 3 SCC 501.
47. *Kalyan Singh* v. *State of U.P.*, AIR 1962 SC 1183.
48. *Ibid.*
49. AIR 1954 SC 592.

(4) *The right must be subsisting on the date of the petition.*—If the right is not subsisting on the date of petition, mandamus cannot be issued. Therefore, while a High Court upheld the unconstitutionality of a law and directed interim payment, the Supreme Court in appeal, disagreeing with the High Court, upheld the validity of the law and further provided that interim payment could be made only until the date of determination by the Director under law. The Supreme Court held that the High Court committed serious error in issuing mandamus for the enforcement of the so-called right which never subsisted on the date of issue of mandamus in view of the decision of the Supreme Court to the contrary.[50]

1.3.2 *Grounds for the grant of mandamus*

Mandamus can be issued on all those counts on which certiorari and prohibition can be issued. Therefore, mandamus can be issued for lack of jurisdiction, excess of jurisdiction, abuse of jurisdiction, violation of the principles of natural justice, and error of law apparent on the face of the record. Mandamus may be issued not only to compel the authority to do something but also to restrain it from doing something.[51] Therefore, it is both negative and positive and, hence, can do the work of all other writs. It provides a general remedy in administrative law.

Like any other extraordinary remedy, the grant of mandamus is discretionary. The court may refuse it if there is unreasonable delay in filing the petition, or if there is adequate alternative remedy, or if it is premature, or if its issuance would be infructuous and futile. It may also be refused on equitable considerations, *i.e.* where there is a misstatement or suppression of facts in the petition. In view of the provisions of Articles 122(2) and 212(2) of the Constitution, mandamus will not lie against any officer or Member of Parliament or State Legislature in whom powers are vested for regulating the procedure or conduct of business for maintaining order. Mandamus would also not lie against the President or Governor of any State for the exercise and performance of powers and duties of his office.[52] Articles 327, 328 and 329 preclude the jurisdiction of the court in matters of election process to Parliament or State Legislature except on a petition as provided by a law passed by Parliament; therefore, the remedy of mandamus will not be available against any person involved in the election process.[53]

50. *Director of Settlements* v. *M.R. Apparao,* (2002) 4 SCC 638.

51. *Tapendra Nath Roy* v. *University of Calcutta*, 1953 SCC OnLine Cal 200: AIR 1954 Cal 141. Mandamus was issued against the University to restrain it from giving effect to an order passed in violation of its own rules. See also, *Nagpur Kshatriya Khatik Samaj* v. *Nagpur Corpn.*, 1955 SCC OnLine MP 59: AIR 1956 Nag 152. Mandamus was issued to restrain the Municipality from collecting an illegal tax.

52. Art. 361, Indian Constitution.

53. *Shankar Nanasaheb Karpe* v. *Returning Officer.*, 1951 SCC OnLine Bom 133: AIR 1952 Bom 277.

A writ of mandamus cannot be issued to compel an authority to pass an order in violation of a statutory provision. Where the Income Tax Officer has no power to make assessment beyond the prescribed period, mandamus cannot be issued to make him extend his assessment order beyond that period.[54] Where the administrative authority refused an application for licence without any notice and hearing, the High Court is not justified in issuing mandamus to grant licence to the company.[55] Mandamus can also not be issued to refrain an authority from enforcing the law.[56] In the same manner, mandamus cannot be issued to compel the authority to reach a particular decision.[57]

In hearing the petition for mandamus, the court does not sit as a court of appeal. The court will not examine the correctness or otherwise of the decision on merits.[58] It cannot substitute its own wisdom for the discretion vested in the authority unless the exercise of discretion is illegal.[59] This is true for other writs also.

Exercising its power in a creative manner, the court has now developed the concept of "continuous mandamus" so that it can supervise the performance of duty ordered by the court.

1.4 Writ of quo warranto

Quo warranto means "by what warrant or authority". It is a judicial order issued by the Supreme Court or a High Court by which any person, who occupies or usurps an independent public office or franchise or liberty, is asked to show by what right he claims it, so that the title to the office, franchise or liberty may be settled and any unauthorised person ousted.

It is a method of judicial control in the sense that the proceedings practically review the actions of the administrative authority which appointed the person. Furthermore, it tunes the administration by removing inefficient and unqualified personnel and impostors from public offices. Thus, the writ of quo warranto gives the judiciary a weapon to control the executive, the legislature, and statutory and non-statutory bodies in matters of appointments to public offices. Conversely, it protects a citizen from being deprived of a public office to which he has a right.

Originally, quo warranto was a high prerogative writ. The essence of the procedure was calling a subject to account for an invasion or usurpation of the royal prerogative or the right of franchise or liberty of the Crown. At that period of time it was the King's weapon, and subjects were not allowed to use it. The Statute of 1710 extended this remedy to the public.

---

54. *Hope Textiles Ltd.* v. *Union of India*, 1995 Supp (3) SCC 199.
55. *State of Maharashtra* v. *Pooja Brew-Chem Industries (P) Ltd.*, 1995 Supp (4) SCC 179.
56. *State of U.P.* v. *Harish Chandra*, (1996) 9 SCC 309; *State of Bihar* v. *Ramdeo Yadav*, (1996) 3 SCC 493.
57. *Mansukhlal Vithaldas Chauhan* v. *State of Gujarat*, (1997) 7 SCC 622.
58. *Utkal University* v. *S.K. Ghosh*, AIR 1954 SC 217.
59. *Ibid.*

1.4.1 *Conditions for the grant of quo warranto*

(1) *Office must be a public office.*—In *Anand Bihari Mishra* v. *Ram Sahay*[60], the court held that a public office is one which is created by the Constitution or a statute and the duties of which must be such in which the public is interested. In this case, it was held that the office of the Speaker of the legislative assembly is a public office. In *G.D. Karkare* v. *T.L. Shevde*[61], it was held that the office of Advocate General is a public office. In the same manner, the office of members of a municipal board[62] or the office of a university official[63] are public offices. Therefore, quo warranto would not be issued against a managing committee of a private school,[64] or against a member of the working committee of the Arya Samaj Pratinidhi Sabha[65], because these are private offices not created by law.

(2) *Public office must be substantive in nature.*—A substantive office is one which is permanent in character and is not terminable at will. In *R.* v. *Speyer*[66], the word "substantive" was interpreted to mean an "office independent of title". Therefore, quo warranto would be granted even when the office is held at the pleasure of the State provided it is permanent in character. In other words, the official must be an independent official and not merely one discharging the functions of a deputy or servant at the pleasure of another officer.[67]

(3) *The person must be in actual possession of the office.*—Mere declaration that a person is elected to an office or mere appointment to a particular office is not sufficient for the issue of quo warranto unless such person actually accepts such office.[68]

(4) *The office must be held in contravention of law.*—There must be a clear violation of law in the appointment of a person to a public office. If there is a mere irregularity, quo warranto will not lie. In *State of Assam* v. *Ranga Muhammad*[69], the court found the transfer and posting of two District judges contrary to law; but did not issue quo warranto, as it was a case of mere irregularity that did not make the occupation of office wrongful.

Quo warranto will also be issued when a person validly occupies the office but acquires a disqualification later on.

60. 1951 SCC OnLine MP 142: AIR 1952 MB 31.
61. 1950 SCC OnLine MP 67: AIR 1952 Nag 330.
62. *Shiam Sunder* v. *State of Punjab*, 1957 SCC OnLine Punj 120: AIR 1958 Punj 128.
63. *Rajendrakumar* v. *State of M.P.*, 1957 SCC OnLine MP 66: AIR 1957 MP 60. See also, *Ram Singh Saini* v. *H.N. Bhargava*, (1975) 4 SCC 676, where the post of a university professor was held to be a public office.
64. *Amarendra Chandra* v. *Narendra Kumar Basu*, 1952 SCC OnLine Cal 37: AIR 1953 Cal 114.
65. *Jamalpur Arya Samaj* v. *D. Ram*, 1954 SCC OnLine Pat 3: AIR 1954 Pat 297.
66. (1916) 1 KB 595.
67. *Ibid.*
68. *Puranlal Lokhanpal* v. *P.C. Ghosh*, 1969 SCC OnLine Cal 51: AIR 1970 Cal 118.
69. AIR 1967 SC 903.

1.4.2 *Locus standi for the writ of quo warranto*

The proposition that a writ can be issued on the petition of a person whose rights are adversely affected has no application to the writ of quo warranto. A petition for quo warranto is maintainable at the instance of any person, although he is not personally aggrieved or interested in the matter.[70] However, he must not be a man of straw set up by anyone. For example, in order to challenge a municipal office, the person must at least be the resident of the area where the municipality governs.

Like any other extraordinary remedy, quo warranto is also a discretionary remedy. It can be refused on the ground of unreasonable delay. Therefore, when a person has held office for a long time without challenge, the writ may be refused. However, in *K. Bheema Raju* v. *Govt. of A.P.*[71], the court remarked that in a matter which involves a fundamental right to a public office and violation of a legal procedure to be adopted in the matter of public appointments to a public office, the delay should not deter the court in granting the relief and rendering justice because the usurper's continuance in office gives cause of action each day and every hour till he is ousted. Furthermore, a usurper does not cease to be one by lapse of time.[72]

Normally, acquiescence is no ground for refusing the remedy in cases of public office appointments, but it may be a relevant factor in cases of election.[73]

The writ may also be refused if there is an adequate alternative remedy. Therefore, in *V.D. Deshpande* v. *State of Hyderabad*[74], the court refused the writ against Members of legislatures who had become disqualified since they held offices of profit, as Article 192 of the Constitution provided an adequate remedy. However, in *State of Haryana* v. *Haryana Coop. Transport Ltd.*[75], the Supreme Court issued the writ against the appointment of a presiding officer of a Labour Court on the ground that the officer did not possess the prescribed qualifications, holding that the remedy provided under Section 9(1) of the Industrial Disputes Act, 1947 cannot detract the High Court from exercising its jurisdiction to issue the writ under Article 226 of the Constitution.

In cases where the issue of writ would be futile in its result, the court may refuse it. In *P.L. Lakhanpal* v. *A.N. Roy*[76], the Delhi High Court refused the writ against the former Chief Justice of India, Ray J, on the ground that on the resignation of three senior judges, Ray J becomes the seniormost and, therefore, can be reappointed even if it is held that Article 124(2)

70. *Gadde Venkateswara Rao* v. *State of A.P.*, AIR 1966 SC 828.
71. 1980 SCC OnLine AP 76: AIR 1981 AP 24, 29.
72. *Pushpa Devi M. Jatia* v. *M.L. Wadhawan*, (1987) 3 SCC 367.
73. *Ruttonjee & Company* v. *State of W.B.*, 1966 SCC OnLine Cal 62: AIR 1967 Cal 450.
74. 1954 SCC OnLine Hyd 151: AIR 1955 Hyd 36.
75. (1977) 1 SCC 271.
76. 1974 SCC OnLine Del 28: AIR 1975 Del 66.

embodies the seniority rule. The court further observed that the motive of the appointing authority is not relevant for the grant of the writ.

While issuing the writ of quo warranto, the court will at the outset determine whether a case for the issuance is made out. The jurisdiction of the court to issue quo warranto can be exercised only when the appointment is contrary to statutory rules. While issuing such a writ, court cannot consider the respective impact of the candidates and other such factors.[77]

1.5 Writ of habeas corpus

Habeas corpus is a Latin term, which may be translated into English in some such form as "you must have the body". However, recent developments of law indicate that in a writ of habeas corpus, the production of the body of the person alleged to be unlawfully detained is not essential.[78]

Habeas corpus may be defined as a judicial order issued by the Supreme Court or a High Court by which a person who is confined by any public or private agency may secure his release. The writ in the form of an order calls upon the person, in whose confinement a person is, to let the court know the legal justification for the detention, and in the absence of such justification to release the person from his confinement. The efficacy of this writ lies in its promptness and effectiveness in securing the release of persons illegally detained.

The true origin of the writ in the common law is still to be traced,[79] but it is certain that the present writ developed out of the prerogative writ of ad subjiciendum by which people could secure their release from illegal detention in jails.

A writ of habeas corpus can be filed by any person on behalf of the person detained or by the detained person himself. However, every petition must be supported by an affidavit stating the facts and circumstances of detention and, where relevant, the reasons as to why the prisoner is unable to make an application. In the case of a minor, any person entitled to the minor's custody can file a petition. If no such person is available, any other person may file such petition.

In *Icchu Devi Choraria* v. *Union of India*[80], the Supreme Court held that in case of a writ of habeas corpus, the court does not, as a matter of practice, follow strict rules of pleadings nor does it place undue emphasis on the strict observance of the rules of burden of proof. Even a postcard by a *pro bono publico* is sufficient to galvanise the court into examining the legality of detention.

---

77. *High Court of Gujarat* v. *Gujarat Kishan Mazdoor Panchayat*, (2003) 4 SCC 712.
78. *Kanu Sanyal* v. *Distt. Magistrate, Darjeeling*, (1973) 2 SCC 674.
79. According to Maitland, "Origin Lies in Feudal Custody"; Jenk, "In the Vague Assertions of Civil Liberties"; Holdsworth, "Procedural Law"; Cohen, "Norman Origin".
80. (1980) 4 SCC 531. See also, *Veena Sethi* v. *State of Bihar*, (1982) 2 SCC 583.

In order to maintain a petition for habeas corpus, physical confinement is not necessary. It is sufficient if some kind of control, custody or restraint is exercised over the person. Thus, if a child is forcibly kept away from his parents, if a man is wrongly kept in confinement as a lunatic, if a nun is alleged to be prevented from leaving her convent, the court will always issue the writ of habeas corpus.[81]

The purposes for which the writ of habeas corpus may be issued may include 1) testing the regularity of detention under preventive detention laws and any other law; 2) securing the custody of a minor; 3) securing the custody of a person alleged to be a lunatic; 4) securing the custody of a marriage partner; 5) testing the regularity of detention for a breach of privilege by the House; 6) testing the regularity of detention under court-martial; and 7) testing the regularity of detention by the executive during emergency, etc.

Besides these traditional grounds for which the writ of habeas corpus may be issued, Krishna Iyer J in *Sunil Batra* (2) v. *Delhi Admn.*[82] [*Sunil Batra* (*II*)] opened new vistas for the issuance of this writ. *Sunil Batra* (*II*) arose out of a letter written by a convict to one of the judges of the Supreme Court alleging inhuman torture to a fellow convict. Krishna Iyer J treated this letter as a petition of habeas corpus filed on behalf of Prem Chand, though the latter had not demanded his release from the jail. The learned judge followed a series of American cases[83] employing the writ of habeas corpus for the neglect of State penal facilities like overcrowding, understaffing, insanitary facilities, brutality, constant fear of violence, lack of adequate medical and mental health, censorship of mail, inhuman isolation, segregation, and inadequate or non-existent rehabilitative or educational opportunities. The writ was also issued when a ban was imposed on law students to conduct interviews with prisoners for affording them legal relief.[84] Thus, this new dynamics of the writ of habeas corpus is a high benchmark of judicial creativity in India which has made the writ coextensive with growing human rights jurisprudence.

In India, as in England, successive applications to different judges and Benches of the same court are not allowed if the order on the first application has been made on merit.[85] However, if the petition has been heard and rejected by the High Court, a fresh petition under Article 32 can still be filed in the Supreme Court.[86] Therefore, this is an exception to the principle of res judicata which applies to other writs. In the same manner, in *Lallubhai Jogibhai* v. *Union of India*[87], the Supreme Court held that when

81. Dicey, *Law of the Constitution*, 219.
82. (1980) 3 SCC 488.
83. *Ibid*, SCC 501–02.
84. *Ibid*, SCC 502. *See also*, Mohammad Ghouse, "Constitutional Law-I", (1980) 16 ASIL 193–94.
85. *Bansi* v. *Consolidation of Holdings*, 1966 SCC OnLine Punj 121: AIR 1967 Punj 28.
86. *Ghulam Sarwar* v. *Union of India*, AIR 1967 SC 1335.
87. (1981) 2 SCC 427.

a writ petition challenging an order of detention is dismissed by a court, a second petition can be filed on additional grounds to challenge the legality of continued detention and it will not be barred by res judicata. In the same manner, constructive res judicata also does not apply to habeas corpus proceedings as it would whittle down the wide sweep of this constitutional protection.[88]

In England, no appeal lies against the order if the petition of habeas corpus has been accepted. In India, there is no such restriction and appeal would lie to the Supreme Court under Article 136 against the order of the High Court granting or rejecting the petition for the writ.

Writ of habeas corpus provides security against administrative and private "lawlessness" but not against judicial "foolishness". Therefore, if a person has been imprisoned under the order of conviction passed by a court, the writ would not lie. The normal procedure in such case is appeal. In exercise of its discretion, the court may refuse the petition if there is a special alternative remedy available. But it is not a rule of the limitation of jurisdiction. The court may still grant relief in appropriate cases.[89]

In a habeas corpus writ proceeding, not only the fact of detention but the constitutionality of the law can also be challenged. In *A.K. Gopalan* v. *State of Madras*[90], the court examined the constitutionality of the Preventive Detention Act, 1950.

1.5.1 *Constitution and the writ of habeas corpus*

The writ of habeas corpus gives meaning and colour to the rights of personal liberty guaranteed under Article 21 of the Constitution. Without the remedy of habeas corpus, the right to personal liberty would be merely a tale told by an idiot full of sound and fury, but signifying nothing.

Judicial behaviour before 1978 gave not only a restricted meaning to the term "personal liberty" but did not allow the importation of the principles of natural justice or procedural due process into the words "procedure established by law".

The decision of the Supreme Court in *Maneka Gandhi* v. *Union of India*[91] electrified the whole concept of liberty by making two significant innovations with far-reaching consequences: 1) The court gave a wide, extended meaning to the term "personal liberty" as including everything that makes life worthwhile, including the right to education, involving the right to participate in the activities and the corporate life of an university,[92] and the right to legal aid in cases of criminal convictions with long loss of

88. *Ibid.*
89. *Gopal Ji* v. *Shree Chand*, 1954 SCC OnLine All 197: AIR 1955 All 28.
90. 1950 SCC 228: AIR 1950 SC 27. See also, *Kanu Sanyal* v. *Distt. Magistrate, Darjeeling*, (1973) 2 SCC 674.
91. (1978) 1 SCC 248.
92. *Anand Vardhan Chandel* v. *Delhi University*, 1978 SCC OnLine Del 74: AIR 1978 Del 308.

liberty.[93] 2) The court imported the element of fairness and justness in the "procedure established by law" depriving a person of his liberty. Therefore, now a writ of habeas corpus would lie if the law which deprives a person of his liberty is not fair, just and equitable.

Before the Constitution (44th Amendment) Act, 1978, the President of India could suspend the enforcement of Article 21 during an emergency—under Article 359(1)—and, therefore, courts were debarred from considering the legality of an executive detention during the emergency even on the ground that it was ultra vires the Act, or palpably wrong or mala fide. But now after the amendment of the Constitution in 1978, the right to personal liberty under Article 21 cannot be suspended even during an emergency, therefore, the writ of habeas corpus will be available to people against any wrongful detention during an emergency proclaimed under Article 352 of the Constitution. Thus, the 1978 constitutional amendment overrules *ADM, Jabalpur* v. *Shivakant Shukla*[94] (also known as the *Habeas Corpus case*) decided during the 1975 Emergency which remains a blot on the glorious history of the Supreme Court.

2. PRIVATE LAW REVIEW/NON-CONSTITUTIONAL REVIEW

Private law review refers to powers of ordinary courts of the land, exercised in accordance with ordinary law of the land to control administrative action. Private law review is exercised through injunction, declaratory action, and suit for damages. This non-constitutional mode of judicial review of any administrative action can be exercised by the civil and criminal courts, tribunals, special courts like the one constituted under the Scheduled Castes, Scheduled Tribes (Prevention of Atrocities) Act, 1989, Consumer Courts and environmental authorities, etc.

In countries like the US where the administrative process has grown tremendously, emphasis on writs as a strategy for the control of administrative acts is shifting in favour of more speedy and flexible remedies like injunction and declaration. This demonstrates the inherent virtue of private law review.

The instrumentalities of private law review, being ordinary remedies, are free from technicalities of writs with regard to locus standi, nature of administrative authority and action. Private law remedies are broad-based when compared with writs insofar as these allow production of evidence and examination of witnesses as a fundamental requirement for a decision. Private law review is cheaper and easily available. However, one difficulty with this kind of judicial review is the requirement of two months' notice under Section 80, CPC before any suit can be filed against the government.

93. *M.H. Hoskot* v. *State of Maharashtra*, (1978) 3 SCC 544.

94. (1976) 2 SCC 521. In this case, the Supreme Court had taken the view that during an emergency, a detention order cannot be challenged even on the ground that it is ultra vires the Act, or illegal, or mala fide, or based on extraneous considerations.

This created a difficulty where immediate injunctive relief was required. But after the amendment of Section 80 by the Civil Procedure Amendment Act, 1976, this difficulty has been removed as courts have now been authorised to waive the requirement of notice in suitable cases.

2.1 Injunction

The jurisdiction of Indian courts to issue injunctions is statutory. Sections 36 to 42 of the Specific Relief Act, 1963 govern the grant of injunctive relief.

Injunction may be defined as an ordinary judicial process that operates in personam by which any person or authority is ordered to do or to refrain from doing a particular act which such person or authority is obliged to do or to refrain from doing under any law. The remedy is coercive but not rigid and can be tailored to suit the circumstances of each individual case. It can be negative or affirmative, absolute or conditional, temporary or perpetual, or it can operate immediately or at a future date. The court in its proceedings for injunction can review all actions—judicial, quasi-judicial, administrative, ministerial or discretionary. Its equitable nature leaves a discretion with the court to prevent its abuse. It can operate against any authority or person, constitutional, statutory, non-statutory or private.

Injunction is more incisive than certiorari. Certiorari can quash an action, which can be restarted, but injunction, if perpetual, may forbid the authority from taking that action in perpetuity. Injunctive relief is not only negative but also positive and can compel an authority to do something which under law it is obliged to do and may, therefore, be very effective as a control mechanism of administrative action.

Temporary injunction is granted as an interim measure on an application by the plaintiff to preserve the status quo until the case is heard and decided. The grant of temporary injunction is governed by Order 39, CPC. In granting temporary injunction, the court takes into consideration the prima facie case of the plaintiff, nature and the extent of his injury, balance of convenience and the existence or otherwise of an alternative remedy.

Perpetual injunction is granted on the final determination of the case to prevent the infringement of those rights to which the plaintiff is entitled permanently. Under Section 38 of the Specific Relief Act, 1963, perpetual injunction may be granted to prevent the breach of an obligation existing in favour of the plaintiff, either expressly or by necessary implication, or to prevent a breach arising from a contract, or to prevent the invasion of the right to or enjoyment of the property, if the defendant is a trustee; or where there exists no standard to ascertain damages or money, and compensation would not be an adequate relief; or where it is necessary to prevent the multiplicity of suits.

Injunction will not be granted

(1) to restrain a person from instituting or prosecuting any judicial proceeding, civil or criminal;

(2) to restrain any person from petitioning to any legislative body; and
(3) to prevent the breach of a contract which cannot be specifically enforced, *i.e.* service contracts.

Since it is an equitable relief, the court may refuse it in exercise of its discretion if the plaintiff has acquiesced in the matter, or an equally efficacious relief is available, or the conduct of the plaintiff is objectionable.

Under Section 39, the court may grant a mandatory injunction as a final decision in a case to prevent a person from continuing with a wrong action as also to compel him to do a positive act, necessary to remedy the harm already done. Therefore, an improvement authority can be issued a mandatory injunction not only to restrain the construction of a building, if it interferes with the easementary rights of the plaintiff, but also to pull down the construction already made in contravention thereof.

The court under Section 42 may grant an injunction restraining the breach of a negative contract, express or implied, in those cases where according to clause (*e*) of Section 41 an injunction cannot be granted to prevent the breach of a contract, the performance of which could not be specifically enforced. Therefore, where there is an affirmative agreement to do a certain act, coupled with a negative agreement, express or implied, not to do a certain act, and the court cannot compel the specific performance of the affirmative agreement, it can still grant an injunction to perform the negative agreement. Suppose *A* contracts to play the piano in *B*'s orchestra in a particular hotel for the whole summer season and not to play the piano with any other orchestra elsewhere. *B* cannot obtain specific performance of the contract to play the piano in his orchestra by an affirmative injunction because the contract of personal service is not specifically enforceable. *B* is still entitled to get an injunction restraining *A* from playing the piano at any other hotel.

The court, in its discretion, may grant damages in lieu of or in addition to injunction.

Injunction can be granted on the petition of a person who has a personal interest in the matter. This is interpreted to mean that either there must be an existing obligation in favour of the applicant, or the person has suffered some injury. Does this mean that no person can enforce a public right which he shares with everybody else? In such situations, Section 91, CPC provides that any two persons with the consent of the Advocate General or by leave of the court may file a suit for the removal of a public nuisance, whether or not they have suffered special damage. In this manner a person can, through injunction, enforce his public right against any administrative authority for doing or refraining from doing certain acts which cause any injury, damages or annoyance to the public.

In *A. Venkatasubbiah Naidu* v. *S. Chellappan*[95], the Supreme Court ruled that a litigant has a right to appeal against an ex parte injunction

95. (2000) 7 SCC 695.

passed by the court if it did not finally dispose of the stay application within 30 days of making the order. If it is not possible to decide the matter within 30 days, the court must record reasons. Therefore, where the mandate of Order 39, Rule 3-A, CPC is flouted, the aggrieved party is entitled to appeal notwithstanding the pendency of the application for grant or vacation of a temporary injunction against the order remaining in force.

Nuisance may be of fact or of law. Nuisance of law refers to ultra vires acts of the administrative authority. Therefore, in such situations, any member of the public must be allowed to file a suit for its abatement by right even without the permission of the Advocate General.

The Constitution (42nd Amendment) Act, 1976[96] had considerably curtailed the powers of the High Court under Article 226 in matters of making interim orders whether by an injunction or stay or in any other manner. The High Court could not issue interim orders by way of injunction or otherwise unless the opportunity was given to the other party to be heard, except in exceptional circumstances for reasons to be recorded in writing. Even in such exceptional circumstances, the order ceased to have effect on the expiry of 14 days from the date on which it was made, unless before the expiry of this period the other party had been heard. Clause (6) of the 42nd Amendment had further imposed a blanket ban on interim orders if it had the effect of delaying an enquiry into any matter of public importance, or any offence punishable with imprisonment, or any execution of any project of public utility, or any acquisition of property by the government. These restrictions were, however, removed by the 44th Amendment.[97] Now, under clause (3) of Article 226, the High Court shall have the power to issue ex parte interim orders, whether by way of injunction or stay or in any other manner; however, the court shall have to decide the matter within a period of two weeks from the date when the application for the vacation of the order is made or received whichever is later, failing which such order shall stand vacated.

Injunction is an effective method of judicial control of administrative action where the authority has acted without jurisdiction, or has abused its jurisdiction, or has violated the principles of natural justice.

Injunction is also an effective instrument in controlling the exercise of administrative discretion. Therefore, if the administrative authority has either not exercised its discretion at all, or has exercised it at the discretion of some other body, or it is arbitrary, or has been exercised on extraneous considerations, or for an improper purpose, or where its exercise is mala fide, injunction would lie. *Ganga Narain* v. *Municipal Board of Cawnpore*[98] is an illustrative case on the efficacy of injunctive relief in cases of abuse of discretion by the administrative authority. In this case, the

96. S. 38, cls. (4), (5) and (6).
97. S. 30.
98. 1897 SCC OnLine All 25: ILR (1897) 19 All 313.

Kanpur Municipality constructed a market, but because of high rent, traders shifted to an old market owned by the plaintiff. In order to earn profit for its own market, the Municipality served a notice to the plaintiff to close down the market as it was a nuisance. In a suit filed by the plaintiff, the court held that the market was not a nuisance. Thereafter, the Municipality got the regulation amended and secured for itself the power to close down any market on the ground of nuisance. The plaintiff was prosecuted for not removing a nuisance, *i.e.* the market. In a suit, the plaintiff claimed the remedy of injunction and declaration on the ground of abuse of discretion which was granted. In practice, injunction has proved to be a suitable remedy for the control of administrative action, but it is not frequently resorted to because people have placed much faith in extraordinary remedies. If the remedy of injunction is to secure its due place, it is necessary that every person should be allowed to establish his rights without showing special injury or the consent of the Advocate General.

In granting relief, courts have consistently taken the view that law must always have precedence over any consideration of administrative convenience. *B. Prabhakar Rao* v. *State of A.P.*[99] is an illustrative case on this point. In this case, the reduction in retirement age for government servants from 58 to 55 years had been challenged by those who had been retired under the new dispensation. However, later on the retirement age was again raised to 58 years. The question before the court was whether petitioners were entitled to reinstatement with back wages? The contention of the government was that there would be considerable chaos in the administration if those already retired were again reinducted into the service. The court negativated the contention by holding that "those that have stirred up a hornet's nest cannot complain of being stung"[100]. Thus, it was firmly established that the Constitution must always take precedence over administrative convenience.

In some countries, a greater use of injunction is being made in public law. In the US and England even in cases of administrative rule-making, the court examines an application for injunction to find out if the rule-making power has been properly exercised or not. As mentioned earlier, within the federal jurisdiction in the US, writs have been completely replaced by injunction and declaration. In England, injunction is freely used against administrative authorities. In *Bradbury* v. *Enfield London Borough Council*[101], an injunction was granted against the local education authority on an application by a parent restraining the authority from converting a grammar school into a comprehensive school in violation of the Education Act, 1944, and the fact that the parent had no legal right to enforce was not treated as a disqualification.

99. 1985 Supp SCC 432.
100. *Ibid*, 463.
101. (1967) 1 WLR 1311 (CA).

2.2 Declaration

A declaratory action may be defined as a judicial remedy which conclusively determines the rights and obligations of public and private persons and authorities without the addition of any coercive or directory decree.

In the words of Jennings, declaratory action is a symbol of the 20th century conception of law because it is highly democratic. In an age where more and more an individual's action is liable to bring him in conflict with the administration, declaratory action satisfies the need of a simple but all-embracing method of redress against the administration. Sometimes coercive relief is unnecessary against public authorities where merely a declaration is enough to keep the authority within the bounds of legality. In England, under the Crown Proceedings Act, 1947, every claim against the government may be by a declaratory action. Being an ordinary law remedy, it is free from the technicalities of writs relating to locus standi, choice of remedy, character of administrative action and the nature of the administrative authority.

The history of declaratory action in India begins with the Act of 1854 by which the provisions of the Chancery Procedure Act, 1852 relating to the grant of declaratory relief were made applicable to the Indian Supreme Court in Presidency Towns. At that initial stage, courts declared the rights of parties as introductory to the directory relief which they ultimately granted. In 1859, the same provisions found place in Section 19 of the Civil Procedure Code, 1859. In 1877, this declaratory relief was transferred to Section 42 of the Specific Relief Act, 1877 and, thereafter, to Sections 34 and 35 of the Specific Relief Act, 1963.

2.2.1 *Conditions for the grant of declaratory relief*

(1) *The person must be entitled to a "legal character" or a "right to any property"*.—The term "legal character" is not in frequent use in legal drafting, but if interpreted in its wide connotation, may include every jural relationship of an individual which is recognised by law. In juristic parlance, legal character is equivalent to legal status which may include official position, profession, sex, marital status, minority, legitimacy, nationality, franchise, etc. Therefore, the right to stand for a public election or the right to get an election declared invalid may be a subject of declaratory relief.

In the same manner, the "right to any property" may include any right which is not a mere hope or chance or which is not contractual in nature.

There seems to be no reason, except multiplicity of suits, why this remedy cannot be made more broad-based by using only the word "right" which would include the right of status, property rights and other rights also. The term "right" would comprehend both "liability" and "immunity". Therefore, it would be possible for a person to obtain a declaration to the effect that a certain statute does not apply to him.

(2) *There must be some danger or detriment to such right or character.*—There must be some person or authority, public or private, either interested in denying such character or right or must have actually denied it.

(3) *Plaintiff must seek further relief if he is entitled to it.*—This places a restriction on the power of the court to grant a mere declaration. In situations where the plaintiff is entitled to consequential relief and does not claim it, the court will not grant declaratory relief.[102]

Consequential relief is that relief which directly flows from the declaration. In a suit for declaration in a case of wrongful dismissal, the consequential relief would be reinstatement and arrears of salary. Injunction may be a consequential relief in certain situations. In England and the US, courts are entitled to grant "mere declaration", and the plaintiff may reserve further relief for a separate action.

In the area of public law, consequential relief ought not to be of significance. The very nature of a declaratory proceeding is not compensation or restitution but prevention. As in the case of writs, the question of consequential relief does not arise, so in a declaratory action it should not be relevant. In a case of administrative inaction, a person may be interested in a mere declaration that the inaction is void and may not necessarily be interested in an action in a particular manner.

The essential role of declaratory action in public law as a means of judicial control of administrative action is yet to be appreciated in India. It is largely considered and utilised as a mode to regulate private relationships rather than the relationship between citizens and the administration. This perspective is the moving spirit behind the loading of this remedy with the restrictions mentioned earlier. However, this does not mean that the use of declaratory action in public law is wholly absent. In all cases where the administrative authority lacks, exceeds or abuses jurisdiction, or violates the principles of natural justice, declaratory action provides the required relief.

In *Rai Brij Raj Krishna* v. *S.K. Shaw and Bros.*[103], the Supreme Court applied the principles of certiorari in the disposal of a declaratory suit by a tenant for the declaration that the eviction order of the House Rent Controller under the Bihar Buildings (Lease, Rent and Eviction) Control Act, 1947 was ultra vires. In the same manner in *Joseph* v. *Calcutta Corpn.*[104], where

102. *Qabool Singh* v. *Board of Revenue*, 1972 SCC OnLine All 322: AIR 1973 All 158; *Dumpala Ramachandra Reddy* v. *Dumpala Kanta Reddy*, 1971 SCC OnLine AP 121: AIR 1973 AP 189.

103. 1951 SCC 102: AIR 1951 SC 115.

104. 1916 SCC OnLine PC 49: AIR 1916 PC 123.

the Calcutta Corporation had issued a notice to the plaintiff to remove certain projections under the Calcutta Municipal Act (III of 1899), a declaration was granted.

In *State of M.P.* v. *Mangilal Sharma*[105], the court held that a declaratory decree merely declares the right of the decree-holder and does not direct anybody to do or refrain from doing any particular act or thing, hence a declaratory decree is beyond the purview of execution proceedings. In this case, the respondent had filed a suit for declaration under Section 34 of the Specific Relief Act, 1963 that he continues to be in service but did not claim consequential benefits like arrears of salary, etc. The court granted a declaration but the respondent in execution proceedings had claimed consequential benefits.

In *Vemareddi Ramaraghava Reddy* v. *Konduru Seshu Reddy*[106], the Supreme Court added a new dimension to this remedy by allowing a declaration for the enforcement of a public right. In this case, the petitioner prayed for a declaration to the effect that certain properties belonged to the deity. Though this claim was not for a legal character or a right to property, the declaration was given. The remedy is also available to a taxpayer for getting a declaration against a municipality for misapplication or misappropriation of property. But whether a declaration could be given regarding the unconstitutionality of a statute is still unclear. If the limitations of "consequential relief", "legal character" and "property rights" are eliminated from the precincts of declaratory relief, it would do the work of certiorari, mandamus, prohibition and quo warranto insofar as judicial control of administrative action is concerned. Declaration and injunction may be proper relief in a petition under Article 32 of the Constitution.[107]

Declaration is a discretionary remedy and may be refused if it would be infructuous, or if an adequate alternative exists, or on other equitable consideration.[108]

After the Federal Declaratory Judgments Act, 1934, declaratory relief as a measure of control for administrative action in the US has greatly increased. Though in England, it has not reached that level of efficacy and utility, it is in constant use along with other writs.

2.3 Suit for damages

Whenever any person has been wronged by the action of an administrative authority, he can file a suit for damages against such authority. Such a suit is filed in the civil court of first instance and its procedure is regulated by the CPC. The requirement of two months' notice is mandatory under

105. (1998) 2 SCC 510.
106. AIR 1967 SC 436.
107. *K.K. Kochunni* v. *State of Madras*, AIR 1959 SC 725.
108. *H. Mathewson* v. *Gobardhan Tribedi*, 1900 SCC OnLine Cal 224: (1900) 5 CWN 654; *Mohd. Israil* v. *Patna Municipality*, 1942 SCC OnLine Pat 223: AIR 1943 Pat 34.

Section 80 of the amended Code before filing the suit, unless it is waived by the court in special circumstances. The extent of liability of the administration in contracts entered into with private individuals for torts committed by its servants has been discussed in Chapter VIII. Principles determining the quantum of damages are the same that govern private individuals.[109]

2.4 Affirmative action for the enforcement of public duties

During the last few years, the Indian Supreme Court has certainly developed a fine jurisprudence of right mobilisation. Affirmative action for the enforcement of public duties is one of the areas where the genius of the Indian judiciary has been registered in a unique manner. It is a fact that judicial redress can more readily be available for wrongful acts than for wrongful omissions of public bodies, and the effectiveness of the judicial remedies is also limited either by their intrinsic characteristics or by restrictive technical rules.[110] However, *Municipal Council, Ratlam* v. *Vardichan*[111] is a unique testimony of a new judicial dynamism, unhampered by these limitations, which has produced new "enforcement" dimensions to public duties owed by administrative bodies to people at large.

The Ratlam Municipality is a statutory body constituted to undertake and make reasonable and adequate provisions for cleaning public streets and public places, abating all public nuisances, and disposing night soil, rubbish, etc. The Ratlam Municipality, however, neglected its public duties and created unbearable insanitary conditions. When nothing could move the Municipality to remedy the deplorable conditions, one of the residents filed a suit against it under Section 133 of the Criminal Procedure Code, 1973 (CrPC) for the removal of nuisance to the public which were "unhygienic conditions" in this case. The Magistrate ordered the Municipality to abate the nuisance within 15 days. The Municipality instead of doing its duty which was its legal and moral responsibility decided to challenge the Magistrate's order. The case ultimately reached the Supreme Court which not only expressed appreciation for the "activist" application of Section 133, CrPC by the Magistrate but also characterised this case as a "pathfinder in the field of people's involvement in the justicing process"[112].

To everybody's dismay and surprise, the Municipality pleaded not only insufficiency of funds to carry out its duties but also requested for more time for doing its duty which it neglected to do for the last many years. Turning down both these tactical manoeuvres by the Municipality, the Supreme Court emphasised that a public body cannot extricate itself from public duties and responsibilities on the pretext of financial inability. The court observed:

109. *Thawardas Pherumal* v. *Union of India*, AIR 1955 SC 468.
110. De Smith, *Judicial Review of Administrative Action* (1980) 526.
111. (1980) 4 SCC 162
112. *Municipal Council, Ratlam* v. *Vardichan*, (1980) 4 SCC 162, 163.

> The criminal procedure code operates against statutory bodies and others regardless of the cash in their coffers, even as human rights under Part III of the Constitution have to be respected by the State regardless of budgetary provision. Likewise, Section 133 of the Act has no saving clause when the municipal council is penniless. Otherwise, a profligate statutory body or pachydermic governmental agency may legally defy duties under the law by urging in self-defence a self-created bankruptcy or perverted expenditure budget. That cannot be.[113]

Turning down the plea for extension of time, the court pointed out that eight years had passed since the Magistrate made the order but the Municipality had done nothing to implement the same. This was perhaps the most shocking request coming from a public body charged with the public duty of maintaining sanitation on which public health depends.

Maintaining its activist posture, the Supreme Court sought to frame a scheme and fix a timetable to implement the same and even to supervise the implementation of the scheme. It directed the Magistrate to supervise the implementation of the scheme and to prosecute the Municipality if the scheme was not fully implemented within a period of one year. The court also exhorted the State Government to provide sufficient funds to the Ratlam Municipality to enable it to implement the scheme.

Assuring its aid to people in similar situations, the Supreme Court categorically asserted that the heads of public bodies whether appointed or elected "will have to face the penalty of the law if what the Constitution and follow up legislation direct them to do are defied or denied wrongfully. The wages of violation is punishment, corporate and personal"[114].

In this case, a provision of the CrPC was used for the enforcement of public duties. But, as the trend in judicial behaviour indicates there seems to be no reason why mandamus cannot be used for this purpose.[115]

Judging by past experience, however, one salutary judicial rap on the knuckles will not move the establishment out of traditional inertia and apathy, but it does indicate a "writing on the wall" which public bodies cannot afford to ignore. This decision shall also remain a refreshing example of how an enlightened judiciary, even within the limitations of law, can enlarge and enrich the concept of citizens' rights in a democracy.

3. NON-BINDING (ADVISORY) REVIEW

This kind of review of administrative action can be exercised by Human Rights Commissions, Lokayukta (Ombudsman), and various other statutory commissions like Women Commissions, Child Commissions, Minority Commissions, Scheduled Castes and Tribes Commissions, etc. Jurisdiction of these bodies is advisory but not without any effect. Sanction behind the

113. *Ibid*, SCC 170, para. 12.
114. *Ibid*, SCC 174.
115. *See*, (1980) 16 ASIL 435, comment by Professor M.P. Jain.

advisory jurisdiction, over any administrative action, is "public opinion" which, in any democratic society, is the real sanction.

4. ALTERNATIVE DISPUTE RESOLUTION MECHANISMS IN ADMINISTRATIVE PROCESS

Deciding administrative disputes through judicial process is highly dilatory, expensive and thus not in public interest. Therefore, a need to employ alternative dispute resolution in the administrative process cannot be overemphasised. There is an urgent need to use alternative dispute resolution mechanisms. These alternative dispute resolutions may include besides others, conciliation, facilitation, mediation, fact-finding, minitrials, arbitration and use of ombuds or any combination thereof. With the consent of the parties arbitration may be a viable means for speedy justice in administrative disputes.

4.1 Appointment of administrative law judges

Section 1305 of the USA Administrative Procedure Act provides for the appointment of administrative law judges. Each administrative authority shall appoint as many administrative law judges as are necessary to conduct proceedings required to be conducted under Sections 556 and 557 of the Act which includes cases where there is involved military or foreign affair functions or a matter relating to authority's management or personnel or public property, loan, grants, benefits and contracts or where law requires adjudication on the record after a hearing. Administrative authority, in certain situations, may use administrative law judges selected by the Office of Personnel Management. Such an administrative law judge may be removed or suspended by the authority, where the judge is employed, only for a good cause established and determined by the Merit Systems Protection Board, on the record after opportunity for hearing before the Board. The pay and level of appointment shall be determined by the Office of Personnel Management. Practice in the USA suggests that every administrative authority should have its own quasi judicial mechanism to decide administrative disputes to ensure quality administrative justice. This practice will also ensure minimum judicial interference in the functioning of the administrative authority by ensuring fair administrative justice which is a necessity of today's administrative process legitimacy.

POINTS FOR DISCUSSION

1. The prophecy of Lord Denning, written in 1949, that as the pick and shovel is no longer suitable for the winning of coal, so also the procedures of writs are not suitable for the winning of freedom in the new age, has come true. Perhaps Lord Denning's prophecy was founded

on the technicalities from which these writs suffered. Against this backdrop, procedural technicalities and inconveniences of writ jurisdiction in India may be discussed. The discussion should aim at exploring a simple but effective technique for providing judicial review of administrative action. Students may consider the suggestion of the Law Commission in England that an "application for review" by the court should replace the present complex remedies.[116]

2. In India, the importance of injunction and declaratory action as the general utility remedy by which the legality of an administrative action may be determined is still to be recognised. One of the reasons is the statutory constraints of "relator action" and "further relief requirement". Discussion must review the efficacy of these remedies in the public law area with the aim of evolving certain principles by which the use of these less technical remedies in protecting not only the personal but public, economic, aesthetic and environmental rights may be increased.
3. The above discussions on various aspects of judicial review of administrative action should enable students to review existing remedies with a view to evolving simpler and effective system. In this behalf, the following options may be discussed.
   (*a*) Creation of an administrative division of High Courts and the Supreme Court. Assessors experienced in administrative matters and professional skills would assist where necessary.
   (*b*) Engrafting an administrative jurisdiction of the continental type for our legal system administered by a court corresponding to the Conseil d'Etat.
   (*c*) "Application for review" procedure to replace the existing restrictive remedies which would also obviate the need to specify any specific remedy to be sought.
4. The Constitution and the writ of habeas corpus may be discussed against the backdrop of the *Habeas Corpus case*[117]. Special attention may be paid to the dissent of H.R. Khanna J which set the tone for future development of the law.
5. "Instead of being astute to discover reasons for not applying this great constitutional remedy [Mandamus] for error and misgovernment, we think it our duty to be vigilant to apply it in every case to which, by any reasonable construction, it can be made applicable."[118] Students may discuss the use of mandamus in India in the light of this statement.
6. Writs of prohibition and certiorari are complementary writs, but certiorari is remedial whereas prohibition is preventive. In the light of this statement, students may discuss the scope of both these writs.

116. "Remedies in Administrative Law", (1971) Law Commission Working Paper No. 40.
117. (1976) 2 SCC 521.
118. *Rochester* v. *R.*, 1858 EL BL&EL 1024: 120 ER 791, *per* Martin J.

7. An union of injunction and declaration can completely replace technical writs. Against this backdrop, students may discuss the relative merits of both the systems of review of administrative action.
8. Do you think that judges play a political role while exercising power of judicial review? If yes, what is the legitimacy?
9. Do you think that a judge exercising power of judicial review should be independent and impartial only or should he also be an active judge who firmly believes in the culture of the Constitution?
10. What do you think is the basic purpose of judicial review of administrative action? Is it *a*) to protect the Constitution and enforce its culture; *b*) to supervise the working of the administration; *c*) to do justice to the litigant.

SUGGESTED READINGS

1. A.T. Markose, *Judicial Control of Administrative Action* (1959).
2. A.T. Markose, "Certiorari Certified", (1965) 16 Northern Ireland Legal Quarterly 239.
3. B.L. Strayer, "Injunctions Against Crown Officers", (1964) Can Bar Rev 1.
4. C.K. Thakker, *Administrative Law* (Eastern Book Company 2012) 967–1054.
5. D.C.M. Yardley, "Certiorari and the Problems of Locus Standi", (1955) 71 LQR 388.
6. D.C.M. Yardley, "Prohibition and Mandamus and Problems of Locus Standi", (1957) 73 LQR 534.
7. D.C.M. Yardley, "The Grounds of Certiorari and Prohibition", (1959) 37 Can Bar Rev 294.
8. D.C.M. Yardley, "The Purpose of Mandamus in English Law", (1959) Judicial Rev 1.
9. D.L. Keir and F.H. Lawson, *Cases in Constitutional Law* (5th Edn., Clarendon Press 1967) Chap. II.
10. D.M. Gordon, "Certiorari and Declaration as Alternative Remedies", (1959) 75 LQR 455.
11. D.M. Gordon, "Certiorari and the Problem of Locus Standi", (1955) 71 LQR 483.
12. D.T. Warren, "The Declaratory Judgments: Reviewing Administrative Action", (1966) 44 Can Bar Rev 610.
13. G.J. Borrie, "The Advantages of the Declaratory Judgment in Administrative Law", (1955) 18 Mod L Rev 138.
14. H.W.R. Wade, "The Future of Certiorari", (1958) Cambridge LJ 218.
15. Huang Su Mien, "Judicial Review of Administrative Action by the Prerogative Order", (1960) 2 University of Malaya LR 64.
16. I. Zamir, *The Declaratory Judgment* (1962).
17. I. Zamir, "Declaratory Judgment v. Prerogative Orders", (1958) Public Law 341.

18. Indian Law Institute, *Judicial Review Through Writ Petitions* (N.M. Tripathi 1962).
19. J.F. Garner, "Locus Standi in Actions for a Declaration", (1968) 31 Mod L Rev 512.
20. J.F. Garner and A.R. Galbraith, *Judicial Control of the Administrative Process* (Ditchley Foundation 1969).
21. J.M. Fitzgerald and I.D. Elliot, "Certiorari: Errors of Law on the Face of the Record", (1964) Melb UL Rev 552.
22. M.A. Fazal, *Judicial Control of Administrative Action in India and Pakistan* (Clarendon Press, 1969).
23. Markandey Katju, "Administrative Law and Judicial Review of Administrative Action", (2005) 8 SCC J-25
24. Mark Elliot, *The Constitutional Foundations of Judicial Review* (Hart Publishing 2001).
25. S.A. deSmith, "The Prerogative Writs", (1951) 11 Cambridge LJ 40.
26. S.A. deSmith, "The Province of Declaratory Judgment Redetermined", (1958) 21 Mod L Rev 404.
27. S.M. Thio, "Locus Standi in Relation to Mandamus", (1966) Public Law 133.
28. S.N. Jain, "Bodies to Which Mandamus can be Issued", (1973) 5 JILI 109.
29. S.N. Jain, "Scope of Judicial Review to Correct Errors of Law Through Mandamus and Certiorari", (1964) 6 JILI 316.
30. Sir Francis Vallat, "Declaratory Judgments", Current Legal Problems 1.
31. Sir W. Ivor Jennings, "Declaratory Judgments Against Public Authorities in England", (1932) 41 Yale LJ 407.
32. Trevor Allen, "The Constitutional Foundations of Judicial Review: Constitutional Conundrum or Interpretative Inquiry?" (2002) 61 CLJ 87.
33. V.S. Deshpande, "Judicial Review—Expansion and Self-restraint", (1973) 15 JILI 531.
34. W. Friedmann, "Declaratory Judgments and Injunction as Public Law Remedies", (1949) 22 Australian Law Journal 446.
35. W.S. Holdsworth, *History of English Law*, Vol. IV, 201, Vol. VI, 20, Vol. X, 140.

CHAPTER 10

Public Interest Litigation or Social Action Litigation and Campaign Litigation

It is a fact that in India, today, public interest litigation (PIL) or social action litigation (SAL) jurisdiction of the constitutional courts has grown so much that now courts are drawing their identity and legitimacy largely from the exercise of this jurisdiction, and their traditional role has slipped into background.

The term "public interest litigation" was first used by Prof. Abram Chayes in 1976 to refer to cases seeking social change through court directives, which articulated public norms of governance and also enforced the public norms. Thus, it is free from traditional judicial trappings, legal centralism, precedents, and other procedural inflexibilities. In fact, it is not an "adjudication" in the real sense of the term, but a collaborative effort to bring a socio-economic change in society to make it more equal, just and inclusive. The PIL may thus be described as a litigation in the interest of the "voiceless voices" to secure their legal rights and entitlements.

SAL and PIL are terms which are used interchangeably in India.[1] The term PIL comes to us from the US jurisdiction where it was designed to provide legal representation to previously unrepresented groups and interests. The necessity for this was the recognition that the ordinary market place for legal services fails to provide such services to significant segments of the US population and to significant interests. Such groups and interests include poor, environmentalists, consumers, racial and ethnic minorities, and others.[2] But the term PIL is the one that is currently used indiscriminately in the courts. The term SAL is not much in use.

PIL is a socio-economic movement generated by the judiciary to extend justice, especially, to the weaker sections of society for whom even after so many years of independence, justice is merely a teasing illusion. In other words, it is a long-arm strategy of the judiciary to extend justice to those

1. I am tempted to agree with Prof. Upendra Baxi that the term "SAL" is more appropriate in the Indian context. *See* Baxi, "Taking Suffering Seriously: Social Action Litigation and the Supreme Court", (December 1982) 29 International Commission of Jurists Rev 37–49.
2. "Balancing the Scales of Justice—Financing Public Interest Law in America", A Report by the Council for the Public Interest Law (1976) 6–7, quoted by Prof. S.K. Agarwal, *Public Interest Litigation in India: A Critique* (N.M. Tripathi 1985) 2.

who due to socio-economic handicap cannot reach the doors of the courts. Therefore, it is a judge-led and judge-induced strategy and represents high benchmark of judicial creativity and sensitivity to the problems of the weak and the vulnerable. The idea of PIL came from *actio popularis* of the Roman jurisprudence, which allowed court access to every citizen in matters of public wrongs. In India, inspiration to court for the development of this strategy came from the oath which a judge takes to defend the Constitution, wherein socio-economic justice and equal court access are the prime principles. Thus, this innovative strategy, while providing easy access to justice to the weaker sections of Indian society, also provides a powerful tool in the hands of public-spirited individuals and social action groups for combating exploitation and injustice and securing for the underprivileged segment of society, their social and economic entitlements.[3]

1. NATURE AND PURPOSE OF PIL

PIL which means "litigation in the interest of public" entered judicial process in 1970. This type of litigation was innovated by judges to provide "equal access" to the judicial process to those who could not come to the court for the vindication of their rights due to socio-economic handicaps, for which there was a dire need.

It is not a litigation in the real sense of the term. It is, in fact, a challenge and an opportunity to undo historical injustice done by a few to many. Therefore, it is totally different from ordinary litigation which is essentially of an adversary character. In PIL, litigation is not considered as a battle to be won but a disease to be cured. Unlike ordinary litigation, the purpose of the SAL is not to enforce the right of one person against the other, but to extend justice to the deprived sections of society and, hence, SAL is not so much for the benefit of an individual as it is for a class. Unlike ordinary litigation, it is largely preventive not punitive, corrective not compensatory and, hence, involves the court and the petitioner on a long-term basis, as justice is done through directions. Such litigation involves wider questions of law and policy and provides opportunity to the petitioner to determine the course of litigation. Viewed in that perspective, SAL is a collaborative effort between the petitioner, court and the government and its instrumentalities to make socio-economic rescuer programmes for the disadvantaged and deprived meaningful for them. Therefore, the State must not only welcome it but must also actively participate in this movement because the idea behind the movement is not to tread on the toes of the administration or to usurp its powers, but to extend justice to the darkest and remotest corners of India. Any attempt to undermine this movement would be destructive of the rule of law, which is a basic feature of our Constitution. Rule of

3. *State of H.P.* v. *Parent of a Student of Medical College*, (1985) 3 SCC 169; *Bandhua Mukti Morcha* v. *Union of India*, (1984) 3 SCC 161; *M.C. Mehta* v. *Union of India*, (1987) 1 SCC 395.

law demands equal access to justice, but in our society a vast majority has no access because of socio-economic handicap. Thus, the SAL movement strives to create a rule of law society in India.

1.1 Constitutional habitat

It may be pointed out that in PIL the court is not exercising any extra-constitutional jurisdiction as this strategy is now firmly rooted in Articles 14 and 21 of the Constitution. Article 14 provides protection against all arbitrariness and lawlessness in administrative actions, and Article 21 provides for protection of "life" which embodies everything that goes for a dignified living, including rightful concerns for others. It also encompasses violations of various directive principles of state policy in the Constitution, which are especially for the benefit of the weaker sections of society.

1.2 Locus standi

The PIL strategy has been developed by the court by lowering the threshold level of locus standi. As discussed in Chapter 8 of this book, traditional view of locus standi was that only an "aggrieved person", who has personally suffered a legal injury by reason of violation of his right or legally protected interest, can file a suit for the redress of his grievance.[4] This was the highly restrictive and individualistic view of the Anglo-Indian mould which did not suit to the needs of the present day society and therefore, the phrase has been liberally interpreted in the field of PIL to allow standing to any *pro bono publico*.[5] Thus interpreted, the rule of locus standi has been made broad-based and people-oriented to allow access to justice through "class actions", "representative actions" and "public or social action litigation" so that justice may become easily available to the lowly and lost.[6] Courts have now travelled a long distance from "personal injury" standing to "public concern" standing in order to allow access to public-spirited individuals, groups and organisations on behalf of those who because of their poverty, illiteracy and ignorance cannot come before the court and, thus, continue to suffer injustice and deprivation.[7] For this purpose, courts have allowed "letter petitions" and at times have acted suo moto where the situation is such that shocks the conscience of the court. Thus, even press reports have been turned into PILs.

The strategy of PIL was devised for increasing citizen's participation in the judicial process, for making accessible the judicial delivery system to one who could not otherwise reach court for various reasons. Thus, any member of the public having sufficient interest can maintain an action

4. *S.P. Gupta* v. *Union of India*, 1981 Supp SCC 87.
5. *Ibid.*
6. *Per* Bhagwati J in *People's Union for Democratic Rights* v. *Union of India*, (1982) 3 SCC 235.
7. For detailed discussion *see*, Chap. 8 of this book.

for public injury. This is absolutely necessary for maintaining the rule of law, furthering the cause of justice, and accelerating the pace of realisation of the constitutional objectives. However, it is equally necessary that any busybody or meddlesome interloper who masquerades as crusader for justice should not be allowed to abuse the process of the court for improper motives. Thus, courts will not allow that its process be obstructed or polluted by unscrupulous litigants for oblique reasons under the garb of PIL.[8] Locus standi in PIL, thus, will not be lightly allowed to any one to litigate in the name of public interest to cause damage to others. Therefore, where the union challenged the action of the Vice-Chancellor who had allowed students to appear at the examination through a PIL, the court held that such a union must disclose 1) whether it was authorised to file litigation; 2) if so, then by whom; 3) whether it has sufficient funds to indulge in such type of litigation; and 4) the basis of alleging public harm. This shows that standing in PIL cannot be taken for granted.[9]

In *Malik Bros.* v. *Narendra Dadhich*[10], the Supreme Court clarified beyond doubt that standing in PIL is to be judged keeping in view the purpose of the petition. The purpose of the petition should be the betterment of society and not individual benefit, so that this strategy is not allowed to degenerate into personal, publicity or political interest litigation. According to the court, the real purpose of PIL is 1) vindication of the rule of law; 2) facilitating effective access to justice to socio-economic weaker sections of society; or 3) meaningful realisation of fundamental rights. In other words, a PIL petition can be entertained for redressing public injury, enforcing public duty, protecting socio-economic rights of weaker sections, and vindicating public interest. In this case, a petitioner had purchased a land by auction but as he failed to deposit the amount as stipulated, his security deposit was forfeited. His prayer for referring his case to arbitration was accepted. Nevertheless, he came before the court in a PIL in his capacity as a taxpayer for quashing the award which was nothing but an abuse of judicial process.

The court in this case took the opportunity and issued a warning that if courts do not restrict the free flow of cases in the name of PIL traditional litigation would suffer and the courts of law, instead of dispensing justice, will have to take upon themselves administrative and executive functions. It is only when there is a gross violation of fundamental rights by a group or a class action, or where basic human rights are invaded, or when there are complaints of such acts as will shock judicial conscience, then only such petitions be heard and the court should extend its jurisdiction for remedying the hardships and miseries of the needy, the underdog and the neglected. The court also observed that a PIL petition cannot be filed in the

8. See, *Janata Dal* v. *H.S. Chowdhary*, (1992) 4 SCC 305; *S.P. Gupta* v. *Union of India*, 1981 Supp SCC 87; *Meera Massey* v. *S.R. Mehrotra*, (1998) 3 SCC 88.
9. *Bhartiya Homoeopathy College* v. *Students' Council*, (1998) 2 SCC 449.
10. (1999) 6 SCC 552.

first instance unless all the alternative remedies have been exhausted, so that the time of the court is not wasted. Whether a person who is himself not a candidate for the post can challenge appointments to certain posts under the government by way of a PIL on the ground that appointments were secured on the basis of forged experience certificates? This question was left open by the court.[11] In *National Council for Civil Liberties* v. *Union of India*[12], the court rightly held that private disputes are not maintainable as PILs. In this case, a petition had been filed alleging that Medha Patkar of Narmada Bachao Andolan is involved in subversive activities, in order to obstruct developmental projects of national importance, affecting fundamental rights of the people. The court held that it appears to be a private litigation to discredit and defuse the agitation for rehabilitation of displaced persons from dam sites.

Moving in the same direction, the Supreme Court in *Kalyaneshwari* v. *Union of India*[13] reiterated that a PIL petition can be entertained only if it is a bona fide litigation in public interest, and the litigant approaches the court with clean hands and discloses complete fact. A court must also evaluate the necessity of it. Therefore, the court emphasised that if a PIL lacks bona fide, abuses the process of court, and is merely a proxy litigation for personal gains, exemplary cost must be imposed.

1.3 Procedure

As discussed earlier, social or public action litigation is different from private litigation and, therefore, if the technical rules of procedure applicable to the private litigation are applied to PIL also, it would be counterproductive. Hence, the courts have developed new procedural norms to suit the requirements of this strategy.

A PIL can be initiated by any public-spirited person or group on behalf of any person or persons who, because of any socio-economic handicap, cannot come before the court, or where the right which is violated is a "diffused" right. However, no busybody, meddlesome interloper, wayfarer or officious intervener will be allowed to abuse the process of law by initiating frivolous litigation for personal or political gains, or for mere publicity, or for other oblique reasons.[14] Thus, only a genuine public-spirited person or group will be allowed standing in a PIL. However, drafting of petition should be done by persons having expert knowledge in the field after making proper research, especially, when the petition is concerned with issues of constitutional law.[15] It is also necessary that in a PIL petition, public interest must be prominent. A PIL filed alleging mala fide on the part

11. *Pratap Singh* v. *State of Haryana*, (2002) 7 SCC 484.
12. (2007) 6 SCC 506.
13. (2011) 3 SCC 287.
14. *B. Krishna Bhat* v. *Union of India*, (1990) 3 SCC 65; *Janata Dal* v. *H.S. Chowdhary*, (1992) 4 SCC 305; *S.P. Gupta* v. *Union of India*, 1981 Supp SCC 87.
15. *S.P. Anand* v. *H.D. Deve Gowda*, (1996) 6 SCC 734.

of a Municipal Corporation in demolishing multi-storied building, where family members of the petitioner got trapped, is not maintainable because in the opinion of the court no public interest is involved. Factual disputes cannot be examined under Article 32 of the Constitution.[16]

In a number of cases, courts have entertained "letters" also not only from the aggrieved persons but also from persons acting *pro bono publico* to initiate a PIL.[17] In exceptional cases, courts have even acted suo motu on the basis of a press report. Generally, the PILs are heard on a priority basis, therefore, unless the petitioner has a genuine public interest, he will not be allowed to jump the queue, otherwise it would irk others waiting in the long queue for justice.

No matter, the Supreme Court and the High Courts have by rules prescribed procedures for moving the court under Articles 32 and 226, but in a PIL the cause of justice is not allowed to be thwarted by procedural technicalities.[18] Therefore, the court does not insist on a regular writ petition and sworn affidavits. Evidences are generally taken on commission at the State expense. No matter, the jurisdiction of the Supreme Court is confined to the violation of fundamental rights, but if there is a breach of a social legislation, or a matter of serious public concern is involved, the court has allowed access.[19] Even in cases where the court is called upon to give effect to the directive principles or fundamental duties under the Constitution, it will not shrug its shoulders and say that these are not enforceable rights and it will issue directions.[20] Regarding withdrawal of petitions, the court developed a unique procedural norm when it held that the petitioner can withdraw but the petition would stay, and the court will ask any other person to represent the case.[21] However, the court may grant permission to withdraw keeping in view the consideration of public interest and to check abuse of process of the court.[22] In the area of PIL, justice is done mostly through court's directives. No matter it is open to the court to supplement the prescribed procedure by evolving its own rule in this area, nevertheless, the supplement procedure must conform at all stages to the principles of natural justice, and other accepted procedural norms characteristic of judicial proceedings.[23] Therefore, where the number of persons affected by the PIL is large and indeterminate, public notices issued in large number of newspapers in English and local language about the pendency of the litigation and the date of next hearing will be considered as sufficient notice to all those who would be affected by the decision of the court and, in such

16. *Daljit Singh Dalal* v. *Union of India*, (1997) 4 SCC 62.
17. *S.P. Gupta* v. *Union of India*, 1981 Supp SCC 87; *Bandhua Mukti Morcha* v. *Union of India*, (1984) 3 SCC 161, 239–40.
18. *Bandhua Mukti Morcha* v. *Union of India*, (1984) 3 SCC 161.
19. *Sheonandan Paswan* v. *State of Bihar*, (1987) 1 SCC 288.
20. *Sachidanand Pandey* v. *State of W.B.*, (1978) 2 SCC 295.
21. *Sheela Barse (2)* v. *Union of India*, (1986) 3 SCC 632.
22. *S.P. Anand* v. *H.D. Deve Gowda*, (1996) 6 SCC 734.
23. *Bandhua Mukti Morcha* v. *Union of India*, (1984) 3 SCC 161, 230–31.

cases, principles of Order 1, Rule 8 of the Civil Procedure Code (CPC) are not invocable and no one can say to have received no notice.[24]

In a pace-setting judgment, the Supreme Court held that while exercising the power under Article 32 of the Constitution for the enforcement of fundamental rights under a PIL, it can issue guidelines and norms to fill up the vacuum in an existing legislation. Thus, in *Vishaka* v. *State of Rajasthan*[25], the court issued detailed directions to protect working women from sexual harassment and to make their fundamental rights meaningful to them.

Court has also allowed a writ against inertia of pollution boards for their failure to check pollution by private units which is their statutory duty.[26]

However, one cannot deny the fact that in recent times, in increasing instances, the PIL strategy has been abused. This special type of litigation which was essentially meant to protect basic human rights of the weak and the disadvantaged—who on account of poverty, helplessness, or social and economic disabilities could not approach the court for relief—has now become private or publicity litigation in a number of cases. Increasingly, it is becoming a weapon in the hands of persons who are not disadvantaged or deprived to protect their entitlements. Therefore, the Supreme Court thought it proper to re-emphasise the parameters within which a PIL could be resorted to by the petitioner and entertained by the court in *BALCO Employees' Union* v. *Union of India*[27] (*BALCO*). The court emphasised that a PIL is meant to protect the violation of Article 21 of the Constitution (Right to life and personal liberty) and other human rights. It can be initiated for the benefit of the poor and the under-privileged who are unable to come before the court. In such cases, also it is the legal rights which are secured by the court as a PIL cannot be a panacea for all wrongs. Thus, the court concluded that a PIL cannot be used to challenge the financial or economic decisions taken by the government. No doubt a person who is personally aggrieved by such decisions can himself come before the court, but a PIL at the behest of the stranger ought not be entertained. Such a litigation cannot per se be on behalf of the poor and the downtrodden, unless court is satisfied that there has been a violation of Article 21 of the Constitution and persons adversely affected are unable to come before the court. The court further emphasised that a PIL is available if there is an injury to public because of dereliction of constitutional or statutory obligation on the part of government. The court restated that every matter of public interest or curiosity cannot be a subject of PIL, because courts are not expected to conduct the administration of the country.

Explaining the scope of enquiry of the constitutional court, while hearing a PIL, the Supreme Court held that after giving notice to the parties, the

24. *Gopi Aqua Farms* v. *Union of India*, (1997) 6 SCC 577. See also, *S. Jagannath* v. *Union of India*, (1997) 2 SCC 87.
25. (1997) 6 SCC 241.
26. *Indian Council for Enviro-Legal Action* v. *Union of India*, (1996) 3 SCC 212.
27. (2002) 2 SCC 333. See also, *Mohd. Aslam* v. *Union of India*, (2003) 4 SCC 1.

court may enter issues wider than those raised in the PIL. Technicalities do not deter the court in wielding its power to do justice, enforcing the law, and balancing equities. The court is obliged to see, while scrutinising the conduct and activities of a public body, that its activities bear no colour, except being transparent, and are guided with the object of public good, and are within the four corners of law. These observations were made by the court in *Padma* v. *Hiralal Motilal Desarda*[28], wherein the High Court after framing questions, put all the parties on notice before it that it proposed to enter into issues wider than those raised in the petition. Non-petitioners, including appellants, were allowed full opportunity of defending themselves. The court also called for the record of the authority and scrutinised it. Thus, while hearing a PIL, the constitutional court acts as a custodian of constitutional morality, ethics and code of conduct. In another case, the Supreme Court recommended that the PIL should be disposed of at the earlier as delay may cause further injury to the public.[29]

Nevertheless, the principle of res judicata (finality of litigation) shall apply to a PIL in the same manner as applied to other writ proceedings. Therefore, a PIL is not maintainable where matters have already been completely and effectively adjudicated upon in individual petitions. Thus, in *Joydeep Mukharjee* v. *State of W.B.*[30], the court did not entertain a PIL relating to illegal and arbitrary allotment of government land in Salt Lake City, Calcutta from the Chief Minister's discretionary quota, as the issue had already been adjudicated upon in the High Court and the Supreme Court in individual petitions.

In retrospect, PIL in India has developed in three phases:[31]

1. In the first phase court exercised power to protect the fundamental rights and to reach socio-economic justice to the deprived and marginalised sections of society who could not reach the court because of their socio-economic handicap.
2. In the second phase court exercised power for the protection, preservation and development of ecology, environment, forests, marine and wildlife, rivers and historical monuments. These are the manifestations of public property in a state of neglect.
3. In the third phase court exercised power for enforcing probity, transparency and integrity in the governance. Thus, focus of the court was good governance wherein human rights were identified with human development. In this phase court is also being used by politically entrenched groups for serving their political and sectional interests.

---

28. (2002) 7 SCC 564.
29. *BALCO Employees' Union* v. *Union of India*, (2002) 2 SCC 333.
30. (2011) 2 SCC 706.
31. *State of Uttaranchal* v. *Balwant Singh Chaufal*, (2010) 3 SCC 402.

1.4 Complexities and problems of PIL

One of the distinctive features of the PIL movement has been that from its very inception it became a hypersensitive area and generated a lot of controversies and apprehensions. One such controversy is that the PIL strategy is a status quoist approach of the court to avoid any change in the system, and so it is a painkilling strategy which does not treat the disease. It is argued that the problems of the poor, disadvantaged and the deprived cannot be solved by any trickle down method and, therefore, whatever the court is doing in a PIL is merely symbolic, simply to earn a legitimacy for itself which it has lost over the years. There may be truth in this assertion, and whatever little the court is doing through a PIL may be just straws floating in the air, but one thing is certain that they are floating in the right direction.

It is further argued that by extending its jurisdiction through a PIL, the court is trying to bite more than what it can chew. Lawyers have started complaining that much of the court's time is being consumed by PILs and, hence, for the court a postcard has become more important than a 50-page affidavit. It is further argued that at a time when the figures of pending cases before the courts are astronomical, this new area of litigation would spell a total collapse of the judicial system in India as it would open floodgates of litigation. However, the history of PIL in India does not support this apprehension. Indian litigation system is a very tiresome process, therefore, no one would like to litigate for the lark. In the Supreme Court, 35,000 cases were filed in 1985 and in comparison to this, only 200 PILs were filed. It is important to note that if 35,000 cases benefited 35,000 persons, perhaps 200 PILs may have benefited millions.[32] Contrary to the popular belief, fresh PIL filing has registered a decline in the subsequent years. It is ironical that decline started exactly when the doors of the courts were open wide to the common man. The reasons for this trend are many. The tribe of conscientious citizens who regularly moved social action cases is feeling discouraged because of frequent adjournments and long delays in the grant of final relief, and whatever relief is granted, in many cases, stops at the gates of the court because of the indifferent attitude of the administration. Furthermore, well-intentioned persons feel insulted and discouraged when administration imputes motives to them. Lawyers who readily offered their services for a laudable cause are retracing their feet because of the realisation that it is not all publicity and glamour but time and money also. Furthermore, those who have been sending letters as petitions in the past to a particular judge have found that it may not be heard by him. A new practice developed by the court is to refer such letters to legal aid committees which would convert them into writs. It is also now being increasingly recognised that leading evidence is more difficult than sending newspaper clippings to the court. Added to this is the time consumed in waiting upon

32. *Indian Express* 27-10-1986, 6.

lawyers, where for some of them SAL is only a cosmetic touch to their public image.[33] Division among judges on the desirability of PIL, some of whom do not even hesitate in making a sardonic remark in the open court, is also responsible for this backlash effect.

Without being exhaustive, other popular criticisms of the opponents of PIL are as follows:

(1) It is an attempt at picking a judge and making him a commercial item.
(2) It is a politics of liberation wherein court seeks social legitimacy for itself.
(3) In a country which is full of injustices, it is nothing but don quixote forays in the harsh realities of life.
(4) It is an attempt to pre-empt legislation and administrative initiative.
(5) It is an attempt at using a system against system which would hit back.
(6) It is leading to class conflicts and social tension.
(7) It is an attempt at disturbing the constitutional balance between legislature, executive and the judiciary..
(8) It is a shift away from the democratic system as the people instead of looking up to their elected representatives look up to the court.
(9) It is a tool of blackmail.

Even in the US, the PIL is not without hostility. In *United States* v. *B. Richardson*[34], Powell J observed, "Relaxation of standing requirements is directly related to the expansion of judicial power and that such relaxation would significantly alter the allocation of power at the national level, with shift away from the democratic form of government."[35]

According to one opinion, the misuse of PIL has reached ridiculous limits, and petitions are being filed all over the country before the writ courts for matters like monkey menace, students and teachers strike, shortage of buses, lack of cleanliness in hospitals, irregularities in stock exchange, painting of road signs, dengue fever, examinations and admissions in universities and colleges, etc. One can go on but the list will not be exhaustive. A classic case came up when a PIL was filed in the Delhi High Court for a direction to the United Front Government at the Centre (1997) to form a coalition cabinet with the Congress. A petition (1999) was filed for invalidating the no-confidence vote against the Vajpayee government. In 2003, a PIL was filed challenging the decision of the U.P. Governor inviting Mulayam Singh Yadav to form a government in the State of Uttar Pradesh. In most situations, lawyers file PIL petitions for themselves and not for other PIL petitioners. More than half of the PIL work of courts answers the description of the "Hyde Park" syndrome, where petitions are more like

33. *Indian Express*, Chandigarh 6-9-1983, 7.
34. 1974 SCC OnLine US SC 147: 41 L Ed 2d 678: 418 US 166 (1974).
35. *Ibid*, US 188.

ill-prepared public speeches or memoranda than judicial petitions. Power and publicity apart, many judges have to entertain PIL because of the liberalisation of the rule of locus standi and the concept of social justice for the poor, oppressed and exploited sections of society. Thus, indiscriminate use of this strategy is bringing it into disrepute because it has become the privilege of the privileged to have access to the court.[36] In fact, majority of the petitions either should not have been filed or should not have been entertained. PIL must be confined to cases where justice is to be reached to that section of society which cannot come to the court due to socio-economic handicap, or where a matter of grave public concern is involved.

While PIL is being hailed as a strategy to reinforce the rule of law in the administrative process and as a unique innovation of judicial statesmanship, the Supreme Court expressed its anguish at the manner in which a useful strategy of extending justice to the disadvantaged sections of society on equal basis is being misused by unscrupulous litigants for everything, except genuine public interest for which it was designed. In this case, a lawyer had filed a PIL to blackmail people and was caught red-handed accepting "blackmailing" money.[37]

Explaining the meaning of "public interest", which is at the heart of the PIL, the court quoted with approval the definition as given in *Stroud's Judicial Dictionary*[38], which lays down that public interest or general interest matter does not mean that which is interesting or gratifying curiosity or a love of information or amusement, but that in which a class or the community have a pecuniary interest or some interest by which their legal rights or liabilities are affected.

Giving further guidelines to the courts for entertaining a PIL, the Supreme Court opined that besides public or general interest which must be present in the petition, the court has to be satisfied about 1) the credentials of the applicant; 2) prima facie correctness or nature of information given by him; and 3) the information not being vague or indefinite. The information should show gravity and seriousness involved. The court then should strike a balance between two conflicting interests: 1) nobody should be allowed to misuse the judicial process by making wild and reckless allegations besmirching the character of others; and 2) avoidance of public mischief to avoid mischievous petitions seeking to assail, for oblique motives, justifiable executive actions. In such cases court cannot be liberal and court must watch that under the guise of redressing a public grievance, it does not encroach upon the sphere reserved by the Constitution to the executive and the legislature.[39] It was further emphasised that the court must

36. Sangeeta Ahuja, *People, Law and Justice*, Vol. 2 (1997). Anupam Gupta, "There was mass rejection of PILs by the Rajasthan High Court (1997)", *The Tribune, News Review* 10-12-1997, 11.
37. *Dattaraj Nathuji Thaware* v. *State of Maharashtra*, (2005) 1 SCC 590.
38. Vol. 4 (4th Edn.).
39. *Ashok Kumar Pandey* v. *State of W.B.*, (2004) 3 SCC 349; *B. Singh* v. *Union of India*, (2004) 3 SCC 363.

be ruthless while dealing with impostors and busybodies or meddlesome interlopers, impersonating as public-spirited holy men, who masquerade as crusaders and *pro bono publics*. The court also advised that in situations where serious questions of law are involved like the one in service matters, a PIL should not be allowed.[40] Unfortunately, today PIL has become middle class interest litigation (MIL), therefore, there is a need to revert PIL to its original design of reaching justice to the disadvantaged sections of society whose rights suffer from atrophy and waste.

Even if all criticism is valid, no one would suggest to abolish this strategy which the courts have innovated to extend justice to the deprived sections of society. Anything contrary would be like suggesting the abolition of marriage in order to solve the problem of divorce. This socio-economic movement generated by court has at least kept alive the hope of the people for justice and, thus, has weaned people away from self-help or seeking redress through a private system of justice. It is necessary for sustaining the democratic system and the establishment of a rule of law society. Therefore, one has to be both adventurous and cautious in this respect and the judiciary has to keep on learning mostly by experience.[41]

PIL must not be allowed to degenerate into private publicity, or political or paisa interest litigation. Finding the delicate balance between ensuring justice and maintaining institutional legitimacy is the continuing challenge before the higher judiciary.

Needless to emphasise that the strategy of PIL must be used by the courts carefully, prudently, and with discrimination because any indiscriminate use of it would bring it into contempt, both from the public and the government.[42] Therefore, the correct approach of the court in PIL cases should be a judicious mix of restraint and activism determined by the dictates of existing realities. Any misuse of this strategy must be strongly discouraged by the courts.[43]

1.5 Changing perspective

With the introduction of the policy of liberalisation, privatisation and globalisation of economy in 1990s, the court's perspective on PIL has also changed. It is more sensitive to fast economic development and considerations of planning and execution. Human rights of the people have been

40. See also, *Duryodhan Sahu* v. *Jitendra Kumar Mishra*, (1998) 7 SCC 273.
41. S. Rangarajan, *Some Thoughts on Legal Research* (Mimeo 1982) 6.
42. In *J.P. Sanghi* v. *State of M.P.*, 1984 SCC OnLine MP 144: AIR 1985 MP 109, A PIL was used for getting the road signs painted. In *Sathyalaya Social and Cultural Organisation* v. *Madras Doordarshan*, 1984 SCC OnLine Mad 94: AIR 1985 Mad 186, PIL was used for the deletion of a few songs from a film. See also, *Chhetriya Pardushan Mukti Sangharsh Samiti* v. *State of U.P.*, (1990) 4 SCC 449.
43. Mukharjee CJ, *Chhetriya Pardushan Mukti Sangharsh Samiti* v. *State of U.P.*, (1990) 4 SCC 449, 452.

pushed in background. In *BALCO*[44], the Supreme Court held that the economic policy of disinvestment cannot be challenged in a PIL unless there is a violation of the right to life and personal liberty of persons who cannot approach the court due to their socio-economic handicap. Lack of sensitivity of the court is visible in areas of rights of the workers and slum dwellers. In *Almitra H. Patel* v. *Union of India*[45], court adversely commended on the government's policy to allot land to slum dwellers.

Exercising its powers of judicial review under PIL, court has generated a huge movement of judicial activism which has grown in four directions—constitutional activism, legislative activism, interpretative activism and executive activism. All the four dimensions have become controversial on the ground of violation of the delicate constitutional balance between different organs of the State.[46]

Unfortunately today, PIL has become MIL. The strategy which had been developed to provide excess to justice to the disadvantaged sections of society has been hijacked by middle classes to protect their rights and entitlements. There is a need that PIL be restored to its original purpose.

It is absolutely true that the courts through PILs cannot take care of all the problems of the poor. The ultimate guarantee of one's right, however, lies in self-assertion. The poor and the weak must, therefore, be organised and made self-reliant.[47] Bhagwati J rightly emphasised:

> We must always remember that social action litigation is a necessary and valuable ally in the cause of the poor but it cannot be a substitute for organisation of the poor, development of community, legal self-reliance and establishment of effective organisational structures through which the poor can combat exploitation and injustice, protect and defend their interests and secure their rights and entitlements.[48]

In the US, where the requirement of locus standi has been liberalised and has already reached maturity, courts have recognised not only taxpayers' or competitors' or consumers' standing—asserting economic or uneconomic interests—but also the standing of those asserting aesthetic and environmental interests.[49] The courts have recognised standing in citizens' groups concerned with protection of natural, scenic and historic resources; a national conservation organisation challenging the construction of expressway,[50] a public benefit corporation bringing a class action against

44. (2002) 2 SCC 333.
45. (2000) 2 SCC 679.
46. See, *Rameshwar Prasad* (5) v. *Union of India*, (2005) 7 SCC 625; *Centre for Public Interest Litigation* v. *Union of India*, (2005) 8 SCC 202; *Union of India* v. *Assn. for Democratic Reforms*, (2002) 10 SCC 111.
47. C.K. Thakker, *Administrative Law* (Eastern Book Company 1992) 607.
48. "Law, Justice and Underprivileged", Keynote address at the National Seminar on Unorganised Rural Labour held at New Delhi on January 5–8, 1984; cited by C.K. Thakker, *ibid*, 607.
49. *Sierra Club* v. *C.B. Morton*, 1972 SCC OnLine US SC 83: 31 L Ed 2d 636: 405 US 727 (1972).
50. *Citizens Committee for Hudson Valley* v. *Volpe*, 425 F 2d 97 (2nd Cir 1970).

a proposed nuclear detonation;[51] an organisation devoted to environmental protection, challenging the use of the DDT;[52] a citizens' group attacking a model cities programme;[53] and a conservationist organisation challenging mining and timber cutting in a national forest.[54]

In England,[55] the PIL movement started with the *Blackburn cases*. Blackburn, a former Member of Parliament (MP), took up many cases before the Court of Appeal which involved matters of public concern. The court granted him locus standi to challenge the governmental action relating to the joining of European Economic Common Market,[56] police inaction in prosecuting big gambling houses[57] and enforcing the pornography law.[58] Similarly, the court allowed standing to Ross McWhirter (he was one of twin brothers who produced the Guinness Book of Records) to file petition for injunction restraining the Independent Broadcasting Authority from telecasting a film, which according to him was outrageous—"a shocker, the worst ever"[59].

The era of liberalising the strict rule of locus standi was also heralded by the rule of the Supreme Court, Order 53 Rule 3(5), which replaced the judiciary-created rule of "aggrieved person" with the rule of "sufficient interest"[60]. However, this rule was narrowly interpreted by the House of Lords in *IRC* v. *National Federation of Self-Employed and Small Businesses Ltd.*[61] In this case, about 6000 casual workers, called "Fleet Street Casuals", who were doing casual work for the newspapers did not sign their true names on pay packets and, thus, by hiding their true identity defrauded the tax authorities to the tune of about one million pounds. After the fraud was detected, a settlement was arrived at according to which arrears of past taxes were written-off, but they were made liable for the payment of tax on all future earnings. The settlement was challenged by the Federation of Self-Employed and Small Shopkeepers on the ground that the writing-off of the tax was illegal and sought mandamus for the collection of tax according to law. The Court of Appeal held that the Federation had "sufficient interest" in the matter. Lord Denning, who was a champion of the liberal rule of locus standi, held that the Federation has a genuine grievance because the "Fleet Street Casuals" are getting out of

51. *Crowther* v. *Seaborg*, 312 F Supp 1205 (1970).
52. *Environmental Defense Fund Inc.* v. *M. Hardin*, 428 F 2d 1093 (1970).
53. *North City Area-Wide Council Inc.* v. *Romney*, 428 F 2d 754 (1970).
54. *West Virginia Highlands Conservancy* v. *Island Creek Coal Co.*, 411 F 2d 232 (1971).
55. *See*, Denning, *The Discipline of Law* (1979) Part III.
56. *Blackburn* v. *Attorney General*, (1971) 1 WLR 1037 (CA).
57. *R.* v. *Metropolitan Police Commr., ex p Blackburn*, (1968) 2 QB 118: (1968) 2 WLR 893 (CA).
58. *R.* v. *Metropolitan Police Commr., ex p Blackburn (No. 3)*, 1973 1 QB 241: (1973) 2 WLR 43 (CA).
59. *Attorney General, ex rel McWhirter* v. *Independent Broadcasting Authority*, 1973 QB 629: (1973) 2 WLR 344 (CA).
60. *See*, S.N. Jain, *Standing and Public Interest Litigation* (Mimeographed) 15.
61. 1982 AC 617: (1981) 2 WLR 722 (HL). See, *ibid*, 15.

paying their back taxes because of their industrial muscle power. However, in appeal, the House of Lords reversed for various reasons.[62]

In India, until the PIL was developed by the Supreme Court, justice was only a remote and even theoretical proposition for the mass of illiterate, underprivileged and exploited persons in the country. They were unaware of the law or even of their legal rights, unacquainted with the niceties of procedure involved, and too impoverished to engage lawyers, file papers and bear heavy expenditure on dilatory litigation. Thus, the vested interests that exploited them were emboldened to continue with their cruel and even illegal practices with cynical contempt for the law. This vast underprivileged section of society found themselves utterly helpless. Nor could anyone else take up their case for lack of locus standi or any direct interest in the matter.

By propounding the thesis that citizens should be enabled to enjoy the right to life and liberty guaranteed under Article 21 of the Constitution, the Supreme Court enlarged the scope of locus standi to include the rightful concern of other citizens willing to espouse the cause of their less fortunate countrymen. Understandably an increasing number of cases have come up before the Supreme Court and in some instances, it has acted suo motu in converting newspaper reports and letters, recounting incidents of gross exploitation and inhumanity into writs.[63] The effect of this has been quite electrifying and has truly brought justice to the last man as never before. Today justice to the "little man" is not a teasing illusion but a reality.

At a time of crucial, social and economic transformation, the judicial process has a part to play as a midwife of change. The issue of PIL touches a matter of the highest importance literally affecting the quality of life of millions of Indians.[64] Besides this, it will also spread wide the canvas of judicial popular support and moral authority, specially at a time when other institutions of governance are facing a legitimate crisis.[65]

In underlining the need for judicial activism to end class and ethnic exploitation, the International Workshop on the Role of the Judiciary in Plural Societies has echoed the emerging sentiment in favour of PIL. The

62. Majority held that the Federation had not shown sufficient interest. Lord Diplock reversed on the ground that the Federation could not show that the action of the tax authorities was illegal. According to Lord Scarman, the Federation failed to show any ground for believing that the Revenue had failed to do its statutory duty. Lord Roskill reversed both on the ground of locus standi and the Federation having no case. *See also*, 1978 AC 435.

63. Rajinder Sachar and R.N. Aggarwal JJ have suo motu taken notice of a news report about convicts sentenced to simple imprisonment in Tihar Jail being forced to serve rigorous imprisonment. A Newspaper reported the cases of convicts who had been asked to affix their thumb impression on the convict history ticket. Below the thumb impression, a jail officer had allegedly written in Hindi, which on translation in English would read, "I want to get my simple imprisonment changed into rigorous imprisonment."

64. See, *Indian Express* Editorial, Chandigarh 11-12-1982.

65. *See*, Upendra Baxi, "Taking Suffering Seriously: Social Action Litigation and the Supreme Court", (Mimeographed) 1, quoting from his book *The Indian Supreme Court and the Politics* (Eastern Book Co. 1980) 246–48.

workshop adopted a report calling upon the judiciary to give up its traditional self-restraint and passive interpretation and to take a direct and active interest to ensure human rights and socio-economic welfare for the exploited classes, ethnic and other minorities, including women. The judiciary should encourage public interest bodies and social action groups to expose variegated exploitation and, as P.N. Bhagwati J said in his opening remarks, functionally involve itself in the process of emerging social and economic justice to the deprived and the exploited. The need for judicial activism was also stressed in the task of balancing interests of ethnic groups, as both the executive and the legislature would invariably reflect the aspirations of the majority community. Judicial inaction in such circumstances could aggravate perceptions of injustice and eventually lead to violence. It was, perhaps, as much a recognition of these dangers as it was a response to considerations of social justice that witnessed the growth of the PIL in India. Until it was taken up by the Indian Supreme Court, justice even in its obvious and elementary form was mostly a theoretical proposition for the mass of the illiterate, dispossessed and exploited persons. Nevertheless, the problems are colossal, and only a more active concern on the part of the enlightened citizens and the higher judiciary can change this dispensation.[66]

It is true that independence of the judiciary is the first concern of the Constitution, but how far a judge can go is not without limits. A court is called upon to dispense justice according to the Constitution and the law of the land. Therefore, in activity, it must not forget the limits of its power that call for self-restraint, and in periods of restraint it must not be unmindful of its constitutional duty and obligation. Fact remains that the judiciary in India has performed well, lapses notwithstanding.[67]

Today, the PIL jurisdiction of the constitutional courts has grown so much that there is a clear divide within the judiciary itself about its dimension and reach. One view suggests that the PIL represents the last hope of the people against administrative apathy, indifference and abuse of power, while the other view suggests that in the garb of PIL, court is usurping the powers of the executive and the legislature. Against this backdrop recently (April 2008), the Supreme Court decided that it will lay down broad guidelines and parameters for itself and the High Courts to entertain PILs. For this purpose, the court issued notice to the Supreme Court Bar Association and also asked Senior Counsel, Fali Nariman to render assistance. While directing that the matter be listed for August 2008, the Chief Justice of India, though agreed that the court should not interfere in policy decisions and in trivial issues, yet asserted that the court will protect the rights of common man if the executive fails to do its duty.

PIL is a good strategy to provide access to justice to a large disadvantaged sections of society and decide "diffused" constitutional and statutory

66. See, *Indian Express* Editorial, Chandigarh 26-8-1983.
67. A.G. Noorani, "Judicial Activism v. Judicial Restraint", (April–May 1997) SPAN 15.

rights which affect the whole society and, therefore, it should not be allowed to be wasted. PILs have been filed seeking to ban the Quran and Miss World from marrying a tree, to avoid astrological consequences, and punish Richard Gere who kissed actress Shilpa Shetty, etc. PILs should not be allowed to degenerate to the level of a farce or joke. While breaking new ground, the court should not allow the "middle class" to hijack the PIL process at the cost of its original intention of providing access to justice to the disadvantaged and deprived sections of society. Recently a trend is visible in which court is being used by politically entrenched groups for serving their political and sectional interests. This besides eroding the legitimacy of PILs, pushes the court into gravitational orbit of competitive politics with negative consequences. Bold lines of the Constitution bind the judiciary also in the same manner as they bind the executive and the legislature. These bold lines must not be crossed. Courts should not rush in where judicially manageable standard do not exist for the sake of creating hype only.

1.6 Notable case laws

(1) *S.P. Gupta* v. *Union of India*[68] *(popularly known as the Judges' Transfer case)*.—In this case, the Supreme Court entertained petitions by lawyers challenging the constitutionality of a Law Minister's circular regarding transfer of judges of High Courts and non-confirmation of sitting Additional Judges of High Courts. Standing was allowed on the ground that the independence of the judiciary is a matter of grave public concern.

(2) *People's Union for Democratic Rights* v. *Union of India*[69] *(popularly known as the Asiad case)*.—In this case, the Supreme Court entertained petition from a public-spirited organisation on behalf of labourers belonging to socially and economically weaker section and employed in the construction work of various projects connected with the Asian Games of 1982, complaining violation of various labour laws including non-payment of minimum wages, and granted relief.

(3) *D.S. Nakara* v. *Union of India*[70].—It was held that a registered cooperative society consisting of public-spirited citizens seeking to espouse the cause of old and retired infirm pensioners, unable to seek redress through tardy and expensive judicial process, can approach the court through a PIL petition.

(4) *Bandhua Mukti Morcha* v. *Union of India*[71].—A public-spirited organisation approached the court for the release of bonded labourers working in stone quarries.

68. 1981 Supp SCC 87.
69. (1982) 3 SCC 235.
70. (1983) 1 SCC 305.
71. (1984) 3 SCC 161.

(5) *People's Union for Democratic Rights* v. *State of Bihar*[72].—The Supreme Court entertained petition by a public-spirited organisation for compensation on behalf of persons who were victims of unjustified police atrocities.

(6) *D.C. Wadhwa* v. *State of Bihar*[73].—The Supreme Court held that a professor of political science—who is deeply interested in ensuring proper implementation of the constitutional provisions—can approach the court through a PIL petition against the practice of issuing ordinances on a large scale to bypass legislature, as being a fraud on the Constitution.

(7) *Sunil Batra (2)* v. *Delhi Admn.*[74].—Court allowed access to a prisoner complaining about brutal attack and assault by a head warden on a fellow prisoner on the ground of class standing.

(8) *Municipal Council, Ratlam* v. *Vardichan*[75].—Court held that public duties are owed not by any individual but by the public, therefore, for the enforcement of any public duty, any public-spirited person will be granted standing. The Supreme Court issued directions to the Municipal Council on a PIL petition by a citizen to construct public conveniences and drains, etc. and to keep the streets clean.

(9) *Parmanand Katara* v. *Union of India*[76].—In order to provide immediate relief to the Bhopal gas tragedy, on a PIL petition, the court upheld the validity of the Bhopal Gas Leak Disaster (Processing of Claims) Act, 1985 and the settlement arrived at between the Union of India and the Union Carbide Company.

(10) *M.C. Mehta* v. *Union of India*[77].—On a PIL petition by a lawyer of the Supreme Court, the court granted relief to the victims of gas leak from the Shriram Fertiliser and Chemical Plant at Delhi, and also liberated the Indian tort law from the bondage of *Rylands* v. *Fletcher*[78] by holding that no exception to strict liability laid down in this case will be applicable if any hazardous activity is undertaken.

(11) *Parmanand Katara* v. *Union of India*[79].—On a PIL petition, the court directed the government that every injured person brought for medical treatment should instantaneously be given medical aid, without waiting for the completion of police procedural formalities, in order to avoid negligent death of an accident victim.

72. (1987) 1 SCC 265.
73. (1987) 1 SCC 378.
74. (1980) 3 SCC 488.
75. (1980) 4 SCC 1623.
76. (1989) 4 SCC 286.
77. (1987) 1 SCC 395.
78. (1868) LR 3 HL 330 (HL).
79. (1995) 3 SCC 248.

(12) *Banwasi Seva Ashram* v. *State of U.P.*[80].—On a PIL petition, the Supreme Court granted relief to *adivasis* and other backward people using forest as their habitat and means of livelihood against their eviction from the forest land by the government.

(13) *Sampat Singh* v. *State of Haryana*[81].—A writ petition as PIL was filed by Members of the legislative assembly (MLAs) and MPs seeking direction for a CBI enquiry on the basis of a first information report (FIR), alleging serious charge of corruption and misuse of power by a person holding cabinet rank in the Central Government, and for setting aside the order of the Magistrate discharging that person. Court held that since petitioners were not a party to earlier proceedings at any stage, hence they have no locus standi to file the PIL petition.

(14) *Indian Council for Enviro-Legal Action* v. *Union of India*[82].—Where the court relied on expert reports and no objection was taken immediately regarding absence of cross-examination of the experts, the court held that no such objection can be raised at a belated stage.

(15) *Sudip Mazumdar* v. *State of M.P.*[83]—The court directed the government to remove inadequacies of safety precautions in army's ammunition test firing range resulting in death and maiming of tribals who stray into the range for collection of scrap of ammunition.

(16) *Vellore Citizens' Welfare Forum* v. *Union of India*[84].—Court issued suitable directions to give relief to people against pollution of tanneries and asked the Madras High Court to establish a Green Bench to monitor further progress.

(17) *Vishaka* v. *State of Rajasthan*[85].—In the absence of a legislation, the court filled in the gap by giving wide directives to protect working women from sexual harassment.

(18) *Kanhaiya Lal Sethia* v. *Union of India*[86].—Where the relief claimed is not based on any fundamental right, court cannot grant relief. Thus, the court refused to issue direction to the government to include Rajasthani language in the Constitution.

(19) *Daljit Singh Dalal* v. *Union of India*[87]. Court refused relief where in the petition no public interest was involved. Court held that factual disputes cannot be raised and examined under Article 32 of the Constitution.

80. (1993) 2 SCC 612.
81. (1993) 1 SCC 561.
82. (1996) 3 SCC 212.
83. (1996) 5 SCC 368.
84. (1996) 5 SCC 647.
85. (1997) 6 SCC 241.
86. (1997) 6 SCC 573.
87. (1997) 4 SCC 62.

(20) *Malik Bros.* v. *Narendra Dadhich*[88].—Court refused relief where no public interest was involved and the consequence was frustration of any law of the land.

(21) *BALCO Employees' Union* v. *Union of India*[89].—In this case, Union had challenged the disinvestment policy and implementation thereof through a PIL. The Supreme Court held that the decision to disinvest and the implementation thereof is purely an administrative decision, relating to economic policy of the State, and challenge to the same at the instance of a busybody cannot fall within the parameters of the PIL.

(22) *T.K. Rangarajan* v. *State of T.N.*[90]—Court held that there is no fundamental or legal right to strike or bandh (complete shut down), whether by a political party or otherwise, even for a genuine expression of grievance if causes inconvenience to the public.

(23) *National Council for Civil Liberties* v. *Union of India*[91].—In this case, a petition had been filed alleging that Medha Patkar and others of the Narmada Bachao Andolan are involved in subversive activities in order to obstruct developmental projects of national importance. Dismissing the petition, the court observed that it appears to be a private litigation to discredit and diffuse the agitation for rehabilitation of displaced persons from a dam site.

(24) *Dattaraj Nathuji Thaware* v. *State of Maharashtra*[92].—Dismissing the PIL petition filed by a lawyer, who had blackmailed people and was caught red-handed accepting blackmailing money, the court expressed its anguish at the misuse of this strategy by unscrupulous litigants, and exhorted courts to be ruthless while dealing with such impostors.

(25) *Anil Kumar Pandey* v. *Union of India (All, 2011)*[93].—A PIL was filed in the Lucknow Bench of the Allahabad High Court challenging the constitutional validity of the proposed Jan Lokpal Bill, 2011, which was prepared by the civil society and now presently under consideration of the Joint Committee, consisting of members of the government and the civil society.

(26) In *Umedsinh P Chavda* v. *Union of India*[94], there was mala fide PIL against sale and use of soft drinks like Coca Cola, Thums Up, allegedly in the interest of public health but without any expert report. An exemplary cost of ₹ 5,00,000 was imposed.

88. (1999) 6 SCC 552.
89. (2002) 2 SCC 333.
90. (2003) 6 SCC 581.
91. (2007) 6 SCC 506.
92. (2005) 1 SCC 590.
93. *The Hindu* 21-4-2011, 3.
94. (2020) 6 SCC 684.

(27) In *Janhit Manch* v. *State of Maharashtra*[95], the Supreme Court noted that the elected government has to take care of policy matters unless they are in contravention of the Constitution. Individual ideals cannot supersede policy formulating elected bodies.

(28) In *Campaign for Judicial Accountability and Reforms* v. *Union of India*[96], where successive writ petitions were filed intending to scandalise highest judicial functionaries with frivolous allegations, the Supreme Court observed that as the prayer for constitution of Special Investigation Team (SIT) headed by retired Chief Justice with regard to the same FIR has already been dismissed by earlier writ petition, the present petition is held to be wholly frivolous, contemptuous, unwarranted and without any accountability by the petitioner who professes to espouse the cause of accountability. Hence, the writ petition was dismissed with costs of ₹25 lakhs and a warning was also issued that such petitions/contemptuous conduct can result in debarring the petitioner from filing PILs in future.

(29) In *State of H.P.* v. *Ravinder Kumar Sankhayan*[97], it was held that re-auction of leased municipal property directed by the High Court without adverting to efficacy of the existing lease or the reliefs prayed for in the writ petition, was not proper.

(30) In *Exploitation of Children in Orphanages in State of T.N., re*[98], a PIL raised the issue of sex abuse of children in orphanages and government schools; the Supreme Court held that a broader and purposeful interpretation to the definition of "child in need of care and protection" in Section 14(2), Juvenile Justice (Care and Protection of Children) Act, 2015, must be given. The said definition in addition to child in conflict with law must also include victims of sexual abuse/assault/harassment under the Protection of Children from Sexual Offences Act, 2012 (POCSO) Act as also victims of child trafficking. The said definition is illustrative and benefits envisaged for children in need of care and protection should be extended to all such children in fact requiring State care and protection. Such children must also be given protection under the Juvenile Justice (Care and Protection of Children) Act, 2015, being victims of crime under the POCSO Act and the Immoral Traffic (Prevention) Act, 1956.

(31) In *Supreme Court Women Lawyers Assn. (SCWLA)* v. *Union of India*[99], on the issue regarding the rape of young girl children, the Supreme Court noted that when statutory provision regarding the rape of minor girls and punishment therefor exists under Section 376(2)(*i*) IPC, the court can neither enhance punishment so provided nor can it create a new offence and prescribe punishment in that regard. This is a legislative function and

95. (2019) 2 SCC 505.
96. (2018) 1 SCC 589.
97. (2018) 5 SCC 584.
98. (2017) 7 SCC 578.
99. (2016) 3 SCC 680.

the court can only make suggestions to the legislature. Having regard to increasing incidents of rape of girl children, observed, in present social situation, Parliament should define "child" in context of rape by prescribing upper age limit, may be, of 10 years so as to distinguish girl children from minors generally [falling within the expression "woman when she is under 16 years of age" under Section 376(2)(*i*) IPC] and providing for more severe punishment for those committing rape on girl children.

(32) In *Lok Prahari* v. *State of U.P.*[100], the Supreme Court held while it is true that ordinarily Article 32 can be invoked for infringement of fundamental rights of citizens/non-citizens, as the case may be, but there is a paradigm shift therefrom to infringement of rights of a class, developing into independent and innovative stream of jurisprudence called "public interest litigation" or class action; hence, the petition filed by the petitioner registered society challenging the validity of Section 4(3), U.P. Ministers (Salaries, Allowances and Miscellaneous Provisions) Act, 1981, allocating official accommodation to former CMs of the State of U.P. for their lifetime after demitting office, was maintainable. The court further held that the U.P. Ex-Chief Ministers Residence Allotment Rules, 1997 which permitted ex-CMs to continue occupation of government bungalows for lifetime after demitting office were invalid and ultra vires U.P. Ministers (Salaries, Allowances and Miscellaneous Provisions) Act, 1981.

2. CLASS ACTIONS

In class actions, a plaintiff asks relief not only for himself but for all others similarly situated. By its nature, class action asks for more than *inter partes* relief. It is far beyond the mere settlement of disputes between private parties. Class actions are governed by Section 91 and Order I, Rule 8, CPC. After the amendment of Section 91 in 1976, the courts have been given discretion to entertain suits at the instance of two or more persons against public authorities for public nuisance or other public wrongs. Before the amendment, the scope of the remedy was highly restrictive, because even a suit for the removal of public nuisance could not be brought except with the consent of the Advocate General. The Law Commission of India in its 54th Report had suggested a wide amplitude of Section 91 by doing away with the consent requirement and also by including all public wrongs, besides nuisance, within its scope. The government accepted the recommendation of the Law Commission, and the amended section now provides that in case of a public nuisance and any other public wrong, a suit for a declaration and injunction and any other appropriate relief can be filed either by the Advocate General, or by two or more persons, with the leave of the court, even though no damage has been caused to such persons. There is also no obligation to give notice to all the persons affected by such public

100. (2016) 8 SCC 389.

nuisance or wrong. The court shall grant leave for the filing of such a suit according to the well-defined principles.

Order 1, Rule 8 also provides for the filing of a representative suit subject to the conditions that it must be filed by two or more persons acting on behalf of the class, and that a notice to this effect must be served, at the plaintiff's expense, to the persons who are affected.

The inclusion of general class action in the CPC is certainly a welcome step. This is also an indication of the mood of the legislature on PIL for its continuation either as an ordinary or constitutional remedy strategy.[101]

American history of class action is not very inspiring. Some of the problems which have been created are—increase in court arrears, main beneficiaries being the attorneys and not the class, legalised blackmail by unscrupulous lawyers, difficulties in the ascertainment of a class and the disbursement of damages, and adverse economic constraints. These problems may be peculiar to the US, therefore, development of class action in India, which is in its infancy, is to be watched carefully.[102]

It was held by the Supreme Court in *Anjum Hussain* v. *Intellicity Business Park (P) Ltd.*[103] that in the plain language of Order 1 Rule 8 CPC, the principal requirement to bring a suit within that rule is the sameness of interest of the numerous persons on whose behalf or for whose benefit the suit is instituted. The court, while considering whether leave under Order 1 Rule 8 CPC should be granted or not, should examine whether there is sufficient community of interest to justify the adoption of the procedure provided under the rule. The object for which this provision is enacted is really to facilitate the decision of questions in which a large number of persons are interested without recourse to the ordinary procedure. The provision must, therefore, receive an interpretation which will subserve the object for its enactment. The persons who may be represented in a suit under Order 1 Rule 8 of CPC need not have the same cause of action and all that is required for application of the said provision is that the persons concerned must have common interest or common grievance. What is required is sameness of interest. The same principle is applicable in respect of class actions brought under the Consumer Protection Act.

2.1 Campaign litigation

It is a litigation initiated by a pressure group that has members or supporters. For example "Greenpeace", a global campaign organisation which acts as a pressure group for environment protection to safeguard the health and safety of the people. Such recognised campaign litigant is granted standing if: 1) the issue has public importance; 2) no one else can make a responsible challenge; and 3) the group has a prominent role in the field. In campaign

101. *See*, S.N. Jain, *Standing in Public Interest Litigation* (Mimeographed) 28.
102. *Ibid.*
103. (2019) 6 SCC 519.

litigation, a group may not have a personal interest in the matter but as an expert group it may help the court to come to a right decision in the case which will serve an important public interest.[104] Therefore, even a pure campaign litigation is a step in the right direction because a campaign for a special interest may serve an important public interest.

POINTS FOR DISCUSSION

1. Prof. Baxi uses the term "social action litigation" in preference to the more voguish term "PIL" because according to him, PIL represents for America a distinctive phase of socio-legal development for which there is no counterpart in India. Students may discuss the growth of PIL concept in the US in order to appreciate the use of the term "SAL" in the Indian situation.
2. It is now firmly established that there is a new activist of the Indian Supreme Court. Causes for this new role perception and performance may be discussed.
3. PIL is not an extra legal strategy as it has now a constitutional habitat. Students may discuss this constitutional habitat.
4. PIL has been possible only by lowering the threshold level of the locus standi principle. Gradual lowering the level of the locus standi principle may be discussed.
5. PIL in India is still in a developing state and, therefore, the whole process is confronted with various personal and institutional complexities. Students may discuss their complexities.
6. There is a shade of opinion in India which does not favour judicial adventurism in an area which is a legislative and executive domain. Students may discuss the legitimacy of PIL against this backdrop.
7. "The process (SAL), like all political institutions, promises more than it could deliver and is severely exposed to the dynamics of disenchantment."[105] Against this backdrop, a socio-legal audit of judicial role performance may be made.
8. There are clear dangers in the indiscriminate use of PIL. Students may demarcate area where this strategy can be most suitably used.
9. PIL cannot solve all the problems of the poor. Therefore, unless the poor and the weak are organised and made self-reliant, there is no guarantee for the solution of their problems. Students may discuss this proposition.
10. Students may discuss the future of PIL in India.
11. Students may discuss the statement of Mukharji CJ, which he made in the context of PIL, "Article 32 of the Indian Constitution is not the nest for all the bees in the bonnet of 'public-spirited persons'".

104. See generally, *R* v. *Inspectorate of Pollution, ex p Greenpeace (No. 2)*, (1994) 2 CMLR 548.
105. Baxi, "Taking Suffering Seriously: Social Action Litigation in the Supreme Court of India", (Mimeographed) 1.

12. Students may develop guidelines necessary for entertaining PIL petitions by the court so that misuse of this strategy may be minimised.
13. If the concept of class action as provided in the CPC is encouraged and other grievance mechanism like the ombudsman is strengthened, the PIL may not be necessary. Students may discuss the validity of this statement.
14. Students may discuss the legitimacy and legality in granting standing to any "pressure group" to litigate cause in which though no personal interest is involved but huge public interest is being served in a globalised world.

SUGGESTED READINGS

1. A.M. Bhattacharjee, "Judicial Activism and the World Judges' Conference", (1984) 3 SCC J-1.
2. B.K. Nehru, *Thoughts on our Present Discontent* (1986) Introduction to B.K. Nehru by M. Hidyatullah.
3. "Balancing the Scales of Justice—Financing Public Interest Law in America", A Report by the Council for Public Interest Law (1976).
4. Carol Harlow, "Public Standing and Popular Justice" (2002) 65 MLR 1.
5. D.C. Jain, "The Phantom of 'Public Interest' ", (1986) 3 SCC J-30.
6. Deepak Kumar, "Review of Courting the People : Public Interest Litigation in Post-Emergency India", (2018) 5.1 GNLU L. Rev. 210.
7. Filzah Belal, "Role of Public Interest Litigation in Advancing Fundamental Rights of Have-Nots in India", (2018) 8 GJLDP (April) 118.
8. Lord Denning, *The Discipline of Law* (1982) 106–09.
9. Louis Chaffe, "The Citizen as Litigant in Public Actions: The Non-Hohfeldian or Ideological Plaintiff", (1986) 116 U Pa L Rev 1033.
10. M. Cappelletti, *Vindicating Public Interest through the Courts: A Comparativists' Contribution* (1979) Chap. III, "Access to Justice".
11. M. Gobinda, "Public Interest Litigation: A Silent Revolution", (1985) 1 SCC J-1.
12. M.M. Blecher, "Is the Class Action Doing the Job?" (1975) 55 Fed Rules Decisions 365.
13. Madhavan Menon, "Public Interest Litigation: A major breakthrough in the delivery of Social Justice", (1982) 9 Journal of Bar Council of India 150.
14. Madhvi Divan, "The Viability of Public Interest Litigations", (2008) 2 SCC J-7.
15. Mercer, "The Gouriet Case v. Public Interest Litigation in Britain and Canada", 1979 Public Law 214.
16. Michael Fordham, "'Public Interest' Intervention" (2007) PL 410.

17. Mihika Poddar and Bhavya Nahar, "'Continuing Mandamus' - A Judicial Innovation to Bridge the Right-Remedy Gap", (2017) 10 NUJS L Rev 555.
18. P.N. Bhagwati, "Unorganised Labour", (1984) 3 SCC J-40.
19. P.N. Bhagwati and C.J. Dias, "The Judiciary in India : A Hunger and Thirst for Justice", (2012) 5 NUJS L Rev 171
20. P.N. Bhagwati J talks to Dina Vakil, "How the Supreme Court enforces Citizens' Rights", Indian Express, Sunday Magazine, 31-1-1982.
21. P.N. Singh, "Promises and Perils of Public Interest Litigation in India", (2010) 52 JILI 172.
22. P.N. Singh, "Thinking About the Limits of Judicial Vindication of Public Interest", (1985) 1 SCC J-3.
23. P.N. Singh, "Vindicating Public Interest through Judicial Process: Trends and Issues", (1983) 10 Journal of Bar Council of India 23.
24. R. Sachar, "Social Action Litigation: Activist and Traditional Judges", (1987) 1 SCC J-13.
25. Rajeev Dhavan, "Law as Struggle: Public Interest Law in India", (1994) 36 ILIJ 302.
26. S.K. Agarwala, *Public Interest Litigation in India: A Critique* (N.M. Tripathi 1985).
27. S.N. Jain, *Locus Standi and Public Interest Litigation* (Mimeographed).
28. Sangeeta Ahuja, *People, Law and Justice*, Vol. 2 (1997).
29. Upendra Baxi, "Demosprudence and Socially Responsible/Response-Able Criticism: The NJAC Decision and Beyond", (2016) 9 NUJS L Rev 219.
30. Upendra Baxi, "Taking Suffering Seriously: Social Action Litigation in the Supreme Court of India", (December 1982) 29 International Commission of Jurists Rev 37–49.
31. W. Simon, "Class Actions—Useful Tool or Engine of Destruction?", (1973) 55 Fed Rules Decisions 375.
32. Zafar A. Khan,, "Public Interest Litigation : A Tool for Providing Ends of Justice", 20 ALJ (2012–13) 271.

CHAPTER 11

Liability of the Administration

In any democratic country where government assumes the role of a "welfare and service state", the question of government liability evokes a serious response. On the one hand, the concept of an intensive form of government requires active participation of the State in welfare and service activities, but on the other, the concept of governmental liability may have a chilling effect on such participation. Therefore, a very delicate balance has to be drawn.

If any person has been wronged or made to suffer any loss, there may be two courses open to him. He may either proceed against the officer concerned, or he may sue the government on whose behalf the officer was acting. Early common law firmly recognised the principles of liability of the officers concerned because they were treated as ordinary citizens. With the growth of governmental powers, the shift has been from the "officer's liability" to "State liability", on whose behalf he acts. The main reason for such a shift could be the apprehension that the concept of "officer's liability" may dampen the independence and initiative of the officers. However, the recent trend shows a judicious mix of both these concepts.

1. LIABILITY OF THE ADMINISTRATION IN CONTRACT

1.1 Constitutional provisions and the development of the concept of liability

Articles 294, 298, 299 and 300 complete the constitutional code of contractual liability of the government. Article 294 makes provision for the succession by the present governments of the Union and the States to property, assets, rights, liabilities and obligations vested in the former governments. Article 298 lays down that for carrying out the functions of the State, the government can enter into contracts. Article 299 contains essential formalities which a government contract must fulfil. Article 300 provides the manner in which suits and proceedings against, or by the government may be instituted. However, the constitutional code for public contract is not complete, therefore, it is supplemented by the provisions of the Contract Act, 1872. A government contract, in order to be valid, besides satisfying the requirements of Article 299, must also fulfil the requirements of Section 10 of the Contract Act, 1872 dealing with the essentials of a valid contract.[1] In the same manner, the principles for determining the quantum of damages contained in Sections 73, 74 and 75 are also applicable in case of government contracts.[2] Nevertheless, all the provisions of the Contract Act, 1872 are not applicable to government contracts. The provisions relating to capacity as to age and mind have no relevance to such contracts.

The extent of governmental liability is in direct succession of the liability of the East India Company in similar situations. Article 300 of the Constitution points out that the extent of liability of the Union of India and the States will be same as that of Dominion of India and the provinces under the Government of India Act, 1935. The Act of 1935 refers to the Act of 1915 which in turn refers back to the Government of India Act, 1858. Thus, one must refer back to the times of the East India Company in order to determine the extent of liability of government today.

Before 1947, the Crown in England enjoyed immunity from being sued in its own courts. This immunity of the Crown was further fortified by the doctrine of feudalistic origin signifying that the "king can do no wrong". However, even during the heyday of Crown immunity, a person could seek redress against the Crown through a "petition of right".

There was never any doubt that the East India Company, which was essentially a commercial concern, was not entitled to any immunity which the Crown may enjoy from the liability arising out of contracts. In *Bank of Bengal* v. *United Co.*[3] (*Bank of Bengal*), Sir Charles Grey and Franks J of the Bengal Supreme Court clearly held that the East India Company had no sovereign character to prevent it from being sued for the recovery of interest on three promissory notes on the basis of which the Company borrowed money for the efficient prosecution of war for defending and extending the territories of the Crown in India.

Unfortunately, in *Nobin Chunder Dey* v. *Secy. of State for India*[4] (*Nobin Chunder Dey*) a doubt was cast on the extent of liability of the East India Company, respecting contract. In this case, a ganja licence was auctioned. Nobin Chunder, the highest bidder, sued for specific performance of the contract. It was held that the suit for specific performance could not succeed because the auction of ganja licence was a method of collecting tax which was a sovereign function. It is gratifying to note that this proposition of immunity of the government from liability arising out of contract

1. *State of Assam* v. *Keshab Prasad Singh*, AIR 1953 SC 309; *Kalyanpur Lime Works Ltd.* v. *State of Bihar*, AIR 1954 SC 165; *Govt. of U.P.* v. *Nanhoo Mal Gupta*, 1959 SCC OnLine All 147: AIR 1960 All 420.
2. *Thawardas Pherumal* v. *Union of India*, AIR 1955 SC 468; *Dhulipudi Namayya* v. *Union of India*, 1957 SCC OnLine AP 294: AIR 1958 AP 533; *Union of India* v. *Natabarbal Jayshankar*, 1962 SCC OnLine Ori 53: AIR 1963 Ori 66.
3. (1831) 1 Bignall's Reports 87–181.
4. ILR (1875) 1 Cal 11.

entered into in exercise of its sovereign power was not followed by the courts in India.

There is no denying the fact that government, because of its special responsibilities and position, cannot be equated with any other individual and, therefore, the Government of India Acts, 1858, 1919 and 1935 made special provisions prescribing the manner in which government contracts are to be made. The formal requirements in these Acts were always considered mandatory and their non-fulfilment rendered the whole contract invalid. The mandatory character of these formal requirements is evident from the fact that in 1870, the government had to pass a special statute to validate those contracts which were deficient in these formal requirements.[5] Maintaining the same tradition, the Indian Constitution also lays down certain formal requirements for contracts in Article 299(1). These requirements are mandatory. These have not been provided merely for the sake of form but to protect the government against unauthorised contracts, so that public funds may not be wasted on unauthorised contracts. The formal requirements laid down in Article 299(1) are as follows.

(1) *The contract must be expressed to be made by the President or the Governor, as the case may be.*—This requirement is not a mere formality. In *Chatturbhuj Vithaldas Jasani* v. *Moreshwar Parashram*[6], the court held that the constitutional provisions were inserted not merely for the sake of form but to safeguard the government against unauthorised contracts. In this case, the question which arose for consideration was whether a person who has entered into a contract with the government in violation of the form prescribed in Article 299 was disqualified to be elected to the legislature under Section 7(*b*) of the Representation of the People Act, 1951. This contract had been entered into by a person authorised in this behalf, but was not expressed in the name of the President. The court held that the contract was void. The Supreme Court maintained the same position in *Karamshi Jethabhai Somayya* v. *State of Bombay*[7]. In this case, the appellant entered into a contract with the Minister of Public Works Department (PWD) for the irrigation of his landholdings. Subsequently, the contract was repudiated on the ground that it was not expressed in the name of the Governor. A suit was filed for the specific performance of the contract. The court dismissed the appeal holding that the mandatory requirements of Article 299 had not been complied with.

Though the word "expressed" in Article 299(1) might suggest that the government contract must be in some particular form, the Supreme Court in *Union of India* v. *A.L. Rallia Ram*[8] (*A.L. Rallia Ram*) held that no formal document need be executed. In this case, the Chief Director of Purchase

5. 33 and 34 Vict. C 59.
6. AIR 1954 SC 236.
7. AIR 1964 SC 1714. See also, *Govt. of U.P.* v. *Nanhoo Mal Gupta*, 1959 SCC OnLine All 147: AIR 1960 All 420.
8. AIR 1963 SC 1685.

(Disposals), Food Department, Government of India had invited tenders for the purchase of American cigarettes. In the tender of the respondent, the agreement provided for arbitration in case of dispute between the parties. The government challenged the arbitration award on the ground that it was not executed in a proper manner. The Supreme Court held that the contract was entered into by an authorised person and on a fair reading of the letter of acceptance, it would be reasonable to hold that the contract was entered into in a proper manner. However, if there is any other statutory requirement for the execution of a formal deed, it must be complied with. In *State of Madras* v. *R. Ranganatham Chettiar*[9] the High Court held that in view of a statutory provision requiring formal execution of a deed, the contract as it stood was inchoate and, therefore, unenforceable. In this case, the rule required that a formal contract had to be entered into by the government and the highest bidder at the auction. Though the respondent was the highest bidder and deposited the security amount, he did not execute any formal document. Later, when the suit was filed against the government to restrain it from holding another auction, which became necessary owing to complaints from the public, the court refused to oblige on the ground that there was no formal contract. A contrary view has, however, been taken by the Patna High Court in *Chandra Dhan Singh* v. *State of Bihar*[10].

Article 299 though provides that the government contracts must be expressed in the name of the President or the Governor, as the case may be, yet clause 2 states that they shall not be personally liable in respect of any contract or assurance.

(2) *The contract must be executed on behalf of the President or the Governor, as the case may be.*—Another formality of Article 299(1) is that the competent authority must execute the contract on behalf of the President of India or the Governor of the State, as the case may be. If such authority by mistake or otherwise does not sign on behalf of the Chief Executive, the contract shall become invalid, as it also belongs to the category of mandatory conditions.[11] However, the court has mitigated the harshness of this rule by holding in *Davecos Garments Factory* v. *State of Rajasthan*[12] that in the absence of any specific rule, if the competent authority has signed the contract deed in its official capacity, the requirement of the formality of Article 299(1) shall be deemed to have been complied with. In this case, the contract for the supply of police uniforms was signed by the Inspector General of Police (IG) who did not write after his signatures "signed on behalf of the Governor".

(3) *The contract must be executed by a person authorised by the President or the Governor, as the case may be.*—The condition that government

9. 1974 SCC OnLine Mad 121: AIR 1975 Mad 292. See also, *Union of India* v. *Uttam Singh Dugal & Co. (P) Ltd.*, 1971 SCC OnLine Del 186: AIR 1972 Del 110.
10. 1975 SCC OnLine Pat 112: AIR 1976 Pat 15.
11. *Chatturbhuj Vithaldas Jasani* v. *Moreshwar Parashram*, AIR 1954 SC 236.
12. (1970) 3 SCC 874. See also, *Union of India* v. *A.L. Rallia Ram*, AIR 1963 SC 1685.

contracts must be signed by "authorised person" only is certainly very fundamental if State is to be protected from spurious claims made on the strength of unauthorised contracts.[13] Article 299 does not lay down any specific mode of authorisation and, therefore, the normal governmental procedure of notification in the Official Gazette may be considered as proper authorisation. Lack of proper authority would render the contract invalid.[14] However, again in order to avoid hardship which this requirement may entail, the court has held in *State of Bihar* v. *Karam Chand Thapar & Bros. Ltd.*[15] that in the absence of any specific authorisation, implied authorisation may be considered as substantial compliance with this requirement of Article 299(1). In this case, the respondent-company entered into certain construction contracts with the Government of Bihar. After the completion of the contract, a dispute arose in respect of certain payments and the matter was referred to arbitration by an agreement between the parties. On the basis of the award, the company filed a petition for decree in terms of the award. The suit was contested on behalf of the government on the ground that the arbitration agreement was not executed by the Secretary to the government for PWD, who was the only authorised person. The company contended that the Executive Engineer signed the document after necessary instructions from the Secretary. The whole process of correspondence and negotiations showed that the Secretary was in the picture all the time. Under these circumstances, the court came to the conclusion that the Executive Officer, though not specifically authorised, was impliedly authorised on an ad hoc basis. The Supreme Court followed the same approach in *Bhikraj Jaipuria* v. *Union of India*[16]. In this case, in pursuance of the order placed by the Divisional Superintendent, food grains were supplied to the Railways. The Divisional Superintendent was not authorised to sign the contract. The proper authority in this case was the Secretary to the Railway Board. However, the evidence showed that an officer of the Railway Board was authorised to take delivery, transport it and distribute it to Railway ration shops. The Board also fixed programmes for inspection, allotted wagons, accepted railway ration and made payments. On the basis of these facts, the court held that the Divisional Superintendent had the implied authority from the Railway Board to execute the contract. However, in the absence of such evidence from which implied authority cannot be inferred, the court held in *Union of India* v. *N.K. (P) Ltd.*[17] that if the contract has

13. *State of W.B.* v. *B.K. Mondal & Sons*, AIR 1962 SC 779. See also, *Chiranji Lal Multani R.B. (P) Ltd.* v. *Union of India*, 1963 SCC OnLine Punj 353: AIR 1963 Punj 372.
14. *Thawardas Pherumal* v. *Union of India*, AIR 1955 SC 468. See also, *Municipal Corpn. of Bombay* v. *Secy. of State*, 1932 SCC OnLine Bom 13: AIR 1934 Bom 277; *K. Perumal Mudaliar* v. *Province of Madras*, 1949 SCC OnLine Mad 104: AIR 1950 Mad 194; *Raipada Pramanik* v. *State of W.B.*, 1976 SCC OnLine Cal 204: AIR 1977 Cal 7; *Mangalji Chhotey Lal* v. *State of Rajasthan*, 1970 SCC OnLine Raj 53: AIR 1972 Raj 1.
15. AIR 1962 SC 110.
16. AIR 1962 SC 113.
17. (1973) 3 SCC 388. See also, *Karamshi Jethabhai Somayya* v. *State of Bombay*, AIR 1964 SC 1714.

not been signed by a person authorised by the President or the Governor, as the case may be, the contract is absolutely void.

The act of entering into a contract is an executive act, and therefore, if a contract has been entered into not in exercise of executive powers but statutory powers, the requirements of Article 299(1) will not apply. Consequently, if the liquor licence is to be granted by auction under excise law, the formality formulations of Article 299(1) of the Constitution shall not apply.

(4) *Ratification.*—The question whether an agreement which does not fulfil the requirements of Article 299(1) can be ratified by the government has been answered in the negative by the Supreme Court in *Mulamchand* v. *State of M.P.*[18] (*Mulamchand*). Therefore, the government cannot ratify a contract if it does not comply with the requirements of Article 299(1) as to enable it to enforce it against a private party. However, if the parties to the contract agree to ratification, there seems to be no reason why ratification may not be allowed.

(5) *Enforcement of liability.*—The question then arises that if a government contract is void for its non-compliance with the requirements of Article 299(1) and it cannot be ratified either, can the party claim the benefit of Sections 70, 230(*iii*) or 235 of the Contract Act, 1872. Application of Section 70 does not pose much problem. In *New Marine Coal Co.* v. *Union of India*[19], the Supreme Court held that the government must make compensation for the coal supplied which has been consumed by it, even though the contract does not comply with the requirements of Article 299 of the Constitution. Therefore, if a person has done something for government under an invalid contract without doing it gratuitously and the government has obtained any benefit out of it, then the government is bound to make compensation.

However, a more complicated question of liability arises in situations where a person has done something for the government under a void contract, but the government has not obtained any benefit under it. In *State of U.P.* v. *Murari Lal & Bros.*[20] (*Murari Lal*), such a situation came before the Supreme Court. In this case, an officer of the government department of agriculture, who was not authorised to sign contracts on behalf of the government, contracted for a space in the cold storage for potatoes from the Agriculture Department, which never came. The proprietors sued for damages which they suffered for keeping the space vacant. The Supreme Court held that since the requirements of Article 299 are not complied with, the contract was void and was also not capable of ratification, which presupposes a valid contract. Section 70 of the Contract Act, 1872 was also not applicable as the government had not derived any benefit under the

18. AIR 1968 SC 1218; *State of U.P.* v. *Murari Lal & Bros. Ltd.*, (1971) 2 SCC 449.
19. AIR 1964 SC 152.
20. (1971) 2 SCC 449.

contract. In such a situation, the court considered the question of liability of the officer concerned under Section 230(*iii*) or 235 of the Contract Act, 1872. Section 230(*iii*) provides that an agent may be personally bound under a contract in cases where the principal, though disclosed, cannot be sued. The court held that the officer concerned, acting as agent on behalf of the government, cannot be held personally liable under Section 230(*iii*) because the section presupposes a valid contract. However, the Supreme Court did not express any opinion as regards the applicability of Section 235 of the Contract Act, 1872 in this case. However, the observations of the Supreme Court seem to favour the view that even Section 235 will not be attracted because that section also presupposes a valid contract. Section 235 lays down that where a person, untruly representing himself to be the agent of the other party thereby, induces a third party to deal with him, he will be liable if this alleged principal does not ratify his act to make compensation to the other party for the loss or damage suffered by him in such dealing.

Therefore, the position of the government as it emerges is that the contracts which do not comply with the requirements of Article 299 are absolutely void, not even capable of ratification, and the party shall have no claim whatsoever, either against the government or the officer, except where the government has taken any benefit under such contract.

Murari Lal[21] makes one think that there is something wrong with the law relating to public contracts in India; because for no fault of his, a person may be compelled to suffer a loss without a remedy. In this age of an intensive form of government, it is not humanly possible for any person to keep himself up-to-date with the list of government officials authorised to negotiate public contracts in various departments.

The difficulty with the law relating to public contracts in India seems to be that the separate entity of public contracts is not being fully recognised. A public contract, besides the provisions of Article 299 of the Constitution, is also governed by the general law of contract. Therefore, when the provisions of a general law governing private contracts is applied to public contracts, which have a special status because of the public interest involved therein, injustice and arbitrariness is bound to arise. It is for this reason that in France the law governing public contracts is entirely different and exclusive from the law governing private contracts. In France, if the formalities of a public contract are not complied with, it is void; but is capable of ratification by the administration, and it is always open to the private party to question the authority of the administration to withhold ratification in a court of law. The courts in France have also developed a viable principle of "public interest", which must always be protected even if it demands variations in the express terms of the contract. Therefore, when the administrative law recognises the right of the administration to modify the terms of a contract, or to upset the economic basis of the contract, it

21. *State of U.P.* v. *Murari Lal & Bros. Ltd.*, (1971) 2 SCC 449.

also recognises the right of the other party to claim compensation. Both these aspects can be equally justified on grounds of "public interest". In the same manner, the courts exercise power to modify the express terms of standard contracts, through their power of interpretation, and to allow release from the obligation of the contract under hard circumstances on the ground of public interest.

The administrative courts have further developed the doctrine of imprevision which implies that if unforeseen circumstances arise which make it uneconomical for the private party to perform the contract, the court will allow action against the administration for the extra cost. This doctrine is different from the common-law doctrine of "frustration" of the contract, which provides relief by determining the contract if it is physically or legally incapable of performance. The French doctrine applies even in cases where the economic contents of the contract are changed to the disadvantage of the private party by unforeseen circumstances. However, in the public interest the contract is not determined, but is made to be performed subject to compensation for the extra economic burden.

Interestingly, in common-law countries whatever law has been developed, besides the ordinary law of contract governing public contracts, it heavily leans in favour of the government. The doctrine of "executive necessity" developed in England in *Rederiaktiebolaget Amphitrite* v. *R*[22] (*Amphitrite*), which allows the administration to rescind the contract in its discretion under certain circumstances without any remedy to the other contracting party, may be cited as an illustration. The same doctrine still holds ground in England. Thus, in *Commissioners of Crown Lands* v. *Page*[23], where the question was whether an implied covenant for quiet enjoyment in a lease granted by the Crown was broken when the Crown requisitioned the premises under wartime legislation, the Court of Appeal held, unanimously, that it was not. The judgment was based on the ground that an implied covenant would not extend to prevent the future exercise by the Crown of powers and duties imposed on it in its executive capacity by statute. Devlin LJ went a step further to hold that the same conclusion would follow even if such covenant is expressly laid down in unqualified terms. This doctrine has thus clearly been accepted into law and applies both to the Crown and other statutory authorities, invested with discretionary powers, because there is as much impingement on the "public good" in commercial contracts as there is in such matters as the defence of the realm involved in *Amphitrite* itself. It is gratifying to note that this doctrine has no application in India.[24]

22. (1921) 3 KB 500. See also, *Robertson* v. *Minister of Pensions*, (1949) 1 KB 227 doubted the rationale of the doctrine.
23. (1960) 2 QB 274: (1960) 3 WLR 446 (CA). *Also see,* Mitchell, *The Contracts of Public Authorities* (1954) 27–32, 52–65.
24. *Union of India* v. *Indo Afghan Agencies Ltd.*, AIR 1968 SC 718.

(6) *Contractual obligation and the constitutional power of the government.*—A contract cannot clog the government's constitutional power of eminent domain. In the same manner, the legislature acting within the scope of its legislative competence may vary the terms of a contract. In *Secy. to Govt. Public Works and Transport Deptt.* v. *Adoni Ginning Factory*[25], when the electricity rates were enhanced, contrary to the provision in the contract for the supply of electricity, the court held that the existence of a contract cannot foreclose the authority of the legislature to legislate on subjects within its competence. The courts in England have also held that it is not within the competence of the Crown to make a contract which would have the effect of limiting the executive power in future.[26]

(7) *Government contracts and doctrine of waiver.*—"Waiver" means abandonment of right and it may be either expressed or implied from the conduct, but its basic requirement is that it must be an intentional act with knowledge. Waiver is a question of fact and it must be properly pleaded and proved. No plea of waiver can be allowed to be raised unless it is pleaded and a factual foundation is laid for it. In *Motilal Padampat Sugar Mills Co. Ltd.* v. *State of U.P.*[27] (*Motilal Padampat Sugar Mills*), the court did not allow the government to raise the plea of waiver for the first time at the hearing of the writ petition because it had not been taken in its affidavits. In the case, the court also held that in the absence of any substantial evidence to show that the appellant intentionally abandoned the right of a sales tax holiday, mere acceptance of the concessional rate of tax would not amount to waiver of such right.

Since the requirements of Article 299 are mandatory, these cannot be waived by the government. In *A.L. Rallia Ram*[28], the Supreme Court held that even if the contention that the arbitration agreement did not satisfy the requirements of Article 299 was not raised before the arbitrator, it can be raised in the judicial proceedings and the doctrine of waiver shall not apply.

In a welfare state, the government undertakes to provide various services for the benefit of the people. A question may generally arise regarding the applicability of the Contract Act, 1872 in governing the relationship between an individual and a public service instrumentality. This question of far-reaching practical significance came before the Supreme Court in *Union of India* v. *Mohd. Nazim*[29]. In this case, an Indian resident had sent a value payable post (VPP) to an addressee in Pakistan. The Pakistan government, though realised the amount, did not remit it to the Government of India because it had suspended the VPP service between the two countries.

25. 1958 SCC OnLine AP 271: AIR 1959 AP 538.
26. *Rederiaktiebolaget Amphitrite* v. *R.*, (1921) 3 KB 500.
27. (1979) 2 SCC 409.
28. AIR 1963 SC 1685. See also, *State of M.P.* v. *Firm Gopichand Sarju Prasad*, 1970 SCC OnLine MP 65: AIR 1972 MP 43; *State of Bihar* v. *R.B. Ojha*, 1977 SCC OnLine Pat 129: AIR 1977 Pat 258.
29. (1980) 1 SCC 284.

The appellant sued the Union of India for the amount. The Supreme Court ruled that the Post Office, which had been established under the Post Office Act, 1898, is not a common carrier or an agent of the sender for postal articles. It is a branch of public service providing postal service. The Pakistan government for that matter is not a sub-agent and the money received by it cannot be said to have been received by the Government of India. Under the arrangement, entered into between two sovereign powers, none of them could be said to be employed by, or acting under the control of the other. This settles at least one point of public law of contract.

(8) *Whether a writ can be issued for the enforcement of contractual obligation.*—The jurisdiction of the Supreme Court to issue writs under Article 32 is confined only to enforcement of fundamental rights, therefore, the Supreme Court cannot issue writ for the enforcement of a contractual obligation.[30] The power of the High Court to issue writs under Article 226 is much wider than that of the Supreme Court. A High Court can issue writ for the enforcement of fundamental rights and also for the enforcement of private rights. Normally, a civil suit remedy is available for the enforcement of contractual obligation, therefore, a High Court will not exercise its writ jurisdiction in such matters. Nevertheless, in some cases where the State or its instrumentalities commit a breach of contractual obligations, the High Court may issue a writ.[31]

Cases involving breach of contractual obligation by the State or its authorities and agencies may be divided into four categories:

(1) Where promissory estoppel applies against the State.
(2) Where breach of a statutory rule or regulation is alleged by the petitioner.
(3) Where public law element is involved which the party seeks to invoke.
(4) Where breach of a contractual obligation is alleged which arises only out of the terms of the contract.[32]

In the first three cases, a High Court may exercise its writ jurisdiction. The Supreme Court in *Gujarat State Financial Corpn.* v. *Lotus Hotels (P) Ltd.*[33] held that the writ of mandamus can be issued against the government or its instrumentalities for the enforcement of contractual obligations because promissory estoppel applies against the government. In this case, Lotus Hotels had entered into a contract with the State Financial Corporation for a loan of ₹30 lakhs for the construction of a hotel. Based on this agreement, the petitioner had incurred certain liabilities. However, acting on two pseudonymous letters attacking the character of the proprietors, the loan was refused which had been previously sanctioned. The highest Bench

30. *Satish Chandra* v. *Union of India*, AIR 1953 SC 250; *Premji Bhai Parmar* v. *DDA*, (1980) 2 SCC 129. See also, *Ramesh Sanka* v. *Union of India*, (2019) 3 SCC 589.
31. *Radhakrishna Agarwal* v. *State of Bihar*, (1977) 3 SCC 457.
32. *Joshi Tecnhologies International Inc.* v. *Union of India*, (2015) 7 SCC 728.
33. (1983) 3 SCC 379.

ruled that it is too late in the day to contend that the government can commit breach of a solemn undertaking on which the other side has acted, and then contend that the party may sue for damages in a civil court and cannot compel specific performance of the contract through mandamus.[34] In the same manner, the Supreme Court held in *K.N. Guruswamy* v. *State of Mysore*[35] that where a liquor contract has been given in violation of a statutory provision, the aggrieved party can question the action through a writ petition.

In the fourth category of cases, where neither any promissory estoppel applies against the government nor is there a violation of any statutory rule and the basis of the claim is only a term of a contract, the court held that the petitioner cannot invoke the writ jurisdiction under Article 226 for the enforcement of a pure contractual obligation because the proper remedy in such cases is a civil suit. Therefore, in *Har Shanker* v. *Excise and Taxation Commr.*[36], when the liquor contractors challenged the demand made by the department through a writ petition under Article 226, the Supreme Court held that the writ jurisdiction of the High Court is not intended to facilitate avoidance of obligations voluntarily incurred. However, the recent trend of cases show that in situations where petitioner alleges arbitrariness, absence of fair play, and the breach of natural justice, the writ jurisdiction of the court can be invoked. Thus, in *Mahabir Auto Stores* v. *Indian Oil Corpn.*[37], the Supreme Court observed that even though the rights of the citizens are in the nature of contractual rights, the manner, the method, and motive of a decision of entering or not entering into a contract are subject to judicial review on the touchstone of relevance and reasonableness, fair play, natural justice, equality and non-discrimination.[38] In this case, the Indian Oil Corporation had abruptly stopped supply of material, without any notice and hearing, to the petitioner firm which was carrying on business of sale and distribution of lubricants for the last 18 years. In the same manner, normally the contract of personal service cannot be enforced through writ, but when the statutory bodies act in breach of mandatory obligation imposed by a statute, the writ can be issued.[39]

Keeping in view the liberalisation and globalisation of the economy, the Supreme Court in *Food Corporation of India* v. *SEIL Ltd.*[40] held that contractual disputes involving public law elements are amenable to writ jurisdiction. In this case, supply of sugar was made in terms of a statutory order

34. *Gujarat State Financial Corpn.* v. *Lotus Hotels (P) Ltd.*, (1983) 3 SCC 379, 385.
35. AIR 1954 SC 592; *DFO* v. *Ram Sanehi Singh*, (1971) 3 SCC 864.
36. (1975) 1 SCC 737. See also, *Divl. Forest Officer* v. *Bishwanath Tea Co. Ltd.*, (1981) 3 SCC 238.
37. (1990) 3 SCC 752.
38. *Ibid*, SCC 760–61 (*per* Mukherjee CJ); see also, *Shrilekha Vidyarthi* v. *State of U.P.*, (1991) 1 SCC 212.
39. *S.R. Tewari* v. *District Board, Agra*, AIR 1964 SC 1680. See also, C.K. Thakker, *Administrative Law* (Eastern Book Company 1992) 486–98.
40. (2008) 3 SCC 440.

under Essential Commodities Act, 1955 and there was no factual dispute also. Thus, court held that writ petition is maintainable for securing payment arbitrarily withheld. In contrast, the Supreme Court was of the opinion in *Chaman Lal Singhal* v. *Haryana Urban Development Authority*[41] that if allotment is cancelled and earnest money is forfeited in terms of the contract because the contracting party did not perform his part under the contract, writ jurisdiction cannot be exercised because no question of public law is involved.

1.2 Grant of government largess

The government is the biggest businessman, therefore, the question arises: Whether the government, like any private individual, is absolutely free to enter into a contract with any person at its own sweet will? Answering the question in the negative, the courts have always held that government is still a government, hence, when it acts in the matter of granting largess, it cannot act arbitrarily because it does not stand in the same position as a private individual. Therefore, when the government enters into a contract or is administering largess, it cannot, without adequate reason, exclude any person from dealing with it, or take away largess arbitrarily.[42] Reiterating its earlier position the Supreme Court in *Union of India* v. *Hindustan Development Corpn.*[43] held that distribution of State largess should be reasonable, fair, non-arbitrary and in accordance with social and economic justice and directive principles. In this case, the Railways had issued tenders for the supply of cast steel bogies. Tenderers included big as well as small manufacturers. Big manufacturers identically quoted lower price in order to push small manufacturers out of competition. The Railways, considering such price quoted by big manufacturers as predatory and also taking the view that they have formed a cartel, adopted a dual pricing system giving a counter-offer of a lower rate to the big manufacturers and a higher rate to the smaller manufacturers, and also suitably adjusted the allotment of quantity of order to make them viable for a healthy competition. The court held the action of the Railways as bona fide, reasonable and non-arbitrary. The Supreme Court observed that the government, while entering into contract or issuing quotas, is expected not to act like a private individual, but should act in conformity with certain healthy standards and norms. Such actions should not be arbitrary, irrational or irrelevant, and must be justifiable on the basis of some policy or valid principles. Therefore, government's right to adopt dual pricing system was upheld because under the circumstances, it was reasonable and in conformity with the ideal of social and economic justice, which emanates from the directive principles of state policy.

41. (2009) 4 SCC 369.
42. *Ramana Dayaram Shetty* v. *International Airport Authority of India*, (1979) 3 SCC 489.
43. (1993) 3 SCC 499.

Taking the same approach, the Supreme Court in *LIC* v. *Consumer Education and Research Centre*[44] held that in the sphere of contractual relations the State, its instrumentality, public authorities and those whose acts bear insignia of public element, action to public duty or obligation, are enjoined in a manner that is fair, just and equitable, after taking into consideration all the relevant options, and in a manner that is reasonable, relevant and germane to effectuate the purpose of public good and, in general, public interest, and it must not take any irrelevant or irrational factors into consideration or appear arbitrary in its decisions. It is on this rationale that the court held that the power of the Life Insurance Corporation to enter into contract and prescribe terms and conditions for life insurance does not include the power to confine its policies for salaried class from government, semi-government or reputed commercial firms. It is discriminatory offending Article 14 of the Constitution. However, the power of judicial review on the question of awarding licences and contracts shall rest only on grounds of bad faith, irrational or irrelevant consideration, non-compliance with the prescribed procedure or violation of any constitutional or statutory provision.[45]

The law relating to government contracts is deficient in India. This deficiency arises from the fact that special significance which such contracts assume due to the element of public interest involved therein is yet to be recognised. Furthermore, when a law chiefly designed to govern the contractual relationship of private parties is applied to a public contract, the matter becomes still more complex. Therefore, the courts must aim at developing special public law doctrines to govern public contracts until the matter is taken up by the legislature.

2. LIABILITY OF THE ADMINISTRATION IN TORT

The term "administration" is used here synonymously with "State" or "Government". To what extent the administration would be liable for the torts committed by its servants is a complex problem, especially, in developing countries with ever widening State activities. The liability of the government in tort is governed by the principles of public law inherited from British common law and the provisions of the Constitution.

The whole idea of vicarious liability of the State for the torts committed by its servants is based on three principles:

(1) *Respondeat superior* (let the principal be liable).
(2) *Qui facit per alium facit per se* (he who acts through another does it himself).
(3) Socialisation of compensation.

44. (1995) 5 SCC 482; *G.D. Zalani* v. *Union of India*, 1995 Supp (2) SCC 512.
45. See also, *Asia Foundation & Construction Ltd.* v. *Trafalgar House Construction (I) Ltd.*, (1997) 1 SCC 738.

Article 300 of the Indian Constitution, which deals with the extent of liability of the Union of India and the government of a State, instead of laying down the liability in specific terms, refers back to Section 176 of the Government of India Act, 1935. Section 176 of the Act of 1935 refers, in turn, to Section 32 of the Government of India Act, 1915 which, in its turn, refers to Section 65 of the Act of 1858. Section 65 of the Act of 1858 laid down that on the assumption of the Government of India by the British Crown, the Secretary of State for India-in-Council would be liable to the same extent as the East India Company was previously liable. Therefore, in order to determine the extent of liability of the government in tort, one has to find out the extent of liability of the East India Company. This is certainly a strange way of determining the liability of a State governed by a Constitution. It is because of this "strange way" with resultant confusion and complexity that the Law Commission recommended a legislation on the subject. Accepting the recommendation, the government introduced two Bills on "the government liability in tort" in the Lok Sabha in 1965 and 1967 respectively, neither of which emerged as an Act. The government allowed the Bills to lapse on the ground that they would bring an element of rigidity in the determination of the question of liability of the government in tort. Consequently, one has to uncover the extent of liability of the East India Company in order to understand the liability parameters of the administration today, as the liability of the administration today is in direct succession to that of the East India Company.

The East India Company launched its career in India as a purely commercial corporation, but gradually acquired sovereignty. Therefore, in the beginning, the Company did not enjoy the immunity of the Crown. It was only when it acquired political powers that a distinction was made between sovereign and non-sovereign functions. As a result of this, in *Bank of Bengal*[46], the Supreme Court of Judicature at Calcutta rejected the Company's plea of exemption from suit on the ground of sovereignty. It was an action brought by the Bank of Bengal to recover interest due on promissory notes written by the East India Company to borrow money for the prosecution of war. Likewise, in *P.&O. Steam Navigation Co.* v. *Secy. of State for India*[47] (*P.&O. Steam Navigation Co.*), the Supreme Court allowed an action against the Secretary of State for the negligent act of the government workers. In this case, the workers employed by the Kidderpore Dockyard, which was a government dock, were carrying iron bars across a public way passing through the port, which bars they dropped on the road. The noise so created scared the horses of the carriage in which the plaintiff was sitting and he sustained injuries. Sir Barnes Peacock CJ, who delivered the judgment of the court, held that the Company had been invested with sovereign functions but this did not make it a sovereign authority. It may be

46. (1831) 1 Bignall's Reports 87.
47. (1861) 5 Bom HCR 1, Appendix "A".

noted that after 1833, the East India Company was acting in a dual capacity, exercising commercial functions as also the sovereign powers, with respect to the newly-acquired territories as trustees of the Crown. The use of the terms "sovereign" and "non-sovereign" function which created confusion in the later development of the law was made clear by Peacock CJ in the judgment when he said:

> It is clear that the East India Company would not have been liable for any act done by any of its officers or soldiers in carrying on hostilities, or for the act of any of its naval officers in seizing as prize property of a subject, under the supposition that it was the property of an enemy, nor for any act done by a military or naval officer or by any soldier or sailor, whilst engaged in military or naval duty, nor for any acts of any of its officers or servants in the exercise of judicial functions.[48]

However, even after such a clear enunciation of law, the judgment in the above case was interpreted in two different ways. In *Nobin Chunder Dey*[49], the court held that the government is not liable in suit for anything done in exercise of sovereign functions. In this case, the plaintiff sued the government for specific performance of the contract of sale of ganja licence as he was the highest bidder at the auction. The court based its decision on the rationale that since the auction of ganja licence was a method of raising revenue (tax), it was a sovereign function which no private individual could undertake and, hence, the action was not maintainable as the government was immune from any such action.

The other interpretation of the *P.&O. Steam Navigation Co. case*[50] was that the immunity extended only to cases which may be covered within the definition of the term "acts of State". This line of reasoning was adopted by the court in *Secy. of State for India in Council* v. *Hari Bhanji*[51] (*Hari Bhanji*). On the basis of this interpretation, the government could not claim any immunity for its acts done under the colour of municipal law. In this case, a suit was filed to recover the excess excise duty collected by the State on a consignment of salt. Rejecting the plea of immunity, the court held that no immunity attaches to actions done under the colour of municipal laws. The same principle was confirmed in *Salaman* v. *Secy. of State in Council of India*[52].

The Law Commission of India also accepted the *Hari Bhanji* view as correct and recommended legislation giving effect to this view.[53] However, the court did not follow this view in later cases.

After independence, in *State of Rajasthan* v. *Vidhyawati*[54] (*Vidhyawati*), the Supreme Court held the State vicariously liable for the tort committed

48. *Ibid*, Appendix "A", 14 and 15.
49. ILR (1875) 1 Cal 11.
50. (1861) 5 Bom HCR 1, Appendix "A".
51. ILR (1882) 5 Mad 273.
52. (1906) 1 KB 613 (CA).
53. "Liability of the State In Tort", First Report of the Law Commission.
54. AIR 1962 SC 933.

by its servants. The facts of this case were that in February 1952, a driver of a government jeep, while driving back from the workshop, knocked down a person on the footpath, causing multiple injuries including fracture of the skull and the backbone, which resulted in his death. A suit by the widow of the deceased and her minor daughter for compensation was decreed by the trial judge against the driver, but not against the State. On appeal, the High Court decreed the suit against the State also. Hence, the State of Rajasthan went in appeal before the Supreme Court. The main argument on behalf of the State was that it was not liable for the tortious acts of its employees, for in similar circumstances the East India Company would not have been liable, as the jeep was maintained in exercise of sovereign powers and not as a part of commercial activity of the State. B.P. Sinha CJ dismissing the appeal by the State of Rajasthan held that the immunity rule of the Crown in England was based on the old feudalistic notions of justice. In India, ever since the time of the East India Company, the sovereign had been held liable to be sued in tort or in contract, and the common-law immunity never operated in India. He went on to say that India has now been constituted as a socialistic state with varied welfare activities employing a large army of servants and, therefore, there is no justification in principle or in the public interest that the State should not be held liable vicariously for the tortious acts of its servants. It was thought that this decision has abolished the distinction between sovereign and non-sovereign functions for the purpose of determining State liability and that, henceforth, the government would be liable for the torts committed by its servants in all cases, except "acts of State".

Unfortunately, only three years later, the development of law in this area suffered a setback in *Kasturi Lal Ralia Ram Jain* v. *State of U.P.*[55] (*Kasturi Lal*). In this case, the plaintiff was going to Meerut to sell gold, silver and other goods. As he was passing through the city, he was taken into custody by three policemen. His person was searched and all the gold and silver was taken into custody, and he was put in the lock-up. On his release, his gold was not returned, though silver was immediately returned. The gold had been misappropriated by the head constable who fled to Pakistan. Kasturi Lal filed a suit against the Government of Uttar Pradesh for the return of the gold or value. There was a clear finding on record of gross negligence on the part of the police authorities in the matter of safe custody of the gold. However, Gajendragadkar CJ, as he then was, reintroduced again the vague distinction of sovereign and non-sovereign functions, and held that the State is not liable because the functions of arrest and seizure of the property are sovereign functions. The court further held that if the act is sovereign, no act of negligence on part of the employees of the State would render the State liable.

55. AIR 1965 SC 1039. *See also*, Alice Jacob, "Vicarious Liability of the Government in Torts", (1965) 7 JILI 247 and Blackshield, "Tortious Liability of Government: A Jurisprudential Case-note", (1966) 8 JILI 643.

In this case, the court wrongly applied the ratio of *P.&O. Steam Navigation Co.*[56] A close reading of the case shows that Sir Barnes Peacock, while writing about the sovereign functions, had in mind only the functions which could be technically termed as "acts of State" and, therefore, cannot be done under the colour of municipal law. This becomes clear from the fact that "acts while carrying on hostilities" or "seizing enemy property" were the expressions used as illustrations to demonstrate "sovereign acts". This is also a wrong decision because by no stretch of imagination could such flagrant violation of the U.P. Police Regulations be termed as a "sovereign function". Facts of the case showed that the officer in charge of the police station allowed the constable to keep the gold in his private custody, whereas the law required its deposit in the local government treasury.

In *State of M.P.* v. *Chironji Lal*[57], a new question came before the court relating to the payment of damages for the loss caused by a policelathi-charge in a situation where it was unauthorised and unwarranted by law. It was alleged that the police resorted to lathi-charge wilfully and without any reasonable cause and, thus, damaged the plaintiff's property. The claim was rejected on the ground that the function of the State to regulate processions and to maintain law and order is a sovereign function. It may be pointed out that under similar circumstances, the government would have been liable under French jurisdiction on the ground of "fault" and "risk" theories. With the growing governmental lawlessness, it is no denying the fact that the law in this area requires restatement.

It is heartening to note that *Lala Bishambar Nath* v. *Agra Nagar Mahapalika*[58] is a pointer in the right direction. In this case, the firm of Lala Bishambar Nath was in possession of 2048 bags of *atta* (flour) which was unfit for human consumption and a sign to this effect was pasted on the bags. The firm intended to sell this *atta* for the consumption of animals and other purposes, such as *lei* (adhesive) used in the manufacture of shoes. The Health Officer, while exercising powers under Section 244(1) of the Municipalities Act, 1916 took possession of the *atta* and prosecuted the appellant. Section 244(1) provided that if in the course of inspection of a place, an article of food or drink for an animal appears to be intended for consumption of human and to be unfit therefor, the Board may seize and remove the same or may cause it to be destroyed or disposed of so as to prevent it from being exposed for sale or use for such consumption. The Health Officer acted under a wrong interpretation of Section 244(1) believing that this section covers a case where an article of food is for the consumption of animals also. The lower court dismissed the suit on the ground that Section 244(1) does not admit such interpretation. On appeal, the High Court reversed the decision of the lower court. The Supreme Court on appeal by the appellant held that the language of the section cannot be

56. (1861) 5 Bom HCR 1, Appendix "A".
57. 1980 SCC OnLine MP 35: AIR 1981 MP 65.
58. (1973) 1 SCC 788.

strained as to include what is not there and held the State liable for damages for the illegal acts of its servants. The court further observed that if an action is illegal, the good motives of the officer cannot make it valid. It may be noted that the court, while holding the State liable for the illegal acts of its servants, did not bring in the vague concept of sovereign and non-sovereign functions, which is responsible for all the confusion in this highly-sensitive area of law.

The trends in judicial behaviour in the direction of government accountability have become more visible in subsequent cases. In *Shyam Sunder* v. *State of Rajasthan*[59], K.K. Mathew J vehemently pleaded for discarding the feudalistic doctrine of government immunity in the exercise of sovereign functions, in view of the changed socio-economic context.

Basavva Kom Dyamangouda Patil v. *State of Mysore*[60] represents another step in the right direction. In this case, a theft was committed and property worth ₹ 10,000 was stolen. Five persons were arrested. The recovered property was produced before the Magistrate who asked the police to keep it in safe custody. Later on, the recovered property was stolen from the police station. The application to the Magistrate under Section 517 of the Criminal Procedure Code for return of the recovered property was refused on the ground that the property was not in the custody of the Magistrate, *i.e.* the Treasury. The same view was taken by the High Court on the ground that the recovered ornaments never reached court's custody. On appeal, the Supreme Court reversed the decision and held it wrong to suppose that once the property is not available with the court, the court would disclaim all responsibility. Where the property is stolen or destroyed and there is no prima facie defence of due care, the court can order the payment of the value of the property in order to meet the ends of justice. These trends in governmental accountability may be just straws, but they are floating in the right direction.

The distinction between sovereign and non-sovereign functions is a juristic blasphemy which leads to absurd and arbitrary conclusions. A brief survey of various High Courts' decisions proves this fact beyond all reasonable doubt. In *Satya Wati Devi* v. *Union of India*[61], the Delhi High Court held that the carrying of a hockey team in a military truck to the Air Force Station to play a match is not a sovereign function. The Bombay High Court held in *Union of India* v. *Sugrabai Abdul Majid*[62] that the transporting of military equipment from the workshop of the Artillery School is not a sovereign function. The Mysore High Court in *State of Mysore* v. *Ramchandra Gunda Kulkarni*[63] came to the conclusion that the construction of a reservoir by the State for the purpose of supplying drinking-water

59. (1974) 1 SCC 690. It was a case under Fatal Accidents Act.
60. (1977) 4 SCC 358. *See,* B.B. Pande, "Perforating the Escutcheon of Sovereign Immunity", (1974) 2 SCC J-9.
61. 1967 SCC OnLine Del 7: AIR 1967 Del 98.
62. 1967 SCC OnLine Bom 75: AIR 1969 Bom 13.
63. 1970 SCC OnLine Bom 102: AIR 1972 Bom 93.

is not a sovereign function. The Allahabad High Court held in *State of U.P.* v. *Hindustan Lever Ltd.*[64] that the government sub-treasury's banking function is not a sovereign function. The Punjab High Court in *Union of India* v. *Harbans Singh*[65] came to the conclusion that the State is not liable for compensation to a person who is run over by a military truck carrying meals for military personnel on duty in the forward area, as it is a sovereign function. However, the same High Court in *Union of India* v. *Jasso*[66] came to the conclusion that the carrying of coal to the army headquarters is not a sovereign function. In view of the above facts, the need for the development of a more viable principle to determine governmental accountability cannot be overemphasised. A comprehensive legislation on the subject is the only right answer.

In *Khatri* (2) v. *State of Bihar*[67], an important question was raised regarding liability of the government for wrongful arrest and detention. Moving ahead in the direction of new dimension of the right to life and personal liberty, Bhagwati J said, "Why should the court not be prepared to forge new tools and devise new remedies for the purpose of vindicating the most precious of the precious fundamental rights to life and personal property." It may be noted that the Government of India has not signed the treaty which provides for compensation for wrongful arrest and detention. This amply proves the lack of government's concern for the precious of the precious rights of the people for the sake of discounting its own inefficiency and lawlessness.

It is heartening to note that the desire of Bhagwati J for forging new tools to provide compensation for illegal detention was fulfilled in 1983 by Chandrachud CJ who, in *Rudul Sah* v. *State of Bihar*[68], laid down a most important principle of compensation against government for wrong action of its officials. This important judgment was handed down by the Supreme Court against the Bihar government for the wrongful and illegal detention of Rudul Sah in Muzaffarpur jail for as many as 14 years, after he was acquitted by the Sessions Court in June 1968. The court ordered compensation of ₹30,000 for the injustice and injury done to Rudul Sah and his helpless family. In this case, the Bihar government had taken the plea that the prisoner was not released even after acquittal because he had been declared insane. Rejecting the contention as "sordid and disturbing", the court opined that insanity could well be the consequence rather than the cause of detention. Moving forward, the Supreme Court in *Bhim Singh*

64. 1972 SCC OnLine All 28: AIR 1972 All 486.
65. 1957 SCC OnLine Punj 133: AIR 1959 Punj 39.
66. AIR 1962 Punj 315. See also, *Nandram* v. *Union of India*, 1978 SCC OnLine MP 16: AIR 1978 MP 209, where the court held that bringing back officers from the place of military exercises is not a sovereign function.
67. (1981) 1 SCC 627, 630.
68. (1983) 4 SCC 141. In another case, the Bihar government agreed to pay ₹300 per month to Ramchandra who was kept in jail for 30 years on the unfounded plea that he had become a criminal lunatic while in prison.

v. *State of J&K*[69] awarded exemplary cost of ₹50,000 on account of the authoritarian manner in which the police played with the liberty of the appellant. Similarly, in *Mahavir Singh* v. *State of Rajasthan*[70], the court granted ₹1 lakh for the custodial death of a young boy who had been arrested on a theft charge. In fact, these measures are not damages in the strict sense of the term for which only the ordinary civil court process is the remedy. These measures are only for making the fundamental rights of the people meaningful and effective. It is now well settled that Article 32 is not limited by a particular kind of proceedings, except that it must be appropriate with reference to the purpose of enforcing fundamental rights.

Moving in the right direction, the Supreme Court in *Saheli* v. *Commr. of Police*[71] quoted with approval its decision in *Vidhyawati*[72], where it held that the State is responsible for the tortious acts of its servant committed within the scope of his employment like any other employer. It further clarified that the doctrines of sovereign immunity, "king can do no wrong", "king cannot be sued in the courts of its own creation" are feudalistic origin and, hence, cannot be applied to a democratic country like India. The court further observed that ever since the time of the East India Company, sovereign has been held liable to be sued in tort or contract and the common-law liability never operated in India. In this case, a women's organisation known as SAHELI had filed a writ against the government for compensation on behalf of two poor women who had been mercilessly beaten by the landlord in collusion with the police. The court not only awarded ₹75,000 as compensation but also opined that the amount can be recovered from the police officers responsible for the tort. Therefore, the classification of governmental functions into sovereign and non-sovereign for the purpose of determining governmental liability in tort is no longer a valid classification.

The Supreme Court reiterated the same principle of law in *N. Nagendra Rao & Co.* v. *State of A.P.*[73] In this case, the appellants were carrying on business in fertiliser and foodgrains. The Vigilance Cell raided the premises of the appellants and seized huge stocks. Orders were issued to dispose of the stocks pending investigations. However, no action was taken. Later on, it was found that there was no irregularity, except in accounting, so the stocks were to be returned to the appellants but by then the stocks had been rendered unusable. The trial court decreed the suit for compensation, but the Andhra Pradesh High Court reversed it on the basis of ratio of *Kasturi Lal*[74]. On appeal, the Supreme Court upheld the trial court's decision and held that the doctrine of sovereign immunity stands diluted in the context

69. (1985) 4 SCC 677.
70. (1987) 2 SCC 342.
71. (1990) 1 SCC 422.
72. *State of Rajasthan* v. *Vidhyawati*, AIR 1962 SC 933.
73. (1994) 6 SCC 205.
74. AIR 1965 SC 1039.

of modern concept of sovereignty and, thus, the distinction between sovereign and non-sovereign functions no longer survives. The court further observed that the State is immune from liability only in cases of acts of State like defence of the country, administration of justice, maintenance of law and order, and repression of crime, except when Article 21 is breached. In this case the court also confirmed the principle of personal liability of the negligent officer.[75] Expounding the philosophy behind this principle of law, the court observed that no civilised system can permit the executive to play with the lives of the people of its country and claim that it is entitled to act in any manner as sovereign. No legal or political system can place the State above the law. There is shift from the concept of sincerity, efficiency and dignity of State as a juristic person to liberty, equality and rule of law. The concept of public interest has also changed with the structural change in society. Thus, the Supreme Court concluded that any compartmentalisation of functions of State into sovereign and non-sovereign, or governmental or non-governmental is not sound as it is contrary to modern thinking.[76]

In *Common Cause* v. *Union of India*[77], the Supreme Court emphatically stressed that *Kasturi Lal*[78] has, apart from being criticised, not been followed by the court in subsequent cases and, therefore, much of its efficacy as a binding precedent has been eroded. Same remark was also made in *Railway Board* v. *Chandrima Das*[79] (*Chandrima Das*).

Expanding the application of the principle of vicarious liability of the State for the torts committed by its servants in *State of Maharashtra* v. *Kanchanmala Vijaysing Shirke*[80], the Supreme Court held that even when an authorised act has been done in an unauthorised manner by the servant of the State, the State will be vicariously responsible. In this case, the driver of a government vehicle had allowed another government employee, having no driving licence, to drive the vehicle in connection with official purpose. An accident took place due to the negligence of the driver. It was held that the government is responsible. In the same manner, the court has held that the government is responsible for the misfeasance and non-feasance on the part of its servants. Misfeasance is wilful, reckless, or heedless conduct in commission of a positive act lawfully done, but with improper conduct. Non-feasance means non-performance of some act

75. See also, *LDA* v. *M.K. Gupta*, (1994) 1 SCC 243. Where the Supreme Court held that when public servant by mala fide, oppressive and capricious acts in performance of official duty causes injustice, harassment and agony to common man and renders the State or its instrumentality liable to pay damages to the person aggrieved from public fund, the State or its instrumentality is duty-bound to recover the amount of compensation so paid from the public servant concerned. In this case, compliance was to be reported to the Supreme Court.
76. *N. Nagendra Rao & Co.* v. *State of A.P.*, (1994) 6 SCC 205, 235.
77. (1999) 6 SCC 667.
78. AIR 1965 SC 1039.
79. (2000) 2 SCC 465. See also, *State of A.P.* v. *Challa Ramkrishna Reddy*, (2000) 5 SCC 712.
80. (1995) 5 SCC 659.

which ought to be performed, or an omission to perform a required duty, or a total neglect of duty.[81]

When a person died while going on a scooter in Delhi because a branch of a dead Neem tree standing near the road accidentally fell on him, rejecting the plea of accident or an act of God, in a suit for damages against the Municipal Corporation, the Supreme Court held that the authority was negligent in the performance of its duties under the common law for not removing a dead tree and for not making the road safe for the users, and therefore liable for damages to the members of the deceased family.[82] This landmark ruling if properly used may achieve the same object which legendary Ralph Nadar achieved fighting single-handed to make public and private enterprises adopt zero danger norms in the US.

In yet another landmark decision, the Supreme Court in *Chairman Chandrima Das*[83]—where a woman, a foreign national, was gang raped by railway employees in Railways Yatri Niwas—held that the Union of India, which runs the Railways as a commercial activity, would be vicariously liable to pay compensation to the victim of the rape.

Several High Courts have also echoed this sentiment when faced with situations where equity demanded compensation for the victims of the State's wrongful acts, but the hangover of the British common law prevented any relief being given. So far only "ex gratia" payments were given by the courts. What is remarkable about these cases is that the Supreme Court has used the writ jurisdiction to award compensation to victims of State's wrongful acts. Usually a victim has to start from the lower court to reach the highest Bench. By using writ jurisdiction, the remedy has been made cheap and fast. Those cases will have a salutary effect on the governments which have become immune to strictures and public condemnation, because now a new burden may be added to their already depleting resources.[84]

The government's effort in 1967 in introducing the Bill on government liability in tort was a step in the right direction, though abandoned before they finished. The proposed Bill made the State liable in the following cases:

(1) Tort committed by an employee while acting in the course of his business.

(2) Tort committed by an employee while acting beyond the course of his employment, if the act was done on behalf of the government and is ratified by it.

(3) Tort committed by an independent contractor employed by the government provided—

(*a*) the government assumes control of the act contracted to be done;

81. *Rajkot Municipal Corpn.* v. *Manjulben Jayantilal Nakum*, (1997) 9 SCC 552; *Shivsagar Tiwari* v. *Union of India*, (1996) 6 SCC 558.

82. *The Tribune* 5-5-1999, 10.

83. (2000) 2 SCC 465.

84. M.J. Antony, "Compensation for Illegal Detention", *Indian Express* 8-8-1983.

(*b*) the government has ratified the tortious act;
(*c*) reasonable care is not taken under the circumstances where though the act is lawful but is of such a nature that it may cause injury;
(*d*) the government is under a duty to do the act itself; and
(*e*) the government is under an absolute duty to ensure the safety of persons or property in the doing of the act contracted to be done and there has been a failure to comply with that duty.

(4) Where there is breach of common-law duties attached to the ownership, possession, occupation or control of immovable property.
(5) Where the government is in possession of any dangerous thing which when escapes causes injury.
(6) Where there is breach of duty to the employees which the government owes by reason of being the employer.

However, the Bill had exempted the government from liability in the following cases:

(1) Acts done by any member of the armed or police force in discharge of his duties or which are natural consequences thereof, and acts done for the purpose of training or maintaining the efficiency of the armed forces, as also the acts done for the prevention of breach of peace or damage to the public property.
(2) Acts of State.
(3) Any act done by the President or the Governor in discharge of their constitutional functions.
(4) Judicial acts and acts done in execution of judicial process or claims arising from defamation, malicious prosecution or arrest.
(5) Acts done under proclamation issued under the various provisions of the Constitution.
(6) Any claim arising from the operation of any guarantee law.
(7) Any claim arising in a foreign country.
(8) Any claim arising from injury done by doing an act authorised by law, where such injury is a natural consequence of the act.
(9) Any claim arising from any act for which immunity is provided under the Telegraph Act, 1885; Indian Post Office Act, 1898 and the Indian Railways Act, 1890.

It is apparent from the above provisions of the Bill that the government did not fully appreciate the significance of governmental accountability in a democratic welfare state. The escape clauses are so wide that in many cases a person would find himself without remedy in case of injury to his person or property. In a democratic welfare state, the government must not fight the people like a cantankerous litigant, but must have the courtesy to settle disputes outside court in the best interests of social justice. Today, the Government of India has become the biggest litigant. Deprecating this trend, Krishna Iyer J observed:

> Here is a case of a widow and daughter claiming compensation for the killing of the sole bread-winner by a State Transport bus; and the Haryana Government, instead of acting on social justice and generously settling the claim, fights like a cantankerous litigant, even by avoiding adjudication through the device of asking for court-fee from the pathetic plaintiffs.[85]

Before 1947 in Britain, the old maxim that the "king can do no wrong" was never allowed to run riot. In the beginning, though the immunity of the Crown was no defence to the servant personally, yet the government adopted the practice of conducting the defence and paying the damages wherever the official was acting in the course of employment. In those cases, where the actual tort-feasor was not identifiable, *i.e.* in accident cases, the government would supply the nominated defendant.[86]

In 1947, Britain codified the law by enacting the Crown Proceedings Act, 1947, which makes the Crown subject to all those liabilities in tort to which it would be subject if it were a private person of full age and capacity.[87] The Act makes the Crown liable for torts committed by its servants and agents and for the breach of the common-law duties owed by employers and by owners or occupiers of property. The Act further provides for the liability of the Crown for the breach of statutory duty, whenever the statute binds the Crown, and for dangerous operations without negligence on the principle of strict liability. The escape clauses are few and limited. The Crown is not liable for judges, officers not appointed by the Central Government, post offices and its employees, etc. Unlike in the US, there is no immunity for discretionary functions. If the discretion is exercised negligently, or any tort is committed while exercising discretionary functions, the government cannot escape liability. The distinction between sovereign and non-sovereign functions to which the Indian courts are so tenaciously glued has no relevance in Britain. Thus, the Home Office has been held liable in negligence for allowing dangerous prisoners to escape, although only the government can keep prisoners.[88]

In 1998, the UK passed the Human Rights Act as a Convention obligation which has added a new dimension to liability of the State. Section 6 of the European Human Rights Convention, which mandates effective remedy by domestic courts in cases of human rights violations, has added a new principle of tort based on the "duty of care". The EU Human Rights Court held that immunity to police and public authorities violates Section 6 of the Convention. Thus, where the police failed to prevent a murderous attack by a mentally deranged teacher, who had formed an obsessional attachment of a student, court attached liability of the State.[89] However, "policy

85. *State of Haryana* v. *Darshana Devi*, (1979) 2 SCC 236, 237.
86. *Adams* v. *Naylor*, 1946 AC 543 (HL). The House of Lords criticised the practice of government departments putting up "nominated" or "nominal defendants", as "whipping-boys". See also, *Royster* v. *Cavey*, (1947) 1 KB 204 (CA).
87. S. 2(1), Crown Proceedings Act, 1947.
88. *Dorset Yacht Co. Ltd.* v. *Home Office*, (1969) 2 QB 412: (1969) 2 WLR 1008 (CA).
89. *Osman* v. *United Kingdom*, (2000) 29 EHRR 245.

decisions" of local authorities are not open to challenge on the ground of negligence, while "operational matters" are actionable.

The liability of the US for the torts committed by its servants is governed by the Federal Tort Claims Act, 1946. This Act makes the US liable, respecting tort claims, in the same manner and to the same extent as a private individual under like circumstances. Though, the basics of the Act are similar to the basic provisions of the Crown Proceedings Act, 1947, yet the US statute is much narrower and restrictive in its operation because of extensive escape clauses contained therein. The exceptions in the Federal Tort Claims Act, 1946 are of three kinds: 1) There are exceptions for specific administrative functions or agencies, as well as for all claims arising in foreign countries. 2) There are exemptions for claims arising out of assault, battery, false imprisonment, false arrest, malicious prosecution, abuse of process, libel, slander, misrepresentation, deceit or interference with contract rights. This broad category chiefly covers intentional torts. 3) There are exemptions for acts or omissions of the employees exercising due care in giving effect to statutes or regulations, whether they be valid or not, and acts of discretion by government employees in the performance of their duties, whether or not the discretion is abused. This exception is a very serious flaw in US law. This exempts the government from liability in all cases where its employees exercise discretionary powers, even though the act causing the damage was done negligently. This was the basis of the decision in *Dalehite* v. *United States*[90]. In this case, a large cargo of ammonium nitrate fertiliser exploded on board a ship docked at Texas City in 1947. The result was a gutting of the entire dock area; more than 560 persons were killed and some 3000 injured; property damaged ran into hundreds of millions of dollars. The fertiliser itself had been manufactured in plants owned by the federal government as per its order and specifications. It was being shipped to Europe at the government's discretion under the Marshall Plan. Over 300 suits were brought against the government under the Federal Tort Claims Act, 1946 on the ground of negligence in the handling of the fertiliser by the government. The lower court found negligence in the production, transportation and storage of the fertiliser. However, the Supreme Court by 4:3 held that this did not make the government liable since the wrong was done in exercise of its discretionary authority. Therefore, in the US, neither the government nor the officer concerned is liable for the tort committed in exercise of his discretionary powers, even in case of negligence or abuse of discretion. This exception renders it just to say that the Federal Tort Claims Act, 1946, despite a high-sounding title, in substance accomplishes very little.

Of all the developed systems of jurisprudence, perhaps the French system is the most logically satisfying in the area of governmental liability, which deserves our attention.

---

90. 1953 SCC OnLine US SC 76: 97 L Ed 1427: 346 US 15 (1953).

2.1 Governmental liability in tort—the French model

At the time when the common-law jurisdictions were still lost in the darkness of the feudal principle of governmental immunity, a progressive idea of governmental liability was flourishing in some major countries of the continent which had recognised the principle of governmental liability, though on a basis comparable with that of private law. However, a gradual unfolding of this idea of liability ultimately led not only to the rationalisation of the law but also to the development of an independent public law of governmental liability. It is rather unfortunate that not only in India but in the UK and the US also, courts have not tried to develop any principle of public law relating to governmental liability, but are still busy in stretching the private law principles to a domain for which they were not designed. This is the root cause of all confusion in this area of high social visibility and practical efficacy.

The French model is discussed below.

2.1.1 *Personal faults*

Contemporary French law of State liability for tortious actions is based on the distinction between *faute de service* (service fault) and *faute personnelle* (personal fault).[91] This is construed liberally to include within *faute personnelle* not only action clearly outside the scope of authority,[92] as the use of government vehicle for private use, but also any act characterised as malicious or grossly negligent.[93] Therefore, a government official is not absolutely immune from personal liability even for acts which under the common-law jurisprudence are in exercise of public functions. This keeps the government officer at his best all the time because there is penalty for all his actions unworthy of public office as not to be properly attributable. For such actions, he may be sued personally in the ordinary courts. It is true that in some cases it may be a worthless right against a penniless official, yet its importance in keeping the administration on tabs cannot be overemphasised.[94] It is also true that the distinction between *faute personnelle* and *faute de service* is a difficult one, especially, in the complexities of a modern administration, however, this does not undermine the efficacy of a principle but merely illustrates the basic difficulty of applying a general principle to concrete cases.[95]

91. Brown and Garner, *French Administrative Law* (2nd Edn.) 101.
92. *Affaire Pastor*, CE 28-11-1947.
93. Commitment, in error, of persons to a mental instead of ordinary hospital. Waline, *Droit Administratif* (9th Edn.) 199.
94. Schwartz, *French Administrative Law and the Common Law World* 260. It may be noted that in a majority of cases, including even most cases of excess of authority, the personal liability of the individual official before ordinary courts is being replaced by State liability before administrative courts.
95. *Ibid*, Chap. 9.

2.1.2 *Service fault*

The liability of the administration is primarily based on *faute de service*. This consists of some defect or failure in the operation of public service. The distinction between personal fault and service fault is not an easy one. However, a service fault is one which is committed in exercise of a public function for service. Therefore, the official preserves his immunity by reason of the principle of separation of powers, which prohibits the ordinary court receiving actions against the administration or its official. Instead, the injured party must sue the administration before the administrative courts.[96]

2.1.3 *Service-connected fault*

Between these two extremes lies an intermediate category in French law of "service-connected torts". The principle that responsibility for illegal interference with the protected interests of the citizen is primarily a responsibility of the public authority, in whose service the officer stands rather than of the individual concerned, is firmly and irrevocably established in the continental jurisprudence.[97]

With the development of the concept of welfare and service state, the concept of faults connected with the service is expanding tremendously, and courts are recognising "combination of faults" (*cumul*) in situations where a tort could not have been committed by the officer but for the fault of service and, therefore, the State could be held liable for the whole damages claimed.[98] The concept of *cumul* was further elaborated in *Lemonnier*[99], where the Conseil d'Etat held the State liable for the negligence of the Mayor in permitting a shooting competition in which a person was hit, in spite of the complaint by a person of the possible risk to life, because the Mayor's negligence constituted at one and the same time a combination of personal and service fault. The concept is expressed in the oft-quoted conclusion of Leon Blum, Commissaire du Gouvernement, as he then was:

> If the personal fault has been committed in the public service, or on the occasion of the service, if the means and instruments of the fault have been placed at the disposition of the party at fault by the service, if in short the service has provided the conditions for the commission of the fault, the administrative judge will and must then say: the fault may be severable from the service—that is for the ordinary courts to decide; but the service is not severable from the fault.[100]

96. Brown and Garner, *French Administrative Law* (2nd Edn.) 101.
97. Schwartz, *French Administrative Law and the Common Law World* 260.
98. In August (CE 3-2-1911), a visitor to a post office was assaulted and his leg was broken by two members of the post office staff because he left by the staff entrance, the entrance for public having been prematurely closed. The court held that it was a combination of faults (*cumul*).
99. CE 26-7-1918.
100. Quoted in Brown and Garner, *French Administrative Law* (2nd Edn.) 101, 102.

The *cumul* doctrine was extended to its logical conclusion in the trio of cases (Mimeur, Defaux and Besthlsemer) decided on the same day.[101] In all these cases, the complainants suffered injuries by negligent driving of the government officials. The motor cars involved belonged to the administration, but were being used by officials on private and unauthorised trips. The Conseil d'Etat held the administration liable on the ground of combination of personal and service faults. Hence, the accident was not deprived of all connection with the service.[102]

The doctrine of "service fault" and "service-connected fault", though originally limited to feasance, was progressively expanded to cover cases of non-feasance and late-feasance, as Prof. Schwartz puts it. Moreover, the service is held to be at the fault not only when its action is open to criticism, but a fortiori when such mishandling of public affairs has expressed itself in an illegal decision.

2.1.4 *Contribution*

Recognising the danger inherent in holding the administration responsible on the ground of extended doctrine of *cumul,* even in cases where the officer is "on a frolic of his own", the Conseil d'Etat gradually evolved the concept of "contribution" to check the irresponsible and reckless behaviour of the officers in dealings with the public. Consequently, in *Delvile*[103], where a government vehicle was involved in an accident partly because the driver was drunk and partly because of the defective brakes, the Conseil d'Etat allowed a direct action by the administration for 50 per cent contribution by the official.[104] The quantum of contribution is determined according to the official's duties and responsibilities in the particular service, in which he is employed, rather than by reference to the actual part played by him in the cause of the damage.

2.1.5 *Risk theory*

The principles of State liability discussed above are still based on the principle of private law of tort where "fault" remains a primary factor, since

101. CE 18-11-1949.
102. See also, *Benard* (CE 1-10-1954). If a policeman is on duty outside a bar, goes in to have a drink, becomes involved in an argument and injures a customer with his revolver, the service will be at fault and responsible. However (*Litzler,* CE June 1954), service was not held responsible where a customs officer in uniform but off duty used his service revolver to commit a murder.
103. CE 28-7-1951.
104. See also, *Laurell* (CE 12-3-1948), where the Conseil d'Etat allowed a contribution suit filed by the administration against the army officer who took away the army vehicle without authority on a private trip and knocked down a pedestrian. In its view, the administration was entitled to contribution from the officer for although there was a combination of service and personal fault, it does not lie in the officer's mouth to allege the service fault since he was guilty of fraud.

these principles are mainly concerned with the problem of adjustment of a burden between two parties; hence it is still generally a proper principle that as between two innocent parties, the burden should lie where it falls. However, the Conseil d'Etat has made a significant contribution to the concept of governmental liability by developing a principle of public law of tort with far-reaching ramifications. The central idea of this principle is that damage to private persons arises often from actions taken in public interest. Therefore, the prejudice caused to the private party is, in such cases, a kind of a public charge, which in accordance with the principle of equality should not accidentally rest with one or the other persons involved, but be redistributed among the members of the community through the responsibility for compensation attached to the public authority.[105]

The jurisprudential basis for liability without fault is that of the risk theory. The activities of the State, even when conducted without fault, may in certain circumstances constitute the creation of risk; if the risk materialises and an individual has suffered injury or loss, it is only just that the State should indemnify him.[106]

The moving spirit behind this "no fault liability" is perhaps the fundamental principle of equality of all citizens in bearing public burdens. Duguit was referring to the same principle when he wrote:

> The activity of the State is carried on in the interest of the entire community; the burden that it entails should not weigh more heavily on some than on others. If then State action results in individual damage to particular citizens, the State should make redress, whether or not there be a fault committed by the public officers concerned. The State is, in some ways, an insurer of what is often called social risk....[107]

This shouldering by the community of a burden which in English Law lies where it falls (because even if a tort had been committed there would be lawful authority) is one of the most striking and laudable aspects of French droit administratif.[108]

State responsibility on the ground of "no fault" theory has been identified in various typical spheres of governmental activity which are as follows:

(1) *Responsibility for damages arising from dangerous operations or responsabilite du fait des choses.*—Where a public authority creates an abnormal risk in the neighbourhood, then it must be prepared to compensate if any person suffers damage. It was on this basis that the Conseil d'Etat held the State liable when during the First World War a grenade dump in a residential neighbourhood exploded causing extensive damage to person and property. Disagreeing with the argument that the State was liable because of the negligent operating

105. Brown and Garner, *French Administrative Law* (2nd Edn.) 103.
106. *Ibid*, 105.
107. *Ibid*, 105.
108. Prof. Thompson, 1968 JSPTL 470; *Ibid*, 105.

of the dump, the court held the State liable on the ground of "risk" and in that case it was unnecessary for the victims to establish "negligence" or "fault"[109].

The same principle has been extended to dangerous operations. If the operation is such which involves abnormal risk, the court would grant a right of indemnity without proof of any fault. Therefore, when a bystander suffered injuries through the use of firearms by the police, the court granted damages against the State.[110] Under English Law, however, in similar circumstances, "negligence" had to be established to enable the court to find the administration liable for damages.[111] This principle has also been extended to cover the consequences of general measures justified by public necessity.

(2) *Workmen's compensation principle in public law of tort or risque professionals.*—Even before the concept of social security became a reality in France, the administrative courts had developed the principle of compensation for the workmen, without the necessity of proving fault.[112] This principle was based on governmental obligation to indemnify against the risk of employment. Later on, this principle was extended to cover even those cases where a person is assisting in public services in a voluntary capacity. Therefore, in Saint-La-Plaine, the Conseil d'Etat granted compensation to a person who had injured himself while helping to set off fireworks at a village carnival, without proving "fault" on the part of the commune.[113]

The same principle of social security has been benevolently extended to cover risks arising out of "public service actions". Consequently, if a man was injured while trying to apprehend a thief,[114] or when a person injured himself while helping an old woman out of a ditch where she had fallen accidentally, the Conseil d'Etat granted compensation.[115]

(3) *Risk from society or risque social.*—Extension of "risk without fault" liability covers also the cases of public disorders of varying magnitude. If a person suffers in person or property due to any public

109. *Regnault—Desroziers* (CE 28-3-1919). *See also*, Saulze (CE 6-11-1968), where a school teacher was able to recover damages from the State because she runs a special risk when attending to her duties if any of the pupils are suffering from measles, and therefore a baby which suffered injuries because his mother had contracted the disease while she was carrying him in the womb.

110. See, *Lecomte and Daramy* (CE 24-6-1949). In *Lecomte*, the complainant's wife was shot dead accidentally when the police was pursuing the assailant. In *Daramy*, the person was hit by the bullet when police opened fire at a motorist evading a roadblock.

111. *Dorset Yacht Co. Ltd.* v. *Home Office*, (1969) 2 QB 412: (1969) 2 WLR 1008 (CA).

112. *Cames* (CE 21-6-1895). Court allowed compensation to an employee who injured himself while working in the State arsenal.

113. CE 22-11-1946.

114. *Pinguet*, CE 17-4-1953.

115. *Gaillard*, CE 8-10-1970.

disorder without his fault, administrative courts allow compensation again on the principle of equality in bearing burdens.[116]

2.1.6 *Compensation for governmental refusal to protect the legal interests and rights of the people*

To combat essential inertia of the government and to protect the principle of equality, the administrative courts in France have developed another principle of far-reaching consequences within the area of public law of governmental liability by allowing compensation to private individuals in cases where the government either refuses or delays action to protect the legal rights and interests and, thereby, causes loss to such persons. Therefore, in *Couiteas*[117], when the government showed its inability to get the land of the plaintiff vacated by the nomadic tribes because of the fear of civil war, the Conseil d'Etat allowed damages against the government. In the same manner, when the decree of ejectment against the tenant could not be executed for four years because of administrative indifference, court awarded damages.

2.1.7 *Compensation for governmental action imposing statutory unequal sacrifice*

Generally the statute causing prejudice to the proprietary or financial interest of a person provides for compensation. However, where the statute is silent, the administrative courts, again enforcing the principle of equality in bearing public burdens, award compensation.[118] Therefore, if the business interests of any person have been adversely affected because either the State has opted for State monopoly or controlled activity, the administrative courts shall award compensation.[119]

2.1.8 *Some observations for the future development of the law in India*

(1) The doctrine of "sovereign immunity" is an anachronism without any rational basis. It is amazing that even today this feudalistic and authoritarian doctrine is still persisting obscuring the proper understanding of the role and functions of a government in a welfare democratic society.

116. "No fault liability" in French administrative law goes much farther than the strict liability principle for animals under Animals Act, 1971 and *Rylands* v. *Fletcher*, (1868) 3 HL 330.
117. CE 1-11-1923.
118. *Mergui* (CE 19-3-1971).
119. *La Fleurette* (CE 14-1-1938) and *Compagnie Generale D'Energie Radioelectrique* (CE 30-5-1966). Right to compensation arises only when the activity is not injurious to public health, order or morals.

(2) Any welfare democratic society presupposes equality between the governors and the governed and the socialisation of compensation. In this context, any immunity granted to the State from compensation for the harm done to its citizens would lead to an anatomical impairment of the concept of "welfare".

(3) The laboured distinction between "sovereign" and "non-sovereign" functions of the State to which the Indian courts are so tenaciously glued is based on logical fallacy and practical absurdity and derives its justification, if any exists, from extra-legal consideration of protecting the impecunious authority from liability. In view of the multitude of business like operations which are conducted by the government for the general welfare of its people, the test artificially divides and truncates the ubiquitous functions of the State.

(4) It is only desirable and equitable that an attempt to protect an "impecunious State" from liability should be through budgetary reorganisation and not through shifting the burden to the helpless victims.

(5) The trauma of the development of law in the common-law world has been that it hinges on the private law of tort which was not designed to solve problems of public law area. This created a quagmire, well illustrated by various decisions of the courts in India. Solution lies in the efforts designed to develop a public law of tort for which blueprints have been provided by the French jurisprudence.

(6) One such principle of the public law of tort, relating to governmental liability, may be that in a welfare democratic society damage to any private citizen arises often from actions taken in public interest, hence the prejudice caused to the private party is a kind of a public charge which in accordance with the principles of equality, should not accidentally rest where it falls, but be redistributed among the members of the community. Thus, socialisation of compensation must be the foundation on which the infrastructure of the law relating to governmental liability in tort must be built.

(7) In any developing and welfare state, "financial implications" for public bodies arising out of tort liability may be a matter of serious concern. Tort claims may have detrimental effect on public services. Therefore, emphasis must also be on statutory regulations, openness and institutional mechanisms which may prevent litigation for tort claims.

No one has any misgivings about the creativity of the Indian judiciary, but this creativity has failed to develop even a single viable principle within the area of governmental liability in tort. Our courtrooms are still haunted by doctrines which are long dead. It is only hoped that the genius of the Indian judiciary would also be registered in this area of high social visibility by developing the principles of "public law of tort", satisfying the claims of "socialisation of compensation".

2.2 Liability of private individuals to the State for committing a tort against its servants

The discussions on the liability of the government for torts committed by its servants brings us to an inevitable question: Whether the government can also recover damages from any private individual for the tort committed by such individual against its servants? Within the realm of domestic relations, the master is entitled to an action *per quod servitium amisit* for damages when his servant has been injured. However, this principle of tort has not been firmly engrafted within the area of public law. In England, in *IRC* v. *Hambrook*[120], Denning LJ was of the view that the action *per quod servitium amisit* must be confined to domestic relations and it does not lie, therefore, at the instance of the government, to corporations and other employers who do not keep a household. This approach, however, has not been accepted in Australia. In *Commr. for Railways (NSW)* v. *Scott*[121], the High Court held that the Commissioner could recover damages from a rider of a motor cycle whose negligence caused its engine driver to suffer a breakdown. These days it is common in welfare societies to provide for sick pay, medical expenses and other forms of compensations in their statutes, if their employees are injured in the course of employment. When apart from the action *per quod servitium amisit,* the employer has no general law means of recovering the sum paid by it to its employees, this action has, therefore, assumed importance from an economic point of view, which it perhaps did not have in some earlier periods of its history. The application of the action *per quod servitium amisit* in public law is still in its ante-natal stage in India and deserves serious consideration from the Bench and the Bar.

3. PRIVILEGES AND IMMUNITIES OF THE ADMINISTRATION IN SUITS

Though the equality clause of the Constitution envisages absence of any special privileges to anyone including government, but since government is a government in contradistinction to a private individual, law allows certain privileges to the government as a litigant. From among the numerous privileges available to the government under various statutes, a few important ones may be discussed here.

3.1 Privilege of notice

Section 80(1) of the Civil Procedure Code, 1908 (CPC) provides that no suit shall be instituted against the government or a public officer, in respect of any act purporting to be done by such public officer in his official capacity,

120. (1956) 2 QB 641.
121. (1959) 102 CLR 392 (Aust).

until the expiration of two months next after notice in writing in the manner provided in the section has been given. The requirement of notice is mandatory and admits of no exception.[122] However, if the public officer has acted without jurisdiction, the courts have held that the requirement of notice is not mandatory. Therefore, if a public officer seizes property without authority[123] or assaults a witness,[124] no notice is necessary for filing a suit against him in his official capacity. The Allahabad and Calcutta High Courts have further held that notice is unnecessary when a public officer though acts within jurisdiction but in a mala fide manner.[125] The requirement of notice may also be waived either expressly or impliedly by the government.[126]

The requirement of notice applies to all kinds of relief and forms of action, whether injunctive or otherwise. Whatever else may be the merit of the rule, it certainly creates hardships for the litigants seeking injunctive relief against the government. The plight of the litigant is well illustrated in *State of Orissa* v. *Madan Gopal Rungta*[127] (*Madan Gopal*). In this case, the government notified to the lessees of mines, Madan Gopal and others, that their leases had become void and they should remove their assets within a fortnight. The lessees wanted to file a suit for injunction against the government, but the two months' notice rule of Section 80 proved to be an insurmountable hurdle. Therefore, they moved the High Court for the writ of mandamus. The High Court granted the writ on the ground that under the circumstances, the alternative remedy was inadequate, and restrained the State Government from disturbing the possession for three months during which the suit could be filed by the petitioners after complying with the requirement of notice. The Supreme Court reversed the decision of the High Court in appeal. Keeping in view this hardship, the Law Commission recommended the abolition of the requirement of notice as it causes great inconvenience to the litigants, especially when they seek immediate relief against the government.

Keeping in view this hardship, especially, in cases where the person needs immediate and urgent relief, the Civil Procedure Code Amendment Act, 1976 added clause (2) to Section 80 which provides that the court may grant leave to a person to file a suit against the government or a public officer without serving two months' notice in cases where relief claimed is

122. *Sawai Singhai Nirmal Chand* v. *Union of India*, AIR 1966 SC 1068.

123. *Babu Rameshwar Prasad Singh* v. *Mohd. Ayyub*, 1950 SCC OnLine Pat 70: AIR 1950 Pat 527.

124. *Dattatraya Ramchandra* v. *Annappa Pandurang Kokatnur*, 1928 SCC OnLine Bom 41: ILR (1928) 52 Bom 832.

125. *Mohd. Saddiq Ahmad* v. *Panna Lal*, ILR (1903) 26 All 220; *Raghubans Sahai* v. *Phool Kumari*, ILR (1905) 32 Cal 1130. The Madras HC has taken opposite view in *F.H. Wilson* v. *Nathmull*, 1929 SCC OnLine Mad 205: AIR 1930 Mad 458.

126. *Paleti Sivaramakrishnaiah* v. *N.C. Canals Sathenapalli*, 1978 SCC OnLine AP 215: AIR 1978 AP 389.

127. AIR 1952 SC 12.

immediate or urgent. But before granting the exemption, the court must satisfy itself about the immediate or urgent need. After this amendment, the hardship caused to the litigant in cases like *Madan Gopal Rungta*[128] should not recur.

The real purpose behind the privilege of notice to the government is to alert the government to negotiate a just settlement or at least have the courtesy to tell the person why the claim is being resisted. If the government does not act to lessen the hardship of the individual and save wasteful litigative expenditure of public money on long-drawn-out litigation, there seems to be no justification in allowing this privilege to the government.[129]

However, the reality test shows that in large number of cases either the notice is not replied or where replied, it is generally vague and evasive, but certainly no effort is made to settle the matter outside the court. This defeats not only the purpose of notice but also puts heavy cost on the exchequer, besides adding to the misery of litigants. Therefore, in *Salem Advocate Bar Assn.* (2) v. *Union of India*[130], the Supreme Court issued directive for the appointment of Special Officer who shall be responsible for sending replies to notices within time and after due application of mind, and must be held responsible if reply is not sent or is vague or evasive or has been sent without due application of mind. The Supreme Court also directed the courts to impose heavy cost which may be calculated after taking into consideration the cost of time spent, all fees, incident cost, including lodging and transportation expenditure. This will certainly make administration responsive, besides reducing the heavy burden on public exchequer and the misery of litigants.

It is common to find in the common-law world that government bodies are entitled to special notice before legal action is taken against them. A fairly typical example is Section 580 of the New South Wales Local Government Act, 1919 which requires one month's notice for filing any suit against the Council. The notice must state 1) the cause of action; 2) the time and place at which the damage or injury was sustained; and 3) the name and place of abode or business of the intended plaintiff and his attorney (if any) in the case. After the notice, a representative of the Council must be permitted to inspect the damaged property and an authorised medical practitioner must be permitted to examine any person injured. A plaintiff will not be permitted to go into evidence of any cause of action not stated in the notice nor to proceed at all unless the notice is served. However, a judge may permit an amendment of a notice and allow its non-compliance if he deems it "just or reasonable in the circumstances". In Victoria, the Limitation of Actions Act, 1958 requires six months' notice of similar nature.[131]

128. AIR 1952 SC 12.
129. See, *State of Punjab* v. *Geeta Iron & Brass Works Ltd.*, (1978) 1 SCC 68.
130. (2005) 6 SCC 344.
131. *See*, Redmond, "Notices Before Action", (1964) 37 Australian LJ 316.

3.2 Privilege to withhold documents

In India, the privilege of the government to withhold documents from the courts is claimed on the basis of Section 123 of the Evidence Act, 1872, which lays down that no one shall be permitted to give any evidence derived from unpublished official records relating to the affairs of the State except with the permission of the head of the department concerned, who shall give or withhold such permission as he thinks fit. Section 124 extends this privilege to confidential official communication also.

The privilege if claimed is not conclusive in the sense that the courts can do nothing except to admit it. This proposition is based on Section 162 of the Evidence Act, 1872 which provides that when a witness is required to produce a document, he must bring it to the court and then may raise an objection to its production and admissibility.

In *State of Punjab* v. *Sodhi Sukhdev Singh*[132], the court had the opportunity of discussing the extent of government privilege to withhold documents where twin claims of governmental confidentiality and individual justice compete for recognition. In this case, a District judge challenged the validity of his dismissal order and wanted the production of the minutes of the meeting of the Council of Ministers, and also a copy of the recommendation of the Public Service Commission to fortify his defence. The court allowed the privilege to withhold these documents. The minutes were not allowed to be produced because of the prohibition in Article 163(3) of the Constitution which lays down that the advice tendered by a Minister cannot be enquired into by any court. As regards the recommendations of the Public Service Commission, the court came to the conclusion that its disclosure would involve injury to public interest. The court further elaborated the extent of privilege by holding that the government documents can be classified into two categories: 1) documents relating to the affairs of the State; and 2) documents not relating to the affairs of the State. For the documents falling in the second category, there is no immunity. But for the documents falling in the first category, the claim of the privilege is not conclusive and the court is required to enquire into the nature of the document in the light of relevant facts and circumstances. However, the court held that in order to determine the claim of privilege, the court cannot inspect the document and the administration shall be the sole judge of the public interest involved in the disclosure.

The court was very alive to the constraints of this privilege on private defence, therefore, Gajendragadkar J delivering the majority judgment cautioned that care has to be taken to see that interests other than that of the public do not masquerade in the garb of public interest and take undue advantage of the provision of Section 123 of the Evidence Act, 1872. In order to guard against the possible misuse of the privilege, the court also developed certain norms:

132. AIR 1961 SC 493.

(1) The claim of privilege should be in the form of an affidavit which must be signed by the Minister concerned or the Secretary of the department.
(2) The affidavit must indicate within permissible limits the reasons why the disclosure would result in public injury, and that the document in question has been carefully read and considered and the authority is fully convinced that its disclosure would injure public interest.
(3) If the affidavit is found unsatisfactory, the court may summon the authority for cross-examination.

Working the formulations still further, the court in *Amar Chand Butail* v. *Union of India*[133] disallowed the privilege where there was evidence to show that the authority did not apply its mind to the question of injury to public interest which would be caused by the disclosure of the document. In *Indira Nehru Gandhi* v. *Raj Narain*[134], the court compelled the production of Blue Books of the police and disallowed the claims of privilege. In *State of Orissa* v. *Jagannath Jena*[135], the Supreme Court again disallowed the privilege on the ground that the public interest aspect had not been clearly brought out in the affidavit. In this case, the plaintiff wanted to see endorsement on a file by the Deputy Chief Minister and the IG.

In *State* v. *Midland Rubber & Produce Co.*[136], the Kerala High Court went a step further and reserved to itself the right even to inspect the document before allowing the claim of privilege. In this case, the court came to the conclusion after inspecting the document that no public interest would suffer from its disclosure. Other High Courts have also followed the same line of reasoning in deciding upon the claims of privilege.[137] The recent trends in judicial behaviour in this area of high social visibility is most welcome.

The decision of the Supreme Court in *ADM, Jabalpur* v. *Shivakant Shukla*[138] may, however, be regarded as highly selective because of the special setting in which the case was decided. Ray CJ observed that Section 16-A(9) of the Maintenance of Internal Security Act, 1971—which provided that the grounds of detention are to be treated as confidential and are deemed to refer to matters of State and to be against public interest to disclose—enacts provisions analogous to a conclusive proof of presumption. Such a provision is a genuine rule of evidence. It is in the nature of an explanation of Sections 123 and 162 of the Evidence Act, 1872. Therefore, when the detaining authority is bound by Section 16-A(9) and forbidden absolutely from disclosing such material, no question can arise for adverse

133. AIR 1964 SC 1658.
134. 1975 Supp SCC 1.
135. (1977) 2 SCC 165.
136. 1971 SCC OnLine Ker 62: AIR 1971 Ker 228.
137. *Mohd. Yusuf* v. *State of Madras*, 1971 SCC OnLine Mad 52: AIR 1971 Mad 468; *Union of India* v. *Lalli*, 1970 SCC OnLine Pat 58: AIR 1971 Pat 264; *Sujit Kantha Neogi* v. *Union of India*, 1969 SCC OnLine Gau 17: AIR 1970 Assam & Ngld 131.
138. (1976) 2 SCC 521, 589.

inference against the authority. The court cannot insist on the production of the file or hold that the case of the detenu stands unrebutted by reason of such non-disclosure. To hold otherwise would be to induce reckless averments of mala fides to force production of the file which is forbidden by law. Maintaining the same pre-Emergency tenor of judicial articulation, the Supreme Court ordered the Government of Bihar to produce copies of the Criminal Investigation Department (CID) reports and other documents relating to the blinding of undertrials in Bhagalpur jail. The judges asserted that it is imperative to the proper functioning of the judicial process and satisfactory ascertainment of truth that all relevant facts must be made available to the court. It is difficult to see how the State can resist the production of these reports and their use as evidence in the proceedings before the court when the reports clearly relate to the issue as to how, in what manner, and by whom the 24 undertrials were blinded. The court pointed out that the country has adopted the adversary system of jurisprudence in which truth emerges from the clash between contesting parties. Therefore, all facts relevant to the investigation must be brought before the court and irrelevant facts must be shut out, for otherwise the court may get a distorted or incomplete picture of the facts and that might result in miscarriage of justice.[139] Similarly, in *S.P. Gupta* v. *Union of India*[140] (*S.P. Gupta*), the Supreme Court rejected the government's claim of privilege over the correspondence relating to the transfer and non-extension of the terms of two judges of High Courts. After studying the documents in the chamber, the judges came to the conclusion that the documents did not belong to the privileged category covering "affairs of State" and their disclosure would not jeopardise public interest. In arriving at this conclusion, the court applied the "balancing of interest" test. It was stressed that in the ultimate analysis the approach of the court, while deciding the question of privilege, would be that it has to balance public interest in just justice and just administration of justice and State affairs and then decide which way the balance tilts. After laying down this test, the court held that in this case a disclosure in the interests of justice far outweighs the possible embarrassment felt by the government. The court also recommended that the century-old provisions of Section 123 of the Evidence Act, 1872 relating to privileged documents enacted to some extent, keeping in view the needs of empire builders, must change in the context of the republican form of government and the open society which the people of India have established.[141] Keeping the same tenor, the court in *Sethi Roop Lal* v. *Malti Thapar*[142] did not allow the claim of privilege by the government for the production of marked copy of electoral roll.

139. *Anil Yadav* v. *State of Bihar*, (1981) 1 SCC 622.
140. 1981 Supp SCC 87.
141. *Ibid*, 700–01, *per* Desai J.
142. (1994) 2 SCC 579.

However, the two-judge Bench in *State of Bihar* v. *Kripalu Shankar*[143] expressed doubt over the decision of the court in *S.P. Gupta*[144] and remarked that the legal milestone in that case "needs a retreat, a bit". In this case of contempt, the Supreme Court held that government files are privileged documents and no contempt proceedings, civil or criminal, can be initiated on the basis of notings on files, as this privilege is necessary in order to maintain the independent functioning of civil services and fearless expression of views. Similarly, the Supreme Court in *Doypack Systems (P) Ltd.* v. *Union of India*[145] held that it is the duty of the court to prevent disclosure of documents where Article 74(2) of the Constitution is applicable. Article 74(2) provides that the advice tendered by Ministers to the President shall not be inquired into in any court. Documents falling within this class are, therefore, entitled to protection in public interest as a "class" because it is necessary for the proper functioning of the State. This class of documents may include Cabinet minutes, minutes of discussions between heads of departments, high-level interdepartment communications, despatches from the Ambassadors, papers brought into existence for the purpose of preparing a submission to Cabinet, noting of the officials leading to the Cabinet decision, and documents which relate to the framing of government policy at the high level.

However, the claim of "class" privilege has always proved a serious obstruction in the administration of justice. It is for this reason that in *R.K. Jain* v. *Union of India*[146] the Supreme Court was quick enough to circumscribe the limit of "class" privilege under Article 74(2) of the Constitution. In this case, a petition had been filed to challenge the appointment of the President of the Central Excise Gold Appellate Tribunal by the government. Rule nisi was issued to the respondents to produce the file relating to the appointment. In the first instance, government claimed privilege under Article 74(2) of the Constitution but later on agreed to the perusal of the file by the court, but claimed privilege to disclose the contents to the petitioner. After perusing the file, though the court allowed the privilege, yet the court thought it proper to lay down the law in its correct perspective, especially, where the privilege claimed was a "class" privilege under Article 74(2). The court made it clear that Article 74(2) of the Constitution, which provides that advice tendered by the Cabinet to the President cannot be enquired into by any court, does not allow a "class" privilege. Immunity can be claimed in respect of those documents only the disclosure of which may result in harm to the nation or to the public interest. This may include information relating to national security, diplomatic relations, internal security or sensitive diplomatic correspondence as "class" documents for which public interest demands complete immunity from disclosure. The bar of judicial

143. (1987) 3 SCC 34.
144. 1981 Supp SCC 87.
145. (1988) 2 SCC 299.
146. (1993) 4 SCC 119.

review is confined to the factum of the advice, its extent, ambit and scope but not the record, *i.e.* the material on which the advice is founded. While deciding the claim of privilege, the court would give utmost consideration to the views of the government but it will not be conclusive.

The court further amplified the law by laying down the factors to be considered in deciding the public interest immunity claims. These factors would include the following:

(1) Interest affected by the disclosure of the document.
(2) In case of "class" protection—Whether the public interest immunity protects the class.
(3) The extent to which the interests referred to have become attenuated by the passage of time or intervening events.
(4) The seriousness of the issue by which production of the document is sought.
(5) The likelihood that production of the document will affect the outcome of the case.
(6) The likelihood of injustice if the document is not produced.

Thus, the claim of a "class" privilege under Article 74(2) of the Constitution was confined by the court to its proper place.

In *Robinson* v. *South Australia*[147], the Privy Council also interpreted the privilege narrowly and the powers of the court broadly. The Privy Council held:

(1) The privilege is a narrow one, to be exercised only where there is some plain overriding principle of public policy.
(2) Only rarely can documents relating to the industrial or commercial activities of the State come within the rule, especially in times of peace.
(3) The mere fact that the production of a document might prejudice the Crown's own case is not a justification for a claim of privilege.
(4) The court is entitled to require, and should require, an actual affidavit from a responsible Minister whose mind has been directed to the questions involved.
(5) In all cases, the court has in reserve its power to inspect the document in question.

In England until the Second World War, it was generally recognised in the courts that the Crown's powers to forbid the disclosure of specified evidence was not absolute. However, the law took a sharp turn in the wrong direction in 1942 when the House of Lords decided *Duncan* v. *Cammell, Laird & Co. Ltd.*[148] (*Duncan*). The House of Lords ruled that if a Minister claims privilege for any document on the ground of public interest, it shall be considered as final and conclusive. This judicial abdication, however,

147. 1931 AC 704 (PC).
148. 1942 AC 624 (HL).

can be justified in view of the special circumstances attending the case. In this case, a submarine sank during trials killing 99 persons. One of the dependants of the killed brought an action against the builders of the submarine on the ground of negligence in the manufacture of the submarine, and in order to prove negligence, wanted the production of blueprints of the design of the submarine. The First Lord of Admiralty claimed privilege on the ground that the blueprints of the design of the submarine was a military secret and its disclosure would jeopardise public interest. The court allowed the claim of privilege as conclusive. This decision opened the door to all kinds of "class" claims which proved a serious obstruction in the administration of justice. As a result, the courts started breaking away from this sweeping rule.[149]

The criticism generated by the broad sweep of the privilege led in 1956 to a statement in the House of Lords by Viscount Kilmuir LC. The statement indicated, first, that the privilege might be claimed not only on the ground that the disclosure of the particular document would injure the public interest; but also on the ground that the document was one of a particular class of documents, disclosure of which would injure the public interest in that it might prejudice freedom and candour of communication with and within the public service. The statement then indicated that, as a matter of policy, privilege would not for the future be claimed in respect of certain classes of documents:

(1) In relation to road accidents, accidents involving government employees and accidents on government premises, reports of the employees involved and other eyewitnesses and subsequent report made by the foreman, superintendent or other official as to such matters as the state of the machinery, vehicle or premises involved. This class does not include reports of a government inspector, etc. investigating an industrial or mining accident.
(2) Ordinary medical reports in respect of the health of civilian employees. This class does not include medical reports and records in the fighting services and in the prison service, though the privilege would not be claimed in proceedings against the medical officer concerned for negligence, or in criminal proceedings.
(3) Statements made to the police (except by "informers"). These would be produced in court on subpoena or furnished earlier with the consent or at the request of the witnesses themselves.
(4) In contract cases, all documents passing between the parties, other documents affecting the legal position (for example, an authority to an agent), and relevant reports on matters of fact (as distinct from comment and advice).[150]

149. *Glasgow Corpn.* v. *Central Land Board*, 1956 SC (HL) 1; *Grosvenor Hotel* (*No.* 2), *re*, 1965 Ch 1210: (1964) 3 WLR 992 (CA).
150. *See*, 197 HL Deb, Cols. 741 and 237; HL Deb, Col. 1063.

The Lord Chancellor pointed out that, as to oral communications, the privilege was available on the same principles as in the case of written communications.[151]

It may be pointed out that in England the privilege to withhold documents cannot be referred to as Crown privilege. A private person may raise the same claim and the court itself may, of its own motion, refuse to permit disclosure. Therefore, it can be rightly called a public interest privilege.

But in 1968, the House of Lords unanimously repudiated its extreme formulation of 1942 and regained judicial control in *Conway* v. *Rimmer*[152]. In this case, a junior police officer who had been prosecuted for theft of an electric torch and acquitted had brought an action for malicious prosecution against a superior officer and desired to see the report made on him in the police service. The Home Secretary intervened with a claim of "class" privilege. The House of Lords disallowed the claim, inspected the document themselves and ordered its disclosure. The House of Lords made it clear that though the courts would naturally respect claims based on genuine secrets of State, they would not allow any claims unless the public interest in secrecy clearly outweighs the public interest in doing justice to the litigant; and that was a matter to be determined by the court and not by the executive.

In England now, Section 28 of the Crown Proceedings Act, 1947 specifically recognises the right of the Crown to withhold documents if in the opinion of the relevant Minister it would be injurious to the public interest to disclose them. However, the claim of privilege is to be decided by the judge and not by the executives and for this purpose, unless the document relates to national security, diplomatic relations, or State secrets of high importance, the court shall have the power to inspect the document. In *R.* v. *Goodchild*[153], the Court of Appeal allowed privilege relating to a commercial document on the ground of possible far-reaching political repercussions. But, the House of Lords after inspecting the document found that it contained nothing of substantial evidentiary value and thus dismissed the appeal.[154]

The American term for government privilege is "executive privilege". In the US, the courts never abdicated their control over the claims of the executive for privilege. The leading case is *United States* v. *Reynolds*[155] (*Reynolds*), which arose out of the crash of a military aeroplane on a flight to test secret electronic equipment. Three civilian observers aboard were killed and their widows sued the government under the Federal Tort Claims

151. *Coonan* v. *Richardson*, 1947 QWN 19.
152. 1968 AC 910: (1968) 2 WLR 998 (HL). See also, *Burmah Oil Co. Ltd.* v. *Governor and Company of the Bank of England*, 1980 AC 1090: (1979) 3 WLR 722 (HL). The House of Lords did not allow absolute protection even to the Cabinet proceedings.
153. (1977) 1 WLR 473.
154. *Burmah Oil Co. Ltd.* v. *Governor and Company of the Bank of England*, 1980 AC 1090: (1979) 3 WLR 722 (HL). *See also*, Administration of Justice Act, 1970.
155. 1953 SCC OnLine Us SC 26: 97 L Ed 727: 345 US 1 (1953).

Act, 1946. The plaintiffs moved for the production of the Air Force's accident investigation report, but the government claimed privilege and refused to produce the report. The court rejected the view that the assertion of the executive privilege was conclusive on the question of production. It recognised that there are State secrets which need not be disclosed. But, the determination of whether such secrets are involved is a judicial function.

In case of other "official information" not involving State secrets, Rule 228 of the Model Code of Evidence Rules clearly lays down that the disclosure of such information must be made and the alternative for the government is one to the case.

The refusal of the US courts to pass executive privilege to suppress information as conclusive received a striking confirmation in *New York Times Co.* v. *United States*[156], popularly known as the *Pentagon Papers case.* In this case, the US sought an injunction against the *New York Times* and *Washington Post* prohibiting them from publishing the contents of a classified study entitled "History of US Decision-Making Process on Vietnam Policy". The history was prepared within the Defence Department and had been classified as "Top Secret". The government contended that its disclosure would jeopardise national security and national defence. The Supreme Court denied injunction. Though the court was divided 6:3, and each of the justices wrote a separate opinion, one can, nevertheless, identify two broad common formulations: 1) that the Constitution bars any restraint upon newspaper publication, regardless of the nature of material published, except under special circumstances where it would result in direct, immediate and irreparable damage to the nation; and 2) that the "damage to the nation" from the publication is primarily for the executive to determine, and the courts should defer to the executive determination.

The difference in English and American approaches may be due to the theory of separation of powers, in general, and to the judiciary, in particular. For the US Supreme Court, having distinguished *Duncan*[157] in *Reynolds*[158], held:

> But we do not regard the [Duncan] case as controlling in any event. For whatever may be true in Great Britain, the Government of the United States is one of checks and balances. One of the principal checks is furnished by the independent judiciary which the Constitution established. Neither the executive nor the legislative branch of the government may constitutionally encroach upon the field which the Constitution has reserved for the judiciary by transferring to itself the power to decide justiciable questions which arise in cases or controversies submitted to the judicial branch for decision. Nor is there any danger to the public interest in submitting the question of privilege to the decision of the courts. The judges of the United States are public officers whose responsibility under the Constitution is just as great as that of the heads of the executive departments.

156. 29 L Ed 2d 822: 403 US 713 (1971).
157. 1942 AC 624 (HL).
158. 1953 SCC OnLine Us SC 26: 97 L Ed 727: 345 US 1 (1953).

At this point it is pertinent to point out that in the US, there is a legally enforceable right to know. In 1966, the Congress passed the Freedom of Information Act which gives to every citizen a legally enforceable right of access to government files and documents generally. The government cannot refuse information unless it is covered in any of the nine specific exceptions given in the Act. The Indian and English law are diametrically opposed to the US law, because of the prohibitions of the Official Secrets Acts in both the countries.

The power of the court to compel production of the document, for which privilege is claimed by the government, has recently thrown up an interesting issue regarding the possible use of such document by the party which asked for its production. This issue came up before the Supreme Court when the Union Government asked the court to take action against the former additional judge of the Delhi High Court, Mr S.N. Kumar, for contempt. Mr Kumar had filed a suit against the Chief Justice of the Delhi High Court, Mr Prakash Narain, seeking damages worth ₹2 lakhs for defaming him in a letter the Chief Justice wrote to the then Law Minister. The confidential letter had alleged that Mr Kumar probably took bribes, was slow at work, and his conduct was not becoming of a judge.[159] The court had compelled the production of this letter in *S.P. Gupta*[160], popularly known as the *Judges' Transfer case*, at the instance of the plaintiff. The contention of the government was that the letter disclosed at the instance of the court cannot be used for any "collateral" purposes and thereby the government put forward the doctrine of implied undertaking, according to which there is an implied obligation on the party which got the document not to make improper use of it in other proceedings. This doctrine is not in much use in England now. The decision of the court would lay down a new rule in India.[161]

4. IMMUNITY FROM STATUTE OPERATION

The general principle of the common law is that the king is not bound by a statute unless a clear intention appears to that effect from the statute or from the express terms of the Crown Proceedings Act, 1947 or by necessary implication. This principle is based on two well-known maxims: 1) the king can do no wrong; and 2) the king cannot be tried in the courts of his own creation. Applying the same principle in India, the Privy Council held in *Province of Bombay* v. *Municipal Corpn. of Bombay*[162] that the government is not bound by the statute. In this case, the government had agreed to the proposal of the Municipality to lay down water pipes through

159. *Indian Express* 26-10-1982.
160. 1981 Supp SCC 87.
161. The case is still pending before the Supreme Court and, therefore, any comment at this stage is not possible.
162. 1946 SCC OnLine PC 34: AIR 1947 PC 34.

government land. Under the provisions of the City of Bombay Municipal Act, 1888, the Municipality had the power "to carry water mains within and without the city". The question was whether the government was bound by the Municipal Act? The Privy Council answered it in the negative.

Applying the doctrine of English Law, which envisages that the Crown is not bound by its own law unless so bound either expressly or by necessary implication, the Supreme Court held in a much-debated judgment delivered in *Director of Rationing and Distribution* v. *Corpn. of Calcutta*[163] that the State in India is not bound by its own statutes unless they are made applicable to it expressly or by necessary implication. In this case, Section 386(1)(*a*) of the Calcutta Municipalities Act, 1923, as substituted by the later Act 33 of 1951, provided that every person storing rice within the municipal limits can do so only under a licence issued by the Corporation. This measure was adopted to avoid the spread of epidemics through rats. The Director of Rationing and Distribution as representative of the Food Department of the Government of West Bengal, when prosecuted for a violation of this provision, pleaded that the State is not bound by a law of its own creation unless expressly mentioned therein, or by necessary implication extended to it. The Supreme Court, by a majority, held that the common-law principle will be adopted as a rule of interpretation and, therefore, the State shall not be bound by its own statute unless made applicable to it either expressly or by necessary implication. The main criticism of the case was that it engrafted a common-law immunity rule which had its roots in feudalistic society in a democratic and welfare society. The decision also missed the point which even the common-law immunity rule recognises as an exception where the statute is for the public benefit. This was a seven-judge decision wherein Subba Rao J recorded his dissent.

Shortly after this decision, Subba Rao J became the Chief Justice of the Supreme Court and constituted a Bench of 11 judges to reconsider this decision in *Supdt. and Remembrancer of Legal Affairs* v. *Corpn. of Calcutta*[164]. He persuaded eight of his colleagues on the Bench that the English common-law theory "king can do no wrong" was subversive of the rule of law, and that it had been given up in England after the Crown Proceedings Act, 1947, hence, it cannot be permitted under the Indian Constitution. Thus, the earlier case was overruled. In this case, Section 218 of the Calcutta Municipalities Act, 1951 provided that any person carrying on the business of running a market can do so only under a licence issued by the Corporation. The State of West Bengal which was running a daily market was prosecuted for not obtaining a licence under the provisions of the Act. The Supreme Court, overruling its earlier decision, held that the State is bound by its own law unless excluded either expressly or by necessary implication. This case has another message that "Howsoever high you

163. AIR 1960 SC 1355.
164. AIR 1967 SC 997. See also, *State of Madras* v. *ESI Corpn.*, 1965 SCC OnLine Mad 163: AIR 1967 Mad 372.

may be, the law is above you". This message had a great influence on the later course of development of administrative law and on the supremacy of the judiciary in testing the validity of all executive and legislative actions.

This principle was affirmed in *Union of India* v. *Jubbi & Dunia*[165]. In this case, the statute provided that the tenants can acquire proprietary rights in the land by paying compensation to the landowner in the manner laid down in the statute. The question was whether the benefit of this statute can be availed of by tenants holding land owned by the State. The Supreme Court held that the statute binds the State because the State is not excluded from its operation either expressly or by necessary implication.

It is not difficult to ascertain if the State has been expressly exempted from the operation of a statute, but where it has been exempted by "necessary implication", it may pose a problem. Nevertheless, it may be mentioned that in cases where a statute provides for criminal prosecution involving imprisonment, or in cases where a penalty of fine is imposed, the money would go to the same coffer, the State is excluded by necessary implication.

In *State of Maharashtra* v. *Indian Medical Assn.*[166], the Supreme Court came to the conclusion that Section 64 of the Maharashtra University of Health Sciences Act, 1998, which provided that all applications for permission to open a medical college should be routed through the University to the State Government, does not bind the government, if it intends to open a government run medical college. The court pointed out that expression "management" occurring in Section 64 refers to private management and, hence, State is not bound by law by any necessary implication.

5. IMMUNITY FROM ESTOPPEL (PROMISSORY ESTOPPEL)

The doctrine of promissory estoppel is premised on the conduct of the party making a representation to the other, so as to enable him to arrange his affairs in such a manner as if the said representation would be acted upon. The core of the doctrine is "faith of the people" in governance, which has assumed tremendous importance in this era of global economy.[167]

Estoppel is a rule whereby a party is precluded from denying the existence of some state of facts which he had previously asserted and on which the other party has relied, or is entitled to rely on. The doctrine of promissory estoppel has been evolved by courts, on the principle of equity, to avoid injustice. A person who himself misled the authority by making a false statement, cannot invoke this principle, if his representation misled the authority into taking a decision which on discovery of misrepresentation is sought to be cancelled. The doctrine of promissory estoppel applies also to government and public authorities, however, it would yield where equity so

165. AIR 1968 SC 360.
166. (2002) 1 SCC 589.
167. *U.P. Power Corpn. Ltd.* v. *Sant Steel & Alloys (P) Ltd.*, (2008) 2 SCC 777.

demands.[168] Thus, if it is shown that it would be inequitable in larger public interest to hold the administrative authority to its promise, assurance or representation, the court may not invoke the doctrine.[169] "Estoppel" in *Black's Law Dictionary* is indicated to mean that a party is prevented by his own acts from claiming a right to the detriment of the other party, who was entitled to rely on such conduct and has acted accordingly. In other words, the principle of promissory estoppel is that where one party has by his words or conduct made to the other a clear and unequivocal promise or representation, which is intended to create legal solutions or affect a legal relationship to arise in the future, knowing or intending that it would be acted upon by the other party to whom the promise or representation is made, and if in fact so acted upon by the other party, the promise or representation would be binding on the party making it and he would not be entitled to go back upon it, if it would be inequitable to allow him to do so, having regard to the dealings which have taken place between the parties. This doctrine is now well established in the field of administrative law.[170] Section 115 of the Evidence Act, 1872 is also more or less couched in a language which conveys the same expression.[171] However, even where the case does not fall under Section 115, promissory estoppel can still be invoked. A man should keep his words, all the more so when the promise is not a bare promise but is made with the intention that the other party should act upon it.[172] Therefore, a promise intended to be binding, intended to be acted upon, and in fact acted upon is binding.[173] It is now settled that the doctrine of promissory estoppel applies equally to government and public authorities. But it is equally settled that this doctrine cannot be used to compel the government or public authority to carry out a representation or promise which is prohibited by law, or which was beyond the power of the officer making it. It will also not apply to government or public authority if a larger public interest so demands. In order to resist the liability under this doctrine, government or public authority would disclose to the court the various events insisting its claim to be exempt from liability, and it would be for the court to decide whether those events are such as to render it inequitable to enforce the liability against the government or public authority.[174] Judicial behaviour clearly indicated that, in India, estoppel would not be available against the government in violation of a statute. In *Amar Singhji* v. *State of Rajasthan*[175], the Supreme Court refused to apply estoppel against the government where the Collector had given an assurance that

168. *Central Airmen Selection Board* v. *Surender Kumar Das*, (2003) 1 SCC 152.
169. *Union of India* v. *Unicorn Industries*, (2019) 10 SCC 575.
170. *Sharma Transport* v. *State of A.P.*, (2002) 2 SCC 188.
171. *Ashok Kumar Maheshwari* v. *State of U.P.*, (1998) 2 SCC 502.
172. *Ibid.* Lord Denning, "Recent Developments in the Doctrine of Consideration", (1952) 15 Mod LR 5.
173. *Central London Property Trust Ltd.* v. *High Trees House Ltd.*, 1947 KB 130.
174. *Sharma Transport* v. *Govt. of A.P.*, (2002) 2 SCC 188.
175. AIR 1955 SC 504.

the *jagir* of the petitioner would not be acquired during his lifetime under the Rajasthan Land Reforms Act, 1952 because the assurance was in clear violation of the provisions of the statute. In the same manner, in *Mathra Parshad & Sons* v. *State of Punjab*[176] and *Narinder Chand Hem Raj* v. *Lt. Governor, H.P.*[177], the Supreme Court held that estoppel is not available against the government if the representation is in violation of a tax law. The same opinion was reaffirmed in *K. Ramadas Shenoy* v. *Town Municipal Council, Udipi*[178]. The facts of this case were that the Madras Legislature passed the Madras Planning Act, 1945 which marked areas for business and residential purposes. The area marked for residential purposes included social and community hall as well. A person applied for the construction of a social-cum-lecture hall, which was permissible and, therefore, allowed in the residential area. Later, he applied to convert the hall into a picture palace. The Municipality by a resolution allowed the conversion even in the face of Section 15 of the Act, which prohibited any commercial building in the residential area except with the permission of a competent authority under the Madras Town Planning Act, 1920. The defendant started work on the cinema. This was challenged by a resident of the area. Among other grounds, the plea of estoppel was also taken. The court held that the resolution sanctioning the plea for conversion of a lecture hall into a cinema was in violation of the Madras Town Planning Act, 1920 and, therefore, in an excess of statutory power and cannot be validated by the operation of the principle of estoppel. The Supreme Court further remarked that the court declines to interfere for the assistance of persons who seek its aid to relieve them against express statutory provisions.

However, while dealing with the question whether a promise or representation made by the government is against the statute or not, the Supreme Court held that a distinction must be borne in mind between a representation which goes clearly contrary to the mandatory provisions of the statute and a case where only irregularities have been committed.[179]

Judicial behaviour in India further indicates that estoppel cannot be applied against the government if it jeopardises the constitutional powers of the government. In *C. Sankaranarayanan* v. *State of Kerala*[180], as a result of an understanding between the employees and the government, a notification was issued under Article 309 of the Constitution raising the age for retirement, but by a subsequent notification it was brought down to 55 years. Rejecting the contention of estoppel, the court held that the power conferred by Article 309 of the Constitution cannot be curtailed by any agreement. Similarly, in *M. Ramanatha Pillai* v. *State of Kerala*[181],

176. AIR 1962 SC 745.
177. (1971) 2 SCC 747.
178. (1974) 2 SCC 506.
179. *LML Ltd.* v. *State of U.P.*, (2008) 3 SCC 128.
180. (1971) 2 SCC 361.
181. (1973) 2 SCC 650.

the Supreme Court held that a contract appointment will not operate as estoppel against the government acting in a public or sovereign capacity. In this case, the government created the post of Vigilance Commissioner and appointed Sri Pillai for a period of five years. However, the post was abolished before the expiry of this period. The same opinion was reaffirmed with greater vigour in *State of Kerala* v. *Gwalior Rayon Silk Mfg. (Wvg.) Co. Ltd.*[182] [*Gwalior Rayon Silk Mfg. (Wvg.) Co. Ltd.*]. The facts of this case were that the Gwalior Rayon Company established its factory in Kerala with the understanding that the government would supply the raw material, *i.e.* pulp. Later when the government showed its inability to supply the necessary raw material, it entered into an agreement with the company to the effect that the company could purchase its own forest land for drawing raw material and that the government would not interfere with such land for a period of 60 years. Acting on this agreement, the company invested ₹5 lakhs and purchased 30,000 acres of land. Later on, acting in pursuance of a law passed by the State Legislature, the government acquired the land for agrarian reforms before the expiry of 60 years. The Supreme Court summarily dismissed the plea of estoppel against the government on the ground that the government cannot abdicate their legislative powers by mere agreement.

The court also did not allow the plea of estoppel against the government if it had the effect of repealing any provision of the Constitution. In *Mulamchand*[183], the Supreme Court did not apply estoppel against the government in cases of contracts not entered into in accordance with the form prescribed in Article 299 of the Constitution. The court held that if the estoppel is allowed, it would mean the repeal of an important constitutional provision intended for the protection of the general public.

Cases like those depicted in *Gwalior Rayon Silk Mfg. (Wvg.) Co. Ltd.*[184] are not difficult to imagine, where non-application of estoppel against the government creates real hardship for the persons who act on its advice or representation. Therefore, in such situations, the court on the basis of equity may grant relief. The most significant judicial decision in which the strict rule of non-availability of estoppel against the government was relaxed is *Union of India* v. *Indo Afghan Agencies Ltd.*[185]. The facts of this case were that the Textile Commissioner published a scheme of export promotion and represented to the exporters of woollen goods that they would be entitled to import raw material of the total amount equal to 100 per cent of the free on board (FOB) value of exports. In the instant case, the respondent exported goods worth ₹5 lakhs, but the Commissioner issued an import licence for

182. (1973) 2 SCC 713.
183. AIR 1968 SC 1218.
184. (1973) 2 SCC 713.
185. AIR 1968 SC 718. See also, *Municipal Corpn. of the City of Bombay* v. *Secy. of State*, ILR (1905) 29 Bom 580; *Collector of Bombay* v. *Bombay Municipal Corpn.*, 1951 SCC 978: AIR 1951 SC 469.

₹1.99 lakhs only. On the order being challenged, the government took the plea that the scheme is merely administrative in character and, therefore, not binding on the government. The Supreme Court rejected the contention and held that even if the scheme has no statutory force, the government is not entitled to break promises at its whim. The court observed that the government on some undefined and undisclosed ground of necessity or expediency can neither refuse to carry out the promise solemnly made by it, nor it can claim to be the judge of its own obligations to the citizen on an *ex parte appraisement* of the circumstances. However, if the government wants to resile from the promise or assurance on the ground that the concessions promised by it are being misused, it may be allowed to resile from it if the misuse is well established by the government before the court.[186]

The softening of the legalistic attitude of the court under the impact of fairness and justice becomes further evident in *Century Spg. and Mfg. Co. Ltd.* v. *Ulhasnagar Municipal Council*[187]. In this case, the Municipality agreed to exempt existing industrial concerns in the area from octroi duty for a period of seven years. Acting on the representation of the Municipality, the industrial concerns expanded their business. However, later on the Municipality sought to impose duty. This was challenged by the industrial concern. The Supreme Court, while remanding the case to the High Court, held that where a private party has acted upon the representation of a public authority, it could be enforced against the authority on the ground of equity in appropriate cases, even though the representation did not result in a contract owing to the lack of proper form.

The whole law relating to the application of promissory or equitable estoppel against the government was discussed afresh by the Supreme Court in *Motilal Padampat Sugar Mills*[188]. In this case, the appellant was a limited company. On 10 October 1968, a news item appeared stating that the respondent-State had decided to give exemption from sales tax for a period of three years under Section 4-A of the U.P. Sales Tax Act, 1948 to all new industrial units in the State. On 11 October 1968, the appellant wrote to the Director of Industries stating that in view of the sales tax holiday announced by the government, the appellant desired to set up a plant for the manufacture of *vanaspati* and sought confirmation of the exemption. The Director of Industries confirmed the position. An assurance to the same effect was given by the Chief Secretary, Government of Uttar Pradesh. In view of these assurances, the appellant went ahead with the setting up of the factory. In May 1969, the State Government had second thoughts on the question of exemption and requested the appellant to attend a meeting. At the meeting, the appellant's representative reiterated that the respondent-government had already granted exemption from sales tax and that on the basis of the assurance, the appellant had proceeded

186. *CCT* v. *Dharmendra Trading Co.*, (1988) 3 SCC 570.
187. (1970) 1 SCC 582.
188. (1979) 2 SCC 409.

with the work of setting up the factory. The State Government, however, on 20 January 1970, took a policy decision that new *vanaspati* units which went into commercial production by 30 September would be given partial concession of sales tax. The appellant's factory went into production on 2 July 1970, but the State Government once again changed its policy and on 12 August 1970 intimated its decision to rescind the concessions. The High Court dismissed the writ and rejected the plea of promissory estoppel against the government. The Supreme Court, allowing the appeal, held that where one party has by his words or conduct made to the other a clear and unequivocal promise, which is intended to create legal relations or affect a legal relationship to arise in the future, knowing or intending that it would be acted upon by the other party to whom the promise is made, and it is in fact so acted upon by the other party, the promise would be binding on the party making it and he would not be entitled to go back upon it, if it would be inequitable to allow him to do so having regard to the dealings which have taken place between the parties, and this would be so irrespective of whether there is any pre-existing relationship between the parties or not. Of course, the basic requirement for invoking the principle must be present, namely, that the factual situation should be such that "injustice can be avoided only by the enforcement of the promise". Application of the doctrine of promissory estoppel in the area of "tax exemptions" by the government had been the most contested area so far. Elaborating the scope of the doctrine in *Bannari Amman Sugars Ltd.* v. *CTO*[189], the Supreme Court held that no vested interest as to tax exemption is acquired by a person who is granted concession by the government. If any concession is given by the government, it can be withdrawn at any time and no time-limit can be insisted upon for withdrawal. The rule of promissory estoppel, court clarified, can be invoked by an industry if on the basis of representation by the government, the industry was established to avail the benefit of exemption. Though, it is now firmly established that the government can change its policy at any time in public interest which must override private interest, however, withdrawal of representation or promise which induced a person to change his position to his disadvantage must not be arbitrary, unreasonable and must satisfy the requirements of Articles 14 and 19 of the Constitution. Reasonableness is to be determined in an objective manner from the standpoint of public interest. In order to determine the reasonableness of the change of policy, the court will see 1) nature of the right infringed; 2) the underlying purpose of change; 3) the extent of evil sought to be remedied; 4) disproportion of the imposition; and 5) prevailing conditions at a given time. The Supreme Court further elucidated that in order to invoke the doctrine, clear, sound, and positive foundation must be laid by the party invoking the doctrine. Mere assertion would not attract the

189. (2005) 1 SCC 625.

application of the doctrine simply because the party has altered its position relying on government assurance.

The doctrine of promissory estoppel is not really based on the principle of estoppel, but it is a doctrine evolved by equity in order to prevent injustice. There is no reason why it should be given only a limited application by way of defence. It can be the basis of a cause of action.[190]

For attracting the doctrine of promissory estoppel, what is necessary is only that the promisee should have altered his position in relying on the promise. It is not necessary that he should suffer any detriment as well. The law of consideration as applicable in contracts cannot be attracted in this area. No doubt, under English Law, still the doctrine of consideration continues to inhabit the judicial mind which has thwarted the full development of this new equitable principle and realisation of its vast potential as a juristic technique for doing justice.[191]

Thus, the decision of the court in *Motilal Padampat Sugar Mills*[192], which marks a significant development in law relating to the doctrine of promissory estoppel, stands for the propositions: 1) the doctrine could be used as a shield or as a sword; 2) the doctrine is not based on any contract and, therefore, even when a government contract is void for non-compliance with Article 299, the government could still be bound by estoppel; and 3) the doctrine cannot be defeated on the plea of executive necessity or freedom of future executive action.

However, in *Jit Ram Shiv Kumar* v. *State of Haryana*[193], Kailasam J tried to cast some shadow on *Motilal Padampat Sugar Mills*, where he held that the doctrine of estoppel is not available against the exercise of executive function of the State and the State cannot be prevented from exercising its functions under the law.

It is gratifying that this doubt was soon removed by the Supreme Court in *Union of India* v. *Godfrey Phillips India Ltd.*[194], when it held that the law laid down in *Motilal Padampat Sugar Mills* represents the correct law on promissory estoppel. This view was further reinforced in *Express Newspapers (P) Ltd.* v. *Union of India*[195], wherein the doctrine was used to preclude the government from quashing the action of a Minister for approval of a lease as it was within the scope of his authority to grant such permission. Thus, the fraud on the exercise of power was checked.

The same point was further explained by the court in *Delhi Cloth and General Mills Ltd.* v. *Union of India*[196], when it held that alteration in position by acting on the assurance or representation is enough and consequent

---

190. *Motilal Padampat Sugar Mills Co. Ltd.* v. *State of U.P.*, (1979) 2 SCC 409.
191. *Ibid.*
192. *Ibid.*
193. (1981) 1 SCC 11.
194. (1985) 4 SCC 369.
195. (1986) 1 SCC 133.
196. (1988) 1 SCC 86.

detriment, damage or prejudice to the promisee is not to be proved. It is also immaterial whether such representation was wholly or partially responsible for such alteration in the position. The Supreme Court rightly observed that the concept of detriment now is not monetary loss but whether it appears unjust, unreasonable or inequitable that the promisor should be allowed to resile from the assurance or representation, having regard to what the promisee has done or refrained from doing in reliance on the assurance or representation.

Applying the above principles, the Supreme Court in *Bhim Singh* v. *State of Haryana*[197] estopped the government from going back on its promises made to the employees on the basis of which they shifted to another department. The court held that the appellants having believed the representation made by the State and having further acted upon cannot be defeated of their hopes which have crystallised into rights by virtue of the doctrine of promissory estoppel and, therefore, the State is bound to confer such rights and benefits as were promised by it in entirety. Extending the doctrine of promissory estoppel further into the area of service jurisprudence, the Supreme Court in *Surya Narain Yadav* v. *Bihar SEB*[198] held that repeated representations made by the Board to its ex cadre trainee engineers that they would be permanently absorbed and encadered without taking any examinations are binding on the Board because relying on the representation, some trainees did not seek employment elsewhere.

However, as the doctrine of promissory estoppel is an equitable doctrine, it must yield when equity so requires. If it can be shown by the government that, having regard to the facts, as they have transpired, it would be inequitable to hold the government to the promise made by it, the court will not raise an equity in favour of the promisee and enforce the promise against the government.[199] Therefore, if the promise is statutorily prohibited or is against public policy, the court will not enforce it against the government. Thus, the doctrine of promissory estoppel cannot be invoked to enforce a promise contrary to law. Where prescribed mode of recruitment is only through direct recruitment, any promise of appointment by promotion if given by the administrative authority cannot be enforced against it.[200] In the same manner, if the representation made by the government though bona fide but is not legally enforceable, the court would not enforce it. *Amrit Banaspati Co. Ltd.* v. *State of Punjab*[201] is a case on this point. In this case, a brochure had been issued by the Punjab government announcing its "new policy" declaring that incentives, one of them being refund of sales tax, would be available to industrialists who would set up industries in focal points. The question was: Whether the government is bound by

197. (1981) 2 SCC 673.
198. (1985) 3 SCC 38.
199. *Motilal Padampat Sugar Mills Co. Ltd.* v. *State of U.P.*, (1979) 2 SCC 409.
200. *Ashok Kumar Maheshwari* v. *State of U.P.*, (1998) 2 SCC 502.
201. (1992) 2 SCC 411.

promissory estoppel to refund sales tax for a period of three years to the company, which it had already transferred to the consumers and which now cannot be refunded to any individual consumers? The court held that refund of sales tax to the company is statutorily prohibited and against the public policy because being an indirect tax, the company has already collected it from the people which cannot be refunded by the company to individual consumers.

As the doctrine is based on equity or obligations, in certain situations, court has to strike a balance between individual rights and the larger public interest. Since "public interest" is the *suprema lex*, it can override individual equity. Applying this principle, the court in *M.P. Mathur* v. *DTC*[202] allowed the Delhi Transport Corporation (DTC), which had promised transfer of certain tenements owned by it but given to the employees on their retirement, to withdraw from the promise because the tenements were needed to provide accommodation for the existing workforce. Thus, by balancing the equities, the court did not apply the doctrine of promissory estoppel. This proves that an administrative authority can change its policy, at any time, in public interest provided there is no bias, discrimination and arbitrariness. Working on the same equity principle further in *A.P. Steel Re-Rolling Mill Ltd.* v. *State of Kerala*[203], the Supreme Court held that where the party itself neglects to fulfil the conditions necessary under the representation, it cannot claim the application of the doctrine of promissory estoppel against the government. Here the State Government, under its industrial policy, had promised concessional power tariff for a period of five year for industrial units which continued commercial production up to 1996, which the appellant in this case could not do. On the same basis, in *U.P. Power Corpn. Ltd.* v. *Sant Steel & Alloys (P) Ltd.*[204] [*Sant Steel & Alloys (P)Ltd.*], the court applied the doctrine of promissory estoppel against the government which had granted concessions for five years for establishing industries in hill area.

The doctrine of promissory estoppel cannot be availed to permit or condone a breach of law. The doctrine cannot be invoked to compel the government or a private party to do an act prohibited by law. There can also be no promissory estoppel against the exercise of legislative power. The legislature can never be precluded from exercising its legislative functions by reverting to the doctrine of promissory estoppel. Therefore, if the U.P. Sales Tax Act, 1948 did not contain a provision like Section 4-A enabling the government to grant exemption, it would not be possible to enforce the representation against the government because the government cannot be compelled to act contrary to the statute.[205] In the same manner, the court

202. (2006) 13 SCC 706.
203. (2007) 2 SCC 725.
204. (2008) 2 SCC 777.
205. *Ibid.* See also, *Excise Commr.* v. *Issac Peter*, (1994) 4 SCC 104.

held that allotment of land contrary to rules cannot be protected by the doctrine of promissory estoppel.[206]

There seems to be no other reason for excluding the legislature from the operation of promissory estoppel except that the legislature cannot be estopped from exercising its legitimate powers in the public interest.[207] It also implies a presumption, and rightly so, that the legislature always acts in the public interest. If this is the basis of such exclusion, there seems to be no reason why it cannot be invoked in favour of executive policy decisions? The ratio of *Motilal Padampat Sugar Mills*[208] is that the executive cannot be so exempted from the rule of promissory estoppel. In fact, what is needed is not so much the pinning down of the government on its policies because some people have relied on it, as the protection of the people from irresponsible or indifferent bureaucrats who may mislead them in their official dealings,[209] and in this respect the law still requires more rationalisation. This process of rationalisation unfolded itself in *STO* v. *Shree Durga Oil Mills*[210], wherein the Supreme Court held that the government is competent to change its policy in the public interest on such basis as resource crunch and that would be sufficient for non-applicability of the doctrine of promissory estoppel. The fact remains that public interest can always override consideration of private loss or gain. Against this backdrop, the Supreme Court allowed the change in the government's medical reimbursement policy wherein reimbursement had been restricted in case of retired employees.[211]

However, if a right has already been vested, it cannot be divested by an executive action exercised under statutory or executive powers. The doctrine of legitimate expectation would preserve such right. Therefore, if the tax exemption is for a fixed period and conditions for exemption have also been fulfilled, withdrawal of that exemption cannot affect the already accrued right.[212] In this manner, a right can be preserved also by the invocations of the doctrine of promissory estoppel. However, it is subject to the provisions of law to the contrary because application of the doctrine against constitutional or statutory provisions is impermissible in law. The doctrine of legitimate expectation is now considered to be a part of natural justice also. If a person is given to understand that a benefit given would not be taken away without complying with the principles of natural justice, benefit cannot be taken away without complying with the requirements of natural justice.

---

206. *Jalandhar Improvement Trust* v. *Sampuran Singh*, (1999) 3 SCC 494.
207. *State of Kerala* v. *Gwalior Rayon Silk Mfg. (Wvg.) Co. Ltd.*, (1973) 2 SCC 713.
208. (1979) 2 SCC 409.
209. *See*, M.P. Singh, "Estoppel against the Government: Is Equity Running Wild", (1978–79) Delhi Law Rev 154.
210. (1998) 1 SCC 572.
211. *State of Punjab* v. *Ram Lubhaya Bagga*, (1998) 4 SCC 117.
212. *Southern Petrochemical Industries Co. Ltd.* v. *Electricity Inspector & ETIO*, (2007) 5 SCC 447.

The trend in all the important jurisdictions is that the doctrine of promissory estoppel is enforceable against the government. In England, the judicially favoured view is that the Crown is not immune from liability under the doctrine of promissory estoppel.[213] In the US, though there is no express decision of the US Supreme Court regarding the enforceability of this doctrine against the government, however, the trend in the State courts is strongly in favour of application of the doctrine against the government and public bodies, where the interests of justice, morality and common fairness clearly dictate such a course.[214]

In applying this doctrine, no distinction can be made between exercise of a sovereign or governmental function and a trading or business activity of the government. Whatever be the nature of the function which the government is discharging, the government is subject to the rule of promissory estoppel and if the essential ingredients of this rule are satisfied, the government can be compelled to carry out the promise made by it.[215]

Besides the application of promissory estoppel based on equity which creates substantive rights in favour of the person who acts on the representation as to the existing facts or to the future course of conduct, estoppel may also arise against the government under Section 115 of the Evidence Act, 1872 which contains a rule of evidence and relates to existing facts only. In *Union of India* v. *Rasul Ahmed*[216], the court allowed the plea of estoppel against the railway authorities who represented to the consignee that his goods had not been received by the Parcel Office.

The reach of the doctrine of promissory estoppel has now been extended to delegated legislation also. In *Sant Steel & Alloys (P) Ltd.*[217], the Supreme Court held that where an administrative authority issues a notification in exercise of its delegated authority, but has no power to revoke, it cannot be said that an unequivocal promise is not made and hence shall bind the authority. In this age of global economy, faith of the people in the governance is very important. Therefore, court further held that promissory estoppel shall apply where administrative order is repugnant to public morality and arbitrary. In this case, electricity concession granted for establishing industries in hill area for five years had been revoked, court opined that the principle that estoppel does not apply against a statute is not applicable in case of delegated legislation.

In *Manuelson Hotels (P) Ltd.* v. *State of Kerala*[218], the Supreme Court revised the doctrine of promissory estoppel once again. In this case Kerala Government, acting on the recommendations of the Government of India suggesting that tourism be declared an "Industry" and an exemption from

213. *Robertson* v. *Minister of Pensions*, (1949) 1 KB 227.
214. *Orennan* v. *Star Paving Co.*, (1958) 31 Cal 2d 409.
215. *Motilal Padampat Sugar Mills Co. Ltd.* v. *State of U.P.*, (1979) 2 SCC 409, 410–15.
216. 1969 SCC OnLine Ori 31: AIR 1970 Ori 157. See also, *University of Delhi* v. *Ashok Kumar Chopra*, 1967 SCC OnLine Del 155: AIR 1968 Del 131.
217. (2008) 2 SCC 777.
218. (2016) 6 SCC 766.

building tax be provided, amended its Building Tax Act in 1990 and added Section 3-A which provided that the government by notification in the Official Gazette may make exemption from the payment of building tax under the Act. However, no notification under the Act was issued. Further Section 3-A providing for exemption was also deleted in 1993. Nevertheless, acting on the provision of Section 3-A, the appellants began construction of a hotel building which was completed in 1991. The Kerala Government issued a demand notice to the appellants for the payment of building tax which is being challenged on the ground of promissory estoppel against the government. It was contested by the government that since no notification was issued under Section 3-A, Building Tax Act, 1990, the doctrine of promissory estoppel is not attracted. It further argued that Section 3-A was also abolished in 1993, so no statutory provision is available for grant of exemption. Under the direction of Kerala High Court, the matter was required to be decided by a committee constituted by the government which decided against the appellants on the ground that Section 3-A has been omitted. On appeal before the Supreme Court, the main issue involved was whether the appellants can claim exemption from the payment of property tax under the Kerala Building Tax Act, 1975, as amended in 1991 by which Section 3-A was added providing exemption from property tax on the application of the doctrine of promissory estoppel. Answering the issue in the affirmative and allowing the appeal, the Supreme Court held:

1. No matter "taxation" is a sovereign function, but no distinction can be made between the exercise of sovereign or governmental and a trading or business activity of the government so far as the application of the doctrine of promissory estoppel is concerned.
2. Where a government makes a promise or intending that it will be acted upon by the other party to whom the promise is made and who while acting upon it alters its position, the government would be bound by it, notwithstanding that it is not recorded in any formal contract as required by Article 299 of the Constitution. It is enough that the petitioner relied on the promise or representation held out to him and altered his position relying upon such assurance.
3. It is an equity doctrine and therefore contains a degree of flexibility which would render justice to the aggrieved party by the court.
4. Promissory estoppel can be the basis of an independent cause of action in which detriment need not be proved. It is enough that the party has acted upon the representation and altered its position.
5. The court cannot compel the executive to frame rules and issue notification as it would be a violation of the division of powers under the Constitution. In this case the court opined that if the government did not issue the notification under Section 3-A of the amended Act, it is an arbitrary Act and hence of no consequence.

6. The doctrine is based on the foundation that an unconscionable departure by one party from the subject-matter of an assumption which may be of law or fact, present or future and which has been adopted by the other party as the basis of some course of conduct, act or omission, should not be allowed to pass muster.
7. The doctrine of promissory estoppel must yield to overriding public interest which must be so overwhelming that the government is justified in resiling from the promise or representation.

On the basis of facts and circumstances of the case, the court came to the conclusion that for the period Section 3-A was in force no building tax is payable by the appellant. The court, however, did not grant any relief post 1 March 1993 when Section 3-A (granting exemption) was deleted being contrary to the provision of law existing at the relevant time.

In a democratic society, governed by the rule of law, every government which claims to be inspired by ethical and moral values must do what is fair and just to the citizens, regardless of legal technicalities. In this context, the judicial behaviour in the area of estoppel against the government is highly decisive.

The Supreme Court has now identified the following principles which must guide the courts regarding applicability of the doctrine of promissory estoppel against government:[219]

1. There must be clear words or conduct which make an unequivocal promise which is intended to create legal relations or affect a legal relationship to arise in the future, knowing that it will be acted upon by the other party.
2. The doctrine will be applied against government/public body where the interest of justice, morality and fairness so requires. It can also be applied to prevent fraud or manifest injustice.
3. The doctrine cannot be applied against the government or a private party against the provisions of law or public policy.
4. It can be used as a sword and shield both.
5. The doctrine will be applicable where the party has changed or altered its position while acting on the promise. However, it is not necessary for the party to prove damage, detriment or prejudice because of alteration of such promise.
6. The doctrine of promissory estoppel cannot be invoked in abstract. There must be strong supporting material to act upon.
7. It is an equity doctrine and must be used with wisdom and responsibility where reasonableness, fairness and justice demand it.
8. Relief based on promissory estoppel can be denied (*a*) if there is deliberate delay and other factors which make this relief inequitable, (*b*) if such relief is against public interest, (*c*) if reasonable notice formal

219. *Monnet Ispat & Energy Ltd.* v. *Union of India*, (2012) 11 SCC 1.

or informal is given affording other party reasonable opportunity of resuming his position.

6. OTHER PRIVILEGES

Besides the privileges and immunities mentioned above, the government enjoys various other privileges through the medium of statutes. Section 46(2) of the Income Tax Act, 1922 allows precedence to State claims for arrears of income tax over private debts. The Limitation Act, 1963 provides for a longer period of 30 years under Article 112 for government suits. The same Act denies the benefit of Section 6 to a person who has been dispossessed of immovable property against the government. Section 82, CPC makes special provision for the State by laying down that a time shall be specified in the decree within which it shall be satisfied; and if it remains unsatisfied within this period, the court shall report the same for the orders of the government. In the same manner, Rule 5-B of Order 27, CPC casts a duty upon the court to assist in arriving at a settlement in suits against the government, and Rule 8-A of Order 27 provides that no security shall be required from the government.

These privileges and immunities of the government have a social function to perform. These privileges are not so much for the protection of the government as for the benefit of the people. Therefore, an organic and not pedantic approach of interpretation in this area must guide judicial behaviour.

POINTS FOR DISCUSSION

1. Development of the concept of State liability in its historical perspective may be discussed with the aim of evolving a viable principle on which governmental liability in a democratic and welfare state can be based.
2. The real problem with the development of law relating to governmental liability in contracts in India is that the courts try to apply the principles of private law of contracts to the public law area. What new principles of public law of contracts can be suggested on which the liability of the government in contracts can be based in an age of intensive form of government?
3. In the area of governmental liability in India, the principle of sovereign and non-sovereign functions of the State is a justice blasphemy which leads to absurd and arbitrary results. What other principles can be suggested to bring an ideal equilibrium between governmental accountability and individual justice? "Fault theory" and "risk theory" developed by the French Administrative Law may be discussed.
4. Desirability and the efficacy of a comprehensive legislation on governmental liability in torts and contract, and the basic philosophy of such legislation which suits Indian conditions may be discussed.

5. Today when public officers come into contact with private individuals very frequently and at various angles of life, would it not be desirable to allow action by the government for loss of service of its servants? In the light of this fact, the desirability of importing private law action *per quod servitium amisit* into public law be discussed.
6. Krishna Iyer J observed, "A government which revels in secrecy... not only acts against democratic decency but busies itself with its own burial."[220] In the light of this observation, would it be desirable to abolish government privilege to withhold official information except in cases of "State secrets"? Even in this situation who should decide, what is a "State secret"?
7. The application of promissory estoppel against the government is a welcome step, but it is argued that the application of this principle in a developing country like India would dampen a viable governmental initiative and action which is necessary if the lot of the poor masses is to be improved. What should be the correct approach?
8. Is there a justification for applying the doctrine of promissory estoppel to administrative decision making, while exempting legislative decision making on the ground of public interest? What is the solution?
9. Students may discuss the basis of public law of tort on which governmental liability in a welfare society may be based.

SUGGESTED READINGS

1. A.R. Blackshield, "Tortious Liability of Government : A Jurisprudential Case Note", 8 JILI (1966) 643.
2. A.T. Markose and V.D. Sebastian, "Liability of the State in Civil Law" in Law and the Commonwealth (1971) 341.
3. Alice Jacob, "Vicarious Liability of Government in Torts", (1965) 7 JILI 247.
4. B.B. Pande, "Perforating the Escutcheon of Sovereign Immunity", (1974) 2 SCC J-9.
5. B.M. Gandhi, "The Proper Place of Promissory Estoppel", (1986) 3 SCC J-46.
6. Blackshield, "Tortious Liability of Government: A Jurisprudential Case Note", (1966) 8 JILI 643.
7. C.K. Thakker, *Administrative Law* (Eastern Book Company 2012) Chap. II.
8. C.P. Gupta, "A Comment on 'State of Rajasthan v. Vidyawati' ", (1962) 4 JILI 279.
9. Campbell, "Commonwealth Contracts", (1970) 44 Australian LJ 14.
10. Clark, "The Last Word on the Last Word", (1969) 32 Mod LR 142.

220. *Maneka Gandhi* v. *Union of India*, (1978) 1 SCC 248.

11. F.C. Newman, "Should Official Advice be Reliable? Proposals as to Estoppel and Related Doctrines in Administrative Law", (1953) 53 Colum L Rev 374.
12. F.S. Nariman, "Governmental Liability in Civil Law" in Law and the Commonwealth (1971) 361.
13. F.S. Nariman, "The Judiciary and the Role of Pathfinders", (1987) 3 SCC J-1.
14. Friedmann, *Law in a Changing Society* (1959) 371ff.
15. Friedmann, "Public Welfare Offences, Statutory Duties and the Legal Status of the Crown", (1950) 13 Mod LR 24.
16. G.H. Treitel, "Crown Proceedings: Recent Developments", (1957) PL 321.
17. Griffith and Street, *Principles of Administrative Law* (4th Edn.) Chap. VI.
18. H. Street, "State Secrets—A Comparative Study", (1951) 14 Mod L Rev 121.
19. H. Street, "Tort Liability of the State: The Federal Tort Claims Act and the Crown Proceedings Act", (1949) 47 Mich L Rev 341.
20. H.W.R. Wade, "Crown Privilege Controlled at Last", (1968) LQR 171.
21. Hogg, "The Doctrine of Executive Necessity in the Law of Contract", (1970) 44 Australian LJ 154.
22. J.E.S. Simon, "Evidence Excluded by Considerations of State Interest", (1955) Cambridge LJ 62.
23. Jain and Jain, *Principles of Administrative Law*, Chap. XV.
24. Jennings, "Tort Liability of the Administrative Officers", (1937) 21 Minn LR 263.
25. "Liability of the State in Torts", Law Commission of India, First Report (1956).
26. Lord Denning, "Recent Developments in the Doctrine of Consideration", (1952) 15 Mod LR 5.
27. M.G. Cown, "Contracts With the Crown", (1965) Current Legal Problems 153.
28. M.P. Singh, "Estoppel Against the Government; Ist Equity Running Wild", (1978–79) Delhi Law Review 154.
29. Mitchell, *The Contracts of Public Authorities* (1954).
30. P.I. Bell, "Crown Privilege", (1957) Public Law 28.
31. P.S. Nirmal, "Governmental Privilege to Withhold Documents from Courts", (1967) 3 Aligarh Law Journal, 29.
32. R. Berger, *Executive Privilege: A Constitutional Myth* (1974).
33. R. Girish, "Law and Development: Public Procurement Law to ensure transparency and fairness in the procurement by Government", (2015) 5 GJLDP (July) 59.
34. R. Ramchandran, "State of Bihar v. Kripalu Shankar: Contempt is What Contempt Does", (1987) 4 SCC J-41.
35. Redmond, "Notices Before Action", (1964) 37 Australian LJ 316.
36. Richardson, "Incidents of the Crown-Servant Relationship", (1955) 33 Can Bar Rev 424.

37. S.N. Jain, "Some Recent Developments in Administrative Law in India", (1968) 10 JILI 531.
38. Salman Khurshid, "Estoppel Advent", (1981) 3 SCC J-3.
39. Sawer, "Crown Liability in Tort and Exercise of Discretions", (1951) 5 Res Judicata 15, n. 7.
40. Sawer, "Non-Feasance Revisited", (1955) 18 Mod LR 541.
41. Sawer, "Per Quod Servitium Amisit and the Crown Servants", (1956) 30 Australian LJ 387.
42. Sir Thomas Barnes, "The Crown Proceedings Act, 1947", (1948) Can Bar Rev 387.
43. Street, *Governmental Liability* (1953).
44. V.G. James, "Equality in Government Contracts", 32 JILI (1990) 200.
45. V. Ramaseshan, "Promissory Estoppel and State Liability", 31 JILI (1989) 482.
46. V.S. Deshpande, "Common Law Liability of States in India, in Some Aspects of Indian Law Today", (1964) 25 Int'l & Comp LQ Supplementary No. 8.
47. Williams Glanville, *Crown Proceedings* (1948).

CHAPTER 12
Statutory and Non-statutory Public Undertakings

The growth of public undertakings, statutory or non-statutory, is a by-product of an intensive form of government. In order to undertake and fulfil multifarious welfare and service commitments, the government may choose from amongst the various forms of organisation. The government may undertake to accomplish its objectives either through its own department, or through an autonomous statutory corporation, or through a government company registered under the Companies Act, 1956. The choice between the various available alternatives would depend on the policy, purpose and the nature of activity.

Before independence, because of the limited ambit of governmental activity, the growth of public undertakings was negligible. But immediately after independence, a phenomenal burgeoning of public undertakings became evident as a result of the socialistic, welfare and service policies of the government. The directive principles of state policy contained in Article 39(*b*) and (*c*) enjoined the State to direct its policy towards ensuring 1) that the ownership and control of material resources of the community are so distributed as best to subserve the common good; and 2) that the operation of the economic system does not result in the concentration of wealth and means of production to the common detriment. This led to the growth of public undertakings as an instrument for the economic structurisation of the country because in a public body accountability, freedom of action, public purpose and conscience corporate spirit, and concern for the consumer could be legitimately expected. Furthermore, these public bodies could also generate resources much needed for the development of the country. In the beginning, the organisational choice for undertaking any activity was in favour of statutory corporations. The industrial policy statement of 1948 clearly indicated that the management of State enterprises will, as a rule, be through the medium of public corporations. But thereafter, a conspicuous shift favouring governmental companies as the organisational model for State enterprises was in evidence. However, a trend favouring statutory corporations was again visible. The Administrative Reforms Commission in 1967 recommended statutory corporations as a mode for organising governmental commercial activities. It is also in conformity with the provisions of the Constitution because Article 19(6) provides for "the carrying on by the State or by a corporation owned or controlled by the State, of any trade, business, industry or service, whether to the exclusion, complete or partial, of citizens or otherwise". However, with the new policy of "free market economy", the role of the government in economic field through public corporation is bound to diminish.

The process of disinvestment began in 1990s, but the progress is still slow and tardy. Except nine public sector undertakings (PSUs), rest give an image of shattered scaffolding of broken reed due to the reasons of lack of efficiency, political interference, protection from competition, lack of accountability, inward looking attitude, pampered work force and corruption. Certainly, privatisation is also not a magic-wand. It has its own problems of exploitation, consumerism, self-centredness, and lack of social responsibility and standard of professional ethics. Thus, the need for an effective and efficient regulatory role of the State cannot be over emphasised. A strong State shall still be necessary to enforce social justice concerns of society.

1. RELATIVE MERITS AND DEMERITS OF VARIOUS ORGANISATIONAL FORMS OF PUBLIC ENTERPRISES

Statutory public corporations and government companies are preferred to departmental organisations because they obviate the increase in government departments and the proliferation of civil servants. Organisational autonomy of public corporations and governmental companies results in a decline of political interference, delay and red-tapism, which may be rampant in bureaucratic departmental organisations. Government departments also lack initiative and push which is necessary for the success of any commercial activity. Financial autonomy, flexibility and commercial accountability are also not within the easy reach of a departmental organisation.

In some situations, government companies as a mode of organisation of an activity is preferred to statutory corporations, for companies obviate the necessity of rushing in a legislative measure every time a corporation is to be established. In case of companies, a greater amount of flexibility in action is possible as the articles of association of the company can be easily amended. Companies also make collaboration and capital participation more easy.

Statutory corporations have definite advantages over other forms of organisations due to their autonomy, financial and managerial, freedom of action, and commercial accountability.

However, no consistent pattern is visible in the choice of the government from these three forms of organisations. The Railways and Posts and Telegraphs systems are run through departmental organisation, airways are managed through a statutory corporation, and State trading is organised through a government company.

Out of these three forms of organisations, through which governmental functions are exercised, departmental organisation does not present much legal difficulty as regards status of the organisation, rights of the employees, and liabilities of the government because the employees of such an organisation are government servants and the State is liable for contracts and torts to the extent laid down under Articles 299 and 300 of the Constitution. This chapter, therefore, mainly deals with the other two forms of organisations:

(1) Statutory public corporations.
(2) Government companies.

2. STATUTORY PUBLIC CORPORATIONS

In the US, it is an age of independent administrative agencies, regulatory or benefactory, but in India the growth is halting because the government does not want to surrender any of its powers, especially regulatory, to any independent agency and lose the definite political advantage it possesses.

Independent statutory agencies discharging governmental functions pose a constitutional problem also. In India, one of the bases of the Constitution is ministerial responsibility to Parliament, which in its turn is responsible to the people. The independent agencies discharging governmental functions may appear to run counter to this basic norm of a democratic Constitution. But the control which Parliament exercises over such agencies in India makes them responsible and responsive.

2.1 Chief characteristics

A statutory public corporation may be defined as an agency created by an Act of legislature, operating a service on behalf of the government, but as an independent legal entity with funds of its own and largely autonomous in management.

Because a public corporation is a hybrid organisation combining features of a government department and a business company, it is difficult to lay down its basic characteristics with exactitude. However, the following points may be noted:

(1) Statutory corporation is a creature of a statute which lays down its rights, duties and obligations. Therefore, a corporation can have those rights and exercise those functions only which are authorised by the statute, either expressly or by necessary implication, provided it is not expressly prohibited. Actions of a corporation outside the authorised area of operation are ultra vires and cannot bind the corporation. Such ultra vires acts cannot be ratified and the doctrines of estoppel or acquiescence do not apply in such cases.

(2) It has a separate legal entity and, therefore, can sue or be sued in its corporate name. It can hold and dispose of property by such name.
(3) Depending on the provisions of the statute of its creation, a corporation is largely autonomous in finance and management. It has funds of its own.
(4) It operates an activity on behalf of the government which may be regulatory, benefactory, commercial or developmental.
(5) The statute may delegate rule-making power to a corporation; such rules and regulations are binding if they are within the authority, made in the manner laid down by the statute and do not violate any provision of the Constitution.
(6) A statutory corporation is a "State" within the definition of the term in Article 12 of the Constitution, and therefore, is subject to the writ jurisdiction of the Supreme Court and High Courts under Articles 32 and 226 of the Constitution.

The logical deduction from this, therefore, is that fundamental rights can be claimed against a corporation.[1] Mandamus would also lie against the corporation to enforce a statutory or public duty.

Whether other public undertakings such as government companies and registered bodies are "State" or not within the meaning of Article 12 would depend on the question whether they are "agency or instrumentality" of the State. If a public undertaking is an agency or instrumentality of the State, then it will be a "State" under Article 12 and, hence, writ jurisdiction of the court shall be extended to it. Private corporations are not "State" within the scope of Article 12 and, hence, are not within the gravitational orbit of the writ jurisdiction of the courts unless these are operating in public space and discharging public functions.

(7) However, a corporation is not a citizen within the meaning of Part II of the Constitution and, therefore, is outside the purview of the Citizenship Act, 1955, which lays down in Section 2 that the word "person" shall not include any company, association or body of persons whether incorporated or not. On this basis, whether a statutory corporation can claim fundamental rights given in Article 19, which are available only to a citizen, is a curious question. The law in this behalf is in a nebulous state. In *State Trading Corpn. of India Ltd.* v. *CTO*[2] and *TELCO Ltd.* v. *State of Bihar*[3], the Supreme Court held that a corporation was not a citizen within the comprehension of Article 19 and, therefore, could not complain of denial of fundamental freedoms guaranteed by Article 19 to a citizen. However, a different note was struck in *Rustom Cavasjee Cooper* v. *Union of*

1. *Rajasthan SEB* v. *Mohan Lal*, AIR 1967 SC 1857; *Ramana Dayaram Shetty* v. *International Airport Authority of India*, (1979) 3 SCC 489.
2. AIR 1963 SC 1811.
3. AIR 1965 SC 40.

India[4], when the Supreme Court held that jurisdiction of the court cannot be denied when by the State action the right of the individual shareholder is impaired, if that action impairs the right of the company as well. In this case, the court entertained the petition under Article 32 of the Constitution at the instance of a director and shareholder of a company and granted relief. These two conflicting trends were noticed by the court in *Bennett Coleman & Co.* v. *Union of India*[5]. Keeping these divergent trends in view, the highest Bench in *Delhi Cloth and General Mills Co. Ltd.* v. *Union of India*[6] favoured the trend in the direction of holding that in the matter of fundamental freedom guaranteed by Article 19, the company can maintain a petition for the reason that the rights of a shareholder and the company which the shareholders have formed are rather co-extensive, and the denial to one of the fundamental freedoms would be denial to the other. This case arose out of a group of writ petitions under Article 32 and appeals by special leave challenging the constitutional validity of Rule 3-A of the Companies (Acceptance of Deposits) Rules, 1975. Overruling the preliminary objection that the petitions are not maintainable because the incorporated company not being a citizen is not entitled to claim the fundamental right under Article 19(1)(*g*), the highest Bench admitted the petitions. Beneath this controversy, whether a company can claim the fundamental rights under Article 19, lies the unending battle between the forces of public control and the individual economic freedom and, therefore, the law must hold the balance even to protect the economic health of society. There is no controversy that a statutory corporation can claim the benefit of Articles 14 and 16 of the Constitution. It is significant to note that the Law Commission of India in its 101st Report has recommended an amendment to the Constitution for making fundamental rights under Article 19(1)(*a*) available to those corporations and other entities which are not regarded as natural persons, provided they are engaged in communication business.

(8) A public undertaking is subject to Article 14 of the Constitution, and thus not entitled to deny any person equality by its treatment. Quashing the differential revised tariff rate laid down by the *Orissa State Electricity Board in Kartik Enterprise (P) Ltd.* v. *Orissa SEB*[7] [*Kartik Enterprise (P) Ltd.*], the court ruled that the Board is to so adjust its treatment that ultimately no inequality resulted.

(9) Without the statutory immunity, the activities of a corporation are liable to tax. It is considered an "assessee" under the Income Tax Act, 1961 and a "dealer" under the Central Sales Tax Act, 1956.

4. (1970) 1 SCC 248.
5. (1972) 2 SCC 788.
6. (1983) 4 SCC 166.
7. 1979 SCC OnLine Ori 162: AIR 1980 Ori 3.

(10) Statutory corporations cannot enjoy the privilege of the government to withhold documents. Though there is no decision of the court on this point, yet there seems to be no rationale in extending the privilege of the government to a corporation which, by and large, undertakes regulatory or benefactory or commercial functions.

(11) Public enterprises are owned by the people and the persons who manage them are accountable to the people. In order to enforce this principle of accountability, the Supreme Court has broadened the doctrine of locus standi. Therefore, if the sale of the property of any public corporation is "unjust, unfair and mala fide", the workers shall have right to challenge it under Article 32 or 226 of the Constitution.[8] In *Fertiliser Corpn. Kamgar Union* v. *Union of India*[9], the highest Bench was faced with the question whether the labour union of the Fertiliser Corporation had locus standi to challenge the sale of old plants by the corporation. Though the Supreme Court dismissed the petition because it found nothing wrong with the sale of old machinery, yet broadening the doctrine of locus standi, the Chief Justice observed:

> But, in an appropriate case, it may become necessary in the changing awareness of legal rights and social obligations to take a broader view of the question of locus [standi], to initiate a proceeding, be it under Article 226 or under Article 32 of the Constitution. If public property is dissipated, it would require a strong argument to convince the court that representative segments of the public or at least a section of the public which is directly interested and affected would have no right to complain of the infraction of public duties and obligations.[10]

(12) Continuing their efforts of broadening the horizons of socialism in India, the Supreme Court showed great sensitivity to the rights of the workers in *National Textile Workers' Union* v. *P.R. Ramakrishnan*[11]. In this case, the question before the court was whether the workers of a company have a right to participate in the winding-up proceedings before a court of law? Curiously enough, the Companies Act, 1956 though it provides that a winding-up order shall be deemed to be a notice of discharge to the employees of the company, yet it does not give workers a right to participate in the winding-up proceedings unless they fall within the categories of creditors or contributaries. The decision of the highest Bench in this area of high socio-economic visibility granted workers the right to appear not only at the hearing of the winding-up proceedings, but also to appear and be heard both before the winding-up petition is admitted and an order for advertisement is made. The workers were further allowed entitlement to

8. M.P. Jain, *Changing Face of Administrative Law in India and Abroad* (1982) 37–38.
9. (1981) 1 SCC 568.
10. *Fertiliser Corpn. Kamgar Union* v. *Union of India*, (1981) 1 SCC 568.
11. (1983) 1 SCC 228.

prefer an appeal and contend that no winding-up order should have been made by the Company Judge, including the right to be heard in the matter of the appointment of a provisional liquidator.[12] The majority decision is based on the ground that the company does not belong to the proprietors alone, it equally belongs to the workers who contribute their labour to it, hence they are equal partners. The court further reasoned that no valid winding-up proceeding can take place unless the workers are given an opportunity to be heard because it is going to cost workers their very means of livelihood.[13] However, Venkataramiah J, in his dissenting opinion, asserted that the workers have no hand at all in any economic enterprise.[14] Commenting on this causa celebre, Prof. Upendra Baxi thought-provokingly writes, "The minority view ignores Marx and the majority view distorts it. Perhaps some day even our Justices would learn that even what they call capital is nothing but accumulated, frozen and congealed labour."[15]

In another pace-setting decision, the Supreme Court held that the wages of workers have first priority and must be paid before the company paid its other liabilities. Thus, the court directed Rohtas Industries to sell its stocks and pay wages to the workers. Categorically rejecting the argument of the financial institutions that as the stocks are pledged with them, so they have priority over it, the court held that no matter banks in law have priority, yet it could not be disputed that these stocks were the products of the hard work of the labour without which no stock could have been produced hence, it is they who must have priority.[16]

2.2 Classification of statutory public corporations

No conventional pattern has been followed in the establishment of statutory corporations. They have grown like mushrooms in the rainy season. However, they may be classified as follows:

(1) *Commercial and Financial*: Corporations which carry on a business or discharge public service on commercial lines. In this category one may include the Air India Corporation, Indian Airlines Corporation, Industrial Finance Corporation, Road Transport Corporations, Life Insurance Corporation, Reserve Bank of India, etc.

(2) *Social*: This classification includes those corporations which undertake welfare activities of the State; for example, the Employees' State Insurance Corporation.

12. *See*, U. Baxi, "Pre-Marxist Socialism and the Supreme Court of India", (1983) 4 SCC J-3.
13. *Per* Bhagwati J. *See*, *National Textile Workers' Union* v. *P.R. Ramakrishnan*, (1983) 1 SCC 228, 244–49. As an astute legal craftperson, he reaches the decision through constitutional mandate in Art. 43-A added by the Constitution (42nd Amendment), 1976.
14. See, *National Textile Workers' Union* v. *P.R. Ramakrishnan*, (1983) 1 SCC 228, 280.
15. *See*, U. Baxi, "Pre-Marxist Socialism and the Supreme Court of India", (1983) 4 SCC J-3,13.
16. *Workers* v. *Rohtas Industries Ltd.*, (1987) 2 SCC 588.

(3) *Commodity*: Under this classification, one may include those corporations which besides regulation, primarily undertake the function of development of a commodity, such as the Oil and Natural Gas Commission, Tea, Coffee and Silk Boards.

(4) *Developmental*: Developmental corporations are those which undertake the developmental work in the country. The Damodar Valley Corporation may be cited as an illustration. This corporation was established under the Damodar Valley Corporation Act, 1948 to control floods and utilise water for irrigation, power, etc.

This classification is not watertight and at various points it may overlap. For example, Tea and Coffee Boards may be classified as commodity, commercial and developmental.

2.3 Liability in tort and contracts

Statutory corporations can be sued for the torts committed by its servants, provided the act is within the powers and the purpose of the corporation and is such that it would be actionable if committed by a private individual. Therefore, the corporation would not be liable if the act of the servant is ultra vires the powers of the corporation, or is such that it could under no circumstances have authorised its servants to commit it. However, the servant would be personally liable for such ultra vires acts. The authority emanating from the corporation cannot be implied if the act is outside the authority of the corporation. The extent of liability of the corporation for the torts committed by its servants will be the same as that of a private person, unless circumscribed by the statute. The statute may exclude liability for acts done by its servants in good faith under the Act, or it may limit the liability to pay compensation from the corporate fund for the torts committed by its servants.

In a unique exercise of substantive judicial activism, the Supreme Court in *M.C. Mehta* v. *Union of India*[17] held that the exceptions to the rule of strict liability as laid down in *Rylands* v. *Fletcher*[18] (*Fletcher*) do not apply to Indian situations and, hence, the liabilities of industries engaged in hazardous or dangerous activities is absolute, even when the injury occurs on account of an accident in such activities. The rule of *Fletcher*[19] laid down a principle of liability that if a person who brings on to his land and collects and keeps anything likely to do harm and such thing escapes and does damage to another, he is liable to compensate for the damage caused. However, this rule does not apply to things which escape either due to an act of God (accident), or an act of a stranger (sabotage). The Supreme Court emphasised that this exception has no application in a present-day highly-industrialised society and in consistence with the constitutional

17. (1987) 1 SCC 395.
18. (1868) LR 3 HL 330 (HL).
19. *Ibid*.

norms in India. Thus, making the rule of strict liability absolutely strict, the court observed that an enterprise which is engaged in hazardous or inherently dangerous industry owes an absolute liability to the community to conduct its affairs with the highest standards of safety and to compensate if harm is caused to anyone due to an accident.

In such cases of compensation, it is very natural for the industry to plead financial incapacity to pay compensations. Commenting on this attitude, the court held that if the enterprise is permitted to carry on hazardous or inherently dangerous activity for profit, the law must presume that such permission is conditional on the enterprise absorbing the cost of any accident as an appropriate item of overheads. However, balancing private and public rights in such cases, the court observed that the measure of compensation must be correlated to the magnitude and capacity of the enterprise because such compensation must have a deterrent effect. It may be recalled that in this case oleum gas had escaped from Shriram Chemical and Fertiliser Company, Delhi causing injury to people.

Yet in another pace-setting judgment, the Supreme Court ordered the prosecution of the Chairman and eight directors of the Modi Industries for discharging highly noxious and polluted trade affluents from Modi Distillery into the Kali river and, thus, set an important precedent on the question of liability of industry for pollution. In this case, the U.P. Pollution Board had sought to prosecute Modi Industries. Though the lower court had granted prosecutions, yet the Allahabad High Court reversed the decision on the technical ground that only the Distillery Unit is to be prosecuted and not the industrial group. Reversing the decision, the Supreme Court stated that every person who at the time of the commission of the offence was in charge of and responsible to the company for the conduct of the business of the company as well as company itself shall be deemed to be guilty of the offence and shall be liable to be prosecuted. The import of the judgment is that the directors and also the parent company, in such instances, cannot escape liability for the actions of its subsidiaries.[20]

A corporation can sue for the torts committed by any person against it. It can maintain an action for libel or slander if it adversely affects its business.[21] However, it cannot sue for torts which are personal in nature, like assault or personal defamation.

Statutory corporations can also incur criminal liability. Corporations have been held to be liable for offences committed by its servants who are the organs of the corporation.[22] The liability even extends to offences involving mens rea, such as libel,[23] fraud,[24] and public nuisance[25]. However,

20. For full details see, *Indian Express*, Chandigarh 10-8-1987, 6.
21. *South Hetton Coal Co. Ltd.* v. *North Eastern News Assn. Ltd.*, (1894) 1 QB 133 (CA).
22. *R.* v. *ICR Haulage Ltd.*, 1944 KB 551 (CCA).
23. *Triplex Safety Glass Co. Ltd.* v. *Lancegaye Safety Glass (1934) Ltd.*, (1939) 2 KB 395 (CA).
24. *South Hetton Coal Co. Ltd.* v. *North-Eastern News Assn. Ltd.*, (1894) 1 QB 133 (CA).
25. *R.* v. *Great North England Railway Co.*, (1846) 9 QB 315.

since it possesses only a corporate identity, it cannot be punished with death or imprisonment. It naturally follows that a corporation cannot be found guilty of an offence for which the prescribed punishment is death or imprisonment. A corporation can also not be found guilty of offences which can be committed by natural persons alone; for example, bigamy.

A corporation can enter into a contract and can sue or be sued for the breach thereof. However, any contract made by it beyond its powers is void, and the corporation incurs no liability. A corporation cannot divest itself of its statutory powers or fetter itself in the exercise of such power by entering into a contract. It cannot also fetter its free exercise of discretion by any contract.

The requirements of a valid government contract as laid down in Article 299 of the Constitution do not apply to corporation contracts. However, if any requirement for a valid contract has been laid down by the rules of the corporation or the statute, it must be complied with.

The requirement of two months' notice as laid down under Section 80 of the Civil Procedure Code, 1908 before filing a suit against the government does not apply to statutory corporations.

2.4 Status of the employees

The employees of the corporation are appointed by the corporation. Their terms and conditions of service are regulated by the rules and regulations framed by the corporation, though in some cases a corporation may adopt the rules which govern the service of government servants. Therefore, employees of the corporation are not government servants and, consequently, not entitled to the protection of Article 311 of the Constitution.[26] Nevertheless, because the protection of Part III of the Constitution applies to such employees, therefore, the distinction sought to be drawn between the protection of Article 311 and Part III has no significance. The fact remains that the employment in public sector has grown to vast dimensions, and employees of the public sector often discharge onerous duties as civil servants and participate in activities vital to a country's economy. It is, therefore, right that the integrity and independence of those employed in the public sector be secured as much as the independence and integrity of civil servants.[27]

However, where the undertaking is not an independent statutory authority but merely a limb of the government, its employees would be government employees. Thus, in *Jaswant Singh* v. *Union of India*[28], the Supreme Court ruled that the persons employed by the Beas Construction Board are government servants entitled to the protection of Article 311.

26. *S.L. Agarwal* v. *Hindustan Steel Ltd.*, (1970) 1 SCC 177.
27. *A.L. Kalra* v. *Project and Equipment Corpn. of India Ltd.*, (1984) 3 SCC 316.
28. (1979) 4 SCC 440.

If the employee of a corporation is subject to the control of the government by way of appointment and removal, he will be deemed to be holding an "office of profit" under the government as to incur disability under Article 102 or 191 of the Constitution and cannot be a Member of Parliament (MP) or the legislature. But in other cases, where the services are not so regulated, an employee of the corporation will not be deemed to be holding an "office of profit"[29].

Being subject to the provisions of the statute and the rules and regulations framed thereunder, an employee of a corporation does not enjoy a "status". His services are purely contractual. Therefore, if an employee of a corporation has been wrongfully dismissed, he cannot claim reinstatement but damages only.[30]

However, in *Sukhdev Singh* v. *Bhagatram Sardar Singh Raghuvanshi*[31], the Supreme Court held that statutory regulations passed by statutory corporations give its employees a statutory status. An ordinary individual in a case of master and servant relationship enforces breach of contractual terms by damages because personal services are not capable of enforcement. In case of statutory bodies, there is no personal element whatsoever because of the impersonal character of statutory bodies.

The employees of public corporations have also been allowed the benefit of industrial laws, especially in the case of wage fixation.[32]

Are the employees of a corporation "public servants" within the meaning of Section 21 of the Penal Code, 1860 (IPC)? The law is not clear on the point. However, the definition is wide enough to cover the employees of a statutory corporation. Sometimes the statute itself may confer the status of "public servants" on its employees.[33] In a questionable ruling, the Supreme Court held that a member of the Indian Administrative Service, whose services are placed at the disposal of the Super Bazaar, a cooperative store, is not a public servant within the meaning of Section 21(2), IPC for the purposes of Section 197 of the Criminal Procedure Code, 1973. Accordingly, the store as well as the manager thereof can be prosecuted under the Prevention of Food Adulteration Act, 1954 without the sanction of the Central Government. The ruling becomes questionable because even in view of the fact that the government holds more than 97 per cent shares in the Super Bazaar and holds power to appoint and remove administrative staff, the court held that Super Bazaar is not the "instrumentality of the State"[34]. Even if the statute creating public corporations confers on its

29. *Bibhuti Bhusan Ghosh* v. *Damodar Valley Corpn.*, 1952 SCC OnLine Cal 271 AIR 1953 Cal 581.
30. *Indian Airlines Corpn.* v. *Sukhdeo Rai*, (1971) 2 SCC 192.
31. (1975) 1 SCC 421.
32. *Hindustan Antibiotics Ltd.* v. *Workmen*, AIR 1967 SC 948.
33. S. 56, Damodar Valley Corpn. Act, 1948.
34. *S.S. Dhanoa* v. *MCD*, (1981) 3 SCC 431. *See also*, M.P. Jain, "Administrative Law", (1981) 17 ASIL 528. This decision is not consistent with *Ajay Hasia* v. *Khalid Mujib Sehravardi*, (1981) 1 SCC 722.

employees the status of public servants, they cannot acquire the status of civil servants. It also makes no difference if such corporations adopt the fundamental rules to govern the service conditions of its employees.

2.5 Control of statutory corporations

Since statutory corporations discharge public functions and use public money as capital, the need for public control over the functioning of the corporations cannot be overemphasised. Such control may be exercised through Parliament, government and the court.

2.5.1 *Parliamentary control*

Parliamentary control is implied in statutory corporations as they owe their origin and continued existence to a statute passed by Parliament. Therefore, initial control is exercised at the time when the Bill proposing the creation of a statutory corporation is introduced for discussion in the House. Members can discuss every organisational, financial and functional aspect of the corporation.

Members can discuss the functioning of corporations by asking questions, moving resolutions and motions in the House. In this manner, Parliament ensures public accountability of the corporations.

Parliamentary control may also be exercised through the technique of "laying". Sometimes, the statute creating a corporation may prescribe that the rules, regulations, financial statements and audit report be laid on the table of the House. This provides an opportunity for Parliament to scrutinise the functioning of a corporation. The laying of the rules and regulations may be subject to either affirmative or negative resolution. The Air Corporations Act, 1953 provides that rules made by the Central Government shall be laid before both the Houses, as soon as may be, after they are made.

However, this general control over the functioning of statutory corporations exercised by Parliament is not very effective; because either the members lack the technical skill needed to scrutinise the rules and regulations framed, and financial and audit statements prepared, or they are indifferent because of their preoccupation with "politics" in the popular sense of the term.

The real and effective parliamentary control is exercised through committees of Parliament. Before 1964, the Estimates Committee and the Public Accounts Committee were doing the work of scrutinising the functioning of corporations. But in 1964, on the recommendation of the Menon Committee, a separate committee known as the Committee on Public Undertakings was established for this purpose. It consists of 15 members, 10 from the Lok Sabha and 5 from the Rajya Sabha. A Minister cannot be its member. It is appointed for a period of one year. Its functions include the examination of reports and accounts of the corporations and the report of the Comptroller and Auditor General on Public Undertakings. It also undertakes the examination of the entire working of the corporations to find out if the affairs of the corporations are being conducted in accordance with the policy of the government and the rules of commercial accountability. Though the functions of the committee are advisory, yet they go a long way in informing the mind of the MPs and, thus, making parliamentary control effective.

2.5.2 *Government control*

In order to ensure that the affairs of statutory corporations are conducted in the best interests of society, a general governmental control over the working of the corporations is highly desirable. However, general control does not mean governmental interference in the day-to-day working of the corporations, which is highly destructive of the idea of autonomy necessary for the success of any commercial or service undertaking. The governmental control is not uniform or in any set pattern over all statutory corporations. The nature and the extent of control depends on the provisions of the statute creating the corporations. However, the techniques of control may take any of the following shapes or a combination of these.

2.5.2.1 *Power of dissolution, removal and appointment*

The statute creating the corporation may provide for the appointment and removal by the government of the authority managing the affairs of the corporation. The Reserve Bank of India Act, 1934 lays down that the Governor of the Bank shall be appointed by the government and may be removed by them.

Going a step further, the statute may also provide that the government shall have the power to dissolve the corporation. The Tea Act, 1953 and the Coffee Act, 1942 contain such a provision. This gives ample power to the government to ensure that the corporation functions according to the policy of the government and in the best interests of society.

2.5.2.2 *Power to issue directions*

The statute may provide that the government shall have the power to issue directions to the corporation. This is done to ensure that the affairs of the corporation are conducted in accordance with the policy pattern of the government. These directions may be specific or general, mandatory or directory, depending on the provisions in the statute. The Delhi Transport Undertaking Act empowers the government to issue specific directions on such matters as wages and terms and conditions of service of the employees. On the other hand, the Tea Act, 1953 makes provisions for the issuance of general directions, but it is obligatory on the Board to follow them. In the same manner, Section 34 of the Air Corporations Act, 1953 authorises the Central Government to give directions to either of the corporations relating to the exercise of its functions, and the corporations shall be bound to give effect to these directions.

The purpose of directions as a technique of governmental control can prove beneficial only if these directions do serve only as directions to the corporation. If the government, through directions, interferes with the day-to-day functioning of the corporation, it would be a self-defeating technique.

2.5.2.3 *Power to control finances*

Financial control provides teeth to governmental control over the affairs of the corporation. Financial control may adorn various shapes depending on the terms of the statute.

Sometimes the whole capital of the corporation may be provided by the government. For example, the total capital of the Life Insurance Corporation is provided by the government. However, at times, the statute may invest the government with the power to control capital formation, borrowings and expenditure. The statute establishing Hindustan Steel Ltd. requires prior approval of the government in case of increase of capital, reduction of capital, and consolidation or division of share capital. The Damodar Valley Corporation Act, 1948 makes provision for the approval of the government in case of borrowings and capital investment. The Air Corporations Act, 1953 provides for control of expenditure by the government. The Act provides for the prior approval of the government for incurring capital expenditure over ₹15 lakhs, or for disposing of property, right or privilege exceeding ₹10 lakhs. Section 36 of the same Act further requires the corporation to submit to the government a statement of their programmes of development and operation at least three months before the commencement of the financial year.

The statute may further provide for audit by the Auditor General or an auditor appointed by the government. The statute may also invest the government with the power to call for the budget, accounts and annual report of the corporation.

2.5.2.4 *Power to institute enquiries*

The statute may empower the government to institute enquiries into the working of the corporation under certain circumstances. This provides sufficient deterrent against any deviation from the norms of public functioning. The Delhi Transport Undertaking Act invests government with such powers.

2.5.3 *Judicial control*

As discussed earlier, a statutory corporation is a "State" within the meaning of Article 12 of the Constitution and is, therefore, subject to the writ jurisdiction of the Supreme Court and the High Courts.[35] A corporation can sue and be sued like any ordinary person. It is liable for the torts committed by its servants and is also liable for damages in case of breach of contract. If a corporation is to discharge a public or statutory duty, mandamus would lie for the enforcement of such duty. In *Corpn. of Nagpur* v. *Nagpur Electric, Light & Power Co. Ltd.*[36], the writ of mandamus was issued against a public utility undertaking to compel it to supply electricity to the corporation. In matters of suit, the statutory corporation is not entitled to any of the privileges and immunities of the State. Fundamental rights can be claimed against a statutory corporation; therefore, in case of a breach of fundamental rights, the Supreme Court or a High Court can exercise its jurisdiction whenever necessary for the ends of law and justice. Courts can also control the actions of the corporation in cases of lack of jurisdiction, excess of jurisdiction, and abuse of jurisdiction at the instance of any person who is adversely affected by such actions.

In *Kartik Enterprise (P) Ltd*[37], the court made a significant observation which may herald a new era of judicial control of public undertakings. In this case, the Orissa State Electricity Board had increased electricity rates for various categories of consumers. While challenging the increased tariff, the petitioners made a unique contention. They argued that the statute casts an obligation on the Board to operate efficiently and economically, therefore, tariff cannot be enhanced unless the corresponding obligations are fulfilled. The court held that "without the corresponding obligation to act efficiently and economically, the Board is not intended to exercise the power to adjust its tariff. We cannot accept a situation where the State or any of its instrumentalities would have power without any correlative duty to exercise such powers...." It was made amply clear that if other control mechanisms (legislative and executive) fail, the judicial control has to be operative. This bold judicial behaviour shall instil a sense of responsibility in public undertakings, many of which are not functioning efficiently and indulge in a lot of wastage.[38]

Courts have never hesitated in quashing the actions of corporations it found to be illegal, arbitrary, unreasonable or discriminatory. Even in the case of grant of largess, jobs, contracts, and issuance of quota and licences, courts have held that the corporations have to act in accordance with the provisions of law.[39] Apart from enforcing statutory regulations

35. See, *Ramana Dayaram Shetty* v. *International Airport Authority of India*, (1979) 3 SCC 489.
36. 1958 SCC OnLine Bom 21: AIR 1958 Bom 498.
37. 1979 SCC OnLine Ori 162: AIR 1980 Ori 3.
38. *Idid*, 9.
39. *Ramana Dayaram Shetty* v. *International Airport Authority of India*, (1979) 3 SCC 489.

and granting relief in case of breach thereof by invoking the provisions of Articles 14 and 16, the courts have declared as unconstitutional the rules and regulations framed by the corporation if found to be illegal, arbitrary and unreasonable.[40] No matter the court is not a competent authority to examine entrepreneurial activities, but in exercise of their constitutional obligation, the courts have never hesitated to interfere if there is a breach of the broad parameters of fairness in the administration, bona fides in action, and the fundamental rules of reasonable management of public business.[41]

2.5.4 *Public control*

Civil servants, corporations, and companies are instrumentalities of the State to undertake various programmes for the benefit of the people. Therefore, it is highly desirable that these instrumentalities must respond to the need and the opinion of the people. It is no denying the fact that the indirect responsibility of these agencies to the public through their elective representatives is marginal and superficial, and the direct responsibility is non-existent because public opinion is uninformed and unorganised. However, effective public control over these agencies may be exercised through the following channels.

2.5.4.1 *Mass media*

Mass media in any free society not only reflects public opinion but also creates public opinion by informative and investigative journalism. Therefore, by exposing political interference, bureaucratic red-tapism, corruption and inefficiency, mass media can go a long way in making these agencies respond to the need of public interest. Sometimes, a single newspaper can influence public bodies' policies and actions by discovering and publishing facts which embarrass or discredit the government and its agencies. In India, this control mechanism is highly weak and sterile because television and radio are government departments and the press is largely dependent on the government for financial assistance (in the form of advertisements) and newsprint and other assistance. The approach of the Indian Press is highly simplistic and the era of investigative journalism is yet to begin. Instances of use of informal means to influence the press through quiet phone calls and unofficial approach are also not wanting, leaving aside the cases of open show of threats. Under these and various other constraint parameters, the mass media in India has not been able to establish its role of exercising control over the affairs of public bodies in the public interest.

40. *Central Inland Water Transport Corpn.* v. *Brojo Nath Ganguly*, (1986) 3 SCC 156.
41. *Fertiliser Corpn. Kamgar Union* v. *Union of India*, (1981) 1 SCC 568.

2.5.4.2 *Consumer organisations and councils*

These organisations may either be established under a statute or be organised on a voluntary basis in the form of unions. In Western countries consumers are well-informed and organised, therefore their organisations provide an effective check on the planning, policies and actions of public bodies. In the US, on various occasions, the corporations had to bring down the prices of their commodities because consumer organisations decided not to purchase their products. Through such organisations, consumers also ventilate their grievances and make their views known to the corporations. In England, consumer councils have been established in the electricity, gas and coal industries under a statute.[42] In India, this control is most feeble, partly because the consumer is unorganised and partly because we have still to learn to work in groups. It is desirable that some pattern of consumer consultative machinery must be evolved for every public undertaking.

It is heartening to note that the first panel discussion on distributive trade, held under the auspices of the Federation of Indian Chambers of Commerce and Industry, recommended the setting up of an autonomous organisation—comprising representatives of trade, industry and consumers with close association of technologists, scientists and media-men—to look after the consumers in the country. The consensus was that India needed a strong and broad-based consumer protection movement, not only to effectively combat various malpractices indulged in by anti-social elements in trade and industry, but also to affirmatively protect consumers, the kingpin of the distribution system, who are the worst victims at the hands of a small but unscrupulous section of the community. It is a harsh reality that the consumer in India is either taken for granted or a ride which has made him a real stoic who, generally, tends to take things philosophically without raising a protest. One of the reasons for this state of affairs seems to be that the consumer movement in India has so far been a private affair and the government machinery was by and large indifferent and callous. However, with the announcement by the Central Government on 25 August 1983 for the setting up of a 28-member Consumer Protection Council with the avowed aim of helping the consumer movement in India, a new era in consumer movement is in the offing. The Council is expected to review trade practices and suggest measures to curb the growth of corrupt practices such as adulteration, short weighment, blackmarketing, and deceptive and misleading advertisements. The actual role perception and performance by this official body in an area of high socio-economic visibility is still to be watched; but since the government has not involved private organisations, who have already contributed to the growth of the

42. *See,* Garner, *Administrative Law* (1963) 266–69. Such bodies have also been established under the Transport Act, 1962 and the Civil Aviation (Licensing) Act, 1960.

consumer movement in India, it may dampen the vigour of the movement.[43] For the present, administrative agencies established under the Consumer Protection Act, 1986 and the Monopolies and Restrictive Trade Practices Act, 1969 are the only official agencies providing control over public bodies in the interest of the consumers in India.

2.5.4.3 *Interest representation*

In order to make public bodies directly responsive to the consumers, it is desirable that real consumers of services and products of these bodies must have some say in the policy planning and actions of such bodies. Therefore, in Britain, Parliament by law requires that members of certain public corporations are to be nominated by local bodies or other bodies interested in the working of a particular corporation.[44] In India, the place of "interest representation" as a strategy to control public corporations is yet to be fully appreciated and recognised.

2.5.4.4 *Consumer grievance redressal forums*

The Consumer Protection Act passed by Parliament in 1986 and amended in 1993 provides for the establishment of Consumer Protection Councils at the Centre and State levels in order to protect the rights of the consumers.[45] The Act also set up a three-tier grievance redressal machinery at the Central, State and district levels. These forums now provide less expensive and quick justice to the consumers of goods and services. By the 1993 amendment, these forums have been invested with the power to pass "cease and desist" order, and order "recall" of defective goods. It is too early to comment, but these forums may provide a very effective control over public corporations providing goods and services to the people.

On the basis of the above analysis, it will not be incorrect to say that the public control of statutory and non-statutory undertakings is feeble and its bite is imperceptible.

3. GOVERNMENT COMPANIES

Besides statutory corporations, the government carries on its commercial and service functions through non-statutory companies registered under the Companies Act, 1956. These are limited liability companies where the

43. *Indian Express*, Chandigarh 29-8-1983. Prof. Manubhai Shah's Consumer Education and Research Centre has done an excellent work in this area.
44. Garner, *Administrative Law* (1963) 267.
45. These rights include 1) protection against goods which are hazardous to life and property; 2) the right to be informed about the quality, quantity, potency, purity and price of goods; 3) the right to access to a variety of goods at competitive price; 4) the right to be heard; 5) the right to seek redressal of grievances; and 6) the right to consumer education.

government holds the majority share capital. They are formed either to start a new venture or to take over an existing business.

Section 617 of the Companies Act, 1956 defines a government company in the following terms:

> 617. *Definition of "Government Company".*—For the purposes of [this Act], Government company means any company in which not less than fifty-one per cent of the [paid-up share capital] is held by the Central Government, or by any State Government or Governments, or partly by the Central Government and partly by one or more State Governments [and includes a company which is a subsidiary of a Government company as thus defined].

After registration a government company, like any other company, is considered a distinct legal person with perpetual succession and common seal. But a government company is different from other companies inasmuch as its capital is subscribed by the government and no other person can purchase its share except with the permission of the government. It is controlled by the government which can appoint and remove its directors.

A government company is not a "State" within the meaning of Article 12 of the Constitution[46] and its employees are not government servants within the meaning of Article 311 of the Constitution.[47]

Since a government company is neither a creation of a statute or a department or an agent of the government, it is not subject to the writ jurisdiction of the High Court under Article 226 of the Constitution.[48] However, a writ of mandamus would lie against a government company to enforce a statutory or public duty required by the statute.[49] Therefore, the Kerala High Court issued a writ against a government company when it acted in violation of a statutory duty imposed upon it by the Import and Export Control Act, 1947 in matters of regulation of import and export in cashew nuts.[50] Some High Courts have also issued writs against government companies for violation of standing orders made under the Industrial Employment (Standing Orders) Act, 1946 on the ground that the standing orders thus made have the force of law.[51]

Though the government company is a distinct legal person separate from its members, yet, in order to mitigate hardship to its members or private individuals, courts may provide the remedy by "lifting the corporate veil" so that the real nature of the company may be determined and the liability may be fixed. Therefore, courts may lift the corporate veil if the number of the members fall below the statutory minimum, or where there has been

46. Vide *Kartick Chandra Nandi* v. *W.B. Small Industries Corpn. Ltd.*, 1966 SCC OnLine Cal 87: AIR 1967 Cal 231.
47. *State of Assam* v. *Kanak Chandra Dutta*, AIR 1967 SC 884.
48. *R. Lakshmi* v. *Neyveli Lignite Corpn. Ltd.*, 1965 SCC OnLine Mad 254: AIR 1966 Mad 399
49. *Praga Tools Corpn.* v. *C.A. Imanuel*, (1969) 1 SCC 585.
50. *K.L. Mathew* v. *Union of India*, 1973 SCC OnLine Ker 65: AIR 1974 Ker 4.
51. *Borhan Kumar* v. *Indian Oil Corpn.*, 1970 SCC OnLine Pat 42: AIR 1971 Pat 174; *Abani Bhusan Biswas* v. *Hindustan Cables Ltd.*, 1967 SCC OnLine Cal 69: AIR 1968 Cal 124.

fraudulent trading, or where the company is a mere "sham", or where it is controlled by enemy aliens, or where it is desired to establish its tax residence. However, the courts in India are of the view that they are not entitled to lift the veil and that it can be done by legislation alone.[52]

A government company would be subject to all those limitations which are imposed by the Companies Act, 1956.

The modern state acts through its own civil service as well as through the instrumentalities of corporations and companies. Such instrumentalities acting as an instrumentality or agency of the government act for the State, though in the eyes of law they possess a distinct personality. Their actions are State actions and, like the State, they are bound to respect fundamental norms of public action. But governmental control will not be the only test to determine whether such instrumentalities are agents of the State. The court propounded several others besides large financial assistance by the State, monopoly status, the functions performed and the like. Specifically, if a department of the government is transferred to such instrumentality, it would be a strong factor supportive of this inference. The Prasar Bharti will, therefore, be bound to respect the fundamentals of public dealings. The tests are not exhaustive. It is the cumulative effect of various factors that determines the character of such instrumentalities. Therefore, these State agencies will be subject to the same constitutional or public law limitations as government. The rule inhibiting arbitrary action by government must equally apply to these instrumentalities in their dealings with the public, whether by way of giving jobs or entering into contracts or otherwise, and it cannot act arbitrarily and enter into a relationship with any person it likes at its sweet will, but their actions must be in conformity with some principles which meet the test of reason and relevance. Therefore, setting aside legal technicalities and dogmas, the courts would do well to exercise effective judicial control over the actions of these instrumentalities.[53]

Of late, the public sector in India has been a subject of vehement controversy because of its inefficiency and consequential sickness. The expectation that the public sector would generate resources for the economic growth of the country has remained unfulfilled. The following statistics would show the real state of PSUs in India:

1.	Total investment in public sector in 2014	₹10,96,057
2.	Return on this investment comes to about less than 6 per cent	
3.	Total number of PSUs	298
4.	Total number of PSUs in operation	235

52. *Sunil Kumar Debnath* v. *Mining and Allied Machinery Corpn. Ltd.*, 1967 SCC OnLine Cal 34: AIR 1968 Cal 322.
53. See, *Ramana Dayaram Shetty* v. *International Airport Authority of India*, (1979) 3 SCC 489.

5.	Total number of PSUs which made profit in 2014–15	157
6.	Total number of PSUs which made losses in 2014–15	77
7.	Total number of PSUs deemed sick	39
8.	Total number of PSUs chronically sick	38
9.	Total number of PSUs without Chief Executives	40

Reasons for this state of affairs are many, but the main reason seems to be as someone from Japan remarked, "[w]e run our government on business lines and you run your business on government lines." For various reasons, public sector became more a blight than a blessing. But, in fact, public sector did not fail us, we failed it. It consumes 20 per cent of domestic credit but generates only less than 6 per cent of the gross domestic product (GDP). Some of the reasons for this state of affairs seem to be 1) lack of efficiency which may include poor returns, poor technology and marketing skills; 2) protection from competition; 3) political interference; 4) artificially depressed prices to appease voters; 5) serious environmental consequences; 6) lack of continuity and autonomy in the administration; 7) lack of accountability; 8) inward looking attitude; 9) disregard of foreign capital; and 10) pampered labour which did not talk of productivity. It is for these reasons that privatisation of public sector is taking place. Fact remains that government can breed bureaucrats and not entrepreneaurs. The government following the policy of disinvestment in 2014–15 disinvested its share in PSUs to the tune of ₹24,277.17 crores as against the target of ₹36,925 crores. Thus, the progress of disinvestment is also slow and tardy. Except for the Seven Maharatna and Seventeen Navratna[54], the PSUs give an image of shattered scaffolding of broken reed.

However, it is wrong to assume that privatisation is a panacea for all ills. It has its own problems which may include 1) exploitation, 2) consumerism, 3) self-centredness, and 4) divorce from norms and ideals. These may lead to a "joyless economy" and "unsocial society" where the people are left with nothing except to go for shopping. Nevertheless, with good governance, vigilant accountability, and regulatory institutions with emphasis on social justice and social growth, it can be harnessed in the service of the people. It is possible that in the short run it may increase inequality, it may be harsh on workers and inefficient producers, but in the long run it may be rewarding in terms of creating more jobs, increasing quality of goods and services and better quality of life. In short, it is as good and as bad as democracy itself. When democracies come in different shapes and sizes, imposing one single economic system on a pluralistic world deserves a serious thought.

54. List of Maharatna and Navratna available at <http://dpe.nic.in/publications/list_of_maharatna_navratna-and_miniratna>.

The fact remains that in a developing country like India where the private sector is capital starved, the public sector undertakings will have to play a significant role in the core sector of the economy, but this is not possible unless PSUs are allowed to run on business lines. It is for this reason that now the government is following the policy of ACA (authority-continuity-accountability) to revitalise this important sector of the Indian economy. Nevertheless, "business" in the context of PSUs should not mean mere "profit earning". It should function in a manner as to promote business potential of the country for the benefit of the people.[55]

POINTS FOR DISCUSSION

1. In India, the mushroom growth of statutory and non-statutory public enterprises defies orderly classification by reference to any meaningful criterion because they have been set up by the government and Parliament ad hoc to discharge a variety of tasks. Discussion on the topic may aim at evolving a meaningful criteria of classification and a consistent pattern of establishment.
2. According to one thesis, the creative genius of the bourgeoisie invented corporate device and, hence, the controversy whether public corporations come within the definition of the term "State" is essentially a part of relentless class struggle. Against this backdrop, the desirability or otherwise of treating public corporations as "State" under Article 12 may be discussed.
3. The legal power vested in the corporations are extensive, and although a person having a sufficient legal interest can impugn the validity of their acts and decisions, successful challenges will be rare, *firstly,* because of the breadth of their powers; and *secondly*, because of the disinclination of courts to afford locus standi to members of the general public. In the backdrop of this observation, the problems of locus standi necessary to challenge the actions and policies of public undertakings, and the difficulties in obtaining mandamus for enforcing legal duties of corporations may be discussed.
4. The main reason for preferring independent public undertakings to undertake various governmental functions over government departments was that civil servants would always be looking over their shoulders, apprehensive of the parliamentary inquisitor. Hence, for a better performance of these undertakings, it is desirable that they must be insulated from the rigours of question time in Parliament. Against this background, the desirability, mode and effectiveness of parliamentary control of public undertakings may be discussed.
5. The main reason which has turned many public undertakings into uneconomic pits is political interference. Against this background,

55. *Mahesh Chandra* v. *U.P. Financial Corpn.*, (1993) 2 SCC 279.

various problems of public undertakings adversely affecting their role performance with special reference to political interference may be discussed.

6. Public undertaking, in general, and those undertaking any public service, in particular, have not been able to meet the people's expectations. One of the reasons for this seems to be that the public control exercised through mass media and consumers' representation and participation is very feeble. Discussion on this topic may aim at evolving norms and patterns of public control in the Indian situation.
7. Main constitutional problems relate to the legal status of public corporations, especially their liability in tort and contract. The problems of the liability of public corporations may be discussed with a view to reconciling the claims of individual justice and social defence.

SUGGESTED READINGS

1. Administrative Reforms Commission Study Team, "Report on Public Sector Undertakings" (1967).
2. Bhambhri, *Parliamentary Control over State Enterprises in India* (1960) Chap. VII.
3. Bureau of Public Enterprises, *A Handbook of Information on Public Enterprises* (1969).
4. C.K. Thakker, *Administrative Law* (Eastern Book Co. 2012) Chap. XII.
5. D.N. Chester, "Boards and Parliament", (1958) 36 Public Adm 87.
6. D.N. Chester, "Public Corporations and the Classification of Administrative Bodies", (1953) 1 Pol Studies 34.
7. E.C.S. Wade, "The Constitutional Aspect of Public Corporations", (1949) 2 Current Legal Problems 172.
8. Friedmann, "The New Public Corporations and the Law", (1947) 10 Mod L Rev 233.
9. Garner, *Administrative Law* (4th Edn.) Chap. X.
10. Griffith and Street, *Principles of Administrative Law* (5th Edn.) Chap. VII.
11. Hansow, *Parliament and Public Sector* (1962).
12. J.A.G. Griffith, "Public Corporations as Crown Servants", (1951) 9 U Toranto LJ 169.
13. J.F. Garner, "New Public Corporations", (1966) Public Law 122.
14. Jain and Jain, *Principles of Administrative Law*, Chap. XVIII.
15. Laxmi Narain and B.S. Murthy, *Public Enterprises and Fundamental Rights* (1984 Edn.).
16. Mascarenhas, "Recent Developments in Public Enterprises", (1964) 10 IJPA 535.
17. Paranjape, "Evolving Patterns in Organisation and Administration of Public Enterprises", (1963) 9 IJPA 396.
18. Potter, "Public Enterprises: Parliamentary Control or Accountability", (1959) 5 IJPA 320.

19. R.S. Arora, "State Liability and Public Corporations in India", (1966) Public Law 238.
20. R.U. Singh, "Public Corporations in India", (1967) JILI 1.
21. Report of the Commission on Public Sector Undertakings (1967).
22. Schwartz and Wade, *Legal Control of Government* (1972) Chap. II.
23. V.K.R.V. Rao, "The Role of Public Enterprises in Indian Economy", (1964) 10 IJPA 412.
24. W.A. Robson, "The Public Corporations in Britain Today", (1959) 63 Harv L Rev 1321.

CHAPTER 13

Citizen and Administrative Faults

Any progressive system of administration presupposes the existence of a mechanism for handling grievances against administrative faults, and the recognition of a right of every member of the public to know what passes in government files. Therefore, the treatment of this subject involves the study of the following four topics:

(1) Ombudsman
(2) Right to know
(3) Discretion to disobey
(4) Central Vigilance Commission

1. OMBUDSMAN

Any good system of administration, in the ultimate analysis, has to be responsible and responsive to the people. But history bears witness to the fact that, more often, the impersonal bureaucratic system advertently or inadvertently tries to overwhelm the "little man". With the proliferation of administrative agencies affecting the life of a citizen in every conceivable aspect, the chances of administrative faults touching the rights of a person, personal or property, have tremendously increased. This has led to the never-ending search for an efficacious mechanism that can protect a person from administrative faults. The search has produced the idea of "ombudsman" which in terms of utility means a "watchdog of the administration" or "the protector of the little man". This institution was first developed in Sweden in 1809 and soon became a cherished importable commodity the world over. It is a unique institution which leads to an "open government" by providing a democratic control mechanism over the powers of the State. Its main catch is its apparent effectiveness despite minimal coercive capabilities. It has its own role to play by bringing "renaissance" and "humanism" in the working of modern governments which have tended to develop an attitude to look to the paper rather than the person behind it.

An ombudsman, or his equivalent, has become a standard part of the machinery of any modern government. In the 21st century, almost all countries have witnessed a change from laissez-faire to regulation. Under the weight of new economic policy, State has assumed the role of a facilitator, enabler and regulator. Therefore, the chances of friction between a government official and a private citizen have multiplied manifold. In these circumstances, in the name of progress and development, individual justice against administrative faults may slip into the low visibility zone. Therefore, the importance of an institution like ombudsman to protect the "little man" against administrative faults by keeping the administration on rails cannot be overemphasised.

Conceptually, an ombudsman is only a non-adversarial adjudicator of disputes. He serves as an alternative to the adversary system for resolving disputes, especially between citizens and government agencies. He is an independent and non-partisan officer who deals with the specific complaints from the public against administrative injustice and maladministration. Certainly, an adversarial adjudication by courts necessarily stands on a higher plane than a decision by the ombudsman. Therefore, if a matter is pending before a court, ombudsman cannot exercise jurisdiction.[1]

While designing Lokpal Bill (Ombudsman), some basic principles derived from the working of this institution elsewhere in the world cannot be ignored. It must be ensured that the law is constitutionally valid. Proposed law must not violate Articles 14, 21, 32, 226 and 311 of the Constitution. It should also not transgress the fundamental rights, doctrine of separation of power, rule of law and other basic features of the Constitution. A Lokpal which is designed to receive complaints, investigate, prosecute and judge would certainly be violative of the "due process" clause which has now been transposed in Article 21 of the Constitution. Bringing judiciary under the jurisdiction of Lokpal would conflict with the text and spirit of the Constitution. Even if the Constitution is amended to allow this change, the amending law would still be constitutionally suspect.

Simply because of the fact that the proposed law is extending its arms wide to cover political class, bureaucracy, judiciary and business, it is essential that Lokpal's investigation must remain confidential. If the investigation is brought into public space, it would harm the legitimacy of these categories of persons even if cleared of all charges. Filing of false complaints on personal considerations cannot be completely negated.

Further, this institution cannot also be structured in a manner as to destroy the democratic ethics of the country. Lokpal cannot be designed as a super legislature, executive and judiciary without any representative and responsive character.

Today, in an era of free market economy, corruption has become a global phenomena with transnational reach. Therefore, the United Nations Convention against Corruption (2004) is a right step in the right direction. It promotes international cooperation for fighting corruption and recovery of property, besides strengthening measures for enforcing integrity, accountability and proper management of public affairs. After initial

1. *Durga Hotel Complex* v. *RBI*, (2007) 5 SCC 120.

hesitation, new India has become a party to this Convention, but how best its benefits can be availed is again a matter of political will.[2]

If high-value corruption in high places is important, then low-value corruption and misuse of power in low places, which takes the form of "extortion" and directly affects majority of the people in their lives which they daily live, is no less important. This component of corruption and misuse of power, which can be tackled without creating any high-end institution, can be ignored only at our own peril. Fact remains that people do not hate democracy but they want it to perform and deliver.

History bears witness to the fact that no matter how meticulously societies may craft their public institutions, lack of political will may make them infructuous. Nevertheless, public power must continue to assert itself.

1.1 Developments in England

Like any other country with an intensive form of government, in England also, the grip of Parliament and the courts over the ever-widening fronts of the administration started showing signs of weakness. The resultant discontentment due to administrative faults also started mounting, and, ultimately, erupted in the Crichel Down episode in 1954. This case, though it had little legal content, focused attention on maladministration of the government in dealing with a citizen's grievance. In this case, the government had acquired a piece of land for use as a bombing range during the war. After the war was over, the owner desired to repurchase it. The claim of the owner was considered by various officials with the usual impersonal attitude and callous indifference. Ultimately, the land was given to the Agriculture Ministry to be used as a model farm. The public criticism and heat which this episode generated led to the appointment of the Franks Committee and on its recommendations the Tribunals and Inquiries Act, 1958 was passed. But the problem of administrative faults was solved only in 1967 when the Parliament Commissioner Act was passed.

Parliamentary Commissioner envisaged under the Act is a permanent appointee with the security of service of a High Court judge. He is appointed by the Crown on the advice of the Prime Minister. His salary is charged on the Consolidated Fund and he holds office during good behaviour, subject to the retiring age of 65. He can only be removed on addresses from both the Houses of Parliament. He has power to appoint his own staff subject to the Treasury's approval. Astonishingly, there is no professional lawyer on his staff. He does not receive complaints directly from the citizens but through the MPs. It is called "MP Fitter". This is done to reconcile the notion of ministerial responsibility with the concept of this institution. He has no other power except to investigate and report. The report is made to the Select Committee of the House of Commons which

2. *See generally*, Kamaljit Singh Grewal, "Don't Make Lokpal a Super Cop", *The Tribune* 28-6-2011, 13.

examines it and proposes action. Ministers are not outside the purview of this jurisdiction. One of the characteristic features of this institution is its non-lawyer character and, therefore, it proceeds with the work in an informal manner without obsession with legal technicalities. However, for legal advice it can always use the office of the Treasury Solicitor. There is no set prescribed procedure of enquiry, but the Commissioner has adequate powers to investigate a complaint thoroughly. The investigations are conducted in private and the officials implicated are given reasonable opportunity to defend themselves. He can administer oath and compel the attendance of witnesses and the production of documents. Contempt of his authority is punishable. His reports on investigations, and communications with the MPs on the subject-matter of complaint, are protected by absolute privilege in the law of defamation.[3] Irrespective of the Official Secrets Act, 1920 and the law relating to Crown privilege, he is entitled access to any relevant document except the one relating to the proceedings of the Cabinet and its committees.[4] However, "Crown privilege" may be asserted to prevent the Commissioner or any member of his staff from disclosing the informations obtained during his investigation.[5] The Official Secrets Act, 1920 may also be used to prevent disclosures for purposes other than investigation and report.[6] The Commissioner is prohibited from investigating an action in respect of which the person has a remedy in a court or tribunal by way of appeal, reference or review, unless he is of the opinion that such remedy would not be adequate. The jurisdiction of the Commissioner extends to the departments given in the Second Schedule of the Act. The Third Schedule lays down the departments which are excluded from his jurisdiction. Prominently external relations; crime investigation; judicial proceedings; prerogative of mercy; governmental, contractual and commercial transactions; award of honours; granting of royal charters; national health service; local government; police and personnel matters in armed forces; and the civil services are excluded from this jurisdiction. This exclusion is the subject of much criticism in England. The jurisdiction of investigation extends to the cases of "injustice in consequence of maladministration"[7]. However, the terms "injustice" and "maladministration" have been deliberately left undefined to make the boundaries of jurisdiction flexible. Nevertheless, "injustice" includes cases of hardship and a sense of grievance, besides legally redressible damage.

Maladministration covers a multitude of administrative faults of commission and omission; corruption; bias; unfair discrimination; harshness; misleading a member of the public as to his rights, failing to notify him properly of his rights, or to explain the reasons for a decision; general

3. S. 10(5), Parliamentary Commissioner Act, 1967.
4. S. 8.
5. S. 11(3).
6. S. 11(1) and (2).
7. Ss. 4, 5(*i*) and Sch. II, Parliamentary Commissioner Act, 1967.

high-handedness; using power for a wrong purpose; failing to consider relevant material; taking irrelevant material into account; losing or failing to reply to correspondence; delaying unreasonably before making a tax refund, or presenting a tax demand, or dealing with an application for a grant or licence and so on.[8]

Judged by international standards, Parliamentary Commissioner has done commendable work and the ratio of his successes is consistently on an increase.[9]

Because of various jurisdictional and operational factors, difficult to quantify, the Ombudsman has been nicknamed by sceptics as an "Ombudsmouse" especially after his special report on Sachsenhausen episode in 1967, when the Foreign Office officials had been guilty of procedural maladministration in dealing with an application by ex-prisoners-of-war for discretionary compensation for the sufferings caused by incarceration in a Nazi concentration camp. The reason for disillusionment is that a finding of maladministration does not necessarily lead to anything more than an expression of official regret or an undertaking that the department will suitably modify its procedures.[10]

Since 1994, the Ombudsman has entertained responsibility for enforcing the Open Government Code of Practice on access to government information. He now investigates complaints forwarded to him by the MPs against government departments and other bodies subject to his jurisdiction which fail to comply with the provisions of the Code.

In the absence of enforcement provisions, the Select Committee of the MPs plays an important role in bringing pressure on the departments to accept the Ombudsman's report. The existence of the Select Committee has strengthened this institution in the sense that there have been a few occasions when the recommendations of the Ombudsman have not been accepted.[11]

The Parliamentary Commissioner is a creation of a statute and therefore, amenable to the jurisdiction of courts. In practice courts exercise self-restraint while dealing with the cases relating to decisions of the Commissioner. However, in appropriate cases, courts do exercise the power of judicial review.[12]

1.2 Developments in the US

Though there is a lot of "ombudsmania" in the US, no "ombudsman" has infiltrated the administration except in the three States of Hawaii,

8. S.A. de Smith, *Constitutional and Administrative Law* (3rd Edn.) 618.
9. *See*, Schwartz and Wade, *Legal Control of Government* (1972).
10. *See*, S.A. de Smith, *Constitutional and Administrative Law* (3rd Edn.) 620–21.
11. *See*, Norman Lewis, "British Ombudsman Experience", in Norman Lewis and S.S. Singh (Ed.), *Ombudsman—India and World Community* (1995).
12. *R.* v. *Local Commr. for Admn. for North and East Area of England, ex p Bradford Metropolitan City Council*, 1979 QB 287 (CA); *R.* v. *Parliamentary Commr. for Admn., ex p Dyer*, (1994) 1 WLR 621.

Nebraska and Oregon for local government agencies. Since 1963, in every session of the Congress, a Bill has been introduced to establish an institution akin to ombudsman, but it never did become an Act. The predominant reason seems to be that in the US, the institution of ombudsman is considered by the members of the Congress as a drag on their status and power, for they consider it their sole prerogative to represent their constituencies and handle the grievances of the people. However, the Congressional investigations and grievance cells established in various departments, like the police review boards, discharge the work of ombudsmen.[13]

1.3 Developments in India

M.C. Setalvad, in his speech at the All India Lawyers' Conference held in 1962, suggested the idea of establishing an institution similar to that of an "ombudsman". The idea was extensively investigated by the Administrative Reforms Commission and a definite suggestion was placed before the government in its interim report dated 14 October 1966. On the basis of the recommendations, the government prepared the Lokpal and Lokayuktas Bill, 1968 and introduced it in Parliament, but eventually it was allowed to lapse. In 1971, the Bill was again introduced but was soon lost in oblivion. In 1977, again an attempt was made and the Bill, as emerged from the Joint Select Committee of Parliament, was to come for the consideration of the House in the 1979 monsoon session, but because of the resignation of Prime Minister Desai, the session was adjourned *sine die*. In 1985, another Lokpal Bill was introduced in Parliament which was restricted to offences punishable under the Penal Code, 1860 (IPC). This Bill drew violent protests from the Opposition and, hence, it was withdrawn by the government on the ground that its jurisdictional reach is highly limited. In 1989, another Lokpal Bill was introduced in Parliament but this Bill also could not see the light of day. After India adopted neo-liberal economic policy in 1990s, due to lack of proper accountability mechanisms and lack of effective institution to investigate and prosecute, strong demand was made for the establishment of Lokpal at the Centre. Once again in the monsoon session of Parliament (1993), the government made a promise to appoint a Lokpal to look into the charges of corruption against the government, but it could not be passed. By introducing the Lokpal Bill, 1997 in the budget session of Parliament, the United Front government can be said to have kept the promise it had made about cleansing public life and injecting an element of accountability at the highest level. However, because of the fall of the government, the Bill could not, once again, see the light of day.

An attempt for the establishment of Lokpal at the Centre was made on 3 August 1998 when a fresh Lokpal Bill was introduced in Parliament. This Bill also could not be passed because of controversy regarding the inclusion

13. Gellhorn, *When Americans Complain* (1966).

of Prime Minister within the jurisdiction of Lokpal. In 2003 "Lokpal Bill" was again introduced in Parliament, but failed to see the light of day. A new Bill was again introduced in 2005. This Bill proposes to include Prime Minister also within the orbit of the Bill. The Bill provides that the institution of Lokpal shall consist of a Chairperson, who is or has been a Chief Justice or a judge of the Supreme Court, and other two members, who are or have been the judges of the Supreme Court or the Chief Justices of the High Courts.[14] They shall be appointed by the President of India after obtaining the recommendations of a committee consisting of 1) Vice-President of India, 2) Prime Minister, 3) Speaker of the Lok Sabha, 4) Home Minister, and 5) leader of the Opposition in the Lok Sabha and the Rajya Sabha. However, no sitting judge of the Supreme Court or sitting Chief Justice of a High Court shall be appointed except after consultation with the Chief Justice of India.[15] Section 5 provides that the Chairman and Member shall not be a Member of Parliament (MP) or a Member of Legislative Assembly (MLA) or that of a Union Territory legislature. They shall also not hold any office of profit or be connected with any political party or carry on any business or profession. The Chairman and Members shall hold office for a term of three years or until the age of 70 years, whichever is earlier. On ceasing to be the Chairperson and Member, he shall be ineligible for reappointment as the Lokpal, and further to any office of profit under the Government of India or the State Government.[16] Their salaries and other conditions of service shall not be varied to their disadvantage after their appointment.[17] The Chairperson and Member shall not be removed from his office except by an order of the President made on the ground of proved misbehaviour or incapacity after an enquiry made by a committee consisting of the Chief Justice of India and two other judges of the Supreme Court next to the Chief Justice in seniority.[18] Lokpal shall appoint a Secretary and other staff necessary for the discharge of its functions as the President may determine in consultation with the Lokpal.[19] Lokpal shall have jurisdiction to enquire into any allegation made in the complaint. Limitation for filing a complaint shall be 10 years from the date alleged on which the offence was committed. However, if bias is alleged against the Chairman or any Members, the President, on application, shall obtain the opinion of the Chief Justice of India and shall decide accordingly.[20] Any person other than a public servant can make a direct complaint to the Lokpal. The complaint shall be made in the prescribed manner and shall be accompanied by prescribed fee and affidavit, except in case of a complaint from a person

14. The Lokpal Bill, 1998, S. 3.
15. S. 4.
16. S. 6.
17. S. 6(3).
18. S. 7.
19. S. 9.
20. Ss. 10, 11, 13.

in jail or other place of custody.[21] Every enquiry shall be conducted by the Chairman and the Members sitting jointly. The enquiry shall be open to which public may have access except in exceptional circumstances and for reasons to be recorded in writing, and such enquiry may be conducted in camera.

The Lokpal shall complete an enquiry within a period of six months, but where it is not possible it shall record reasons in writing.[22] For the purpose of conducting enquiry, Lokpal shall have the powers of a civil court, and proceedings before Lokpal shall be deemed to be judicial proceedings within the meaning of Section 193, IPC. The government or any public servant shall not be entitled to any privilege relating to the production of any document or oral evidence. For the proper conduct of an enquiry, Lokpal shall have power to summon and enforce attendance of any person and to examine him on oath, to enforce discovery and production of any document, to requisition any public record, to issue commissions for examination of witnesses and documents, and to search and seize any document.[23] After an enquiry, if the offence is proved, the Lokpal shall communicate its report and findings to the competent authority. Such competent authority shall be the Speaker in case of Prime Minister and a Member of the Lok Sabha; and Chairman of the Rajya Sabha in case of a Member of the Rajya Sabha. The competent authority shall place the report on the table of the Lok Sabha or the Rajya Sabha, as the case may be, if the House is in session and in case it is not in session, within a period of one week from the reassembly of the House. The competent authority shall communicate to the Lokpal, within a period of 90 days from the date of receipt of the report, the action taken or proposed to be taken on the basis of the report. Lokpal shall present annually to the President of India a consolidated report who shall cause the same to be placed before each House of Parliament as soon as possible, but not later than 90 days from the date of receipt of the report. In computing the period of 90 days any period during which Parliament is not in session shall be excluded.[24] Whoever intentionally offers any insult or causes any interruption to any proceedings before the Lokpal shall be punished with an imprisonment for a term which may extend to six months, or with fine, or with both. Lokpal shall have power to try such offence and any person convicted shall have the right to appeal to the Supreme Court against such conviction.[25] Every person who makes a complaint which is found by the Lokpal to be false shall be punished by it, after summary trial, with imprisonment which shall not be less than one year but which may extend to three years and also a fine, which may extend to ₹50,000.[26] Out of this

21. S. 12.
22. S. 14.
23. Ss. 15, 16.
24. S. 17.
25. S. 21.
26. S. 22.

fine, Lokpal may award compensation to the public functionary against whom the false report was filed.[27] The President of India may also confer additional functions on Lokpal and may require it to enquire into any allegations against any public functionary.[28] If the complaint is wholly or partially substantiated, the Lokpal may make necessary orders to compensate the complainant having regard to the expenses incurred by the complainant in respect of such complaint.[29] Lokpal and its officers shall be immune from prosecution or other legal proceedings in respect of any thing done in good faith, and its proceedings or decisions shall not be called in question in any court of law.[30] It may be mentioned that this provision shall not oust the jurisdiction of the High Courts and the Supreme Court. Lokpal shall have power to make rules for the purpose of carrying out its functions.[31] Administrative expenses of the Lokpal institution shall be charged on the Consolidated Fund of India.

The creation of the office of the Lokpal is basically a Western concept. When Sweden took the initiative to create the institution of the ombudsman in the 60s, it was seen as a device for controlling the bureaucracy. Over the years even the political executive was also placed under its jurisdiction. However, the proposed Lokpal Bill suffers from a major deficiency. The Lokpal Bill (1998) seeks to place unreasonable restrictions on those who may have genuine complaints but do not have the necessary proof to substantiate the charges. The complainant must be absolutely sure of the facts and must have proof to substantiate the complaint. It is like asking the complainant to investigate the case, collect evidence and prepare a foolproof charge-sheet. If the complaint made in good faith is not proved, the complainant may be required to pay a fine up to ₹50,000 and face a jail term up to three years. This provision would certainly deter even a genuine complainant.

Furthermore, there is no specific provision that Lokpal should specify the action to be taken against the public functionary in case charges were substantiated. Placing of the report before Parliament for action would mean that the action would be lost in party politics. If the purpose of this institution is to check corruption in high places, then it is equally necessary that there should be a binding provision for making it obligatory for all public functionaries to file their property returns before the Lokpal soon after becoming a Member of the Lok Sabha or the Rajya Sabha. They should also submit a copy of their annual income tax returns to the Lokpal. Attempts were also made in 2003, 2005 and 2008 and the Lokpal Bill was introduced in Parliament but with no positive consequence.

27. S. 23.
28. S. 24.
29. S. 25.
30. S. 26.
31. S. 29.

It is too early to comment on the working of this institution because it is still in the take-off stage. However, its desirability has been fully realised. In India, the existing machinery for the correction of administrative faults is highly inadequate. The public law review system of administrative action through writs and orders under Articles 32, 226, 136 and 227 is not only technical and expensive, but also involves delay because of congestion in courts which has reached staggering proportions. Private law review by injunction, declaration and suit for damages is also not an adequate remedy due to similar reasons. The vigilance exercised by government vigilance and anti-corruption cells is far from satisfactory because of red-tapism and political overtones by which the big fish always escape the net. The help of the MLAs and MPs is not evenly available to every person because they are partisan politicians. Therefore, the institution of the ombudsman seems to be the only hope for a quick remedy for administrative inertia, corruption and indifference.

The apprehension that the Ombudsman will impair ministerial responsibility has lost its substance. If a Minister can be made responsible to courts, there should not be any unconstitutionality if he is made accountable to the Ombudsman who is a creature of Parliament itself. For policy and efficiency of their departments, Ministers are responsible to Parliament, but for administrative lawlessness they may be made accountable to the Ombudsman. Far from weakening ministerial responsibility, the Ombudsman will help that principle work better. On the basis of investigation, Parliament can reach the bottom of the problem and can hold a Minister responsible and accountable for it. Even in England it is being increasingly felt that direct complaints (now they are routed through an MP to Parliamentary Commissioner would fit in the constitutional structurisation because the Commissioner is necessarily an arm of Parliament.

Ministers in any self-governing country like India belong to a majority party and so long as the popular vote prevails, a party in majority today may become the minority tomorrow. Hence, Ministers who shape the policies of the government should be aware that official inequities if tolerated today may tomorrow oppress yesterday's rulers. Hence, "[E]veryone, whether or not in momentary ascendancy, shares a long-range interest in nurturing evenhanded, effective and honest law administration; the rulers and the ruled alike benefit from devices that correct governmental mistakes and help prevent their occurring again."[32] The existence of the Ombudsman will induce Ministers to a greater degree of accountability and responsibility.

The functioning of the proposed institution of Lokpal may be greatly improved by securing for him a constitutional position like the Election Commission under Article 324. In the absence of this position, his powers

---

32. Prof. Gellhorn quoted by R.L. Narasimhan in "The Indian Ombudsman Proposal: A Critique", *Law and the Commonwealth*, 27.

may conflict with those of the High Courts under Article 226. Though the jurisdiction of the High Courts has been restricted to jurisdictional defects only, the proceedings before the Lokpal may be hampered by invoking the jurisdiction of the High Court.

It must be noted that though the Ombudsman may take pressure off the courts and prevent legal principles being strained, yet he is not a panacea for all the evils of bureaucracy. His function is to tidy up and improve the administration. His success depends on the existence of a reasonably well-administered State. He cannot cope with the situation where the administration is riddled with patronage and corruption.[33] There is also growing pessimism that in developing countries, where public opinion is unorganised, the executive is strong and the civil service is prone to abuse of power, the institution of ombudsman may not give forth the desired results. Another source of uncertainty in India is that a single ombudsman institution may not operate efficiently in so large a country because complaints may be too large for a single institution of three persons to dispose of. According to Mukherjea J, this institution which is "accusatorial and inquisitorial" in nature shall not be suitable in India because such an institution would be unprecedented in a democracy with traditions of independent judiciary. So he concludes that it is an "impracticable and disastrous experiment" which will not fit into the Indian Constitution.[34]

The demand for setting up the institution of Lokpal and Lokayukta got new impetus recently (2011) when social activist Anna Hazare went on fast unto death to push for the "Jan Lokpal Bill" proposed by the civil society in India in view of all pervasive governance deficit in the country. Salient features of the proposed Bill include constitutional position for Lokpal and Lokayukta, *i.e* Lokpal will be independent from executive and political control, completion of investigation within one year and trial within the next year, financial and criminal liability of the guilty, recovery of financial loss to the exchequer from the corrupt person, and compensation to the complainant from the fine imposed. Regarding appointment, the Bill proposes a transparent and participatory process through a selection committee consisting of judges, constitutional authorities and civil society. Bill also proposes a merger of anti-corruption agencies like Central Vigilance Commission (CVC), vigilance departments and anti-corruption branch of the Central Bureau of Investigation (CBI) with the Lokpal. Its jurisdiction would extend to all public officers, politicians and judges and others found guilty of corrupting them. It's jurisdiction will cover cases of misconduct of functionaries and grievance of the people. Though Lokpal will not have

33. Prof. Gellhorn quoted by R.L. Narasimhan in "The Indian Ombudsman Proposal: A Critique", *Law and the Commonwealth*, 35. For an exhaustive analysis *see*, M.P. Jain, *Lokpal: Ombudsman in India* (1970); P.K. Tripathi, "Lokpal: The Proposed Indian Ombudsman", (1967) 9 JILI 135; Rajeev Dhawan, "Engrafting Ombudsman Idea on a Parliamentary Democracy—A Comment on Lokpal Bill, 1977", (1977) 19 JILI 257.

34. Quoted by C.K. Thakker, *Administrative Law* (Eastern Book Company 1992) 474.

judicial powers, but will have power to grant stay and to launch prosecution. It's orders will be subject to review by the High Courts and the Supreme Court. Members of the Lokpal could be removed for misconduct by a five-member Bench of the Supreme Court. Selection committee shall consist of the Vice-President of India, Lok Sabha Speaker, Rajya Sabha Chairman, Comptroller and Auditor General, Chief Election Commissioner, two seniormost judges of the Supreme Court, two seniormost judges of the High Court, Chairman of the National Human Rights Commission and the outgoing members of the Lokpal. Government constituted a joint committee consisting of members of the civil society and the government to give a final shape to the Bill.[35]

However, no agreement could be reached and now the government has decided to circulate both the Bills (its own and Anna Hazare's) for wider consultations with all the political parties.

It is also being argued that it is a clever move to remove public corruption cases in high places from the jurisdiction of the High Courts and the Supreme Court which can give binding and enforceable decisions. If the working of this institution in States is any indication, then it is highly improbable that Lokpal shall succeed in its laudable mission of removing corruption from public life. The most controversial part of the Bill is Lokpal's jurisdiction over the judges of the High Courts and the Supreme Court and the Prime Minister. Contradiction is that judges are associated with the selection and removal of the Lokpal and will exercise review powers over its orders, yet will be subject to its jurisdiction for corruption!

If this institution is created in the manner presently visualised, it will be a supreme authority over legislature, executive and judiciary with no accountability. This will put a question mark on the legitimacy of a constitutional democracy. Constitutionality of the Lokpal Bill has been challenged in various courts in public litigation petitions on various grounds including violation of basic features of the Constitution.[36]

It was four decades after the introduction of the first Bill that ultimately the Lokpal and Lokayuktas Act was passed in December 2013. It was the result of a public movement initiated by Anna Hazare, a social activist. This Act was notified on 1 January 2014.

The Act provides for the establishment of a body called Lokpal which is to be headed by a Chairman, who is or has been a Chief Justice of India or is or has been a judge of the Supreme Court or an eminent person who fulfils the eligibility criteria as specified. It will have other eight members, 50 per cent of whom will be judicial members, provided that not less than 50 per cent of members belong to Scheduled Castes, Scheduled Tribes, OBCs, minorities and women. In the same manner a body known as Lokayukta shall be established by law made by the State Legislature to deal with

35. *The Hindu* 7-4-2011, 4.
36. *Ibid*, 3.

complaints of corruption against certain categories of public servants. If such body does not exist already, it must be established within one year from the date of commencement of this Act.

Lokpal will have "inquiry wing" and "prosecution wing". The inquiry wing will be headed by a Director who will conduct initial inquiry into any offence alleged to have been committed by a public servant under the Prevention of Corruption Act, 1988. In the same manner, the Director of Prosecution will prosecute public servant in relation to any complaint by the Lokpal under this Act. It is to be noted that the Chairperson and members of the Lokpal too shall come under the definition of "public servant".

1.4 Appointments

The Act provides for inviting applications for filling the posts of Chairman and eight members. On 27 September 2018, a Search Committee was constituted headed by Justice Ranjana Desai, a former judge of the Supreme Court and other members. The recommendations of the Search Committee were to be considered by the Selection Committee headed by the Prime Minister. Other members of the Selection Committee include Lok Sabha Speaker, Leader of opposition in the Lok Sabha, Chief Justice of India or a judge of the Supreme Court nominated by him and an eminent jurist nominated by the President of India.

In the same manner, a Lokayukta is to be appointed in every State by State functionaries within one year of passing the Act; however, many States are yet to appoint this institution. Members are appointed for five years or till attaining the age of 70 years. On ceasing office Lokpal/member cannot hold any diplomatic office or contest any election of President, Vice-President or Member of Parliament or State Legislature, among others.

1.5 Jurisdiction

The Act covers a wide range of public functionaries within the jurisdiction of Lokpal. The Act specifically includes, within its jurisdiction, Prime Minister, Ministers, Members of Parliament and Group A, B, C and D officers of the Central Government. The Act does not allow enquiry against the Prime Minister if the allegations relate to international relations, external and internal security, public order, atomic energy, and space. Furthermore, no inquiry against the Prime Minister can be conducted unless at least 2/3rd members approve it. The enquiry if conducted shall be in camera and if the Lokpal comes to the conclusion that the complaint deserves to be dismissed, then the records of the enquiry shall not be published or provided to anyone. Lokpal jurisdiction also extends to autonomous bodies established by law or under the law or funded by the government. It also covers a society or a trust receiving foreign contributions above ₹10 lakhs. The enquiry wing shall submit a report within 60 days, thereafter the Lokpal Bench will decide on further prosecution after giving the party a right to be heard.

Though the institution of Lokpal has come into existence headed by Justice Pinaki Chandra Ghose, yet it has not started functioning because it is still waiting for the Centre's approval on notifying the "format" for receiving complaints which is the requirement of law. The seriousness for checking corruption in high public spaces can be judged from the fact that till date no separate office building has been provided so far and Lokpal is temporarily operating from Ashoka Hotel in New Delhi. Operational limitations have reached a point that made one member of the body to resign. Justice Dilip B. Bhosale tendered his resignation effective from 12 January 2020 for personal reasons without elaborating further.

Any one evaluating the performance of any public institution must take into consideration three main factors: 1) structure of the institution; 2) character of the persons appointed to manage the institution; 3) societal environment in which the institution is to operate. All these factors are not selectively exclusive but mutually exclusive. Nevertheless, the second factor is most important. It is rightly said if an institution is badly structured but the persons appointed to manage the institution are good and well-meaning, the institution can still deliver. However, vice versa is not true. Therefore, one has to wait and watch the performance of the Lokpal institution before passing any final judgment.

The United Nations adopted a convention against corruption in 2004 which supports international cooperation, technological assistance and assets recovery and promotes integrity, accountability and clean administration. India ratified this convention only in 2010. It may fuel economic development due to assets recovery.

1.6 Institution of ombudsman in States

Though the birth of an ombudsman in the Centre is still doubtful, but for the States it has become a cherished institution.

The institution of Lokayukta is functioning in 13 States. These States are Andhra Pradesh, Assam, Bihar, Gujarat, Himachal Pradesh, Karnataka, Madhya Pradesh, Maharashtra, Rajasthan, Uttar Pradesh, Orissa, Punjab and Haryana.

In Tamil Nadu and Jammu & Kashmir, different investigating agencies are functioning [*see*, the Tamil Nadu Public Men (Criminal Misconduct) Act, 1973 and the Jammu & Kashmir Government Servants (Prevention of Corruption) Act, 1975]. A similar proposal is pending in the State of Kerala [*see*, Public Men (Investigation About Misconduct) Bill, 1977]. Delhi has also established the institution of ombudsman.

1.7 Working of Lokayuktas in States

The fact of the establishment of the institution of ombudsman in States proves beyond doubt that the assumption of accepting the "system of responsible government" and the consequential "ministerial responsibility" as a means of providing continuous oversight over the administration is not wholly correct. A Lokayukta can be much more effective than an MP or an MLA because of his freedom from political affiliation and because of access to departmental documents. The following table would show the working of the Lokayuktas in various States.

Year	Complaints Brought Forward	Complaints received	Total	Complaints disposed of	Balance
		State of Andhra Pradesh			
2008	1334	1392	2726	1333	1393
2009	1393	1427	2820	1088	1732
2010	1732	2379	4111	1825	2286
2011	2286	3060	5346	1769	3577
		States of Telangana and Andhra Pradesh			
2012	3577	3807	7384	2733	4651
2013	4651	5874	10525	6527	3998
2014	3998	4661	8649	4980	3669
2016	3669	5358	9027	5022	4005
		State of Haryana			
2012-13	647	785	1432	409	1023
2013-14	1023	692	1715	807	908
2014-15	908	438	1346	615	731
2015-16	731	320	1051	343	708
2016-17	708	650	1358	333	1025
2017 18	1025	647	1642	525	1147
2018-19	1147	599	1746	554	1192
		State of Himachal Pradesh			
2015	43	59	102	60	42
		State of Jharkhand			
2011-12		811	811	455	356
2012-13	356	653	1009	743	266
2013-14	266	661	927	532	395
2014-15	395	606	1001	393	608

Year	Complaints Brought Forward	Complaints received	Total	Complaints disposed of	Balance
		State of Karnataka			
2009-10	3889	812	4701	1350	3351
2010-11	3351	1256	4607	1465	3142
2011-12	3142	1318	4460	477	3983
2012-13	3983	661	4644	817	3827
2013-14	3827	1107	4952	4225	727
2014-15	727	1761	2488	1677	811
2015-16	811	1491	2302	564	1738
2016-17	1738	875	2613	159	2454
2017-18	2454	1455	3909	1452	2457
2018-19	2457	1617	4074	1086	2988
2019-20	2988	1290	4278	1745	2533
		State of Madhya Pradesh			
2009-10	11	3616	3627	3620	07
2010-11	07	4407	4414	4389	25
2011-12	25	4923	4948	4892	56
		State of Maharashtra			
2014	4807	5870	10667	6685	3982
2015	3982	6280	10262	6371	3891
2016	3891	7400	11291	6436	4855
2017	4855	7128	11983	9009	2974
2018	2974	5879	8853	6986	1867
2019	1867	6030	7897	6275	1622
		State of Odisha			
2019	195	1132	1327	714	613
2020	613	1409	2022	1537	485
		State of Rajasthan			
2008-09	1121	1246	2367	1357	1010
2009-10	1010	1147	2157	1307	850
2010-11	850	1408	2258	1401	857
2011-12	857	3495	4352	1846	2506
2012-13	2506	1393	3899	96	3803
2013-14	3803	2854	6657	2928	2729
2014-15	2729	4433	7162	3756	3406

Year	Complaints Brought Forward	Complaints received	Total	Complaints disposed of	Balance
2015-16	3406	6485	9891	4990	4901
2016-17	4901	5384	10285	5973	4312
		State of Uttar Pradesh			
2013	808	309	1117	523	594
2014	594	631	1225	385	840

Though the above statistics are old and incomplete as they do not give the necessary details about all the aspects of the working of the institution of Lokayukta in the States, yet a few generalisations may still be made. It is clear beyond doubt that the number of complaints received by the Lokayuktas is constantly increasing. But a large number of them are filed because of various reasons which may include lack of jurisdiction, triviality, baselessness, anonymity or pseudonymity, etc. This indicates that the people while filing complaints have not acted with restraint and responsibility. Another important reflection from the above tables is that the cases in which grievances were redressed is highly negligible. This establishes the practical ineffectiveness of this institution in the Indian situation where lack of administrative cooperation and the apathy of political high-ups is significantly marked. However, it has no reflection on the Lokayuktic therapy if properly administered.

Much information is not available about the types of complaints received by the Lokayuktas in various States, but whatever information is available clearly indicates that the main areas of grievance include police action or inertia, prison torture, mala fide exercise of power and demand or acceptance of illegal gratification.

A survey of State enactments relating to Lokayukta indicates that there is no uniformity in the provisions of these enactments. In some States, grievances against administration are within the jurisdiction of Lokayukta, while in other States such grievances are kept out of its jurisdiction. In some enactments, jurisdiction of Lokayukta extends to only a limited number of public functionaries, while in others even Vice-Chancellors and Registrars of the universities have been brought under its jurisdiction. In some States, the Chief Minister has been brought within the purview of the Act, while in some cases he is not. Similar is the case with the Members of the legislatures. There is no uniformity in the qualification, emoluments, allowances, status and powers of Lokayukta. Only in some enactments, power of search and seizure and power to take action suo motu have been given to Lokayukta. In some States, budget of the Lokayukta office is charged on the Consolidated Fund of the State, but in others it is not done. The power to punish for its contempt is conferred upon the institution of Lokayukta in some States only. In the same manner, only a few States have put an independent investigative machinery at the disposal of Lokayukta. In some States, Lokayukta has been given some other additional functions to perform also in order to make the institution cost-effective. Besides these, there are various other matters where there is no uniformity in State enactments.

Institution of Lokayukta has not been given any constitutional status, hence, its existence and survival completely depends at the sweet will of the State Governments. For political reasons, the State of Orissa issued an ordinance in 1992 for the abolition of Lokayukta institution. For the same reasons, Haryana repealed the Lokayukta Act, 1997 in 1999.

It is tragic that in some States, this institution was established not for prevention of corruption but for harassing and intimidating political opponents and for protecting the ruling elite. It is for this reason that the governments are keen that the Lokayukta should be their own nominee. The Supreme Court had to quash the appointment of Lokayukta of Punjab, H.S. Rai J, because the Chief Justice of the High Court had not been consulted. In the same manner, Vashisht J was removed from the office of the Lokayukta of Haryana by repealing the Act because the Act had made the removal of Lokayukta cumbersome by the outgoing government. This is a dangerous sign when a good institution is being allowed to be destroyed in party politics. In 2011, Hegde J, Lokayukta of Karnataka, resigned in disgust when the State Government did not cooperate in the investigation of mining scandal in the State.

Whether the recommendations of the Lokayukta or Upa-Lokayukta are mere recommendations or have a binding effect, is a question which deserves serious consideration. The Supreme Court in *Institution of A.P. Lokayukta/Upa-Lokayukta* v. *T. Rama Subba Reddy*[37] opined that since the Lokayuktas or Upa-Lokayuktas are high judicial dignitaries, it would be obvious that they should be armed with appropriate powers and sanctions so that their opinions do not become mere paper directions. These authorities should not be reduced to mere paper tigers but must be armed with proper teeth and claws so that the efforts put in by them are not wasted and their reports are not shelved. For this, the court suggested an appropriate legislation in this behalf so that the confidence of the people in this institution is maintained. However, before more powers are given to the Lokayukta, it is essential to ensure that political influence in the appointment of Lokayukta is eliminated. Fact remains that power is not a self validating value, important is the purpose for which it is exercised.

Another problem worth noticing is that whenever the Lokayukta recommends disciplinary action against a public servant—even after complying with elaborate procedure, it is only the beginning of the beginning inasmuch as the recommendations are no substitute for the report of the enquiry committee under the Civil Services (Classification, Control and Appeal) Rules (CCA Rules) and the whole procedure must commence from

37. (1997) 9 SCC 42.

the very beginning before the government. Even if it may be lawful for the government to take action on the recommendation without any further enquiry, the government may not be bound by the recommendation. In this situation also, the court recommended a proper legislation though any writ court can determine this question in a public interest litigation (PIL).[38]

For the effectivity of the institution of Lokayukata, it is further necessary that the Lokayukta must have the power to make its orders or directions to the government regarding investigation time-bound, failing which the Lokayukta must have the power to punish the authority for contempt. Government apathy and indifference on this behalf makes this institution ineffective.

Foregoing analysis of the working of the institution of Lokayukta clearly shows that this institution has not been successful in curbing corruption in high places of administration and creating awareness among the general public about its functioning. However, while assessing the role performance of this institution, one should take into consideration social, economic, political and cultural millieu in which Lokayukta has to function. Corruption has struck deep roots in society and, therefore, it is not easy for any single individual or institution to uproot it, especially when there is a lack of political will and bureaucratic apathy.

Besides the traditional institution of the ombudsman, in India, keeping in view the compulsions and constraints, other ombudsmanic activities need encouragement so that justice may be given to the poor and the downtrodden in an inexpensive and expeditious manner. Failure on this front would spell dangerous consequences. Terrorists in Manipur and Arunachal Pradesh are reported to have started a drive against corruption and are on the rampage, killing known corrupt officials and politicians. It is against this backdrop that the ombudsmanic role of the print and television mass media needs impetus. Efforts have already been made by the *Indian Express*, Chandigarh and *Femina*, a Times of India publication, in this behalf. The *Indian Express* and *The Tribune* published a regular "complaint box" in which individual grievances of the persons against administrative faults are published. In many cases, the individual gets immediate relief. The paper also publishes the administrative action or explanation or suggestion, if any, on the complaint. The same task is undertaken through the "consumer action" page of the *Femina*, a fortnightly magazine. Jalandhar Television also proposes to start such a programme where complaints of a general nature are proposed to be included. One can only hope that in due course of time, newspapers, radio and television media in India would effectively undertake this new role performance in this area of high social visibility. Private voluntary agencies may also play a vital role in this behalf. In Canada, there has been rapid growth of complaint columns in daily papers

38. *Ibid*. S. 12(3), Andhra Pradesh Lokayukta and Upa-Lokayukta Act, 1983 gives power to the government to take action on the recommendation of the Lokayukta, but this power is not coupled with the duty to take action without further enquiry.

and of radio and television programmes to receive and investigate individual grievances.[39] The Delhi Development Authority has also developed a grievance procedure under which on notified fixed days and time, hearing is held by various heads of departments on matters relating to their departments. All this makes administration public-oriented. Therefore, the need of having an ombudsman in specialised fields cannot be overemphasised. Now, there is a growing awareness of the utility of this institution amongst banks and the office of the ombudsman has come into existence.

It may be noted that in 1983, the then Martial Law Administration in Pakistan has also imported the institution of ombudsman. After months on the anvil, an ombudsman, to be called *Wafaqi Mohtasib*, has finally been appointed. Sardar Muhammad Iqbal J became the first Ombudsman of Pakistan. As he was being inundated with petitions even before he started operating, the government had to issue a press note advising people to wait till the *Mohtasib's* secretariat is established. This simply exposes the dire need for an effective grievance machinery in the face of growing governmental lawlessness everywhere.[40]

The First All-India Conference of Lokayuktas and Upa-Lokayuktas was held at Shimla in May 1986. This conference after due deliberations passed the following resolutions in order to make the institution of the Lokayukta still more effective:

(1) That the institution of the Lokayuktas and Upa-Lokayuktas be given a constitutional status.

(2) That suitable amendments be made in the Representation of the People Act, 1951 and other similar Central and State enactments so as to enable the authorities concerned to take into consideration the findings or recommendations of the Lokayuktas and Upa-Lokayuktas in respect of persons holding elective offices.

(3) That since the jurisdiction of the Lokayuktas and Upa-Lokayuktas in some enactments is restricted to Ministers and public servants in office, it is advisable that ex-Ministers and ex-public servants concerned in regard to the action complained against be also expressly brought within their purview.

(4) That the jurisdiction of Lokayuktas and Upa-Lokayuktas should cover not only allegations or corrupt practices, but also grievances or maladministration as defined in the Central Lokpal and Lokayukta Bill of 1968.

(5) That a time-limit be prescribed for placing the special and annual reports by the Governor before the Houses of Legislature. Such time-limit should not, under any circumstances, exceed four months from

39. *See*, Balram Gupta, "Ombudsmanic Role of the Newspapers", (1982) 3 SCC J-34, 37. "Some of them even use the word 'ombudsman' in their titles and have employed large staff to monitor hundreds of letters and thousands of phone calls."

40. *Hindustan Times* 11-2-1983.

the date of the receipt of the report by the Governor or till the legislatures meet next, whichever is earlier.

(6) That the nomenclature of the institution should be "Lokayukta" in every State.

(7) That there should be uniformity throughout India in regard to the service conditions of the Lokayuktas and the Upa-Lokayuktas.

(8) That there should be no security deposit for making a complaint before the Lokayuktas or Upa-Lokayuktas.

(9) That the Lokayuktas and Upa-Lokayuktas should have discretion to dispense with the requirement of filing an affidavit with the complaint.

(10) That there be a separate independent investigating agency under the direct control of the Lokayuktas and Upa-Lokayuktas.

(11) That in the provision relating to "removal of doubts" in the Lokayukta Acts, the expressions "Court" and "Judge" should mean only "High Court", "Civil and Criminal Courts" and their Presiding Officers, as the case may be.

(12) That the Lokayukta and the Upa-Lokayukta be given the power to sanction search and seizure within the meaning of the Criminal Procedure Code, 1973.

(13) That suo motu power of investigation be conferred on the Lokayuktas and Upa-Lokayuktas.

(14) That the Lokayukta and Upa-Lokayukta be deemed to be a High Court within the meaning of the Contempt of Courts Act, 1971.

This resolution was again adopted unanimously in the second conference held at Nagpur in 1989 and reiterated in the third conference held at Hyderabad in 1991. Implementation Committee appointed at the conference drafted a model Lokayukta Bill and placed it before the fourth conference held at New Delhi in 1994. The Bill not only aims at uniformity but also provides for comprehensiveness in various provisions. The scope of the definition of terms like allegation, maladministration has been widened to include more matters for investigation. The definition of the term "public functionary" has also been widened to include Chief Minister, Ministers, MLAs and Vice Chancellors, etc.

In the matters of appointment of Lokayukta, consultation with the Chief Justice of the High Court and the leader of the Opposition in the legislative assembly has been made mandatory and the criteria of merit, eminence and suitability of the person to be appointed is assured.

The conditions of service, salary, allowance, etc. of the Lokayukta have been clearly spelled out equating his status with that of the Chief Justice of the High Court. A time-limit has also been prescribed for filling up the vacancy. It is also provided that the administrative expenses of the institution to be charged on the Consolidated Fund of the State.

While providing for comprehensive powers of the Lokayukta to facilitate investigations, whether on a complaint or suo motu, into allegations of corruption or grievance of maladministration against public functionaries, the proposed Model Bill provides for

(1) empowering Lokayukta to recommend to the competent authority "stay" or "implementation" of the order or action complained against and to take such mandatory or preventive action as may be specified;
(2) taking such action as is necessary including suspension of the public functionary complained against; and
(3) granting interim relief to the complainant.

It has been further provided that if the action of the public functionary has resulted in any injustice or hardship to the complainant, the Lokayukta may recommend remedial action within a prescribed time-frame. It is also provided that he can award compensation for loss or injury due to arbitrary action of the public functionary. A time-limit is provided for laying the annual reports with an explanatory memorandum before each House of the State Legislature.

A provision is also made for initiation of prosecution of public functionary, if Lokayukta is satisfied that the public functionary has committed an offence. Provision is also made for providing an independent investigative agency to function under the exclusive control and direction of Lokayukta. An important provision relates to submission of property statements of certain public functionaries to the Lokayukta.

The proceedings before Lokayukta are categorised as judicial proceedings with power to punish for its contempt.

The Model Bill also provides for vesting of discretion in the Lokayukta to publish reports in public interest relating to exercise and performance of his functions and duties or any particulars of a case investigated by him.

The committee emphasised the need to give the institution of Lokayukta a constitutional status so that it could discharge its functions effectively and independently.

Some of the reasons responsible for the failure of this institution in India include lack of political will to root out corruption, politicisation of appointment of Lokayukta, lack of infrastructural facilities, lack of administrative cooperation and political apathy, lack of public cooperation for fear of reprisals, lack of independent investigatory machinery and advisory nature of recommendations, etc. To some extent, the institution itself is also responsible for its failure. An impression has been created that Lokayukta is a government nominee appointed to protect the government and to demolish the Opposition. Courts have held the view that any enquiry by the Lokayukta against a public servant for corruption will not be considered as enquiry under CCA Rules and therefore, government cannot take action against any employee indicted by the Lokayukta unless the whole process of enquiry is started afresh. This delays matters, duplicates efforts and emboldens delinquent officer. In conclusion one can say that the "institution has not failed us we have failed the institution". Under the existing constraints, perhaps a special Bench in High Court and the Supreme Court to deal with corruption cases will be a better alternative. Fact remains that any other institution can be easily destroyed by lack of political will and bureaucratic apathy. Personal interest and not the public interest is still the *suprema lex*. Remedy against administrative faults must be preventive and punitive both.

2. RIGHT TO KNOW

Government openness is a sure technique to minimise administrative faults. As light is a guarantee against theft, so governmental openness is a guarantee against administrative misconduct. Brandeis J rightly said, "A government which revels in secrecy ... not only acts against democratic decency but busies itself with its own burial."[41] The right to know the truth is paramount and it must outweigh the right to property and other personal rights.

Information is the core value of democracy and good governance. John Adams said, "Remember a democracy never lasts long. It soon wastes and exhausts itself. There was never a democracy which did not commit suicide." The agent which induces suicide is "secrecy" in the functioning of public offices. Ignorance subverts democracy. Lord Nolan Committee identified openness, objectivity and accountability as fundamental standards in public life. These standards can be enforced only if information on public decisions and actions is available to the people. Louis Brandeis once said that the live wire when snapped, darkness prevails. In darkness, even shadows are not formed. In crooked lights, shadows are also crooked. Information is the "live wire" which illuminates democracy and governance. In spite of this fact, one phenomena, which is common all over the world, is that no government appreciates the "right to information" and creates barriers in free access to information because it feels comfortable under the protected umbrella of secrecy.

The US Constitution, the oldest written Constitution of the world, does not contain specific right to information. However, the US Supreme Court has read this right into the First Amendment of the Constitution and granted access to information where there is a tradition of openness to information in question and where access contributes to the functioning of the particular process involved.[42] The Administrative Procedure Act, 1946 was the first enactment which provided a limited access to executive information. The Act was vague in language and provided many escape clauses which are: 1) Every person had no right to information and only persons

41. *Maneka Gandhi* v. *Union of India*, (1978) 1 SCC 248.
42. M.J. Hayes, "Whatever Happened to the Right to Know? Access to Government Controlled Information since Richmond Newspapers", (1987) 73 Va L Rev IV.

properly and directly connected could have access. 2) Agencies were permitted to withhold information without justification. 3) There was no provision for judicial review.

Taking these deficiencies into consideration, the Congress of the US in 1966 passed the Freedom of Information Act, 1966, which gives every corporate or individual, regardless of nationality, a legally enforceable right of access to government unpublished documents which the administrators may be tempted to keep confidential. If any person is denied this right, he can seek injunctive relief from the court.[43]

However, this right recognises nine well-defined exceptions:

(1) Information specifically required by executive order to be kept secret in the interests of national defence or foreign policy.
(2) Information related solely to internal personal use of the agency.
(3) Information specifically exempted from disclosure by statute.
(4) Information relating to trade, commercial or financial secrets.
(5) Information relating to inter-agency on intra-agency memorandums or letters.
(6) Information relating to personal medical files.
(7) Information compiled for law enforcement agencies except to the extent available by law to a party other than the agency.
(8) Information relating to agency regulation or supervision.
(9) Information relating to geological and geophysical maps.

Besides these nine exceptions, agencies within the intelligence communities are prohibited from making any record available to a foreign government or a representative of the same pursuant to a information request.

After investigating the operation of this Act, Congress of the US in 1974 amended it. Amendments provided for 1) disclosure of "any reasonably segregable portion" of otherwise exempted records; 2) mandatory time-limit of 10 to 30 days for responding to information requests; and 3) rationalised procedure for obtaining information, appeal and cost. Statistics show that maximum (80 per cent) use of this Act is being made by business executives and their lawyers, and editors, authors, reporters and broadcasters whose job is to inform the people have made very little use of this Act. The Act was further amended in 1996 to provide for public access to information in an electronic form or format.

The judiciary in the US shares the same concern of the Congress which is reflected in the Freedom of Information Act, 1966. In *New York Times Co.* v. *United States*[44], Douglas J observed, "Secrecy in government is fundamentally anti-democratic, perpetuating bureaucratic errors. Open discussion based on full information and debate on public issues are vital to our

43. *National Labour Relations Board* v. *Robbins Tyre and Rubber Co.*, 57 L Ed 2d 159: 437 US 214 (1977).
44. 29 L Ed 2d 822: 403 US 713 (1971).

national health." In 1974, the Supreme Court in *United States* v. *Nixon*[45] allowed inter-branch access to President's tape relating to Watergate needed for criminal prosecution.

In order to provide access to federal government meetings, the Congress passed the Sunshine Act, 1977 which mandates open meetings for regular session of federal agencies. However, closed door meetings are allowed in cases of 1) national defence and foreign policy; 2) confidential commercial, financial information; 3) invasion of privacy; 4) law enforcement and criminal investigatory records; 5) pre-decisional discussions of general policy; 6) bank examiners' record; and 7) information which may lead to financial speculation. The Act provides that injunctive relief may be obtained to force a pending meeting to be open and to force closing of a meeting held in violation of law. After the enforcement of the Act, all meetings of federal agencies are to be open with at least one week's public notice unless prescribed exceptions are attracted. In the same manner, the Federal Advisory Committee Act, 1972 contains similar provisions regarding the meetings of outside groups advising federal agencies.

In England, before the Freedom of Information Act, 2005 came into operation, the thrust of the legislation was not on "information" but "secrecy". The law was contained in the Official Secrets Acts, 1911, 1920 and 1939. Under Section 2 of the Act of 1911, it was an offence punishable with up to two years' imprisonment to retain without permission, or failure to take reasonable care of information obtained as a result of one's present or future employment; or to communicate information so obtained, or entrusted to one in confidence by a person holding office under Her Majesty, or obtained in contravention of the Act, to anybody other than a person to whom one is authorised to convey it, or to whom it is one's duty to impart it in the interests of State; or to receive such information, knowing or having reasonable cause to believe that it has been given in contravention of the Act. Under these wide-ranging prohibitions, it may be an offence for a civil servant to pass on, or for a research worker to acquire from him, information even if such information has no bearing on security or is not classified as confidential.[46]

Keeping in view the desirability of "openness" of governmental affairs in a democratic society, the Franks Committee recommended a repeal of Section 2 of the Act of 1911 and its replacement by the Official Information Act. The proposals restricted criminal sanctions to defined areas of major importance—wrongful disclosures of 1) information of major national importance in the fields of defence, security, foreign relations, currency and reserves; 2) cabinet documents; and 3) information facilitating criminal activity, or violating the confidentiality of information supplied to the government by or about individuals, and the use of information for private

45. 1974 SCC OnLine US SC 163: 41 L Ed 2d 1039: 418 US 683 (1974).

46. *See*, S.A. de Smith, *Constitutional and Administrative Law* (3rd Edn.) 472.

gains. Mere receipt of protected information would not be an offence under the Act, but communication to journalists and others would still be an offence if the author or speaker had reasonable grounds for believing that it had been conveyed to him in breach of the Act. Only material classified as "top secret" or "secret" or "defence confidential" would be protected.

In 1993, the government in England published a white paper on "open government" and proposed a voluntary code of practice of providing information. This code is voluntary and, thus, cannot be equated to a statutory law on access to information. It provides policies and principles relating to disclosure of government information. The sanction behind the code is moral and not legal. If a request for information has been refused, then only a complaint can be made to the parliamentary ombudsman through an MP.

The Local Government (Access to Information) Act, 1985 provided a legal right to information against local governments. The Act provides for greater public access to meetings and documents of the major local councils. However, this Act leaves much to the discretion of the councils and mentions at least 15 categories of exempted information. Individual seeking information has no adequate legal redress. Certainly, this situation could not have lasted long because of popular pressure and Citizen's Charter, so British Parliament in 2001 passed the Freedom of Information Act which came into operation in 2005.

Referring to the right to obtain information and to publish it in the US and England, Howard Simpson, Managing Editor of the *Washington Post*, observed:

> In USA, the publishers have a right to print anything. If you get hold of a State secret, it is the editor who has the determining authority whether to hold it or print it. The government has the right to keep secrets, but if we come by it, nobody can stop us. Whereas in Britain, the press believes in national security, which means they can be told to hold a story back, they have Official Secrets Acts, etc.[47]

Indian Constitution does not specifically provide for the right to information as a fundamental right, though the constitutional philosophy amply supports it. The Preamble of the Constitution constitutes India into a democracy and secures for its people, justice—social, economic and political; liberty of thought; expression and belief. This justifies the conclusion that the Indian Constitution is drawn upon the idea of open government. In the same manner, Article 19(*a*)—freedom of thought and expression, and Article 21—right to life and personal liberty would become redundant if information is not freely available. Article 39(*a*), (*b*), (*c*) of the Constitution make provision for adequate means of livelihood, equitable distribution of material resources of the community to check concentration of wealth and means of production. As today, information is wealth, hence, need for its

47. *Indian Express* 22-2-1980.

equal distribution cannot be overemphasised. Taking a cue from this constitutional philosophy, the Indian Supreme Court found a habitat for freedom of information in Articles 19(*a*) and 21 of the Constitution. Certainly, poverty of information depreciates life and stultifies free speech. Thus, in India, the right to information is a basic human right which cannot be abridged, only reasonable restrictions can be imposed and that too on the grounds mentioned in Article 19(2)(1) of the Constitution. Information in public sphere is owned by the people and government is only a trustee.

Unique fact is that in India the right to information is a direct consequence of people's movement for reaching socio-economic justice to the deprived sections of society, whose entitlements under rural development schemes were being deprived due to lack of information on developmental projects.

It is heartening to note that the highest Bench in India while recognising the efficacy of the "right to know" which is a *sine qua non* of a really effective participatory democracy raised the simple "right to know" to the status of a fundamental right. In *S.P. Gupta* v. *Union of India*[48] (*S.P. Gupta*), the court held that the "right to know" is implicit in the right of free speech and expression guaranteed under the Constitution in Article 19(1)(*a*). The right to know is also implicit in Article 19(1)(*a*) as a corollary to a free press which is included in free speech and expression as a fundamental right. The court decided that the right to free speech and expression includes 1) the right to propagate one's views, ideas and their circulation;[49] 2) the right to seek, receive and impart information and ideas;[50] 3) the right to inform and be informed;[51] 4) the right to know;[52] 5) the right to reply;[53] and 6) the right to commercial speech and commercial information.[54] Furthermore, by narrowly interpreting the privilege of the government to withhold documents under Section 123 of the Evidence Act, 1872, the court has widened the scope of getting information from government files. In the same manner by narrowly interpreting the exclusionary rule of Article 72(2) of the Constitution, the court ruled that the material on which cabinet advice to the President is based can be examined by the court.[55] However, this judicial creativity is no substitute for a constitutional or a statutory right to information. Against this backdrop, the provisions of the Official Secrets Act, 1923 suffer from the stigma of unconstitutionality. Strange as it might seem, the 1981 study of the Indian Law Institute, New Delhi on the Official Secrets Act, 1923 is the only competent review of the Act ever undertaken

48. 1981 Supp SCC 87. See also, *Dinesh Trivedi* v. *Union of India*, (1997) 4 SCC 306.
49. *Express Newspapers (P) Ltd.* v. *Union of India*, AIR 1958 SC 578.
50. *Reliance Petrochemicals Ltd.* v. *Indian Express Newspapers Bombay (P) Ltd.*, (1988) 4 SCC 592.
51. *Hamdard Dawakhana* v. *Union of India*, AIR 1960 SC 554.
52. *Indian Express Newspapers* v. *Union of India*, (1985) 1 SCC 641.
53. *LIC* v. *Manubhai D. Shah*, (1992) 3 SCC 637.
54. *Tata Press Ltd.* v. *Mahanagar Telephone Nigam Ltd.*, (1995) 5 SCC 139.
55. *S.P. Gupta* v. *Union of India*, 1981 Supp SCC 87.

in this country.[56] The Act, broadly speaking, falls into two parts. One concerns espionage and the other which affects the press, deals with unauthorised disclosure of official information. Section 5 of the Act lays down that if any person having in his possession any document or information, which has been entrusted to him in confidence by any government official, or which he has obtained as an official, communicates it to any person other than a person to whom he is authorised to communicate it, he shall be guilty of an offence. So also a person who receives such document or information "knowing or having reasonable ground to believe" that it is being communicated in breach of the Act. Later, the Act was amended to penalise disclosure of documents or even information which is "likely to affect friendly relations with foreign States". Considering the gross arbitrary abuse to which this vaguely and widely-worded expression may be subjected, the Act may be regarded as violating the provisions of Article 19(1)(*a*) of the Constitution and hence unconstitutional.

Section 5 is the virtual reproduction of Section 2 of the British Official Secrets Act, 1911 which is now recognised as wholly inappropriate in the context of any modern democracy. While acquitting the editor of the *Sunday Telegraph* from the charge under the Official Secrets Act, 1911 for publishing a confidential assessment of the situation in Nigeria, written by the Defence Advisor at the British High Commission in Lagos, Caulfield J remarked that Section 2 should be "pensioned off"[57]. Soon there was a demand for repeal which led to the appointment of the Franks Committee. The Committee condemned Section 2 and observed:

> The main offence which Section 2 creates is the unauthorised communication of official information (including documents) by a Crown servant. The leading characteristic of this offence is its catch-all quality. It catches all official documents and information. It makes no distinctions of kind, and no distinctions of degree. All information which a Crown servant learns in the course of his official duty is 'official' for the purpose of Section 2, whatever its nature, whatever its importance, and whatever its original source. A blanket is thrown over everything; nothing escapes. The section catches all Crown servants as well as all official information. Consequently anyone, whether newsman or lay person, who receives such information is liable to punishment. Both the giver and the receiver of information are liable to imprisonment for a term which may extend to three years.[58]

However the uniqueness of the Act is that Ministers are, in effect, self-authorising. They decide for themselves what to reveal. Senior civil servants exercise a considerable degree of personal judgment in deciding what disclosures of official information they may properly make and to whom. Such communication is regarded as "authorised". The result is that official leaks, a fertile source of disinformation, are protected but their exposure

56. *See,* A.G. Noorani, "Secrets Act: An Anachronism", *Indian Express* 31-7-1981.
57. *Ibid.*
58. Frank Committee on S. 2 of the Officials Secret Act, 1911.

by unravelling the whole truth is forbidden.[59] Lord Delvin's remark is very apt, "It [S. 2] instals as the judges of what ought to be revealed men whose interests it is to conceal."

It may be pointed out that Section 2 was drafted in haste in times of crisis. The Bill was put forward by the government as a measure against spying and was essential on grounds of national security and, therefore, was passed without debate.[60] Consequently, its repeal due to its unsuitability to the recent times was recommended by the Franks Committee. The Committee also recommended the replacement of "likelihood of harm" test by the "strict proof" test, while determining injury to the public interest. Section 2 of the Official Secrets Act, 1911 has now been repealed by the British Official Secrets Act, 1989. The UK's Freedom of Information Act, 2005 is a major step towards "open government".

All these criticisms apply with added force to Section 5 of the Indian Official Secrets Act, 1923. The Indian Law Institute's study further points out a glaring difference between English and Indian practices. In England, the Attorney General alone decides whether to prosecute or not. As Lord Shaweross pointed out in a letter to *The Times* (19 November 1970):

> Although the Attorney-General is a political appointee, his actions as Attorney-General and the way he exercises his discretion are entirely non-political. I know of no instance (since the Campbell case) in which the Cabinet has been called upon to decide whether or not a prosecution should take place, still less in which it has taken any such decision on political grounds.[61]

In India, the executive controls the launching and as recent experience shows, even the withdrawal of prosecutions.

2.1 Right to Information Act, 2005

With judicial support, the right to information become a cause of public action and there was a strong demand for a formal law on freedom of information. The States of Goa, Tamil Nadu and Rajasthan have, since 1997, enacted laws ensuring public access to information, although with various restraints and exemptions. There was a pressure on the Central Government also to enact law granting the right to information. Various drafts were submitted for consideration by empowered bodies like the Press Council of India and by independent citizens' groups. Ultimately, the Freedom of Information Act, 2002 was passed which was assented to by the President on 6 January 2003. However, on the suggestion of the National Advisory Council and others, for significant changes in the law, government decided to repeal the Freedom of Information Act, 2002 and in its place enacted the Right to Information Act, 2005 to effectuate the right to information recognised under Article 19 of the Constitution. The Preamble

59. *Ibid.*
60. *Ibid.*
61. Lord Shawcross in a letter to the Times dated 19-9-1970.

of the Act provides for setting up the practical regime of the right to information for all citizens to secure access to information under the control of public authorities in order to promote transparency and accountability in the working of every public authority. Thus, the Act aims at making government a participating government. Present law converts the "freedom of information" into a "right to information" for all citizens. "Information" includes any mode of information in any form of record, document, e-mail, circular, press releases, contract, sample, electronic data, etc. The right to information covers inspection of work, document, record and its certified copy and information in the form of diskettes, floppies, video cassettes in electronic forms, tapes or stored information in computers, etc. Information can be provided on written request or request by electronic means with payment of nominal fee. It is incumbent for the authority to supply required information within 30 days from the date of request and if information relates to life or liberty of a person, then it can be obtained within 48 hours. Penalty for refusal of application or for not providing information within stipulated time is ₹250 per day, but the total amount should not exceed ₹25,000. The Act prohibits information in certain specified categories and puts restrictions on third party informations.

Section 8 of the Act provides restrictions on informations, disclosure of which would prejudicially affect the sovereignty and integrity of India, the security, strategic, scientific or economic interest of the State, relations with foreign States; forbidden informations, disclosure of which would cause a breach of privilege of Parliament or State Legislature; informations relating to commercial confidence, trade secrets or intellectual properties, the disclosure of which would harm the competitive position of a third party; information on fiduciary relationship; confidential information of foreign land; information relating to the physical safety of person; cabinet papers; information relating to personal information; and information prohibited under the Official Secrets Act, 1923. Except the reach of these restrictions, exceptions are common to almost all jurisdictions. The Act further restricts information relating to certain governmental organisations listed in Second Schedule. Such organisations include Intelligence Bureau, Research and Analysis Wing of the Cabinet Secretariat, Directorate of Revenue Intelligence, Central Economic Intelligence Bureau, Directorate of Enforcement, Narcotic Control Bureau, Aviation Research Centre, Special Frontier Force, Border Security Force, Central Reserve Police Force, Indo-Tibetan Border Police, Central Industrial Security Force, National Security Guards, Assam Rifles, Special Service Bureau, Criminal Investigation Department, CBI, Dadra and Nagar Haveli and Special Branch, and Lakshadweep Police.

For the administration of the Act, provision is made for the appointment of Public Information Officers (PIOs), State Information Commissions and Central Information Commission. Central Information Commission is a multimember Commission and Mr Wajahat Habibullah has been appointed its first Chairperson. State Commissions are to be constituted by the respective State Governments. These Information Commissions have been constituted into independent and autonomous commissions so that they may discharge their functions without fear or favour. They enjoy immunity from any prosecution or proceedings for anything done in good faith under the Act. Commissions shall have the power of the civil court while enquiring into any matter. Any aggrieved person can appeal against the decision of the PIO to the officer who is senior in rank within 30 days, and a second appeal is also provided before the Central or State Information Commission, as the case may be, within 90 days. At the end of each year, Central and State Information Commissions shall prepare a final report on the implementation of the Act and would submit it to the respective governments, which shall be laid before Parliament or State Legislatures along with the Action Taken Report.

Rule-making power has been vested in the respective governments and rules made under the Act are to be laid before Parliament or State Legislatures, as the case may be. Judicial intervention is prohibited and therefore, court shall have no power to entertain any suit or proceeding in respect of any order made under the Act. This finality clause shall have no application for constitutional courts because judicial review is the basic feature of the Indian Constitution. The Act under Section 8(1)(*i*) tries to balance the right to information and the right to privacy which emanates from Article 21 of the Constitution. Therefore, personal information shall not be disclosed as it would lead to unwarranted invasion of the privacy of the individual.

Though the provisions of the Act are laudable, yet like all openness law, this Act also faces huge problem of implementation because bureaucrats do not relish openness. Bureaucrats give lip services to any attempt at openness. This become clear from the fact that the Administrative Reform Commission on the Right to Information Act, 2005 recommended 1) that the PIOs be given power to refuse a request for information if, in his opinion, it is manifestly frivolous or vexatious; 2) that the PIOs be given power to deny request if work involved in processing the request would substantially and unreasonably divert resources of a public body; 3) that armed forces be excluded from the purview of the Act. These recommendations, if implemented, would certainly be a retrograde step on the road to openness. Bureaucratic insensitivity to openness also becomes clear from the fact that the government for a long time was thinking of amending the law to prohibit "notefiles" from disclosure. Consequences of non-disclosure of "notefiles" would have been disastrous as notings play an important role in understanding the decision and disclose reasoning and nexus with the ultimate decision. Imagine a well-reasoned note presented to a Minister, he must indicates his views if he disagrees with the decision. Thus "notes" are considered as live wires, snap them and darkness prevail.

The Right to Information Act, 2005 if read with the Official Secrets Act, 1923 may restrict the accessibility of information from unpublished records and documents of the administrative authorities. Excessive classification is an impediment to information sharing. Escape clauses are too many and too wide. Though it is too early to pass any final judgment on the functioning of the Act, yet fact is that due to poverty of awareness and hostility of government officials, law has failed to make any dent on the culture of secrecy. Nevertheless, the trend indicates a movement towards more government accountability and transparency. It cannot be overemphasised that while the normative framework for upholding "openness" is now reasonably well established in India, enforcement remains a key challenge. Central Information Commission Report suggests that people generally exercise their right to information for settling personal scores and not for enforcing governmental transparency and accountability.

The "right to know" has a definite implication for courts also.[62] People have a right to access courtrooms and court judgments, irrespective of the fact whether it affects them individually or generally as a member/members of the community. People in an open society do not demand infallibility from judicial institutions, but it is difficult for them to accept a situation when they are prohibited from observing or reading. Bentham has put it thus, "Where there is no publicity there is no justice." Besides the well-recognised exceptions, in no other situation the public may be excluded from the courtrooms, no matter the parties may have agreed to such a course or the judge may have thought it expedient and desirable. It is gratifying to note that this aspect of the right to know has been fully recognised in India. The Supreme Court in *S.P. Gupta*[63] rejected the government's claim for privilege and ordered disclosure of correspondence and documents pertaining to non-confirmation of Kumar J. Thus, the seed of freedoms of information has been planted but it requires careful nurturing by Parliament and the executive. However, after the passing of the Right to Information Act, 2005, access to information regarding judiciary, especially when it exercises administration functions, has become a matter of concern. Though the Act does not exempt judiciary from its scope, nevertheless judiciary has always claimed exemption. Certainly judiciary cannot apply two standards, one for others and one for itself in the same matter. Today judiciary enjoys absolute powers in matters of appointment of judges of the Supreme Court and the High Courts, there seems to be no reason then why the information regarding appointment of a judge be kept secret. It is surprising that the Central Information Commissions, deferring to the wishes of the Supreme Court, ruled that no information relating to any court or tribunal can be accessed under the Act. Fact remains that judicial arbitrariness is perhaps more worse than legislative or executive

62. *See*, Soli Sorabjee, "The Right to Know", *Indian Express* 16-3-1982.
63. 1981 Supp SCC 87.

arbitrariness. In a society like ours where freedom suffers from atrophy and activism, it is essential for participative democracy that the narrow pedantry which now surrounds the privilege to withhold information must be replaced by the "right to know" mobilisation.

Right to know also has another dimension. The Bhopal gas tragedy and its disaster syndrome could have been avoided, had the people known about the medical repercussions and environmental hazards of the deadly gas leaked from the Union Carbide chemical plant at Bhopal. Therefore, the government has a duty to provide people baseline health data around existing hazardous plants. Failure to undertake such studies and to provide information to people must render government liable.

In India, bureaucrats place serious difficulties in the way of the public's legitimate access to information. The reason for this can be found in colonial heritage. Even after independence, a government official feels that he is acting on behalf of the President or the Governor and not on behalf of the public. Hence, he had to remain anonymous and keep his actions secret for the convenience of the government in power. A democratic government, to use the words of Woodrow Wilson, "ought to be all outside and not inside". There is a strong public feeling against secrecy of any kind in the administration of government. The secrecy system has become much less a means by which government protects national security than a means by which the government safeguards its reputation, dissembles its purpose, buries its mistakes, manipulates its citizens and maximises its power and corrupts itself.[64]

Today in India, secrecy prevails not only in every segment of governmental administration but also in public bodies, statutory or non-statutory. There is a feeling everywhere that it pays to play safe. Even routine reports on social issues continue to be treated as confidential long after they are submitted. The result is that there is no debate on important matters and no feedback to the government on the reaction of the people. The stronger the efforts at secrecy, the greater the chance of abuse of authority by functionaries.

There is need for administrative secrecy in certain cases. No one wants classified documents concerning national defence and foreign policy to be made public till after the usual period of 35 years is over. Secrecy may also be claimed for other matters enumerated in the Right of Information Act, 2005. But the claims of secrecy, generally by the government and public bodies, may play havoc with the survival of democracy in India. Because of the constraints of the Official Secrets Act, 1923, which was drafted to suit the needs of a foreign rule in India, the claims of informing the public are ignored. The government has unlimited powers to classify documents as confidential with impunity.

64. K.K. Mathew J, "The Nature and Scope of the Right to Know in a Democratic Republic", (1979) 3 SCC J-19, quoting President Polak.

The government has also in 1986 amended the Commissions of Inquiry Act, 1952 in such a way as to empower the government to suppress reports of any enquiry commission under the Act if it is satisfied that in the interest of sovereignty and integrity of India, security of State, friendly relations with foreign States or in the public interest, it is not expedient to lay the report before Parliament or the State Legislature, as the case may be. This was done in the wake of the Thakker Commission Report relating to the assassination of Mrs Indira Gandhi and also the Ranganathan Commission Report relating to the riots following Mrs Gandhi's assassination. This may also seriously jeopardise the people's right to know if the power of withholding information is not properly exercised.

At a seminar on "press, society and government" organised by the Servants of the People Society at Chandigarh,[65] the "right to know" received mammoth support. B.C. Verghese, Editor-in-Chief, *Indian Express* said that information cannot be doled out like ration and the "executive privilege" was an invasion against democracy which was sustained by the people. In a democracy, the citizen's right to know is assumed rather than guaranteed. In fact, the right is derived from the government's accountability and answerability to the people. Therefore, no government should think that people must be told only that much which it thinks to be good for the people and safe for itself.

Dealing directly with the "right to know", the Supreme Court has held on various occasions that it is a fundamental right of the people covered under Articles 19(*a*), 14 and 21 of the Constitution. Moving forward in the same direction, the court in *Union of India* v. *Assn. for Democratic Reforms*[66] held that voter's right to know antecedents including criminal past of a candidate to membership of Parliament or Legislative Assembly is also a fundamental right. Court observed that voter's speech and expression in case of election would include casting of vote, that is to say, that voter speaks out or expresses by casting of vote and for this purpose information about candidate to be selected is a must. In this case, the Supreme Court had further directed the Election Commission to acquire information about crime and property and education status of the candidates as a part of the nomination paper. Subsequently, Parliament amended the Representation of People (Third Amendment) Act, 2002 by which a candidate was required to supply information about his conviction in a criminal case, however, he was not required to give information about his assets and education. Declaring the amendment as illegal, null and void as violative of voter's fundamental right to know under Article 19(1)(*a*), the court in *People's Union of Civil Liberties* (*PUCL*) v. *Union of India*[67] held that the information allowed by the Amendment Act, 2002 is deficient in ensuring free and fair elections which is the basic structure of the Constitution. Similarly, the court

65. *Indian Express*, Chandigarh 12-12-1982.
66. (2002) 5 SCC 294.
67. (2003) 4 SCC 399.

held that people have a right to know the circumstances under which their representatives got allotment of petroleum retail outlets.[68]

Sometimes, there appears to be a conflict between the right to know and the right to privacy of public figures through whom the machinery of government moves. Our experience in India suggests that a public figure should not be allowed protection against exposure of his private life which has some relevance to his public duties on the plea that he has a right to privacy. The right to privacy should not be allowed as a pretext to suppress information.[69]

3. DISCRETION TO DISOBEY

St. Thomas Aquinas wrote, "Laws may be unjust though being opposed to the divine good; such laws are the laws of tyrants... laws of this kind must no wise be observed." About laws which are ultra vires the authority granted to the lawmaker, St. Thomas says that those are acts of violence rather than laws, and such laws do not bind the conscience. St. Augustine also expressed the view that a law which is not just is no law at all.[70] However, today any talk about discretion to disobey may sound seditious at least to those whose minds are trained in the common-law system. In a country like India where people are disempowered, the judicial process grinds slow and the other grievance procedures are feeble and inefficient, perhaps the discretion to disobey may provide an effective check on the operation of the governmental machinery in a reckless manner. It is gratifying to note that at a time when we are not only governed but administered, the Supreme Court has rightly taken the right foot forward in allowing discretion to disobey void orders. The decision of the Supreme Court in *Nawabkhan Abbaskhan* v. *State of Gujarat*[71] allows every person the discretion to make his own decision and disobey an order of the government, if in his opinion it is void. If he turns out to be wrong in his decision, of course, he is answerable, but if he is right he is not answerable in any way. In this case, the petitioner was prosecuted under Section 142 of the Bombay Police Act, 1951 because he had violated the externment order passed by the Police Commissioner. The accused was acquitted by the trial court, but on appeal by the State, the High Court reversed the order of the lower court. The important fact in this whole process was that the accused had challenged the validity of the externment order before the High Court under Article 226 during the pendency of his criminal trial and the High Court quashed the order on 16 July 1968. The accused took the defence

68. *Onkar Lal Bajaj* v. *Union of India*, (2003) 2 SCC 673.
69. This was also the consensus at a seminar on the Right to Know and the Right to Privacy organised by the Haryana Union of Journalists on 20-8-1983. *Indian Express*, Chandigarh 23-8-1983.
70. *See*, "Summa Theologica", 96, 4 and "De Libero Arbitrio", 1, 5 quoted in review of this book by Joseph Minattur (Dr) in (1982) 9(3) Journal of the Bar Council of India 637–41, 640.
71. (1974) 2 SCC 121.

in criminal appeal proceedings before the High Court that since the order becomes *void ab initio* and there being no externment order in the eye of law, there is no offence when he re-entered the forbidden area on 17 September 1967. The question whether a person can disobey the order with impunity if subsequently that order is quashed was answered by the High Court in the negative. The High Court held:

> There is no principle in upholding the respondent's claim that he has a right to violate an order passed by an authority having jurisdiction to pass it, if subsequently he can persuade the court that there was an inbuilt lacuna or latent defect in the said order. In other words he claims to have the right to judge for himself whether it is legal or illegal and in anticipation of the court upholding his contention, the right to violate it with impunity.[72]

On appeal, the Supreme Court reversed the decision of the High Court and held that the externment order is of no effect and its violation is no offence. The individual decision making by private persons of public actions may be considered as a very radical approach, but the alternative is a travesty of constitutional guarantees. Grave consequences involved in allowing discretion to disobey, someone may argue, may first lead to anarchy and then to tyranny. But what is the remedy available to a person who has been subjected to an illegal order? Our legal system does not recognise the right to compensation for damage suffered by a person in obeying an invalid order. However, the distinction between a "void" and "voidable" order brought in by the Supreme Court obstructed the real thrust of the decisions.

This brings us to another problem which is a necessary corollary to the proposition of "discretion to disobey". The problem is: To what extent a person can resort to "self-help" against a public servant who seeks to enforce an invalid law or order against him. The problem came before the Supreme Court in a slightly different complexion in *Kesho Ram* v. *Delhi Admn.*[73] In this case, the appellant struck a Section Inspector of the Delhi Municipal Corporation on the nose which bled and also got fractured. The Inspector had gone to the appellant to seize his buffalo in discharge of his duties to realise the arrears of milk tax from him. The main contention of the appellant was that the attempt to realise the arrears of milk tax by duress was illegal because no demand notice under Section 154 of the Delhi Municipal Corporation Act, 1957 was ever given, so he had a right of self-defence against illegal action. The Supreme Court negatived the contention because in its opinion the Inspector was acting in good faith and had simply erred in the exercise of his powers. However, the Supreme Court reduced the sentence of the appellant from three years to imprisonment already undergone on the ground that the Inspector acted in an improper manner under a misconception about the mode of exercise of his powers. Though the decision is a pointer in the right direction, yet the course of

72. *Ibid.*
73. (1974) 4 SCC 509.

law in this area is still to be watched carefully. It is strange that the case of *Stroud* v. *Bradbury*[74], a leading English case on the point, was not brought to the notice of the court. In this case, a Sanitary Inspector had entered the house of the appellant under the provisions of the Public Health Act, 1936 without giving prior notice which was the requirement of law. The appellant obstructed the entry of the Inspector. The court held that the appellant had the right to obstruct entry of the Inspector which was not warranted by law.

When the Government of India seriously addresses itself to administrative law reforms, it is necessary that the forms of redress against official conduct must receive priority. There seems to be a strong resistance to any significant change, as we saw in the Law Commission's and Administrative Reform Commission's attempts to instigate widespread reform which was resisted by the government. The canvas of grievance redress strategies must be spread wide to include the "right to know" and the "discretion to disobey", besides other judicial and administrative techniques, if the rampant corruption and the abuse of power is to be checked effectively before the people lose complete faith in democracy in India.

4. CENTRAL VIGILANCE COMMISSION (CVC)

In any system of government, improvements in the grievance redressal machinery have always engaged the attention of the people. Even in parliamentary forms of governments, where the rulers rule with the consent of the people, the need for a viable grievance redressal machinery cannot be overemphasised. Actualities of our times have proved false the assumption that the system of responsible government provides for a built-in continuous review of the activities of the administration. The growth of party discipline and the prominence of partisan attitudes in asserting grievances and defending the performance of the governments by Ministers tend to create an unfavourable atmosphere for the proper consideration of individual complaints against the administration. This system no matter, howsoever ineffective, completely fails when inertia and corruption filter from the top. It was against this backdrop that the establishment of the CVC was recommended by the Committee on Prevention of Corruption, the Santhanam Committee. The Committee known after the name of its Chairman was appointed in 1962. It recommended the establishment of a CVC as the highest authority at the head of the existing anti-corruption organisation consisting of the Directorate of General Complaints and Redress, the Directorate of Vigilance and the Central Police Organisation.[75] The recommendations of the Santhanam Committee were accepted by the government and, thus, the CVC was established on a non-statutory basis under a

74. (1952) 2 All ER 76.
75. Other existing grievance machineries included Special Police Establishment (1943), Vigilance Organisation (1955) and Central Bureau of Investigation (1963).

Resolution No. 24/7/64 dated 11 February 1964. The CVC was attached to the Ministry of Home Affairs of the Government of India. Nevertheless, it is independent in its functioning in the sense the Union Public Service Commission (UPSC) is and no order, direction or instruction can be issued by the Ministry so as to interfere with its independent operation. The Central Vigilance Commissioner was appointed by the President for a term of six years or till he attains the age of 65 years, whichever is earlier. Therefore, the Central Vigilance Commissioner, like other civil servants, does not hold office at the pleasure of the President. He can be removed or suspended from the office by the President on the ground of misbehaviour, but only after the Supreme Court has held an enquiry into his case and recommended action against him. His responsibilities include the operation of the vigilance machinery and coordination of the work of vigilance officers subordinate to him.

The powers and functions of the Commission were set out in the resolution under which it is established. It exercised general control and supervision over the vigilance and anti-corruption work carried on in various Ministries, departments and public undertakings. It had been given jurisdiction and power to conduct an enquiry into transactions in which public servants are suspected of impropriety and corruption including misconduct, misdemeanour, lack of integrity and malpractices against civil servants. The Commission was assisted by the CBI in its operations. The CVC has taken a serious note of the growing preoccupation of the CBI with work other than vigilance. Thus, when the CBI is extensively used for non-corruption investigation work such as drug-trafficking, smuggling and murders, it hampers the work of the CVC. The CVC also advises the Home Ministry on the necessity of departmental disciplinary action against public servants where prima facie charges of corruption and misconduct are established.

But how effective this institution has proved in uprooting corruption depends on various factors, the most important being the earnestness on the part of the government, citizens and institutions to clean public life. Over the years, the independence of the CVC has also been seriously compromised. Originally, the CVC had been equated with the UPSC and its Chairman had a six years' term. However, later on it was reduced to five years which was further reduced to three years in 1977 with a provision for two years' extension at the pleasure of the government. U.C. Agarwal who demitted office on 7 July 1987, after a period of three years, was not only refused extension of two years but the office remained vacant for about one year when C.G. Somiah, former Home Secretary, was appointed in 1988. It is discouraging to note that the CVC has mentioned in its 1982 Annual Report 41 cases where the government did not accept its advice of imposing major penalty on erring officials in various units in the Central sector.[76]

76. *Indian Express*, Chandigarh 29-8-1983, 5.

The Commission has suggested premature retirement as the legitimate handle to be used for weeding out the corrupt among the public servants in higher positions. The Commission in its 1982 Report also suggested that in cases where prosecution cannot be launched due to lack of evidence and other reasons, corrective and deterrent action should be taken at the stage of confirmation or the crossing of efficiency bar.[77] In its 1986 Report, the Commission has reacted sharply to the government decision to limit its role over public sector undertakings where the problem of corruption is by no means negligible.

In its efforts to check corruption in public life and to provide good governance, the Supreme Court recommended measures of far-reaching consequences while disposing a PIL petition on the *CBI* v. *V.C. Shukla*[78] (*Jain Hawala*). The three-judge Bench separated four major investigating agencies from the control of the executive. These agencies are the CBI, Enforcement Directorate, Revenue Intelligence Department and the CVC. The court has shifted the CBI under the administrative control of the CVC. The CVC, until now, was under the Home Ministry entrusted with the task of bringing to book cases of corruption and sundry wrong-doings and suggesting departmental action. Now the CVC is to be the umbrella agency and would coordinate the work of three other investigating arms. The court further directed that the CVC should be made a statutory body and its head is to be selected by a three-man high-powered panel consisting of the Prime Minister, the Home Minister and the leader of the Opposition.

In order to give effect to the views of the Supreme Court, the government issued an ordinance on 25 August 1998. However, this measure had diluted the views of the Supreme Court by pitting one view against the other. Therefore, what ought to have been visualised as a reformative step had begun to be seen as a cleaver bureaucratic legalese. Main objections against the Ordinance related to 1) restricting the membership of the CVC to bureaucrats; 2) making prior permission of the competent authority mandatory before starting investigation against government officers above the rank of Joint Secretary and high ranking officers of nationalised banks and public sector undertakings; and 3) making the Secretary Personnel ex officio member. Objections were also raised against Article 21 of the Ordinance which had authorised the Commission to make rules but in consultation with the government.

It was when the Supreme Court expressed concern over these aspects of the Ordinance in the hearing relating to its validity that the government decided to amend the Ordinance and, thus, on 27 October 1998 the Central Vigilance Commission (Amendment) Ordinance was issued. The Commission was made a four-member body and its membership was opened to "others" besides bureaucrats. In the same manner, the single

77. *Indian Express*, Chandigarh 4-9-1983.
78. (1998) 3 SCC 410. See also, *The Tribune* 19-12-1997.

directive of prior permission was deleted and the membership of Secretary Personnel, Government of India was deleted. Nagarajan Vittal, a retired senior bureaucrat, was appointed the first Chief Vigilance Commissioner after the Commission was given a statutory status. It is too early to comment on the functioning of the reconstituted statutory CVC, but one thing is certain that no commission can root out corruption which has sunk so deep in the body politic. It can only act as a facilitator and propellant in the absence of a strong political will.

To ensure probity in public life and incorruptibility in public officials, government at last brought before Parliament the Central Vigilance Commission Bill, 2003, which was passed amidst doubts expressed by many Members that the law is unlikely to be an effective instrument against corruption in the administration due to many anomalies apparent in the Bill.

An obnoxious feature of the Bill is much-derided single directive provisions contained in Section 6-A which protects officials of the rank of Joint Secretary and above from investigation and prosecution without the permission of the government. This has managed to circumvent even a Supreme Court directive to do away with this provision terming it "arbitrary, unreasonable and overprotective" in *Jain Hawala*[79] . The Law Commission of India, to which the matter was referred, also concurred with the Supreme Court's view. In simple terms, this provision would make it impossible for the police to investigate corruption cases against senior bureaucrats because necessary permission, which will come from upper reaches of bureaucracy itself, may come too late or not at all. Chapter III of the Bill relating to the powers and functions of the CVC restricts it from giving any directive to the CBI or to the vigilance departments of various corporations and government departments inconsistent with the instructions of the government. Furthermore, as presently worded, it is possible for the government to ignore the views of the leader of Opposition while making appointments to the Commission because there is no requirement of a consensus between the Prime Minister, Home Minister and the leader of Opposition in matter of such appointments. This may make the CVC a nominee of the government. All this may rob the CVC of an effective role in ensuring probity in public life.

POINTS FOR DISCUSSION

1. After the birth of the institution of ombudsman in Sweden in 1809, it soon became a most cherished importable commodity the world over. Efforts made in India so far to establish this institution may be discussed with special reference to its desirability and effectiveness in a vast country like India ridden by unprincipled and competitive politics, corruption and inertia.

---

79. (1998) 3 SCC 410. See also, *The Tribune* 19-12-1997.

2. The Report of the Joint Select Committee on the Lokpal Bill, 1977 presented to Parliament on 20 July 1979 recommended to include the MPs within the scope of the Bill. There is a sharp cleavage of opinion on this aspect of the Bill. The points for and against this extension of the Bill may be discussed with reference to the concept of ministerial responsibility.
3. The purpose of the Lokpal is not to adjudicate but to provide a regular machinery for investigating grievances against the administration in a discreet and informal way. Under these circumstances, will it not be a futile institution unless the attitude of the party in power and bureaucrats in position defending the performance of the government is most strong?
4. Generally vague terms like "misconduct", "allegation", "maladministration", "injustice" and "grievance" define the jurisdiction of the ombudsman. The scope and ambit of these expressions may be discussed to fix the boundaries of jurisdiction in Indian situations.
5. The Lokpal Bill, 1977 did not contemplate any constitutional status for the Lokpal. It is generally feared that this may bring the Lokpal within the scope of judicial review and, thus, dilute his authority and effectiveness. Will it be desirable to give the Lokpal a constitutional status and insulate him from the jurisdiction of courts? Discussion may cover growing disenchantment with judicial and parliamentary methods of redress.
6. After reading the Lokpal Bill, 1977, sceptics may refer to the "ombudsman" as "ombudsmouse" because he has not been given teeth and his jurisdiction remains advisory which may have very little or no meaning in partisan politics. A complainant on the other hand may get nothing except an official regret. Against this backdrop, evaluation may be made of jurisdictional limitations of the proposed Lokpal in India.
7. On what grounds the Lokpal and Lokayuktas Act, 2013, can be said to be an improvement on the earlier proposed Bill of 1977? Is it desirable to exempt the ombudsman from the power of judicial review?
8. Parliamentary ombudsman in Finland assumes jurisdiction over armed forces and even courts. Is it desirable to give the ombudsman such a wide jurisdiction?
9. How does the concept of ombudsman conflict with the concept of responsible government under a constitutional democracy?
10. Information is the bloodstream of democracy. Without the "right to know", the freedom of speech and expression which includes freedom of press guaranteed by Article 19 of the Constitution becomes meaningless. Against this background, the constitutionality of the Official Secrets Act, 1923 may be discussed.
11. The American Congress passed the Freedom of Information Act, 1966 which replaced the principle of "need to know" with a "right to

know". This led to the development of investigative journalism and made possible the publication of the Pentagon Papers and the exposure of Watergate. The desirability of a similar type of legislation replacing the Official Secrets Act, 1923 may be discussed.

12. Even the most ardent advocates of the "right to know" realise that a certain area of secrecy, no matter howsoever limited, must belong to the government. It is because of this reason that the American legislation provides nine well-defined escape clauses. These escape clauses are considered to be very wide. The discussion should aim at demarcating escape clauses in the Indian situation in view of the Right to Information Act, 2005.
13. "Discretion to disobey" may sound seditious but in view of the growing disenchantment with the parliamentary, judicial and administrative redress processes, it may be the only alternative left to put the administration on the tab. Against this background, the whole concept of "discretion to disobey" and "self-help against government officials" may be discussed.
14. Central Vigilance Commission Bill, 2003 may be discussed with special reference to Section 6-A which contains single directive provision and has a tendency of robbing the CVC of an effective role in ensuring probity in public life.

SUGGESTED READINGS

1. A.G. Noorani, "Press and Citizen's Right to Know", Indian Express 25-11-1987, 4; "Cult of Secrecy", Indian Express 3-9-1986, 4.
2. A.W. Bradley, "The Redress of Grievances", (1962) Cambridge LJ 82.
3. "Administrative Reforms Commission", Interim Report on Problems of Citizen's Grievances (1966).
4. Balram K. Gupta, "Ombudsmanic Role of the Newspapers", (1882) 3 SCC J-34.
5. C.K. Thakker, *Administrative Law* (Eastern Book Company 2012) 1058–61.
6. C.R. Rawat (Ed.), *The Ombudsman: Citizen's Defender* (1966).
7. Carol Harlow, "Ombudsman in Search of a Role", (1978) Mod L Rev 41.
8. D.C. Rawat, "The Proposed Ombudsman System for India", (1971) 5 Journal of Constitutional and Parliamentary Studies 285.
9. D. Williams, "Parliamentary Commissioner Act", (1967) 30 Mod L Rev 547.
10. Daniel Awdry, "Parliamentary Commissionery", Law and the Commonwealth (1971) 18.
11. Frank Stracy, *Ombudsman Compared* (1978).
12. Frank Stracy, *The British Ombudsman* (1971).
13. G. Borrie, "The Watchdog Barks", (1962) 112 Law Journal 432.

14. Gellhorn, *When Americans Complain* (1966).
15. Gellhorn and Others, *Citizens' Protectors in Nine Countries* (1967).
16. H.C. Dholakia, "The Lokpal: A Comparative View", (1978) 7 Journal of the Bar Council of India 750.
17. H.W.R. Wade, "The Ombudsman: The Citizen's Defender", Law and the Commonwealth (1971) 3.
18. I.M. Pedersen, "Parliamentary Commissioner: A Danish View", (1962) Public Law 15.
19. I.P. Massey, "Discretion to Disobey Invalid Orders", (1978) 1 SCC J-32.
20. J.D. Michell, "Ombudsman Fallacy", (1962) Public Law 24.
21. K.K. Mathew, "The Nature and Scope of the Right to Know in a Democratic Republic", (1979) 3 SCC J-19.
22. Kadish and Kadish, *Discretion to Disobey* (1973).
23. Lord Lloyd , "Parliamentary Commissioner", (1968) Current Legal Problems 53.
24. M.P. Jain, Lokpal: *Ombudsman in India* (1970).
25. M.P. Jain, "The First Year of Ombudsman in England", (1972) 14 JILI 159.
26. M.P. Jain, "The Ombudsman in New Zealand", (1963) 6 JILI 307.
27. Dr. Madhubrata Mohanty, "The Lokpal Act, 2013 - Still Waiting for the Sunrise", 2018 SCC OnLine Blog OpEd 24.
28. N.D. Vandyk, "A Collective Ombudsman", (1960) 104 Solicitors' Journal 357.
29. *Official Secrecy and the Press* (Indian Law Institute Publication 1982).
30. P.K. Tripathi, "The Proposed Indian Ombudsman", (1967) 9 JILI 135.
31. Pragya Jain and Akshita Singh, "XII. Down the Rabbit Hole of India's Anti-Corruption Practices", 8.1 RFMLR (2021) 270.
32. Prakriti Bhatt, "Whistle Blowing: A Hobson's Choice? Cherry-Picking Between State Authorities and Third-Party Internet Platforms", (2019) 10 Law Rev GLC 1.
33. R.L. Narasimhan, "The Indian Ombudsman Proposal—A Critique", Law and Commonwealth (1971) 24.
34. Rajeev Dhavan, *Contempt of Court and the Press* (1982) Chap. V.
35. Rajeev Dhavan, "Engrafting Ombudsman Idea on a Parliamentary Democracy—A Comment on the Lokpal Bill", (1977) 19 JILI 257.
36. Richard Kirkham, Brian Thompson, and Trevor Buck, "When Putting Things Right Goes Wrong: Enforcing the Recommendations of the Ombudsman" (2008) PL 510.
37. Richard Kirkham, "Challenging the Authority of the Ombudsman" (2006) 69 MLR 792.
38. "Right to Rebellion and Obedience to Superior Orders" in K.K. Mathew, Three Lectures (1983) Lecture 3.

39. S.K. Agrawala, *The Proposed Indian Ombudsman* (1971).
40. S.P. Sathe, "Lokpal and Lokayukta: The Indian Ombudsman", (1969) 38 Journal of the University of Bombay 265.
41. S.R. Maheshwari, *Open Government in India* (1981).
42. Sir Edmund Compton, "Parliamentary Commissioner for Administration", (1968) Journal of the Society of Public Teachers of Law 101.
43. "The Citizen and the Administration: the Redress of Grievances", A Report by Justice Stevens (1961).
44. T.E. Utley, *Occasion for Ombudsman* (1961).
45. Tanya Ganguly and Deeya Mittal, "IV. "A Switch in Time, Saves Nine" - Minimizing Corporate Crime by Maximizing Corporate Whistle-Blower Protection in India", (2020) 3.2 JCLG 70.
46. V.R. Krishna Iyer, *Freedom of Information* (Eastern Book Company, Lucknow 1990).

Chapter 14

Constitutional Protection to Civil Servants and the Administrative Services Tribunal

In India, government is the biggest provider of jobs to the people. According to an estimate in 1947, the strength of civil servants was 10 lakhs which rose to 20 lakhs in 1978 and became 30 lakhs in 1993. However, this does not include the jobs in public sector undertakings. Maximum number of jobs provided by the government are in defence, Railways and post offices.

This tremendous growth in civil services was mainly due to the fact that without a big army of civil servants, it was not possible to realise the dream of a welfare state which was the cornerstone of the Indian Constitution. After independence in order to achieve the goals of social welfare, economic and social justice, government passed various socio-economic legislations and prepared various schemes and programmes to provide social and economic justice to the people, especially the weaker sections of society, which could not have been operationalised without an expansion of the civil services.

India is the only country where law relating to service matters of the civil servants is provided in the Constitution. The reason for this was that the members of Indian Civil Service (ICS), who were considered to be the steel-frame of the British Government of India, wanted that their salaries and conditions of service be protected through the Constitution, and that the civil services of independent India be also protected by the Constitution so that the services in India could remain immune from the political vagaries. Therefore, Chapter XIV, containing Articles from 308 to 323 providing protection to civil servants, was included in the Constitution. However, Article 314 which provided protection to the members of the ICS was repealed by the Constitution (28th Amendment) Act, 1972 after the last member of the service retired.

India also tops the list of the countries where suits filed by its servants against their master-State are the maximum. Litigation increased so much that on the one hand it clogged the wheels of justice and on the other it made the government servants dissatisfied, inefficient and demoralised. Therefore, in 1985 by-pass surgery was done to clear the arteries of the administration by passing the Administrative Tribunals Act, 1985 which aimed at establishing service tribunals at the Centre and the State levels to decide service disputes of the Central and State Government employees. But will this surgery restore the health of the administration to the normal position is still an open question. It is self-evident that the tribunals have not been able to perform to the expectation as substitutes to the High Court, therefore, these tribunals have been brought under the jurisdiction of the High Court to play only supplemental role in service matters.[1]

Civil services play a crucial role in the administration of a State in every country, but in a welfare state like India civil services play a still more important role because it is the duty of civil servants to execute policies and programmes of the government and also to provide necessary inputs for future policy planning. Therefore, it is expected that a civil servant would be imaginative, dynamic, effective, committed, objective, independent, fair, reasonable and non-political. However, unfortunately the popular image of a civil servant has gone down considerably. Today, the general impression is that civil servants have become political, useable and pliable and that there is corruption, indifference and inertia in the services, besides maladministration, non-administration and abuse of power. Therefore, civil servants cease to be a second line of defence in case political executive fails.

Civil services in India, modelled on British pattern, are based on "tenure system" in contradistinction to American model which is based on "spoil system". Hence the nature of civil service in India is "status" and not "contract". No matter the conditions of service of civil servants can be changed unilaterally by the government and a civil post can be created, abolished and filled at its discretion, yet in case of illegal termination of service, a government servant can claim reinstatement.[2]

Provisions of Chapter XIV of the Constitution apply to established civil services of the Union and the States and to civil posts under the Union and the States. Article 308 of the Constitution provides that the expression "State" in this chapter does not include the State of Jammu and Kashmir.[3] The definition of the word "State" as given under Article 12 of the Constitution is also not applicable to define the scope of the term "State" in Chapter XIV because here the scope of the term "State" is very much narrow. Thus, in the context of Chapter XIV, "State" shall not include panchayats, local bodies, public corporations and government companies unless the law provides otherwise.[4] Therefore, the word "State" in Chapter XIV means only a State as specified in Part A or Part B of the First Schedule of the Constitution.[5]

1. *L. Chandra Kumar* v. *Union of India*, (1997) 3 SCC 261.
2. *C. Sankaranarayanan* v. *State of Kerala*, (1971) 2 SCC 361.
3. Constitution (7th Amendment) Act, 1956.
4. In the State of Gujarat, Panchayats are "State" within Art. 308.
5. Constitution (7th Amendment) Act, 1956.

1. SERVICE RULES

Under the provisions of Article 309, appropriate legislature has been empowered to frame service rules regarding recruitment and conditions of service of persons appointed to public services and posts in connection with the affairs of the Union or of any State. The proviso to Article 309 further provides that until the legislature has legislated on the subject, the executive may frame rules in this behalf. Rule-making powers of the legislature and the executive is thus coextensive.[6] Nevertheless, the power of the government to make rules is subject to the legislative power of the legislature.[7]

Opening words of Article 309, "Subject to the provisions of this Constitution", clearly indicate that the service rules whether legislated by the legislature or framed by the government must conform to the mandatory provisions of Articles 310, 311 and 320 of the Constitution. Similarly, the service rules should also not violate the provisions of Articles 14 and 16 of the Constitution. Thus in *Moti Ram Deka* v. *North East Frontier Railway*[8], the court held that the Rules 148(3) and 149(3) of the Railway Code, which provided for termination of services of permanent employees by giving them notice for the period mentioned in the rules, violate Article 311. In the same manner, in *W.B. SEB* v. *Desh Bandhu Ghosh*[9], the Supreme Court ruled that the service rule providing for termination of service on three months' notice on either side is arbitrary and, hence, violative of Article 14 of the Constitution.

Subject to the provisions of Article 20(1), rules under Article 309 can be made with retrospective operation,[10] however there must be a nexus between rules and retrospectivity.[11] Therefore, it is not enough that the statute should authorise retrospective operation of rules, the government must also show that there was sufficient reasonable and rational justification for applying the rules retrospectively. However, the power under Article 309 to make laws with retrospective effect cannot be exercised to nullify a vested right.[12] Besides making rules, government, in exercise of its administrative powers, can issue instructions also in order to fill a gap. Such instructions are binding provided these are not contrary to any existing law or rule.

Under Article 309, rules can be framed by the legislature or the government relating to recruitment and conditions of service of the civil servants. No matter the words "conditions of service" are comprehensive enough, but a rule validating a past illegal retirement was held to be beyond the authorisation of Article 309.[13] However, the rules dealing

6. *Ram Autar Pandey* v. *State of U.P.*, 1961 SCC OnLine All 223: AIR 1962 All 328 (FB).
7. *Katyani Dayal* v. *Union of India*, (1980) 3 SCC 245, 260–61.
8. AIR 1964 SC 600, 617.
9. (1985) 3 SCC 116.
10. *B.S. Vadera* v. *Union of India*, AIR 1969 SC 118.
11. *B.S. Yadav* v. *State of Haryana*, 1980 Supp SCC 524.
12. *Union of India* v. *Tushar Ranjan Mohanty*, (1994) 5 SCC 450.
13. *State of Mysore* v. *Padmanabhacharya*, AIR 1966 SC 602.

with compulsory retirement were held to be rules relating to conditions of service.[14]

It is surprising that though Article 309 had contemplated that the legislature would make service rules, yet it has not been done and the civil services continue to be governed by the rules made by the executive. The reason for this seems to be that it is comparatively easy to change service rules to suit the requirements of the government and the services. But this logic has made the service rules a plaything in the hands of the government,[15] which are frequently changed; sometimes, just to suit the convenience, sometimes to tide over a temporary crisis, sometimes to appease a class of officers who shout louder, and sometimes to strike at an individual.[16]

1.1 Tenure of office: The doctrine of pleasure

Clause (1) of Article 310 lays down that every person who is a member of a defence service, or a civil service of the Union, or of an All-India service, or holds any post connected with defence or any civil post under the Union, holds office during the pleasure of the President and in the same manner, any person who is a member of a civil service of a State or holds any civil post under a State shall hold office during the pleasure of the Governor. Thus, Article 310 makes the tenure of civil servants at the pleasure of the President or the Governor, as the case may be.

This "pleasure" doctrine has been imported from England. Common-law doctrine of pleasure is based on the principle of public policy in order to make civil servants responsible to the government and responsive to the people. In common law, this doctrine implies that the civil service is not a contract and, hence, service can be terminated at any time without assigning any reason, and a civil servant cannot enforce any condition of his service in a court of law and cannot claim damages or arrears of salary against the government. In this common-law doctrine, Parliament has now made many inroads by legislation relating to employment, social security and labour relations.[17]

The doctrine of pleasure as developed in England has not been accepted in full in India. It is subject to the provisions of Article 311 which lays down procedural safeguards for civil servants. Thus, Article 311 becomes a proviso to Article 310. Therefore, services of any civil servants cannot be terminated at pleasure unless the mandatory provisions of Article 311 have been observed. The doctrine of pleasure is further restricted by the general law of the land which empowers any civil servant to file suit in a court of law for enforcing any condition of his service and for claiming arrears of

14. *Shyam Lal* v. *State of U.P.*, AIR 1954 SC 369.
15. *B.S. Yadav* v. *State of Haryana*, 1980 Supp SCC 524.
16. *Ibid*, SCC 536–37, AIR 569.
17. *Om Prakash* v. *State of U.P.*, AIR 1955 SC 600. Now Central Administrative Tribunal is the forum for this purpose.

pay. The power to dismiss at pleasure any civil servant is not a personal right of the President or the Governor, as the case may be. It is an executive power which is to be exercised at the advice of Council of Ministers.[18] Doctrine of pleasure as contained in Article 310, being a constitutional provision, cannot be abrogated by any legislative or executive law, therefore Article 309 is to be read subject to Article 310. This is not the case in England where Constitution is unwritten and, hence, the common-law doctrine of pleasure can be whittled down by any act of Parliament.

The doctrine of pleasure only applies to civil services and posts held under the State. Therefore, this doctrine has no application to various constitutional posts of judges of the Supreme Court and High Courts, Chairman and members of Public Service Commissions, Chief Election Commissioner, and Comptroller and Auditor General of India. These functionaries hold office for the term as laid down in the Constitution and can be removed only according to the procedure as also laid down in the Constitution.

Clause (2) of Article 310 especially empowers the government to enter into service contracts with persons having special qualifications. The doctrine of pleasure can be qualified or limited by such service agreements. Thus, in order to secure the services of any person, the government may include in the service agreement a provision for compensation in case of premature abolition of the post or retirement not due to misconduct.

Defence personnel fall under the category where President of India has absolute pleasure to terminate their services under Article 310(1). Pleasure doctrine can be invoked by the President at any stage of inquiry on being satisfied that continuance of any officer is not in the interest of security of the State. In such situation though court has the power to review the pleasure of the President but it cannot substitute its own conclusion on the basis of material on record keeping in view the imperatives of national security and safety.[19] Thus, judicial review available to defence personnel in such situation is highly limited.

1.2 Limitations on pleasure doctrine

(1) Articles 14, 15 and 16 place limitations on the free exercise of pleasure doctrine. Article 14 prohibits any discriminatory and arbitrary termination of service. Article 15 prohibits termination of service on grounds of religion, race, caste, sex or place of birth or any of them. Article 16(1) obligates equal treatment and bars arbitrary discrimination in public employment.

(2) Article 320(3)(c) places another limitation on the pleasure doctrine by providing that in all disciplinary matters affecting civil servants,

18. *Samsher Singh* v. *State of Punjab*, (1974) 2 SCC 831.
19. *Union of India* v. *S.P. Sharma*, (2014) 6 SCC 351.

Union or State Public Service Commission, as the case may be, is to be consulted.

(3) Article 311 places two more limitations on the free exercise of pleasure doctrine—(*a*) no dismissal or removal from service by an authority subordinate to the appointing authority; and (*b*) fair hearing.

(4) Statutory appointments.[20] In such cases, appointment and termination is governed by the terms of the statutory provisions.

(5) Even in case of removal of constitutional functionaries, "pleasure doctrine" is not unlimited. Therefore, a Governor cannot be dismissed on whims and caprice. In *B.P. Singhal* v. *Union of India*[21], the Supreme Court opined that a Governor cannot be dismissed on the basis of ideology, change in government, making way for other or loss of faith.

1.3 Constitutional safeguards to civil servants

Article 311 is a limitation on the doctrine of pleasure as laid down in Article 310 and, thus, places two limitations on the power of the government to dismiss a civil servant at pleasure. These limitations are

(1) that no civil servant can be dismissed or removed from service by an authority subordinate to that by which he was appointed; and

(2) that no civil servant can be dismissed or removed or reduced in rank, except after an enquiry in which he has been made aware of the charges against him and also given a reasonable opportunity to defend himself.

These two limitations lay down the constitutional code of procedural safeguards for civil servants in India. For the first time in India, constitutional protection to government servants was provided by the Government of India Act, 1919 which was followed by the Government of India Act, 1935 and continued by the Constitution of India in Article 311.

1.4 Constituency of Article 311

Two procedural safeguards provided in Article 311 apply only to persons who are members of a civil service of the Union, or of an All-India service, or of a civil service of a State, or to persons who hold a civil post under a Union or a State. The expression "civil post" means an appointment on the civil side of the administration as distinguished from the military side. Therefore, these safeguards are not available to the members of the defence forces or to any post connected with the defence which is governed by the Army Act, 1950.[22] Even a civilian holding a post in a department connected

20. *Union of India* v. *Shardindu*, (2007) 6 SCC 276.

21. (2010) 6 SCC 331.

22. *V.K. Nambudiri* v. *Union of India*, 1960 SCC OnLine Ker 281: AIR 1961 Ker 155.

with defence, such as military engineering,[23] or farm[24] service cannot claim the protection of Article 311. Furthermore, the term "civil post" signifies that there must exist a master and servant relationship between the holder of the post and the State which may be indicated by the State's right to recruit, appoint, control and payment of wages. A relationship of master and servant can be indicated by all or some of these factors. Therefore, holding of a "civil post" under the State is a question of fact. In *Kendriya Vidyalaya Sangathan* v. *Arunkumar Madhavrao Sinddhaye*[25], the Supreme Court held that a PT teacher appointed in the Sangathan does not hold a civil post under the government.

The protection of Article 311 applies both to permanent and temporary civil servants because Article 311 does not make any distinction between permanent and temporary employees.[26]

Protection of Article 311, however, shall not be available in case of compulsory retirement in public interest,[27] or termination of service during probation,[28] or termination of service which was temporary and for a fixed period,[29] or reversion from an officiating post,[30] provided the termination of service is bona fide and simpliciter which does not attach any stigma to the employee, or where an appointment is found to be void ab initio, *i.e.* a person who was never an employee.[31]

However, when termination of service is punitive or simpliciter, or when it is a "foundation" or a "motive" of the action was explained by the Supreme Court in *Dipti Prakash Banerjee* v. *Satyendra Nath Bose National Centre for Basic Sciences*[32]. The court observed:

(1) If a finding arrived at in an enquiry as to misconduct of the employee is behind his back without any regular enquiry, the simple order of termination will be founded on allegation, hence bad in law.
(2) If no enquiry was held, as employer was not inclined to hold one, an order of termination will be simpliciter and it would be a case of "motive" and not "foundation", hence will not be bad in law.
(3) If employer does not want to enquire into allegations against the employee because of reason of delay in taking action, or if he is

23. *Subodh Ranjan Ghose* v. *Major N.A.O. Callaghan*, 1956 SCC OnLine Cal 222: AIR 1956 Cal 532.
24. *Union of India* v. *Dharampal Chopra*, 1957 SCC OnLine P&H 79: PLR (1957) 59 P&H 472. See also, *Sher Singh* v. *State of M.P.*, 1954 SCC OnLine MP 25: AIR 1955 Nag 175.
25. (2007) 1 SCC 283.
26. *Parshotam Lal Dhingra* v. *Union of India*, AIR 1958 SC 36.
27. *State of U.P.* v. *Madan Mohan Nagar*, AIR 1967 SC 1260. See also, *D. Ramaswami* v. *State of T.N.*, (1982) 1 SCC 510; *Swami Saran Saksena* v. *State of U.P.*, (1980) 1 SCC 12.
28. *State of Maharashtra* v. *Veerappa R. Saboji*, (1979) 4 SCC 466; *Govt. Branch Press* v. *D.B. Belliappa*, (1979) 1 SCC 477.
29. *ONGC* v. *Mohd. S. Iskender Ali*, (1980) 3 SCC 428.
30. *Hartwell Prescott Singh* v. *U.P. Govt.*, AIR 1957 SC 886.
31. *Punjab Urban Planning and Development Authority* v. *Karamjit Singh*, (2019) 16 SCC 782.
32. (1999) 3 SCC 60.

doubtful that adequate evidence will be available, then allegations would only be motive for termination of service and, hence, termination would be simpliciter, not bad in law.

(4) Where there is a stigma on the employee arising out from any record or order or annexure which can be asked for by any future employer, the order of termination will be bad in law.

This distinction has been further explained by the Supreme Court in *Chandra Prakash Shahi* v. *State of U.P.*[33] as follows:

> Important principles which are deducible on the concept of 'motive' and 'foundation', concerning a probationer, are that a probationer has no right to hold the post and his services can be terminated at any time during or at the end of the period of probation on account of general unsuitability for the post in question. If for the determination of suitability of the probationer for the post in question or for his further retention in service or for confirmation, an inquiry is held and it is on the basis of that inquiry that a decision is taken to terminate his service, the order will not be punitive in nature. But, if there are allegations of misconduct and an inquiry is held to find out the truth of that misconduct and an order terminating the services is passed on the basis of that inquiry, the order would be punitive in nature as the inquiry was held not for assessing the general suitability of the employee for the post in question, but to find out the truth of allegations of misconduct against that employee. In this situation, the order would be founded on misconduct and it will not be a mere matter of 'motive'.

"Motive" is the moving power which impels action for a definite result, or to put it differently, "motive" is that which incites or stimulates a person to do an act. An order terminating services of an employee is an act done by the employer. What is that factor which impelled the employer to take this decision? If it was the factor of general unsuitability of the employee for the post held by him, the action would be upheld in law. If, however, there were allegations of serious misconduct against the employee and a preliminary enquiry is held behind his back to ascertain the truth of those allegations and a termination order is passed thereafter, the order, having regard to other circumstances, would be founded on the allegations of misconduct which were found to be true in the preliminary enquiry.

Applying the same principle, the Supreme Court in *Dhananjay* v. *Zilla Parishad, Jalna*[34] held that where the services of a temporary employee could be simply terminated under the rules, without holding an enquiry, mere allegation or suspension order or contemplation of an enquiry culminating in termination order cannot be held to be punitive attaching stigma.

Government has the power to compulsorily retire any government servant in public interest who has put in a specified number of years of service. This gives unfettered power to the government without any counter balancing

33. (2000) 5 SCC 152.
34. (2003) 2 SCC 386.

protection of Article 311 being available to the employee. Therefore, in many a situations this power has been exercised in a mala fide manner for punishing an employee. Therefore, the courts have started extending the protection of Article 311 in cases of compulsory retirement against executive arbitrariness. Hence, if it can be proved that power was exercised in a mala fide manner and action carries any stigma to the employee, then the courts would not hesitate to quash the administrative actions.[35] In *Baldev Rai Chadha* v. *Union of India*[36], the Supreme Court quashed the order of compulsory retirement which had been passed after taking into account old adverse confidential reports and ignoring confidential reports of the last five years. In another case, court quashed the order when an employee was allowed to cross the efficiency bar but was compulsorily retired soon thereafter, even though there was nothing against him subsequent to his crossing the efficiency bar.[37]

In case of compulsory retirement, decision rests on subjective satisfaction, and it is not considered a punishment or any suggestion of misbehaviour. The proceedings are also not quasi-judicial, therefore, the principles of natural justice are not attracted. However, it can be challenged on the ground of mala fide, no evidence or arbitrariness.[38]

Hitherto, the government has unfettered power to terminate the service of a probationer or a temporary civil servant without any protection of Article 311 being available to him. However, courts have also made some inroads into this area of administrative discretion. The Supreme Court in *State of Maharashtra* v. *Veerappa R. Saboji*[39] observed that in case of termination of service of a probationer or a temporary staff, the court may ask the government to produce its records if the government servant makes out a prima facie case that the order was by way of punishment. Thus, where the termination of service of a temporary employee was preceded by a show-cause notice which was not pursued and his services were terminated on the ground that his services were purely temporary, the court quashed the termination order when it was proved that there was nothing on record against the employee except the show-cause notice.[40]

Courts have further held that the protection of Article 311 is available to a quasi permanent employee also.[41] According to government rules, a quasi permanent employee is one who is appointed to a temporary post but continues in that capacity for more than three years and has been certified by the appointing authority as fit for employment in a quasi-permanent capacity.

35. *Union of India* v. *M.E. Reddy*, (1980) 2 SCC 15.
36. (1980) 4 SCC 321
37. *Swami Saran Saksena* v. *State of U.P.*, (1980) 1 SCC 12.
38. *Baikuntha Nath Das* v. *District Medical Officer*, (1992) 2 SCC 299.
39. (1979) 4 SCC 466.
40. (1979) 1 SCC 477.
41. *Champaklal Chimanlal Shah* v. *Union of India*, AIR 1964 SC 1854.

Constitutional protection of Article 311(1) is available in case of "dismissal" or "removal" from service, but the protection of Article 311(2) applies in case of "reduction in rank" also, besides removal and dismissal. Thus, the scope of Article 311(2) is wider than clause (1). "Dismissal" or "removal" are basically the same concepts because in both the cases termination of service takes place. But the difference between the two expressions is that in case of "dismissal", the employee is barred from future employment but not in case of "removal"[42]. "Reduction in rank" does not entail termination of service because it is only a change to lower grade or class. Therefore, if a person has been appointed on the lowest grade, this punishment cannot be awarded to him. If a person is appointed temporarily or to officiate on a higher post, he gets no right to that higher post and, hence, if reverted to his substantive post, Article 311 is not attracted. But if reversion is by way of punishment, then protection of Article 311 shall be available to him.[43]

Suspension of a civil servant pending an enquiry is neither a dismissal nor removal from service so the protection of Article 311 is not available to a suspended employee. However, if the suspension is by way of punishment, or is based on extraneous or irrelevant considerations, or there is a total non-application of mind, then court may grant relief.[44]

In the same manner, if the service of a civil servant is terminated as a result of abolition of his post, then also the protection of Article 311 shall not be available. Creation and abolition of a post is a matter of public interest which is in the sole discretion of the government. Nevertheless, if the post has been abolished mala fide or as a cloak to punish the employee, then court may grant relief.[45]

The Supreme Court has extended court's jurisdiction by ruling that the availability of judicial review even in cases of departmental proceedings cannot be doubted. The principles of natural justice are integral part of administrative jurisprudence; therefore, in departmental proceedings if it is found that the recorded findings are based on no evidence, or the findings are totally perverse or legally untenable, the court will exercise its power of judicial review.

In this manner, there is no absolute right to terminate the services of any government servant even if contractual in nature without the existence of any cause. Expression "without assigning any reason" does not mean "without existence of any reason". Any administrative action without an application of mind or action devoid of any reason renders it arbitrary subject to judicial scrutiny. However, court can direct reconsideration and not reappointment.[46]

---

42. *Mohd. Abdul Salam Khan* v. *Sarfaraz Ahmad Khan*, (1975) 1 SCC 669.
43. *R.S. Sial* v. *State of U.P.*, (1975) 3 SCC 111; *G.S. Gill* v. *State of Punjab*, (1975) 3 SCC 73.
44. *State of T.N.* v. *P.M. Belliappa*, 1984 SCC OnLine Mad 62: 1985 Lab IC 51.
45. *K. Rajendran* v. *State of T.N.*, (1982) 2 SCC 273.
46. *State of U.P.* v. *Ashok Kumar Nigam*, (2013) 3 SCC 372.

2. PROCEDURAL SAFEGUARDS

2.1 No termination by subordinate authority

Article 311(1) provides the first safeguard to a civil servant in case of his dismissal or removal from service. Article 311(1) provides that no member of a civil service or holding a civil post can be dismissed or removed from service by any authority subordinate to the authority by which he was appointed. The reason behind this safeguard is that the dismissed employee may not have faith in the judgment of a subordinate officer. Therefore, where a member of the Calcutta police force who had been appointed by the Commissioner of Police was dismissed by the Deputy Commissioner of Police, it was held that the order is violative of Article 311(1).[47] In the same manner, dismissal of a civil servant by the Deputy Secretary who had been appointed by the Secretary was held to be in violation of the provisions of Article 311(1).[48] However, it does not mean that appointing and dismissing authorities must be the same. It is enough if both the authorities are of the same rank and grade.[49] Whether an authority is of the same rank or not will be determined with reference to the date of appointment because it is from the date of appointment that the constitutional guarantee becomes available to him.[50] However, there is no bar for conducting an enquiry by a subordinate authority which may ultimately lead to a dismissal or removal of a civil servant.[51]

2.2 Reasonable opportunity to defend

Another safeguard which Constitution gives to a civil servant is pre-decisional hearing. Article 311(2) provides that no civil servant shall be dismissed or removed or reduced in rank except after an enquiry in which he has been informed of the charges against him and given a reasonable opportunity to defend himself against those charges. "Reasonable opportunity" means opportunity to deny guilt and establish innocence. It also implies that all relevant material must be disclosed to the other party whether obtained before, after or during the hearing. Before 1976, Article 311(2) had provided another safeguard of post-decisional hearing against the proposed punishment as a result of the enquiry, but this safeguard was taken away by the Constitution (42nd Amendment) Act, 1976. This protection will be available only when dismissal or removal or reduction in rank is by way of punishment and not otherwise.[52] Therefore, if a person is dismissed as a consequence of the abolition of his post, the protection of Article 311(1) will not be available.

47. *Santosh Kumar Dutta* v. *Commr. of Police*, 1954 SCC OnLine Cal 158: AIR 1955 Cal 81.
48. *Satish Chandra Das Gupta* v. *State of W.B.*, 1958 SCC OnLine Cal 52: AIR 1960 Cal 278.
49. *Mysore SRTC* v. *Mirza Khasim Ali Beg*, (1977) 2 SCC 457.
50. *Krishna Kumar* v. *Divl. Asstt. Electrical Engineer*, (1979) 4 SCC 289.
51. *Registrar of Coop. Societies* v. *F.X. Feranando*, (1994) 2 SCC 746.
52. *S. Sukhbans Singh* v. *State of Punjab*, AIR 1962 SC 1711.

An enquiry begins with the service of charge-sheet on the delinquent civil servant. The charges given in the charge-sheet must be clear, sufficient and not vague. The test of sufficiency of charge-sheet is that it must give the employee sufficient information to enable him to defend himself. Therefore, sufficiency of the charge-sheet is a question of fact and is also a justiciable issue.

The concept of "reasonable opportunity to defend" is synonymous with natural justice. A full discussion on the principles of natural justice has been made in Chapter 7 of this book, nevertheless a few salient principles may be discussed here.

The concept of "reasonable opportunity" is also the same as that of "procedural due process" in the US Constitution, therefore, the final authority is vested with the courts to determine whether an "opportunity" was "reasonable" or not. The legislature or the executive may by law lay down the elements of a "reasonable opportunity", but the final authority to pronounce on the validity of the enquiry procedure rests with the court.

If the law under which an enquiry is held lays down a procedure, then it must be faithfully followed failing which the order of the administrative authority will be declared void.[53] If the law does not lay down any procedure for the enquiry, then the enquiry must be conducted according to the principles of natural justice. Therefore, the Supreme Court in *State of Bombay* v. *Nurul Latif Khan*[54] held that Rule 55 of the Civil Services (Classification, Control and Appeal) Rules, 1967 (CCA Rules), which made oral hearing mandatory if demanded by the civil servants, is binding and must be strictly followed and the denial of it would make the final order of the authority void.

An enquiry must be specific and not general. Therefore, if a general statutory enquiry was held on the basis of which an action was taken against the Assistant Station Master without serving him any show-cause notice, court held the action of the authority as void.[55]

A delinquent employee has a right to know all the evidences against him. Government cannot rely on any evidence which has not been brought to the notice of the employee and he has not been given a reasonable opportunity to rebut those evidences. A delinquent employee has also right to bring all relevant evidence, oral or documentary, before the enquiry officer. Therefore, an enquiry officer should provide an opportunity for the production of documentary evidence and also attempt to secure the attendance of defence witnesses.[56]

Under Rule 15(5) of the CCA Rules, a civil servant has a right to present his case before the disciplinary authority through any government

---

53. *Ranendra Chandra Banerjee* v. *Union of India*, AIR 1963 SC 1552.
54. AIR 1966 SC 269.
55. *Amalendu Ghosh* v. *North Eastern Railway*, AIR 1960 SC 992.
56. *Mohd. Hanif Ashan Ullah Khan* v. *Supt. of Police*, 1957 SCC OnLine All 272: AIR 1957 All 634.

servant, approved by the authority, or through a lawyer with its permission. This rule is mandatory and any denial of it would vitiate the enquiry. The Supreme Court has further fortified this right by holding that the disciplinary authority must bring this right to the notice of the employee. Therefore, when the enquiry against a class IV employee preceded without any assistance, though the government was assisted by a presenting officer, the Supreme Court quashed the order of dismissal because the employee had not been informed of his right of representation through another government servant.[57]

No matter though the oral hearing is not a part of natural justice; yet if the delinquent employee insists on oral hearing, he cannot be denied the right because the courts have held that personal hearing is a part of reasonable opportunity.[58]

In the same manner, though the right of cross-examination is not a part of natural justice, the Supreme Court has held that the delinquent employee must be given a chance to cross-examine the witnesses who have deposed against him.[59]

Departmental proceedings and the case in the law court can simultaneously proceed against the delinquent employee. He can be punished by the government if found guilty in departmental proceedings, no matter he may have been acquitted by the criminal court.[60] The reason for this is that the standard of burden of proof required by the criminal court is much higher than in the departmental enquiry.

Article 311(1) and (2) only provide for procedural safeguards to a civil servant, therefore, courts only ensure that the enquiry is held according to the principles of natural justice. Courts generally do not interfere with the punishment awarded. Nevertheless, courts have held that in cases where penalty imposed is arbitrary, grossly excessive or out of proportion to the offence committed, or not warranted by the facts and circumstances of the case, it will strike down the impugned order.[61] Court further held that in dealing with government servant, State must also conform to the constitutional requirement of Articles 14 and 16 which guarantee just and fair treatment.[62]

Regarding disciplinary action against government an enigmatic problem worth noticing is that whenever Lokayukta or Lokpal recommends disciplinary action against a public servant even after complying with the

57. *A.L. Kalra* v. *Project & Equipment Corpn. of India Ltd.*, (1984) 3 SCC 316. See, *Harinarayan Srivastava* v. *United Commercial Bank*, (1997) 4 SCC 384.

58. *State of Punjab* v. *Karam Chand*, 1958 SCC OnLine Punj 72: AIR 1959 Punj 402; *C.S. Sharma* v. *State of U.P.*, 1960 SCC OnLine All 270: AIR 1961 All 45; *Nripendra Nath Bagchi* v. *State of W.B.*, 1960 SCC OnLine Cal 188: AIR 1961 Cal 1.

59. *Bhagat Ram* v. *State of H.P.*, (1983) 2 SCC 442.

60. *Corpn. of the City of Nagpur* v. *Ramchandra*, (1981) 2 SCC 714; *Govind Dass* v. *State of Bihar*, (1997) 11 SCC 361.

61. *Union of India* v. *Tulsiram Patel*, (1985) 3 SCC 398.

62. *Nepal Singh* v. *State of U.P.*, (1985) 1 SCC 56.

elaborate procedure, it is only the beginning of the beginning inasmuch as the recommendations are no substitute for the report of the enquiry under the CCA Rules and the whole procedure must commence afresh from the very beginning. Even if it may be lawful for the government to take action on the recommendation without any further enquiry, government may not be bound by the recommendation. The Supreme Court did not give its opinion on this curious problem and recommended a proper legislation.[63] Same is the situation where a Human Rights Commission recommends action against a public servant for the violation of human rights. A proposal for the amendment of the Protection of Human Rights Act, 1993 is in the offing to make the recommendation of the Commission binding on the government so that the duplication of enquiry is avoided and action is taken immediately.

2.3 Whether the report of the enquiry be shown to the delinquent civil servant?

This topic has been exhaustively dealt within Chapter 7 of this book. Here it will suffice to point out that the conflicting law laid down by the Supreme Court in *Kailash Chander Asthana* v. *State of U.P.*[64] and *Union of India* v. *Mohd. Ramzan Khan*[65] has now been finally settled by the court in *ECIL* v. *B. Karunakar*[66]. The court finally ruled that a person has a right to the copy of the enquiry report before the authority takes decision on the question of his guilt. This rule will apply to all authorities, whether public or private, and the failure to ask for the report will not be considered as waiver. However, this law will have no retrospective operation[67] and a person cannot take the advantage of the law laid down in this case, no matter the proceedings challenging the dismissal order are still continuing in a court of law.[68]

2.4 Can disciplinary action be taken against an enquiry officer exercising quasi-judicial powers for misconduct?

An enquiry officer conducting an enquiry exercises quasi-judicial powers, therefore, as a general rule, he is not amenable to any disciplinary action for his actions as a judge. However, the Supreme Court in *Union of India* v. *K.K. Dhawan*[69] held that where an officer in exercise of judicial or quasi-judicial powers acts negligently or recklessly, or, in order to confer

63. *Institution of A.P. Lokayukta/Upa-Lokayukta* v. *T. Rama Subba Reddy*, (1997) 9 SCC 42.
64. (1988) 3 SCC 600.
65. (1991) 1 SCC 588.
66. (1993) 4 SCC 727.
67. See, *Union of India* v. *Mohd. Ramzan Khan*, (1991) 1 SCC 588.
68. *Food Corporation of India* v. *Narendra Kumar Jain*, (1993) 2 SCC 400.
69. (1993) 2 SCC 56. In this case, the court explained in *Union of India* v. *R.K. Desai*, (1993) 2 SCC 49 holding that in this case enquiry officer had found nothing wrong against the officer exercising quasi-judicial powers.

undue favour on a person, he is not acting as a judge, he can be subjected to disciplinary action. Elaborating the point further, the court observed that such action can be taken against the officer in the following cases:

(1) Where the officer has acted in a manner as would reflect on his reputation for integrity or good faith or devotion to duty.
(2) If there is a prima facie material to show recklessness or misconduct in the discharge of duties.
(3) If he has acted in a manner which is unbecoming of a government servant.
(4) If he had acted negligently and omitted the prescribed conditions necessary for the exercise of the statutory powers.
(5) If he has acted in a manner to unduly favour a party.
(6) If he has been actuated by corrupt motives, however small the bribe may be.

2.5 Consequential benefits on reinstatement

A government servant suspended on corruption charges is not entitled to consequential benefits as a matter of course even if he is acquitted and reinstated in job. The Supreme Court held that the purpose of prosecution of a public servant is to maintain discipline in service, integrity, honesty and truthful conduct in the performance of public duty. His conduct must be an open book. Though legal evidence may be insufficient to bring home the guilt beyond all reasonable doubt, reinstatement would send ripples among the people in office and locality and would give wrong signals. This is the valiant effort of the judiciary to bring back the lost discipline in the service.[70]

Furthermore, the government may decide as a part of executive policy the date from which arrears would be granted to its employees. The matter being an executive policy in character, cannot be considered as arbitrary violating Article 14 of the Constitution. Therefore, where the High Court had allowed selection grade with consequential benefit, the Supreme Court held that the government can fix a date from which consequential benefits would be available.[71]

2.6 Suspended employee must follow service rules

Upholding the dismissal of a Punjab police officer for abstaining from duty while under suspension, the Supreme Court, rejecting the argument that an employee under suspension need not apply for leave, held that the employee under suspension has to follow the service rules as they were applicable to him while in regular service.[72]

70. *The Times of India* 26-3-1997, 1.
71. *State of Haryana* v. *Rai Chand Jain*, (1997) 5 SCC 167. The government had allowed arrears for 38 months prior to the decision of the court.
72. *The Tribune* 23-9-2003, 2.

2.7 Protection of employees who acquire disability during service

Persons with Disabilities (Equal Opportunities, Protection of Rights and Full Participation) Act, 1995 provides that no person can be dispensed with, reduced in rank, if he acquires disability during his service. If he is not suitable for the post he was holding, he could be shifted to some other post with same pay scale and service benefits. If no such post is available, he may be kept on a supernumerary post unless a suitable post is available or he attains the age of superannuation, whichever is earlier. However, government may exempt, by notification, any establishment from these provisions.

2.8 Judicial review of departmental proceedings

In *Kumaon Mandal Vikas Nigam Ltd.* v. *Girja Shankar Pant*[73], the Supreme Court extended court's jurisdiction to departmental proceedings. This will go a long way in protecting government servants from any possible harassment. In this case, the enquiry officer had finalised the report against the alleged delinquent government servant without giving him the copies of the documents which showed irregularities committed by him and was given no chance to defend himself in the proceedings. Upholding the Allahabad High Court order quashing the departmental enquiry findings against the employee, the Supreme Court observed that judicial review of administrative actions is feasible and same has its application to the fullest extent in even departmental proceedings where it is found that the recorded findings are based on no evidence, or the findings are totally perverse or legally untenable. Judicial review cannot be ousted by any "finality clause" of Article 311.[74]

2.9 Exceptions to the rule of reasonable opportunity to defend

Proviso to Article 311(2) lays down three exceptions to the rule of reasonable opportunity to defend. Therefore, a civil servant can be dismissed or removed or reduced in rank without any notice and hearing in the following three cases:

(1) Where a civil servant is dismissed on conduct which led to his conviction in a criminal charge, conviction means the final conviction because an appeal is merely the continuation of the original proceeding, therefore, if a person is acquitted by the appellate court, he is not convicted at all.[75] This provision applies even if a person is released on probation after he has been found guilty.[76] The Supreme

73. (2001) 1 SCC 182.
74. *Raja Ram Pal* v. *Lok Sabha*, (2007) 3 SCC 184.
75. *R.S. Dass* v. *Divl. Supt., Allahabad*, 1960 SCC OnLine All 207: AIR 1960 All 538.
76. *Southern Railway* v. *T.R. Chellappan*, (1976) 3 SCC 190; *Union of India* v. *Tulsiram Patel*, (1985) 3 SCC 398.

Court held that the word "penalty" under Rule 14(*i*) of the Railway Servants (Discipline and Appeal) Rules, 1968, which provides for the same exception as is provided in Article 311(2)(*a*), does not refer to a sentence awarded to the accused on his conviction; but it merely indicates the nature of penalty which could be imposed by the disciplinary authority, if the delinquent employee had been found guilty of conduct, which led to his conviction on a criminal charge.[77]

However, acquittal in criminal case does not automatically entitle a person to reinstatement. It is open to the competent authority to direct an enquiry before reinstatement.[78]

Under clause (*a*) of the second proviso to Article 311(2) if a government servant has been convicted on a criminal charge by the court, but if the sentence has been suspended or a bail has been granted by the appellate court, it should not be a bar for taking action by the administration. In the same manner, if a government servant has been convicted by the trial court, there is no prohibition that the administration should wait for the result of appeal or revision before taking action so that the employee may not continue in service if he has been convicted on a criminal charge.[79]

In *Southern Railway* v. *T.R. Chellappan*[80] (*Chellappan*), the highest Bench further held that even after his conviction by a criminal court, the delinquent civil servant is entitled to hearing, no matter summary in nature, at least on the quantum of punishment. The rationale behind this proposition was that it is just possible that the employee may have been convicted on a minor or technical charge. However, the correctness of this law was doubted by many from the very beginning. Therefore, in *Union of India* v. *Tulsiram Patel*[81] (*Tulsiram Patel*), the Supreme Court overruled *Chellappan*[82] and held that before punishing a delinquent civil servant on this conviction by a criminal court, the punishing authority must consider the circumstances of the case, judgment of the criminal court, entire conduct of the civil servant, gravity of the offence committed, impact on the administration—whether the offence is of technical or trivial nature, and extenuating circumstances, if any, but this has to be done ex parte by the authority himself without hearing the employee.

However, even after *Tulsiram Patel*, the doors of the court are not completely closed. The order of the government dismissing an employee, without hearing, on his conviction on a criminal charge can still be challenged in a court of law if the impugned order is

77. *Southern Railway* v. *T.R. Chellappan*, (1976) 3 SCC 190.
78. *Dhananjay* v. *Zilla Parishad, Jalna*, (2003) 2 SCC 386.
79. *Director of Collegiate Education (Admn.)* v. *S. Nagoor Meera*, (1995) 3 SCC 377.
80. (1976) 3 SCC 190.
81. *Union of India* v. *Tulsiram Patel*, (1985) 3 SCC 398.
82. (1976) 3 SCC 190.

arbitrary, or grossly excessive or out of all proportion to the offence committed, or not warranted by the facts and circumstances of the case. The impugned order can also be challenged on the ground of non-application of mind by the government to the factors laid down by the court in *Tulsiram Patel* as mentioned in the above para. Therefore, the Supreme Court, even after its decision in *Tulsiram Patel* denying any hearing to the civil servants in case of their dismissal, removal, or reduction in rank on the basis of their conviction by a criminal court, has not left them without a remedy.

The power of disciplinary authority to dispense with an enquiry under relevant rule "on conviction on criminal charge" does not mean that irrespective of the nature of the case or punishment imposed by the court, the order of dismissal can be passed. The doctrine of proportionality will be applied by the reviewing court, if the penalty is disproportionate to the conduct of the employee which led to his conviction.[83]

(2) Second exception to the rule of reasonable opportunity is that where it is impracticable to hold enquiry, a civil servant can be dismissed, or removed or reduced in rank without any notice or hearing. But, before taking action under this exception, it is necessary that disciplinary authority must be satisfied on the question of impracticability and the reasons for its satisfaction must be recorded in writing. "Impracticability of hearing" is a question of fact and hence a justiciable issue. Therefore, if it can be shown that the hearing was practicable, the order of disciplinary authority shall be quashed. No matter clause (3) of Article 311 makes the decision of the government on the question of "impracticability of hearing" as final, nevertheless, "final" is not so final that the courts cannot do anything within the parameters of law relating to the privilege of the government to withhold documents, court can decide on the question of impracticability of hearing. The Supreme Court in *Tulsiram Patel*[84] observed:

> Whether it was practicable to hold the inquiry or not must be judged in the context of, whether it was reasonably practicable to do so. It is not a total or absolute impracticability which is required by clause (*b*). What is requisite is that the holding of the enquiry is not practicable in the opinion of a reasonable man taking a reasonable view of the prevailing situation.

Discretion dispensing with the enquiry on the ground of impracticability should not be exercised improperly, or for insufficient reasons or reasons which are not germane to the issue of dispensing with the enquiry.[85] However, the authority has to reach the decision of dispensing with the enquiry ex parte. Therefore, even in this area of denial

83. *State of M.P.* v. *Hazarilal*, (2008) 3 SCC 273.
84. (1985) 3 SCC 398.
85. *Workmen* v. *Hindustan Steel Ltd.*, 1984 Supp SCC 554.

of reasonable opportunity, a civil servant is not without a remedy. The same law was reiterated by the Supreme Court in *Satyavir Singh* v. *Union of India*[86]. In this case, the appellants who were employees of the Research and Analysis Wing (RAW) resented the introduction of identity card system introduced by the Counter Intelligence Section (CIS), a branch of RAW, for going from one floor to the other as a security measure. This resentment later on took an ugly turn. There were violent demonstrations and the officers were made hostages. Situation became so tense that the police had to be called in to release the hostages. Under these circumstances, witnesses were not available and service of the notice was not practicable. Therefore, delinquent employees were dismissed without hearing under Rule 19 of the Central Services Rules read with clause (*b*) of Article 311(2) of the Constitution. Court came to the conclusion that where an atmosphere of violence or general indiscipline and insubordination prevails, action under Article 311(2)(*b*) can be legitimately taken.

The Supreme Court in *UT of Chandigarh* v. *Ajay Manchanda*[87] further held that unless there are sufficient evidences on record to prove that departmental enquiry is not practicable, the plea cannot be lightly accepted otherwise lower ranking officers will have no protection against senior officers who will always accept the easy course. In this case, in pursuant of a complaint of extortion, the government had passed the order of dismissal against a police officer dispensing with the departmental enquiry on the ground of unpracticability. The enquiry officer confirmed the complaint as true and also confirmed that due to threats, complainant is reluctant to pursue the case and witnesses are not willing to depose and therefore, opined that enquiry is not practicable. It was held that it is not a sufficient material to conclude that enquiry is not practicable. The Supreme Court held that proviso 2 of Article 311 of the Constitution is based on public policy and is conceived in public interest to be employed in public good subject to judicial review. This proviso will apply where government servant deserves the punishment of dismissal, removal or reduction in rank. Every case is to be treated on its own merit. The authority must record reason that why an enquiry is not practicable. These reasons may not be communicated to the delinquent public servant. The finality clause in Article 311 does not mean final as to bar judicial review. Even when power is subjective, it is not beyond judicial review.[88]

However, in such cases, court does not sit as an appellate authority so as to substitute its own view for that of the disciplinary authority. But, court can direct the authority to exercise its discretion, though

86. (1985) 4 SCC 252.
87. (1996) 3 SCC 753; *UT of Chandigarh* v. *Mohinder Singh*, (1997) 3 SCC 68.
88. See, *S.R. Bommai* v. *Union of India*, (1994) 3 SCC 1; *A.K. Kaul* v. *Union of India*, (1995) 4 SCC 73.

it cannot direct it to exercise its discretion in a particular manner where the reasons for dispensing with the enquiry are found to be not proper. Court would normally direct the authority to hold the enquiry, keeping in view the facts and circumstances of each case.[89]

(3) The third exception to the rule of reasonable opportunity to defend is given in Article 311(2)(*c*). It lays down that where the President or the Governor, as the case may be, is satisfied that in the interest of the security of State it is not expedient to provide hearing, then hearing may be dispensed with. "Satisfaction" of the President or the Governor is in the constitutional sense which means that such satisfaction may be arrived at by anyone authorised under the Rules of Business.[90] The President or the Governor need not record reasons for their decision as is required under Article 311(2)(*b*). Security of State, amongst other, may involve situations like disobedience and insubordination on the part of the members of police.[91] The Supreme Court further clarified that what is required under clause (*c*) is not the satisfaction of the President or the Governor, as the case may be, that the interest of the security of the State is or will be affected; but his satisfaction that in the interest of the security of the State, it is not expedient to hold an enquiry as contemplated by Article 311(2).[92]

No matter, there is no requirement for recording of reasons by the President or the Governor for their satisfaction that it is not practicable to hold enquiry; but this does not dispense with the obligation to satisfy the court or tribunal that the satisfaction was arrived at after taking into account relevant facts and circumstances and was not vitiated by mala fides and was not based on extraneous or irrelevant considerations. The government is obliged to produce such material, which may justify its decision, even if it claims a privilege to produce certain documents under Sections 123 and 124 of the Evidence Act, 1872. The court will be within its right to look into the record for the purpose of determining whether the satisfaction has been vitiated for any reasons mentioned by the appellants. Thus, satisfaction of the President or the Governor under Article 311(2)(*c*) is not immune from judicial review, however, the scope of judicial review shall be limited as indicated in *S.R. Bommai* v. *Union of India*[93] to the situations of mala fide and extraneous or irrelevant considerations.[94]

89. *Indian Railway Construction Co. Ltd.* v. *Ajay Kumar*, (2003) 4 SCC 579.
90. *Samsher Singh* v. *State of Punjab*, (1974) 2 SCC 831. See also, *Union of India* v. *Sripati Ranjan Biswas*, (1975) 4 SCC 699, overruling *Sardari Lal* v. *Union of India*, (1971) 1 SCC 411.
91. *Satyavir Singh* v. *Union of India*, (1985) 4 SCC 252.
92. *Union of India* v. *Tulsiram Patel*, (1985) 3 SCC 398.
93. (1994) 3 SCC 1.
94. *A.K. Kaul* v. *Union of India*, (1995) 4 SCC 73.

Therefore, in cases falling under clauses (*a*), (*b*) and (*c*) of Article 311(2), hearing of any kind to the delinquent employee is prohibited. Court further held that no matter Article 14 is the constitutional guardian of the principles of natural justice; but when it is expressly excluded by Article 311(2) clauses (*a*), (*b*) and (*c*), its requirement cannot be read in Article 14 simply because it is not just possible to afford an enquiry under the circumstances. However, if the decision in any of the three clauses is based on extraneous grounds, or the grounds have no nexus to the situation envisaged in that clause, or are mala fide, the doors of the court shall be open wide. In such situations, Article 14 which guarantees protection against arbitrary State action will also be attracted.

Rule-making power of the legislature or the executive under Article 309 is subject to Article 311, therefore, any attempt to negativate the exclusionary effect of Article 311(2) will be void. What the Constitution has prohibited cannot be allowed by any ordinary law-making power.[95]

Now *Tulsiram Patel*[96] though has completely overruled *Chellappan*[97], which had allowed a limited enquiry on the question of nature and extent of the penalty imposed and had also legitimised of possibility of service rules conferring a right of hearing in situations covered under clauses (*a*), (*b*) and (*c*) of Article 311(2), yet judicial review of governmental action under Articles 32 and 226 is not completely barred and, hence, a civil servant can still be sure of court's protection from the arbitrary and mala fide exercise of governmental power. At the most, *Tulsiram Patel* sounds like the bell of a fire-brigade which wakes up people at midnight and causes annoyance but it also saves them from burning alive. Fact remains that without discipline, no nation can progress.

2.10 Disciplinary proceedings against judges of the subordinate courts

Article 235 lays down that the control over District Courts and courts subordinate thereto, including the posting and promotion of and the grant of leave to persons belonging to the judicial service of a State and holding any post inferior to the post of District judge, shall be vested in the High Court. Article 227 further provides that every High Court shall have superintendence over all courts and tribunals throughout the territories in relation to which it exercises jurisdiction. The combined effect of these articles is that the High Courts have been vested of disciplinary control over members of State judicial services in the subordinate courts. This was necessary in order to maintain independence and integrity of the judiciary.

No matter the members of the State judicial services are appointed by the Governor and, hence, in view of Article 311(1), only the Governor has the

95. *Ibid.*
96. (1985) 3 SCC 398.
97. (1976) 3 SCC 190.

authority to impose major penalties of removal or dismissal or reduction in rank; yet in view of Article 235, a Governor cannot conduct disciplinary proceedings apart from the High Court. Therefore, the power to institute enquiry against members of State judicial services vests in the High Court, and on the basis of the recommendations of the High Court, Governor will take action. Governor has no discretion to disagree or modify the recommendations of the High Court. Even Public Service Commission need not be consulted. This was clarified by the Supreme Court in *Baldev Raj Guliani* v. *P&H High Court*[98]. In this case, after an enquiry against a sub-judge, High Court had recommended removal, but the government in consultation with the Public Service Commission reinstated the judge. The Supreme Court held that the recommendation of the High Court is binding on the government. Similarly, the government has no power to order compulsory retirement of a judicial officer unless the High Court recommends so.[99]

3. ADMINISTRATIVE SERVICES TRIBUNALS

For a long time, a search was going on for a mechanism to relieve the courts, including High Courts and the Supreme Court, from the burden of service litigation which formed a substantial portion of pending litigation. As early as 1958, this problem engaged the attention of the Law Commission which recommended for the establishment of tribunals consisting of judicial and administrative members to decide service matters.[100] In 1969, Administrative Reform Commission also recommended for the establishment of civil service tribunals, both for the Central and State civil servants.[101] Central Government appointed a committee under the Chairmanship of J.C. Shah J of the Indian Supreme Court in 1969 which also made similar recommendation. In 1975, Swaran Singh Committee again recommended for the setting up of service tribunals.[102] The idea of setting up service tribunals also found favour with the Indian Supreme Court, which in *Kamal Kanti Dutta* v. *Union of India*[103] advocated for setting up of service tribunals to save the courts from avalanche of writ petitions and appeals in service matters. In the meantime, various States[104] had established their own service tribunals. Service tribunal was also established in Andhra Pradesh in 1973 by the Constitution (32nd Amendment) Act, 1973.

It was against this backdrop that Parliament passed the 42nd Amendment which added Part XIV-A in the Constitution. Articles 323-A and 323-B

98. (1976) 4 SCC 201.

99. *State of Haryana* v. *Inder Prakash Anand*, (1976) 2 SCC 977.

100. Fourteenth Report of Reform of Judicial Administration (1958).

101. Report on Personnel Administration (1969).

102. "Perspective", (1986) 1 SLJ (Journal Section) 1–5.

103. (1980) 4 SCC 38.

104. Gujarat, 1973; Uttar Pradesh, 1975; Rajasthan, 1976; Assam, 1977. In Bihar, Act was passed in 1982 but the tribunal was never established.

enabled Parliament to constitute administrative tribunals for dealing with certain matters specified therein. Article 323-A provided that Parliament may by law provide for the adjudication or trial by administrative tribunals of disputes and complaints with respect to recruitment and conditions of service of persons appointed to public services and posts in connection with the affairs of the Union, or of any State, or of any local or other authority within the territory of India or under the control of the Government of India, or of any corporation owned or controlled by the government. Parliament was further empowered to prescribe by law the jurisdiction, power, authority and procedure of such tribunals and also to exclude the jurisdiction of all courts except that of the Supreme Court under Article 136.[105] Empowered by these enabling provisions of the Constitution, Parliament enacted Administrative Tribunals Act, 1985[106] for the establishment of administrative service tribunals for deciding service disputes of civil servants of the Centre as well as of the States which was amended in 1986.

Section 4(1) of the Act provides for the establishment of Central Administrative Tribunals (CATs). It also empowers the Central Government to establish an administrative tribunal for any State on receipt of such a request to establish an administrative tribunal for any State by the State Government. Section 5 provides for the composition of tribunals and Benches thereof. According to sub-section (*i*) of Section 5, each tribunal shall consist of a Chairman and such number of Vice-Chairman and other members as the appropriate government may deem fit. Section 5(2) further provides that a Bench shall consist of one judicial member and an administrative member. Section 5(4)(*b*) authorises the Chairman to transfer the Vice-Chairman of a Bench or other members thereof to any other Bench.

Section 6(1)(2) and (3) of the Act prescribes qualifications for appointment as Chairman, Vice-Chairman, Judicial Member and Administrative Members. A person shall not be qualified for appointment as the Chairman unless he is or has been a judge of the High Court or has, for at least two years, held the post of a Secretary to the Government of India, or any other post under the Central or State Government carrying a pay scale which is not less than that of a Secretary of the Government of India. Therefore, a retired person can also be appointed as Chairman of the administrative tribunal if he fulfils any of the above qualifications.

Similarly, a person shall not be qualified for appointment as Vice-Chairman unless he is or has been a judge of a High Court, or Secretary to the Government of India or of any State, carrying the pay scale of not less than that of the Secretary to the Government of India; or held the post as Additional Secretary to the Government of India, or has, for a period of not less than three years, held office as a Judicial Member or an Administrative Member.

105. Arts. 323-A(2)(*d*) and 323-B(3)(*d*).
106. Act came into effect on 1-11-1985.

The qualifications for appointment as Judicial Member are laid down in sub-section (3) of Section 6 of the Act. It lays down that a person shall not be qualified for appointment as a Judicial Member unless he is, or has been, or is qualified to be, a judge of a High Court; or has been a member of the Indian legal service and has held a post of Grade I of that service for at least three years.

For the appointment of an Administrative Member, it is necessary that he has for at least for two years held the post of an Additional Secretary to the Government of India, or any other post under the Central or State Government, carrying a scale of pay which is not less than that of an Additional Secretary to the Government of India; or has, for at least three years, held the post of a Joint Secretary to the Government of India, or any other post under the Central or State Government, carrying a pay scale which is not less than that of a Joint Secretary to the Government of India. In addition, he must have adequate administrative experience.[107]

The appointment of Chairman, Vice-Chairman and every other member of CAT is to be made by the President of India in consultation with the Chief Justice of India. Similarly, the appointment of Chairman, Vice-Chairman and other members of an administrative tribunal for a State is to be made by the President of India in consultation with the Chief Justice of India and the Governor of the concerned State.[108]

The tenure of the office of the Chairman and Vice-Chairman has been fixed as five years or 65 years of age, whichever is earlier, and 62 years for members. Central Administrative Tribunal (Salaries and Allowance and Conditions of Service of Chairman, Vice-Chairman and Members) Rules, 1985 framed under Section 35(2)(*c*) of the Act provide under Rule 5 that Chairman, Vice-Chairman and Members on appointment to the tribunal, if they are in Central or State service, would seek retirement from that service and that in the case of a sitting judge of a High Court, who is appointed as Chairman or Vice-Chairman, his service in the tribunal shall be treated as actual service within the meaning of paragraph 11(b)(*i*) of Part D of the Second Schedule to the Constitution. Rule 5 further provides that on retirement he shall be entitled to receive pension and gratuity in accordance with the retirement rules applicable to him. Under Section 10 of the Act, Central Government has power to prescribe by rules the salaries, allowances, and other terms and conditions of service, including pension, gratuity and other retiral benefits. However, these cannot be changed to the disadvantage of the person after his appointment as Chairman, Vice-Chairman or Member of the tribunal.

Chairman, Vice-Chairman or Member of a tribunal can resign from office by notice in writing under his hand addressed to the President of India. However, the resigner shall continue to hold office until the expiry

107. 6(3-A) and (B) of the Act.

108. 6(4) to (7). See also, *S.P. Sampath Kumar* v. *Union of India*, (1987) 1 SCC 124.

of three months from the date of receipt of such notice by the President, or until a person is duly appointed as his successor enters upon his office, or until the expiry of his term of office, whichever is the earliest, or unless he is permitted by the President to relinquish his office sooner.[109]

In the same manner, sub-section (2) of Section 9 of the Act lays down the procedure for removal. It lays down that the Chairman, Vice-Chairman or any Member could be removed from office by the President of India on ground of proved misbehaviour or incapacity. For this purpose, an enquiry is required to be made by a judge of the Supreme Court after such Chairman, Vice-Chairman or other Member had been informed of the charges against him, and he has been given a reasonable opportunity of being heard in respect of those charges. Procedure for such an enquiry can be regulated by the Central Government by framing rules.[110]

Section 11 of the Act further provides that the Chairman, Vice-Chairman and any Member of a State or Central tribunal, on ceasing to hold such office, shall become ineligible for further employment under the Government of India, the Government of State, including employment under any other authority within the territory of India or under the control of the government, or under any corporation or society owned or controlled by the government. However, a Chairman, Vice-Chairman or any Member of CAT can be appointed as Chairman, Vice-Chairman or Member of the State tribunal and vice versa. Furthermore, after ceasing to hold office, such functionaries cannot appear, act or plead before any tribunal where they were Chairman, Vice-Chairman or Member.

Besides the establishment of Central and State administrative tribunals, the Act makes provision for the establishment of joint administrative tribunal for two or more States on the request of such States.[111] Sub-section (5) of Section 4 inserted by the Administrative Tribunals (Amendment) Act, 1986 provides that the Central Government may designate all or any of the members of Bench or Benches of the State administrative tribunal as member of the Bench or Benches of CAT and vice versa.

According to Section 5(1), each tribunal shall consist of a Chairman, and such number of Vice-Chairmen and Judicial and Administrative Members as the appropriate government may deem fit. However, subject to the other provisions of the Act, the jurisdiction, powers and authority of the tribunal may be exercised by Benches of such tribunal. Each Bench is to consist of one Judicial Member and one Administrative Member.[112] Chairman has also been given the power to transfer a member from one Bench to another.

Section 14 of the Act confers jurisdiction, powers and authority on CAT and provides that from 1 November 1985, the tribunal shall exercise all the jurisdiction, powers and authority exercisable immediately before that day

109. S. 9 of the Act.
110. S. 9(3) of the Act.
111. S. 4(3) of the Act.
112. S. 5(2) of the Act.

by all courts, except the Supreme Court, in relation to recruitment, matters concerning recruitment and all service matters of Central civil servants. Section 15 confers similar jurisdiction on State administrative tribunal. Even the pending cases on 1 November 1985 stand transferred to the tribunal.[113] The language of Section 14(1) is wide enough to cover all service matters concerning the persons covered under the Act where the allegation is the violation of Article 311 or any service rule framed under Article 309 of the Constitution, including Articles 14 and 16. Therefore, even in cases of infringement of fundamental rights of the civil servants, the forum will be the tribunal. Thus, the tribunal has authority to decide the constitutionality of any statute, rule, regulation or notification.[114] For this purpose, the tribunal can exercise all jurisdiction, power and authority exercisable by all courts, including the writ jurisdiction of High Courts under Article 226 of the Constitution.

Ordinarily, the tribunal shall not admit an application unless the applicant has exhausted the remedy available under the service rules.[115] A period of limitation of one year is also provided for making an application from the date on which the final order was made by the government against the civil servant.[116] The tribunal has power to punish for its own contempt.[117]

The tribunal can be moved by filing an application before the Registrar of the tribunal along with the prescribed fee of ₹50 and relevant documents.[118] On receipt of an application, the tribunal shall, if it is satisfied after such enquiry, as it may deem necessary, that the application is a fit case for adjudication or trial by it, admit such application; but where the tribunal is not so satisfied, it may summarily reject the application after recording its reasons.[119] An applicant can even send an application through post and can plead the case with or without an advocate.[120]

The Act provides for an informal and non-technical trial procedure. The tribunal is not bound by the technical rules of Civil Procedure Code, 1908 (CPC), but is only required to act in conformity with the rules of natural justice.[121] However, the tribunal shall have the powers of a civil court under the CPC in respect of matters specified in the Act.[122] Normally, the tribunal cannot pass ex parte interim order but under certain circumstances, it can grant interim order for a period not exceeding 14 days.[123] On application,

113. S. 29. See also, *Union of India* v. *Ganesh Khalashi*, 1990 SCC OnLine CAT 443: (1990) 13 ATC 747. It was held that transfer took place by operation of law irrespective of actual transfer.
114. *J.B. Chopra* v. *Union of India*, (1987) 1 SCC 422.
115. S. 20.
116. S. 21.
117. S. 17.
118. S. 2.
119. S. 19(3).
120. S. 23.
121. S. 22.
122. S. 22.
123. S. 24.

Chairman has the power to transfer a case from one Bench to another.[124] The decision of the tribunal shall be by majority, but if the members are equally divided the matter may be referred to the Chairman.[125] Because the tribunal exercises the jurisdiction of the High Court, it can issue writs, but generally tribunals do not issue writs. Order passed by the tribunal shall be final and shall not be called in question in any court including High Court, except the Supreme Court by way of special leave petition under Article 136 of the Constitution,[126] because an administrative tribunal set up under the Act is a substitute of and supplemental to the High Court in service matters.[127]

As a necessary consequence to this, the tribunals are not under the writ jurisdiction of the High Court and are not bound by their decisions, no matter they may have a persuasive value.

With the deletion of Section 2(*b*) from the Administrative Tribunals Act, 1985 by the 1986 Amendment, the jurisdiction of the tribunal has been extended to "workman" within the meaning of the Industrial Disputes Act, 1947, provided that at the same time he is also a government servant. Thus, it created a little confusion because in such a case a workman, who is also a government servant or an employee of an institution notified under Section 14(2) of the Administrative Tribunals Act, 1985 has been brought under the dual jurisdiction of the tribunal and the Industrial Tribunal and Labour Courts. This duality of confusion was, however, settled by CAT in *A. Padmavalley* v. *CPWD and Telecom*[128]. The tribunal clarified that the administrative tribunals are not substitute for the authorities under the Industrial Disputes Act, 1947 and, hence, their jurisdictions cannot be regarded as concurrent, therefore a person seeking relief under the labour law must exhaust the remedies available under that law before approaching the administrative tribunal. As regards the extent of power of the tribunal, it was held that as a substitute of the High Court, the tribunal can exercise the power of judicial review as was exercised by the High Court under Article 226 of the Constitution.

The tribunal has inherited the jurisdiction of the High Court in service matter, therefore, in exercise of its power of judicial review, it cannot interfere with the penalty imposed by the disciplinary authority on the ground that it is disproportionate to the proved misconduct, if the findings as to misconduct are supported by legal evidence.[129]

The Act does not provide for any appeal or review of the order of the tribunal except that a person aggrieved may file a special leave petition before the Supreme Court. However, after the decision of the Supreme Court in

124. S. 25.
125. S. 26.
126. S. 27.
127. *J.B. Chopra* v. *Union of India*, (1987) 1 SCC 422.
128. (1990) 14 ATC 914: (1990) 3 SLJ 544 (CAT).
129. *Union of India* v. *Parma Nanda*, (1989) 2 SCC 177.

L. Chandra Kumar v. *Union of India*[130] (*L. Chandra Kumar*), service tribunals have been brought under the jurisdiction of High Courts and their decision now shall be appealable before the High Courts also.

Even though the judgment in the above case does not ipso facto apply to the Jammu and Kashmir Constitution, but the ratio of the case applies to the exercise of jurisdiction by the Jammu and Kashmir High Court. Thus, the Central Government employees working in the State of Jammu and Kashmir cannot bypass the jurisdiction of CAT.[131] CAT has exclusive jurisdiction, as a court of first instance, in relation to service matters concerning employees of the Kendriya Vidyalaya posted in the State of Jammu and Kashmir.

Under Section 15, an administrative tribunal has power to interfere with the findings of an inferior tribunal; however, such power is limited to cases where inferior tribunal has allowed inadmissible evidence, or has prevented evidence, or has based its conclusion on an erroneous view of law, or the conclusion reached is such which no reasonable man can draw on the existing material on record.[132]

Section 3(*q*)(*v*) of the Act gives wide jurisdiction to the tribunal by using the expression "any other matter whatsoever". But wide does not mean unlimited. The Supreme Court in *Union of India* v. *Rasila Ram*[133] held that matter relating to eviction of unauthorised occupants from government quarters does not come within the purview and jurisdiction of administrative tribunals. In the same manner, a tribunal cannot interfere with the discretionary jurisdiction of the State in matters relating to determination of conditions of service; alteration thereof by amending rules, Constitution, classification or abolition of posts, cadres, or categories of service; amalgamation; bifurcation of departments; reconstitution; restructuring of patterns etc. However, this is subject to limitations and restrictions envisaged in the Constitution.[134]

In order to provide expeditious justice, the Act does not provide for any execution proceedings. The orders of the tribunal are implemented in the same manner in which the impugned order would have been implemented. The legal sanction behind an order of the tribunal lies in the power of the tribunal to punish for its own contempt.

3.1 Constitutional validity of the Administrative Tribunals Act, 1985

The constitutional validity of this Act was challenged before the Supreme Court in *S.P. Sampath Kumar* v. *Union of India*[135] on the ground that the

130. (1997) 3 SCC 261.
131. *Kendriya Vidyalaya Sangathan* v. *Subhash Sharma*, (2002) 4 SCC 145.
132. *State of T.N.* v. *Thiru M. Sannasi*, (2001) 10 SCC 517.
133. (2001) 10 SCC 623.
134. *P.U. Joshi* v. *Accountant General*, (2003) 2 SCC 632.
135. (1987) 1 SCC 124.

exclusion of judicial review of the High Court violated the basic structure of the Constitution. Negativating the contention, the court held that no matter the judicial review, which is the basic feature of the Constitution, cannot be violated; but it is within the power of Parliament to amend the Constitution so as to substitute, in place of High Court, another alternative mechanism of judicial review, provided it is not less efficacious than the High Court.

The whole question of constitutionality of the Administrative Service Tribunals Act, 1985 once again came under the scrutiny of the Supreme Court in the pace-setting case of *L. Chandra Kumar*[136]. The court in this case held that Sampat Kumar was decided against the background and that the litigation before the High Courts had exploded in an unprecedented manner and, therefore, an alternative inquisitional mechanism was necessary to remedy the situation. But it is self-evident and widely acknowledged truth that tribunals have not performed well, hence drastic measures were necessary to elevate their standard ensuring that they stand up to constitutional scrutiny. The court further held that because the constitutional safeguards, which ensure the independence of the judges of the Supreme Court and the High Courts, are not available to the members of the tribunals, hence, they cannot be considered full and effective substitute for the superior judiciary in discharging the function of constitutional interpretation. Against this backdrop, the court came to the conclusion that administrative tribunals cannot perform a substitutional role to the High Court, it can only be supplemental. Therefore, clause 2(*d*) of Article 323-A and clause 3(*d*) of Article 323-B of the Constitution, to the extent they exclude the jurisdiction of the High Courts and the Supreme Court under Articles 226, 227 and 32 of the Constitution, were held unconstitutional; and for the same reason Section 28 of the Administrative Tribunals Act, 1985 which contains the "exclusion of jurisdiction" clause, was also held unconstitutional.[137]

It was further observed by the court that the power of judicial review of the constitutional courts is a part of the inviolable basic structure of the Constitution which cannot be ousted. However, service tribunals shall continue to be the courts of first instance in service matters, and no writ can be directly filed in the writ courts on matters within the jurisdiction of tribunals. Though the two-judge Bench, one of whom must be a judicial member of the tribunal can determine the constitutionality of any statutory provision, yet it cannot determine the constitutionality of the Administrative Tribunal Act, 1985. But the exercise of this power shall be subject to the scrutiny by the Division Bench of the High Court within whose jurisdiction the tribunal is situated. By bringing back the tribunals

136. (1997) 3 SCC 261.
137. Same applies to W.B. Taxation Tribunal Act, 1987; Rajasthan Taxation Tribunal Act, 1995; T.N. Land Reforms (Fixation of Ceiling on Land Amendment Act), 1985; and T.N. Taxation Special Tribunal Act, 1992.

within the jurisdiction of the High Courts, the court served two purposes. While saving the power of judicial review of legislative action vested in the High Courts under Articles 226 and 227 of the Constitution, it will ensure that frivolous claims are filtered out through the process of adjudication by the tribunal. The High Court will also have the benefit of a reasoned decision on merits which will be of use to it in finally deciding the matter. In view of this decision, the existing provision of direct appeals to the Supreme Court under Article 136 of the Constitution also stands modified. Now the aggrieved party will be entitled to move the High Court and from the decision of the Division Bench of the High Court, he can move the Supreme Court under Article 136 of the Constitution. The court saved the constitutionality of Section 5(*b*) by providing that whenever a question involving the constitutionality of any provision arises, it shall be referred to a two-member Bench, one of whom must be a judicial member.

Through this classical case, the court has, in one sense, tried to save the jurisdiction of constitutional courts from encroachment by the legislature by invoking the doctrine of "basic features of the Constitution".

Moving in the same direction, the Supreme Court in *State of T.N.* v. *S. Thangavel*[138] held that the members of the tribunal are not judges and their order is not a judgment or decree under Section 2(9), CPC. At best their statements can be construed to be only orders for the purpose of decision arrived at by the tribunal under the Administrative Tribunal Act, 1985. Keeping in view the subordinate status of the tribunal, the Delhi High Court recently held that CAT cannot entertain a public interest litigation.[139]

The Supreme Court has now finally settled the question of jurisdiction of the tribunals in labour matters by holding that an administrative tribunal has no jurisdiction to adjudicate upon the finding of an Industrial Tribunal that a person is a workman. A tribunal cannot assume jurisdiction by holding that the department in which the employee was working was not an industry.[140] Thus, the duality of jurisdiction in labour matters has now been abolished.

It is also now authoritatively laid down that the doctrine of precedent applies to the administrative tribunals also. The court held that whenever an application under Section 19 of the Administrative Tribunals Act, 1985 is filed which involves a question already concluded by an earlier decision, the tribunal must take into account that decision as precedent and decide accordingly. If the tribunal dissents then the matter must be referred to a larger Bench.[141]

138. (1997) 2 SCC 349.
139. *Cabinet Secretary extension case* (*T.S.R. Subramanian, re*), 31-1-1998 (Del).
140. *Ajay D. Panalkar* v. *Pune Telecom Deptt.*, (1997) 11 SCC 469.
141. *K. Ajit Babu* v. *Union of India*, (1997) 6 SCC 473.

3.2 Working of the administrative services tribunals

The system of administrative service tribunals has now come to stay. Service tribunals started functioning in November 1985, and since then 35 years have passed which is a sufficient period for any meaningful evaluation of system. Unfortunately, much research has not been undertaken in this area. However, from whatever material is available, a few significant from whatever trends in the working of service tribunals, especially CAT, may be discussed.[142]

At present there are two categories of service tribunals, one constituted by the States under their own legislations and the other constituted under the Central legislation, Administrative Tribunals Act, 1985. There was a third category also in which a service tribunal had been established in Andhra Pradesh through the amendment of the Constitution in 1976 which was abolished in 1989. While the States of Uttar Pradesh, Rajasthan, Gujarat and Assam have established service tribunals under their own laws, the States of Orissa, Himachal Pradesh, Karnataka, Madhya Pradesh, Tamil Nadu and Maharashtra have established tribunals for their employees under the Central legislation. CAT has also been established for Central Government employees. The Central Administrative Tribunal was set up on 1 November 1985. As on 31 March 2020, it has 17 regular Benches, 15 of which operate at the principal seats of High Courts and the remaining two at Jaipur and Lucknow. A statement showing the location of Central Administrative Tribunal Benches, the dates of their establishment and the number of courts in each of these Benches along with a list of places where they hold circuit sittings is given below:

Name, date of setting, no. of courts and addresses of various Benches of Central Administrative Tribunal (As on 31-3-2020)

S. No.	Name of the Bench	Date of setting	No. of courts	Address
1.	Principal	1-11-1985	6	New Delhi
2.	Ahmedabad	30-6-1986	1	Ahmedabad
3.	Allahabad	1-11-1985	4	Allahabad
4.	Bangalore	3-3-1986	2	Bangalore
5.	Chandigarh	3-3-1986	2	Chandigarh
6.	Madras	1-11-1985	2	Chennai
7.	Cuttack	30-6-1986	1	Cuttack
8.	Ernakulam	1-9-1988	2	Ernakulam
9.	Guwahati	3-3-1986	1	Guwahati

142. One such research in the area is "Tribunalisation of Justice in India: A study of Growth and Development of Service Tribunals". A doctoral thesis by Dr O.P. Chauhan under the supervision of the author (1992).

S. No.	Name of the Bench	Date of setting	No. of courts	Address
10.	Hyderabad	3-6-1986	2	Hyderabad
11.	Jabalpur	30-6-1986	1	Jabalpur
12.	Jaipur	15-10-1991	1	Jaipur
13.	Jodhpur	30-6-1986	1	Jodhpur
14.	Calcutta	1-11-1985	2	Kolkata
15.	Lucknow	15-10-1991	1	Lucknow
16.	Mumbai	1-11-1985	2	Mumbai
17.	Patna	30-6-1986	2	Patna

Statement showing the name of Bench and places where circuit sittings are held (As on 31-3-2020)

S. No.	Bench		Places
1.	Allahabad Bench	-	Nainital
2.	Calcutta Bench	-	Port Blair, Gangtok
3.	Chandigarh Bench	-	Shimla, Jammu, Srinagar
4.	Madras Bench	-	Pondicherry
5.	Guwahati Bench	-	Shillong, Itanagar, Kohima, Agartala, Imphal, Aizawl
6.	Jabalpur Bench	-	Indore, Gwalior, Bilaspur
7.	Bombay Bench	-	Nagpur, Aurangabad, Panaji
8.	Patna Bench	-	Ranchi
9.	Ernakulam Bench	-	Lakshadweep

The basic purpose behind the establishment of these tribunals was to provide expeditious justice to the civil servants which was not available through the traditional system. How far this purpose has been achieved is the moot question. If available data is any indicator, the trend which was discouraging in the beginning has now shown encouraging trends.

Since its inception in 1985 and up to 28 February 2020, the Central Administrative Tribunal received 8,18,886 cases for adjudication (including those transferred from High Courts), out of which 7,70,645 cases have been disposed of, leaving a pendency of 48,241 cases. On average, more than 94.1 per cent of the cases instituted are disposed of and for the calendar year 2019, the percentage of disposal is 104.36 per cent. A statement indicating the institution, disposal and pendency of cases since the inception of Central Administrative Tribunal is shown below:

Statement showing the position of institution, disposal and pendency of cases in the Central Administrative Tribunal since inception upto 31 October 2019.

(As provided by Central Administrative Tribunal, Principal Bench from time to time)

S. No.	Period	Institution	Disposal	Pendency at the end of the year
1.	1985	2963	30	2933
2.	1986	23,177	8934	17,176
3.	1987	19,410	15,084	21,502
4.	1988	19,425	13,769	27,158
5.	1989	18,602	13,986	31,774
6.	1990	19,283	15,495	35,562
7.	1991	21,623	17,552	39,633
8.	1992	25,184	23,782	41,035
9.	1993	27,067	28,074	40,028
10.	1994	26,230	26,409	39,849
11.	1995	25,789	23,668	41,970
12.	1996	23,584	20,667	44,887
13.	1997	23,098	21,981	46,004
14.	1998	21,911	18,394	49,521
15.	1999	22,944	24,566	47,899
16.	2000	25,146	31,398	41,647
17.	2001	25,977	31,953	35,671
18.	2002	25,398	29,514	31,555
19.	2003	25,089	28,076	28,568
20.	2004	23,825	27,735	24,658
21.	2005	21,528	22,408	23,778
22.	2006	18,722	17,774	24,726
23.	2007	17,725	18,674	23,777
24.	2008	18,287	20,352	21,712
25.	2009	24,496	23,681	22,527
26.	2010	26,620	25,477	23,670
27.	2011	25,869	24,750	24,789
28.	2012	27,733	24,206	28,316
29.	2013	27,442	21,654	34,104
30.	2014	27,913	24,739	37,278
31.	2015	29,089	25,150	41,217

S. No.	Period	Institution	Disposal	Pendency at the end of the year
32.	2016	26,984	26,266	41,935
33.	2017	25,402	20,055	47,282
34.	2018	26,309	23,538	50,053
35.	2019	24,952	26,040	48,965
36.	Upto Feb, 2020	4090	4814	48,241
37.	Total	8,18,886	7,70,645	

Figures given above indicate that after initial hesitation, disposal rate has shown encouraging trends. Out of the total cases filed till date more than 90 per cent of the cases have been disposed of. It is indicated that around 10 per cent cases which are pending are for the reasons beyond the control of the tribunal. The main reason seems to be that for the past seven or eight years a good number of posts of Vice-Chairman and other members have not been filled by the government. The working of the State service tribunals shows a similar trend.

Nevertheless, for the survival of service tribunals as a system, it is of paramount importance that the substitute institution "the Tribunal" must be a worthy successor of the High Court in all respect.[143]

It is widely acknowledged that due to infirmities in the appointment process of the members of the tribunals and the absence of constitutional safeguards which can ensure their independence, administrative tribunals have not been able to perform a substitutional role to the High Courts whose jurisdiction was transferred to them. Therefore, in order to improve the functioning of the tribunals, besides bringing them under the jurisdiction of the High Courts, the Supreme Court has made some significant suggestions.[144]

(1) The appointment of administrative members may continue but there is a need for changes in respect of appointments and supervision of their functioning by an independent authority. Since the selection committee is now headed by the judge of the Supreme Court to be nominated by the Chief Justice of India, there is reason to believe that the administrative members will be selected on the basis of merit and suitability.

(2) Until a wholly independent agency for administration of all tribunals can be set up, it is desirable that all such tribunals should be under a single nodal ministry like the Law Ministry.

(3) It would be open to the Ministry to appoint an independent supervisory body to oversee the working of the tribunals.

143. *Per* Misra J in *S.P. Sampath Kumar* v. *Union of India*, (1987) 1 SCC 124, 139.
144. *State of T.N.* v. *S. Thangavel*, (1997) 3 SCC 261.

(4) If need arises there may be separate supervisory authorities for the Central and State tribunals.

(5) Such a supervisory authority will ensure that the independence of the members of the tribunals is maintained. To that extent, the procedure for selection of the members of the tribunal, the manner in which funds are allocated for the functioning of the tribunals and all other consequential details will have to be taken care of.

After the administrative tribunals have been brought back within the jurisdiction of the High Courts, the suggestion of the Supreme Court for the constitution of an administrative supervisory authority, if operationalised, would go a long way in firmly establishing tribunals as a supplemental dispute resolution mechanism.

POINTS FOR DISCUSSION

1. Desirability of providing measures for the protection of civil servants through the medium of the Constitution may be discussed.
2. The doctrine of pleasure is feudal in origin and, therefore, has no relevance in democratic India. The doctrine of pleasure may be discussed as imparted into the Indian Constitution.
3. The right to reasonable opportunity of hearing may be discussed with the help of changing contents of the rules of natural justice.
4. It is said that *Tulsiram Patel*[145] is like a fire-brigade truck which though awakens people during night but also saves them from burning. The case may be discussed in all its aspect. After this case, whether any constitutional amendment is desirable may also be discussed.
5. If an enquiry officer misconducts himself, can any enquiry be instituted against him even if he is exercising a quasi-judicial function? The concept of accountability in the exercise of quasi-judicial function may be discussed.
6. After the abolition of second opportunity from the disciplinary proceedings against a government servant by the 42nd Amendment, is it necessary that the report of the enquiry officer be supplied to the delinquent government servant and he be given an opportunity to represent against it? The constitutionality of such a measure, if provided by an ordinary law of the legislature subordinate legislation, may be discussed.
7. Administrative Tribunals Act, 1985 is a boon for the civil servants. In the light of this statement, working of the administrative service tribunals may be discussed. Suggestions may be discussed for improving the working of these tribunals.

145. (1985) 3 SCC 398.

8. The role of Central Administrative Tribunal whether confined to judicial review? Against this backdrop, jurisdiction of the service tribunals may be discussed.

SUGGESTED READINGS

1. Alice Jacob, "Bar on Tribunal's Discretion to Examine the Adequacy of Punishment in Disciplinary Cases", (1989) 31 JILI 250.
2. Aman Preet Dhingra, "Administrative or Judicial Tribunal?", 30 JILI (1988) 103.
3. Anupa V. Thapliyal, "Role of Central Administrative Tribunal: Whether Confined to Judicial Review?" (1990) 1 SCC J-11.
4. B.R. Ghaiye, *Employment, its Terms and Conditions* (Eastern Book Company 1981).
5. B.R. Ghaiye, *Law and Procedure of Departmental Enquiries in Private and Public Sectors*, (Eastern Book Company 1976).
6. B. Shiva Rao, *The Framing of India's Constitution: A Study* (1968).
7. C.R. Attlee, "Civil Servants, Ministers, Parliament and Public", (1955) IJPA 95.
8. Chakravarti, *Law of Employees' Victimisation* (1966).
9. D. Bhowmik, "Political Developments in India and Bureaucracy: An Attitude Study", (1975) 21: 1 IJPA 109.
10. D. Bhowmik, "The Commitment of Bureaucracy: A New Philosophy", (Summer 1974) 19: 2 Journal of the Lal Bahadur Shastri National Academy of Administration 233–39.
11. D.D. Basu, *Commentary on the Constitution of India*, Vol. V (1970).
12. D.D. Seth, *Service Laws and the Constitution* (1981).
13. D.K. Srivastava, *Disciplinary Action Against Government Servants and its Remedies* (Eastern Book Company 1977).
14. Ejas Ahmed, *Services in India* (1979).
15. H.L. Kumar, *Commentaries on the Administrative Tribunals Act, 1985* (1986).
16. K.C. Joshi, "Service Tribunals under Administrative Tribunals Act", 28 JILI (1986) 207.
17. K.I. Vibhute, "Administrative Tribunals and the High Courts: A Plea for Judicial Review", 29 JILI (1987) 524.
18. K.N. Goyal, "Procedural Safeguards to Civil Servants and Employees of Public Undertakings: A Survey with Plea for New Service Jurisprudence", (1982) 3 SCC J-45.
19. K. Ramaswami, "Effectiveness of Administrative Tribunals", (1986) 2: 54 An LT 73.
20. Kanchan Lavania, "Revisiting the Indian Constitutional Law : The Role of Governor and the Grey Area in the Doctrine of Pleasure in the Indian Constitution", 3 RSRR 110 (2016).
21. Lakshmi Swaminathan, "A Civil Servant's Right to Be Represented in Disciplinary Proceedings", 16 JILI (1974) 282.

22. M.A. Aleem, "Justice by Tribunals—A Case Study of Andhra Pradesh Administrative Tribunal", (1988) 34–1 IJPA 86.
23. M.P. Jain, *Indian Constitutional Law*, Chap. XXXI.
24. M.P. Jain, "The Legal Status of Public Corporations and Their Employees", (1976) 18 JILI 1.
25. Mohammed Imam, "1 Notes and Comments: Reviewability of Compulsory Retirement Order", 2 JILI (1970) 633.
26. Mohammed Imam, "Power to Initiate and Conduct Disciplinary Proceedings: (A Comment on State of Madhya Pradesh v. Shardul Singh", 12 JILI (1970) 170.
27. N. Narayan Nair, *The Civil Servants under the Law and the Constitution* (Academy of Legal Publications 1973).
28. P.M. Bakshi, "Administrative Tribunals—Some Juristic Reflections", (1986) 1 SCJ 15.
29. P.M. Bakshi, "Administrative Tribunals—Some Legal Issues", (1986) 2 SCJ 9.
30. P.S. Chopra, "Doctrine of Pleasure: Its Scope, Implications and Imperatives", 1975 IJPA 92.
31. P. Leelakrishnan, "Reviewing Decisions of Administrative Tribunal: Paternalistic Approach of the Indian Supreme Court and Need for Institutional Reforms", 54 JILI (2012) 1.
32. P. Leelakrishnan* and Mini S., "Procedural Fairness in Administrative Decision-Making : Approach of the Supreme Court in a Decade", 59 JILI (2017) 335.
33. P. Kalpakam, "Dispensing with Departmental Enquiry", 28 JILI (1986) 246.
34. "Politicians and Civil Servants: Areas of Conflict", Syndicate Report (Autumn 1974) in 19 JLSAA 347.
35. R.C. Saksena, "Adjudication by Tribunals in India : Landmark in Field of Natural Justice", 37 JILI (1995) 222.
36. R. Deb, "Public Services Under the Rule of Law", (1978) 20 JILI 574.
37. S. Bala Krishan, *Law Relating to Services and Dismissals* (1971).
38. Sanjeev Sirohi, "Should Article 311 of Our Constitution Be Amended?", 2010 PL June 8.
39. Sindhu Thulaseedharan, "Right to Public Services in India-A New Legal Scenario", 55 JILI (2013) 59.
40. "The Civil Services", The Report of Expenditure Committee, (1978) JPI (JI-S) 24, JPI 371.
41. V.K.T. Chari, "A Note on Civil Servants", (1963) 5 JILI 148.
42. V.N. Shukla, *Constitution of India* (Eastern Book Company) Part XIV.
43. Y.R. Reddy, "Administrative Tribunals vis-à-vis the Jurisdiction of the High Courts", (1986) 13 Ind Bar Rev 201.

CHAPTER 15
Global Administrative Law

Today, administrative law has moved beyond the narrow domestic walls and has become a global mechanism for regulating global governance. Despite difficulties in generalising about "globalisation", which is a complex and contradictory phenomenon, evidence suggests that it has come to stay and is affecting States and peoples in various ways and varied measures. It is now reshaping fixed ideologies, norms and boundaries between domestic and international spheres and is changing our conceptions of national and international law and politics.

For some "globalisation" signifies that "world is a huge market" but for some, it signifies that "world is a big family". Globalisation connects people across borders, yet binds people within borders hence, individualism and interdependence go together. The term "globalisation" is not a value neutral concept, there are winners and losers in it. In economic sense, it is based on "free competition" and not "fair competition". It has created super highways of economic growth without caring to demarcate safe pedestrian crossings. Hallmarks of globalisation in economic sense include liberalisation, privatisation and integration of domestic economy with world economy. It also includes large-scale delegation of public functions and responsibilities to private players. State withdraws from vast areas of its traditional responsibilities confining its role only as facilitator, enabler and regulator. This makes the government, as is generally called, "third-party government". According to Prof. Baxi, globalisation signifies denationalisation, disinvestment and deregulation. Denationalisation signifies dismantling State ownership; disinvestment signifies selling-off public sector; and deregulation indicates incremental yet substantive, abdication of human rights oriented governmental oversight, invigilation and superintendence.[1] As a consequence, in many situations, people, especially the deprived sections of society, become "victims of development rather than beneficiaries". Only a strong administrative law regime can reconcile economic development with human development. Unfortunately, in order to provide additional flexibilities to the government, courts are also deviating from fundamentals of labour and human rights jurisprudence.

1. *See*, Introduction by Prof. Upendra Baxi, p. XVII.

Another significance of "globalisation" is a tremendous increase in the reach and form of trans-governmental regulation and administration structured to deal with the consequences of globalised inter-dependence. This inter-dependence is clearly visible in fields like security, trade and investment, environment, crime control, law enforcement, financial regulation, information, intellectual property, air and space regulation, labour standards, biodiversity, migration and human rights, etc.[2] This global interdependence requires that transnational equity be built in "globalisation" in a manner that leads to national self-reliance rather than dependency. Therefore, the need to develop a strong body of global administrative law to regulate the forces which globalisation has unleashed cannot be over emphasised. This is necessary to make "globalisation" inclusive based on common but differentiated equality. This aspect of global administrative law has not yet been assumed in legal thought and practice. Global administrative law must address problems of global law-making, global administration, global adjudication and global accountability. The purpose of global administrative law may be to develop principles and norms necessary for reconciling claims of globalisation with the claims of human development over the whole spectrum on equal basis.

Against this backdrop, global administrative law can be described as a study of structures, principles, practices and supporting social understandings that promote or otherwise affect the accountability of global administrative bodies, in order to ensure that they meet adequate standards of transparency, participation, reasoned decisions and legality, while exercising rule-making, rule-application and rule-decision functions. Conceptualisation of global administrative law presumes existence of global or transnational administration which has domestic ramifications.[3]

Sources of global administrative law include classical sources of public international law which may include treaties, customs, general principles of natural justice and proportionality where there is a high degree of convergence. It may be something like *jus gentium* emerging from wide variety of public actions in diverse situations. Global administrative law may thus include law-making process, administrative process and administrative adjudicatory process global in nature in order to infuse fairness, transparency and justice in these processes necessary to create a global Rule of Law Society.

Efforts at developing international administrative law began from the mid-19th century and became more focused in 1920s and 1930s. The idea of analysing transnational governance through administrative law principles and norms did appear in the work of late 19th century social reformers and institution builders. They adopted a broad notion of global administration that included both international institutions and national players,

2. *See*, Richard B. Stewart, "US Administrative Law: A Model for Global Administrative Law", (Summer/Autumn 2005) 68 Law & Contemp Probs 63.

3. *Ibid.*

while taking actions with transboundary significance. However, for various reasons, this attempt faded away. The present interest in global administrative law, in one sense, is the revitalisation of earlier vision and approach.[4]

Moving away from domestic governance as a consequence of globalisation, there is emerging what may be called "global governance". Players in global governance may include 1) formal international organisations like United Nations Organisation (UNO), World Trade Organisation, International Monetary Fund, World Bank, World Health Organisation, International Labour Organisation, UNICEF, UNESCO, etc; 2) transnational network of cooperative arrangements; 3) administration conducted by national regulators under treaty network and other cooperative regimes; 4) hybrid intergovernmental and private arrangement; and 5) private institutions with regulatory functions including multinational corporation with huge economic powers.[5] Global governance impacts in various and varied ways individuals, collectivities and States. The level of impact is directly proportionate to the level of social, economic and political strength of the regime. Sometimes, global domestic governance is indirect through the domestic regime with its consent and approval; but sometimes, it is direct in which global regulatory regimes can be enforced on a domestic regime without its consent and approval. Environmental and financial global regulations may be cited as examples.

Subjects of global governance may be individuals, collectivities or States. Global administration has significant impact on these subjects. Therefore, global administrative law does not only relates to States alone, it is also concerned with private individuals and collectivities like corporations, unions and non-governmental organisations, etc. Today, domestic policies, planning, execution and regulation are no longer fully domestic, as these can be controlled often by transnational regulatory regimes. Powerful presence of private players acting either directly or indirectly as instrumentality or agency of State sharing public authority further complicates governance. This makes development of global administrative law jurisprudence imperative to infuse efficiency, fairness and accountability in global governance.

Growth of global governance has certainly reduced the local democratic control over resources and social and economic life of the people. Its operative values are drawn from capitalist ideology. Thus "corporate liberalism" and "profit maximisation" followed by deregulation, privatisation, formal equality and free competition are operative values of global governance. Only soft shades of rule of law, human rights, social responsibility and ethical values are visible. Fact remains that constitutionalisation of these values in global agenda for governance is necessary for economic growth on

4. *See generally*, Paul S. Reinsch, "International Administrative Law and National Sovereignty", (1909) 3 Am J Int'L L 1–45; C Wilfred Jenks, *The Proper Law of International Organisations* (1963).
5. *See generally*, S. Yamamoto, "The Positive Basis of International Administrative Law", (1967) The Journal of International Law and Diplomacy 1.

equal basis as an imperative for world peace. Transnational regulatory and adjudicatory mechanisms can be legitimised only if based on transparency, participation, negotiated political settlement and accountability. These are the values of classical administrative law. Thus, global administrative law must aim at developing adequate standards of legality, transparency, participation, equity, fair procedure, effective review of rules and decisions, accountability and enforcement.

Today, two approaches for constructing global administrative law are visible. According to one approach, domestic administrative law is transposed into global regulation. International Sports Federation, a non-State actor, uses domestic administrative law to correct private governance to ensure legality, participation and compliance in global regulation. However, this is not embedded in any formal legal mechanism. The second approach transposes global administrative law norms in domestic administrative space to enforce openness, participation and compliance. This approach is generally followed by formal international organisations like the UNO.[6]

Therefore, the need for developing a global Administrative Procedure Code laying down minimum "due process" norms—procedural and substantive—for global rule-making, rule-adjudication and rule-application cannot be overemphasised. Procedural due process must include principles of natural justice, transparency, participation and consensus in dispute resolution mechanisms. Substantive due process must take into consideration special needs and concerns of the developing world such as development, environment, technology transfer, public distribution of goods and services, trade in agriculture, labour standards, human rights, pharmaceutical trade and inclusiveness. Contentment with softer aspects of these concerns will be counter-productive.

Global administrative law must also focus on principles, norms and mechanisms for enforcing responsibility and accountability in global administrative space, necessary for infusing efficiency and fairness in the operations of global economic players. Accountability must be enforced at various levels which are interrelated and mutually supportive levels.[7] First level may refer to internal and external scrutiny of concept, aims, objects and terms of agreement for undertaking transnational operations. Second level may refer to their relationship with Member States, their collectivities, staff members, third party and international organisations. Third level of accountability must relate to the scrutiny of preventive measures undertaken to avoid possible damage caused by lawful operations in any State. Fourth level may relate to compensation for the actual harm suffered by the people by their lawful operations. Fifth level may relate to observance of international human rights, humanitarian law and principles of social

6. *See generally*, Richard B. Stewart, *Administrative Law: A Resource for Global Administrative Law.*
7. "Global Administrative Law Workshop", New York University, report by Juliet Tompkins, Balliol College, Oxford.

responsibility. Sixth level of accountability must refer to State accountability because accountability of global players cannot be viewed in isolation with State responsibility, especially within the areas of environment, human rights, land use, displacement of population and economic consequences. Global administrative law must aim at providing empowerment and avoiding exploitation in global administrative space.

Though, it is still not desirable to pass any final judgment on the desirability and efficacy of "globalisation" as an ideology and mechanism for global economic development, because "globalisation" is a process which is still in an evolving stage; yet considerable evidence suggest that the way in which global administrative space is being administered, it has intensified national and transnational inequalities. The game of free competition has undermined the position of developing world in the absence of level playing field. It is for this reason that the demand for a global administrative law based on freedom, equality, justice and accountability often comes from developing countries because such a law is necessary for infusing fairness in global administration. This is imperative for ushering in a new world order based on inclusiveness and equity. Fact remains that people are the ultimate end of any dispensation. In this context the idea of global system of courts and tribunals may be worth considering as independent and impartial mechanism for enforcing fairness, accountability and inclusiveness, deficient in transnational governance by global administrative authorities.

SUGGESTED READINGS

1. Akshaya Kamalnaath, "A Global Administrative Law Approach to Regulating Transnational Corporations with Respect to Human Rights Violations in Developing Countries", 1.3 CALQ (2013) 3.
2. Aniruddha Rajput, "Notes and Comments: Advent of Investment Arbitration and Evolution of International Administrative Law", 54 JILI (2012) 232.
3. P. Puneeth, "Interface Between Global Regulatory Regime and the Indian Constitution : Issues and Concerns", CNLU LJ (4) [2014] 98.
4. Suchi Jain, "Reconsidering Comparative Methodology in Administrative Law", 10 CPJLJ (2020) 32.

Subject Index

Law Books for Students of LL.B. (3 & 5 Yr. Courses), LL.M. & Competitive Examinations

Standard and Authoritative books from

Website: www.ebcwebstore.com

EBC

August, 2024

- **Eastern Book Company (HO)**
  34, Lalbagh, Lucknow-226001
  Helpline: (0522) 4033621, 4033620, 09935096019
  Ph: (0522) 4033601 (30 lines)
  Fax: (0522) 4033633
  E-mail: salesebc@ebc.co.in
- Eastern Book Company, Delhi
  1267, Kashmere Gate,
  Delhi-110006
  Ph.: (011) 23917616, 23921656
  E-mail: sales.delhi@ebc.co.in
- Eastern Book Company, Bangalore
  25/1, Anand Nivas, 3rd Cross,
  6th Main, Gandhi Nagar,
  Bangalore-560009
  Ph.: 080-41225368
  E-mail: sales.bglr@ebc.co.in
- Eastern Book Company, Ahmedabad
  Ground Floor -07, Satyamev Complex-1,
  Opp. High Court, Sarkhej- Gandhinagar
  Highway Road, Sola, Ahmedabad-380060
  Ph.: 9228012539 Email: sales.ahmd@ebc.co.in
- Eastern Book Company, Nagpur
  F-9, Girish Heights, 1st Floor,
  Near LIC Square, Kamptee Road, Nagpur - 440001
  Ph.: 7028924969 Email: sales.nagpur@ebc.co.in
- Eastern Book Company, Guwahati
  Advika, Unit No. 205,
  Second Floor, M.G. Road, Pan Bazaar,
  Guwahati - 781001
  Ph.: (0361) 2730577
  Email: sales.guwahati@ebc.co.in
- Manav Law House
  Near Prithvi Garden,
  Opp. Dr. Chandra's Eye Clinic,
  Elgin Road, Civil Lines, Allahabad - 211001
  Ph.: (0532) 2400877

Buy online: www.ebcwebstore.com

Author	Title	ISBN	Price	Qty.
	Administrative Law			
Massey, I.P.	Administrative Law, 10th Edn., R/P 2024 (P/B)	9788119868322	845	
Takwani, C.K.	Lectures on Administrative Law, 8th Edn., 2024 (P/B)	9788119868377	795	
	Arbitration			
Subramoniam, Rohith M. & Jain, Navya	International Commercial Arbitration: An Introduction, 1st Edn., R/P 2022 (P/B)	9789351452966	395	
Singh, Avtar	Law of Arbitration and Conciliation, 12th Edn., R/P 2023 Revised by Saurabh Bindal (P/B)	9788119114511	775	
Taly, Mallika	Introduction to Arbitration, 2015 Edn. (P/B)	9789351452447	395	
	Autobiographies, Biographies and Collected Essays			
Iyer, V.R, Krishna	Social Justice – Sunset or Dawn, 1st Edn., R/P 2019 (H/B)	9789388206396	445	
Khanna, H.R.	Neither Roses Nor Thorns, 1st Edn., R/P 2023 (H/B)	9788119114115	795	
Mahajan, V.D.	Chief Justice Mehr Chand Mahajan – Biography of the Great Jurist, 1st Edn., R/P 2014 (H/B)	9789351450764	595	
Malik, L. & Anjum, Shabeea A.	A Philosopher of Raisina – Dr Zakir Hussain Memorial Lectures, 2016 Edn. (H/B)	9789361163383	975	
Manohar, S.V.	Dimensions of Justice: Justice K.T. Desai Memorial Lectures 2004-2017, 1st Edn., 2018 (H/B)	9789387477895	995	
Mathew, K.K.	Three Lectures, 1st Edn., R/P 2012 (H/B)	9789350286975	350	
	Banking			
Patel, Bimal N. Jabbal, Dolly & Motiyani, Prachi V.	Banking Law and Negotiable Instruments Act, 2015 Edn. (P/B)	9789351452683	395	
Patel, Bimal N. Jabbal, Dolly & Motiyani, Prachi V.	Banking Law for Managers, 2018 Edn. (P/B)	9789387487093	295	

Author	Title	ISBN	Price	Qty.
Patel, Bimal N. Jabbal, Dolly & Motiyani, Prachi V.	Eazy Cases: Banking Law, 2014 Edn. (P/B)	9789351451181	325	
Patel, Bimal N. Jabbal, Dolly & Motiyani, Prachi V.	MCQ on Banking Law, R/P 2015 (P/B)	9789351452485	245	
Singh, Avtar	Banking & Negotiable Instruments, 4th Edn., R/P 2023 (P/B)	9788119114443	675	
Bar Exam				
EBC	All India Bar Examination Guide, 3rd Edn., 2023 (P/B)	9789394364875	1895	
Business Law				
Singh, Avtar	Business Law, 12th Edn., 2023, R/P 2024 (P/B)	9788119114818	1625	
Singh, Avtar	Competition Law, 2nd Edn., 2024 (P/B)	9788119868339	495	
Singh, Avtar	Law of Sale of Goods (Sale of Goods Act 1930; Hire Purchase Act, 1972), 9th Edn., R/P 2024, Revised by Deepa Paturkar (P/B)	9789390715640	465	
Child and Law				
Pinho, Emidio A. Desouza & Pinho, Andryusha D'costa	Child Abuse: Law Practice and Prevention, 1st Edn., 2021 (P/B)	9789390715657	495	
Rao, Mamta	Law Relating to Women & Children, 4th Edn., R/P 2024 (P/B)	9788197869822	845	
Civil Procedure				
Takwani, C.K.	Civil Procedure with Limitation Act, 1963, 10th Edn., 2024 (P/B)	9788119868896	1095	
Company Law				
Das, Rinita	Company Law, 1st Edn., 2022 (P/B)	9789390715671	495	
Singh, Avtar	Company Law, 17th Edn., R/P 2024 with Supplement 2021 (P/B)	9788119868131	995	
Singh, Avtar	Company Law: An Introduction, 13th Edn., 2022, R/P 2024 Revised by Rinita Das (P/B)	9788119868407	495	
Constitutional Law and Constitution				
Chandrachud, A.	Due Process of Law, 1st Edn., R/P 2024 (H/B)	9788119868667	895	
Kartikeya, K.	Article 12 – Meaning, Scope and Emerging Judicial Trends, 1st Edn., 2020, R/P 2023 (H/B)	9788196167028	1195	
Kulshreshtha, V.D.	Landmarks in Indian Legal and Constitutional History, 12th Edn., 2019, R/P 2024 Revised by Sumeet Malik (P/B)	9788197869815	845	
Mahajan, V.D.	Constitutional Law of India, 8th Edn., 2023, Revised by Sanjay Jain (P/B)	9789394364547	995	
Rai, Udai Raj	Constitutional Law: Governance Structure, 2nd Edn., 2022 (P/B)	9789394364561	825	
Rao, Mamta	Constitutional Law, 2nd Edn., R/P 2023 (P/B)	9788119114474	945	
Rao, Mamta	Public Interest Litigation – Legal Aid and Lok Adalats, 5th Edn., R/P 2024 (P/B)	9789390715480	525	
Singh, M.P.	Comparative Constitutional Law, 2nd Edn., 2011 (H/B)	9789350281383	1500	
Shukla, V.N.	Constitution of India, 14th Edn., 2022 with Supplement 2024 Revised by Mahendra Pal Singh (P/B)	9788119868353	1395	
Contract				
Aston, Joshua	MCQ on Contract Law (in 2 volumes), 2018 Edn.	9788193547229	550 per set	
Rab, Ajar	Drafting Contracts: Basic Principles, 1st Edn., 2022, R/P 2024 (H/B)	9789390715893	395	
Singh, Avtar	Contract Law (Easy Law Series), 1st Edn., 2012 (P/B)	9789350287194	195	
Singh, Avtar	Law of Contract & Specific Relief, 13th Edn., 2022, R/P 2024 Revised by Rajesh Kapoor (P/B)	9788119868803	1095	
Singh, Avtar	Textbook on Contract & Specific Relief, 8th Edn., 2022 Revised by Varun Malik (P/B)	9789390715862	545	
Vishwanathan, S.	Simply, Legal! – Contracts, 1st Edn., 2021, R/P 2024 (P/B)	9789390715725	345	
Conveyancing, Precedents, Pleadings & Drafting				
Murli Manohar	Art of Conveyancing and Pleading, 2nd Edn., 2004, Revised by R. Prakash (P/B)	8170128080	675 POD*	

Author	Title	ISBN	Price	Qty.
Criminal Law and Procedure				
EBC	Criminal Manual (Three Major Acts, CrPC, IPC & Evidence), Large: 31st Edn., 2020 (H/B)	BB/2458	695	
Gandhi, B.M.	Indian Penal Code, 5th Edn., 2023, Revised by K.A. Pandey (P/B)	9789394364288	1095	
Kelkar, R.V.	Criminal Procedure, 7th Edn., R/P 2023 Revised by K.N.C. Pillai (P/B)	9788195917969	1045	
Kelkar, R.V.	Lectures on Criminal Procedure-Including Probation & Juvenile Justice, 6th Edn., R/P 2023, Revised by K.N.C. Pillai (P/B)	9788195917976	545	
Pillai, K.N.C.	Criminal Law: General Principles, 3nd Edn., 2024 (P/B)	9788119114863	1095	
Srivastava, O.P.	Principles of Criminal Law, 8th Edn., 2023, Revised by Kumar Askand Pandey (P/B)	9788119114412	395	
Takwani, C.K.	Indian Penal Code, 2nd Edn., 2022 (P/B)	9789351452324	495	
Vishwanathan, S.	Simply, Legal! – Penal Code, 1st Edn., 2023 (P/B)	9789394364783	395	
Criminology and Penology				
Siddique, Ahmad	Criminology, Penology & Victimology, 8th Edn., 2024 Revised by Sanjay Vashishtha (P/B)	9788119114542	795	
Cybercrimes				
Fatima, Talat	Cyber Crimes, 3rd Edn., 2021 R/P 2023 (H/B)	9788119114399	1495	
	R/P 2024 (P/B)	9788197116155	945	
Dictionaries				
Chopra, K.	Law Dictionary English to Hindi (Pocket), 4th Edn., R/P 2017, Revised by SCC Editorial Staff (P/B)	9789351454540	245	
Chopra, K.	Law Dictionary English-Hindi (Large) , 4th Edn., 2014, Revised by SCC Editorial Staff (H/B)	9789351451204	450	
Economics and Law				
Nagar, Ranita	Law and Economics: Breaking New Grounds, 2017 Edn. (H/B)	9789351454625	995	
Environment and Pollution				
GNLU	Environmental Law: Contemporary Issues, 2019 (H/B)	9789388822527	895	
GNLU	Environmental Law: Decentralised Environmental Governance, 2019 (H/B)	9789388822114	895	
Patel, Bimal N. Motiyani, Prachi V.	Eazy Cases on Environmental Law, 2017 Edn. (P/B)	9789351455066	295	
Patel, Bimal N. Motiyani, Prachi V.	MCQ on Environmental Law, 2015 Edn. (P/B)	9789351452454	195	
Shastri, S.C.	Environmental Law, 7th Edn., 2024 (P/B)	9788119868735	845	
Singh, Gurdip	Environmental Law, 3rd Edn., 2024 (P/B)	9788119868933	895	
Tandon, Usha	Climate Change: Law, Policy and Governance, 1st Edn., 2016 (H/B)	9789351453376	895	
Equity				
Gandhi, B.M.	Equity, Trusts and Specific Relief, alongwith a chapter on Fiduciary Relationships, 4th Edn., 2007, R/P 2024 (P/B)	9788119868421	695	
Entrance Examination				
Bhattacharya, Aniruddha & Jaiswal, Utkrisht	Legal Aptitude for CLAT and Other LLB Entrance Examinations, Foreword by Justice Imtiyaz Murtaza, 3rd Edn., 2018 (P/B)	9789387487260	650	
CLAT Possible	Clat Solved Papers, 2nd Edn., 2017 (P/B)	9789351454724	395	
EBC	All India Bar Examination Guide, 3rd Edn., 2023 (P/B)	9789394364875	1895	
EBC	EBC's Master Guide to Judicial Services Examination, 2nd Edn., 2020 (P/B)	9789389656091	1395	
Prakash, Vaibhav	Legal Reasoning for CLAT & Other Law Entrance Exams, 1nd Edn., 2023 (P/B)	9788119114866	695	
Sahai, Surabhi Modi	Guide for LLB, CLAT, AILET, SET, DU and Other Law Entrance Exams, 5th Edn., with Solved Paper of CLAT 2022 (P/B)	9789394364509	1045	
Evidence				
Sarathi, V.P.	Law of Evidence, 8th Edn., 2021, R/P 2024 Revised by K.A. Pandey (P/B)	9788197869860	695	

Author	Title	ISBN	Price	Qty.
Family Law				
Gandhi, B.M.	Family Law (in 2 vol.) (P/B) 2nd Edn., 2019, R/P 2023 Vol. 1	9788119114788	545	
	2nd Edn., 2023, Vol. 2	9789390715596	395	
Gandhi, B.M.	Hindu Law, 4th Edn., 2016, R/P 2023 Revised by Sumeet Malik (P/B)	9788119114061	645	
Rashid, Syed Khalid	Muslim Law, 6th Edn., 2020, R/P 2022 (P/B)	9789394364479	475	
Food Security				
Nagar, Ranita	Food Security Law – Interdisciplinary Perspectives, 2014 Edn. (H/B)	9789351450269	485	
Hindu Law				
Gandhi, B.M.	Hindu Law, 4th Edn., 2016, R/P 2023 Revised by Sumeet Malik (P/B)	9788119114061	645	
Human Rights				
Joshi, K.C.	International Law & Human Rights, 4th Edn., 2019, R/P 2024 (P/B)	9788197116148	745	
Pathak, Puneet	International Humanitarian & Refugee Law, 1st Edn., R/P 2023 (P/B)	9788119114931	545	
Rao, Mamta	Law Relating to Women & Children, 4th Edn., R/P 2024 (P/B)	9788197869822	845	
Insolvency				
Singh, Avtar	Law of Insolvency, 5th Edn., 2014 (P/B)	9789350288481	295	
Insurance				
Singh, Avtar	Law of Insurance, 3rd Edn., 2017, R/P 2023 (P/B)	9788119114160	745	
Intellectual Property				
Bindal, Saurabh	Intellectual Property Law: An Introduction, 2nd Edn., 2023 (P/B)	9788119114726	595	
Bindal, Saurabh	MCQ on Intellectual Property Law, 2nd Edn., 2024 (P/B)	9788119868582	345	
Gopalakrishnan, N.S. & Agitha, T.G.	Principles of Intellectual Property, 2nd Edn., 2014 (P/B)	9789351450191	535	
Rao, R. Anita & Rao, V. Bhanoji	Intellectual Property Rights - A Primer, R/P 2013 (P/B)	9789350289204	260	
Thomas, Mathew	Understanding Intellectual Property, 2016 Edn. (P/B)	9789351454212	595	
Verkey, Elizabeth	Intellectual Property, 2nd Edn., R/P 2024 (P/B)	9788197116186	795	
Internship				
Aston, Joshua	Acing Internships-A Practical Guide, 1st Edn., 2018, R/P 2023 (P/B)	9788119114085	295	
International Law				
Jain, Shilpa	An Introduction to Public International Law, 1st Edn., 2016 R/P 2021 (P/B)	9789390715343	360	
Joshi, K.C.	International Law & Human Rights, 4th Edn., R/P 2024 (P/B)	9788197116148	745	
Mujawar, Fatima	Crisp Introduction to International Law, 2016 Edn. (P/B)	9789351453659	125	
Mujawar, Fatima	MCQ on International Law, 2017 Edn. (P/B)	9789351455080	275	
Murthy, B.S.	International Relations and Organisation, 2nd Edn., R/P 2024 Revised by V. Rajyalakshmi (P/B)	9788197116131	345	
Pathak, Puneet	International Humanitarian & Refugee Law, 1st Edn., R/P 2023 (P/B)	9788119114931	545	
Rajyalakshmi, V.	International Organisations, 2018 Edn. (P/B)	9789388206143	495	
Singh, Gurdip	International Law, 4th Edn., 2024 (P/B)	9788119868513	895	
Interpretation of Statutes				
Gandhi, B.M.	Interpretation of Statutes, 2nd Edn., R/P 2024 (P/B)	9788119114764	415	
Sarathi, V.P.	Interpretation of Statutes, 6th Edn., 2024 (P/B)	9788119114832	795	
Judicial Entrance Exam				
EBC	EBC's Master Guide to Judicial Services Examination, 2nd Edn., 2020 (P/B)	9789389656091	1395	
Jurisprudence and Legal Theory				
Mahajan, V.D.	Jurisprudence and Legal Theory, 6th Edn., R/P 2024 Revised by VB Coutinho (P/B)	9788119868391	825	

Author	Title	ISBN	Price	Qty.
Pillai, P.S.A.	Jurisprudence and Legal Theory, 3rd Edn., R/P 2022 (P/B)	9789351452478	345	
Subbarao, G.C.V.	Jurisprudence and Legal Theory, 9th Edn., R/P 2024 (P/B)	9788119114917	445	
Labour and Industrial Law				
Coutinho, V.B.	Lectures on Labour Law, 2019 Edn. (P/B)	9789388206532	295	
Malik, PL	Handbook of Labour and Industrial Law, 18th Edn., 2018, Revised by Editorial Staff of SCC (H/B)	9789388206150	1195	
Legal Aptitude				
Bhattacharya, Aniruddha & Jaiswal, Utkrisht	Legal Aptitude for CLAT and Other LLB Entrance Examinations, Foreword by Justice Imtiyaz Murtaza, 3rd Edn., 2018 (P/B)	9789387487260	650	
Legal Education				
Menon, N.R.M.	An Idea of a Law School Ideas from The Law School, 2019 Edn. (H/B)	9789388822794	995	
Menon, N.R.M.	Clinical Legal Education, R/P 2023 (P/B)	9788119114047	445	
Legal Fictions				
Varadachari, V.K.	Legal Fictions, 2nd Edn., 2012, Revised by V.P. Sarathi (H/B)	9789350285190	350	
Legal History				
Chauhan, S.P.S.	Britishers' Rule in India, 2020 Edn., R/P 2022 (H/B)	9789390715459	1295	
Jatar, Nilakshi & Paranjape, Laxmi	Legal History - Evolution of The Indian Legal System, 2012 Edn. (P/B)	9789350286852	395	
Kulshreshtha, V.D.	A Textbook of English Legal History, 3rd Edn., R/P 2007 (P/B)	8170129950	90	
Kulshreshtha, V.D.	Landmarks in Indian Legal and Constitutional History, 12th Edn., 2019, R/P 2024 Revised by Sumeet Malik (P/B)	9788197869815	845	
Mulchandani, R.R.	Cities of India: A Legal History, 2018 Edn. (H/B)	0780387487001	895	
Legal Language				
Gandhi, B.M.	Legal Language, Legal Writing & General English, R/P 2024 (P/B)	9788197116100	545	
Legal Method				
Ajjappa, G.V. & Malik, Sumeet	Legal Method: An Introduction, 1st Edn., 2023 (P/B)	9788196167004	345	
Legal Research				
Mahalakshmi, J. & Balamurugan, P.	Legal Research Methodology, 1st Edn., 2023 (P/B)	9788119114498	395	
Vibhute, K.I.	Legal Research: Approaches, Methods and Techniques 1st Edn., 2024 (P/B)	9788119868445	695	
Legal Studies				
Kaushik, S. Krishan	Legal Studies: Class XI - CBSE, 2nd Edn., 2021 (P/B)	9789390715251	295	
Paturkar, Deepa	Legal Studies: Class XII - CBSE, 2nd Edn. 2023 (P/B)	9788119114245	225	
Singh, Vijay Kumar	Learn the Law, 1st Edn., 2022 (P/B)	9789394364271	425	
Singh, Vijay Kumar	Legal Studies: Class XI - ISC, 1st Edn., 2022, R/P 2024 (P/B)	9789390715152	495	
Singh, Vijay Kumar	Legal Studies: Class XII - ISC, 1st Edn., R/P 2023 (P/B)	9788119114405	325	
Life and Law				
Aston, Joshua	Higher Studies In Law: How and Where to Apply, 2020 Edn. (P/B)	9788194284833	395	
Bansal, Avani	Life at Law School, 2020 Edn. (P/B)	9789389656169	425	
Menon, N.R.M.	An Idea of a Law School Ideas from The Law School, 2019 Edn. (H/B)	9789388822794	995	
Moot Court				
Malik, Abhinandan	Moot Courts and Mooting, 2nd Edn., 2023, R/P 2024 (P/B)	9788119868414	725	
Media				
Divan, Madhavi	Facets of Media Law, 3rd Edn., 2022 (H/B)	9789351452003	1495	
	Facets of Media Law, 3rd Edn., 2023 (P/B)	9788119114078	945	
Muslim Law				
Rashid, Syed K.	Muslim Law, 6th Edn., 2020, R/P 2022 (P/B)	9789394364479	475	

Author	Title	ISBN	Price	Qty.
	Negotiable Instruments			
Patel, Bimal N., Jabbal, Dolly and Motiyani, Prachi V.	Banking Law and Negotiable Instruments Act, 2015 Edn. (P/B)	9789351452683	395	
Singh, Avtar	Banking & Negotiable Instruments, 4th Edn., R/P 2023 (P/B)	9788119114443	675	
Singh, Avtar	Negotiable Instruments: An Introduction, 9th Edn., 2022, Revised by Deepa Paturkar (P/B)	9789390715664	325	
	Partnership			
Singh, Avtar	Law of Partnership: An Introduction, 11th Edn., R/P 2024 (P/B)	9788197116162	395	
	Property			
Sarathi, V.P.	Law of Transfer of Property, Revised by Mallika Taly, 6th Edn., Reprinted 2024 (P/B)	9788119868780	675	
	Public Interest Litigation			
Rao, Mamta	Public Interest Litigation – Legal Aid and Lok Adalats, 5th Edn., R/P 2024 (P/B)	9789390715480	525	
	Refugee Law			
Pathak, Puneet	International Humanitarian & Refugee Law, 1st Edn., R/P 2023 (P/B)	9788119114931	545	
	Social Justice			
Bhat, P. Ishwara	Law and Social Transformation, 2nd Edn., 2022 (H/B)	9789390715909	1495	
	Social Sciences for Law Student Series			
Agarwal, D.	Sociology, 1st Edn., 2022 (P/B)	9789390715930	495	
Gopalakrishnan, K.C. & Ramdass	Economics (for Law Students) Reprinted, 2012 (P/B)	9789350282397	245	
Gopalakrishnan, K.C.	Legal Economics (Interactional Dimensions of Economics and Law) Reprinted, 2021 (P/B)	9789394364035	395	
Murthy, B.S.	International Relations and Organisation, 2nd Edn., R/P 2024 Revised by V. Rajyalakshmi (P/B)	9788197116131	345	
Murthy, H.V. Sreenivasa	History of India (Part I), Reprinted 2024 (P/B)	9788119868223	425	
Murthy, H.V.S. Elizabeth, V.S.	History of India (Part II), Reprinted 2021 (P/B)	9789389656305	275	
Oommen, T.K. Venugopal, C.N.	Sociology for Law Students, Reprinted 2023 (P/B)	9788119114153	395	
Rathore, L.S. Haqqi, S.A.H.	Principles of Political Theory and Organisation, Reprinted 2021 (P/B)	9789389656480	325	
	Taxation			
Suseela Vasudevan, Jaya	Indirect Taxes: GST and other Indirect Taxes, 2019 Edn. (P/B)	9789388822381	525	
	Torts			
Gandhi, B.M.	Law of Torts with Law of Statutory Compensation & Consumer Protection, 4th Edn., Reprinted 2022 (P/B)	9789351452362	545	
Pillai, P.S.A.	Law of Tort, 9th Edn., R/P 2024, Revised by Abhinandan Malik (P/B)	9788119114740	675	
Vishwanathan, S.	Simply, Legal! – Torts, 1st Edn., 2021 (P/B)	9788194800415	245	
	Women and Law			
Dhanda, A. & Parashar, A	Engendering Law, 1999 Edn., W/S 2007 (H/B)	8170126665	400	
Parihar, Lalita Dhar	Women and Law: From Impoverishment to Empowerment–A Critique, 2011 Edn., R/P 2016 (P/B)	9789351453529	495	
Rao, Mamta	Law Relating to Women & Children, 4th Edn., R/P 2024 (P/B)	9788197869822	845	
Sagade, J.; Jivan, V. & Forster, CC	Feminism in The Subcontinent and Beyond, 2014 Edn. (H/B)	9789351451259	990	

Author	Title	ISBN	Price	Qty.
Law Books in Hindi				
Babel, B.L.	A Guide to Civil Practice, 2013 Edn. (P/B)	9789350289006	525	
Babel, B.L.	Apkritya Vidhi (Law of Torts in Hindi), 2nd Edn., 2009 (P/B)	9788170121855	235	
Babel, B.L.	Apradh Shastra evam Dand Shastra (Criminology & Penology in Hindi), 4th Edn., 2013 (P/B)	9789350285251	275	
Babel, B.L.	Chikitsa Nyayashastra (Medical Jurisprudence in Hindi),6th Edn,2014(P/B)	9789351450801	875 POD*	
Babel, B.L.	Hasthlekh evam Anguli Chhap Vigyan (Handwriting & Fingerprints Science in Hindi), 5th Edn., 2013 (P/B)	9789350287262	210	
Babel, B.L.	Nyayik Vigyan (Forensic Science in Hindi), 5th Edn., 2017 (P/B)	9789351454526	295	
Babel, B.L.	Police Anveshan (Police Investigation in Hindi), 5th Edn., 2017(P/B)	9789351454762	365	
Babel, B.L.	Sampatti Antaran Adhiniyam, 1882 (Transfer of Property Act, 1882 in Hindi), 2nd Edn., 2006 (P/B)	9788170129110	450 POD*	
Babel, B.L.	Van Evam Vanya Jeev Sanrakshan Vidhi, (Law Relating to Forest & Wild Life Protection in Hindi), 4th Edn. 2011 (P/B)	9789350281666	385	
Babel, B.L.	Vivah Evam Talak Vidhi (Law of Marriage and Divorce in Hindi), 2nd Edn., 2017 (P/B)	9789351455509	550	
Chaturvedi, M.D.	Apkrityon ki Vidhi (Law of Torts in Hindi), 2nd Edn., 2008 (P/B)	9788170121510	275	
Chaturvedi, M.D.	Bhartiya Dand Sanhita, 1860 (Indian Penal Code, 1860 in Hindi), 9th Edn., Reprinted 2020 (P/B)	9789388822510	495	
Chaturvedi, M.D.	Prachin Bhartiya Vidhi Vyavastha (Manusmriti ke Vishesh Sandarbh Mein) [Ancient Indian Legal System (with special reference to Manusmriti) in Hindi], 1995 Edn. (H/B)	8170125731	600 POD*	
Chaturvedi, M.D	Sampatti Antaran Adhiniyam, 1882 aur Bharatiya Sukhachar Adhiniyam, 1882 (Transfer of Property Act, 1882 alongwith Indian Easement Act, 1882 in Hindi) 2nd Edn., 2011 (P/B)	9789350280553	295	
Chaturvedi, M.D.	Sakshya Vidhi (Law of Evidence in Hindi), 3rd Edn., 2011 (P/B)	9789350280614	265	
Chaudhary, R.N.	Kanoonon Ke Nirvachan Ke Siddhant (Principles of Interpretation of Statutes in Hindi), 2010 Edn. (P/B)	9788170128762	295	
Chaudhary, R.N.	Paryabaran Vidhi (Environmental Law in Hindi), 2021 Edn. (P/B)	In Press		
Chopra, K.	Law Dictionary (English to Hindi) 4th Edn., 2014 (H/B)	9789351451204	450	
Chopra, K.	Law Dictionary (English to Hindi) 4th Edn., R/P 2017 (Pocket) (P/B)	9789351454540	245	
Fatima, Talat	Internet Vidhi Evam Cyber Apradh (Internet Law and Cyber Crime in Hindi), 2018 Edn. (P/B)	9789388206273	545	
Joshi, K.C.	Antarrashtriya Vidhi Aur Manvadhikar (International Law and Human Rights in Hindi), 3rd Edn., 2017 (P/B)	9789351455257	395	
Kulshreshtha, V.D.	Bharat ka Vaidhanik Evam Samvaidhanik Itihas (Indian Legal & Constitu-tional History in Hindi), 2nd Edn.,2004, Revised by M.D. Chaturvedi(P/B)	8170128064	195	
Malhotra, I.J.	Hindu Vivah Adhiniyam (Hindu Marriage Act in Hindi), 3rd Edn., 2006 (P/B)	8170129028	295	
Malhotra, I.J.	Madhyastham aur Sulah Adhiniyam (Arbitration & Conciliation Act in Hindi), 2nd Edn. W/S, 2005 (P/B)	8170126703	160	
Murli, Manohar	Abhivachano Ke Prarupan Aur Abhihastantaran Lekhan Ki Kala (Art of Conveyancing & Pleading in Hindi), 4th Edn., 2005, Revised by M.D. Chaturvedi (P/B)	8170127807	860 POD*	
Prasad, Aniruddh	Vidhishastra ke Mool Siddhant (Principles of Jurisprudence in Hindi), 5th Edn., 2016 (H/B)	9789351453314	1000 POD*	
	Vidhishastra ke Mool Sidhant (Principles of Jurisprudence in Hindi), (Shorter Edn.), 2016 Edn. (P/B)	9789351454236	1000 POD*	
Rashid, Khalid	Muslim Vidhi (Muslim Law in Hindi), 2nd Edn., Reprinted 2018, Revised by Prof. V.P. Bhartiya (P/B)	9789388206068	375	
Sharma, Y.S.	Dand Shastra (Penology in Hindi), 1999 Edn. (P/B)	8170126525	95	
Sharma, Y.S.	Kanoonon Ka Nirvachan(Interpretation of Statutes in Hindi),2010 Edn(P/B)	817012980X	250	

Author	Title	ISBN	Price	Qty.
Shiva Gopal	Hastantaran Lekhan ke Drishtant aur Prapatra, (Conveyancing, Precedents and Forms in Hindi) 3rd Edn., 2005 (with CD ROM containing Precedents & Forms), Revised by J.V.N. Jaiswal(H/B)	8170128528	325	
Singh, Avtar	Bank-kari Vidhi Evam Parkramya Likhat Adhiniyam (Law of Banking and Negotiable Instruments in Hindi), 6th Edn., 2011 (P/B)	9789350281796	350	
Singh, Avtar	Bhagidari Vidhi evam Seemit Dayitva Adhiniyam(Law of Partnership & Limited Liability Partnership in Hindi), 8th Edn., 2018 (P/B)	9789387487314	295	
Singh, Avtar	Company Vidhi (Company Law in Hindi), 10th Edn., W/S 2021, Reprinted 2024 (P/B)	9788119114504	595	
Singh, Avtar	Company Vidhi - Ek Parichay (An Introduction to Company Law in Hindi), 6th Edn., 2019 (P/B)	9789388222206	295	
Singh, Avtar	Mal Vikraya Evam Avkraya Vidhi (Sale of Goods & Hire Purchase in Hindi), 7th Edn., 2018 (P/B)	9789387487253	395	
Singh, Avtar	Madhyastham, Sulah Evam Anukalpi Vivad Niptan Vidhi (Law relating to Arbitration, Conciliation & Alternative Disputes Resolution in Hindi), 4th Edn., Reprinted 2018 (P/B)	9789388206136	345	
Singh, Avtar	Parkramya Likhat (Negotiable Instruments in Hindi), 6th Edn,2012 (P/B)	9789350286999	195	
Singh, Avtar	Samvida Vidhi evam Vinirdist Anutosh Adhiniyam – Ek Parichay [Law of Contract & Specific Relief Act(An Introduction)in Hindi], 2nd Edn., 2013 (P/B)	9789350289839	325	
Singh, Avtar	Samvida Vidhi Ke Siddhant Tatha Vinirdisht Anutosh Adhiniyam, 1963 (Law of Contract & Specific Relief Act,1963 in Hindi), 11th Edn. R/P 2024(P/B)	9788119114870	725	
Chaudhary, R.N.	Suchna Ka Adhikar Adhiniyam, 2005 (Right to Information Act, 2005 in Hindi), 2013 Edn. (P/B)	9789350289914	225	
Singh, Avtar	Vanijyik Vidhi ke Sidhant (Principles of Mercantile Law in Hindi), 5th Edn., 1996 (P/B)	9788170126300	250	
Singh, R.P.	Uttar Pradesh Bhoomi Vidhi (U.P. Land Laws in Hindi), 2nd Edn., 1995	8170125677	75	
Som, Adheer	Gumnami Baba (in Hindi), 2019 Edn. (P/B)	9789388822138	195	
Subbarao, G.C.V.	Vidhi Shastra evam Vidhi Ke Sidhant (Jurisprudence & Legal Theory in Hindi) Reprinted, 1997 (P/B)	8170121086	125 POD*	
Srivastava, O.P.	Apradhik Vidhi Ke Sidhant (Principles of Criminal Law in Hindi), 5th Edn., 2012, Revised by R.N. Chaudhary (P/B)	9789350287187	675 POD*	
Takwani, C.K.	Prashasanik Vidhi (Administrative Law in Hindi) Translated & Updated, 3rd Edn. 2019 Revised by K.C. Joshi (P/B)	9789388206389	395	

All disputes and complaints are exclusively subject to the jurisdiction of the courts/tribunals/forums at Lucknow only.
Prices quoted herein is/are subject to change without prior notice.

EBC Reader

EBC Explorer